# Exploring Southeast Alaska

1. East Dixon Entrance, Portland Canal, Revillagigedo Channel to Ketchikan
2. Misty Fiords to Wrangell via Behm Canal, Meyers Chuck and Ernest Sound
3. Clarence Strait, Prince of Wales East Coast and Stikine Strait
4. Sumner Strait to Frederick Sound via Wrangell Narrows and Petersburg
5. Stephens Passage, Port Houghton and Gambier Bay to Juneau and Lynn Canal South
6. Lynn Canal North and Icy Strait to Glacier Bay and Cross Sound to Icy Point
7. Chichagof Island Outer Passage to Sitka, North Chatham Strait and Peril Strait
8. Baranof Island, Lower Chatham Strait and Keku Strait, including Rocky Pass
9. Prince of Wales Island West Coast to Craig
10. Prince of Wales Island West Coast to Cape Chacon, including Dall Island

©2018 Don and Réanne Douglass • Diagram not for navigation

*The authors, Don and Réanne, in the Research Vessel* Baidarka, *glide past the majestic arch at Boussole Bay—north of Cape Spencer.*

# Exploring SOUTHEAST ALASKA

## Dixon Entrance to Skagway

**3RD EDITION**

Don Douglass &
Réanne Hemingway-Douglass

**Fine Edge**
*Nautical & Recreational Publishing*

Anacortes, Washington

Editor, Third Edition: Lisa Wright
Editor, Second Edition: Linda Lewis, Ph.D.
Book Design: Melanie Haage
Graphics: Sue Athmann

Front cover photo by Elsie Hulsizer.
Back cover photos by Réanne Hemingway-Douglass
Photos and sidebars in this book are the copyright of the individuals credited for the photo and/or sidebar and have been licensed for use in this book.
Front cover from Chart 17326
Back cover from Chart 17403

Quotations from the U.S. *Coast Pilot* are for illustrative purposes; such information is not to be used for navigation. Appropriate and updated *Coast Pilot* and charts must be used for navigation.

**Important Legal Disclaimer**

This book is designed to provide experienced skippers with planning information for cruising Southeast Alaska. Every effort has been made, within limited resources, to make this book complete and accurate. There may well be mistakes, both typographical and in content; therefore, this book should be used only as a general guide, not as the ultimate source of information on the areas covered. Much of what is presented in this book is local knowledge based upon personal observation and is subject to human error.

The authors, publisher and local and governmental authorities make no warranties and assume no liability for errors or omissions, or for any loss or damage of any kind incurred from using this information.

**Library of Congress Cataloging-in-Publication Data**

Douglass, Don
 Exploring Southeast Alaska: Dixon entrance to skagway / by Don Douglass and Réanne Hemingway Douglass. — 3rd ed.
    p.      cm.
 Includes bibliographical references and index.
 ISBN-13: 978-1-934199-31-2 (pbk., 3rd edition)
    1.Pilot guides--Alaska--Alaska, Gulf of.   2. Pilot guides--Alaska--Alexander Archipelago.   I. Hemingway-Douglass, Réanne.   II Title.

ISBN 978-1-934199-31-2

Copyright ©2018 Don Douglass and Réanne Hemingway-Douglass
All rights strictly reserved under the International and Pan-American Copyright Conventions.
No part of this work may be reproduced or transmitted in any form or by any means, electronic or mechanical, including photocopying, or by any information storage and retrieval system, except as may be expressly permitted by the Copyright Act or in writing from the publisher.

Address requests for permission to:
Fine Edge, PO Box 726, Anacortes, WA 98221
www.FineEdge.com

# Contents

Foreword by *Professor Roderick Frazier Nash* . . . . . . . . . . . . . . . . . . . . . . viii

Introduction . . . . . . . . . . . . . . . . . . . . . . . . . . . . . . . . . . . . . . . . . . . . . . . x

Chapter 1    Dixon Entrance, Portland Canal, Revillagigedo Channel to Ketchikan . . 1

Chapter 2    Misty Fiords to Wrangell via Behm Canal, Meyers Chuck & Ernest Sound . . . . . . . . . . . . . . . . . . . . . . . . . . . . . . . . . . . . . 83

Chapter 3    Clarence Strait, Prince of Wales Island East Coast & Stikine Strait . . . 103

Chapter 4    Sumner Strait & Frederick Sound via Wrangell Narrows & Petersburg . . . . . . . . . . . . . . . . . . . . . . . . . . . . . . . . . . . . . . 118

Chapter 5    Stephens Passage, Port Houghton & Gambier Bay to Juneau & Lynn Canal South . . . . . . . . . . . . . . . . . . . . . . . . . . . . . . . . . 152

Chapter 6    Lynn Canal North, Icy Strait & Glacier Bay, Cross Sound to Icy Point . . . . . . . . . . . . . . . . . . . . . . . . . . . . . . . . . . . . . . . . 188

Chapter 7    Chichagof Island, Chatham Strait & Peril Strait to Sitka . . . . . . . . . . 240

Chapter 8    Baranof Island South of Sitka, Lower Chatham Strait & Keku Strait . . . . . . . . . . . . . . . . . . . . . . . . . . . . . . . . . . . . . . . 296

Chapter 9    West Sumner Strait & Prince of Wales Island West Coast to Craig . . . . 354

Chapter 10    Prince of Wales Island West Coast to Cape Chacon, including Dall Island . . . . . . . . . . . . . . . . . . . . . . . . . . . . . . . . . . . . . . . . 382

## Appendices and References

A. Suggested Itineraries for the Inside Passage from Seattle, Washington, to Southeast Alaska. . . . . . . . . . . . . . . . . . . . . . . . . . . . . . . . . . . . . 416

B. Distance Table—Seattle, Washington to Cape Spencer, Alaska . . . . . . . . . 422

C. Key VHF Radio Channels . . . . . . . . . . . . . . . . . . . . . . . . . . . . . . . . . . 423

D. Summer Wind Reports . . . . . . . . . . . . . . . . . . . . . . . . . . . . . . . . . . . 424

E. Duration of Daylight . . . . . . . . . . . . . . . . . . . . . . . . . . . . . . . . . . . . . 424

F. Sources for Fishing Regulations . . . . . . . . . . . . . . . . . . . . . . . . . . . . . 425

| | | |
|---|---|---|
| G. | Documenting Local Knowledge | 425 |
| H. | Sources of Books and Nautical Charts | 425 |
| I. | Provincial and Federal Agencies; Guides and Air Transportation; Visitors Centers: Alaska | 426 |

Bibliography and References . . . . . . . . . . . . . . . . . . . . . . . . . . . . 428

Acknowledgments . . . . . . . . . . . . . . . . . . . . . . . . . . . . . . . . . . 430

About the Authors . . . . . . . . . . . . . . . . . . . . . . . . . . . . . . . . . . 431

Index . . . . . . . . . . . . . . . . . . . . . . . . . . . . . . . . . . . . . . . . . . 432

Nautical Titles from FineEdge.com . . . . . . . . . . . . . . . . . . . . . . . . 439

Baidarka *exploring the upper reaches of Southeast Alaska—Cape Spencer*

# Foreword

## Professor Roderick Frazier Nash

The floor-to-ceiling map on the wall of the U'Mista Cultural Centre in Alert Bay, British Columbia, had to be over 15 feet high. It covered Puget Sound to Glacier Bay, and there was one of those little red "you are here" dots way down near the floor. It chilled my heart. That was back in the early 1990s and I was a week out of Anacortes, Washington, on my first cruise to Alaska. I had prepared as best I could with the information available at the time, but there in my face was the reality: a thousand miles to go, enormously complex coastline, myriad islands, few human settlements, current, wind, fog, rain—the whole maritime enchilada. Lots of decisions; lots of opportunities for wrong ones.

Sure, I had charts on that first trip, and now there are electronic charting miracles, but in a way, they only make Northwest boating more daunting. Where do you actually want to go on those wonderful charts? What I needed was a way to "get inside" the charts; advice on what they really meant for my voyage. As I walked tentatively down the hill to my boat and headed out into Queen Charlotte Strait, I thought about the value of a navigational psychologist, or just a hand to hold.

What I needed back then was exactly what you are holding right now. Think of it this way—you have just bought years of boating experience from two of the most accomplished explorers and map-makers in maritime history. Well over a thousand anchorages are precisely located and described in this book. It's based on primary research (the Douglasses have been everywhere!), and it is organized in an "open navigation" format. The old-style "recommended route" cruising guides were useful, but discouraged spontaneity. Don and Réanne know that wherever you go, "there you are"; and their book will help you with local knowledge everywhere in Southeast Alaska. They have done a lot of the physical and mental grunt work necessary for a voyage that is safe and special.

This book concerns part of the largest, most complex and most isolated cruising ground in the temperate latitudes of this planet. Thanks to glaciation and a rise in sea level over the last 15,000 years, there is a staggering amount of islands and radically varied coastline in Southeast Alaska. Settlements are few, far between and not accessible by motor vehicle. There is some logging and hydropower development in evidence, but the country swallows it up—we are talking about wilderness boating here. People are visitors who do not remain. There are outstanding opportunities for solitude; chances to interact with the biggest and wildest carnivores of land (grizzly) and sea (whales). You might even see an orca pick off a swimming wolf or grizzly!

Get off the main cruising corridors and you can go days and weeks without seeing another boat. Walk a few hundred yards into the rainforest and it is likely you are standing where no human has ever been. The ridges along the fiords are unclimbed. In general, the coastline looks the same as it did for the first Native peoples and for the Russian, Spanish and English seafarers. Forget about reaching a tow-boat service on Ch 16: Southeast, like all wilderness, puts a premium on self-reliance. If your idea of a lonely anchorage is Catalina Island on a weekday or Puget Sound in the off-season, you are in for a big—and potentially scary—but also exhilarating surprise. It's comforting under these circumstances to have this book close to your pilot station.

There are no trails, only wakes, on the water. Wilderness boating in a place like Southeast Alaska allows every mariner the chance to be a discoverer. Above all, this is an environment of personal exploration: a place to test your skill, your courage and your capacity for wonder. And the Douglasses will help you to—in Henry David Thoreau's words—"go confidently in the direction of your dreams."

*Authors' Note:*
Professor Roderick Frazier Nash, retired from the University of California, Santa Barbara, has cruised waters of the Inside Passage and Southeast Alaska for two decades. He is a creator of the field of environmental history and the author of such classics as *Wilderness and the American Mind* and *The Rights of Nature*. Over thirty years ago, Rod was instrumental in reviving Don Douglass's passion for the Inside Passage on a cruise from Juneau to Seattle on his Nordic Tug, *Forevergreen*.

*Kasnyku Falls in Waterfall Cove, Chatham Strait*

# Introduction

## Important Southeast Alaska Cruising Considerations

It is said that "Experience is what you get right after you need it."

We encourage you to read this chapter carefully. It will help you build an invaluable base of experience and guide your use of this book.

Every summer, Southeast Alaska—called simply "Southeast" by Alaskans—draws a wide variety of pleasure craft, from solo kayakers, trailerable sport-fishing boats, houseboats and small sailboats with outboards, to motorsailers, trawler-style cruisers, and world-class yachts.

They all head north through the Inside Passage following the paths of Canada geese, whales, and salmon. The enjoyment and safety of their trips do not seem to be correlated to boat size, speed, or cost. Rather, the boaters who successfully cruise these waters all have certain values in common—they are well prepared and self-reliant, with the desire to explore this beautiful saltwater wilderness.

To help you plan your cruise, this book includes detailed route and anchoring information on almost every named—and many unnamed—anchor sites in Southeast, providing the vital "local knowledge" missing from charts and other sources. Our philosophy in publishing our comprehensive guidebooks is this: within the more than 3,000 miles of pristine summer cruising offered by the Inside Passage, you should always be able to find a nearby place where you can drop your hook to wait out the fog or chop, or pause for the wind to die down or the tide to turn. You are seldom more than an hour away from safety,

*Research Vessel* Baidarka *in Berg Bay*

so you don't have to over-stress your boat or crew just to make it to a town 50 miles away.

A multitude of wonderful, intimate coves await exploration—or exist as places to enjoy a calm night's sleep. Some of the coves are along ferry routes while others lie along the more remote passages. Some of the places or anchorages mentioned in this guide require advanced piloting skills or risk taking. Such places should be attempted only by qualified skippers who feel comfortable in accepting risk. Any time a passage or an anchor site is too small or tricky, or other than you were expecting, turn around and return to a known safe place, or try another anchor site. By understanding your own abilities and interests and matching these to the almost unlimited outdoor opportunities found in Alaska, you will indeed experience a rewarding adventure.

If you are a newcomer to cruising, we recommend that you prepare by consulting local experts—cruising instructors, yacht clubs, experienced Alaska boaters, commercial fishermen, the Power Squadron, the Coast Guard Auxiliary—and that you read many of the texts listed in the bibliography. We recommend the additional volumes in our Exploring series, especially *Exploring the North Coast of British Columbia* and *Exploring the South Coast of British Columbia*. Internet sources also contain lots of cruising information. (See sidebar on Internet Resources.) Make this the cruise of a lifetime. Plan now, and by all means, go!

## Planning Tips for Cruising to Southeast Alaska

1. For many boaters, cruising to Southeast Alaska is a dream voyage. It is a serious undertaking, so test your vessel and crew well before you start your trip. The better you prepare for your cruise, the bigger the dividends you'll reap in safety, comfort, and enjoyment. A solid plan, executed with good judgment, minimizes potential surprises and has more to do with a successful voyage than the size or speed of your boat or the number of crew you have aboard.

2. Our suggested itineraries (see Appendix A) include information for trips from Washington state through British Columbia to Southeast Alaska. These itineraries do not include layover days for bad weather or relaxation, so you should plan some downtime in your schedule. Fog—prevalent on the Inside Passage during late summer—may affect your travel time. Current, sea, or weather conditions at Seymour Narrows, Yuculta and Dent Rapids, Johnstone Straits, Queen Charlotte Sound, and Dixon Entrance may require you to alter your schedule. Chop caused by current flowing against a contrary wind can also slow you down, so always have a plan for an alternative anchor site. Pre-plotting your route and some alternatives on detailed paper charts or electronic charts before you set out will save you hours each day as well as anxiety in case of emergency.

3. Weather and anchoring conditions grow more challenging the farther north you go, and you will probably become more proficient at monitoring and forecasting local weather than you were at the start of your trip. For a safe and enjoyable cruise, remain flexible and don't become a slave to a schedule. Visit some of the more intricate coves and passages described in this book, but use good judgment. Turn around and head back to a known anchorage if you find you've exceeded your level of comfort or ability to cope. Of increasing importance, as you leave civilization behind, are robust anchor gear (preferably chain rode), engine spares, and the ability to use such gear competently.

4. Newcomers to northwest cruising frequently undertake a series of preliminary or "shakedown" cruises, first to British Columbia and then on to Southeast Alaska as they gain experience. Before you head to the Far North, practice in Puget Sound, the San Juan Islands in Washington, or the Gulf Islands in British Columbia. Test your boat, its equipment, and your

skills and crew. The more practice you get, the better. Practice cruises are strongly recommended, especially for owners of newly purchased boats. Many people trailer their sport fishing boats to places such as Port Hardy, Bella Coola, Prince Rupert or to Southeast Alaska by road and ferry, which allows them to gain experience one segment at a time.

Floatplanes with connections to major airports can reach you and your boat within an hour almost anywhere along the Inside Passage. Consider picking up crew or guests along the route. They can be morale-boosters, bringing news from home or providing delivery of spare parts. (Note that any packages from the U.S. to Canada will have to clear Canadian Customs, which may delay delivery.) We generally pick up and drop off crew or guests two or three times on each of our north- and southbound trips (they arrive in one port, but depart from another), and we've been able to do this from many ports in Southeast Alaska without leaving anyone stranded overnight. This strategy maintains your journey's progress. A few owners even leave their cruising boats in Alaska with a caretaker during the winter and resume their

*With the many floatplane companies available, your guests can fly into one location and out of another.*

voyage the following spring. (We suggest you check out Hoonah Harbor and Sitka for storing your boat.)

5. Before commencing a Southeast Alaska trip, leave a float plan (a proposed itinerary and a description of your boat) with an associate back home. Give instructions to be followed in case you're overdue by a specified length of time. Be sure to update your plans and timeline with your associate during your journey.

6. If you are inexperienced in running saltwater rapids, plan your trip to transit such areas in slack water on a Neap Tide (first and third quarters of the moon's monthly cycle), or when adjacent tidal differences are minimal. (Velocities at neap tides are considerably less than those at spring tides.) This advice especially applies to narrow but important passages, like Sergius Narrows (in Peril Strait) on the way to Sitka, as well as for dinghy adventures, such as in the upper reaches of Very Inlet behind Foggy Bay.

*Hoonah Harbor is a favorite marina for leaving your boat over the winter in Southeast Alaska.*

*A picture-perfect full moon tells you it is a Spring Tide, which means greater tidal ranges and faster currents.*

Radio behind on-the-s quick so sary. Be su VHF conv names of l where VHF to terrain in ers frequentl ssages for one another, so don't hesitate to hail a nearby boater for a report on the wind and sea conditions they are currently experiencing. There is a real sense of community among boaters in these waters; become a participant and use it to your benefit.

7. You may have difficulty obtaining parts, special tools, and instruction manuals en route, so be sure to carry spares for any critical items. If you plan to approach glaciers at close hand, we recommend that you carry a spare prop, both for your primary boat and for your dinghy. Haul-out facilities are limited, but many villages have useful tidal grids where you can inspect your hull or do your own work. (For tips on using haul-out grids, see the sidebar in Chapter 4: "Haul-out Grids in Southeast Alaska.")

8. You will seldom find sand beaches in Southeast Alaska, so a sturdy dinghy is important if you want to explore the many secluded beaches and trails. A good quality, hard-bottom dinghy (such as aluminum or fiberglass) makes it possible for you to pull onto shores that are rocky and barnacle-encrusted. We prefer an inflatable dinghy with a hard bottom (an RBI or Rigid-Bottom Inflatable) because it adds some safety in case of sinking. Don't tow any dinghy in windy weather or through chop if you want to keep it.

9. Don't hesitate to contact the U.S. Coast Guard via VHF radio for weather updates or alternate destinations if conditions deteriorate.

10. It is important to carry large-scale (large detail) charts, tide, and current tables on board. Guidebooks and waypoint guides are also useful. Many chartbooks and marine atlases are out-of-date and of a scale useful only for planning a center-of-the-channel route. Unless you're pressed for time, you'll get the greatest enjoyment traveling along the shore and poking your bow into intimate, secluded anchorages that require more sophisticated navigational information.

Lay out your courses at least the day before a transit (using the largest-scale charts possible)—not after you are underway, when you need to focus on looking at your surroundings. Situational awareness is essential at all times. Careful preliminary chart work will familiarize you with the route's hazards and special requirements. On your large-scale paper charts, use a yellow marker to highlight every rock and hazard that is within a quarter mile either side of your intended course. Use comparable hazard-highlighting methods with your electronic charts (such as alarm circles or electronic boundary lines).

Entering waypoints from guides or from other cruisers can be helpful, but you must examine the details of the course minutely and

your own course decisions. to pay attention!

are challenging waters to navigate, so because Southeast Alaska's nautical charts are not as accurate as those along the lower Inside Passage. If you need to revisit your navigation skills, make it a priority. Do you really know what "cross track error" (XTE) means? And what "course made good" means? If you are linking your GPS/electronic charting and autopilot together, you will need to understand these concepts.

Keep in mind that electronic charting, though efficient and easy to use, must be used with caution. For example, most chart plotters "quilt" charts, but the edges of two quilted charts will not match on the screen if they are at different scales. A prime example of this is in Keku Strait (Rocky Pass): the chart mismatch occurs in exactly the most difficult stretch of the passage.

While both electronic charting and GPS facilitate safe journeys, again we stress the importance of carrying paper charts for all of the waters you plan to travel. These paper charts should be out, opened and stacked in the order of the day's passage. They provide a "big-picture" context that is lost on computer

*Coauthor, Réanne, makes serious use of her paper chart in Rocky Pass.*

screens, as well as being an essential back-up for your electronic navigation systems. If your software freezes or your electronics fail and you don't have your paper charts instantly ready, you will literally be lost.

There is yet another reason for you to use your paper charts diligently. Southeast Alaska's charts frequently contain printed "Notes" about particular areas. These notes often contain critical information that is easy to overlook on electronic charts.

Read the Sidebars placed throughout the book. They are based on personal experience and provide many cruising tips from cruisers who have gone before you and who share their joys and challenges. Some offer practical advice, such as how to work with haul-out grids, stay clear of fishing nets, or meet some of the anchoring challenges in Southeast Alaska. Others discuss how to have fun and stay safe near glaciers, the glories of whale watching, the Zen of carving totem poles, and many other experiences Southeast Alaska offers.

Don't put off your cruise until everything

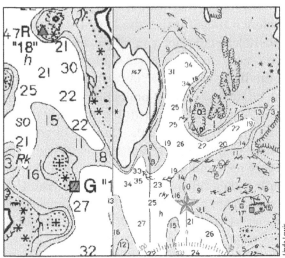

*Note the small-scale/large-scale mismatch in this electronic-chart-quilting example from Rocky Pass, near the Devils Elbow.*

is perfect. The docks are full of boaters who are forever planning their ultimate trip but never leave the harbor. All you need for a safe, satisfying and successful trip is a well-found boat, a good plan, and careful navigation backed by a vigilant skipper and an alert crew. Set a date, and by all means, go for it. You won't regret it!

## How to Use this Book

Each of the following chapters in this book covers a separate cruising area. We start from the area of Prince Rupert, B.C. and Dixon Entrance and proceed from south to north all the way to Skagway and Glacier Bay. Then we return, traveling from north to south, following the west coast of Baranof Island to Cape Chacon. An area map at the beginning of each chapter shows most of the common routes and anchorages, and serves as a quick reference to the location of channels, passages and coves found within the text. Some of the smallest coves and inlets are not shown on the chapter maps, but their entries reference a prominent landmark and you will find them on your charts. Maps on the inside front and back covers provide a graphical overview of Southeast Alaska and the areas covered by the corresponding chapters.

Each geographical entry in this book follows the same user-friendly layout as the other volumes of our *Exploring* series of guidebooks. Place name comes first, followed by the island or major body of water on which that place is located, then general location and distance from a more prominent place. *Note:* Mileages given between geographical locations are straight-line measurements, not actual course distances. Also, be aware that in the accompanying schematic diagrams, the route from an entrance waypoint to an anchor waypoint is normally *curvilinear*. This means it can rarely be followed in a straight line. You must choose your cruising route by visual means and with the use of a depth sounder. If you blindly follow a straight-line course

## Sample Layout Selection

**Still Harbor** (Whale Bay) — Place name (bay)
Still Harbor, at the entrance to Whale Bay, is 4 miles southeast of North Cape. — Distance from known point
Chart 17328 — Largest-scale chart listed first
Entrance: 56°33.91' N, 135°03.49' W
Anchor: 56°32.50' N, 135°00.96' W

> *Still Harbor . . . is about 1.5 miles N of Point Lauder. . . . The NE shore at the entrance is foul.*
>
> *The only anchorage is at the head of the harbor, and even there the swell is felt in heavy weather; this anchorage is not recommended.* (CP)

— Excerpts from official government publications (CP-*Coast Pilot*, SD-*Sailing Directions*) for emphasis or when we disagree

Still Harbor is indeed still; the entrance islets, reefs and rocks do a good job of knocking down the swells and dispersing their energy. (Our Petersburg fishing friend loves to anchor here.) We found no signs of shore stress from swell or chop and would feel free to call this a "summer home." Good anchorage can be found anywhere from north of island (30) to the head of the bay. We have seen lots of wildlife here. Avoid the rocks on the west shore; the southernmost rock extends farther from shore than charted!

— Our own recorded local knowledge based on personal experience

The fishing boat, *Mary Gene*, rode out a 95-knot storm here, proving that, when a storm is blowing in the Gulf, this anchorage may be underrated. Once again, we like the outside environment, where we can hear the surf pounding, yet we feel safe where there is no evidence of storm damage along shore—no logs at the head of the bay—and where the bottom is shallow, flat and sticky mud!

Anchor in 4 to 8 fathoms over sticky brown mud with very good holding.

— Describes in fathoms anchor position given above along with holding power

between the entrance and anchor waypoints, you may find intervening land in your path!

Each geographical entry is followed by the nautical chart number(s) for that place, with the largest-scale chart mentioned first. We provide an entrance waypoint (the lat/long for the center of the preferred channel when approaching from seaward), and recommended anchor position(s), many of which we have used ourselves.

The main body of our text comprises local knowledge, as derived by our own personal observations or obtained from other sources we believe to be reliable and knowledgeable, such as the U.S. *Coast Pilot*.

The last entry for each place-name consists of specific anchoring information for the anchor site waypoint(s) given below the heading and/or on the schematic diagram for that location. As you gain experience, you will be able to judge what consists of a protected anchorage for you and your vessel. Some anchor sites are steep-to or have limited swinging room, in which case a stern-tie to shore is required. If you find conditions different from those described in this book, double-check your position on the chart and make your own judgment about suitability for anchoring. Conditions change over the years and may have altered since the last survey. Use caution and multiple sources of information to make anchoring decisions for your vessel.

It is important to recognize that NOAA is constantly updating navigational information, based on citizen reports as well as on survey voyages. *Coast Pilot's* on-line information is updated twice monthly. Good electronic systems and/or online access let you see updates as soon as they are published. In this guide, rather than quoting *Coast Pilot* directions that may have been updated since printing, we strongly recommend using on-line resources as well as the latest print edition to stay aware of the latest information.

Some specific entries do quote *Coast Pilot* directions (shown in italics at the start of an entry), especially if we want to reinforce the remarks or if our observations differ from the information published at the time we went to press (2018).

## Anchoring

Cruising in Southeast Alaska and along the waterways of the Inside Passage is all about anchoring: once you leave the marinas and fishing resorts of lower British Columbia, finding a safe, secluded anchor site is one of the challenges and pleasures of cruising.

Indispensable equipment includes a conventional, over-sized cruising anchor (not a lightweight folding version). The CQR and Bruce anchors are common favorites of recreational boaters in Southeast Alaska. On small boats, a boat-length of chain and good nylon rode works well. On yachts 40 feet or larger, generally all-chain rodes are used. We also carry a smaller "lunch hook" to use during temporary stops or to restrict our swinging room. For security in close quarters or in deep, steep-to anchorages, we sometimes use a stern-tie to shore. Although we usually prefer to swing on a single CQR anchor, in popular

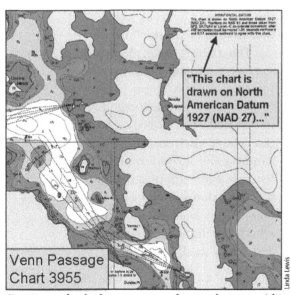

*Don't overlook the notes on charts; they provide important information.*

anchorages we try to minimize our impact by matching the mooring technique and swinging radius of other boats. Note that many larger vessels use an all-chain rode, which provides a different turning radius than boats with mostly nylon rode. (Throughout this book the term "large" vessel generally refers to those 40 feet and over: the term "small" vessel refers to boats 30 feet and under.)

Choosing your anchor site carefully and setting your anchor well assures you of a good night's sleep, even when there are occasional downslope winds or williwaws. Refer to the sidebar "Anchoring Challenges in Southeast Alaska" in Chapter 2 for a more detailed discussion. We have anchored in over 4,000 sites from Seattle to the Gulf of Alaska. The following rating system is based on our observations and experiences.

Royal Sounder *at anchor next to their own private glacier in Reid Inlet, Glacier Bay National Park*

## Definitions Used for Holding Power

**Excellent—very good holding**
Anchor digs in deeper as you pull on it—the preferred bottom in a blow, but a rare find—usually thick, sticky mud or clay.

**Good holding**
Generally sufficient for overnight anchorage in fair weather—anchor digs in but may drag or pull out on strong pull. Common in mud/sand combination or hard sand.

**Fair holding**
Adequate for temporary anchorage in fair weather, but boat should not be left unattended. Bottom of light sand, gravel with some rocks, grass or kelp or a thin layer of mud over a hard bottom. Anchor watch desirable.

**Poor holding**
Can be used for a temporary stop in fair weather only. Bottom is typically rocky with a lot of grass or kelp, or a very thin layer of mud and sand—insufficient to properly bury anchor. Anchor watch at all times is recommended.

**Steep-to**
Depth of water may decrease from 10 fathoms to ½ fathom in as little as one boat length! (Approach at dead-slow recommended.) Use a shore tie to minimize swinging and to keep anchor pulling uphill.

## Anchor Diagrams

We have included anchor diagrams for sites we feel would be helpful. These diagrams show simply the approximate routes we took, the typical depths we found and the places

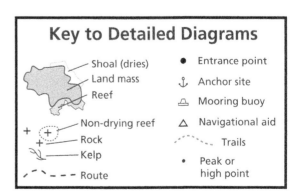

we anchored. Please note that these diagrams, which are non-representational and not to scale, do not include all known or unknown hazards and should always be used with caution and self-verification.

## Measurements and Other Conventions Used in this Book

Unless otherwise noted, the depths listed in this book's text or shown on diagrams are always given in fathoms, regardless of the measurement units on cited charts; depths are also reduced to approximate zero tide (mean lower low water). When you use the depth numbers on our diagrams, you should add the amount of tide listed in the tide tables. If there is a minus tide, you subtract the number from the depth number. Be sure you know how to correct times in the tide tables for the exact time you are there. *Note:* U.S. Chart 17372 in the Rocky Pass area is the only chart in Southeast Alaska that measures depths in feet.

Bearings and courses, when given in this book by the authors, are generally magnetic and identified as such. (Please note that the bearings given in the occasional *Coast Pilot* quotes—in italics—are always stated in true bearings.) Courses are taken off the chart compass rose; they are approximate and are to be "made good." No allowances have been made for deviation, current or drift. Monitor cross track error if using GPS and "crab" as necessary to stay on proper track over ground. When compass cardinal points are used (e.g., NW or SE), these refer to true bearings and should be taken as approximate only.

Unless otherwise stated, distances are expressed in nautical miles and speed is expressed in knots. Scales on the diagrams are expressed in yards, meters and miles as noted and are approximate only. Time is given in four-digit, 24-hour clock numbers; all courses are given in three digits.

Latitude and longitude in the text are cited in degrees, minutes and decimal minutes to the nearest hundredth of a minute and are taken from the largest-scale chart available, (Seconds are not used.) These lat/longs are to be treated as approximate only. Many of the referenced charts are not accurate—nor can

---

### NAVIGATIONAL DATUM ISSUES

The horizontal datum on almost all of the U.S. charts in Southeast Alaska is NAD83 (North American Datum), which is basically or very nearly the same as the GPS system default of WGS84 (World Geodetic Survey). All waypoint entries in this book are NAD83 (WGS 84), except the insets on Chart 17372 for Rocky Pass (which are NAD27).

If you are attempting to plot a NAD83 fix from GPS coordinates onto a NAD27 paper chart, you must adjust for the difference between the two horizontal datum systems. This difference increases with latitude. See the Notes on your paper-charts for the exact offset, as it differs from chart to chart.

Be alert when exiting from Prince Rupert to Dixon Entrance via Venn Passage. The Canadian paper chart for Venn Passage (3955) is based on the NAD27 horizontal datum. If your GPS is not also set to NAD27 for this short passage, you can be longitudinally off-position by as much as 300-600 feet! Mariners using traditional paper-chart navigation methods must make this GPS adjustment themselves. A number of electronic charting systems automatically "convert" to the WGS84 horizontal datum in areas where the NAD27 datum is encountered.

Note that many Canadian charts throughout B.C. waters are based on NAD 27 horizontal datum. A word of caution: it has been reported by experienced mariners that not all electronic charting systems automatically adjust for horizontal datum. In addition, some vendors will tell you the electronic charts themselves have been adjusted for horizontal datum, while other vendors will tell you the software does the adjusting. Be prudent and check with your charting software vendor before you begin your cruise through the Inside Passage.

—DD

they be read accurately—to one-hundredth of a minute. We have approximated this last digit to provide as complete a picture as possible.

Spelling and usage of place names follows, as closely as possible, local tradition and the lead of the *U.S. Coast Pilot*. We have documented many small, unnamed coves and bays and, in each case, have tried to use local names. However, where we could find no reference to an anchor site, we assigned a new name that seemed appropriate.

## U.S. Customs and Border Protection

NEXUS is a mechanism for expediting your border crossings in both directions—between the U.S. and B.C.—by telephone check-in. To use it, every person on your boat must have a NEXUS card. www.getnexus.com Only certain designated ports qualify for NEXUS entry https://www.cbp.gov/travel/pleasure-boats-private-flyers/pleasure-boat-locations/ak. When you phone the customs control number on your NEXUS card, you will receive an entry clearance number that must be displayed on your boat. Proceed directly to your designated entry port—generally Ketchikan, although there are other southeast Alaskan entry ports in Wrangell, Skagway, Juneau, and Sitka. You may have a possible inspection at the discretion of the Customs service, but you are not required to wait at the Customs dock for that inspection.

Without NEXUS check-in, all boats (U.S. and foreign) heading from Canadian waters to Southeast Alaska must clear customs in Ketchikan, approximately 120 miles northwest of Prince Rupert, B.C., and obtain a clearance number. All persons on board must have a passport, regardless of age.

Most boaters heading from Prince Rupert to Ketchikan do not want to (or cannot) make the long trip in one day. However, U.S. Customs and Border Protection does not permit northbound boats to anchor in U.S. waters without having cleared Customs. If you anchor, you have touched land and may be subject to penalties.

Several solutions exist to this Southeast Alaska challenge. One is to anchor overnight as far north as possible in British Columbia (e.g., in Brundige Inlet on Dundas Island), and make the transit to Ketchikan the next day.

Alternatively, you may anchor in Foggy Bay as an interim stop. This option requires prior approval from the U.S. Customs office in Ketchikan, which requests that recreational cruisers plan ahead and do the following:

1. Telephone the Ketchikan Customs office from Prince Rupert using a land line between 6 a.m. and 6 p.m. (907.225.2254).

U.S. cell phones may not work in Prince Rupert; Canadian cell phones may not work in Alaska. (If you have a cell phone and cruise close to Cape Fox at the northeast edge of Dixon Entrance, you may be able to pick up a U.S. cell signal.)

2. Ask the Ketchikan Customs officer to approve anchoring in U.S. waters. Foggy Bay is their approved location for interim anchoring. They will ask you for specific information and give you permission to anchor.

3. You still must clear Customs upon your arrival in Ketchikan. It is not permissible to take side trips until you do so. Ketchikan does not have a Customs dock so once you reach your destination marina, call Customs from your cell or land line. Don't forget to post your clearance number in your window and record it in the ship's log. No one may leave or board the boat, other than Customs officers, until clearance has been given.

4. Ketchikan has a 100 percent boarding policy for recreational boaters. However, if every person on board your vessel has a NEXUS card, at their discretion, Ketchikan Customs can choose to accept your NEXUS information by telephone and will likely give you a clearance number and elect not to board you.

# Internet Resources on Navigation, Weather, Tides, U.S. Customs, and Cruising Information

The websites listed below cover a variety of topics, beginning with the more technical navigation, Customs, and weather sites, followed by Southeast Alaska cruising information. Many towns and harbors in Southeast Alaska also have websites. Additional websites are referenced throughout this book. Please remember that website addresses change over time and may not always work. You are responsible for checking the timeliness and reliability of any information you find.

Remember that you may not have internet access in remote areas. Plan accordingly and download information to your laptop or storage device, and consider printing paper copies of critical information like tide tables and charts updates.

## U.S. *Coast Pilot* 8—includes Southeast Alaska
As mentioned in the text, U.S. *Coast Pilot* is updated biweekly. Download the most recent .pdf files and use word search to find and review your areas of interest.
https://nauticalcharts.noaa.gov/publications/coast-pilot/index.html

## The U.S.C.G. Navigation Center of Excellence
This site provides links to current operations and safety information, as well as notices to mariners.
http://www.navcen.uscg.gov/

## American Practical Navigator—Bowditch
This is a highly regarded, technical navigation reference published by the U.S. Government and periodically updated. The links below go to the 2002 version; a new version is expected in 2018. Download it to your laptop and use the search function.
https://en.wikisource.org/wiki/The_American_Practical_Navigator
http://www.1yachtua.com/nauticalcharts/downloads/Practical_navigator.pdf

## NOAA Charts
This easy-to-use site includes links to chart locaters for both paper and electronic charts (locate both graphically and by name/location) and the Coast Pilot. Each chart link lists the scale, edition, and print date, so you can keep track of latest versions. You can view charts on line, download .pdfs, or purchase paper copies from a list of approved vendors. NOAA sites are undergoing reorganization, so links may have changed since press time.
http://www.charts.noaa.gov/InteractiveCatalog/nrnc.shtml

## Chart No. 1—Symbols, Abbreviations & Terms
It is important to be familiar with U.S. chart symbology and terms, and the keys are found on Chart No. 1. A U.S. government edition is available for free download at: https://www.nauticalcharts.noaa.gov/publications/us-chart-1.html

A paper copy may be easier to use and commercial versions of Chart No. 1 are widely available.

## National Data Buoy Center
This website gives you the current-time wind speed and sea states at specific buoys. For example, to help you make choices about the timing of your Dixon Entrance crossing, look up: Station 46145—Central Dixon Entrance Buoy. You can search by buoy name, number, location, or graphically.
http://www.ndbc.noaa.gov/

## National Dial-a-Buoy
This is an excellent telephone source for wind and wave measurements taken within the last hour at specific locations. Dial-a-Buoy can also read the latest NWS marine forecast for most station locations. Dial 888.701.8992 and enter a station name or a lat/long. Visit the website for instructions and station names.
http://www.ndbc.noaa.gov/dial.shtml

### National Weather Service Weather Radio Station Coverage map:
http://www.nws.noaa.gov/nwr/Maps/PHP/AK-se.php

### National Weather Service Weather Radio Station Listings:
http://www.nws.noaa.gov/nwr/Maps/PHP/AK-se.php - Station

### NOAA National Weather Service Marine Forecasts
The link below goes to the entrance portal for marine forecasts. Review to find the forecast for your area of interest.
http://www.weather.gov/om/marine/alaska.htm

A low band-width version is also available at
http://www.nws.noaa.gov/om/marine/wxiakcwf.htm

### Tides Predictions in Alaska
The website includes information about how tides work, as well as tabular and graphical representation of tide predictions at many Alaskan sites.
https://tidesandcurrents.noaa.gov/tide_predictions.html?gid=1391

### Current Predictions in Alaska
The website includes graphical and tabular current data for many Alaskan sites.
https://tidesandcurrents.noaa.gov/noaacurrents/Stations?g=693

### U.S. Customs and Border Protection
Abundant information, but a challenge to navigate. This is the site where you can purchase your "User Fee Decal" online. Customs information is changing all the time: https://www.cbp.gov/

## SOUTHEAST ALASKA CRUISING RESOURCES:

### Alaska Marine Highway
Ferry system information.
http://www.dot.state.ak.us/amhs/

### General Alaska Information
Information by location; phone numbers; links to other websites.
www.alaskajourney.com/southeast/index.html

### Alaska Recreation Areas and Parks
Guide to Alaska state parks and cabins, with information on trails, reservations, etc.
http://www.dnr.state.ak.us/parks/units/southeast/seindex.htm

### Alaska Department of Fish and Game Sport Fishing
Information on sport fishing in Southeast Alaska: regulations, areas, tips and tricks
http://www.adfg.alaska.gov/index.cfm?adfg=fishingSport.main

### Alaska Rainforest Islands
Website with trip ideas, activities, event calendars, merchants, lodging, outfitters, etc. for the area around Prince of Wales and Wrangell Islands: http://www.alaskarainforestislands.org/

### Fine Edge Nautical & Recreational Publishing
This website is hosted by Fine Edge, the publishers of this book. Along with a wide array of other cruising guidebooks and planning maps, both for Southeast Alaska and worldwide, the website includes boaters' experiences and cruising tips.
Fine Edge now publishes the annually updated Waggoner Guide. Although focused on cruising the Inside Passage from Washington through British Columbia to Ketchikan, the Guide is rich with information for cruisers ultimately headed for Southeast Alaska. There is no better online source for the most up-to-date, understandable information on U.S. and B.C. Customs issues for Inside Passage cruisers.
http://fineedge.com/

### Cave Art Press
This website is hosted by the authors of this book. The site lists cruising maps for the west coast of North America, from Baja to Prince William Sound, as well as other interesting books, including Don Douglass's autobiography and Réanne Hemingway Douglass's survival story of a pitchpole in the Great Southern Ocean.
www.caveartpress.com

—LW

If you enter U.S. waters and encounter serious weather that endangers your vessel and/or crew, or other circumstances (e.g., illness) that prevent you from completing your journey to Ketchikan, contact the USCG via VHF radio. They will relay your request for permission to anchor to Ketchikan Customs. (The USCG does not routinely involve itself in Customs issues.)

## Internet and Other Resources

You will find references to internet websites throughout this book. Of course, website addresses change over time. You are responsible for checking the timeliness and reliability of any information you find on a website. See the sidebar "Internet Resources" for some of these references related to navigation, weather, U.S. Customs, and general cruising information.

While you are underway in Southeast Alaska, your ability to find a wifi internet connection from your boat will depend a great deal upon your geographical location (major ports) and even where your boat is moored in a particular marina.

Here is a communications tip: Try your cell phone whenever you are in the vicinity of a "MICRO" tower, as indicated on your nautical chart. Cell equipment is being systematically added to these existing structures. You will be surprised how often you can get a signal while far from a port. Examples include Cape Fox, Kake, outside the entrance to Baranof Warm Springs, and outside Hoonah Harbor to about a mile away from the entrance to Glacier Bay National Park.

Additional resources include published guidebooks and promotional literature from Chambers of Commerce and similar organizations. Useful information on events and attractions can be found, but make sure your source is current before planning a long side trip to attend an event that may no longer be happening. Numerous specialty guidebooks address

*Fend off bergie bits and proceed very slowly.*

particular interests such as kayaking, fishing, archeology, and ethnology. The Bibliography at the end of this book includes notes on many additional sources of information.

## Navigating the Inside Passage

Navigation to Alaska through the Inside Passage consists largely of selecting appropriate point-to-point routes and avoiding traffic, logs and other flotsam, and reefs and rocks. You can usually spot any hazards visually, since even low clouds do not greatly interfere with visibility, except in fog. Pre-setting GPS waypoint routes using paper or electronic charting is recommended in case visibility decreases; this also gives you a useful monitor on your progress and an idea of current, drift, or distance remaining on your route.

For lengthy crossings of open water, it's best to start very early in the morning after you've received a favorable weather report and before the prevailing wind comes up. (Remember, light comes early in these latitudes.) Visible landmarks may be too far away to be helpful, so GPS-guided charting is useful to keep you on track and help you judge your progress.

Most fjords and protected inside channels are steep-to. Stay near the center of the channel to take maximum advantage of a favorable current, or follow the shore to pick up back eddies when currents are against you. In long channels that are open on both ends, such as Wrangell Narrows and Keku Strait (Rocky Pass), opposing currents meet midway through the passage. With proper timing, you can ride the last of the flood to enter and catch the first of the ebb on the "downhill" to exit.

Except for Wrangell Narrows, which has the highest concentration of buoys and aids to navigation anywhere in the Inside Passage, the number of buoys and lighthouses decreases the further north you go. Boaters looking to get away from well-traveled commercial waterways can find areas in Alaska where it's possible to go for days or weeks without passing an aid to navigation. Your GPS receiver and electronic charting can offset this sparseness of nav-aids.

## Global Positioning System (GPS)

Over the last decade, GPS has become a major factor in the safe navigation of the Inside Passage, and particularly in Southeast Alaska. For old-timers like us, who learned to navigate the hard way, it's an unbelievable tool with magic powers. In the hands of a trained skipper, a GPS receiver is easily worth two full-time navigational assistants on the bridge (one giving you accurate full-time positions,

---

### Cell Phone and Internet Access in Southeast Alaska
#### Elsie Hulsizer

Phone and internet access is important in SE Alaska, not only for communicating with family and friends, but also for applying for permits for Glacier Bay and bear observatories, for buying fishing licenses, and for ordering parts.

On one of our first trips to SE Alaska, I read the mystery, *Murder at Five Finger Light* by Sue Henry. The resolution of the mystery depended on a cell phone call from the lighthouse area. I was skeptical. Was there really cell phone service out in the middle of Stephens Passage? But later that year we met volunteers who worked at the light. They assured me the author had visited the light and confirmed it had cell service.

Five Finger isn't the only cellphone hotspot in remote locations in SE Alaska's waters. We've found service in Ratz Bay on Prince of Wales Island, offshore Gambier Bay on Admiralty Island, near Sisters Island in Icy Strait, in Cross Sound within view of Cape Spencer, in Chatham Strait offshore of Warm Springs Bay and off the lighthouse on Tee Point. There are probably others.

Most towns in SE Alaska have cell service. Some very small towns that don't have real service do have accidental hot spots: the helicopter pad at Meyers Chuck, the boat ramp at Edna Bay and the boardwalk in Elfin Cove. We've heard reports of service at the dump in Pelican (watch out for bears). To find a hotspot, look for groups of people standing around.

Check with your cellphone provider before leaving for Alaska to make sure you have coverage. Depending on the provider and plan, U.S. cellular companies may have no service in either Alaska or Canada (or both), or partial service, such as talk and text only. Service maps can be misleading or confusing so check in person. Some U.S. providers charge a fee for service in Canada, so it's best to arrange that before leaving. For Canadians, buying a U.S. prepaid phone in Alaska may be a good solution to getting service.

In large ports with cruise ship docks, cell phone service can be appreciably slower when ships are in port.

Alaska also has an excellent library system with wifi and/or computers with internet. Once we walked into the empty library at Coffman Cove on Prince of Wales Island, sat down at computers and checked our email – all without seeing a librarian.

Depending on your provider, and if your cell phone is setup as a personal wifi hotspot, you may get internet access almost anywhere there is cell phone service.

the other giving you steering, course headings, distance to go, drift, heading, distance made good).

In unfamiliar territory, GPS readings can verify your position. For cruisers who use electronic charting, the GPS-indicated position (in the form of your boat's icon) moves along the chart itself, giving you more freedom to watch outside the boat. In conditions of limited visibility, you can use GPS readings to determine which direction to head and the distance to travel. But, while GPS and electronic charting are excellent navigational tools—essential for any boat on a tight schedule and a desirable tool for everyone else—you should use them only in conjunction with other means of navigation and allow for their limitations.

One of the specific constraints on cruising with GPS in Southeast Alaska is the issue of GPS signal reception in this mountainous region; the other is the issue of GPS accuracy versus Southeast Alaska charts' accuracy. Both issues should be viewed as important limitations when cruising these waters.

Whether you have GPS equipment that is un-enhanced, or augmented by DGPS, WAAS, or other systems, you face an important GPS signal problem, because Southeast Alaska is a mountainous area with many high-walled fjords. This kind of terrain results in a loss of GPS satellite signals on low orbits and signal refraction throughout these abundant high-mountain walls, resulting in transmission-induced errors. These circumstances compromise your ability to rely entirely on your GPS. Remember also that the GPS system as a whole is certainly not foolproof.

In Alaska, you will also find many instances where the GPS and the chart do not agree. Your GPS latitude and longitude read one way, but your boat icon (or your position fix on your paper chart using the GPS figures) is near or sitting on land! What to trust? Of the two, in Southeast Alaska, it is more likely that the chart is inaccurate. That message is worth underscoring: Southeast Alaska charts are frequently small scale, based on old surveys, and have many inaccuracies. It is important to remember that Southeast Alaska is a geologically dynamic area subject to seismic activity, uplift, and rapid sedimentation. Many coves and inlets are shallower than their chart data indicates, especially in areas where seismic

*Birds don't stand on the water! Keep a vigilant watch for logs.*

*The march of the navigation aids in Wrangell Narrows*

events have modified the bottom configuration or glaciers have recently receded, like Glacier Bay. Practice great caution.

The important point in this discussion is that in Southeast Alaska you cannot rely as heavily on chart accuracy and GPS signal as you do in less remote areas. You need to be vigilant, surveying your surroundings at all times and processing information from a variety of instruments and other sources. Practicing constant situational awareness is the only way to safely navigate these waters.

Don't wait until you're surrounded by a fog bank to program your route. It's too nerve-racking, and the chances of your making an error are greatly increased. Furthermore, you should maintain an adequate margin of safety in all GPS work, so you don't encounter any nasty surprises.

GPS and electronic charting, like radar, require that you have adequate proficiency before you try to push the limits, so make a point of practicing with your instruments in port or in home waters. Competence in GPS and electronic charting can be one of the more important skills you develop for safe navigation.

As a check on GPS signal data, especially in limited visibility, compare your depth sounder readings against the depths indicated on the charts for a given GPS lat/long. If the data differ very much, start asking why, and try to determine the reason. If nothing makes sense, slow down and head to deeper waters until you're sure of your data. Obviously, in tight situations, you should not rely on GPS alone, but should use traditional techniques—an alert bow watch, radar, sightings by hand compass or binoculars with internal compass to track land reference points, and a depth sounder. Remember, a good pair of binoculars can be your best investment!

## U.S. Chart Symbols and Charts

At press time in 2018, NOAA (National Oceanic and Atmospheric Administration) information is available for free download from the NOAA website. NOAA responsibilities include the National Weather Service, coastal information including tides, currents and charting, and fisheries regulation. Spend some time reviewing the website to see what's available. Charts are available for online or downloaded viewing.

Familiarize yourself with existing American chart symbols and abbreviations, by referring to *Chart No. 1 United States of America Nautical Chart (Symbols, Abbreviations and Terms)*.

In this book, we specify the charts needed and/or recommended for cruising in Southeast Alaska. The online version of the NOAA nautical chart catalog that allows users to search by area or chart number may be found at: http://www.charts.noaa.gov/InteractiveCatalog/nrnc.shtml

The catalog and online charts are updated weekly; existing versions go quickly out of date. For the most up-to-date information on charts and their latest editions and corrections dates, visit the NOAA website: https://www.nauticalcharts.noaa.gov

Many other U.S. government navigation-related documents are available for free download. Having the current edition of the *Coast Pilot* for Southeast Alaska downloaded to your laptop can be a real asset: the U.S. government's free, downloadable version is in .pdf format, with its attendant easy word-search function. Go to: https://nauticalcharts.noaa.gov/publications/coast-pilot/index.html for the most current edition of U.S. *Coast Pilot 8—Pacific Coast Alaska: Dixon Entrance to Cape Spencer.*

The bible of navigation: *American Practical Navigator—Bowditch* is available for free download from numerous sites: search for Download Bowditch Free.

## Canadian Charts and Symbols

For B.C. waters, study Canadian Chart 1 (*Symbols, Abbreviations and Terms*) to become familiar with Canadian Chart symbols. Remember that Canadian charts report depths in metric units, U.S. charts *report depths in **fathoms**.*

Canada does not make its publications or nautical charts available for free download.

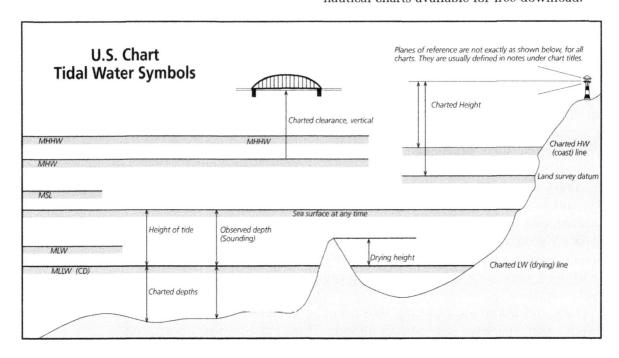

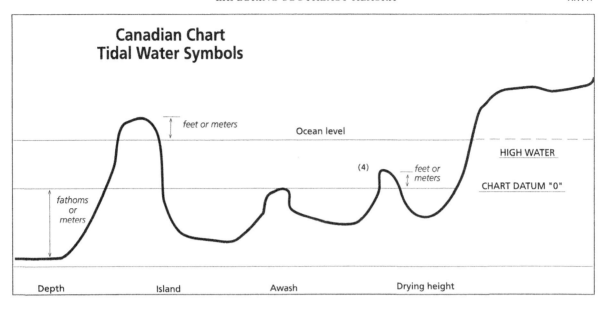

## Weather and Sea Conditions

Contrary to its reputation among outsiders, Southeast Alaska enjoys a mild summer climate, although it also receives its fair share of rain—some places measure rain in feet rather than in inches. The summer season between May and early September usually brings periods of exceptionally beautiful weather, however each summer season is unique. We have experienced some weeks with 90 percent rain and 10 percent sun, and others just the opposite. Horizontal visibility is generally good unless you encounter fog. The North Pacific high usually brings mornings of calm seas and light breezes, which allow you to move toward your next destination before the afternoon prevailing breezes pick up and the "rippled" seas give way to 1- to 3-foot chop. Additional climate information may be found in a brochure from the National Weather Service at: http://www.weather.gov/media/ajk/brochures/Summer%20Climate%20Guide%202016.pdf

Sea conditions, along with fog, clouds and rain, can be important hazards to cruising boats. Tidal current opposing a wind can cause sharp, breaking seas and uncomfortable conditions for a boat and its crew. Winds of 5 to 15 knots opposing a tidal current can cause the chop to double in height to the point where it starts to break. As winds increase to near-gale force (20 to 30 knots) against an opposing current, seas build to a nasty, breaking chop that can become dangerous for small craft. Although these conditions are infrequent in summer, it is best to anticipate the weather and be prepared to seek shelter until conditions ease. If you plan to cross open waters, set out in the early morning before prevailing winds come up to ensure a more comfortable crossing. This applies particularly to Dixon Entrance, Clarence Strait, Chatham Strait, Peril Strait and Lynn Canal.

*VHF reception becomes limited in steep-walled fiords and mountainous terrain.*

## Beware of Paralytic Shellfish Poisoning

The shellfish of the Pacific Northwest, including bivalves like clams, mussels, oysters, scallops, as well as some whelks and snails, are filter feeders. They pump sea water through their digestive systems, filtering out and consuming algae and other food particles. This process can make shellfish dangerous to humans and other creatures that eat shellfish, because certain species of algae produce poisonous biotoxins. These single-celled dinoflagellates are generally present in sea water at low concentrations year-round. However, during algal "blooms," the concentration of toxin-producing algae in the water increases, and large amounts of biotoxin accumulate in shellfish tissues. It can take several days to months, or even longer, for shellfish to flush the toxins from their systems. Although there are anecdotal accounts of lower-risk months, the exact combination of factors that contribute to algal blooms is not yet known.

Paralytic Shellfish Poisoning (PSP) results from consumption of these biotoxins. The biotoxins block normal neuron function and can lead to death from paralysis of the breathing muscles. Some biotoxins are 1,000 times more potent than cyanide, and the toxin levels contained in a single shellfish can be fatal to humans. In 1793, PSP poisoned members of Captain George Vancouver's survey crews after the men gathered and consumed mussels. PSP deaths have also been documented in wildlife populations such as sea otters and humpback whales.

In humans, symptoms of PSP include tingling or numbness that starts around the lips and mouth and spreads to the face and neck. Prickly sensations occur in the fingertips and toes, accompanied with headache and dizziness. Muscle weakness, nausea, and vomiting can also occur. Severe poisoning can produce tingling or burning in the arms and legs, incoherent speech, lack of coordination and breathing difficulties.

Do not underestimate the seriousness of PSP. There is no antidote. If you suspect that someone has PSP, seek immediate medical attention. Induce vomiting to expel shellfish from the stomach. Treat for shock and transport the victim as quickly as possible to a medical facility. Life support services may be necessary to sustain the victim's life. Once treated, the reduction of symptoms usually occurs within 9 hours, with complete recovery in 24 hours.

To reduce your risk of PSP, you should not eat self-harvested shellfish, but purchase it from a reputable seafood retailer or shellfish farm that is required to sell only tested products. Neither cooking nor freezing eliminates the biotoxin from shellfish. Since crabs feed on shellfish, the guts/butter of crabs has been found to contain the biotoxin, although it is not known to accumulate in crab meat. Therefore, consumers of non-commercially harvested crab should clean the meat thoroughly, discard the guts/butter before boiling, and avoid drinking the broth in which the crab was boiled.

If you consider harvesting shellfish, you should take into account the recent history of PSP in the area, the species harvested and their ability to concentrate and retain biotoxins, and the method of cleaning and preparing the shellfish. You should also be aware that the color of the seawater is not a reliable indicator of toxic shellfish. Just because red tide is not present does not mean absence of danger. Listen regularly for local PSP alerts on the weather channel. There is no Alaskan closure hotline, but Canadian shellfish closure notices are updated on the Fishing Information Lines at 604-666-2828 / 1-800-431-3474; and notices are available online. Consult the map of Biotoxin Management Areas and be aware of closure notices.

—LW

### State of Alaska Shellfish Poisoning Resources:
http://dhss.alaska.gov/dph/Epi/id/Pages/dod/psp/default.aspx

Alaska PSP fact sheet:
http://dec.alaska.gov/eh/pdf/fss/resources-shellfish-guide-paralytic-shellfish-poisoning.pdf

Map of Biotoxin Management Areas for Canada:
http://www.pac.dfo-mpo.gc.ca/fm-gp/contamination/biotox/index-eng.htm

Biotoxin and Sanitary Contamination Closure notices for Canada:
http://www-ops2.pac.dfo-mpo.gc.ca/fns-sap/index-eng.cfm?pg=view_notice&lang=en&ID=recreational&ispsp=1

BC Centre for Disease Control
http://www.bccdc.ca/health-info/diseases-conditions/paralytic-shellfish-poisoning

Washington State Department of Health: http://www.doh.wa.gov/CommunityandEnvironment/Shellfish/BiotoxinsIllnessPrevention/Biotoxins/ParalyticShellfishPoison

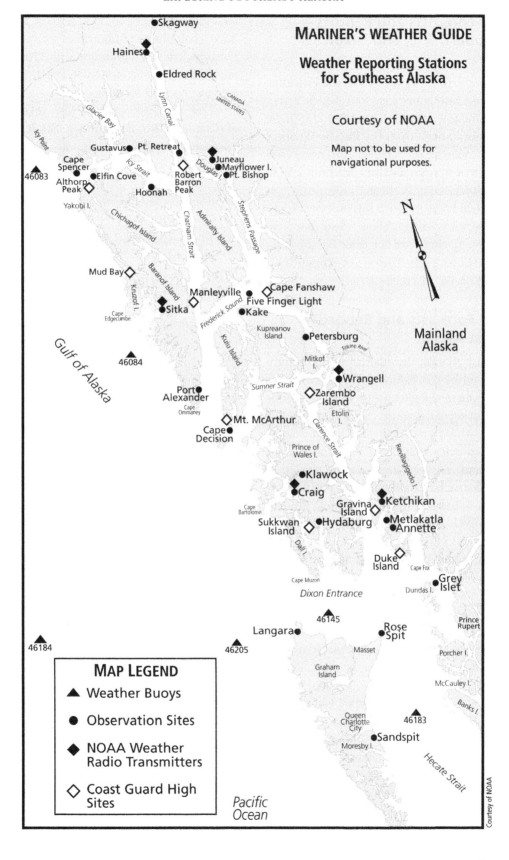

## Weather Forecasts and Reports—Prince Rupert, B.C., and Dixon Entrance

Forecasts for Prince Rupert and Dixon Entrance are prepared and broadcast four times a day (at approximately 0400; 1030; 1600; 2130) by Environment Canada from the Pacific Weather Centre in Vancouver. These forecasts are rebroadcast 24 hours a day on continuous VHF weather channels and through repeater stations, and can be heard with satisfactory reception all the way to Ketchikan. You can also receive B.C. marine weather forecasts by telephoning 604.664.9010. (Please see Appendix C for key VHF radio channels.)

## Weather Forecasts and Reports—Southeast Alaska

In Southeast Alaska, the marine weather forecast is issued by the National Weather Service (NWS) in Juneau at 0400 and 1600 for a 24-hour period, then repeated about every five minutes on VHF Weather Channel 1 or 2. This forecast is also repeated twice a day by the U.S. Coast Guard (morning and evening) and—during the summer—by Glacier Bay National Park. NWS transmitters are located in Yakutat, Haines, Juneau, Sitka, Wrangell, Annette Island (Ketchikan) and Craig. The working range of each broadcast station is only about 20 to 40 miles; the mountainous terrain of Southeast Alaska generally limits VHF reception. The NOAA website shows a map of likely weather radio reception https://www.weather.gov/nwr/alaska-se, but variations in local conditions make such maps unreliable. Repeater stations are located at Mt. Robert Barron, Althorp Peak, Duffield Penninsula, Cape Fanshaw, Manleyville, Zarembo Island, Mt. McArthur, Sukkwan Island, Gravina Island and Duke Island. These repeater stations increase the ability of boaters to hear VHF weather transmissions. Throughout the day each one provides hourly observations of wind, temperature and barometric pressure at their respective locations, and they include buoy reports. If you have a cell phone connection, you can also hear these reports by telephoning 907.790.6850 and navigating a menu until you reach the forecast for your desired location.

The forecast covers the inside waters of Clarence Strait, Sumner Strait, Stephens Passage, Chatham Strait, Frederick Sound, Lynn Canal, Icy Strait, Cross Sound and Glacier Bay, as well as the outside waters from Dixon Entrance to Cape Fairweather.

Once you leave the main channels and venture out on your own, you're usually out of range of VHF weather broadcasts. Misty Fiords, Glacier Bay, the west coast of Prince of Wales Island and a number of other places—as much as half of Southeast Alaska—have little or no VHF broadcast reception. If you urgently need weather information and have no VHF reception, it is permissible to contact the Coast Guard and ask for a weather update, although in some areas, you may not even be able to reach the Coast Guard by VHF.

However, you can generally manage quite well by making your own educated guesses, by contacting other boats to ask what conditions they're experiencing or by telephoning the NOAA weather numbers where possible. Some boaters carry satellite phones for emergency use, however similar caveats apply: high cliffs surrounding narrow waterways inhibit signal transmission and reception.

If you have an Internet connection, the National Data Buoy Center at http://www.ndbc.noaa.gov provides information on the current-time wind and sea states. You may be particularly interested in Buoy 46145—Central Dixon Entrance (54°38' N-132°45' W) for planning your initial entry (from the Prince Rupert area) into Southeast Alaska across Dixon Entrance.

You can also get a Southeast Alaska four-day weather forecast in text format from the National Weather Service Marine Forecast site at http://www.nws.noaa.gov/om/marine/wxiakcwf.htm

## Semi-annual Weather Patterns: Spring and Summer

The weather in Southeast Alaska follows a general semi-annual pattern. Changes are associated with the building up or breaking down of the North Pacific High around the times of the spring and fall equinoxes.

Following the late winter storms, from about March 21, the North Pacific High begins to build up far off the western shore of Vancouver Island. This more or less permanent high-pressure zone deflects most summer lows into the Gulf of Alaska, where they either dissipate or take a varied path that affects Southeast weather. We recommend waiting until the Pacific High is well established—generally early to mid-May—before you head north of Dixon Entrance.

During the summer months, in times of stable high pressure, Southeast Alaska experiences a daily pattern of diurnal micro-weather that is quite predictable. Nights are usually quite calm and quiet over the entire length of Southeast Alaska, with fog or low clouds moving on shore. In the afternoon, moderate northwest breezes pick up, dissipating the fog and clouds and creating 1- to 3-foot chop until evening, when conditions become calm again. During such periods, most weather stations report a high percentage of light winds with little or moderate precipitation—conditions that provide for good cruising.

Although low pressure fronts do manage to evade the North Pacific High and hit the West Coast, they usually occur at intervals of one to three weeks in Southeast Alaska. These fronts are usually announced by a falling barometer and a change in both the direction and intensity of the wind, as well as by clouds and precipitation. They normally last just a day or two and are well forecast. It is best to remain securely in a sheltered harbor or cove during the approach of unstable weather.

*Fog is ubiquitous in Southeast Alaska; hone your radar skills before you go.*

Sometimes in Southeast, these fronts stall out and linger before picking up strength and heading north. When this happens, their timing and path are less predictable than the fronts that occur farther south.

Summer storms are not as intense as winter storms, but they can still pack a dangerous wallop to small craft. Although gale force winds of up to 40 knots do occur, they are infrequent.

The farther north you go in Southeast Alaska, the lower the (barometric) pressure can become, and the more the wind intensifies. Winds of 30 knots are not uncommon, and occasional gale force winds occur in the summer. (From autumn to spring, gale force winds occur frequently.) In certain east-west channels, such as Peril Strait, Cross Sound, Icy Strait, Frederick Sound, and Sumner Strait, you may experience strong easterlies at the very time a southerly is shrieking up the north-south channels. After the passage of the front, local channel winds generally reverse 180 degrees and blow hard for a day or two.

Take all these summer storms or deep, low-pressure fronts seriously. Record barometric pressure and monitor weather broadcasts frequently. Make a practice of taking written notes on forecasts to use as you travel beyond the range of weather radio. When you observe signs that a storm is developing or hear a report of an impending storm, head directly for an anchor site that offers protection from south or east winds. Take appropriate precautions for safety, such as maintaining sufficient swinging room and a well-set anchor. It is always a good idea to record bearings on fixed objects to detect if your anchor is dragging.

## Semi-annual Weather Patterns: Fall and Winter

Near the autumnal equinox (about September 21), the North Pacific High begins to collapse and the first major low pressure fronts return, bringing foul weather and precipitation. Without the protection of a strong North Pacific High, about 10 to 20 low-pressure fronts per month affect Southeast Alaska. During some of these storms, barometric pressure drops as low as 960 millibars, bringing hurricane force winds of over 60 knots. In winter, prevailing winds are from the southeast, with heavy precipitation and high, dangerous seas. For this reason, we suggest that you head south of Dixon Entrance by early September and, if you're planning to continue south on the outside of Vancouver Island, it's a good idea to round Cape Scott by late August or early September to avoid being caught north of Brooks Peninsula in a series of lows. Although both the west and east coasts of Vancouver Island normally have fine weather in September and October, it's a good idea to head to protected waters south of Estevan Point or Chatham Point.

## Barometric Pressure and Wind Velocities

Wind velocity tends to occur in direct proportion to the barometric pressure gradient—the rate of rise or fall of pressure. Falling barometric pressure that descends 1 millibar per hour usually means strong winds of 20 to 30 knots; a drop of 2 millibars per hour means gales of 35 to 45 knots; a drop of 3 millibars per hour brings storm force winds of 50 to 60 knots. On the contrary, a rising barometer of 1 millibar per hour brings strong to gale-force winds of 25 to 40 knots.

By noting barometric pressure hourly in your ship's log, or by using a recording barometer, you can visualize this gradient of pressure and prepare for expected wind and sea conditions.

## Wind Rotation

In the Northern Hemisphere, winds flow clockwise around a high-pressure cell and counterclockwise around a low-pressure cell. In other words, in the Northern Hemisphere, with the wind to your back, the low pressure is on your left, while the higher pressure is on your right. This simple test, and observation of the barometric pressure gradient, can give you an idea of the path of a storm cell and the strength and direction of upcoming winds. However, local topography can greatly affect the direction of the wind; by studying the movement of clouds aloft, you can get a better idea of true wind direction and strength.

## Wind Direction and Cloud Cover

Winds that arrive in advance of a low-pressure front generally blow from the south or southwest, then back (counterclockwise) to the southeast as the front approaches. The strongest winds and highest seas usually occur just ahead of the low-pressure front. With the approaching front, clouds thicken and lower, taking on an ominous appearance;

precipitation is heavy and may last for several hours. In some cases, with the passage of a low-pressure front, the wind veers (moves clockwise), first to southwest, then to northwest. During the summer after the wind veers to its prevailing northwesterly direction, it may blow hard for a day or two, as if to send all the southern air back where it originated. We have experienced our lumpiest crossings of Dixon Entrance when we set out too soon after the barometer "bottomed out" and the wind veered to the west.

If high pressure over the interior sends strong outflow or arctic winds—with cold dry winds building from the northeast along with a rising barometer—quickly seek shelter from down-channel winds and seas. The eastern edge of Dixon Entrance, Portland Canal and Douglas Channel are notorious for such conditions.

In addition, during times of strong runoff caused by heavy rainstorms or snowmelt, ebb currents tend to be quite strong. In some cases, they may completely override the direction of the flood on the surface of the water. It's a good idea to stay put during periods when strong currents oppose the wind.

## Micro-climatic Conditions

Since wind forecasts usually cover a wide general area and are given for the strongest winds expected, local winds—influenced by the topography of an area—may vary significantly from the forecast. We frequently hear stories of boats that stay put longer than they need to because of small craft warnings or high wind notices. Weather forecasts are conservative by nature. You won't hear a forecast calling for a beautiful calm day; instead, it predicts the worst weather expected to occur any time during that period.

*Corner wind* is the effect of increased wind speed when a wind blows past a headland, such as off Dundas Island or headlands facing the Gulf of Alaska. A corner wind is usually

*Wind opposing the current creates very difficult sea conditions.*

stronger than that experienced on either side of its land mass.

*Gap winds* (or funnel winds) are caused by a funneling effect between islands—such as the directional shift the wind makes to follow an inlet or channel, or the increase in wind speed that occurs in Peril Strait, Lynn Canal or Clarence Strait. When gap winds blow against tidal currents, they can cause dangerous, steep, breaking waves. These conditions occur on Baranof Island where outside inlets almost connect through a low pass to inlets on Chatham Strait.

*Lee effect* occurs along a steep shoreline where a turbulent and gusty offshore wind meets an opposing wind at the top of a cliff. Reversed eddies, along with onshore winds, may create confused, steep seas along the base of the cliffs.

During periods of light prevailing winds, *sea breezes* blow from sea toward land during the heat of the day (usually in the afternoon). In Dixon Entrance and Cross Sound, the prevailing inflow and afternoon sea breeze can combine to reach 30 to 40 knots. Sea breezes may contribute to the prevalence of moderately strong afternoon southerlies in north-south facing bodies of water such as Clarence and Chatham Straits, despite forecasts of light-to-moderate northwest winds over Southeast Alaska. These winds may intimidate a skipper new to the area who interprets them as winds that arrive in advance of a low-pressure front. Check your barometer to verify whether these south winds are prevailing afternoon sea breezes or a more serious change requiring you to seek alternative shelter.

*Land breezes* blow from land toward sea during the night and can be gusty, but—except for outflow winds—their velocity is usually less than that of a sea breeze. Both sea and land breezes die quickly, as does the chop they generate.

*Anabatic winds*, upslope winds caused by rising warm air, occur during the daytime in valleys and inlets.

*Katabatic winds* (also known as williwaws) are downslope winds that occur at night and are caused by falling cool air. They are usually stronger than upslope winds, and often blast down a fjord or the steep slope of a high, snow-laden ridge, giving you good reason to set your anchor well on an otherwise calm evening. Williwaws can reach frightening velocities when the sides of a fjord are steep and capped by ice or snow; they are usually of short, but intense duration and may affect just a small area. Since they are cyclonic in nature, the actual direction of williwaws vary, and they frequently whip up chop or foam when they hit the water.

*Surge winds* are strong winds generated occasionally in the summer during periods of high barometric readings (1008 to 1012 millibars). These winds disturb the stable weather off the Pacific Coast and can surprise a cruising boat. Caused by a lee trough that forms off the coast during during prolonged periods of heating of the interior land mass, this phenomenon causes prevailing light easterlies adjacent to the coast, but it can cause gale force northwesterlies farther offshore. A potentially more dangerous condition called *stratus surge* occurs when a larger lee trough off northern California shoots north along the Oregon and Washington coasts, picking up speed as it surges, and bringing with it low clouds and fog. During a stratus surge, winds shift abruptly from light easterlies to southerlies of gale force or stronger. These winds can strike suddenly without much movement in the barometer, but they bring a sharp drop in air temperature. Local fishermen call these "fog winds," as fog or low, dark stratus clouds from the south are the only reliable signs of their approach. However, when such conditions do occur, they are usually forecast on the continuous weather broadcasts.

If you are in doubt about any weather forecast, or if you witness any unusual or rapid changes in prevailing conditions that could affect the safety of your boat, call the U.S. Coast Guard on Ch 16 at once. Ask for a clarification or, if you need it, for assistance. The Coast Guard would rather give you the information you need for a wise decision than risk a dangerous and costly operation to rescue you.

## Marine Fog

Marine fog—formed when warm Pacific air moves over relatively colder seas during late summer and early autumn—causes greatly reduced visibility a good part of the late summer, making navigation dangerous. At times in Southeast Alaska, visibility can be reduced to zero. Cruising boats without radar often find they have to wait until the fog burns off before they can move on. Fog can be forecast quite well as the dew point approaches the temperature of the environment; local marine weather stations broadcast such conditions.

Marine fog frequently forms offshore, moves inland in early evening, remains all night, and then lifts or dissipates in the late morning. Many weather stations report the highest percentage of fog in their 7 a.m. observations, the least in their 4 p.m. observations. With the lengthened hours of daylight in summer, you can frequently get a late start after the fog lifts and still maintain your planned schedule.

During foggy periods, many sport fishing and commercial boats continue to fish, creating congestion and navigational hazards (or challenges!) for cruising boats, particularly near harbor entrances and across fishing grounds. It's a good idea when you approach congested areas to station a lookout on your bow and to listen carefully for fog horns, bells or the sound of other propellers. Remain especially alert in shipping channels. Ferry boats and other commercial high-speed craft rarely slow down, and there's nothing quite so alarming as hearing the horn of a large ship as it bears down on your little vessel. Good radar reflectors and radar sets are critical in these situations, as is bridge-to-bridge contact on VHF (Ch 13).

"Tag scanning" VHF radios allow you to monitor Ch 16, Ch 13, and the local Vessel Traffic Service channel simultaneously. You should also consider using an Automated Information System (AIS) receiver, as this is a superb way to keep in touch with the positions of commercial vessels.

Since the frequency of fog varies somewhat along the Inside Passage, with Dixon Entrance being strongly affected in late summer, we advise you to study the tables in the appendices of Canada's *Sailing Directions* and read the comments in U.S. *Coast Pilot*.

Radiation fog is primarily a problem in harbors and inlets. It forms over land during the early mornings on windless days and generally dissipates after the sun or wind comes up. During prolonged spells of radiation fog, winds are usually (but not necessarily) light, and the seas are nearly flat.

When fog moves offshore during the day, it is called sea fog. Formed when winds are moderate, sea fog moves back onshore in the evening and may persist as winds become stronger, lasting just a day, or continuing without a break for several days at a time.

*A bank of fog can await you just around the corner.*

## Rain

Rain—accompanied by low, dark clouds, and often lasting for several hours at a time—reduces visibility, although usually to a lesser extent than fog. Drizzle (fine precipitation) also occurs with the passage of a front. Rain showers cover a small area for short periods and fall from cumulus clouds, the heaviest usually occurring after a front has passed and cold northwesterly winds have set in.

Much of Southeast Alaska is located in a temperate rainforest zone. Rain is less pervasive in summer than in winter. North of Queen Charlotte Sound, B.C., rainfall averages 100 inches or more per year, peaking near Ketchikan, which gets nearly 160 inches. In summer, we have experienced from as few as two to as many as twenty rainy days in a month while cruising from Anacortes, WA, to Juneau, AK.

## Strategies for Coping with the Variables of Weather

To make your voyage more comfortable, here are some additional practical tips:

1. Monitor weather broadcasts on VHF (or on continuous recordings by telephone as noted above) before you arrive in a critical

area. Pay particular attention to this and adjacent areas to give you an idea of the state and speed of an approaching front.

2. Monitor actual conditions at lighthouses and reporting stations to see if the forecast is materializing. Since forecasts are given for the worst weather expected over a certain area, you may frequently encounter lesser conditions on your actual route.

3. Track barometric pressure, wind direction and strength, cloud cover and sea conditions, and develop your own skills for monitoring and interpreting weather. Use every opportunity to check your findings against what is being reported and what you observe.

4. Maintain radio schedules with cruising boats ahead of you and monitor their inter-boat transmissions on working channels. Break in to ask for a report of local conditions from time to time.

5. Delay or advance your daily runs to arrive at critical passages when stable conditions are expected. We find that under normal conditions, starting early in the day gives us an advantage before prevailing winds kick up. Be sure your boat is secure and shipshape before you leave.

6. Prepare alternative plans for safe anchorages in case the weather and seas exceed your expectations or the crew becomes uncomfortable. Don't be afraid to implement these changes.

7. Through critical passages, talk with Coast Guard (via channel 16 and working channel 22A or VTS Traffic Control) about weather updates and solicit their observations if you need to, particularly if unexpected changes occur.

*This Tlevak Narrows buoy is being towed by the current—situational awareness is critical.*

## Sea Conditions

"Sea" is defined as that segment of a wave riding on top of the prevailing swell and caused by winds arising from sources outside the local region.

The ocean swells you encounter crossing Dixon Entrance can be alarming if your only experience is on inside waters. Shoaling water (such as that found in Queen Charlotte Sound, B.C.) can cause the background swell to reach 3 or 4 meters. However, the wavelength of such swell is generally about 100 yards, and while the swells may appear large, they are usually not threatening. However, if a strong ebb current meets a moderate southwest wind, the swells are much closer together, causing an uncomfortable jostle and a wet, hazardous crossing. These conditions may be confined to local areas—such as the east end of Dixon Entrance.

## Tides and Currents

The farther north you go, or the farther removed you are from the open ocean, the greater the tidal range. In general, human-powered kayaks and low-powered craft will need to pay close attention to tides and currents.

In Glacier Bay and heads of remote inlets, an extreme tidal range of over 20 feet is not uncommon. As standard daily procedure, check tide tables and allow for changes in tide levels, especially when anchoring or transiting narrows.

Most electronic charting programs include tide and current tables. You should update your electronic tides and current data as you do your charts. NOAA periodically updates their observation network with new stations and recalculates their tables for Southeast Alaska, so make sure your electronic systems are up to date.

Always carry appropriate paper chart backups as well as hard copies of tide and current tables, including correction factors for different locations. One hard-copy backup strategy is to use your (up-to-date) electronic tables in advance: call up the tide and current for locations and months of interest and make printouts before your trip starts. NOAA tide and current predictions may be found at: https://tidesandcurrents.noaa.gov/tide_predictions.html?gid=1391 and https://tidesandcurrents.noaa.gov/map/index.shtml?region=Southeastern Alaska

*A final caution:* These tables provide predictions only and may not reflect what you actually experience in a given location at a given moment. Outside of the major locations, such as Sergius Narrows, you may find many occasions in Southeast Alaska when the table says one thing but you experience something different. (For example, see the entry and the sidebar on current speed at Devil's Elbow in Rocky Pass in Chapter 8). Accurate timing of currents in Southeast Alaska is particularly suspect. In restricted channels and at lagoon entrances, slack water is typically one to three hours later than in outside waters. Use your eyes and learn to recognize different tide and current situations.

## Steep Waves

Waves become steeper near shore, or when a current opposes the direction of the waves. This steepness presents the most danger for small craft. A current flowing in the same direction as the wind has the opposite effect. The swell height is diminished and the period lengthened, cutting wave steepness dramatically.

Dixon Entrance, Cross Sound and Peril Strait are areas known for strong tidal currents that can create steep, breaking waves. On the north side of Dundas Island, in Dixon Entrance, we have seen two-meter wind waves roughly double in height and steepen to the breaking point against an opposing ebb current of several knots. Strong outflow winds from Portland Canal, lasting several hours, frequently build up nasty chop that steepens to the breaking point on flood tides as far west as Dundas Island. In conditions like these, when the current is unfavorable, it's a good

*Train your eye to roughly recognize the stage of the tide—such as the "low" tide at this island.*

*Don Douglass, always ready to discover new territory*

idea to hole up for a few hours, rather than stressing your boat and crew unnecessarily.

Fortunately, the passages with significant exposure to ocean swells, or to the outlets of major fjords, are of rather short duration (a few hours in most cases). It's comforting for a crew to know that prevailing swells and seas die down quickly in protected waters and don't affect the coves where you anchor each night.

## Narrows and Rapids

Uncomfortable or dangerous seas also occur in tidal narrows and rapids and across channel or inlet bars. Rips are turbulent agitation of the water caused by the interaction of currents and wind waves. In shallow water, irregular bottom rips can create short breaking waves. The entrances to Holkum Bay, Endicott Arm, and Tracy Arm are notorious examples of this phenomenon.

Overfalls are areas of turbulent water caused by currents setting over submerged ridges or shoals. A severe overfall can produce a sharp rise or fall in water level and may even create whirlpools. Short, closely spaced, standing waves ("dancing waters") are also seen where currents meet. A small boat may be tossed from side to side in overfalls. Note the indications of rips and overfalls on your nautical charts and heed the warnings and instructions in Canada's *Sailing Directions* or the U.S. *Coast Pilot* when you transit such areas. Many narrows, such as Sergius Narrows, Hole in the Wall, Tlevak Narrows and others, have overfalls and turbulent water. Once again, try to plan your transit at or near slack water to reduce the severity of these conditions.

Just as with tide tables, check your current tables daily. Aboard *Baidarka*, we found it convenient to write down key tides and currents data for each day on a small re-writeable tablet or post-it note. Predictions for major locations like Sergius Narrows are more likely to be accurate than less-travelled locations. However, always remain ready to react to the actual conditions you experience rather than assuming the tables will be accurate.

## Tsunamis

Tsunamis are waves generated by the displacement of a large volume of water due to earthquake, landslide, or other disturbance. They occur occasionally along the Alaska coast and may present hazards to small boats from strong currents that break moorings and drive boats ashore.

Tsunami warnings for the West Coast of North America in the U.S. are issued by the West Coast and Alaska Tsunami Warning Center (WCATWC) and broadcast by the USCG on channel 16. Any vessel in danger should clear harbor and head for open waters where the effect of the waves is reduced and navigation is less hazardous.

## Floating logs, ice, and other hazards

As previously mentioned, the Inside Passage is a wild and remote region. But with adequate planning and skill you can deal with the challenges of weather, navigation, and so forth. However, one additional hazard needs special mention—encounters with floating debris, especially floating logs, as well as ice.

Constant vigilance by a skipper and crew will minimize the danger posed by flotsam. In all Pacific Northwest waters, including Southeast Alaska, collision with a floating log can occur at any time and place. Small, high-speed runabouts that collide with a log may be flipped over, with occasionally fatal results. Slower cruising boats with protected or enclosed propellers tend to glance off or roll over a log, which may still cause damage to the propeller, the drive train or the rudder. Exposed props are more vulnerable to collisions with logs. Bending or breaking a prop means severe vibration and sometimes flooding when the drive train or rudder is overstressed.

Floating logs become particular hazards after storms that produce heavy runoff, especially during extreme spring tides when beach logs float free or in areas of active logging operations. Floating logs tend to bunch together in eddy currents or to spread out in a long line where tidal currents from different directions meet—such as in Wrangell Narrows. Long lines of floating logs and debris also occur where fresh water flowing out from creeks and rivers "floats" on top of the saltwater.

When you pass through such areas, look for gaps in the lines of debris and head through these gaps with a slow approach, shifting into neutral and gliding through. Also, notice the quantity and age of logs on south-facing beaches; this will indicate the seriousness of the local hazard.

Of particular danger is a "deadhead"—also called a "sinker" or "black floater." This is a vertical log, semi-submerged and bobbing up and down slowly with the chop of swells. A collision with one of these can actually hole a vessel.

Areas of icebergs may create similar possibilities for damage, since ice does not always protrude above the water surface. Boaters need to be aware of the risk of damaging hulls and props by collision not only with visible icebergs, but also with dense ice floating just under the surface. Large icebergs are known to invert without warning, sometimes swamping nearby boats. The active front of a calving glacier is spectacular, but the impact of huge masses of ice can create waves that capsize nearby boats. Chunks of ice may break off underwater from glaciers that reach the ocean. These bergs will rocket to the surface without warning and with great destructive power. Use caution in the vicinity of glaciers.

The best defense against collision with a log or an iceberg is to keep a constant watch on what's ahead. Use binoculars to check the route frequently and travel at a speed that clearly allows you to spot and avoid such potential threats. Binoculars are one of your most important navigation tools, so you should have good ones. Make sure yours have at least a 7 x 50 rating (magnification and field of vision). Ask your guests to bring their own binoculars for sightseeing purposes.

The recent decrease in Southeast Alaska's logging activity has somewhat reduced the hazards of floating logs compared to decades ago.

Most of the boats we have seen with collision damage have been models with exposed and highly vulnerable shafts, props and rudders—particularly twin-engine, high-speed vessels. Displacement or semi-displacement hulls with an enclosed prop and rudder fair considerably better.

In Southeast Alaska, beyond the cities and major towns, damage to a prop usually means flying in a new one and paying a substantial diving charge for its replacement. If you have an exposed prop or if you travel in areas of logging activity or icebergs, it's a good idea to

---

## Responsible Marine Mammal Viewing

Whales begin their northbound migration to Alaska in February with most cows and calves migrating between April and May. Cruisers who visit Southeast Alaska between June and early September are most likely to see Humpback, Gray, and Minke Whales, Orcas (Killer Whales), Pacific White-Sided Dolphins, and Dall's and Harbour Porpoises. Whales begin their southbound trek in late October and continue through December.

The Marine Mammal Protection Act prohibits harassment of all marine mammal species in U.S. waters.

See the Alaska Marine Mammal Viewing Guidelines and Regulations at: https://alaskafisheries.noaa.gov/pr/mm-viewing-guide

Harassment means any act of pursuit, torment, or annoyance which has the potential to injure a marine mammal, or has the potential to disturb a marine mammal by causing disruption of behavioral patterns, including migration, breathing, nursing, breeding, and feeding.

Humpback Whale viewing regulations require boaters to

- Not approach within 100 yards of a humpback whale.
- Not place your vessel in the path of oncoming humpback whales causing them to surface within 100 yards of your vessel.
- Not disrupt the normal behavior or prior activity of a whale.
- Operate your vessel at a slow, safe speed when near a humpback whale.

Limit observation times to 30 minutes. Whales should not be encircled, trapped between vessels, or trapped between a vessel and the shore. You may not place your vessel in the path of on-coming whales causing them to surface. You should reduce speed to less than 7 knots when within 400 yards of a whale. If approached by a whale, put your engine in neutral and allow the whale to pass.

To safely observe porpoises and dolphins, observe all guidelines for watching whales. Do not steer through groups of porpoises or dolphins to encourage them to bow ride. Should a porpoise or dolphin choose to ride your bow wave, reduce speed gradually and avoid sudden course changes.

These voluntary guidelines are recommended when viewing Harbor Seals in their glacial fjord habitat

- Remain 500 yards (~1/4 mile) from all seals without compromising safe navigation.
- Practice no wake, avoid abrupt changes in course or engine pitch, and avoid loud noises.
- Avoid traveling through waters with greater than 50% ice cover.
- When possible, target visits during early morning and evening hours when fewer seals are hauled out.

—LW

*Réanne Hemingway-Douglass, happy at the helm of* Baidarka's *speedy dinghy*

carry a spare prop or the means for making your own repairs on a local tidal grid. The risks of colliding with a log are significant and the costs of repair are high! (See sidebar on how to use Haul-out Grids in Southeast Alaska.)

## Conclusion

In conclusion, remember the quotation at the beginning of this Introduction: "Experience is what you get right after you need it." Your voyage to Southeast Alaska may be just the first of many exciting experiences. There's a lifetime of exploring awaiting you, and we hope that the topics we've covered here have given you enough basic knowledge to keep you in your comfort zone and help you "get it right" *before* you need to. Happy cruising!

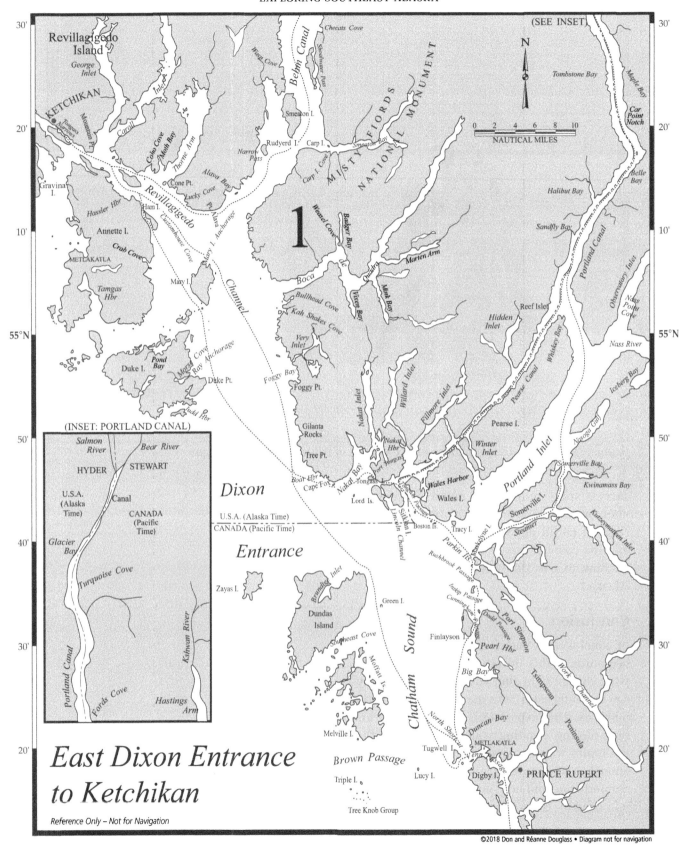

# 1

# DIXON ENTRANCE, PORTLAND CANAL, REVILLAGIGEDO CHANNEL TO KETCHIKAN

## INTRODUCTION

Dixon Entrance—the gateway to Alaska's magnificent cruising wilderness—is the second of two main bodies of water to be crossed when cruising the Inside Passage to Southeast Alaska (or, as Alaskans say, "Southeast"); the other main body of water being Queen Charlotte Sound in British Columbia. Dixon Entrance marks the international boundary between the United States and Canada. Open to the prevailing swells and winds from the west, it also receives large flows of fresh water and occasional high winds that can whistle down the inlets from the east. While the swells in Dixon Entrance originate in the Gulf of Alaska, they are frequently less noticeable than those in Queen Charlotte Sound. However, due to strong and confused tidal flows and complex wind and weather fronts, nasty chop or breaking waves can develop, so it is best to cross during a period of benign weather (stable barometer).

For the most direct route from Prince Rupert to Ketchikan, go west through Venn Passage, passing Metlakatla (3 miles west of Prince Rupert) on your starboard, then head north via either the east or west side of Tugwell Island. Turn north in Chatham Sound and head for Revillagigedo Channel, passing the west side of Green Island. If the weather turns nasty or swells are uncomfortable, Brundige Inlet on Dundas Island provides good refuge at the south side of Dixon Entrance; on the north side, Foggy Bay, Judd Harbor or Morse Cove are good anchor sites.

Note, however, that northbound boats leaving from Prince Rupert and planning to anchor overnight in Alaskan waters must obtain prior

*Call Green Island Lighthouse for a real-time report on wind and sea state in Dixon Entrance.*

permission from Ketchikan Customs to anchor in Foggy Bay—the only designated anchorage. U.S. Customs asks that you call during normal office hours to make your request (tel: 907.225.2254). A U.S. cell phone connection is possible near Cape Fox, but the most reliable strategy is to call before you leave Prince Rupert.

Most pleasure boats that cruise at slower speeds (5-9 knots) take two days to make the trip from Prince Rupert to Ketchikan, leaving near dawn on the first day and anchoring by noon before the chop builds up in Revillagigedo Channel. Faster boats should also consider a two-day trip strategy because arriving in Ketchikan in early afternoon will improve your chances for finding moorage.

There is no Customs dock in Ketchikan. All boats (U.S. and foreign) must first obtain moorage from the harbormaster who will then notify Customs to send an agent to your boat to obtain clearance. If every person aboard has a NEXUS card, you may obtain entry clearance by phone (see U.S. Customs information in the Introduction).

If you wish to return to some areas of interest (such as Misty Fiords), you can do so only *after* you have received your clearance number from Ketchikan Customs. All persons on board must have a passport. (Please see the Introduction of this book for more U.S. Customs details.)

During conditions of easterly outflow winds in Portland Inlet, B.C., hug the mainland shore and dart across from one secure anchorage to another; this allows you to escape the uncomfortable beam seas and chop near Green Island, and you can move forward while other boats are still waiting in Prince Rupert for calm weather. On this route, rough water is reduced to about three miles across the entrance to Portland Inlet. Convenient layover sites can be found on either side of the inlet, allowing you to wait for an optimum crossing time.

If you want to hug the mainland shore, visit Khutzeymateen Grizzly Bear Reserve, or head for the remote waters of Portland Canal. We find the following route to be the most protected:

From Port Simpson, exit via Inskip Passage or Rushbrook Passage, and pass east of Parkin Islets to the west side of Maskelyne Island. The lee of Maskelyne Island is the last of smooth-water until you cross Portland Inlet to the lee of Wales Island. If Portland Inlet looks forbidding, wait and watch from the south side of Maskelyne Island, or return to Port Simpson for shelter.

As you cross northbound to Alaska, set your clocks back one hour to the Alaska time zone; southbound, advance your clocks an hour to Pacific Time. (Southeast Alaska does observe Daylight Savings Time.)

As you proceed farther north, you will notice more than just time zone and international boundary changes. The scenery is on a grander scale, the islands are higher, the channels deeper and the number of small, convenient anchorages decreases. The area around Ketchikan has some of the heaviest rainfall in Southeast Alaska, providing some of the most dense temperate rainforests on Earth.

If you can take the time before crossing into Southeast Alaska, a foray up British Columbia's Portland Canal will treat you to turquoise waters, waterfalls and gorgeous overhang-

*Baidarka's brief encounter with long-distance paddlers off Cape Fox*

ing cliffs. Measured from Dixon Entrance to Stewart, this fjord—71 miles long (114 kilometers)—is perhaps the longest on the North American continent. Many of the inlets in the area, such as Observatory Inlet, have barely been surveyed and are a delight to explore. Hyder, Alaska, and Stewart, British Columbia, share an almost non-existent border at the head of this remote, isolated fjord. Largely pristine, and infrequently visited, the canal named by Vancouver after William Bentinck, Duke of Portland, is deep, with sheer mountain sides. Anchorages—marginal at best and far apart—depend entirely on the weather. The farther north you go in Portland Canal, the more difficult it is to receive VHF weather reports or radio reception of any kind.

The international boundary between Canada and Alaska runs mid-channel through Pearse and Portland Canals, north to Stewart. Floating trees or flotsam, common past Fords Cove, call for caution. Between Blue Point and Glacier Cove, the water in Portland Canal is an unusually bright turquoise blue, becoming increasingly opaque at the upper end of the canal, with underwater visibility very limited. Snowcapped peaks and hanging glaciers rise above Stewart, providing a lovely setting for the small community.

Narrower and more intimate than Alaskan fjords, Portland Canal generally has benign weather in the summer and is relatively easy to navigate. At its entrance and central section, you can receive weather broadcasts only on Ch 21B (on some receivers Weather Ch 8). North of Glacier Cove there is no reception. (See Stewart Marine Rescue under Stewart.) Locals report that upslope winds predominate in the summer, and downslope winds in the winter. The winds tend to die off as you near Stewart; this phenomenon becomes apparent near Hattie Island or a little farther north. Most summer nights are quiet and calm. Other than a few Stewart sport fishing vessels, you are unlikely to see any other pleasure craft.

In Alaska, as in Portland Canal and other British Columbia fjords, VHF weather and Ch 16 (Coast Guard) coverage is spotty or non-existent when you leave the express or ferry routes. Don't be surprised if, in Behm Canal and many other areas of Southeast Alaska, there is no VHF radio reception.

*Note:* For Portland Canal, Pearse Canal, and Tongass Passage, we recommend the use of Canadian charts, which are more detailed than the U.S. charts in some locations.

It is important to remember, also, that charts for Alaska are in fathoms (1 fathom = 6 feet) rather than meters (1 meter = 3.28 feet).

As you head north of Dixon Entrance, Port Tongass, Foggy Bay, Judd Harbor and Morse

## WHO WAS PRINCE RUPERT?

Most of the non-native place names in coastal British Columbia and Southeast Alaska were bestowed by European explorers and settlers, including the Russian navigators Bering and Chirikov (who visited in 1741), an assortment of Spanish mariners (1790s), and George Vancouver (1792-4). Prince Rupert is a notable exception. The Canadian port city was founded in the first years of the twentieth century as the western terminus of the Grand Trunk Pacific Railway. It superseded Port Essington, on the Skeena River, as the commercial hub of the northern B.C. coast. "Prince Rupert" was the winning entry in a name-that-town competition (with a prize of $250!) sponsored by the Grand Trunk Railway. The name honors Rupert, Count Palatine of the Rhine, Duke of Bavaria, Duke of Cumberland and Earl of Holderness (1619-1682), commonly known as Prince Rupert of the Rhine. In an era when all members of European royal families were related to one another, the German-born Rupert (1619-1682) was a grandson of King James I of England, a nephew of Charles I, and an uncle to King George I. In a varied and illustrious career that reflected his many interests and accomplishments, Prince Rupert's professional exploits included that of Royalist cavalry officer in England, mercenary general in France, privateer in the Caribbean, and head of the Royal Navy. He also served as the first governor of the Hudson's Bay Company—which is why the name "Rupert" appears quite frequently among Canadian place names.

—AC

Cove (the first anchor sites you come to) afford good anchorage in most weather. As mentioned above, however, Ketchikan Customs will give you permission to anchor only in Foggy Bay; no other anchoring location is acceptable for northbound boats. It is best to obtain this permission ahead of time by calling Ketchikan Customs before you leave Prince Rupert.

Port Tongass, a small harbor between Tongass Island and the mainland, is the site of an 1870 fort and an abandoned Tlingit community.

In Foggy Bay, the best anchor site is within Very Inlet to its immediate north (see diagram

*Totem pole imagery—turned upright the figures emerge*

## Kaleidoscope Magic

Linda Lewis—Journal Notes—M/V *Royal Sounder*

All cruisers have their own favorite scenes of magic. For me, nothing is quite as mysterious and wonderful as seeing the land reflected in very still water at low tide. Nature is the supreme artist in these moments. I am the blessed observer. I have heard it said that native peoples were inspired to create totem poles by these same visions. When I turn my head to the side I can see the figures emerge.

When I was a child I had a kaleidoscope that I loved. Today, when I am on the water, I discover these images and know that I am privileged to see, first hand, nature's kaleidoscope magic.

*Land reflected in very still water at low tide*

*It's an alien, or an insect, or a cruiser gone bad*

*A bird in flight—or a stealth airplane when turned upright*

later in this chapter). Foggy Bay is worth at least a day's exploration. Paddling a kayak or quietly rowing your dinghy can give you the full sensation of a rainforest environment. This is the home of muskeg ponds, pools and lagoons and of cedar trees, the bark of which is the source of the deep brown water. Walking here is difficult and rubber boots are a necessity.

## Venn Passage and Metlakatla Bay, B.C.
Charts 3955 metric, 3958 metric
East entrance: 54°18.68′ N, 130°22.88′ W
South entrance (Metlakatla Bay): 54°18.40′ N, 130°30.40′ W

Although narrow and intricate with strong currents, Venn Passage offers a good shortcut for small boats heading north from Prince Rupert into Chatham Sound. The passage is marked by a couple of ranges and several buoys. Be aware, however, that the buoys in Venn Passage are often dragged out of position after being hit by tows.

Be sure of your route before attempting Venn Passage and in all narrow, passages, be sure to check for recent chart corrections. Use Chart 3955 to identify turning points, and line up with the range marks (at the southeastern part of Venn Passage, in Shkgeaum Bay) and the three sector lights throughout the rest of Venn Passage.

Electronic vector and raster charts have all been converted to the WGS 84 horizontal datum, so mariners using this method do not need to alter their GPS. Check with your electronic charting vendor to be sure this applies for your software.

Notice that, as you transit from the Prince Rupert end of Venn Passage towards Chatham

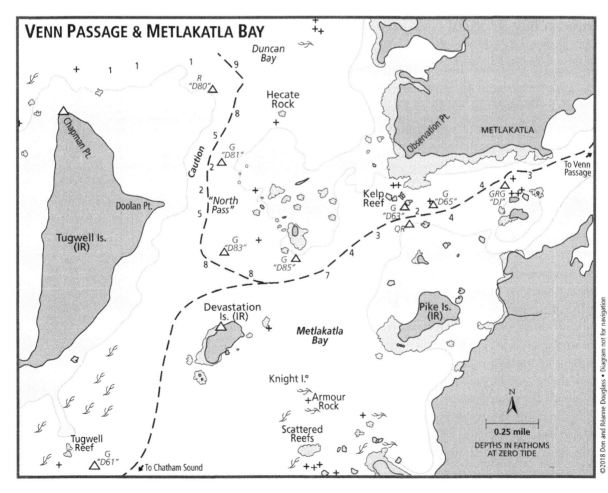

Sound, you will have the range marks and the sector lights *behind* you, which requires very careful helming skills.

When you pass the airport ferry dock at Du Vernay Point (where most locals slow down) and again off the Metlakatla float (where most locals do *not* slow down), please DO slow down.

If you leave Prince Rupert near or ahead of high water, you have favorable current all the way to Green Island.

In summer, after a favorable weather forecast, there is frequently an early morning exodus (0400 to 0500 hours) of boats from Prince Rupert heading north. Venn Passage is heavily used by fishing vessels. Their skippers are not always the most courteous during this limited-space passage, so plan accordingly and be ready to give way a bit—safely.

## Duncan Bay Shortcut (west of Venn Passage)
1.6 mi W of Metlakatla float
Chart 3957, 3955
Entrance (S) 54°19.70′ N, 130°29.40′ W
Entrance (N) 54°20.57′ N, 130°29.15′ W

*Please note:* When using paper Chart 3597 through the Duncan Bay Shortcut, the horizontal datum is WGS 84. If you are doing paper charting and used paper Chart 3955 through Venn Passage, your GPS was set for NAD 27. For the Duncan Bay Shortcut you will use paper Chart 3957 and you must re-set your GPS to WGS 84. Cruisers using electronic charting will find that their program makes the adjustments for these issues. (Check with your software vendor.)

Don't bury yourself in the chart. This is a *piloting* passage: look out the window. As you make the transit, watch your depth sounder and the many nav-aids which provide good guidance for your passage.

By leaving the west end of Venn Passage and entering Duncan Bay, you can gain a half hour when northbound using a shortcut across the sand bar. We call this route "Duncan Bay Shortcut." Larger yachts (approximately 40 feet and over) may find this route too shallow and/or narrow; however, smaller yachts can safely cross the bar during the upper half of most tides, staying close to the buoys and monitoring the depth sounder carefully. A professional skipper advises us that *at the appropriate tide*, vessels up to 80 feet with an 8-foot draft can also make this passage. Plan carefully and proceed cautiously.

## Brundige Inlet (Dundas Island)
Brundige Inlet is 5 miles northwest of Green Island Light.
Chart 3909 metric (inset)
Entrance: 54°36.86′ N, 130°50.73′ W
Anchor (bitter end): 54°35.30′ N, 130°53.50′ W

Brundige Inlet, a narrow, 3-mile-long channel on the north side of Dundas Island, affords excellent shelter from all outside swells and chop. When you're anchored deep in the inlet, everything is still, and it's difficult to tell whether a tempest is blowing outside or not. The inlet has long been a favorite refuge for both north- and southbound cruising boats.

The only negative we've heard is the presence of pesky black flies when winds are slight or non-existent. However, we've been so thankful for this shelter after a rough crossing of Dixon Entrance that either we didn't notice the flies or else they weren't there. (There are no

*Public floats, Port Simpson (Lax Kw' Alaams)*

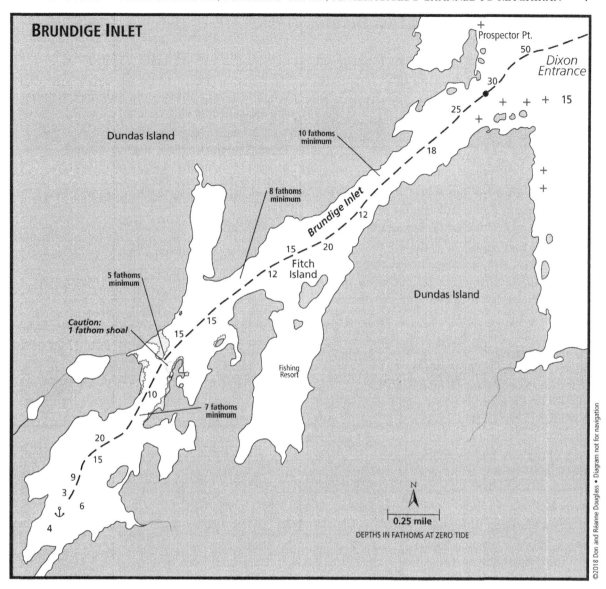

deer on Dundas Island. It is said that if there were, the black flies would drain them of all their blood.)

Although entering Brundige Inlet is not difficult, it is easy to overshoot the entrance; if you're arriving from the north, it helps to take a fix on Prospector Point. Stay mid-channel for the entire 3 miles, then favor the west shore at the beginning of the last narrows; there is a rock mid-channel with about 6 feet over it at zero tide. The entrance is quite narrow and Chart 3909 is helpful for entering.

We have anchored at the bitter end of the inlet and been perfectly comfortable during a major blow. There is shallower water and more swinging room on the south side of the lagoon south of Fitch Island.

Returning from Alaska, obtain permission from Canadian customs via CACG on VHF prior to entry. *This can be considered only as an emergency option, since it is not a port of entry.*

Anchor (bitter end) in 4 to 6 fathoms over a mud bottom with very good holding.

## Mainland Route across East Dixon Inlet via Portland Inlet

(Recommended during periods of northeast outflow winds from Portland Inlet.)

When strong winds funnel down Portland Canal and kick up a nasty chop in Chatham Sound and East Dixon Entrance, consider hugging the mainland coast for a smooth-water route. Although longer than the direct route, this route is more scenic. By staying in Port Tongass, you can divide your trip to Ketchikan into two easy segments. Rough water on this route is reduced to about 3 miles across the entrance to Portland Inlet. Convenient layovers can be taken on either side of the inlet to allow for an optimum crossing time.

## Pearl Harbour

Charts 3959 metric, 3963 metric
Entrance (Boat Passage): 54°30.16' N, 130°28.30' W
Anchor: 54°30.29' N, 130°26.83' W

Very good protection from northeast winds can be obtained on the east side of Pearl Harbour.

After clearing Sparrowhawk Rock, enter Pearl Harbour via the deep-water route on the west side of Flat Top Island. Small boats can use narrow Boat Passage, but the reef south of Mist Island must be identified and avoided. If passing north of Mist Island, be careful to avoid the drying spit to the north. Many boats have gone aground there, expecting the reef to terminate farther south. Stay close to Buoy "DK."

Anchor in the far east side of Pearl Harbour, due north of Pearl Point. The "pearl" in Pearl Point is a large glacial boulder 200 yards northwest of the point.

Anchor in 4 fathoms, sand and mud bottom, fair-to-good holding.

## Port Simpson (Lax Kw' Alaams)

Port Simpson is 15 miles northwest of Prince Rupert.
Charts 3963 (inset), 3959
Breakwater light: 54°33.71' N, 130°25.78' W

Port Simpson has three finger-floats for small boats on the south side of the breakwater, but the floats are frequently crowded with sport fishing and commercial boats. Avoid the shallow water east and south of the floats (see inset in Chart 3963). Fuel and propane are available on a part-time basis; good water can be obtained from a hose at the foot of the gangway; electricity is available for a reasonable fee. The village has a grocery store.

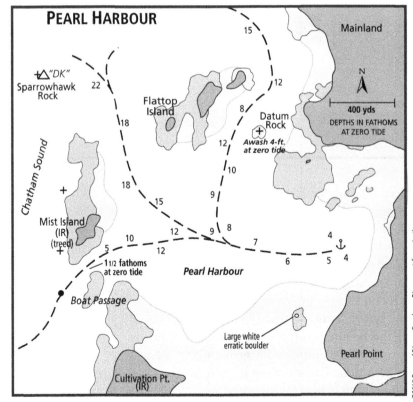

## Tongass Passage

Tongass Passage, between Sitklan and Wales islands, is 28 miles northwest of Prince Rupert.
Chart 17437
Southeast entrance (0.3 mile east of Boston Islands): 54°42.10' N, 130°32.72' W
South entrance (0.54 mile northwest of Haystack Island): 54°43.50' N, 130°37.72' W
North entrance (mid-channel between Bartlett Point and Point Mansfield): 54°45.83' N, 130°39.60' W

Tongass Passage is the smooth-water route into Alaska that crosses the entrance of Portland Inlet and leads northwest into a narrow channel east of Boston and Proctor islands. The passage between these islands is clear and well protected. Both sets of islands have beautiful sandy beaches that provide excellent kayak haulouts and campsites. The head of the bay, on the south end of Wales Island, offers protection from downslope winds from Portland Inlet. The south entrance between Island Point and Haystack Island is easier to enter in poor visibility.

Sitklan Passage can be followed to Port Tongass or Nakat Harbour.

## Lincoln Channel

Lincoln Channel, between Kanagunut and Sitklan Islands, is 2 miles south of Port Tongass.
Chart 17437
South entrance (0.5 mile east of Garnet Point): 54°43.12' N, 130°40.27' W
North entrance: 54°45.61' N, 130°43.09' W

Lincoln Channel can be used by small craft as a shortcut to Port Tongass. Anchorage can be found on the southwest side of the channel on the northwest side of the island labeled 260. The north end of the channel is very narrow and shallow with less than 10 feet in the fairway at low water. The bottom is clearly visible in the shallowest parts.

Lincoln Channel makes an interesting passage for shallow-draft boats; shelter can be found in the small west bight on the north side of the island just inside the south entrance. The head of the bight has the makings of a good campsite for kayakers.

The northeast side of the mid-channel islet has several fishing floats and a possible anchor site in southerlies. The north entrance has a flat bottom with kelp, and depths of about 7 feet at zero tide. The bottom is visible most of the way through the shoal area.

## Port Tongass

Port Tongass, on the east side of Tongass Island, is 3.8 miles east of Cape Fox.
Chart 17437
South entrance (0.09 mile west of Dark Point): 54°45.90' N, 130°43.39' W
North entrance (0.19 mile north of the Tongass Reef beacon): 54°47.40' N, 130°44.68' W
Anchor: 54°46.52' N, 130°44.06' W

The south shore of Tongass Island was once the site of a Tlingit village. The totems from the abandoned village were removed to Ketchikan in the 1970s. Most of the inhabitants had already moved to Saxman by the early 1900s. Fort Tongass, on the east side of the island—established in 1868 as a border station to prevent smuggling and to maintain peace among the tribes and traders—was abandoned in 1870. There are few signs of either the village or the fort, except for a few old bricks, scattered logs and old engine parts. The only residents of Port Tongass now are seals, loons, and bald eagles.

There is a good landing beach of mud and

*Anchorage, Port Tongass*

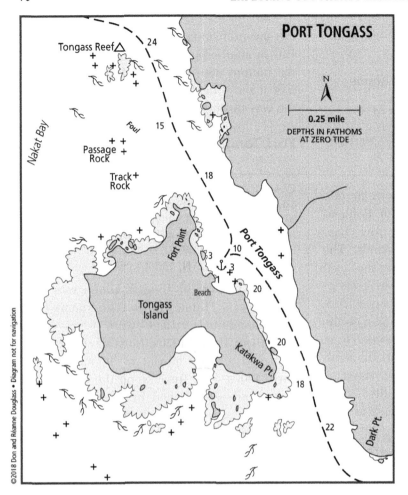

find good holding. Ebb current flows southeast at one knot, with some back eddies in the cove. On the last of the flood that flows northwest at about 2 knots, small whitecaps develop off North Point and a slight swell is felt in the cove.

Anchor in 2 to 4 fathoms over a mud, sand, shell and grass bottom with good holding.

To regain the direct route to Ketchikan, head north from Port Tongass, rounding Tongass Reef, and turn southwest for Cape Fox. Cross Nakat Bay before resuming your northbound route to Revillagigedo Channel.

## Pearse Canal

Pearse Canal, which connects Tongass Passage to Portland Canal, is 32 miles north of Prince Rupert.
**Chart 17437**

Pearse Canal, narrower and more sheltered than Portland Inlet, has interesting places to explore at its southern entrance.

## Wales Harbour (Wales Island)

Wales Harbour is entered 0.5 mile south of Pearse Canal Island Light.
**Chart 17437**
**Entrance (0.28 mile east of Phipp Point): 54°46.59′ N, 130°36.85′ W**
**Anchor: 54°45.27′ N, 130°34.50′ W**

A small anchorage can be found on the east side of an unnamed island southeast of Safa Islands on the British Columbia side of Pearse Canal. The south entrance is very narrow and should be entered only after you reconnoiter with a dinghy to ensure adequate depths. The anchorage is very well protected but it has limited swinging room and a shore tie should be used.

shell in front of the brambles that fill the old fort site. The rocks on the north side of the cove hold a colony of giant barnacles, a variety that grows up to 4 inches in diameter!

A good walk from the fort site follows the shoreline around Katakwa Point to the former village. The rocks and reefs of the south side are full of shellfish, and the view to seaward is fantastic. Unless you have a war canoe to get through the reefs, do not approach the village site from the south.

Anchoring near the landing beach will give you protection from most winds except northerlies. Anchor off the beach in 2 fathoms, or as close as your draft allows. Eel grass grows along the 1-fathom line. By anchoring close-in you can avoid most of the current and

Anchor in 8 fathoms over mud and sand with good holding.

## Southwest Arm of Wales Harbour (Wales Island)

The cove in the southwest arm of Wales Harbour is 1.6 miles southeast of Pearse Canal Island Light.
Chart 17437
Entrance (0.83 mile southeast of Safa Islands): 54°45.61' N, 130°35.67' W
Anchor: 54°45.27' N, 130°35.79' W

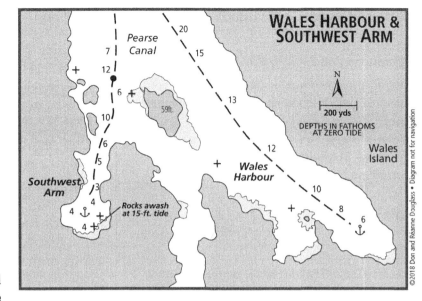

Anchorage can be found deep in the small basin in the southwest arm, avoiding the submerged rock on the east side of the basin. This intimate cove is shaped like a keyhole and offers very good protection from southerly weather. It has room for one or two boats over a flat bottom with steep-to, rocky shores.

Anchor in 4 fathoms over a soft bottom with good holding.

*First mate Réanne's work is never done.*

*. . . But Captain Don plays on!*

### Regina Cove (Fillmore Island)
Regina Cove is 2.1 miles northeast of Pearse Canal Island Light.
Chart 17437
Entrance 54°48.23' N, 130°33.54' W

Regina Cove, which is exposed to the south, has an irregular bottom and many submerged rocks. We do not recommend it for cruising vessels.

Wales Harbour and Winter Inlet are preferred anchorages in this region.

### Wales Passage
Wales Passage, between Pearse and Wales islands, is 1 mile southwest of Winter Inlet.
Chart 17437
South entrance (mid-channel between Swaine Point and York Island): 54°45.57' N, 130°25.86' W
North entrance: 54°49.64' N, 130°29.52' W

When there's a blow in Portland Inlet or Pearse Canal, the water is generally smooth in Wales Passage. This passage frequently contains a number of crab pots marked by small floats.

### Manzanita Cove (Wales Island)
Manzanita Cove is 5 miles south of the entrance to Winter Inlet.
Charts 17437, 17427
Entrance: 54°45.67' N, 130°26.20' W
Anchor: 54.45.45' N, 130°26.29' W

Manzanita Cove has a steep-to bottom with depths inconvenient for anchoring and no flat areas. The little nook on the south side, immediately west of Swaine Point, is protected in most weather and is useful for just one or two small craft, using a stern-tie to shore.

At the head of the nook, you can see the ruins of one of the four original stone masonry cabins built for the initial surveys of the Alaska border in 1896, under the direction of Captain Gaillard, U.S. Army Corps of Engineers. A stone plaque on the north corner of the building says ". . . property, Do not Injure." The U.S.-Canada border was established north of Wales and Pearse islands by a later tribunal and, since then, someone has chiseled out the "US" in the stone marker.

Anchor off the former U.S. Customs House in 6 fathoms, rocky bottom, poor holding, with a stern-tie to shore recommended.

### Wales Passage Cove (Pearse Island)
Wales Passage Cove, on the east side of Wales Passage, is 1.3 miles north of Manzanita Cove.
Chart 17437
Entrance: 54°46.79' N, 130°25.77' W
Anchor: 54°46.96' N, 130°25.77' W

"Wales Passage Cove" is what we call the small bay in Wales Passage, on the south side of Pearse Island. Temporary shelter may be found here when downslope winds are blowing in Portland Inlet. Depths in the cove are irregular, indicating a rocky bottom. Winter Inlet, just north, provides superior all-weather protection.

Anchor in about 6 fathoms over a largely rocky bottom with poor-to-fair holding.

*Exploring the former U.S. Customs House, now on Canadian soil (Manzanita Cove)*

## SE Alaska's Marinas

We think of SE Alaska as a land of wilderness: of glaciers, mountains and bears. But SE Alaska is also a land of small towns. And that means totem parks, museums, stores, restaurants and bars with local color: all reasons to visit and spend more than a few hours.

Visiting a town by boat in SE Alaska usually means tying up at a marina. Anchorages near towns are scarce: either the currents are too strong, the waters too deep or cruise ship traffic too busy.

Marinas in SE Alaska are built and managed for fishing boats. But fishermen leave in the summer, making their spaces available to transient boats. When you tie up at a SE Alaska marina, chances are you are "hot berthing"—using someone else's slip while they are away. It's an efficient use of space and helps keep marina prices low.

But hot berthing can create challenges. Harbormasters rarely know when a slip will become vacant, nor do they always know when a tenant will return. If a permanent tenant returns unexpectedly, you may have to move. If commercial fishing opens nearby, moorage could be crowded. And you may not be able to plug in if the permanent tenant pays the utility bill directly. Despite these complications, the system works. In six trips to SE Alaska, we have always found moorage when we needed it.

To arrange a slip, call the town harbormaster on Channel 16 when you are within sight of the marina, not before. The harbormaster (or a staff person) will then ask you to shift to a working channel. Give your boat's name, length, sailboat or powerboat, whether you want electricity, how many nights you plan to stay and if you prefer port or starboard tie-up. If the town has several marinas and you have a preference, tell them. They'll then assign you to a slip. It's helpful to have this guidebook open to the appropriate page to identify the slip's location.

You'll usually pay by the foot, no matter the size of the slip. Some marinas charge moorage fees for dinghies left in the water. Hoonah once required us to put ours on deck.

Once tied up, be sure to plan grocery shopping, laundry and refilling propane tanks at high tide. Tidal range is large in SE Alaska. It reaches twenty-five feet, in Juneau for example, and ramps at low tide can be steep.

Most SE Alaska marinas have sturdy wooden docks, rock breakwaters and wide slips and fairways for safe navigation in strong winds. The State of Alaska built the marinas then transferred them to the towns. Unfortunately, not all towns have the resources to maintain them. As a result, docks in smaller towns may have occasional missing cleats or canting floats. But we've also encountered brand new rebuilt docks where we least expected them, a sign of how important marinas are to the economic livelihood of Alaska's towns.

The no-frills nature of Alaska's marinas means they may not have showers, laundry or even restrooms. Private businesses fill the voids and chances are you'll find a coin-operated laundromat with showers nearby. Fuel docks are also separate businesses. Most marinas do have dumpsters for garbage and a dumpsite for waste oil.

Marina staff in the larger, busier harbors work long hours. Petersburg answers calls 24/7. But harbormasters at smaller towns, such as Kake and Klawock, work for only a few hours a week. If no one answers your call at a small marina, go into the marina and find a vacant slip, but don't plug in without permission. If you take someone's slip and they return, they may ask you to move. We once tied up at the slip belonging to the mayor of Klawock. Everyone in town wanted to tell us what a mistake we'd made, but the mayor just took another space.

Once tied up, look for the harbormaster's office. You may find a number to call or a drop box for the fee. Or you may get a free night of moorage.

One of the advantages of Alaska marinas is that your neighbors may be fishermen, recreational boaters or a mixture. Staying at a SE Alaska marina is a great opportunity to meet friendly people willing to share experiences and information. And you may get a free fish.

—EH

## Winter Inlet (Pearse Island)

Winter Inlet is 6.75 miles northeast of the entrance to Wales Harbour.
**Chart** 17437
Entrance: 54°50.50' N, 130°27.67' W
Anchor: 54°48.26' N, 130°25.85' W

Winter Inlet is one of the most well-sheltered anchorages east of Dixon Entrance. It is a long, scenic inlet where total protection can be found anywhere in reasonable depths past the small, well-treed islets along the west shore. Porpoises and seals like to play in the strong

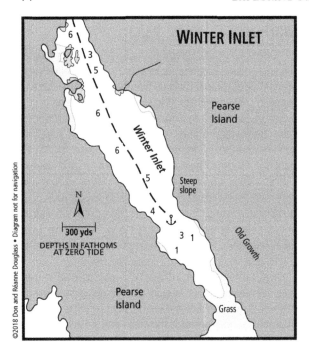

Gwent Cove, off the south entrance to Hidden Inlet, provides fair-weather anchorage directly in front of the old white cannery building with two smoke stacks. There is a 5-fathom flat area off the old wharf and a small private float. The float is sometimes used as a sport fishing outstation.

West of the wharf, the head of the cove shoals rapidly. Since the water is dark brown muskeg, there is no more than a foot or two of visibility.

Anchor in 5 fathoms over sand and mud with shells; good holding.

### Hidden Inlet (Pearse Canal)
Hidden Inlet is 0.25 mile northeast of Gwent Cove.
Chart 17437 (inset)
Entrance: 54°56.72' N, 130°19.85' W
Anchor: 54°57.14' N, 130°20.27' W

Hidden Inlet is located on the northwest side of Pearse Canal, 8 miles northeast of Winter Inlet. The entrance is narrow, set back from the canal, and easy to miss. The tree-covered Yelnu Islets, 300 yards off the west shore, are a leading mark.

Enter the inlet on or near slack, staying mid-channel. The fairway is quite wide, but favor slightly west of center at the south entrance, and east of center in the narrows. The fairway has a fairly even bottom, bouncing between 3 and 5 fathoms. One hour after a low water of 6 feet, we measured a flood current of 2 knots. Thirty minutes later, it had increased to 3-plus knots, with moderate turbulence forming.

Just beyond the narrows, on the west side of the inlet, is a grassy shore, off of which lies a 2- to 3-fathom shoal where temporary anchorage can be found. The bottom is rocky and there are kelp patches on either side of the beach area. The shores are steep, with rocky slabs, and high peaks can be seen nearby.

currents off the entrance. The creek outlet on the east shore has grassy margins, and the head of the inlet is a large grassy meadow.

Anchor in 3 to 5 fathoms over sticky black mud, small broken shells and wood debris; very good holding.

### Gwent Cove (Pearse Canal)
Gwent Cove is 8.7 miles northeast of Winter Inlet.
Chart 17437 (inset)
Entrance: 54°56.57' N, 130°20.02' W
Anchor: 54°56.55' N, 130°20.25' W

*The majestic eagle rules Southeast Alaska*

CHAPTER 1 — DIXON ENTRANCE, PORTLAND CANAL, REVILLAGIGEDO CHANNEL TO KETCHIKAN   15

*Portland Canal, looking north at head*

Anchor in 3 fathoms over a rocky bottom with kelp; poor holding.

## Portland Canal

Portland Canal, which forms the international boundary between Alaska and Canada for over 100 miles, terminates in Hyder, Alaska, and Stewart, British Columbia.
Charts 17427, 17425
Entrance: (1.45 miles north of Tree Point): 55°03.47' N, 130°11.54' W

Portland Canal is a long, narrow fjord, perhaps the longest on the entire North American continent. When measured from Dixon Entrance to Hyder, it is 130 miles long. Its sides are sheer and steep and its waters are deep. This is a remote and isolated channel with an appearance of rugged wilderness.

Anchorage is marginal at best and depends entirely on the weather. VHF weather reports are difficult to receive; VHF Ch 21B is useful in the central part of Portland Canal.

## Whiskey Bay (Pearse Island)

Whiskey Bay is at the north tip of Pearse Island, near the junction of Pearse and Portland canals.
Chart 17427
Entrance: 55°02.09' N, 130°11.10' W
Anchor: 55°01.93' N, 130°11.15' W

Whiskey Bay is a good lunch stop, or an overnighter if no downslope winds are expected. The head of the bay has a grassy meadow with a huge stump. The shoreline has a constant slope that can be used as a kayak haul-out. Upon entering, avoid the rocks awash on the east side of the bay and anchor in convenient depths.

Anchor in 4 to 6 fathoms over sand and mud with good holding.

## Reef Island (Portland Canal)

Reef Island is 3.0 miles northwest of Whiskey Bay.
Chart 17427
Anchor (south cove): 55°04.78' N, 130°12.64' W
Anchor (west Reef Island): 55°04.93' N, 130°12.35' W

Reef Island, on the west side of Portland Canal, has two coves that provide some relief from down-slope winds, but both are exposed to the south.

The south cove is steep-to and temporary anchorage can be taken in 6 to 8 fathoms off the drying beach. Small craft can also find some protection directly west of Reef Island, off the stony beach. The fairway on the west side of Reef Island has a minimum depth of about one fathom. There is a 1- to 2-fathom area in the passage between Reef Island and the shore. The level of the tree limbs indicates that the area is mostly free of chop. If you anchor in this passageway, a stern-tie to shore may be effective.

Anchor (south cove) in 6 to 8 fathoms. The bottom is sand, stones and iridescent seaweed; fair holding.

Anchor (west Reef Island) in about 3 fathoms, mixed bottom, predominantly sand; fair-to-good holding.

### Sandfly Bay (Portland Canal)
Sandfly Bay is 7.9 miles north of Whiskey Bay.
Chart 17427
Entrance: 55°09.52' N, 130°09.07' W
Anchor: 55°09.75' N, 130°09.28' W

Some temporary protection from downslope winds can be found in scenic Sandfly Bay. It is a good place for small craft to anchor in fair weather only. Sandfly Bay is steep-to off the creek outlet. The foreshore slope on the west side of the bay is less steep, and its grassy margins have little driftwood to indicate severe weather or chop. Avoid the charted rocks near the east shore.

Anchorage can be found about 100 yards from the white granite rocks on the west shore, 50 yards south of the drying gravel flat. This spot can provide reasonable anchoring for one or two boats in fair weather. There is easy landing access.

Anchor in 3 to 5 fathoms over sand with fair-to-good holding.

### Halibut Bay (Portland Canal)
Halibut Bay is 11.6 miles northeast of Whiskey Bay.
Chart 17427
Entrance: 55°13.02' N, 130°05.50' W
Anchor (east shore): 55°13.73' N, 130°05.69' W
Anchor (west shore): 55°13.40' N, 130°05.94' W

Halibut Bay affords the best protection between Whiskey Bay and Maple Bay or Fords Cove. Convenient anchorage can be found in the entrance on the east shore, just off a tiny creek

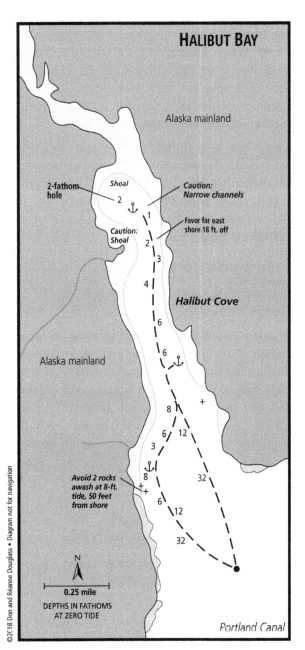

## RUSSIANS IN ALASKA

The first Europeans to set foot in Alaska were Russians. This may have happened as early as 1648, when the explorer Semyon Dezhnev was reportedly blown off course on a voyage through the Arctic Ocean around the eastern tip of Asia; however, no evidence exists to confirm this. In 1732, the Russian navigator Ivan Fedorov sighted Cape Prince of Wales, on the eastern side of what is now called the Bering Strait. He did not land, but settled the question posed by Tsar Peter the Great as to whether Siberia was connected to North America. Russia laid claim to the northern Pacific Coast of the Americas at this time.

In June 1741, two ships set sail from the port of Petropavlovsk, on the Kamchatka peninsula, to explore the possibilities of Russian colonization. (Earlier expeditions that had set forth on this undertaking had been unsuccessful.) Commanded by Vitus Bering and Alexei Chirikov, respectively, the *Sv. Petr* and the *Sv. Pavel* lost sight of one another almost immediately, but both vessels continued sailing eastwards. Chirikov sighted what is thought to have been Prince of Wales Island on July 15, 1741, and sent ashore a landing party—the first known instance of Europeans setting foot on the northwest coast of North America. On almost the same day, Bering and his crew sighted Mount St. Elias, on the Alaska mainland. Both captains set course for Russia shortly afterwards to report their discoveries. However, the *Sv. Petr* came to grief on what is now Bering Island, at the western end of the Aleutian chain. Bering died shortly afterwards, but his crew survived the winter on the island and reached Kamchatka aboard a boat constructed from the wreckage of their ship.

Both Bering's men and Chirikov's *Sv. Pavel* returned to Russia with cargos of fine sea otter pelts. This led to the establishment of a series of Russian fur trading posts in the Aleutians, coastal southeast Alaska, and northern California. Aleuts and other natives were co-opted to harvest the pelts. Cruelly exploited or enslaved, and decimated by their exposure to infectious diseases, the natives tried and failed to repel the colonists, who responded with punitive acts of violence. Meanwhile, some of the trading posts became permanent settlements—among them, Unalaska (from 1774), Three Saints Bay (1784), and New Archangel, now Sitka (1804).

As various Russian fur companies tussled for supremacy, their outposts remained dependent on provisions obtained at great expense from British and American merchants. By the 1860s, the supply of furs was in decline; competition from British and American trappers was on the rise despite several treaties signed in the 1820s that recognized exclusive Russian rights to the fur trade above 54° 40' North; and the colonial settlements (home to no more than 700 Russian citizens) remained costly to maintain. In 1867, the Russian government sold "Russian America" to the United States for $7.2 million, despite protests from Alaskan natives who argued that the land wasn't Russia's to sell, and from other Americans who saw the purchase as a waste of taxpayers' money. The Russians who remained in Alaska were offered US citizenship, but few chose to stay. Their legacy as colonists survives in the onion-domed Russian Orthodox churches that still stand in places like Sitka, and in the Russian surnames of some native Alaskans, notably on Kodiak Island.

The canceled check signed by US Secretary of State William Seward to purchase Alaska (for 2 cents an acre!) now resides in the US National Archives in Washington DC.

—AC

---

and stony beach, or on the west shore between a small creek and the rocky point. While the bay is open to the southeast, most of the summer up- and downslope winds blow by the entrance.

In the inner bay, there is a 3-fathom hole north of the large creek. The passage to this hole is very shallow. We found as little as 2 feet in the fairway at zero tide, with rapidly shoaling flats on either side.

Anchor (east shore) in 8 fathoms over sand, gravel and stones with good holding.

Anchor (west shore) in 6 fathoms off a tiny creek over sand, gravel and stones with good holding.

### Car Point Notch (Portland Canal)
Car Point Notch is 19.4 miles northeast of Whiskey Bay.
Charts 17427, 17425
Position: 55°20.30' N, 130°00.14' W

The head of the notch at Car Point holds a wonderful surprise—a stunning waterfall that tumbles vertically over somber, angular, gray-

and rust-colored granite. Although many lovely cascades adorn the eastern shore of Portland Inlet, this one received raves from all our crew. As we approached the notch, the water grew calm and we were able to come within 10 feet of the waterfall. Ferns and delicate white flowers grow out of every small crevice, while hemlock and spruce sprout from unlikely vertical faces.

At the south end of Portland Canal, the water is tea-colored but it becomes progressively greener as you proceed northward.

## Tombstone Bay (Portland Canal)
Tombstone Bay is 23.25 miles northeast of Whiskey Bay.
Chart 17425
Float position: 55°24.36' N, 130°03.30' W

On the north side of Tombstone Bay there are overhanging cliffs from which hemlock and cedar grow. The bottom is steep-to with a rocky beach. This bight could offer shelter from north winds with an anchor placed close to the drying flat at its head.

The south end of Tombstone Bay is the watershed for an unnamed creek that flows from a perfect, U-shaped valley. Protection from southerly weather can be obtained here; however, avoid the charted rocks and the drying flat off the creek.

Anchor off the drying flat, in about 10 fathoms over an unrecorded bottom.

## Maple Bay (Portland Canal)
Maple Bay is 24.1 miles northeast of Whiskey Bay.
Chart 17425
Entrance: 55°25.36' N, 130°01.17' W
Anchor: 55°25.28' N, 130°00.66' W

Maple Bay lies 1.5 miles north of Tombstone Bay at the foot of Mt. Tourney. The bay offers good protection from southerlies if you tuck just inside Columbia Point on the south end, and moderate protection from northerlies behind Maple Point on the north end. Avoid the rocks near shore.

On one visit we saw three mobile homes on log floats moored in the bay. An old cabin and pilings from a former pier are located at the north end of the bay. Several streams and waterfalls drop from snow fields on Mt. Tourney.

Anchor in 3 fathoms off the edge of the drying bank over stone and gravel with poor holding. Be sure to check the set of your anchor.

## Fords Cove (Portland Canal)
Fords Cove is 35.9 miles north of Whiskey Bay.
Chart 17425
Entrance: 55°37.80' N, 130°06.02' W
Anchor (small boats): 55°37.67' N, 130°05.84' W

Fords Cove affords good protection in southerly weather. Small boats can anchor between the float and the sandy beach in 3 fathoms; larger boats can anchor just outside the float in 5 to 7 fathoms.

Anchor (small boats) in 3 fathoms over sand with very good holding.

## Turquoise Cove (Portland Canal)
Turquoise Cove is 43.5 miles north of Whiskey Bay.
Chart 17425
Entrance: 55°45.36' N, 130°08.12' W
Anchor: 55°45.20' N, 130°07.97' W

What we call "Turquoise Cove," on the east side of Portland Canal, 0.5 mile south of

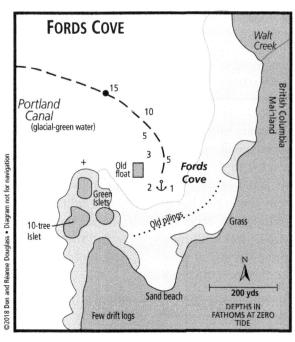

Round Point, can provide anchorage for one small boat only. It is out of the southerly chop and has good protection from most summer weather. The V-shaped cove is deep, with continuous shoaling to the small beach at its head. A stern-tie to shore is recommended.

You have a first-class view of high snowfields on the mountains to the west, and the color of the water is an exquisite light turquoise, thus our name for it. However, visibility through the water is only about a foot.

Anchor in the head of the cove in about 5 fathoms over soft silt with fair holding.

### Glacier Cove (Portland Canal)
Glacier Bay and Cove is 47.4 miles north of Whiskey Bay.
Chart 17425
Entrance: 55°49.13' N, 130°07.55' W
Anchor (east cove): 55°49.38' N, 130°07.08' W
Anchor (west bay): 55°49.44' N, 130°07.61' W

The large bay south of Glacier Point is known locally as Glacier Bay. However, we call it Glacier Cove in order not to confuse it with Glacier Bay National Park. The cove has two possibilities for anchorage in stable weather or downslope winds. The easterly cove, just behind Glacier Point, is steep off the rocky shore with room for one or two boats in about 7 fathoms. A stern-tie to shore can be used effectively here.

The western part of the bay is steep-to and more open, with swinging room for a number of boats. Water visibility is limited to about a foot due to silt from the large glacier to the northwest. Both anchor sites are completely open to the south.

An unnamed river enters the south end of Glacier Cove through a 40-foot cleft in a 100-foot-high cliff. It's an impressive sight to view from a dinghy. Caution: shoal water exists a quarter-mile off the shore of the river, contrary to what is indicated

*Enjoying Glacier Cove*

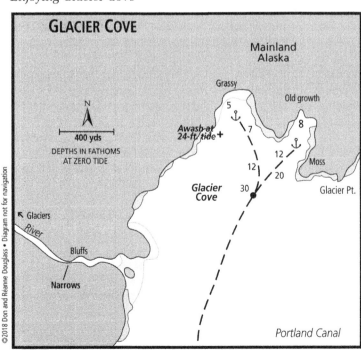

on the chart. The waters here take a close second in beauty to Turquoise Cove.

Anchor (east cove) in 9 fathoms over sand or glacial silt, with fair holding.

Anchor (west bay) in 7 fathoms over sand or glacial silt, with fair holding.

**Hyder** (Portland Canal—U.S. side)
Hyder is 52.7 miles north of Whiskey Bay.
Chart 17425
Float position: 55°54.22' N, 130°00.64' W

Hyder advertises itself as the friendliest ghost town in Alaska, though it actually has about 80 year-round residents, as well as a couple of sourdough saloons where tourists go to get "Hyderized" (i.e., drunk)! The most attractive building in town is the Orthodox Church with its golden ornaments. The town, with its pot-holed road, largely exists as a duty-free zone for residents of neighboring Stewart, B.C. Ketchikan, Alaska, has the nearest U.S. customs and immigration facilities; there are

## HYDER

Though a landlubber, not a boater, I've visited Stewart, B.C., and Hyder, Alaska, twice in the past ten years, both times by Subaru. The approach to the twin towns by road (Provincial Highway 37A) may rival that of the water route, as it passes through a long valley draped with glaciers. One of them is the famous Bear Glacier, 20 miles out of Stewart, which descends in spectacular fashion down a wide cleft to dip its frozen toes into a gray lake at the bottom.

The needs of car-campers are not so different from those of cruisers: my diary records Stewart as a pleasant, peeling-painted sort of place in which to satisfy cravings for Canadian junk food (sausage rolls!) and stock up on basic groceries, including 'smores fixings for my two boys and a bottle of something more bracing for me.

Hyder is a further three miles down the road. There's an old U.S. Customs house at the border, but no U.S. Customs agents on duty, so you don't have to bother with border formalities—though the Canadians will get you on your way back. On our 2013 visit, we were appalled to have to wait in line behind two other vehicles—veritable gridlock! to have our passports checked on our departure from Hyder.

Hyder itself is a ragtag collection of buildings in various states of decay; the most robust among them is probably the town's one hostelry, the SEALASKA Inn, which is also the place to get "Hyderized" if you feel compelled to do so. My boys and I camped in the rustic campground (though it had hot showers!) at the north end of town and accepted the manager's assurances that bears only visit occasionally. Adjacent campsites housed several sets of Harley riders, who had set themselves the goal of visiting all 49 of the continental American states in 10 days or less, and were either at the end of their journey or just about to set out. Because of its location, Hyder sees a lot of these long-distance bikers, who, if successful in their endeavor, are entitled to bestow upon themselves the unofficial but glorious title, "Iron Butt"!

Hyder's lure derives in part from its remoteness for car travelers and boaters alike, and its frontier ambience adds to its charm. However, the best reasons to visit—assuming you have land transport (boaters can take a bus tour out of Stewart)—are the salmon-eating bears and the Salmon Glacier. In August, when Coho salmon are running, grizzlies and black bear alike can be seen up close from the Fish Creek Wildlife Viewing Platform. A few miles north of town, this is essentially a fenced boardwalk from which you can look down upon bears fishing in the stream below. The animals tend to come and go, but our experience from several visits has been that if we don't see bears at the viewing platform, we're just as likely to see them along the road.

Fifteen miles further along from Fish Creek is the Salmon Glacier. This is the fifth largest glacier in Canada, and even from the spectacular vantage points afforded by the road you can only see a small part of it. If you drive far enough you eventually arrive at a height at which you can look down over a tremendous sweep of crevassed ice—which, unless you're an alpine climber, is a unique perspective, since most glacier views (as with the aforementioned Bear) tend to be from the bottom up. A Fish Creek ranger warned us, incidentally, that the mosquitoes above the Salmon Glacier "tend to be pretty bad by afternoon." For Alaskans, "pretty bad" is evidently a relative thing when referring to mosquitoes. If you're a non-Alaskan, and you plan to visit Hyder, Fish Creek, the Salmon Glacier or anywhere else in the general locale, pack bug spray!

—AC

none in Hyder, though it has a U.S. post office.

The State of Alaska upgraded the Hyder floats in recent years, installed new pilings and a seaplane dock, and it has dredged the harbor. However, the area is still subject to shoaling and cruising boats are advised to enter at high tide; at low tide a boat may find its keel aground.

Hyder's main attractions are its remoteness and its rustic saloons. The Fish Creek Wildlife Viewing Area—an excellent place to watch bears when the salmon are running in August—is three miles out of town along the Salmon Glacier road. The Salmon Glacier itself is some 20 miles up the road and well worth a look if you can get there. Another pot-holed road connects Hyder to Stewart, B.C., approximately two miles to the north, and to all other places in mainland B.C. from Stewart via Highway 37A.

*Stewart: public dock and yacht club floats*

### Stewart (Portland Canal)
Stewart is 53.6 miles north of Whiskey Bay.
Chart 17425
Entrance (Stewart Yacht Club public float):
55°55.20' N, 130°00.47' W

The beautiful setting of Stewart and the upper canal make the lengthy cruise up Portland Canal worthwhile. The mountains become more precipitous, glaciers are more prominent, and waterfalls increase.

As in so many former logging and mining towns, Stewart's economy is now dependent on tourism. Its attractions are the nearby Bear and Salmon Glaciers, Fish Creek Wildlife Viewing Area (accessible via Hyder), fresh- or saltwater sport fishing and the town's rustic northern ambience, which has attracted a number of filmmakers. Although most visitors arrive by automobile on Highway 37A, curious cruising boaters also wend their way up Portland Canal.

About 800 residents make their home in Stewart and they welcome visitors. However, the Stewart Yacht Club has a locked gate with a barbed wire fence, so if you wish to stay there, make prior arrangements by calling the Harbor Lights General Store at (250.636.2626). The floats have electricity but no other amenities (including water). It's a two-mile walk into town, where you can find provisions, post office, gift shops and several eateries. For

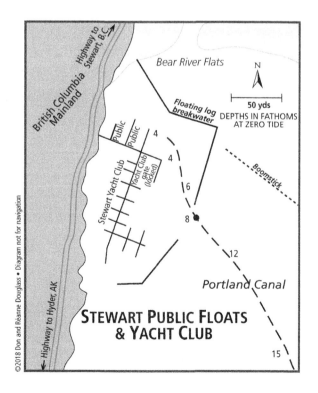

weather conditions in the area, CBC broadcasts radio reports. However, you probably won't have reception until you're nearly to the end of the Portland Canal and can determine the weather for yourself.

Stewart is connected by road to Hyder, Alaska, and the residents of both communities come and go freely. However, there is no U.S. Customs clearance in Hyder. Canadian Customs clearance is available by phone through Prince Rupert, but any vessels coming from Alaska should contact Prince Rupert ahead of time for the possibility of clearing in Stewart.

There are two cargo ship facilities in Stewart, so be aware of ship traffic.

For additional information, contact the Stewart-Cassiar Tourism council at 866.417.3737 or see the Stewart-Hyder Community Website: www.stewart-hyder.com.

# SOUTHEAST ALASKA

## Nakat Inlet
Nakat Inlet, northeast of Nakat Bay, is 4.7 miles northeast of Cape Fox.
Chart 17437
Entrance (0.16 mile west of Surprise Point): 54°49.13' N, 130°44.06' W
Anchor (8.3 miles north of Surprise Point): 54°57.41' N, 130°45.06' W

Anchorage can be found at the head of the inlet, northwest of three islets, off the drying sand flat.

Anchor in 8 fathoms over sand and mud.

## Nakat Harbor, Baidarka Arm (Nakat Inlet)
Nakat Harbor is 2.8 miles northeast of Port Tongass.
Chart 17437
Entrance (southwest arm Nakat Harbor, 0.58 mile southeast of Surprise Point): 54°48.67' N, 130°43.15' W
Anchor (1.35 miles southeast of Surprise Point): 54°47.79' N, 130°43.54' W

The un-named arm in the southwest end of Nakat Inlet is what we call "Baidarka Arm." The lower two-thirds of this arm is shallow and constricted, however, excellent shelter from southeast weather can be found at the head of the arm.

The fairway is narrow and winding and an approach should be made slowly with a bow watch and using a depth sounder alarm. The small scale of the chart does not show all hazards. The first half of the fairway is 4 to 5 fathoms minimum; favor the west shore. The last third of the fairway is 2 to 3 fathoms; also favor the west shore. Because the depths change due to creeks flowing into the vicinity, you are on your own to identify the fairway and find your route to the anchorage.

A dinghy passage at high water can be used to enter Nakat Bay.

Anchor in 2 to 3 fathoms over soft brown mud with clam shells and twigs; very good holding.

## Fox Island Cove (Fox Island)
Fox Island Cove is 3.8 miles southeast of Tree Point Light.
Charts 17437, 17434
Entrance: 54°45.83' N, 130°50.40' W
Anchor: 54°45.96' N, 130°50.77' W

Fox Island Cove—the small boat channel off Cape Fox—has provided us with comfortable anchorage in moder-

*Old boilers in Nakat Harbor gather moss.*

CHAPTER 1 — DIXON ENTRANCE, PORTLAND CANAL, REVILLAGIGEDO CHANNEL TO KETCHIKAN   23

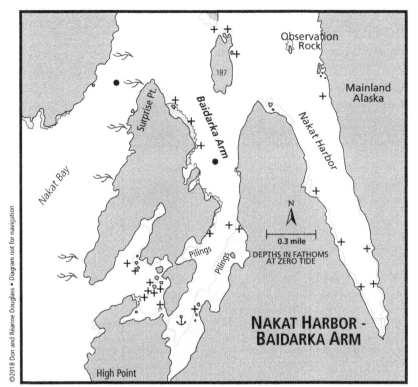

## Revillagigedo Channel
Revillagigedo Channel connects East Dixon Entrance to Ketchikan.
Chart 17420
South Entrance (Tree Point Light brg 090°T): 54°48.20' N, 131°01.35' W
North Entrance (Potter Rock brg 090°T at 0.25 Nm): 55°18.09' N, 131°35.11' W

## Tree Point
Chart 17434
Tree Point is 10.4 miles north of Dundas Island.
Tree Point waypoint (1 mile west of Tree Point Light): 54°48.17' N, 130°57.81' W

A shoal and foul area extending a half-mile or so offshore southeast of Tree Point cause the prevailing westerly swells to heap up. Keep well clear of the area in limited visibility

ate weather. Although technically not a cove, when you are tucked inside, it has the feel of a cove. It makes a good lunch stop, and it is a favorite layover spot for kayakers "doing" the coast. Enter from the east, avoiding the charted mid-channel rock. The west entrance is chock-full of kelp that provides shelter in prevailing northwest winds.

Anchor on the north side of Fox Island in 2 to 3 fathoms over sand and mud with good holding.

and particularly during fishing season. During this time gill netters set extensive series of nets close to Tree Point where there's excellent salmon fishing, so be alert for these. From Cape Fox to Tree Point you can make faster time by staying west of the action and following the 40- to 50-fathom curve.

## Gilanta Rocks
Gilanta Rocks are 2.75 miles northwest of Tree Point Light.
Chart 17434
Entrance: 54°50.89' N, 130°56.84' W
Anchor: 54°50.75' N, 130°56.39' W

Behind Gilanta Rocks, there's an intriguing cove that makes a great lunch stop in fair weather. A lovely sand beach rings the cove, and old-growth forest is thick above the beach. Don's uncle Phil, who canoed the Inside Passage in 1936, said this was the largest beach he and his friends had come across since Puget Sound. At that time, there were also a number of totems still standing in the village site above the beach. The totems have long been removed to museums, but as you explore the clearings

*Cove at Gilanta Rocks*

## AVOIDING FISH NETS WHILE UNDERWAY
### Linda Lewis and Dave Parker—M/V *Royal Sounder*

No one wants to have a "fishing-net-meets-prop" encounter. Good vigilance at the helm means being ever-watchful for fishing vessels with their nets deployed. OK, how do you know what vessels to look for? And what strategies can you use to spot and avoid the nets?

Although there are many types of fishing vessels in SE Alaska waters, the most likely ones a cruiser will encounter are gill netters and purse seiners, with the former being your biggest challenge.

Both vessels use a weighted net that extends down into the water from a "float line." Small, usually white, floats, which are only about six inches long, are dispersed along the float line. The small floats create a major challenge. Spotting them running along the water's surface can be very difficult, especially when the water is choppy or when you are looking into the sun.

Gill net fishing vessels are usually 30–40 feet long with a large drum on the stern to deploy and store the net. The float line, with its net hanging below it, is strung along the water in a more or less straight line, with one end remaining attached to the boat. Often after sitting awhile in the current, this line takes on a snake-like configuration along the top of the water. The "free" end of the float line usually has a large, orange, ball-shaped float. The goal is to avoid going between the fishing vessel and the orange float at the end of

*This is how small the net-floats are—hard to spot in the water.*

the net. When you see more than one gill netter in an area, you need to figure out which orange ball goes with which fishing vessel. Here's a tip we received from a fisherman: If you can't see enough of the float line to determine where it is coming from, very carefully head directly towards the big orange ball. As you get closer you will be able to determine what boat the net is leading from and steer a path to avoid it.

Purse seiners are larger vessels; about 50–60 feet long. They can be identified by the large "crane-like" power block used to winch the net onboard and there is always a skiff that helps set the net. The net is deployed in approximately a circle. This deployment (or "set") is usually done relatively close to shore. The proximity to shore and the (approximately) circular pattern of the set make these nets easier for the cruiser to spot.

The Alaska Deptartment of Fish and Game has a small brochure with pictures of these (and other) fishing vessels in PDF format that you can print out and carry with you on your boat. Go to: http://cf.adfg.state.ak.us/geninfo/about/faq/cf_faq.php#PurseSeiners.

*Gill netter's large orange ball—but where are the net floats?*

*(Continued on next page)*

# CHAPTER 1 — DIXON ENTRANCE, PORTLAND CANAL, REVILLAGIGEDO CHANNEL TO KETCHIKAN

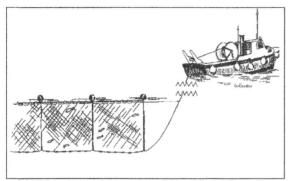
*Schematic of a gill netter operation*

*A small white line of floats snakes from the gill netting vessel to the large ball.*

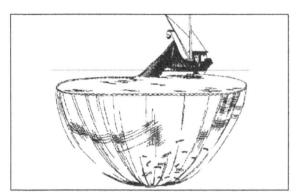
*Schematic of a purse seiner operation*

*Purse seiner checking gear*

Photos: Linda Lewis
Schematics: Courtesy of Alaska Department of Fish and Game

behind the beach you can imagine the marvelous culture that once thrived here.

Hike the beach, walk inside the forest or climb on the outlying rocks, but beware—we found fresh bear and wolf tracks on shore.

Enter from the north of Gilanta Rocks, passing close to a rock with white paint on its leading edge. There is good fair-weather anchorage anywhere from this rock to the sandy beach.

Anchor in 2 fathoms over sand and grass with fair-to-good holding.

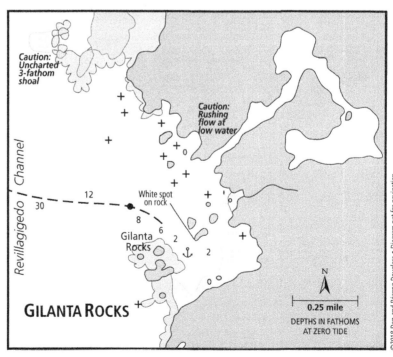

## Foggy Bay, Outer Cove

Foggy Bay, Outer Cove is 7.9 miles north of Tree Point Light.
Chart 17434 (inset)
Entrance: 54°56.40' N, 130°58.92' W
Anchor: 54°56.00' N, 130°56.86' W

Foggy Bay, the first and best anchorage north of Dixon Entrance, offers very good protection in most weather. Since its entrance is encumbered with rocks and reefs, consult the inset on Chart 17434 before entering and use extreme caution, even if you've entered it before.

Fishing boats use the outer cove in the southeast corner of Foggy Bay for convenient anchorage, and that site gets crowded at times. Most cruising boats head for the inner cove. Although it takes longer to enter and is more intricate, it offers complete shelter from all chop.

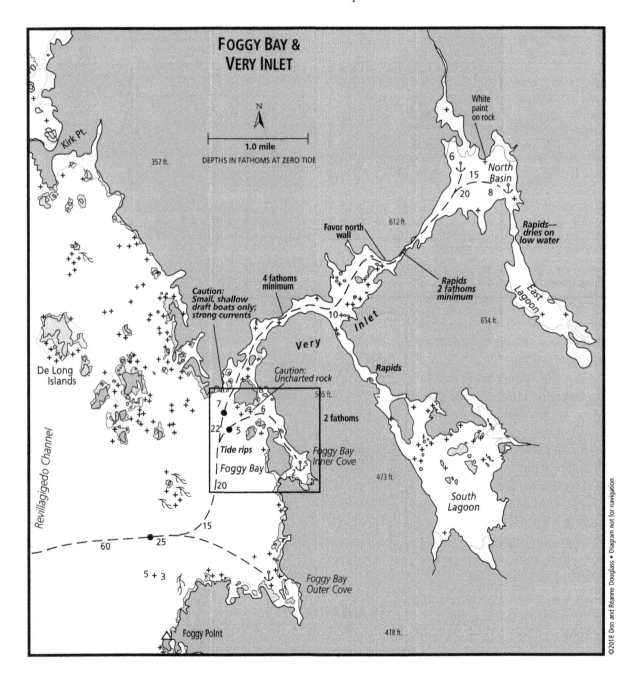

*Special entertainment—throw a fish in the water and watch a nearby eagle swoop down to pick it up.*

your exit from the inner cove plot your course carefully from the Inner Cove to Revillagigedo Channel to avoid the numerous rocks and reefs in the outer bay area. Exit Foggy Bay using the same course by which you entered it. Then, when you reach Revillagigedo Channel, turn north. This strategy will keep you away from the rocks and reef. More than one cruising boat has hit these rocks, with serious consequences!

Note that the bay is called "Foggy Bay" for obvious reasons—be ready. Foggy Bay is also a favorite of commercial fishing boats. (See the sidebar in this chapter for tips on "Avoiding Fish Nets While Underway.") You should also anticipate the westerly swell from Dixon Entrance as you exit Foggy Bay and head north in Revillagigedo Channel. This westering swell will place you in beam seas if you head directly north. If you do not have stabilizers, you may have a more comfortable trip if you proceed in a more westerly direction from Foggy Bay toward Duke Island, then turn north as you gain the protection of its lee shore.

Some cruisers become complacent about exiting a harbor after a successful entry. Be particularly careful in Foggy Bay. If you plan to head north to Ketchikan, when making

Anchor (Outer Cove) in 5 fathoms, deep in the southeast corner over mud and gravel with fair holding.

### Foggy Bay, Inner Cove

Foggy Bay, Inner Cove, is 8.8 miles north of Tree Point Light.
Chart 17434 (inset)
Entrance: 54°57.41' N, 130°57.47' W
Anchor: 54°57.00' N, 130°56.48' W

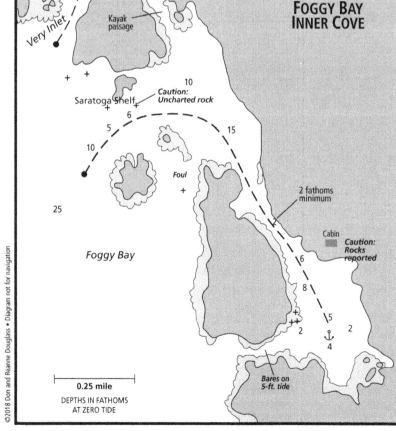

After crossing Dixon Entrance, the inner cove of Foggy Bay is a good place to unwind. The harbor on the far eastern side of the bay is well protected from all weather and receives no swell or chop. Rainforest surrounds the basin, and wildlife, including bear and

*Transiting the narrow entrance to Foggy Bay's Inner Cove.*

little martens, poke about its shores searching for food.

Entrance to the inner cove is a bit tricky and requires a cautious approach with sharp lookouts. As you head northeast for the small, round island with tall cedar trees, avoid Saratoga Shelf on your port. The shoal extends farther north and south than shown on the chart. An uncharted rock is located at 54°57.52' N, 130°57.24'W; leave this shelf well to your north. Loop around the small island and the reef on its east side before turning south through a narrow, shallow channel. The protected anchorage lies behind the long ham-shaped island on the extreme east side of the bay. Caution: depths may be reported incorrectly on electronic charts. Note that there have also been uncharted rocks reported at the anchor site off the cabin.

Anchor in 4 to 6 fathoms over sand and mud with good holding.

## Very Inlet
Very Inlet is 9.5 miles north of Tree Point Light.
Chart 17434
Entrance: 54°57.63' N, 130°57.69' W
Anchor (North Basin, west side): 54°59.81' N, 130°54.00' W

Very Inlet is a good place for a day's exploration by small boat, dinghy or kayak; however, the route is narrow and currents can be strong. Paddling quietly along the rocks you may come face to face with a marten or two. This is a particularly good place to experience the full sensation of a rainforest environment.

We recommend Very Inlet only for boats under 35 feet in length, and then only under favorable conditions and with an experienced crew. We suggest checking it out by dinghy first before you enter. It is safest to pass through at high-water slack, which occurs after that of Ketchikan. If you're in a kayak or a canoe, it's easy to get caught inside and have difficulty getting out until the next tide, so keep an eye on the time.

Although the entrance to Very Inlet is narrow, good water is carried through to the north basin. The fairway tends to favor the north wall, especially in the turn before the rapids. The bottom is irregular and you can expect your depth sounder to bounce around. But we have encountered no particular shoal area, unless you turn right too soon at the small islets midway through the inlet.

The rapids carries a minimum of about 4 fathoms, and the entrance the same or more. The rapids before the inner cove can drop at least a foot on spring tides, so use caution. The north basin has room for several boats to anchor. The water is mostly deep, though shallow enough for anchoring at the two places indicated in the diagram.

We do not recommend entering the south or east lagoons. The south lagoon is shallow and has a tricky passage. The east lagoon dries on low tides, and the current flows at a high rate.

Anchor (North Basin), as indicated, in 6 to 10 fathoms over mud and rocks with fair-to-good holding.

## Kah Shakes Cove
Kah Shakes Cove is 6.5 miles north of Foggy Bay.
Chart 17434
Entrance: 55°02.90' N, 131°00.09' W
Anchor (outer cove): 55°02.61' N, 130°59.90' W
Anchor (inner cove): 55°02.37' N, 130°59.01' W

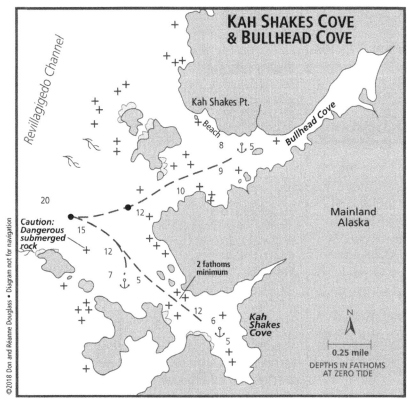

Kah Shakes Cove offers very good protection from southerly storms in picturesque surroundings. A fair-weather anchorage is located outside the narrow entrance, against the north side of the island west of Kah Shakes Cove. Enter the cove from the northwest; the southwest entrance is foul. Post an alert lookout on your bow, approach slowly, and follow a careful mid-channel course between the islets and rocks that nearly close the entrance.

If you are using passive stabilizers, be sure to raise them fully before entering or exiting the cove.

Minimum depth in the fairway is about 2 fathoms, and the bottom and underwater rocks are clearly visible. Avoid the mid-cove underwater rock, as well as the two rocks to the south end of the cove.

Anchor (outer cove) in 4 fathoms over sand with fair holding.

Anchor (inner cove) in 5 to 6 fathoms over mud with very good holding.

## Bullhead Cove

Bullhead Cove is 7 miles north of Foggy Bay.
Chart 17434
Entrance: 55°03.04' N, 130°59.90' W
Anchor: 55°03.33' N, 130°58.89' W

Bullhead Cove is another good anchorage offering very good protection in all but strong southwesterly weather. It has a fine beach on the south side of Kah Shakes Point and a deep inlet to explore by dinghy.

Bullhead is easier to enter than Kah Shakes and carries much more water. The fairway follows a mid-channel course, as indicated on the diagram. Avoid the numerous rocks en route to the anchor site. You can anchor on either side of the eastern island.

Anchor in 5 fathoms over sand and mud with good holding.

## Boca de Quadra

Boca de Quadra entrance is 6.8 miles southeast of Mary Island Light.
Charts 17434, 17427
Entrance (mid-channel between Kah Shakes and Quadra points): 55°04.64' N, 130°59.33' W

*Boca de Quadra has its entrance on the E side of Revillagigedo Channel between Kah Shakes Point and Quadra Point. . . . It extends NE to*

*It's a male—see the narrow "arrowhead" profile on its underbelly?*

the flat that extends 0.8 mile from its head. (See chart 17427.) The sides are steep-to and densely wooded, and there are no outlying dangers. (CP)

## Weasel Cove (Boca de Quadra)
Weasel Cove is 6.7 miles northeast of the Boca de Quadra entrance.
Chart 17434
Entrance: 55°08.52' N, 130°49.80' W
Anchor: 55°09.32' N, 130°49.95' W

> Weasel Cove indents the N shore ... and affords anchorage in 17 to 19 fathoms, mud bottom, about 0.5 mile above the E point at the entrance. The entrance and anchorage are clear, but vessels must keep clear of the flat that extends 700 yards from its head. (CP)

Anchor in 10 fathoms over a mud bottom.

## Vixen Bay (Boca de Quadra)
Vixen Bay is 6.4 miles east of the entrance to Boca de Quadra.
Charts 17434, 17427
Entrance (0.15 mile northwest of Gannet Island): 55°04.64' N, 130°48.22' W
Anchor (Gosling Island): 55°02.30' N, 130°46.91' W

Anchor in about 5 fathoms.

## Mink Bay (Boca de Quadra)
Mink Bay is 2.8 miles northeast of the entrance to Vixen Bay.
Chart 17427
Entrance: 55°05.57' N, 130°43.53' W
Anchor: 55°05.11' N, 130°43.80' W

Anchor in 5 to 7 fathoms in the west side passage.

## Duke Island
Duke Island, on the north side of Dixon Entrance, is 8 miles west of Foggy Bay.
Chart 17434

We like the isolation of Duke Island and find Judd Harbor and Morse Cove outstanding secure anchorages.

## Judd Harbor (Duke Island)
Judd Harbor, on the south side of Duke Island, is 13 miles northwest of Tree Point.
Chart 17434
Entrance (2 miles west of East Island Light): 54°52.49' N, 131°15.27' W
Anchor: 54°53.11' N, 131°15.74' W

Pay close attention to Chart 17434 since numerous submerged rocks lie on both sides of the fairway. The fairway carries 6 fathoms or more all the way into the anchorage. Kelp Island and the foul area on its north side give complete protection to Judd Harbor in all weather.

While this is an excellent anchorage, it is difficult to assess actual sea conditions outside the harbor. As always, be willing to weigh anchor and venture out, take a look and turn around and re-anchor if you don't like what you encounter.

Anchor in 4 fathoms over sand and mud with very good holding.

## Kelp Island Anchorage (Kelp Island)
Kelp Island Anchorage is 1.9 miles west of East Island Light.
Chart 17434
Entrance: 54°52.24' N, 131°15.22' W
Anchor: 54°52.15' N, 131°15.58' W

Anchor in about 6 fathoms over rock and sand with fair holding if your anchor is well set.

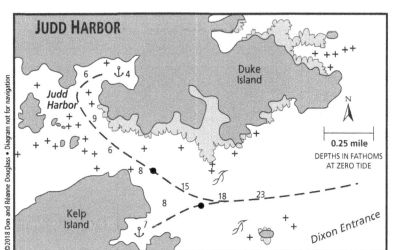

## Ray Anchorage (Duke Island)
Ray Anchorage is 9 miles west of Foggy Bay.
Chart 17434
Entrance: 54°56.25' N, 131°12.86' W

Ray Anchorage has a rocky shore and offers marginal anchorage. Protection from southerlies can be found along the south shore near the entrance to Morse Cove.

## Morse Cove (Duke Island)
Morse Cove, at the southwest corner of Ray Anchorage, is 10 miles west of Foggy Bay.
Chart 17434
Entrance: 54°55.78' N, 131°13.90' W
Anchor: 54°55.17' N, 131°17.07' W

Morse Cove, one of our favorite anchor sites, is bombproof in all weather. The narrow entrance has rocks along its edges and a dangerous mid-channel rock. Favor the north shore as you pass through the narrows; the minimum depth in this section is about one fathom. Note that there are strong currents in the narrows on spring tides. (See the Morse Cove Adventure sidebar.)

Once you have navigated the narrows, you enter a secure anchorage where you can spend a restful night or two. We once spent two days here with a curious Minke whale that awakened us early each morning with his blowing.

Anchor in 7 fathoms over mud and some gravel with good holding.

## Reef Harbor (Duke Island)
Reef Harbor is 3 miles north of Ray Anchorage.
Chart 17434
Entrance: 55°00.08' N, 131°14.22' W
Anchor: 54°58.78' N, 131°15.15' W

Anchorage can be found at the head of the harbor with good protection from westerlies, but it is open to southeast weather, depending on tide level, with marginal protection from the submerged rocks.

Anchor in 10 fathoms.

## Cat Passage
Cat Passage lies between Duke and Dog islands on the south and Double Islands and Cat Island on the north.
Chart 17434
East entrance (0.29 mile north of Grave Point): 55°00.47' N, 131°14.57' W
West entrance (0.4 mile west of Double Islands): 55°00.01' N, 131°19.34' W

> *The best approach to Pond Bay is from Revil-la-gi-gedo Channel through Cat Passage between Grave Point and three islets off the SE point of Cat Island. The best water leads about 0.3 mile off Grave Point until up to a reef that extends SW from a small highwater island off the NE point of the entrance to the bay, thence it leads about midchannel. It is advisable for strangers to enter at low water and with caution. Rocks in depths of 41/2 and 6 feet have been reported in the W end of Cat Passage. (CP)*

## Pond Bay (Duke Island)
Pond Bay is on the north side of Duke Island, 2 miles southwest of Grave Point.
Chart 17434
Entrance 54°59.78' N, 131°17.39' W
Anchor: 54°58.02' N, 131°20.64' W

> *Pond Bay, SE of Dog Island between it and Duke Island, affords good anchorage when once inside, but is little used because of the dangerous approach. The entrance from Felice Strait and Dog Bay, W of Dog Island, bares about 2 feet. A 6-fathom passage leads N*

*of Dog Island into Pond Bay, but it is obstructed by rocks and requires local knowledge to enter safely.* (CP)

Pond Bay offers very good protection in all weather. The best approach is through Cat Passage (see Coast Pilot description above).

Anchor in 6 fathoms over mud, shells, cobble and eel grass with fair-to-good holding.

## Morse Cove Adventure
### Kris Jensen

I was on my way home to Ketchikan, with my dad aboard, in a new sailboat I'd bought in Anacortes, Washington. Although I was using your suggested "Ultra-Marathon" Itinerary [26-day trip], I had only 16-days to get back to work. (Not bad for a 5.5-knot cruise and never sailing at night!) Your book definitely played a large part in my enjoyment of this entirely too short trip, but I ran into a minor problem in Morse Cove on our next-to-last night.

My dad and I anchored overnight in Morse Cove (Duke Island) and, as we entered, I noticed the current was near 4 knots in the narrowest spot. I needed to plan my departure for near slack water the next morning to ensure I'd be able to push out against the current. Low tide on 22 June was a minus 3.75 feet at 0810 at Ketchikan, so I was concerned about the depth. My chart showed 1.25 fathoms near the rock but the diagram in your book showed 2 fathoms.

Hmmm. I figured I'd put down there at low slack and see if you were right, since I didn't want to hang around till high slack. If the chart was right I'd be right on the bottom; if you were right I'd have about 4 feet under the keel, no sweat.

So, in the morning, we head down the narrow passage just after 0800. Very quickly I notice we're moving faster than I'd like to and I throttle back. My dad is on the bow spotting the channel; the bottom is very visible as we slide by the rock. Kelp is visible all across the channel beyond the rock.

I aim for the thinnest spot. We run aground in gravel, sand and large rocks approximately 150 feet to seaward of the rock. The dink slams into the stern and fills about a quarter with water before it bounces back up and slides around to the side.

I get this great idea to spin the boat sideways and increase our drag and heel to—hopefully to lessen our draft and carry us over this high spot. Just 20 feet ahead deeper water is plainly visible. I allow the current to pull the rudder to one side and we slew quickly broadside to the current and heel approximately 20 degrees.

It feels like we're moving but it's just the rushing of the water against the hull. Yep, definitely stuck—the rudder is jammed hard over against a rock. I'm worried about it, so we stand on the bow waiting for slack water. My dad wonders aloud why we came down here at 0700 and I suddenly realize I forgot to change my watch over to Alaska time when we crossed the line! Arrggh!

We didn't see any bugs during the evening in Morse Cove. But now that we're sitting ducks, they descend in clouds as we wait on the bow. After significant loss of blood we say "screw the rudder" and run for the cabin.

At about 0815 (Alaska Time), the boat stands up and we wait for the tide to turn. Watching from the companionway hatch we see the tide reverse at 23 minutes after low slack in Ketchikan.

Now the concern is how fast the current will be running when there's enough water to float us out of the pocket our keel is now sitting in. I really don't want to be carried backwards by the current and find a big rock with my rudder.

As the current begins to flow and the boat rises, we're able to spin back around into the current with a shot of throttle against a hard-over rudder. Thirty minutes after slack we're lifted free, and I feel us slip backwards a few inches and bump another rock.

I pop the engine in gear and slowly motor forward against the current until the keel hits the sand again. I figure I'll hold it against the ground as long as possible and try to do a 180-degree turn if I can't outrun the current. Soon we're running at cruising RPM, which usually nets about 5.5 knots, and I have only a little throttle left.

My dad is up on the bow looking for a path through the rocks. He says it looks a little deeper to starboard once I get around this big rock. I back off the throttle about 3 RPM and we slide back a few feet and maneuver around a large rock. I have to go to full power to get moving forward again. Slowly, we crawl past the kelp and the large rocks toward deeper water. Finally our speed begins to increase over the ground and the depth finder has something to report.

So now, I can accurately report that on a minus 3.75-foot tide there is somewhat less than 4 foot 7 inches in the channel at Morse Cove, and it looks like the chart was closest!

## Danger Passage

Danger Passage (on the southwest side of Mary Island) connects Revillagigedo Channel to Felice Strait. The passage lies between Lane Island and Danger Island (and its associated reefs).

Chart 17434

East entrance (0.45 mile east of Lane Island): 55°02.07′ N, 131°12.19′ W
West entrance: 55°02.72′ N, 131°14.72′ W

Danger Passage requires a curvilinear route to avoid the dangers southeast and west of Danger Island. It is possible that small vessels can use the narrow passage between Cat Island and Fripo Island with a minimum of 2 to 3 fathoms in the fairway; however, this passage is largely choked with kelp during the summer. Note that all dangers are marked by kelp.

## Mary Island Anchorage (Mary Island)

Mary Island Anchorage is 0.7 mile northwest of Mary Island Light.

Chart 17434

Entrance: 55°06.63′ N, 131°11.70′ W
Anchor: 55°06.46′ N, 131°11.73′ W

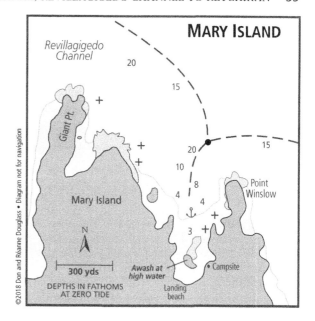

Mary Island Anchorage, although a rather rocky site, is strategically located. We have taken refuge here in pea soup fog, but it offers protection

## METLAKATLA

Metlakatla is a tribal community on the west (Clarence Strait) side of Annette Island, 15 miles south of Ketchikan. It is located within the 132,000-acre Annette Islands Reserve—the only Indian reservation in Alaska. Most of Metlakatla's 1,400-plus residents are Tsimshian, though some individuals have affiliations to other Alaska Native tribes. Collectively, the population comprises the Metlakatla Indian Community. Its members have exclusive commercial and subsistence fishing rights to all waters surrounding the island within a half-mile of shore.

The site of an abandoned Tlingit village, Metlakatla ("saltwater passage") was settled in 1887 by a group of Tsimshian people who were followers of an English lay missionary, William Duncan. Duncan was a former tannery company employee who brought Christianity to the Hudson's Bay Company trading post of Fort Simpson (now Lax Kw'alaams), near Prince Rupert in British Columbia. From 1857 onwards, he made converts of at least 800 of the natives—approximately one-third of the Fort Simpson population at that time—and persuaded them to leave the fort and its many temptations and relocate to Metlakatla (now Old Metlakatla, B.C.) a few miles to the south. After a dispute with B.C. church authorities in 1886, Duncan petitioned the US government for a new site in Alaska and was given land on Annette Island by President Cleveland.

Duncan and his flock built a settlement on Port Chester, on the west side (Clarence Strait) of the island. Laid out on a grid, New Metlakatla (the "New" was eventually dropped) had a church, a school, a cannery and a sawmill. In 1891, Congress granted Duncan's request that Annette Island be designated an Indian reserve. Duncan remained there until his death in 1918.

During World War II, the Metlakatla Indian Community allowed the US to build a military airbase on Annette Island. In exchange, a road was constructed to the east (Inside Passage) side of the island, making possible a year-round ferry connection to Ketchikan. The airfield was manned during the war by Canadian personnel—the only instance in which Canadians have assisted in the defense of the US from a US base. The facility later served as a Coast Guard search and rescue base, and as a regional commercial airfield.

Present-day Metlakatla is a thriving community with a large fishing fleet and a rich native culture. Boaters are encouraged to visit the community art center, local totem poles, and a longhouse by the boat harbor, where Tsimshian songs and dances are performed in full regalia, in the traditional (and all but extinct) Sm'algyax language.

—AC

from southerly weather only. There is a landing beach and campsite as noted in the diagram.

Entering is not a problem. Head due south, halfway between Point Winslow on the east and the islet to the west. Do not go deep into the cove—there is a reef and a rock awash at high water. Set your anchor well since the bottom is somewhat irregular.

Anchor in 4 fathoms over sand and rock with fair-to-good holding.

## Felice Strait

Felice Strait, which joins Clarence Strait to Revillagigedo Channel, lies between Duke, Dog, Cat, and Mary Islands on the southeast and Annette Island on the northwest.
Chart 17434
North entrance (1.5 miles west of Twin Islands Light): 55°08.54' N, 131°15.67' W
Southwest entrance (1.2 miles northwest of Percy Point and 1.7 miles
Southwest entrance to Sealed Passage (2.7 miles southeast of Percy Point and 1.2 miles north of Bee Rocks): 54°54.60' N, 131°34.50' W
Northeast entrance to Sealed Passage (0.5 mile north of the north end of Vegas Islands and 0.9 mile southwest of Tamgas Reef): 54°58.73' N, 131°26.73' W

## Ryus Bay (Duke Island)

Ryus Bay, on the northwest corner of Duke Island, is 6 miles south of Tamgas Harbor and 7 miles northwest of Judd Harbor.
Chart 17434 (inset)
Entrance: 54°58.37' N, 131°25.51' W
Anchor: 54°57.80' N, 131°25.20' W

Enter Ryus Bay between Form Point and Goose Tongue Island. Anchor northwest of Roy Island at the south end of the bay.

Anchor in 8 fathoms over sand and shells with fair-to-good holding.

## Harris Island

Harris Island, off the northwest tip of Hotspur Island, is 2.8 miles east of Point Davison Light.
Charts 17435, 17434
Anchor (0.22 mile southeast of the Harris Island Light): 55°00.16' N, 131°31.78' W

Anchor in 3 fathoms over sand and shells with rocks and kelp. Fair holding.

## Tamgas Harbor (Annette Island)

Tamgas Harbor, on the southwest side of Annette Island, is 11 miles west of Mary Island and 25 miles northeast of Cape Chacon.
Charts 17435, 17434
Entrance (0.32 mile west of Mule Rock Light and 0.35 mile east of Grass Rock): 55°01.30' N, 131°31.39' W
Anchor (0.35 mile northwest of Crab Point): 55°04.22' N, 131°33.59' W

For boating or emergency facilities, Tamgas Harbor is the closest major shelter to Cape Chacon and the lower part of Clarence Strait.

Anchor in 5 fathoms over sand with good holding.

## Crab Bay (Annette Island)

Crab Bay is 9 miles northeast of Ryus Bay and 5.5 miles west of Mary Anchorage.
Chart 17434
Entrance: 55°06.49' N, 131°21.30' W
Anchor: 55°06.36' N, 131°21.82' W

Anchorage can be found at the south end of Crab Bay, protected by the reef that extends north from the peninsula. Avoid shoals on either side of the entrance when entering Crab Bay. The upper bay is interesting to explore by dinghy, but it is shoal and largely dries on low water.

Anchor in about 2 fathoms over sand and mud with very good holding.

## Cascade Inlet

Cascade Inlet lies between the east side of Annette Island and Ham Island.
Charts 17434, 17428
Entrance (1.1 mile south of Middy Point and 0.4 mile south of Ham Island): 55°09.47' N, 131°21.19' W

Cascade Inlet is a deep and narrow inlet. A dangerous rock bares on a 1-foot tide, 0.45 mile southeast of the entrance waypoint to Cascade Inlet.

## Ham Island Bight (Ham Island)

Ham Island Bight is 2 miles southeast of Hassler Harbor.
Charts 17434, 17428
South entrance: 55°11.49' N, 131°23.28' W
North entrance: 55°11.95' N, 131°23.23' W
Anchor (south section): 55°11.68' N, 131°23.33' W

We like the protection and intimate feeling of the channel between Ham Island and Annette Island, which we call "Ham Island Bight." Both the north and south bends allow you to get off to the side of the channel and find sheltered waters. You will experience some current here, so set your anchor well and maintain an anchor light—some small local fishing boats zoom through at high speed in the dark.

The north entrance requires that you avoid the long spit extending northwest from Ham Island, as well as the rocks farther north that extend 100 yards off the Annette Island shore. Favor the Annette shore until you are west of the north end of Ham Island.

Anchor in either bend in about 5 fathoms over sand with good holding.

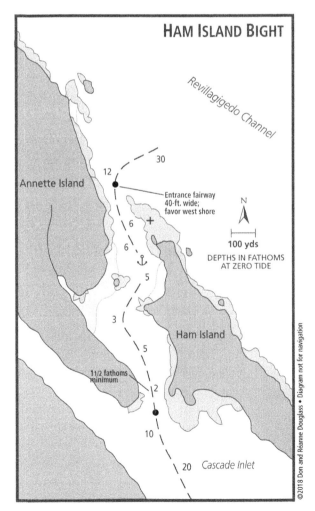

## Nichols Passage
Nichols Passage separates Annette and Gravina Islands.
Charts 17432, 17434
South entrance (1.4 miles northwest of Hid Reef buoy R"2" and 1.8 miles south of Point Mc-Cartey Light): 55°05.00' N, 131°42.47' W
North entrance: (Potter Rock brg 090°T at 0.25: 55°18.09' N, 131°35.11' W

Nichols Passage connects the lower end of Chatham Strait to the south end of Tongass Narrows.

## Canoe Cove (Annette Island)
Canoe Cove is 3 miles north of Point Davison and 3 miles south of Cedar Point.
Chart 17434
North entrance (1.7 miles southeast of Hid Reef buoy R"2"): 55°03.15' N, 131°38.14' W
Anchor: 55°02.75' N, 131°37.48' W

When entering Canoe Cove, avoid the rocks and reefs on either side of the entrance. Anchorage can be found east of the two major islets.

Anchor in 4 to 6 fathoms. Bottom and holding are unrecorded.

## Port Chester (Annette Island)
Port Chester, on the west side of Annette Island, is at the village of Metlakatla.
Chart 17435
Entrance (small craft basin 0.3 mile west of Village Point): 55°07.87' N, 131°35.07' W
Entrance (small craft basin close southeast of City Pier): 55°07.76' N, 131°34.23' W

## Sylburn Harbor (Annette Island)
Sylburn Harbor is on the west side of Annette Island, 3.1 miles north of Metlakatla.
Charts 17435, 17428
Entrance (0.73 mile northeast of Driest Point Light): 55°11.31' N, 131°36.10' W
Entrance (Japan Bay): 55°10.91' N, 131°34.68' W
Anchor: 55°10.62' N, 131°35.68' W

Sylburn Harbor is a very narrow, shallow channel with one-half fathom or less in the fairway leading to the inner basin. Best to enter at low water when you can see the dangers.

Anchor in 6 to 8 fathoms over sand and gravel with some rocks; fair holding.

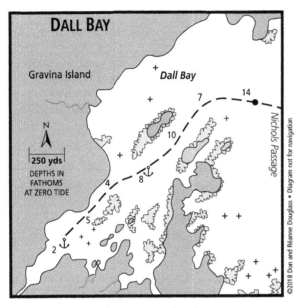

Dall Bay offers excellent protection for cruising boats. However, its narrow entrance is shallow and complex. It is best entered with Chart 17432.

Anchor (between two islands) in 8 fathoms, mud bottom.

Anchor (small craft) in 3 fathoms, mud bottom.

### Seal Cove (Gravina Island)
Seal Cove is 1.8 miles north of Dall Bay.
Charts 17428 (inset), 17434
Entrance: 55°10.53' N, 131°43.16' W

Favor the Gravina Island shore to avoid the extensive rock and reef system in the entrance. Anchorage can be found anywhere in the bay over a flat bottom of 5 to 7 fathoms of sand, mud and lots of rocks with good swinging room. The cove is exposed to southeast winds but offers good protection in prevailing northwesterlies.

### Annette Bay (Annette Island)
Annette Bay is 5 miles southeast of Ketchikan.
Chart 17428
Entrance: 55°16.81' N, 131°34.89' W
Anchor: 55°15.25' N, 131°31.55' W

Anchor in 8 fathoms over mud, shells and gravel with fair holding.

### Dall Bay (Gravina Island)
Dall Bay, on the west side of Nichols Passage, is 11.5 miles south of Ketchikan.
Charts 17432, 17434
Entrance: 55°09.41' N, 131°43.02' W
Anchor (between two islands): 55°09.33' N, 131°44.86' W
Anchor (small craft): 55°09.13' N, 131°45.32' W

### Black Sand Cove (Gravina Island)
Black Sand Cove is 0.6 mile west of Gravina Point.
Charts 17428, 17434
Entrance: 55°17.00' N, 131°37.70' W
Anchor: 55°17.06' N, 131°37.98' W

Black Sand Cove affords protection from northwest winds only. The sizeable number of logs on shore indicates that this cove is exposed to southeast winds.

Anchor in about 1 fathom.

### Lucky Cove (Revillagigedo Island)
Lucky Cove is 5.5 miles east of Hassler Harbor.
Chart 17434
Entrance: 55°12.74' N, 131°16.32' W
Anchor: 55°12.70' N, 131°16.10' W

Lucky Cove is a stopping place for local fishermen. Some temporary shelter can be found here from southeast weather. Anchor close to the drying mud flat in the lee of the small island. Note, however, that we found the cove marginal and uncomfortable when the wind shifted to the northwest in the middle of the night, and we had to proceed to Ketchikan under radar.

*Calm waters at Dall Bay*

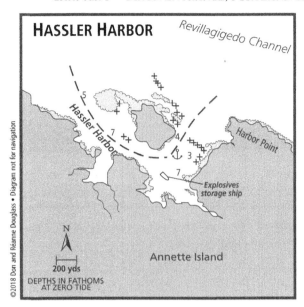

Anchor in about 10 fathoms on a somewhat steep-to sand and mud flat with fair holding.

### Camp Cove (Ham Island)
Camp Cove is 0.3 mile northwest of Middy Point.
Charts 17428, 17434
Entrance: 55°10.41′ N, 131°20.05′ W
Anchor: 55°10.34′ N, 131°20.12′ W

Camp Cove is a small cove suitable for anchorage in fair weather with limited swinging room, but the bottom is rocky with poor holding.

### Hassler Harbor (Annette Island)
Hassler Harbor, on the northeast side of Annette Island, is 1.4 miles southwest of Bold Island Light.
Charts 17428, 17434
Northwest entrance (0.7 mile northwest of Pow Island): 55°13.32′ N, 131°27.14′ W
East entrance (0.33 mile northeast of Pow Island): 55°13.13′ N, 131°25.22′ W
Anchor: 55°12.86′ N, 131°25.68′ W

Hassler Harbor is not one of our favorite anchorages. The east entrance is foul, although it is navigable by staying close to the Pow Island shore, 0.27 mile southwest of Harbor Point, to avoid a series of rocks that extend from Annette Island. The harbor has a very irregular bottom and we have experienced difficulty in getting a good anchor bite in the hard bottom. However, if a southeast gale were to spring up on south-bound itinerary in Revillagigedo Channel, we would not hesitate to use it.

Anchor in 7 fathoms southeast of Pow Island over a hard bottom with poor-to-fair holding.

### Nadzaheen Cove (Annette Island)
Nadzaheen Cove is 1.7 miles northwest of Hassler Harbor.
Charts 17428, 17434
Entrance: 55°13.64′ N, 131°27.28′ W
Anchor: 55°13.81′ N, 131°28.33′ W

Nadzaheen Cove provides shelter from northwest winds but it is fully exposed to the southeast.

Anchor in 6 to 8 fathoms.

### Coho Cove (Thorne Arm)
Coho Cove, at the entrance to Thorne Arm, is 1 mile northeast of Round Island.
Chart 17428
Entrance: 55°15.80′ N, 131°22.11′ W
Anchor: 55°16.38′ N, 131°22.13′ W

Anchor in 10 fathoms at the head of the cove.

### Moth Bay (Thorne Arm)
Moth Bay is 1.2 miles east of Coho Bay and 2 miles northeast of Round Island.
Chart 17428
Entrance: 55°15.96′ N, 131°19.83′ W
Anchor: 55°16.89′ N, 131°20.46′ W

As you enter, keep the two small islets to your west. Anchor in a soft-bottomed, 12-fathom hole near the head of the bay.

### Carroll and George Inlets (Revillagigedo Island)
These inlets are shown on the chapter map, but the coves listed below are too small to show on the map. Please use chart 17428.

### Carroll Inlet (Revillagigedo Island)
Carroll Inlet extends 24 miles northeast of Mountain Point.
Chart 17428
Entrance (0.83 mile northeast of Cutter Rocks Light): 55°17.76′ N, 131°30.19′ W

### Gnat Cove (Carroll Inlet)
Gnat Cove, on the east side of Carroll Inlet, is 5 miles northeast of California Cove.
Chart 17428

Entrance: 55°23.06' N, 131°19.98' W
Anchor: 55°22.67' N, 131°19.78' W

Gnat cove is the best sheltered anchorage in Carroll Inlet. With the absence of log rafts, good anchorage can be found west of the islet on the south side of the bay. Avoid the mud flat and rock ledges.

Anchor in about 7 fathoms over a mixed bottom, fair holding.

**Shelter Cove** (Carroll Inlet)
Shelter Cove is 10 miles north of Gnat Cove.
Chart 17428 (inset)
Position: 55°32.15' N, 131°20.90' W

Some protection from upslope winds can be provided at Shelter Cove, tucked in between the east point and the drying mud flats in about 5 fathoms.

## Ketchikan
### Don Douglass & Réanne Hemingway-Douglass

Ketchikan is the first Alaskan stop for boaters heading north, hence the nickname, "the First City." Its population is about 8,200, but the summer influx of visitors gives it a bustling atmosphere. This working community is known for its salmon and totem poles. Bring rain gear—Ketchikan gets about 160 inches of "liquid sunshine" a year.

The community began with a Tlingit fishing village located at the mouth of Ketchikan Creek. That's a good place to orient yourself. From there, Ketchikan stretches out in both directions along the coast like the wings of an eagle.

The bridge at Steadman Street crosses the creek along which lies Ketchikan's most famous attraction, Creek Street. Pastel buildings, formerly brothels, now house gift shops, galleries and book stores. You can get a glimpse of the former occupants' lifestyle by taking the tour at Dolly's House Museum and Gift Shop at number 24.

Near the top of Creek Street is the Married Man's Trail, a leafy "back door" into the red-light district. Climb the mossy, wooden staircase for a view of the harbor, then come back down to Ketchikan Creek and see the salmon ladder. Cross the creek to visit the Tongass Historical Museum at 629 Dock Street.

Inside, you'll peruse an eclectic mix of artistic and historical objects. There are bentwood boxes, tools, adornments, baskets, clothing, even a medical examination chair. You'll see the bullet-perforated skull of "Old Groaner," a massive bear brought down in 1935, and an assortment of photographs from the Victorian era to the present that illustrates how the city and its people have changed.

Another hub of activity is the waterfront. The Ketchikan Visitors Bureau provides maps and bus schedules, and volunteers to answer your questions. Concessionaires can set you up with excursions and conveyances, including horse-drawn trolleys, Jeeps, kayaks, Harley-Davidson, and "duck tours" on amphibious vehicles.

Many cruise ships dock here so there are lots of shops. If shopping isn't your cup of tea, visit the spacious U.S. Forest Service Southeast Alaska Discovery Center, a good place to learn about the Tongass rainforest and the Tlingit, Haida and Tsimshian cultures. Aside from its nature and wildlife exhibits, you can watch short videos of Alaskan residents talking about their lives and livelihoods.

Other attractions in town include the Totem Heritage Center with its collection of nineteenth-century totems and the Deer Mountain Tribal Hatchery and Eagle Center.

Two and a half miles southeast from Ketchikan is Saxman Native Village, a Tlingit community named for a teacher from Pennsylvania who drowned in 1886. You can see carving demonstrations and dance performances at the Beaver Clan House.

Ten miles northwest from the city is Totem Bight State Historic Park. See totems, a clan house and learn about cedar carving and other aspects of Native culture.

Pristine wilderness surrounds Ketchikan. Take a backcountry trip to see the abundant animal life—bears, wolves, martens, deer, minks—of Tongass National Forest, or a floatplane trip to Misty Fiords National Monument to see its glaciers, waterfalls and wildlife. The U.S. Forest Service building located near the harbormaster's office at Bar Harbor has excellent literature on Southeast Alaska recreational resources and a map of all the Forest Service buoys, floats and cabins.

For visitor information go to Ketchikan Visitors Bureau, 131 Front St., tel.: 907.225.4250 or 800.770.3300; www.visit-ketchikan.com.

## George Inlet (Revillagigedo Island)
George Inlet extends 14 miles north of Mountain Point.
Chart 17428
Entrance (0.83 mile northeast of Cutter Rocks Light): 55°17.76' N, 131°30.19' W

## Coon Cove (George Inlet)
Coon Cove, on the east shore of George Inlet, is 10 miles north of Mountain Point.
Chart 17428 (inset)
Entrance: 55°27.33' N, 131°29.40' W
Anchor: 55°27.42' N, 131°28.82' W

Coon Cove provides good anchorage in southeast weather. The upper part of the cove is a tidal flat.

Anchor in 5 to 8 fathoms over mud with good holding.

## Leask Cove (George Inlet)
Leask Cove, on the west shore near the head of the inlet, is 3 miles northwest of Coon Cove.
Chart 17428 (inset)
Entrance: 55°30.08' N, 131°30.77' W
Anchor: 55°30.33' N, 131°30.80' W

Anchor in 10 fathoms over sand and gravel.

## Bat Cove (George Inlet)
Bat Cove is 3 miles north of Coon Cove.
Chart 17428 (inset)
Entrance: 55°30.17' N, 131°30.16' W
Anchor: 55°30.42' N, 131°29.38' W

Anchor in 10 fathoms over black mud with very good holding.

*Tongass Narrows cruise ship traffic; one exiting and two at the dock in the distance.*

## Tsa Cove (George Inlet)
Tsa Cove, on the east shore of the inlet, is 2.5 miles northeast of Coon Cove.
Chart 17428 (inset)
Outer entrance (0.12 mile southwest corner of Granite Island): 55°29.97' N, 131°28.92' W
Inner entrance (in the narrow fairway between Granite and Bull islands): 55°29.89' N, 131°28.49' W
Anchor: 55°30.00' N, 131°27.68' W

Although Tsa Cove has a tricky entrance the best route to take is between Bull Island and Granite Island, favoring the Granite Island shore, avoiding shoals and rocks.

Anchor in 10 fathoms over black mud and shells with very good holding.

## Tongass Narrows
Tongass Narrows separates Gravina Island from Revillagigedo Island.
Charts 17428, 17430
Southeast entrance to East Channel (0.12 mile southwest of buoy N"2"): 55°18.49' N, 131°35.42' W
Southeast entrance to West Channel (0.20 mile southwest of buoy R"2"): 55°17.88' N, 131°36.62' W
Northwest entrance to West Channel (0.17 mile southwest of Pennock Reef buoy): 55°20.19' N, 131°40.33' W
Northwest entrance to East Channel (0.275 mile northeast of Pennock Reef buoy): 55°20.50' N, 131°39.78' W

*A typical sight along the cruise ship dock*

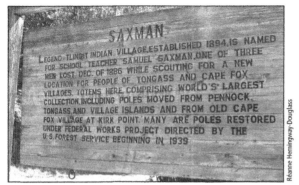
*A sign at Saxman Park tells of the legend.*

*The longhouse at Saxman Park*

*One of the many faces on the totems*

*Maintaining the totems*

*Creative, colorful totems fill the grounds.*

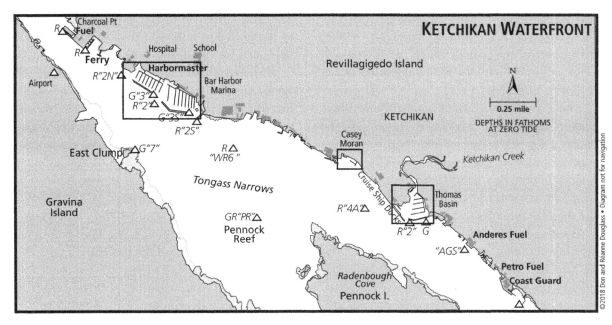

Tongass Narrows is the main thoroughfare for large cruise ships that berth at Ketchikan. It is not unusual to find three of these huge ships tied up at the dock and they come and go frequently. An additional cruise ship may also be anchored in Tongass Narrows, just west of the cruise ships dock. Keep a careful ear and eye out for traffic and stay well to your side of the fairway.

## Saxman Native Village (Revillagigedo Island)
Saxman Village is 2.5 miles northwest of Mountain Point.
Charts 17430, 17428
Position: 55°19.12' N, 131°36.08' W

## Ketchikan (Revillagigedo Island)
Ketchikan is on the south side of Revillagigedo Island and on the east side of Tongass Narrows.
Charts 17430, 17428

Ketchikan, once a rough town full of miners and loggers, calls itself the First City since it is the first port of call entering from the south and the necessary Customs clearance center.

In summer, Tongass Narrows hums to the noise of cruise ships coming and going, tenders zooming southward to Misty Fiords and float planes taking off. Creek Street, which used to be the largest red light district west of the Mississippi, is full of smart boutiques and restaurants. Nearby Stedman Street is home to Parnassus Books, one of the best bookstores in Southeast Alaska.

Contact the harbormaster on Ch 73 or 16 or by phone at (907) 228-5637 for instructions on where to moor. Be sure to mention your AC power needs. When you are assigned a moorage, the harbormaster will phone Customs, give them your slip location and a Customs official will come to your boat. Be patient, this is a busy waterfront and it is very possible that you will be "hot-berthing"—meaning that you will be assigned to a slip that has been temporarily vacated, most likely by a fishing-vessel owner.

The Port & Harbors Department operates and maintains five boat harbors: Bar Harbor, Thomas Basin, Casey Moran, Knudson Cove, and Hole-In-The-Wall. Thomas Basin or Casey Moran Harbor are both in the center of town, Bar Harbor is a mile north of town, while Knudson Cove is several miles north of town and Hole-in-the Wall marina is about 10 miles southeast, on George Inlet. There are transient moorage areas in all the harbors.

All vessels using the harbors must register with the Harbormaster's office at Bar Harbor, located at 2933 Tongass Avenue, or submit a registration via email. When registering, official vessel numbers must be provided. All vessels mooring in the harbors must pay a user fee based on the overall length of the vessel. This includes auxiliary skiffs and seine skiffs, if they are in the water.

Check out time is 12:00 p.m. (noon). Boats remaining in the harbor after noon will be charged for that day. For less than two hours moorage, vessels may use the loading zones. Loading zones are painted white and located near harbor ramps. There is no charge for use of the loading zones for a maximum of two hours.

For "super" yachts of virtually any size, another moorage option can be found at the private, full-service Doyon's Landing (400-foot dock), just south of the Coast Guard Station. Although expensive, it gives first-class service with ample power, fuel, Internet, covered ramps, a seaplane float and 24-hour security. Call on Ch 16 or telephone 907.225.5151; Website: www.doyonslanding.com.

Within a short distance of both Thomas Basin and Casey Moran Harbor you can find all services, as well as gift shops, art galleries and museums. Chief among the latter are the Tongass Historical Museum and the Totem Heritage Center. The Visitors Bureau, located at 131 Front Street along the quay, offers a wealth of brochures to help you decide what to visit. (Request their Walking Tour brochure.)

There are three markets on the north end of town. Alaskan & Proud to Be (known as A & P), three blocks south of the airport Ferry Terminal, will deliver you and your groceries to the harbor (tel: 907.225.1279). A gigantic Safeway supermarket is located in the Plaza Mall Shopping Center, a block south of Bar Harbor Basin (tel: 907.228.1900); pharmacy (tel: 907.228.1960). For a fee of $5.00, the store will box your groceries and deliver them to you. WalMart is located north of Bar Harbor, on the bus line.

In the south end of town you can provision at Tatsuda's IGA (ice available) at the corner of Stedman and Deermount (tel: 907.225.4125); they will deliver your groceries. There is also a laundromat near Tatsuda's. Tongass Trading Company, on the dock, has tourist items. They have moved their marine supplies and charts to west of Plaza. For additional marine supplies go to Pacific Pride, 1050 Water Street (tel: 907.225.3135), or Madison Marine (division of Madison Lumber and Hardware), 2557 Tongass (tel: 907.225.9828).

Gasoline, diesel and propane are available

*Thomas Basin puts you right in the heart of the downtown area and adjacent to the cruise ship docks.*

south of town (near the Coast Guard base) at Anderes Oil, 900 Stedman (tel: 907.225.2163), or Petro Marine, 1100 Stedman (tel: 907.225.2106). Another fuel dock (with propane available) is located near Bar Harbor, north of the Alaska Ferry Dock (across from the airport). Propane is also available at White Pass Alaska, a mile south of town.

If you're picking up or dropping off crew, Ketchikan has a convenient airport (with an Alaska Airlines terminal) just across Tongass Narrows (north of Bar Harbor); city buses run from downtown to the Airport Ferry dock. In good weather, we have tied up at the small float south of the terminal to await crew. The float adjacent to the terminal is reserved for the ferry and for float planes. Be alert for the very active Airport Ferry crossing as you cruise north out of Ketchikan.

The Ketchikan area provides you with your first opportunity in Southeast Alaska to query your computer for a WiFi hotspot. Try this while at any of the marinas mentioned below and you will probably bring up the site of an area-owned service provider. You can purchase varying amounts of time on a secured connection. (See the Introduction of this book for a more complete explanation.) Although there are cybercafés in Ketchikan, they are frequently packed with people, especially staff from the cruise ships. (Although the Ketchikan Public Library used to provide computer time for visitors, this is no longer true.)

Be patient, this is a busy waterfront and you will likely be "hot-berthing"—meaning that you will be assigned to a slip that has been temporarily vacated, most likely by a fishing-vessel owner.

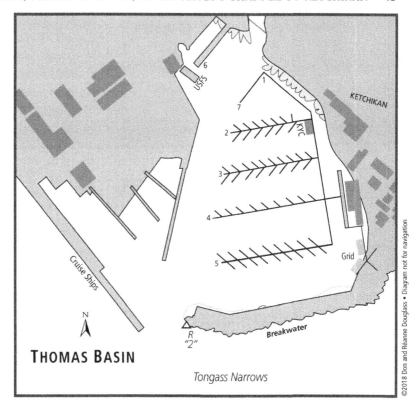

*Watch for the small USCG base on your starboard as you approach downtown Ketchikan from the south.*

## Thomas Basin (Ketchikan Harbor)
Thomas Basin is 0.65 miles northwest of the Coast Guard Base.
Chart 17430
Entrance: 55°20.30′ N, 131°38.59′ W

Thomas Basin may have accommodations for transients. Call the harbormaster on Ch 73 to inquire. Some of the docks have been upgraded in the past several years—the finger floats are much more stable—and general

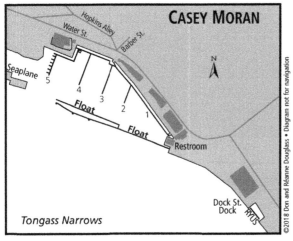

improvement work is ongoing. 30A power is available throughout the harbor, with 30A/50A on floats 4 and 5 where larger vessels moor. Note that all power pedestals now have GFI receptacles, so if your vessel has any sort of fault in your electrical system you will not be able to utilize the power grid in Thomas Basin. Thomas Basin floats are often filled in the summer and you may have trouble finding space in this tight basin. Note that in heavy weather or high winds, it may be difficult for boats over 36 feet to maneuver in the basin. Float number 2 is the Ketchikan Yacht Club transient float; if you can find space, tie up and check instructions on the outside of the club house.

### Ryus Float (Ketchikan Harbor)
Ryus Float is 0.9 mile northwest of the Coast Guard Base.
Chart 17430
Float: 55°20.49' N, 131°38.88' W

Ryus Float is an unloading zone, reserved exclusively for the use of cruise ship tenders and tour boats.

### Casey Moran Harbor (Ketchikan Harbor, labeled "City Floats" on charts)
Harbor is 1.1 miles northwest of the Coast Guard Base.
Chart 17430
Entrance: 55°20.63' N, 131°39.18' W

Casey Moran Harbor, formerly called City Floats, is conveniently located near the center of town, and has the only sewage pump out in town. However, with the increase in cruise ship traffic and the noise of float planes taking off all day long, most cruising boats prefer the quieter Bar Harbor. Since the floats are crowded in summer, you may have to raft. But be forewarned that, if you raft on the outside of a fishing vessel, you may have to move early in the morning or late at night.

### Bar Harbor (Ketchikan Harbor)
The middle entrance to Bar Harbor is 2.25 miles northwest of the Coast Guard Base.
Chart 17430
East entrance: 55°20.87' N, 131°40.75' W
Middle entrance: 55°20.96' N, 131°41.14' W
West entrance: 55°21.11' N, 131°41.43' W

Bar Harbor is the main cruising-boat moorage in Ketchikan. The Harbor has water, showers, laundry, and some power (be sure to specify your needs when you inquire about a slip).

## WHO WAS CASEY MORAN?

There are two Casey Morans in Southeast Alaska history. They were father and son. Casey Moran Harbor in Ketchikan is named after the son, Captain Casey Moran (1902-1990), a locally famous marine pilot and a visionary who in the 1970s encouraged the development of Ketchikan as a port of call for cruise ships. Co-author Don Douglass, who spent his late-teenage years in Ketchikan, recalls meeting him on at least one occasion.

The elder Casey Moran had no particular connection to Ketchikan, but his story is colorful enough to be worth mentioning. Bernard "Casey" Moran was an Alaska pioneer, a bootlegger, newspaperman and entrepreneur, who earned a fortune during the Klondike Gold Rush, not from mining but from bringing ice to Alaska. According to a *Popular Mechanics* story from August 1907, Moran "rented a tugboat to haul a small iceberg to Juneau. When he arrived he was reportedly greeted by hundreds of sweltering Alaskans, all willing to trade gold for cold beer." He was additionally famous for publishing a newspaper story claiming that Noah's Ark had come to rest in Alaska. In 1910, he testified before a congressional committee in Washington DC in favor of Alaskan home rule. He also anticipated the Alaska oil boom and ran a newspaper for a time in Venezuela.

Casey Moran Harbor was formerly known as City Floats and has long been home to Ketchikan's commercial fishing fleet.

—AC

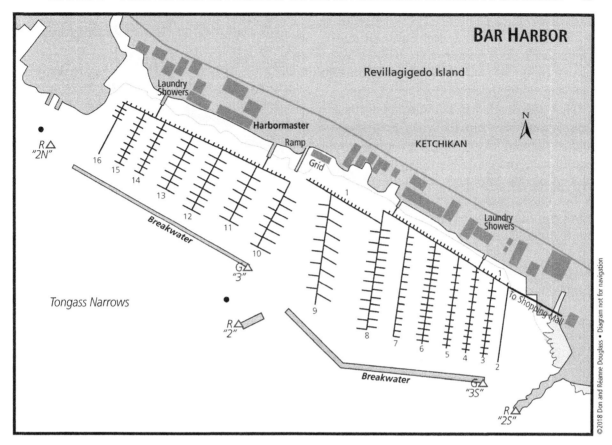

*Don't forget to watch for cruise ship traffic as you exit Ketchikan—fairway space can get tight.*

Bar Harbor is close to the main road with its heavy traffic. You trade the noise for convenient access to a laundromat, a liquor store, restaurants, and supermarkets, including the Safeway, which has free WiFi.

This large harbor is home to many fishing vessels and may provide your first up-close look at the real life of those who still work the sea. In fact, you are likely to be "hot-berthed" in a space that belongs to a fishing vessel that is out on the water. Take time to watch the labor and consider the long hours involved in the fishing life. It's a real education.

## Airport Small-craft Passenger Float
(Ketchikan Harbor)

Airport small-craft passenger float is 0.2 mile southeast of the airport tower and 0.7 mile northwest of Bar Harbor.
**Chart 17430**
**Float: 55°21.27' N, 131°42.24' W**

The small-craft float south of the passenger terminal is part of Seattle's old Lake Washington floating bridge. This is short-time moorage only, intended for vessels taking on or dropping off flight passengers.

## Bald Headed Cove (Pennock Island)
Bald Headed Cove is in the East Channel on Pennock Island and across from Saxman Village.
**Chart 17430**
**Entrance: 55°19.01' N, 131°36.72' W**

Bald Headed Cove is a small cove on the southeast side of Pennock Island.

---

## Alaskan Eyes
### Don Douglass

*Note:* In the days before Alaska became a state, most of the pink and chum salmon were taken from nets attached to floating fish traps anchored offshore. The traps were tended by watchmen who lived in a crude shack built on top of the float. These traps were outlawed after Alaska attained statehood.

It was July 1950, and I was a teenager fresh from the Lower 48. I had hired on for the summer season as an assistant watchman on a salmon fish trap. The trap, anchored off the southern tip of Revillagigedo Island, was tethered to shore by its 600-foot-long net, and it sat square in the face of whatever weather came blasting north from Dixon Entrance, a few miles away.

Since the trap tenders came just once a week to pick up the fish, other than fending off an occasional fish pirate and keeping up with maintenance, there wasn't a lot to do. I could spend my time rowing, fishing, diving, or—if the weather was lousy—reading.

One beautiful day, I had taken the 16-foot working skiff to a small bight a half-mile to the east and was free diving for king crab along the sandy bottom. I had managed to pull one up on my improvised hook before it slid off and scrambled quickly into the eel grass 20 feet below the drifting skiff.

I took a deep breath, preparing to dive after it, when I was stopped by the sight of a big rack of antlers bearing down on me. I grabbed the transom of the skiff, ready to hop out of the water as a five-pointer raced by, just twenty yards away, heading for the other end of the bight. Clearly, a bear or a pack of wolves had cornered the deer on one end of the spit, and he had decided to beat a fast retreat to the north side of the bight.

My heart pumped. This was my buck, and his rack would make a beautiful trophy. I quickly pulled myself into the skiff, and rowed in hot pursuit. Only two days to the opening day of hunting season: everything would be legal, I thought, if I could just catch him and keep him alive till then. Joe, my partner on the fish trap, would know how to dress the carcass, and instead of the canned and smoked stuff the trap owner provided, we could have fresh meat.

But I couldn't risk being caught with a poached deer—it would cost me my fishing license and summer income for college. How to pull it off?

First, I had to get him on board. Pulling alongside him, I looked at those horns and realized they're made for fighting males stronger and faster than I was. Trying to capture him with my bare hands was out of the question. Along with dreams of fresh meat, my courage waned.

But, wait! The skiff painter, twenty-five feet of rough manila line, might just make a lasso and even up my odds for a capture. A quick bowline-on-a-bight and I lassoed him, grabbed him by the horns, hauled him on board, tied his hoofs with the line, and rowed back to the trap.

Joe and I heaved "Big Deer"—as we soon named him—into our six-by-ten-foot shack, tied his thrashing

### Whisky Cove (Pennock Island)
Whisky Cove, on the east side of Pennock Island, is across from the Coast Guard Base.
Chart 17430
Position: 55°19.73' N, 131°37.95' W

### Radenbough Cove (Pennock Island)
Radenbough Cove is immediately across from Thomas Basin.
Chart 17430
Position: 55°20.05' N, 131°38.66' W

### Clam Cove (Gravina Island)
Clam Cove is in West Channel, 0.9 mile south of Pennock Reef.
Chart 17430
Position: 55°19.50' N, 131°39.77' W

Clam Cove is a log booming area. Some shelter can be found from southeast weather close to the drying mud flats in the cove or in the unnamed cove 0.6 mile to the north. Both anchorages are temporary at best and subject to the wake of passing ships.

### Ward Cove (Revillagigedo Island)
Ward Cove is 3.3 miles northwest of Bar Harbor.
Chart 17428 (inset)
Entrance (0.25 mile east of East Island): 55°23.73' N, 131°44.35' W

Ward Cove (known locally as Wards Cove) was the site of a large pulp mill and log storage area.

### Guard Islands Light (Tongass Narrows)
Guard Islands Light is at the northwest entrance to Tongass Narrows.
Chart 17428
Northwest entrance to Tongass Narrows (0.75 mile east of Guard Island Light): 55°26.75' N, 131°51.54' W

---

feet to his antlers and settled down for a 48-hour wait.

That night, a southeast gale off Dixon Entrance came up and assaulted the 100-foot square trap with breaking seas. Two- to three-foot water spouts began shooting up between the cracks in the floor, wetting everything inside. Joe got nervous.

There was a shack on shore that provided shelter in case we had to evacuate the fish trap, but reaching it would be suicidal. Joe couldn't swim, and rowing the 600 feet to that rocky shore in these conditions was impossible.

The storm increased during the night, and Joe began talking to God. I stared out the small window, watching the breakers sweep across the trap. Then I spotted running lights. I figured it was a cruise ship; no small boat could make it through seas like this, tonight. I grabbed our powerful flashlight and began sending a slow SOS signal into the dark. Soon, a large local fishing boat pulled alongside and Joe and I were taken on board by the daring crew—good-hearted Ketchikan folk who were out raiding fish traps vacated due to the storm. (Later, we learned two lives were lost that night.)

The crew treated us for hypothermia, filling us with hot soup and booze as the boat shook and rolled at anchor in nearby Lucky Cove. Thirty-six hours later, they returned us to our fish trap which, amazingly, was still in one piece, with the deer now lying exhausted and passive in a corner.

Forty-eight hours had passed, and according to the plan, it was time to dispatch Big Deer. But he was a pitiful sight. In the pounding from the storm, and his efforts to escape, he had worn his skin raw. He couldn't move a muscle. He was beat, and he knew it was the end. He'd evaded a savage attack by bear, only to die by slow torture at the hands of his two-legged captors.

I couldn't escape his stare. His big, dark eyes, alert and beautiful, followed me everywhere. His brain processed my slightest move. And in that tiny room, there was no place to hide.

Finally, Joe looked at Big Deer and said, "Okay, this guy's history. I've got my knife. You get the gun, and let's move him outside for the slaughter."

My stomach tightened. My throat thickened. This was the biggest, easiest kill of my life but those big dark eyes kept watching my every move. Eyes pleading with me for a fair chance to do combat—man to man, like when I hauled him aboard the skiff—just one more chance. I couldn't pull the trigger on him. Not me. Not now. "No!" I told Joe. "We'll load him in the skiff, and I'll row him ashore."

I rowed him back to the bight, beached the skiff and searched the sand for fresh bear or wolf tracks. There weren't any.

I laid the buck gently on the sand and carefully untied his bindings. All the time he just kept staring at me, with those beautiful dark eyes. Finally, I stepped back 10 yards and said, "Go for it!"

He stood up slowly, wobbling like a newborn fawn. "Go for it!" I repeated. He glanced at me once more, shook himself and took off, leaping and bounding into the brush. And all I could see were those big dark eyes.

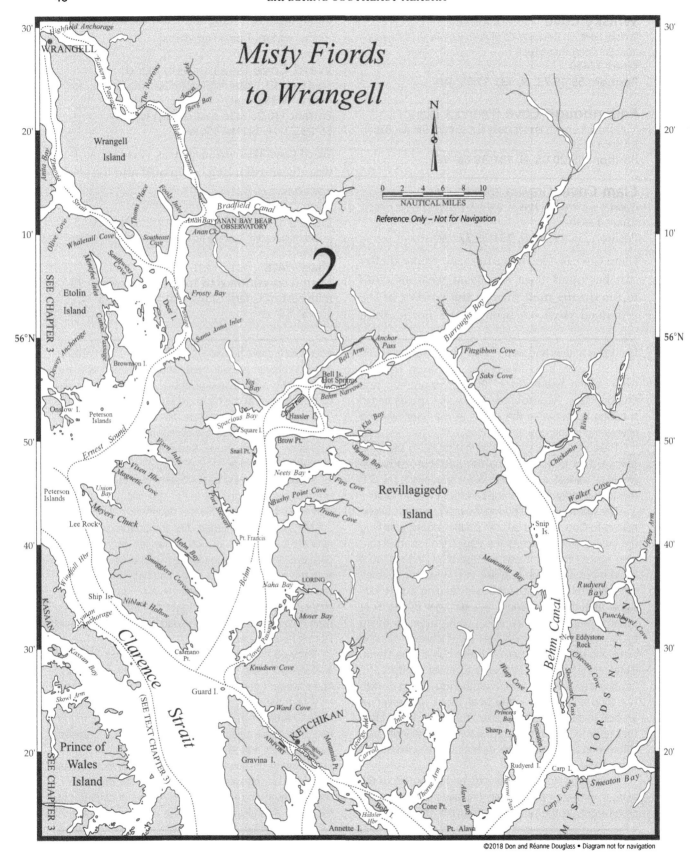

# 2
# MISTY FIORDS TO WRANGELL VIA BEHM CANAL, MEYERS CHUCK AND ERNEST SOUND

## INTRODUCTION

The area from Ketchikan and Misty Fiords to Wrangell is often called the "banana belt" by native Southeasterners. Although it gets a lot of precipitation, summer temperatures are usually mild, and wind and seas are less changeable and extreme than farther north. This region is popular with hunters, anglers, miners and explorers of all kinds. In recent years it has become something of a tourist mecca, but you can still get a real sense of the frontier spirit once you venture away from the cruise ship ports.

A circumnavigation of Revillagigedo Island via Behm Canal and a visit to hauntingly beautiful Misty Fiords National Monument gives you an excellent introduction to the rainforests and fjords of Southeast Alaska. Magnificent scenery and wildlife are the rewards for putting up with the rain, which averages over half an inch per day! Remote and intensely beautiful, this area is also known for its world-class salmon fishing. You can immerse yourself in solitude and primitive surroundings and fish to your heart's content!

Located to the east and south of Revillagigedo Island, Misty Fiords National Monument encompasses 2.2 million acres of unspoiled wilderness. You'll see beautiful, deeply cut fjords, glacier-fed streams and rivers and waterfalls that careen off 3,000-foot sheer cliffs, plummeting directly into the sea. This is an excellent spot to watch for Alaska's abundant coastal wildlife—humpback whales, orcas, sea lions, bald eagles and, in August, spawning salmon.

Wrangell, historically the jumping off point to the goldfields up the mighty Stikine River, has the feel of old Alaska. Fewer cruise ships

*Research Vessel* Baidarka *in Misty Fiords*

## Anchoring Challenges in Southeast Alaska
### Q & A with Brian Pemberton of NW Explorations

Most of us who dream of cruising our boat to Southeast Alaska have anchored our boats a fair amount. But we also know that the challenge of anchoring is different up there where the water is deeper, the bottom is rockier, the winds may be bigger and sometimes the williwaws come sweeping down from the mountains straining your boat hard against its anchor rode. You may feel the need for a little extra wisdom. Here are some words of guidance from an expert with lots of Southeast Alaska experience so you can feel better prepared. Brian Pemberton, of NW Explorations, a charter company in Bellingham, WA, has answers to some of the often-asked Southeast Alaska anchoring questions.

**Q:** *I'm nervous about my abilities to anchor in Southeast Alaska. It all seems so complex.*

**Brian:** A little apprehension is healthy but there is no reason to be nervous. Approach anchoring with a soft touch, with ease and gentleness. Anchoring has only one simple purpose: to the hold the boat.

You need to leave behind your preconceived notions about "only this type or weight of anchor is right," or "only this type and length of rode will be found on my boat," or "only certain types of secluded locations will be acceptable for putting my hook down," or "I must always be close to land."

**Q:** *But what do you mean? I thought there was a certain way to do this?*

**Brian:** Burst that balloon before you slip your lines. In truth, all of anchoring is about making choices based on the situation before you. The farther north you go, the more you must deal with anchoring "wherever you can find a place,"… and more likely than not, when you do find that place it will be deep and the wind may be blowing.

**Q:** *How deep is deep?*

**Brian:** At least 50 feet. Every Southeast Alaska cruiser needs to be prepared for anchorages at that depth, for anchorages with wind, big tidal ranges (~25 feet), and occasional 3-knot currents swirling through the anchorage.

**Q:** *Sounds intimidating. How should I prepare for those circumstances?*

*Rocks create anchoring challenges.*

**Brian:** It doesn't need to be daunting. Good planning will take you a long way.

**Q:** *I'd like to start with the anchor. What kind should I get and how heavy?*

**Brian:** I'm going to surprise you. An oversized, heavy anchor hanging off the end of your bow pulpit does not make good sense. That only adds weight to your bow and awkwardly extends the fulcrum point. An anchor is only one part in your ground tackle system. The more important picture is the combined weight of the anchor *and* the rode—usually chain for most Southeast Alaska cruisers.

**Q:** *OK, I'm hearing you: don't overdo the size of anchor for the boat. Do use chain (or a combination of chain and nylon). Tell me more. What anchor do you use on your boat?*

*(Continued on next page)*

*(Continued from previous page)*

**Brian:** Now we're getting into one of boating's most passionate subjects: which anchor and how many pounds. Over-rated debate, folks. I'm not a passionate fan of one type of anchor over another. And I'm not in favor of oversized anchors.

**Q:** *Well what do you use on your boat?*

**Brian:** My boat is a 57-foot LOA [length overall]; I have a 60-pound CQR because I believe it is better in rocks. (My 60 lb anchor would be considered in the mid-range of what manufacturers recommend.) Some folks swear by the Bruce anchor. We have a Danforth for backup, which is best in mud.

**Q:** *If the anchor is not the star of the show, what is?*

**Brian:** The big picture is the combined setup of the anchor and its rode. In Southeast Alaska waters a long chain rode is as important a part of your ground tackle as is the anchor. It's all about getting weight down to the bottom of the ocean, laying it out in a nice line that parallels the bottom as much as possible, then "setting" the anchor into the bottom until it holds well, then taking the next steps.

**Q:** *Talk more about chain. What size, length?*

**Brian:** My 57-foot LOA boat has 400-foot BBB 3/8 chain (11,000-pound breaking strength) and 300 feet of 5/8 3-strand New England rope (12,200-pound breaking strength); total rode equals 700 feet. Between my 60-pound anchor and my 680 pounds of chain, I can withstand just about anything.

**Q:** *What about my smaller boat?*

**Brian:** If your LOA is ~42 feet, you probably use 5/16 chain (most cruisers have this size chain) which has a breaking strength of 7600 pound; your ½-inch nylon 3-strand has a breaking strength of 7500 pounds.

**Q:** *Why nylon? And isn't that little nylon rope a bit small for the job?*

**Brian:** That "little" rope has a 12,200-pound breaking strength. And here is why nylon is really important: it gives. Nylon stretches 40 percent of its length under a load, thus protecting the set, ground tackle and pulpit. When the pull is reduced, the nylon returns to its original length, ready for the next stretch. The load of the boat isn't on your non-forgiving chain, but rather, on your resilient nylon.

*Kelp prevents an easy set. We call the big sheets of kelp that make anchor setting particularly challenging "newspaper kelp."*

**Q:** *I'm convinced. Now what about the "Anchor Bridle" you like so much?*

**Brian:** The anchor bridle gets put in place after you have deployed and set your anchor and played out your desired scope. You start with an anchor chain grabber that gets placed on your anchor chain. The nylon line bridle comes off each side of the grabber and is led up through a convenient fairlead onto the deck of the boat. An anchor bridle should have a minimum of 15 feet of nylon line (use the same size as your nylon rode) on each side of the anchor chain grabber.

**Q:** *Seems like a lot of fuss to have a fancy bridle out there. Why am I doing this?*

**Brian:** It is critical to have an anchor bridle; the advantages are enormous. The entire load of the boat is shifted away from the pulpit that is sticking up high in the air (where we don't want the weight) to a lower

*(Continued on next page)*

*(Continued from previous page)*

spot on the boat (where we do want the weight), then through fairleads where the bridle lines can be well secured. An anchor bridle is especially critical if you have an all-chain rode. It may be the only stretch you have in your entire system.

**Q:** *So far this looks like a lot of money for ground tackle.*

**Brian:** A man whom I very much respect, Mr. Don Douglass, recommends that 5 percent of the value of your boat should go into ground tackle. I agree with him. How much is safety and security worth to you and your crew?

**Q:** *Well, now I'm equipped. Let's get to the anchorage and do something. Walk me through this.*

**Brian:** This is the time for making choices related to the situation you are in. Assess the weather, the wind (current and expected), tidal activity, other boats nearby, rocky bottoms, steep bottoms, very, very deep bottoms, little swinging room, scope issues, chance of wiliwaws, etc. Take a small cruise around your selected anchorage and look carefully. The Southeast Alaska charts are not as accurate as we wish they were. Look out the window; watch your depth sounder. Have a bow watch.

Think to yourself: here is what I have to work with, how can I optimize my situation? For example, if the weather makes you want to seek a "bomb-proof" anchorage, can you get there before dark? Or should you stay where you are and plan to let out much greater scope.

**Q:** *My anchor is in position to deploy; here we go.*

**Brian:** Hold it. Hold it. One more thing to think about: Windlasses draw enormous power. Consider turning your generator on before you start your anchoring maneuvers. It's a good idea to presume that it will take three tries to get a good set.

**Q:** *Three times! You can't be serious.*

**Brian:** Keep your power up; you won't be sorry. It's OK to take three times. This is not a contest; this is about getting a good set that will keep everyone on your boat safe and happy.

**Q:** *I'm really ready now.*

**Brian:** Do yourself a favor and don't dump your anchor and a large amount of chain over the front of the boat like you're trying to build a pyramid down there. Slowly lower your anchor until it touches the ground. Then ever so gently put your boat in reverse, paying out the chain as you idle or drift slowly backwards. Lay a nice trail of chain along the bottom of the ocean. At some point you decide to "set" your anchor. Easy does it. High powered boats should barely bump into reverse and come right back out.

**Q:** *How do I know it's set?*

**Brian:** When an anchor is set, as you are in reverse, the rode will raise up out of the water in a straight line, approaching parallel to the water. The rode (especially chain rode) becomes almost as stiff as a rod. One cruiser with chain suggests that you put your hand lightly on the chain and "listen" to the chain when you are testing for set and you're not sure. You can actually feel the chain bumping and klunking over rocks or fishtailing back and forth over eel grass or kelp if it is not set. If it is set, the chain rises up in that straight line and takes on the feel of a solid, stiff cable. If it's not set, letting out a little more rode and doing setting maneuvers again often does the trick.

**Q:** *I see. I have the chain laid out nicely, I have a good set, and I have let out appropriate scope for the circumstances—I hope.*

**Brian:** Remember that scope decisions are situational. If you anticipate a 50 plus knot gale, you need 7:1 scope. Those are the times you will be glad you have 350 feet of rode.

**Q:** *OK, I'm done now right?*

**Brian:** Not by a long shot. Put that anchor bridle in place as the final and important touch. You firmly attach the chain grabber to the chain, then you lead each line through its fairlead and secure it on a strong cleat or capstan. *Then*, don't forget the next critical step: You now let out additional chain until you have a nice big loop of chain hanging down. For example, if you are anchoring in 25 feet of water, after the bridle has been secured, let out another 50 feet of chain. That way the nylon rope of the bridle is taking all the strain and is doing so closer to the ground.

**Q:** *I think I'm ready to try it.*

**Brian:** Remember to have a soft touch. Don't be in a hurry. Be ready to make repeated tries, and sleep well!

call at Wrangell and it's refreshing to enter a port where working boats outnumber pleasure craft. The Shakes Island longhouse and the petroglyphs along the beach make historic Wrangell a fascinating place to visit.

Anan Bear and Wildlife Observatory, 22 miles southeast of Wrangell, is well worth the stop. A short hike on a boardwalk trail through the rainforest leads to a waterfall where bear can be seen feeding on migrating salmon. Note that passes (obtainable online) are required from July 5 to August 25.

Three main cruising routes lead from Ketchikan to Wrangell: 1) the direct route used by larger vessels through Clarence and Stikine Straits (via Chichagof Pass); 2) the popular, more protected cruising route via Clarence Strait and Ernest Sound, Seward Passage and Zimovia Strait; and 3) the longer, more scenic, most protected of the three routes, which leads through Clarence Strait, Ernest Sound, Seward Passage, Blake Channel and Eastern Passage. This chapter deals only with the latter two routes. The first route through Clarence and Stikine Straits is detailed in Chapter 3.

## Behm Canal and Misty Fiords National Monument

Behm Canal borders the east, north and west sides of Revillagigedo Island; Misty Fiords National Monument extends along the east side of Behm Canal.
Charts 17434, 17424, 17422, 17420, 17423
SE entrance (mid-channel between Point Alava and Point Sykes): 55°11.52' N, 131°07.60' W
Northwest entrance (mid-channel between Caamano Point and Point Higgins): 55°28.60' N, 131°54.22' W

Established in 1978, Misty Fiords National Monument encompasses 2.2 million acres administered by the U.S. Forest Service as part of the Tongass National Forest. [*Note:*

*Entering Rudyerd Bay from Behm Canal brings into view the dramatic wall in Punchbowl Cove; sharing this amazing sight with guests is an added pleasure.*

Although the Monument uses American spelling, we adhere to the Norwegian spelling of fjord throughout this book's text, unless a business name uses the American spelling.]. While most of this is designated as wilderness, a 150,000-acre portion within the Monument, including upper Smeaton Bay and the head of Boca de Quadra, was reserved by Congress for the exploration and development of a potentially commercial molybdenum deposit at Quartz Hill. Hemlock, spruce and cedar grow on vertical granite slopes; numerous waterfalls tumble from snow-filled bowls; and gentle rain gives the area its misty appearance. Accessible only by boat or float plane, the Monument is a popular destination for kayakers. Within the Monument, the U.S. Forest Service maintains 13 recreational cabins, a few mooring buoys, and some hiking trails. For more information, contact the Ketchikan-Misty Fiords Ranger District, 3031 Tongass Avenue, Ketchikan, AK, 99901 (tel: 907.225.2148). Website: <u>mistyfiords.org</u>.

For cruisers who do not plan to travel beyond Ketchikan, a circumnavigation of Revillagigedo Island via Behm Canal may nevertheless be enticing as it takes in parts of the Monument.

Side trips into Smeaton Bay, Rudyerd Bay and Walker Cove provide the most dramatic scenery of the route; however, finding anchorages along the way requires attention. Many cruisers with time-limited schedules head south out of Ketchikan (after clearing Customs), then north up Behm Canal past the landmark New Eddystone Rock, and into Rudyerd Bay (about a 45-mile trip) and Punchbowl Cove. If you can make only one anchorage in Behm Canal, this is the one to choose.

Throughout the Monument the fjords are steep-to and deep, and mud flats shoal rapidly at the head of the inlets, offering few possibilities for anchoring. Most of the anchor sites lie along the shore of Behm Canal, and many offer only marginal shelter. You may be able to pick up one of the public buoys mentioned in this chapter.

Within the Monument, you are out of reach of National Weather Service broadcasts from Annette Island.

The weather, as the name of the National Monument implies, is often overcast with frequent rain or drizzle (over 150 inches per year). Wind and chop are short-lived and benign, and because of the heavy fresh-water outflows, the current is largely a continuous ebb on the surface.

Those who do not have time to visit the Monument by boat can book a flight through MistyFjords Air (1.877.228.4656) or through their website www.mistyfjordsair.com.

### Sykes Cove (Behm Canal)
Sykes Cove is on the east side of the southeast entrance to Behm Canal.
**Chart 17434**
**Entrance: 55°12.04' N, 131°04.82' W**
**Anchor: 55°11.75' N, 131°04.90' W**

Shelter from southerly winds can be found in Sykes Cove on the north side of Point Sykes. Swinging room is limited.

Anchor off the beach at the head of the cove.

### Point Alava (Revillagigedo Island)
Point Alava, on the southern tip of Revillagigedo Island, is the south entrance to Behm Canal.
**Position (0.5 mile southeast of Point Alava): 55°11.11' N, 131°10.58' W**

### Alava Bay (Revillagigedo Island)
Alava Bay, on the west shore of Behm Canal, is about 2.4 miles northeast of Point Alava.
**Chart 17434**
**Entrance: 55°12.78' N, 131°08.23' W**
**Anchor: 55°13.52' N, 131°09.13' W**

Fair-to-good shelter can be found in the far west bight of Alava Bay during stable conditions, but there is little protection in a strong southerly blow.

Anchor in 6 to 10 fathoms near the beach over mud bottom with fair holding.

### Rudyerd Island, Narrow Pass (Behm Canal)
Rudyerd Island and Narrow Pass are on the W side of Behm Canal, 8.5 miles NE of Alava Bay.
**Charts 17434, 17424**
**Entrance (north bight): 55°18.42' N, 131°02.30' W**

A lee from southerly storms can be found on the north shore of Rudyerd Island. However, the bottom is steep-to and there is very limited swinging room. We recommend Sykes Cove to the south or Roe Point Cove and Carp Island to the east for convenience and comfort.

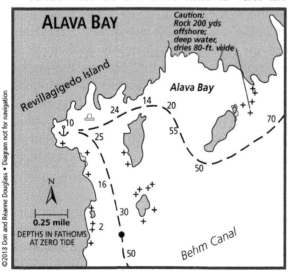

## Roe Point Cove (Behm Canal)

Roe Point Cove, on the E shore of Behm Canal, is 2.7 miles SE of Rudyerd Island.
Chart 17434
Entrance: 55°14.69' N, 131°00.26' W
Anchor: 55°14.55' N, 131°00.13' W

## Carp Island Cove (Behm Canal)

Carp Island Cove is on the south side of the entrance to Smeaton Bay.
Charts 17434, 17424
Entrance: 55°17.99' N, 130°52.85' W
Anchor (south of island) 55°17.86' N, 130°53.24' W

The area off Carp Island is reported to be a very good crabbing area and it is a favorite summer anchorage for local cruising boats that anchor just south of Carp Island or on the shoal closer to Short Point. However, downslope or outflow winds (from the north) can make this a rough anchorage. One cruiser reported to us that they found the bottom in this cove to be very rocky and had to leave after repeated efforts to set their anchor failed.

Anchor in about 6 fathoms, rocky bottom.

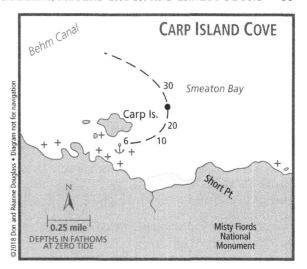

## Smeaton Bay (Behm Canal)

Smeaton Bay, on the east side of Behm Canal, is 9.8 miles northeast of Point Sykes.
Chart 17424
Entrance (Smeaton Bay, mid-channel between Nelson and Trollop): 55°18.56' N, 130°53.49' W
Entrance (Bakewell and Wilson arms, 6.6 miles east of Smeaton Bay entrance): 55°18.80' N, 130°41.97' W

---

## TONGASS NATIONAL FOREST

One of the (many) things that makes cruising in Southeast Alaska so special is that almost all the waterways of the region are situated within either forest or wilderness areas. In fact, all of the Inside Passage and most of the other places described in this book, apart from town sites, fall within one of the nation's largest areas of public lands—the Tongass National Forest.

Encompassing 17 million acres (approximately the size of West Virginia!) the Tongass is the largest national forest in the US. Lush and green, it includes the largest tract of temperate rainforest remaining in the world—as well as mountains, islands, glaciers, salmon streams, and numerous species of notable and endangered flora and fauna, including bears, whales, wolves, salmon and eagles. It is home to over 70,000 people in 32 communities, from the State capital, Juneau, to tiny Meyers Chuck (pop. 12 or less), A number of First Nations communities within the forest, including Tlingit, Haida, and Tsimshian peoples, continue to rely on the natural resources that provide the basis of their economy and cultural traditions.

The Tongass National Forest had its origins as the Alexander Archipelago Forest Reserve, created by President Theodore Roosevelt in 1902. A subsequent presidential proclamation, in 1907, created the Tongass National Forest, which took its name from Tlingit people who inhabited the Ketchikan region of Southeast Alaska. The two Forests were joined in 1908, and expanded in the last days of the Roosevelt Administration the following year. The Forest was again expanded in 1925 by Calvin Coolidge to encompass much of Southeast Alaska.

Almost 6 million acres of the forest are designated wilderness areas. These include Misty Fiords National Monument Wilderness and 18 other preserves, which are administered, along with the rest of the forest, by the U.S. Forest Service. The Tongass National Forest is also known for its extensive and controversial logging industry, and some lands within the forest are privately held by the Sealaska Corporation, a regional native corporation created under the 1971 Alaska Native Claims Settlement Act.

—AC

Smeaton Bay is the first of three majestic fjords cut deep into the mainland shore of Behm Canal.

### Sharp Point (Revillagigedo Island)
Sharp Point is 1.6 miles west of Smeaton Island.
Chart 17424
Entrance (cove west of Sharp Point): 55°20.55' N, 131°01.78' W
Anchor (cove 1.4 miles southwest of Sharp Point): 55°19.47' N, 131°03.09' W
Anchor (lee of Sharp Point): 55°21.03' N, 131°01.82' W
Entrance (cove 1 mile north of Sharp Point): 55°21.59' N, 131°01.49' W
Anchor: (cove 1 mile north of Sharp Point): 55°21.42' N, 131°01.65' W

Sharp Point provides anchorage in three nearby sites—one on the Behm Canal side of the peninsula, one on the bight in the lee of Sharp Point immediately west, and another in the shallow cove 1.5 miles to the southwest. Each site is essentially uncharted and requires a careful approach. The mid-channel charted rock 0.25 miles northwest of Sharp Point is, in fact, two separate rocks. Anchor in depths as required. Swinging room is limited in all three sites.

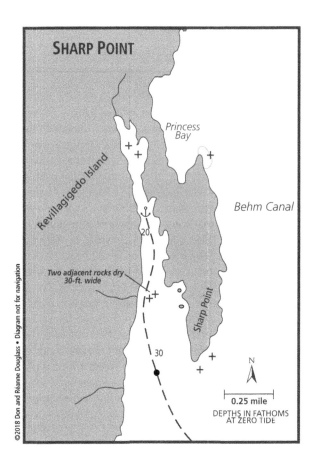

*Co-author, Réanne, in Walker Cove*

### Wasp Cove (Revillagigedo Island)
Wasp Cove, on the west shore of Behm Canal, is about 3 miles north of Smeaton Island.
Chart 17424
Entrance: 55°25.76' N, 130°58.74' W
Anchor: 55°25.64' N, 130°59.21' W

Wasp Cove is reported to provide good shelter in all but northeast winds.

Anchor in about 7 fathoms over soft bottom with fair-to-good holding.

### Shoalwater Pass (Behm Canal)
Shoalwater Pass, on the east side of Behm Canal, separates Winstanley Island from the mainland.

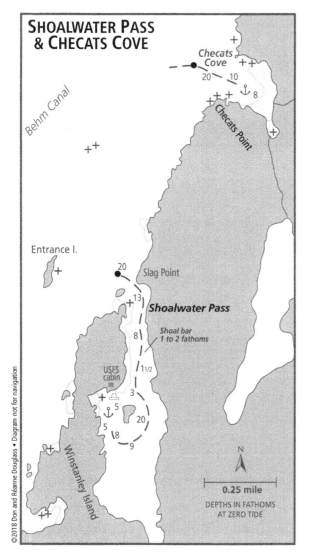

*New Eddystone Rock is a dramatic, 230-foot-high landmark in Behm Canal.*

### Checats Cove (Behm Canal)
Checats Cove, on the east side of Behm Canal, is 2.1 miles southeast of New Eddystone Rock and about 1.7 miles northeast of Winstanley Island.
Chart 17424
Entrance: 55°29.37' N, 130°53.01' W
Anchor: 55°29.26' N, 130°52.66' W

Checats Cove offers good protection in a southerly blow and is easy to access.

Anchor in 8 to 10 fathoms over mud with good holding.

### New Eddystone Rock (Behm Canal)
New Eddystone Rock is 2 miles northwest of Checats Cove.
Chart 17424
Position: 55°30.19' N, 130°56.30' W

New Eddystone Rock owes its name to George Vancouver, who thought that it resembled the lighthouse rock off Plymouth, England. Have your camera ready: this 230-foot, dramatic rock is a much-photographed landmark along Behm Canal.

### Rudyerd Bay (Behm Canal)
Rudyerd Bay is about 23 miles north of Point Sykes and 3.6 miles northeast of New Eddystone Rock.
Chart 17424
Entrance (mid-channel between Louise and Eva points): 55°32.99' N, 130°52.34' W

Rudyerd Bay with Punchbowl Cove is one of the main scenic attractions of Misty Fiords and

Chart 17424
South entrance: 55°23.40' N, 130°53.32' W
North entrance: 55°27.96' N, 130°54.17' W
Anchor (USFS cabin): 55°27.07' N, 130°54.32' W

The U.S. Forest Service maintains a cabin and float on Winstanley Island, at the northwest end of the north anchorage. The shallow water in front of the cabin offers very good shelter from all winds. Enter from the north via Slag Point over a 1- to 2-fathom bar.

Anchor in 5 fathoms south of a U.S. Forest Service buoy over mud with good holding. (The buoy cannot be reserved.)

*The majestic wall at Punchbowl Cove*

*The steep and muddy hike up to Punchbowl Lake is well worth it to see this amazing place.*

well worth a complete tour. The high granite cliffs on the east side of Punchbowl Cove are covered with numerous waterfalls during rainy periods. Deeper inside Rudyerd Bay, you will find a huge snow-filled bowl, overhanging gardens, and waterfalls at every glance.

## Punchbowl Cove (Rudyerd Bay)
Punchbowl Cove is 2.25 miles east of the entrance to Rudyerd Bay.
Entrance: 55°33.13' N, 130°48.36' W
Anchor: 55°31.59' N, 130°46.86' W

The Punchbowl is quintessential Misty Fiords. The 3,000-foot granite face on the east side of the cove is the scene depicted most often in pictures of Misty Fiords National Monument. A steep mud-and-boardwalk trail at the very southeast corner of the cove leads to gorgeous Punchbowl Lake. This hike might be better classified as a "scramble" since the trail has deteriorated; use caution. There are plenty of vantage points from which you can stop and admire the view. About a half-mile up the trail you will reach Punchbowl Creek Waterfall Overlook, which has breathtaking views. Wear boots and be prepared to exert yourself. However, when you get your first glimpse of Punchbowl Lake, you will agree that every minute of effort has been worth it. A small USFS open-sided cabin offers a welcome lunch spot.

A mooring buoy for small and medium watercraft is available on a first come, first serve basis. This buoy provides access to the Punchbowl Lake trail and shelter. Use the buoy for a short stay, or seek anchorage a little south of the buoy, between the buoy and the shore over a deep, hard bottom, avoiding rocks along the south shore. Tourist traffic is brought in by numerous sea planes.

Anchor in about 10-12 fathoms over rocky, hard, mostly mud bottom with fair holding.

### Rudyerd Bay, Upper Arm
The upper arm is about 4.8 miles from Punchbowl Cove.
Chart 17424
Entrance (upper arm): 55°35.82' N, 130°42.56' W
Position (Nooya Lake bight): 55°36.65' N, 130°42.55' W

The far north arm of Rudyerd Bay shoals rapidly, offering little in convenient anchor sites. The sand and mud flats up-river are full of giant stumps and root systems. Crabbing is reported to be good in these cold waters, and we have seen grizzlies combing the shores of the delta.

A private float used by tour boats has 12 fathoms at its south side and one fathom on its north. There is possible temporary anchorage off the outlet to Nooya Lake in 5 fathoms, but we have no record of the bottom. The south arm is reported to offer reasonable anchoring.

### Manzanita Bay (Revillagigedo Island)
Manzanita Bay, on the west side of Behm Canal, is 3.5 miles northwest of the entrance to Rudyerd Bay.
Chart 17424
Entrance: 55°35.46' N, 130°56.89' W
Anchor: 55°34.82' N, 130°57.60' W

Manzanita Bay provides significant shelter from southerly and northerly winds, which makes it a good place to stay when visiting Rudyerd Bay. The water is deep, however, and the drying mud flats are steep-to. A shore tie may be useful along the east shore of the cove.

Anchor in 6 fathoms over a bottom of thin mud and rock.

### Snip Islands (Behm Canal)
Snip Islands, on the west shore of Behm Canal, are 6 miles north of Manzanita Bay.
Chart 17424
North entrance: 55°41.78' N, 130°57.89' W
Anchor: 55°41.29' N, 130°57.87' W

Snip Islands are west of Walker Cove. Southerlies blow right through here, and the water is too deep and the sandy bottom too soft for convenient small-craft anchoring.

### Walker Cove (Behm Canal)
Walker Cove, on the east side of Behm canal, is 2.2 miles northeast of Snip Islands and 9.5 miles north of Rudyerd Bay.
Chart 17424
Entrance (mid-channel between Ledge and Hut points): 55°42.44' N, 130°54.11' W
Walker Cove buoy position: 55°43.90' N, 130°45.29' W

Walker Cove is a spectacular fjord with a classic glacier-carved valley at its head. Upon entering the cove, you pass a snow-filled bowl, high cirques, narrow snow-choked canyons, and a granite quarter-dome. Countless streams and dramatic waterfalls plunge from mile-high summits down these granite walls to the saltwater

*Cascades in Misty Fiords*

*Mossy granite, Misty Fiords*

Except for its entrance bar of 5 fathoms, Walker Cove may be too deep for convenient anchorage by most pleasure boaters. However, Captain Brian Pemberton, of NW Explorations, has reported good holding in depths of 50-70 feet on either side of the buoy. We have used the buoy in the inner bay and spent a wonderful, quiet night after entering under radar.

Another veteran charter boat captain considers Walker Cove to be one of the most beautiful anchorages in Southeast Alaska, and a favorite place to take his guests. He recommends using a special anchoring technique for anchoring off the drying mud flats on the south side of the cove southwest of the buoy. Enter on a high tide. Drop the stern anchor over the mudflat area and run out to an area about 80 feet deep and drop the bow anchor. Winch back between the two anchors to an area where the depth is about 50 feet deep. The next day, depart on a high tide to retrieve the anchor from the mud flats.

### Chickamin River (Behm Canal)
Chickamin River enters Behm Canal 5.8 miles northwest of the entrance to Walker Cove.
Chart 17424
Entrance: 55°47.53' N, 130°58.86' W

This place is rather exposed, and because the water is an opaque green, you can't see any hazards. We prefer Snip Islands or Fitzgibbon Cove as anchor sites.

### Saks Cove (Behm Canal)
Saks Cove is about 10 miles northwest of the mouth of the Chickamin River.
Chart 17424
Entrance: 55°55.80' N, 131°08.74' W

We found Saks Cove too deep for easy anchorage and recommend Fitzgibbon Cove. However, the deep waters of Saks Cove are reported to offer some fine hauls of prawns.

### Fitzgibbon Cove (Behm Canal)
Fitzgibbon Cove, on the northeast shore of Behm Canal, is 2.5 miles north of Saks Cove.
Chart 17424
Entrance: 55°57.81' N, 131°11.58' W
Anchor: 55°58.94' N, 131°10.84' W

Set in a beautiful, remote location, Fitzgibbon Cove offers good shelter from all winds.

Entrance is made to the east of the islets and to the west of Gibbs Rock, which dries. The inner cove has plenty of swinging room over a deep, flat bottom.

Anchor in 12 fathoms over mud with good holding.

### Burroughs Bay (Behm Canal)
Burroughs Bay enters Behm Canal from the northeast, 2.4 miles northwest of Fitzgibbon Cove.
Chart 17424
Entrance (0.8 mile northwest of Point Fitzgibbon): 55°59.63' N, 131°13.86' W
Klahini River USFS mooring buoy: 56°02.67' N, 131.05.94' W

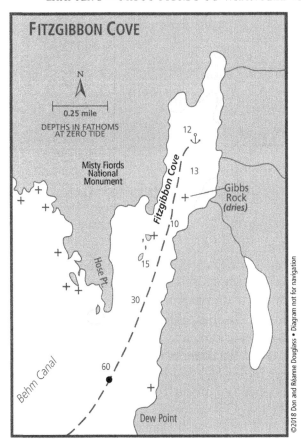

Anchor in 14 fathoms over a hard bottom of unknown holding power.

### Bell Arm (Behm Canal)
Bell Arm separates the northwest shore of Bell Island from the mainland.
Chart 17422
Entrance (0.5 mile north of Snipe Point Light): 55°56.01' N, 131°36.92' W
Anchor: 56°00.02' N, 131°25.77' W

Anchor in about 10 fathoms over sticky mud with very good holding.

### Short Bay and Bailey Bay (Bell Arm)
Short and Bailey Bays are on the northwest side of Bell Arm.
Chart 17422
Entrance (Short Bay): 55°58.60' N, 131°30.92' W
Anchor (Short Bay): 55°59.92' N, 131°31.33' W
Entrance (Bailey Bay): 55°56.24' N, 131°37.30' W
Position (Bailey Bay, mooring buoy): 55°58.05' N, 131°37.23' W

Anchor (Short Bay) in about 15 fathoms.

### Blind Pass (Behm Canal)
Blind Pass separates Black Island from the northwest side of Hassler Island.
Chart 17422
Northeast entrance: 55°54.34' N, 131°37.88' W
Southwest entrance: 55°52.68' N, 131°41.43' W
Anchor: 55°53.04' N, 131°40.91' W

A small cove can be found on the south side with very good anchorage and protection. Enter north of the rocks, staying approximately 30 feet from shore until you reach the anchor site.

### Anchor Pass (Behm Canal)
Anchor Pass, 5.9 miles west of the entrance to Burroughs Bay, separates the northeast end of Bell Island from the mainland.
Chart 17422
South entrance: 55°57.58' N, 131°24.04' W
North entrance: 55°59.87' N, 131°25.73' W

Anchor Pass has been the site of unfortunate small craft groundings.

### Behm Narrows (Behm Canal)
Behm Narrows separates Bell Island from Revillagigedo Island.
Chart 17422
East entrance: 55°56.38' N, 131°26.14' W
West entrance (0.8 mile southeast of Snipe Point Light): 55°55.01' N, 131°35.47' W
Anchor (cove 0.5 mile south of Bell Island Hot Springs): 55°55.21' N, 131°34.03' W

Exposed to westerlies and 100 feet deep, the bight mentioned above appears to be useful in fair weather only. In bad weather, opt for Yes Bay.

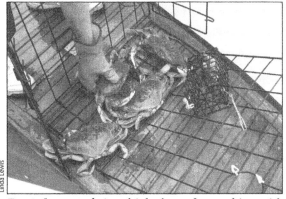

*Don't forget to bring thick gloves for working with the crab catch.*

There is a gravel bar to the northeast up Blind Passage. Continuing up the passage is not recommended, except by kayak.

Anchor in 5 fathoms.

### Hassler Pass and Gedney Pass (Behm Canal)
Hassler and Gedney passes separate Hassler Island from Revillagigedo Island.
Chart 17422
North entrance (Hassler Pass): 55°54.17' N, 131°36.46' W
South entrance (Hassler Pass): 55°51.10' N, 131°34.58' W
West entrance (mid-channel between Brown Point and Gedney Island): 55°50.68' N, 131°42.69' W

### Shrimp Bay, Klu Bay (Revillagigedo Island)
Shrimp Bay is at the head of Gedney Pass; Klu Bay is at the head of Shrimp Bay.
Chart 17422
Entrance (Shrimp Bay): 55°50.33' N, 131°30.98' W
Entrance (Klu Bay): 55°50.10' N, 131°27.99' W
Anchor (Klu Bay): 55°50.56' N, 131°27.20' W

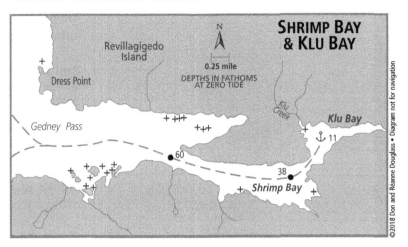

Klu Bay, known locally as Echo Bay, comes highly recommended by Southeasterners who fish and crab here. It is well protected from all weather. There are lots of eagles here and bear gather salmon along the creek bed.

Anchor off the drying flats of Klu Creek in 10 to 14 fathoms (if logging operations allow it); soft bottom with fair-to-good holding.

### Yes Bay (Behm Canal)
Yes Bay, on the northwest side of Behm Canal, is entered between Bluff and Syble points.
Chart 17422 (inset)
Outer entrance: 55°53.13' N, 131°44.54' W
Yes Bay Resort: 55°54.86' N, 131°47.56' W
Inner entrance: 55°54.88' N, 131°47.89' W
Anchor (first basin southeast corner): 55°54.61' N, 131°48.01' W
Anchor (inner basin west of old tramway): 55°56.37' N, 131°50.15' W

Yes Bay, whose name derives from the Tlingit word for mussel (yas), has unbeatable shelter from all weather at the far end of the first basin. The first and second basins are seldom disturbed, and moss hangs heavy on the trees.

Yes Bay Lodge, which is open to the public, has fuel, water and telephone service, as well as a bar and dining room. During high season the lodge recommends that you call ahead for dinner reservations and availability of fuel (907.225.7906). The lodge monitors VHF Ch 10. If you wish to stay at the lodge you must make advanced reservations. Daily air service from Ketchikan to Yes Bay is available.

Entry to the outer bay is easy. To transit the first basin, you must pass directly off the lodge, hugging the shore closely. It is best to do so during low tide when you can sight the rocks. When you have cleared the narrow peninsula on the west side, round up and turn directly southeast until you're deep in the cove. There is not much swinging room at the head of the cove, but you shouldn't need a lot since anchor strain is rare.

If you are heading for the inner basin, follow the directions of *Coast Pilot*: remain about 100 yards off the N shore until you reach the group of islands that separates the two basins. At that point the channel narrows to about 75 yards where there is submerged rock with 3 feet over it and a rock awash at low water, both of which are on the west side of the channel. In passing through this channel, keep the NE shore aboard about 30 yards. The inner basin is clear.

Anchor in the first basin in 7 fathoms over mud with good holding.

## Spacious Bay (Behm Canal)
Spacious Bay is about 22 miles north of Caamano Point.
Chart 17422
Entrance (1 mile north of Snail Point): 55°51.93' N, 131°47.84' W
Anchor: 55°51.28' N, 131°50.94' W

Inner Spacious Bay, which has easy access, provides good protection in settled weather. If southerlies are expected, consider the bight behind Snail Point, 1.9 miles to the southeast of Square Island. The west side of Square Island has a large, shallow area that provides convenient anchorage with good swinging room. Anchor 400 yards or more from shore to avoid the shoal.

Anchor in 2 to 4 fathoms over sand and mud with good holding.

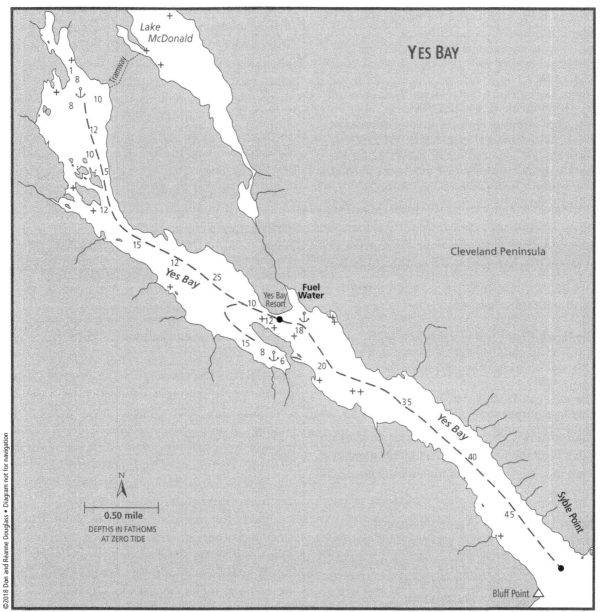

## Snail Point Bight (Behm Canal)
Snail Point Bight, on the west side of Behm Canal, is 1.9 miles southeast of Square Island and 20.6 miles northeast of Caamano Point Light.
Chart 17422
Entrance: 55°49.45' N, 131°46.78' W
Anchor: 55°49.13' N, 131°46.65' W

Snail Point Bight offers good protection for one boat in southerly weather at the head of the bay.

Anchor in about 5 fathoms.

## Neets Bay, Fire Cove (Revillagigedo Island)
Neets Bay, on the east side of Behm Canal, is 19.2 miles northeast of Caamano Point.
Chart 17422
Neets Bay entrance (0.8 mile south of Chin Point): 55°46.48' N, 131°42.15' W
Fire Cove entrance (Fire Cove, 5.4 miles east of Neets Bay entrance): 55°46.58' N, 131°32.23' W
Anchor (Fire Cove): 55°46.30' N, 131°32.44' W
Rock Fish Cove position (2.7 miles east of Neets Bay entrance): 55°45.89' N, 131°37.41' W

Fire Cove, a popular getaway for local cruising boats, is well protected from all weather and is reported to have excellent salmon fishing. A co-op fish hatchery is located in Neets Bay.

Anchor south of island in 4 fathoms over sand with good holding.

## Traitors Cove (Revillagigedo Island)
Traitors Cove is about 2.5 miles southeast of Bushy Point Light and 15.1 miles northeast of Caamano Point.
Chart 17422
Entrance: 55°41.59' N, 131°42.33' W
Entrance (upper cove): 55°43.65' N, 131°37.53' W

Traitors Cove, named by Vancouver after a skirmish with the natives in 1793, offers good bear viewing. We do not recommend anchoring in this cove.

## Marguerite Bay (Traitors Cove)
Marguerite Bay is on the south shore of Traitors Cove, about 2 miles from the entrance.
Chart 17422
Entrance: 55°42.24' N, 131°38.97' W
Anchor: 55°42.17' N, 131°38.33' W

There is a public Forest Service dock in the bay. Please be considerate of float plane operators who use the dock to unload visitors to the USFS Margaret Creek wildlife observation site.

## Port Stewart (Behm Canal)
Port Stewart, on the west side of Behm Canal, is 13.3 miles north of Caamano Point.
Chart 17422
Entrance (0.3 mile east of two islets):
55°42.24' N, 131°49.68' W
Anchor: 55°43.62' N, 131°51.21' W

Port Stewart was named by Vancouver in 1793 for John Stewart—his master's mate on the *Discovery* who drew the charts in Vancouver's atlas. The landlocked basin on the north shore offers excellent protection for small craft. Care must be taken to avoid mid-channel rock and shoals. Chart 17422 is your best guide. Be aware that in the past, the head of Port Stewart has been the site of a major log booming operation.

Anchor in about 6 fathoms.

## Naha Bay (Revillagigedo Island)
Naha Bay is 8.5 miles northeast of Knudson Cove.
Charts 17423 (inset), 17422
Entrance: 55°36.04' N, 131°41.36' W
Position (Loring): 55°36.01' N, 131°38.04' W
Anchor (0.2 mile southeast of Loring):
55°35.85' N, 131°37.78' W
Entrance (Roosevelt Lagoon): 55°35.28' N, 131°37.08' W

Naha Bay is the home of Loring, an early fish cannery and loading site for schooners bound for California with massive hauls of canned salmon. A few private residences with floats remain from this former era. Cruising vessels visiting Loring can find reasonable shelter 0.2 mile to the southeast in the lee of Dogfish Island, as indicated in the diagram.

One of the main attractions in Naha Bay is Roosevelt Lagoon, with its nature trail, wildlife, and fishing. The lagoon is protected by a rapids that is safe to traverse only in a dinghy at, or near, high-water slack. The lagoon is a favorite place to watch for trumpeter swans, some of which are said to over-winter here. Visitors should respect the birds' habitat. Bear and deer are plentiful along the lagoon trail and river and lakes upstream to the east. During the late summer spawning salmon choke the rapids and the outlet of the river.

Loring's seaside gardens and Cannery House Museum, located in in the historic Heckman House, provide additional attractions in Naha Bay. Tours may be scheduled. Open May-September, call 907-254-3506, http://loringalaska.info

The public float just west of the Roosevelt Lagoon rapids makes a great lunch or overnight stop. A poorly maintained trail leads to the rapids and farther east along the lagoon. If the float is full, you can anchor in the rather deep water off the floats in mid-channel.

Anchor (Dogfish Island) in 6 fathoms over sand and some rock bottom with fair holding.

Anchor (off public float) in 8 to 12 fathoms over sand and rocky bottom with fair holding.

## Moser Bay (Revillagigedo Island)
Moser Bay entrance is 7.5 miles northeast of Knudson Cove.
Charts 17423 (inset), 17422
North entrance (between Moser and Cedar islands): 55°34.78' N, 131°40.87' W
South entrance (southeast of Stack Island): 55°33.88' N, 131°41.41' W
Anchor: 55°32.59' N, 131°39.14' W
Entrance (Long Arm): 55°34.22' N, 131°39.48' W

*Public Float, Naha Bay*

Anchorage can be found off the drying mud flat at the head of the bay. This area was used extensively for logging operations in the past and may have slash (logging debris) along the bottom.

Anchor in about 8 fathoms.

## Moser Bay Bight (Revillagigedo Island)
Moser Bay Bight is 6.6 miles northeast of Knudson Cove.
Charts 17423 (inset), 17422
Entrance: 55°33.66' N, 131°40.71' W
Anchor: 55°33.53' N, 131°40.92' W

Shelter can be found on the west side of Moser Bay in a small bight just inside the entrance to the bay. The anchorage is close to the popular fishing grounds of Clover Passage immediately southwest. There may still be some old float houses in Moser Bay.

Entering Moser Bay Bight, favor the southeast shore to avoid the islet and foul ground on the west side of the bight.

Anchor in 7 fathoms over an unrecorded bottom.

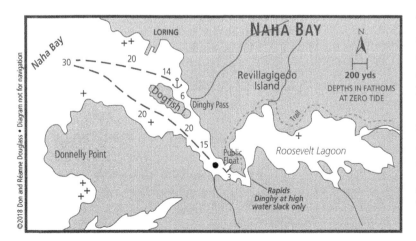

## Clover Passage (Behm Canal)
Clover Passage is 10 miles northwest of Ketchikan.
Chart 17422
North entrance (between Grant and Stack islands): 55°33.97' N, 131°42.26' W
South entrance: 55°28.53' N, 131°49.70' W

Clover Pass Resort and Restaurant, near Survey Point, is open in the summer and has moorage, gas, diesel, shower and laundry facilities, Internet access, a lodge, restaurant, boat rentals, RV sites and fishing charters. Staff monitor VHF Ch 16, or call the resort for more information (888.564.4525, 800-410.2234, https://www.cloverpassresort.com).

## Knudson Cove (Revillagigedo Island)
Knudson Cove, on the southeast side of Clover Passage, is 2 miles northeast of Point Higgins.
Chart 17422
Entrance: 55°28.70' N, 131°47.73' W
Anchor: 55°28.53' N, 131°47.78' W
Float: 55°28.37' N, 131°47.91' W

Knudson Cove, which has public and private floats, is used as a base of operation by the Clover Pass sport fishing fleet and others who troll for its famous salmon. Although busy, it's a good place to run for cover when southeast gales kick up.

Knudson Cove marks the northwest entrance to Behm Canal. From here, it's a short return to Ketchikan for fuel and supplies.

## Raymond and Wadding Coves (Behm Canal)
Raymond Cove is 8.7 miles northeast of Caamano Point Light; Wadding Cove is 7.7 miles northeast of Caamano Point Light.
Chart 17422
Entrance (Raymond Cove): 55°37.48' N, 131°52.13' W
Entrance (Wadding Cove): 55°37.07' N, 131°53.19' W

## Helm Bay Float (Behm Canal)
Helm Bay is 6.2 miles northeast of Caamano Point Light and 8 miles northwest of Knudson Cove.
Chart 17422
Entrance (0.75 mile northeast of Helm Bay Light): 55°35.34' N, 131°54.74' W
Float: 55°37.84' N, 131°58.69' W

An Alaska State float west of the north end of Forss Island is available for use by pleasure craft, but there are no facilities, nor access to land.

# CLARENCE STRAIT FROM KASAAN PENINSULA TO SUMNER STRAIT

## Caamano Point
Caamano Point is 4.5 miles northwest of Guard Island Light.
Chart 17420
Position (0.25 Nm south of Light): 55°29.67' N, 131°59.00' W

Caamano Point—the southernmost tip of Cleveland Peninsula—is on the northeast side of Clarence Strait and the west side of the northwest entrance to Behm Canal.

Clarence Strait, northwest of Caamano Point, is a popular trolling area. Ebb currents are strong, however, and it doesn't take much of a southeast breeze to kick up a nasty chop. Cruising boats can pass inside Ship Island and find some shelter behind Lee Rock, but Meyers Chuck to the north or Lyman Anchorage on the west side of the strait offer better protection in a blow.

*A lowering sky*

*Meyers Chuck is a welcome stop both for cruisers and for float planes; watch for traffic.*

### Lee Rock (Clarence Strait)
Lee Rock is 2.5 miles south of Meyers Chuck.
**Chart 17420**

With no large-scale chart of this area, we recommend entering this cove from the northwest, avoiding several rocks in the vicinity. With Meyers Chuck so close, we would not recommend anchoring here except temporarily in fair weather.

### Meyers Chuck (Meyers Island)
Meyers Chuck is about 40 miles northwest of Ketchikan.
**Chart 17423 (Union Bay inset)**
Outer entrance (0.26 mile southwest of inner entrance):
55°44.49' N, 132°16.23' W
Inner entrance: 55°44.55' N, 132°15.80' W
Public float: 55°44.37' N, 132°15.48' W
Anchor: 55°44.44' N, 132°15.52' W

Clarence Strait often kicks up a nasty chop, so Meyers Chuck can be a godsend for boaters as it offers complete protection from almost all weather. Its narrow entrance can be a bit intimidating to first-timers, but inside all is calm.

The entrance into Meyers Chuck is small and easy to miss. From Clarence Strait, watch for the two-second flashing xenon light on the microwave tower. The island north of the microwave tower is Meyers Island.

The entrance is on the north side of Meyers Island and is marked by G"3" to port and R"4" to starboard. Turn south immediately after

---

## MEYERS CHUCK

Meyers Chuck is a tiny, salt-stained fishing settlement on the Cleveland Peninsula, on the east side of Clarence Strait, about 40 miles north of Ketchikan. It has about 50 houses and a dozen year-round residents, most of whom are fishermen or retirees. There are no roads and no local government. It has a school house, but no students (they all grew up!). "Main Street" is a narrow foot path. At the time of writing (February 2017) the local economy consisted of three small businesses: a lodge offering summer accommodation, an art gallery and a US post office. Mail service is the only regular link to the outside world. Meyers Chuck has no store. Groceries are ordered by phone from Ketchikan and arrive on the weekly mail plane. The isolation is an attraction for the independent souls who choose to live there, but is also the reason there are so few of them.

Meyers Chuck has not always been so small. Commercial fishermen, who appreciated its sheltered natural harbor, began settling there from the late 1800s. Within two decades the area boasted a salmon cannery, a floating clam processor and a herring plant. In the 1920s, Meyers Chuck was home to at least a hundred people, and had a store, a bakery, a barbershop, and other businesses of more dubious repute. But with the onset of World War II, the burning down of the Union Bay cannery in 1947, and the gradual decline in logging and salmon fishing throughout the remainder of the twentieth century, the population declined too. Once the home of colorful characters with names like Halibut Pete, Pike Pole Slim, Lone Wolf Smith, Crackerbox Mack, and Greasy Gus ("an epically sloppy bachelor fisherman," according to Andy Hall of *Alaska Magazine*), Meyers Chuck is still colorful—at least to visiting boaters, who can find refuge there from the chop of Clarence Strait.

—AC

*The old Post Office at Meyers Chuck*

so rafting is encouraged. Note that you can also tie along the shore side of the float; just be sure to stay close to the float. Check with locals before using the untreated water on the float. (Drought conditions do exist in Alaska, believe it or not!)

There's usually room for several boats to anchor well off the float plane dock (no tie ups—this is in constant use).

The small settlement has a small post office on Meyers Island across the bay from the float (open Tuesday and Wednesday), and a little gallery that sells locally-made crafts. You may obtain two bars of cell phone signal at the helicopter platform at the

clearing R"4." The south side of Meyers Island is foul—do not enter there.

The float at Meyers Chuck is owned by the Wrangell Borough, and fees may be charged. It tends to be crowded during the summer,

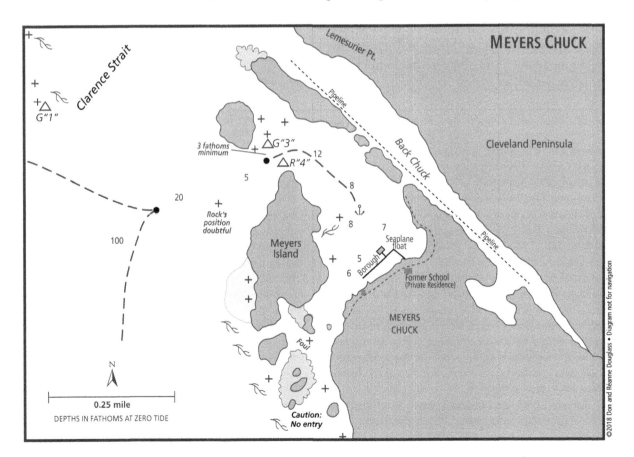

head of the dock. A dirt trail that leads north from the float connects the home sites located along the island.

Anchor off the Borough float in 8 fathoms over a mixed bottom with good holding.

## ERNEST SOUND TO WRANGELL VIA ZIMOVIA STRAIT
Charts 17385, 17423 (inset)
Ernest Sound southwest entrance (1.65 miles northwest of McHenry Ledge buoy): 55°48.26' N, 132°19.81' W

This route is the most popular cruising route between Ketchikan and Wrangell, as it offers better protection and is more attractive than the one through Stikine Strait. Follow instructions given in the prior section for Clarence Strait to Meyers Chuck, then turn northeast into Ernest Sound.

### Union Bay (Ernest Sound)
Union Bay, 1.5 miles east of Meyers Chuck.
Charts 17385, 17423 (inset)
Entrance (1.4 miles northeast of Lemesurier Point): 55°46.64'N, 132°14.71'W

### Magnetic Cove (Union Bay)
Magnetic Cove is 1 mile southwest of Vixen Harbor.
Charts 17385, 17423 (inset)
Entrance (3.3 miles east of Lemesurier Point): 55°46.93'N, 132°11.29'W
Anchor: 55°47.46' N, 132°10.90' W

"Magnetic Cove" is our name for the long narrow cove behind Magnetic Point. It is land-locked and well protected from all weather, with no signs of driftwood along its shore. This place is secluded and pristine, with old-growth forest and inquisitive resident seals. The name Magnetic Point comes from the observance of compass errors as high as 38° due to local underground magnetic disturbance.

The entrance to Magnetic Cove is quite narrow (about 80 feet) and there is a 3-foot bar in the center of the narrows. Time your passage at an adequate tide level, and avoid the tree trunk that extends about 40 feet from the east shore. This tree hides a rocky peninsula. The M/V *Sanctuary* found a rock 50 yards south that is estimated to be 2 feet above MLLW. Favor the west shore and use caution!

Anchor in 2 to 3 fathoms over very soft mud with good holding if your anchor is well set.

### Vixen Harbor (Ernest Sound)
Vixen Harbor is 5.5 miles northeast of Meyers Chuck.
Chart 17423 (inset)
Entrance (0.9 mile east of Union Point): 55°48.29'N, 132°09.60'W
Anchor: 55°47.90'N, 132°10.31'W

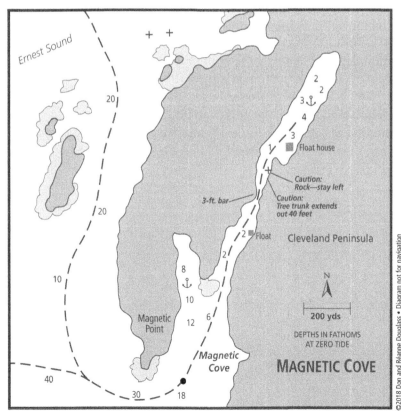

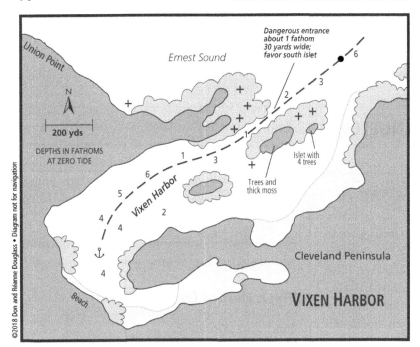

Vixen Harbor offers good shelter, and once you're inside you have a feeling of security. Birds and seals like this shelter, too!

We found entering Vixen Harbor difficult. The entrance channel is quite narrow—about 30 yards or less—and the channel has a minimum depth of about one fathom *or less* at zero tide! You should not enter it in foul weather, in poor visibility, or under radar. Dangerous reefs extend well off the point and off the three small islets. Because the reefs and rocks are dark in color and the water is murky (about 4 feet of underwater visibility), you have little warning if you veer off course. Slightly favor the islands on the south side of the entrance.

The harbor bottom is mostly flat with room enough for several boats. There is a landing beach on the southwest side.

Anchor in 4 fathoms over soft, sticky mud and sand with very good holding.

### Vixen Inlet

Vixen Inlet is 6.5 miles northeast of Lemesurier Point.
Chart 17385
Entrance (0.9 mile northwest of Sunshine Island): 55°49.66' N, 132°06.46' W
Anchor: 55°48.26' N, 132°02.77' W

Anchorage in Vixen Inlet can be found deep in the inlet off the drying mud flats.

Anchor in 7 to 9 fathoms over a mud bottom with fair holding.

### Petersen Islands (Ernest Sound)

Petersen Islands are 4.6 miles west of Easterly Island Light and 3 miles southwest of Brownson Island.
Chart 17385
South entrance: 55°52.98'N, 132°13.76'W

*A friendly fisherman from Meyers Chuck, with his net extended*

*Salmon lovers are everywhere.*

We have found temporary anchorage as a lunch stop at the scenic north end of the narrow channel between the islands.

## Canoe Passage (Ernest Sound)
Canoe Passage separates Brownson Island from Etolin Island.
Chart 17385
South entrance: 55°55.26'N, 132°12.88'W
North entrance (0.3 mile southwest of Menefee Point): 56°02.38'N, 132°10.37'W
Anchor (north end): 56°02.42'N, 132°12.63'W
Anchor (tiny cove, 0.5 mile south of north narrows): 56°01.90'N, 132°12.41'W

## Seward Passage
Seward Passage separates Deer Island from the mainland.
Chart 17385

Cruising boats can find better anchorage in Santa Anna Inlet than in Sunny Bay.

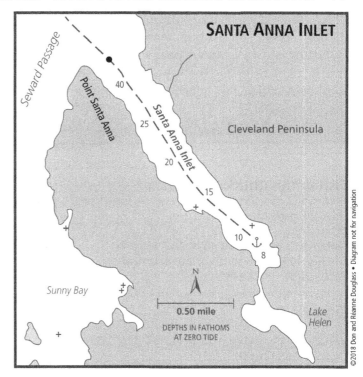

## Santa Anna Inlet (Seward Passage)
Santa Anna Inlet is 18.5 miles northeast of Meyers Chuck.
Chart 17385
Entrance: 55°59.84'N, 131°57.73'W
Anchor: 55°58.64'N, 131°56.04'W

Santa Anna Inlet offers some of the most accessible, well-sheltered anchorage in Ernest Sound. Go deep into the inlet and anchor at its head off the outlet of Lake Helen. From Lake Helen at the head of the bay, it's only three miles overland to the upper basin in Yes Bay. Locals report good crabbing here.

Anchor in 8 fathoms over an unrecorded bottom.

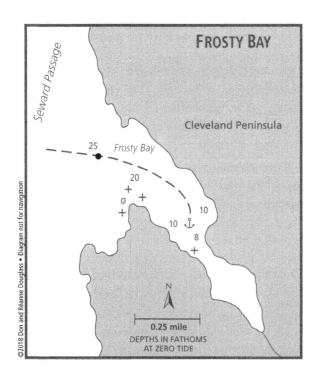

## Frosty Bay (Seward Passage)
Frosty Bay, on the east side of Seward Passage, is 4.5 miles north of Santa Anna Inlet.
Chart 17385
Entrance: 56°04.05'N, 131°58.76W
Anchor: 56°03.86'N, 131°58.10' W

Well protected and scenic, Frosty Bay is worth a visit if only to watch the seals that hang out on the partially submerged rocks off its west entrance.

A loggers' cabin on the southwest shore near the log transfer site has been renovated by the USFS for use as a recreational cabin. There is also a USFS float in the bay. Anchor in the southwest corner just outside the narrows to the inner basin.

Anchor in 7 fathoms over sand and gravel with fair holding.

## Fisherman Chuck (Etolin Island)
Fisherman Chuck separates Menefee Point from Etolin Island north of Canoe Passage.
Chart 17385
North entrance: 56°03.45'N, 132°11.16'W
Anchor (0.16 mile south of north entrance); 56°03.27'N, 132°11.16'W

## Zimovia Strait
Zimovia Strait lies between Etolin and Wrangell islands and connects Ernest Sound with the east end of Sumner Strait.
Chart 17385 (inset)
South entrance: 56°06.06'N, 132°05.42'W
North entrance (Wrangell Harbor brg 013°T at 1.9 Nm): 56°26.31'N, 132°24.09'W

Zimovia Strait, which divides Wrangell and Etolin islands, is a popular, smooth-water route between Ketchikan and Wrangell. More sheltered and attractive than Stikine Strait, it offers several anchor sites along its length. The eastern side of Etolin Island has an intricate shoreline, with narrow inlets and lagoons and steep-sided peaks that rise above 3,000 feet. The southern portion of the island lies within the South Etolin Island Wilderness. The island is almost split in two by Anita Bay and Mosman and Burnett inlets.

The strait is an intricate passage that requires careful navigating, particularly through Zimovia Narrows. The Narrows passes through the center of a once-flourishing tribal village; you can still see evidence of places where the Natives cleared the beaches of rocks in order to land their canoes.

Follow the navigational aids as shown on Chart 17385 (inset), and you should have no difficulty. Pass north of Button Island and make the full jog to southwest before resuming your northwest heading.

## Zimovia Cove (Etolin Island)
1 mi NE of south entrance to Zimovia Strait
Chart 17385
Entrance: 56°06.94'N, 132°06.74'W
Anchor: (cove) 56°06.76'N, 132°07.53'W

Good protection can be found near the head of the unnamed cove we call "Zimovia Cove" on a flat shelf of 12 to 13 fathoms (zero tide) in the center portion of the cove. The north section of the cove may be shallower; however, the shore is steep-to. The shores of the cove show very few signs of stress.

Anchor in about 12 fathoms over fine brown sand and mud with very good holding. The cove has enough swinging room for several boats and it can be entered in the dark, but avoid charted rocks close to north shore.

## Thoms Place (Wrangell Island)
Thoms Place is 3.5 miles from the south entrance to Zimovia Strait.
Chart 17385
Entrance: 56°09.64'N, 132°07.37'W
Anchor: 56°10.44'N, 132°08.33'W

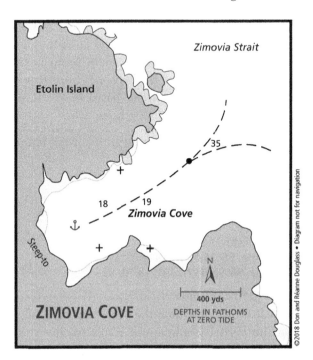

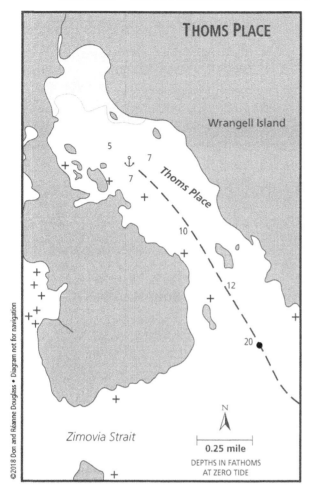

Thoms Place, an undeveloped state marine park, offers shelter in fair weather. The bottom is somewhat irregular, suggesting that it's rocky, but we have found mud holes where the bottom is level. Much of the shore is foul, so be careful when approaching it.

Anchor in 7 fathoms near the head of the bay over mud with good holding.

### Whaletail Cove (Etolin Island)
4 mi NW of Thoms Place
Chart 17385
Entrance: 56°11.32'N, 132°14.22'W
Anchor: 56°11.06'N, 132°14.85'W

Small, completely landlocked Whaletail Cove has very good protection from all weather in its east branch. This anchorage is a challenge for small boats and can be entered only near high-water slack due to strong currents. *Caution:* The entrance, which is narrow, shallow and winding, has several uncharted, below-surface rocks, and it almost dries at zero tide. On approach, the entrance to Whaletail Cove is hidden and difficult to see due to the flat terrain. Use the inset on Chart 17385; electronic charting is also helpful.

Wait for adequate tide before you enter or exit; beware of the current which can carry a boat onto submerged rocks. When entering from Zimovia Strait, avoid Trap Rock to the east, which bares on a 6-foot tide. This large complex of rocks should be given a wide berth.

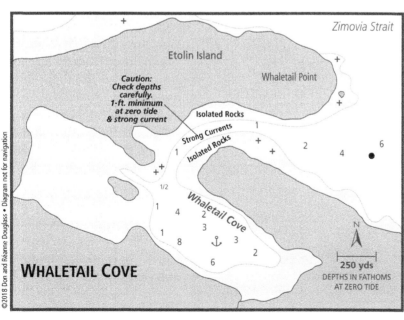

Anchor in the lower center of the east branch in 4 fathoms over sticky mud with very good holding.

### Olive Cove (Etolin Island)
Olive Cove is 2.5 miles west of Whaletail Cove.
Chart 17385
Entrance: 56°11.59' N, 132°18.81' W
Anchor: 56°11.41' N, 132°18.95' W

Olive Cove, near the village sites in Zimovia Strait, is well protected from southerly weather, but it largely dries at low tide. The cove should be entered northwest of Village Island due to foul ground south of the island. Anchorage can be found off the entrance, short of the drying flat.

Anchor in 5 to 8 fathoms over sand with good holding.

## Anita Bay (Etolin Island)
Anita Bay is 5 miles northeast of Whaletail Cove.
Chart 17382
Entrance: 56°14.27'N, 132°22.82'W
Anchor: 56°11.55'N, 132°30.01'W

*Wrangell-Reliance Harbor*

Anita Bay indents Etolin Island almost to its west coast. Its upper end lies just 1.3 miles from the north tip of Burnett Inlet on Etolin Island's west side. The sharp 3,800-foot Virginia Peak, frequently bare of snow in the summer, lies just west of the entrance to Anita Bay, providing a scenic background to the anchorage. For larger boats, Anita Bay is the preferred anchorage in this area.

Anchor in about 12 fathoms over sand with good holding.

## Shoemaker Bay Boat Harbor (Wrangell Island)
Shoemaker Bay Boat Harbor is about 5 miles southeast of Wrangell.
Chart 17384
Entrance: 56°25.01'N, 132°21.22'W

Shoemaker Bay Boat Harbor is located approximately 5 miles south of downtown Wrangell. The harbor has 250 slips for large and small commercial fishing and recreational vessels. There are also tidal grids, a hydraulic hoist, all-tide boat launch and a work float located at the harbor. Power, water, waste-oil collection and garbage collection are provided. Contact the Wrangell harbormaster (next entry) for mooring assignment.

Rainbow Falls Trail takes off across the road from the harbor. It's an easy hike and worth doing. Since this harbor is part of a larger recreational complex (tent and RV camping), recreational facilities include a tennis court, park with shelter, and playground.

*Wrangell, Alaska, welcomes cruisers with open arms.*

## Wrangell (Wrangell Island)

Wrangell is 89 miles north of Ketchikan and 148 miles south of Juneau.

Chart 17384
Entrance (Wrangell-Reliance Harbor): 56°28.06'N, 132°23.10'W
Reliance Float: 56°27.95'N, 132°22.95'W

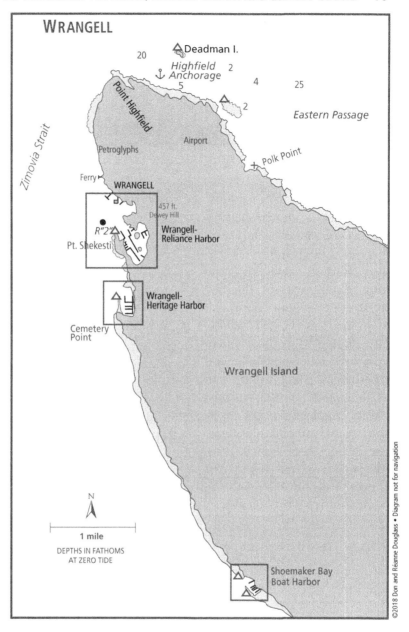

In the past, it has been difficult to find moorage in Wrangell-Reliance Harbor without rafting—sometimes three to four deep! New options are now abundant.

For a slip assignment, call the harbormaster on VHF Ch 16, switch and answer VHF Ch 10 (907.874.3736) http://www.wrangell.com/port/downtown-etolin-harbor Harbor personnel are extremely helpful and they like cruising boats. ("They're good folks!" says the harbormaster).

City Dock, also known as the Cruise Ship Dock, is a t-shaped dock located at the north end of downtown. The dock face is 405 feet with a breasting pier head of 565 feet and an additional stern mooring dolphin 225 feet off the northeast end of the dock, allowing accommodation of ships +/-950 feet. The inside face permits moorage for smaller cruise ships, yachts, and also contains the u-shaped Summer Float, with accommodation for charter vessels to load and unload passengers as well as some transient moorage. Water and electricity are available on the City Dock and Summer Floats.

The Downtown Harbor has three main docking areas. The Inner Harbor Float is primarily reserved moorage for craft under 40 feet, while the Fish & Game Float is reserved moorage for craft from 30-60 feet. The Reliance Float is the primary transient dock. Two fuel docks—Wrangell Oil and Delta Western—are opposite the Reliance Dock. Power, water, waste oil collection and garbage collection is provided at the head of each access ramp. Showers and laundromat can be found in town about 200 yards from the harbormaster's office.

In addition to the harbor expansion and enhancements, the city has installed boat repair facilities with a 150-ton Travel Lift (located at the Marine Repair Center, across from the breakwater) and storage for vessels up to 50 feet. There is a tidal haul-out grid for vessels 45 feet and under within the harbor. The Float Plane Dock is located on your port as you enter the harbor.

The deep-draft Heritage Harbor, about a mile from downtown, in the bay south of Shekesti Point (at approximately °27.46' N, 132°23.18' W), is now open. Reserved moorage stalls and side-tie transient space can accommodate visiting vessels. Utility connections are available in 30, 50, and 100 amps. An all-tides boat launch, potable water on the docks and a new restroom complete the facilities.

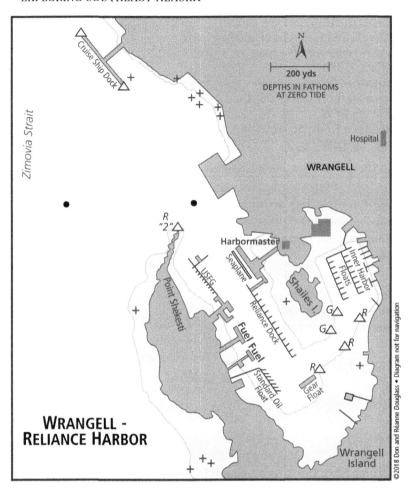

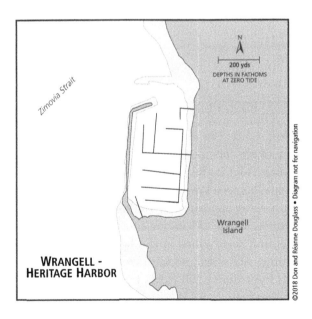

*This petroglyph is now part of a protected park.*

## Wrangell
### Don Douglass and Réanne Hemingway-Douglass

Wrangell had its origins as Redoubt Saint Dionysius—a fort built by the Russians in 1834 to prevent encroachment by Hudson's Bay Company traders. In 1839, the Russians leased part of Southeast Alaska, including the fort, to the British who changed its name to Fort Stikine. Major trading went on between the Tlingits and the Hudson's Bay Company until 1849, when the fort was abandoned. After the U.S. purchase of Alaska, the Army established a military post here in 1867, naming the settlement Fort Wrangell. Boom-bust periods occurred regularly—with each gold strike—until the end of the nineteenth century.

Less sophisticated and more relaxed than other historic Southeast towns, Wrangell has the feel of the Alaska frontier and for that reason is one of our favorite ports of call. (In fact, residents say this is one of the few communities where people look you in the eye as they pass on the street!) Fewer cruise ships call here than at larger towns in Southeast, and it's refreshing to visit a port where skippers of working boats, barges, outboard skiffs and pleasure craft all communicate with one another in a friendly manner.

For visitors, attractions here include the Nolan Museum and Visitor Center (with a movie theatre)—a

*Muskeg Meadows Golf Course—where the view rivals that of Pebble Beach*

handsome addition to Wrangell; Chief Shakes House; Petroglyph Beach Park; picnic areas and some good hiking trails, as well as the Anan Bear and Wildlife Observatory, south of Wrangell. With the requirement of permits and the lack of convenient anchorage for cruising boats at Anan Creek, we suggest docking at Wrangell and taking one of the tour boats to see the bears. Also, if a raft trip on the Stikine River interests you, Stickeen Wilderness Adventures (tel.: 800.874.2085) and Alaska Vistas (tel.: 866.874.3006) offer tours. And if you just happen to need a "golf fix," you can find nine holes at the beautiful USGA Muskeg Meadows Golf Course, north of town (rentals available). When the sun shines, the view from the first tee rivals that of Pebble Beach, California. The Garnet Ledge is no longer open for visits of any kind. The town also has a public swimming pool and a library with Internet service (sign up for your turn).

City of Wrangell Website: www.wrangell.com.

*An example of crafts at Nolan Center in Wrangell*

*Petroglyph faces*

*The breakwaters at Wrangell's Heritage Harbor—south of Pt. Shekesti*

For groceries and other supplies visit the following: City Market, Bob's IGA, Otteson's True Value and Sentry Hardware. All stores are within a short walking distance of Reliance Float. To carry heavy supplies to and from Heritage Harbor, you'll need transportation.

Wrangell is serviced by air and the Alaska State Ferry (north of the cruise ship dock).

*Rafting along the Reliance Dock (center of picture)*

## BRADFIELD CANAL TO BLAKE CHANNEL AND EASTERN PASSAGE
Chart 17385

The most easterly of the three routes from Ketchikan to Wrangell, this is the longest, most protected and, for many, the most scenic. It follows Clarence Strait to Ernest Sound, Seward Passage to Anan Bay, then Blake Channel and Eastern Passage around the north tip of Wrangell Island to the town.

On this route, you can stop to take a hike at the Anan Bear and Wildlife Observatory, then experience the muddy glacier melt of the mighty Stikine River.

### Bradfield Canal
Bradfield Canal extends 13 miles east of Anan Bay.
Chart 17385
West entrance (0.5 mile northwest of Point Warde): 56°10.82'N, 131°58.77'W

### Anan Bay (Bradfield Canal)
Anan Bay is 2.3 miles east of Point Warde.
Chart 17385
Entrance: 56°11.16'N, 131°53.94'W
Public float: 56°11.09'N; 131°53.54'W
*Anan Bay, about 2.3 miles E of Point Warde, is an open bight on the S shore of Bradfield Canal. (CP)*

Anan Bay (pronounced An-An) is located about 30 miles south of Wrangell. From

*Heed our caution: the anchorage at Anan Bay is temporary and an anchor watch should stay onboard.*

Meyers Chuck head northeast into Ernest Sound, then to Bradfield Canal, watching for Anan Bay on your starboard. Fed by Anan Creek, the Bay abounds with pink salmon that draw bears, eagles and seals, as well as humans who want to observe their activity. The Anan Bear and Wildlife Observatory, in Anan Bay, is a highlight for Southeast Alaska cruisers; don't pass it by!

Anchoring is possible for pleasure craft; however, the shoal along shore that drops steeply at a 45-degree angle into much deeper water, as well as the sandy bottom, make holding

## Respect the Bears!
### Don Douglass & Réanne Hemingway-Douglass

Everyone has heard or has a story to tell about Alaska and her bears. For many cruising boaters, just spotting a bear can often be the highlight of the trip.

Black bears are the most common species and you will frequently see them prowling for trout at the mouths of the numerous streams that flow into the ocean. The smallest of the North American bears, black bears grow to about five feet long and weigh between 200 and 300 pounds, although some can reach 500 pounds. These bears are swift of foot and can run up to 25 miles per hour. They are skillful tree climbers and have a well-deserved reputation for being troublesome around campsites. They have often been known to bite (or maul) the hand that feeds them. (Don't try it!)

The brown bear (grizzly) roams Southeast Alaska and Kodiak and Afonak islands among others. They grow to be about eight feet long and weigh 350 to 500 pounds. They can anger quickly but usually don't attack unless threatened in some way. Known as *Silvertips* and *Grizzlies*, these bears use their long, curved claws for digging out ground squirrels and mice, the same claws that also become lethal weapons.

Bears are wild animals and people need to give them their proper respect. Boaters who disembark to sightsee on land need to be bear-conscious. National Park officials offer the following guidelines when entering bear territory:

- Use caution when near natural bear foods. Bears are attracted to areas where there are berries and nuts. Try to avoid these areas when these crops are in season.
- Stay away from carcasses. This is a great food source for a bear and bears will aggressively defend them.
- Watch for signs of bear. Tracks, fresh diggings and droppings may indicate that a bear is still in the area.
- Leave your dog on the boat. Dogs have been known to provoke a bear attack or even return to the unsuspecting owner with an angry bear in pursuit.
- Hike in a group. There is more safety in numbers. While hiking, make loud noises, whistle, sing, talk or carry noise makers. Most bears will leave you alone if they are aware of your presence. It's when you startle them that the trouble begins.
- If camping, always put away food in bear-resistant food storage facilities (when provided) or suspend food between two trees a minimum of 13 feet above the ground and three feet from the tree trunks.
- Avoid cooking or eating smelly foods as odors will attract bears. Bears may also be drawn to hair spray, soaps, toothpaste, shaving cream and cosmetics.
- Use a telephoto lens when photographing bears.
- Always keep children nearby and in sight.

# Anan Bay Bear and Wildlife Observatory
## Linda Lewis—Journal Notes—M/V *Royal Sounder*

The opportunity to see bears, up close—in their own environment, was irresistible to the three mid-westerners on the boat. David stayed onboard to do anchor watch in Anan Bay, as recommended in the Douglass guide. The three of us spent a magical hour watching the bears in their world. We were able to feel safe (*we* were the ones enclosed) and see them in their own world. Anan Creek was so abundant with salmon it resembled a carpet. The bears would just reach in, pull out a fish and then feast on only the brain and roe. Then they would toss it aside for the eagles and ravens to clean up later. In all my trips to Southeast Alaska, this remains one of my most favorite experiences.

*The observatory includes a duck blind-type viewing area for a really up-close look.*

*Choices, so many choices*

*A selected salmon and the carcass pile*

*Anan Creek's carpet of salmon*

*The bears get up close and personal at the observation platform at Anan Creek.*

difficult; in addition, during good weather, a westerly swell sets up in the bay. **If you choose to anchor here, we strongly recommend that you leave a crew member aboard when you go ashore.**

## Blake Channel

Blake Channel connects Ernest Sound with Eastern Passage and the east end of Sumner Strait; its south entrance is 3 miles northeast of Point Warde.
Chart 17385
South entrance (0.2 mile east of Blake Channel Light): 56°12.57'N, 131°55.13'W

## Berg Bay (Blake Channel)

Berg Bay is 11 miles north of Anan Bay and 15 miles southeast of Wrangell.
Chart 17385
Southeast entrance: 56°21.15'N, 132°00.39'W
Anchor: 56°21.70' N, 132°00.52' W

Berg Bay offers very good shelter in a chilly, remote alpine setting. As you proceed up Blake Channel, the water becomes a milky green, currents run strong, and the vegetation grows more dense. Less than 10 miles to the north, there are permanent snowfields on 5,000- to 6,000-foot peaks,

From here you can explore the extensive outflow of Aaron Creek immediately east, being careful to avoid the numerous pilings in the log storage area.

Entry into Berg Bay can be made on either side of the islets as indicated in the diagram. The easterly route has deeper water. Anchor just south of the USFS float near the head of the bay next to the cabin. Avoid kelp and check the set of your anchor. There is a wonderful beach walk here and cruisers report great crabbing in this bay.

Anchor in 9 fathoms; silt and gravel with poor-to-fair holding.

---

## Visiting the Anan Bear and Wildlife Observatory

Anan is a world-class bear viewing area and one of the few places in the world where both black and brown bear feed at the same creek at the same time. Anan Creek is home to one of the largest runs of pink salmon in Southeast Alaska, which supports the high density of black and brown bears that gather there.

A half-mile boardwalk follows the shoreline to a covered observation platform where you can watch black bears feeding near the falls. USFS guides (with firearms) greet you, give talks and answer questions. A maximum of 60 visitors per day is allowed. No domestic animals are permitted on shore and no food or beverages, other than water. A small float off the USFS cabin is strictly reserved for cabin users.

From July 5 to August 25, a day-use permit (small per person fee) is required to visit the Anan Bear and Wildlife Observatory. We recommend checking the official website for permitting information, as procedures change regularly. Plan ahead, because the limited number of permits become available on February 1, and the process is competitive. More information about the observatory may be found at the Tongass National Forest website at https://www.fs.usda.gov/recarea/tongass/recreation/recarea/?recid=79154

There are four ways to obtain a permit

1. Purchase a permit by navigating to the Anan Wildlife Observatory page on the national reservation website www.recreation.gov, or call their toll-free number: 907-874-2323

2. Reserve the Anan Bay Recreation Cabin, also on www.recreation.gov. Your reservation comes with four permits.

3. Make reservations through an authorized guide. A link to authorized guiding companies is found on the Tongass National Forest website noted above.

4. A "last minute lottery" for four permits is held weekly at the Wrangell District Office. Call 907-874-2323 for more information.

Here is an extra tip from the Rangers. Even if the reservations calendar looks full, try calling at the last minute when you are nearby. Someone may have cancelled and you might be lucky.

—LW

## The Narrows

The Narrows, 12 miles northwest of the entrance to Blake Channel, connects Blake Channel with Eastern Passage.
Chart 17385
East entrance: 56°22.01' N, 132°03.97' W
West entrance: 56°21.75' N, 132°07.36' W

In The Narrows, about 5 miles south of Wrangell, you can see a tidal bore and a definite demarcation line where the green water of The Narrows meets the chalky waters of the Stikine River. The water temperature immediately drops several degrees.

## Madan Bay (Eastern Passage)

Madan Bay is 5 miles northwest of Berg Bay.
Chart 17385
Entrance: 56°22.66' N, 132°08.87' W
Anchor: 56°24.09' N, 132°10.28' W

Cruisers enthusiastically report this anchorage as very protected and private.

## Highfield Anchorage (Wrangell Island)

Highfield Anchorage, at the north end of Wrangell Island, is 1.5 miles north of Wrangell Harbor.
Chart 17384
Anchor: 56°29.45' N, 132°22.26' W

After passing through the narrows (easier if you use the flood tide) and proceeding up Eastern Passage, you meet part of the muddy brown outflow of the mighty Stikine River. We once headed straight for the mud flats but lost our nerve when the water became totally opaque and the depth sounder began reacting to all the silt in the water.

Rounding the north tip of Wrangell Island, you can pass safely on either side of Simonof Island. The area south of Simonof Island is fairly shallow, and provides refuge during southerly storms, but it is used extensively for permanent anchorage by some local boats.

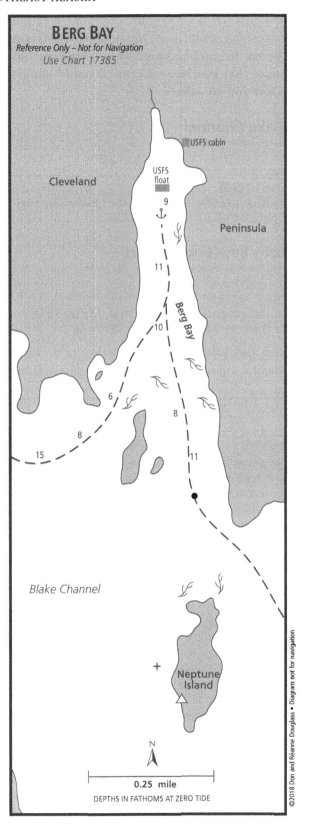

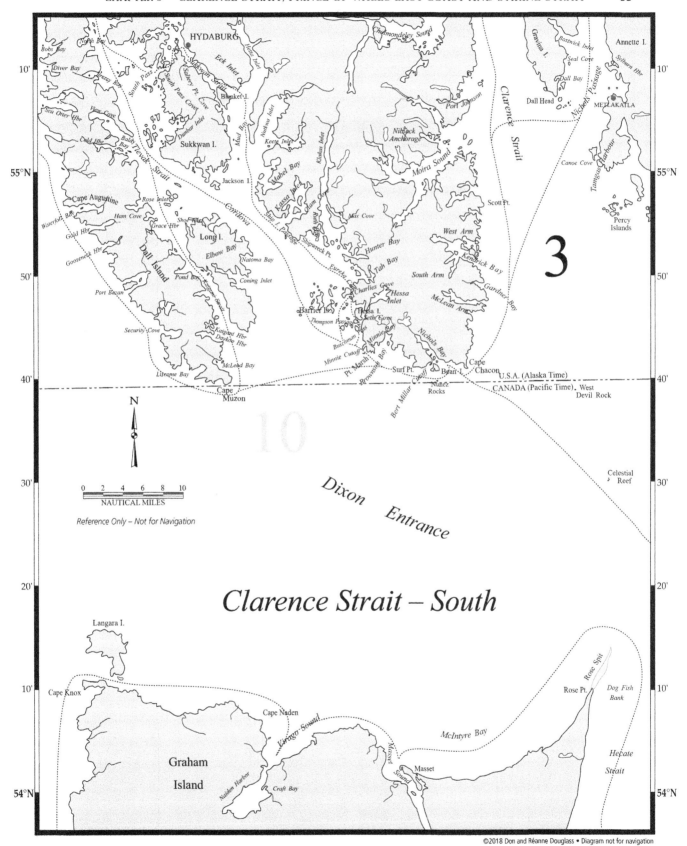

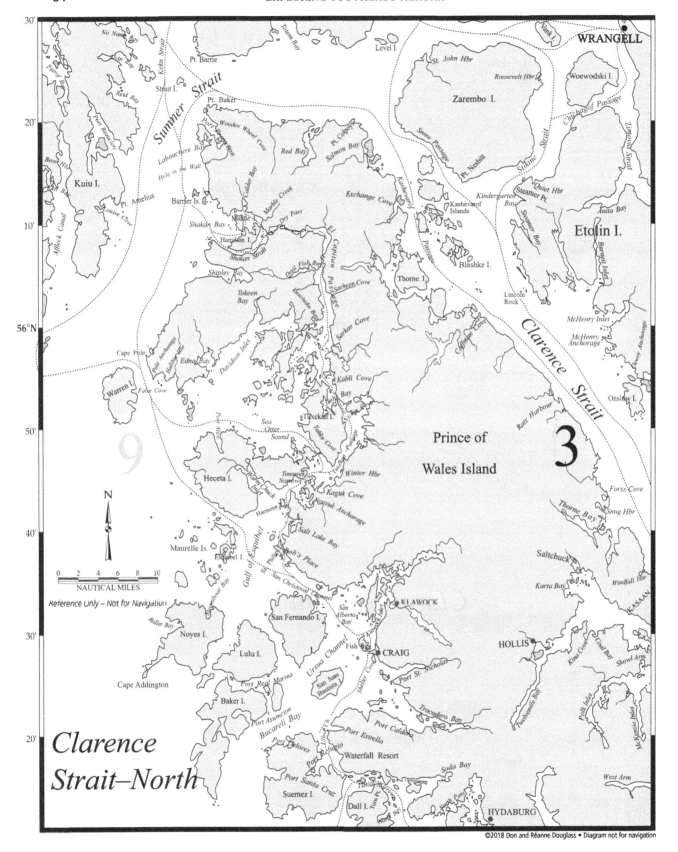

Clarence Strait–North

# 3

# CLARENCE STRAIT, PRINCE OF WALES EAST COAST AND STIKINE STRAIT

## INTRODUCTION

Clarence Strait extends 100 miles north from Dixon Entrance to Sumner Strait where Kuiu, Kupreanof and Mitkof islands separate the southern part of Southeast Alaska from the northern part. We have made this area the subject of an entire chapter because we think it offers outstanding cruising opportunities, yet it is in close proximity to Ketchikan.

Since boats entering Alaska from British Columbia must check in with customs at Ketchikan, the normal northbound route is to follow Revillagigedo Channel. However, this bypasses some wonderful, little-known areas. The east coast of Prince of Wales Island, along the west shore of Clarence Strait, is worth serious exploration by cruising boats. The southern part of Prince of Wales Island also hides some jewels—complex inlets and sounds that are seldom visited. Kendrick Bay, Ingraham Bay, Moria Sound, Cholmondeley Sound, Kasaan Bay, Thorn and Tolstoi bays, and Kashevarof Passage all have sheltered waters and solitary coves that rarely see the wake of pleasure vessels. If you want to test your pathfinding skills in some remote wilderness that is not yet thoroughly charted, this is a good place to start!

The islands along the east shore of Clarence Strait also have some little-known anchor sites worth exploring. The Percy Islands to the south, the west side of Annette Island, the south shore of Gravina Island, and, especially, the west shore of Etolin Island and the Blashke

*Beachcombing provides many hours of pleasure for both photographers and collectors (Kasaan Bay).*

## Clothing in Southeast Alaska
### Linda Lewis

My two favorite clothing words in Southeast Alaska are "fleece" and "layering". Along with silk or poly long underwear and waterproof outer wear, you have the main items you need to stay comfortable in this temperate-zone, rain-forest environment. Add boots for any dinghy expeditions and hiking. Be Alaska savvy and get 16" tall X-traTuf boots (sometimes called Sitka Slippers). Visit www.xtratuf.com.

During June, July, and August, the temperatures range from the mid 40s (F) to mid 60s during daylight hours (as many as 18-20 hours), with an occasional gloriously sunny and warm (70s) day or two. It rains; some summers it really rains—a lot. Some summers it is wonderfully sunny for days at a time, repeatedly. You just never know. So you need the full range of clothing. A few shorts and sun tops, lots of long pants, t-shirts, long-sleeve shirts, warm socks, fleece jackets of all kinds, hats, gloves, and waterproof rain gear. For sailors: full foul-weather gear. For glacier viewing on the outside of your boat, pretend you're going snow skiing and dress accordingly.

Round this out with an inflatable PFD and you're ready to cruise in Southeast Alaska.

*Clothing for glacier watching*

*Don't forget the dog!*

*Xtra-Tuffs—the real Alaska boot*

*It really does get this warm and sunny—sometimes.*

*For most men, this is the uniform of the day.*

*Sailing in full foul weather gear*

Islands on the north, are excellent places to poke around and explore. They also offer world-famous salmon fishing. Be alert to the presence of commercial fishing vessels, which seem abundant in the area of Luck Point in Clarence Strait and in Kashevarof Passage. Stay vigilant to avoid their nets.

Clarence Strait, open to the southeast and northwest, has strong currents of several knots in certain areas and up to four knots in Snow Passage Narrows. Four knot currents have also been reported at the northwest corner of Prince of Wales Island in the vicinity of Point Baker—in Sumner Strait. Clarence Strait is susceptible to southeast gales, which can quickly pick up to dangerous proportions with the passage of a weather front. A nasty chop develops in Clarence Strait any time a wind over 15 knots is blowing, especially against the strong outflowing ebbs at Behm Canal and Ernest Sound. It is best to cross the strait early in the morning when fair weather has been forecast. Once you are inside any of the major inlets or protected coves, chop or swells quickly die down.

## CLARENCE STRAIT SOUTH ENTRANCE

**McLean Arm** (Prince of Wales Island)
McLean Arm is 6.5 miles north of Cape Chacon.
Chart 17433
Entrance: 54°47.71' N, 131°57.15' W
Anchor: 54°47.81' N, 132°02.78' W

McLean Arm has easy access and offers the first reasonable shelter for small craft north of Cape Chacon.

Anchor in 3 to 5 fathoms over a mud and rocky bottom.

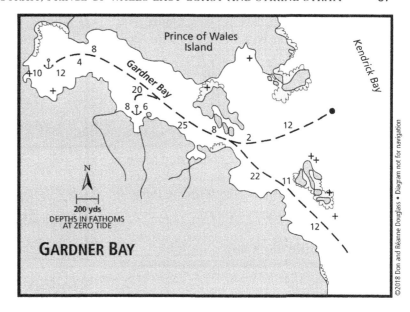

**Gardner Bay** (Prince of Wales Island)
Gardner Bay is 8 miles north of Cape Chacon.
Chart 17433
Entrance: 54°49.44' N, 131°57.37' W
Anchor (nook): 54°49.46' N, 131°59.11' W
Anchor (head of bay): 54°49.64' N, 131°59.93' W

Gardner Bay is landlocked and offers very good shelter for small boats. Enter between two 1-fathom shoals marked by kelp or south of the outer islands. Stay mid-channel in either case. We prefer the small nook for one boat west of the islet and 0.4 mile west of the entrance narrows on the south side of the nook. Summer saltwater temperature is 65° F.

Anchor (nook south side) in 6 to 8 fathoms over sand and mud with good holding.

*Entrance to Gardner Bay*

Anchor (head of the bay) in 10 fathoms over sand, mud and rocks with fair-to-good holding.

## Kendrick Bay (Prince of Wales Island)
Kendrick Bay is 10.5 miles north of Cape Chacon.
Chart 17433
North entrance: 54°54.00' N, 131°58.05' W
South entrance: 54°51.43' N, 131°58.12' W

Kendrick Bay offers cruising boats good protection in either the south or west arms. Entrance is south of the Kendrick Islands; avoid the reef located well within the entrance.

## South Arm (Kendrick Bay)
South Arm is 2.5 miles west of the south entrance to Kendrick Bay.
Chart 17433
Entrance: 54°52.35' N, 132°02.17' W
Anchor: 54°50.44' N, 132°03.43' W

## Short Arm (Kendrick Bay)
Short Arm is 3 miles west of the south entrance to Kendrick Bay.
Chart 17433
Entrance: 54°52.39' N, 132°02.47' W

Short Arm is too deep for convenient anchorage. The two small coves between Short and West arms offer anchorage to small craft, the first in 10 fathoms south of an uncharted 3-fathom shoal in the center of the cove. The second anchorage is tucked around the two-tree islet in the center of the cove in 10 fathoms over a soft-to-hard bottom. Watch for uncharted 3- to 4-fathom shoals in the entrance.

## West Arm (Kendrick Bay)
West Arm is 3.5 miles west of the south entrance to Kendrick Bay.
Chart 17433
Entrance: 54°53.23' N, 132°03.28' W
Anchor (first cove west of Short Arm):
54°53.78' N, 132°03.15' W
Anchor (third cove west of Short Arm):
54°52.89' N, 132°04.03' W
Anchor (head of West Arm): 54°53.97' N, 132°06.31' W

Anchor in 10 fathoms over mud and rocks with fair holding.

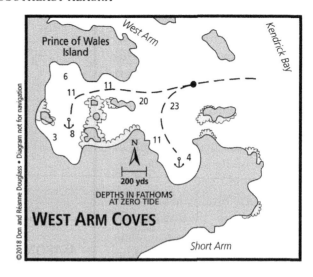

## Kendrick Islands
Kendrick Islands are at the entrance to Kendrick Bay.
Chart 17433
Entrance: 54°53.62' N, 132°00.21' W

The center island on the outside offers potentially good anchorage for small craft at both its

*Rod Nash fishing in Moira Sound*

north and south shores, but the bottom is irregular, resulting in marginal holding.

## Hidden Bay (Prince of Wales Island)

Hidden Bay, on the west side of Clarence Strait, is 5 miles north of Kendrick Bay.
Chart 17432
Entrance: 54°56.08' N, 131°57.73' W
Anchor: 54°56.02' N, 132°01.15' W

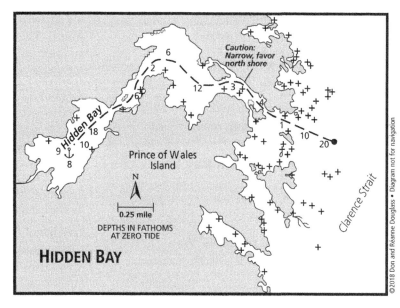

For the explorer, Hidden Bay, Ingraham Bay and North Arm of Ingraham Bay each have a special charm and wild qualities. We found it difficult to pick a favorite. All are landlocked and protected by dangerous rocks and shoals with irregular bottoms until you are well inside. North Arm has the most straightforward entrance and takes less time and effort to enter, but it has poor holding. All three are influenced by currents, especially at spring tides. Keep in mind that these small-scale charts may lack sufficient detail for safe navigation.

Anchor (head of bay) in 7 fathoms over mud and shells with good holding and swinging room.

*No net needed here; he lands this salmon by hand.*

*Réanne and Rod are proud of this fish.*

### Ingraham Bay (Prince of Wales Island)
Ingraham Bay is 2.2 miles north of Hidden Bay.
Chart 17432
Entrance: 54°58.40' N, 131°58.62' W
Anchor (south arm): 54°57.28' N, 132°03.78' W

Anchor in 4 fathoms over sticky mud with very good holding and swinging room.

### North Arm of Ingraham Bay (Prince of Wales Island)
North Arm of Ingraham Bay is one mile west of Ingraham Point.
Chart 17432
Entrance: 54°59.03' N, 131°59.86' W
Anchor: 54°58.99' N, 132°01.80' W

In fair weather, North Arm of Ingraham Bay can be entered or exited through the 6-fathom gap in the middle of the outer island chain. The arm is relatively easy to enter and is totally landlocked. It is very quiet within an old-growth cedar forest and has a slight musty smell. There is room for several boats here, as well as a grassy landing beach and kayak campsite. We found the bottom hard.

Anchor in 7 to 10 fathoms with poor-to-fair holding.

### Chichagof Bay (Prince of Wales Island)
Chichagof Bay is 2.5 miles north of Ingraham Bay.
Chart 17432
Entrance: 55°01.58' N, 131°59.05' W
Anchor: 55°01.42' N, 131°59.64' W

Chichagof Bay is a tiny, intimate bay with relatively good shelter protected by kelp beds and a small inlet. When entering, stay north until close to the east shore, then head southwest to the inlet. This anchorage has a safe feel to it and is close to Clarence Strait.

Anchor in 4 fathoms over sand with fair holding.

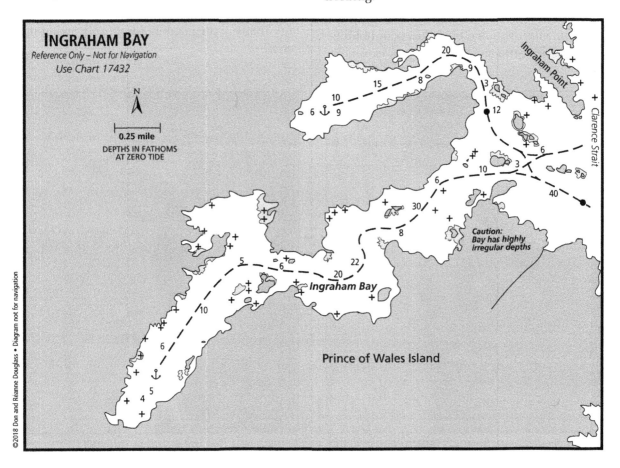

## About Salmon: Alaska's Famous Fish

Most people will agree that the best-tasting salmon comes from Alaskan waters. There are five species of wild Alaska salmon: the chum, pink, silver, sockeye, and King. Alaska salmon are active and thrive on the high levels of oxygen found in cold, rushing streams, estuaries and the upper levels of the ocean. The salmon spawn in fresh water and then migrate to the sea where they mature. Five to seven months after spawning the salmon fry emerge from the gravel where their parents had deposited and fertilized the eggs the previous fall. While some fry travel to sea immediately, others remain in the freshwater lakes and streams for a year or longer. As the fry migrate to sea they metamorphose to prepare for life in the saltwater. During this time of their life they are known as "smolt." In the estuaries where the fresh and salt water mix and the food is abundant, the smolt often double or triple their weight before heading west into the Gulf of Alaska or the Bering Sea.

Following is a brief description of the five species you may find in Alaska.

PINK—This is the smallest and most plentiful of the wild Alaska species. Most are between two and six pounds with the average weight around four pounds. Pinks can be found in all Alaskan streams from the Arctic to the Southeastern. Ocean-bright pinks are slim with silvery skin; semi-bright pinks have a distortion on their backs as the hump develops in the males. Dark bars are slightly apparent on the sides. Dark pink males have a pronounced hump and dark bars on the sides. Pink salmon has a delicate flavor.

CHUM—Most chums grow to be just over two feet long and weigh from 4–13 pounds. Eggs hatch in three to four months. The fry quickly move from their freshwater streambeds to the ocean. They spend three to five years in the salt water before returning home to spawn. Ocean-caught or bright Chums have silver sides and bellies with a dark, metallic, greenish-blue body. While they have no spots, fine, pale bars may be present on the sides. This is a delicately flavored, pink flesh fish with low-to-moderate fat content.

SILVER—Also known as Coho Salmon, Silvers are caught by troll and net fisheries. They are an attractive fish ranging from 25–35 inches and weighing two to 12 pounds. Silver fry stay in fresh water for a year before they turn into smolts. They spend 18-30 months growing in the ocean before they return to the streambeds of their birth. Ocean-caught or bright Silvers are dark, metallic blue on the back and upper sides. Small black spots may be evident on the back or on the top half of the tail. Pink skin or semi-bright Silvers have a slight pink or rose shading along the belly. Dark Silvers have a telltale red skin color with darker backs. Females may be darker than males; both have a pronounced hook of the nose. These salmon are most popular in restaurants because of their superior texture and pleasing orange-red flesh. Silvers make good smoked salmon.

SOCKEYE—Sockeye have a deep, red flesh and are one of the most abundant species of Alaskan salmon. They can grow to almost three feet and weigh up to 15 pounds. Eggs incubate from two to five months then the fry drift or swim to a nursery lake where they remain for one to two years. In their second or third spring they migrate to the sea. They return four years later to their original stream to spawn. Ocean-caught or bright Sockeye (also known as "blueback,") are deep, greenish-blue on their heads and back. Their sides are silver and they have a white belly. When mature they have a bright red back and green head with a pronounced line where the two colors meet at the gill plate. Sockeye flesh retains its deep red color when cooked. It has a high oil content, a moist texture and rich, complex flavor.

KING—The least abundant and most sought-after King (Chinook) Salmon ranges from 30–40 inches and from 5–40 pounds. Ocean-caught or bright Kings have silvery skin and scales and a deeper body than the other species. They have small, black spots on the back and upper sides and on the upper and lower halves of the silvery tail. The inside of a King's lower jaw is black. Most Kings return to their stream of origin after three to five years. King are prized for their red flesh, rich flavor, high oil content and firm texture. King salmon make up less than one percent of the total Alaskan salmon harvest.

## Moira Sound (Prince of Wales Island)

Moira Sound, entered between Rip and Adams points, is 25 miles north of Cape Chacon.
Chart 17432
South entrance (Rip Point bearing 157°T at 0.4 Nm): 55°02.57' N, 131°59.08' W
North entrance (Moira Rock Light bearing 186°T at 0.6 Nm): 55°05.58' N, 131°59.79' W

## Menefee Anchorage (Moira Sound)

Menefee Anchorage is 1 mile west of Rip Point.
Chart 17432
Entrance: 55°02.07' N, 132°00.81' W
Anchor: 55°01.58' N, 132°00.84' W

Menefee Anchorage is not as charted. We found the bottom to be highly irregular, with a 4-fathom shoal where the 25-fathom mark is! However, we found a nice 6-fathom hole near shore on the far steep-to south side that is bombproof if you use a stern-tie to trees.

Anchor in a 6-fathom hole over a hard bottom and poor holding.

## North Arm (Moira Sound)

North Arm is 2.8 miles west of Moira Rock.
Chart 17432
Entrance: 55°04.65' N, 132°04.89' W

North Arm has some exceptional places to anchor and explore. Watch for unmarked shoals, but enjoy the great view of 3,500-foot Eudora Mountain to the west.

## Halliday Nook / Moira Cove (North Arm)

Moira Cove is 2.5 miles northwest of Moira Island.
Chart 17432
Entrance: 55°05.40' N, 132°05.02' W
Anchor: 55°05.30' N, 132°04.77' W

"Moira Cove" is what we call the small well-placed notch 1 mile inside the entrance to North Arm on the east shore, just north of Halliday Point. It is well sheltered and cozy. Avoid the long reef south of the islet.

Anchor in about 3 fathoms over sand, mud and some kelp with good holding.

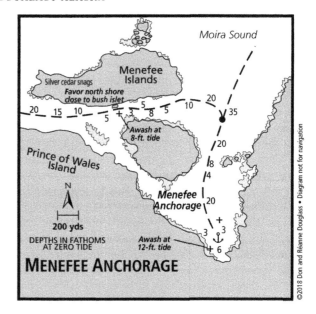

## Nowiskay Cove (North Arm)

Nowiskay Cove is 3.5 miles northwest of the entrance to North Arm.
Chart 17432
Entrance: 55°07.35' N, 132°08.70' W
Anchor (head of bay): 55°07.62' N, 132°08.99' W

Larger boats will find good protection from northwest winds at the head of Nowiskay Cove, but it is somewhat open to southeast chop. One or two small boats can find more complete shelter in the tiny west arm formed by a large submerged rock awash at high water.

Anchor (head of bay) in 8 to 10 fathoms over sand and gravel with fair holding.

*A careful entry through Hideaway Inlet Narrows brings you to full shelter.*

Anchor (tiny cove) in 2 fathoms over sand and gravel with fair holding.

## Clarno Cove (North Arm)
Clarno Cove is 4 miles northwest of the entrance to North Arm.
Chart 17432
Entrance: 55°07.09' N, 132°08.91' W
Anchor: 55°07.53' N, 132°10.63' W

Anchor in 8 to 10 fathoms over mud with good holding.

## Hideaway Inlet (Clarno Cove)
Hideaway Inlet is on the south shore of Clarno Cove.
Chart 17432
Entrance: 55°07.26' N, 132°10.07' W
Anchor: 55°06.98' N, 132°09.83' W

Hideaway Inlet, the landlocked basin on the south side of Clarno Cove, is one of our favorites. Completely sheltered from all weather, it is quiet and peaceful and the entrance is narrow and shallow. Enter carefully and reap your reward.

Anchor in four fathoms; sand and mud with good holding.

*Watch for dead heads that have become stuck in the bottom—like this one at Aiken Cove, complete with its own parasitic tree.*

## Aiken Cove (North Arm)
Aiken Cove is 4.5 miles northwest of the entrance to North Arm.
Chart 17432
Entrance: 55°07.41' N, 132°10.60' W
Anchor (larger boats, 0.08 mile southwest of entrance): 55°07.36' N, 132°10.70' W
Anchor (leaping salmon, 0.45 mile west of entrance): 55°07.34' N, 132°11.40' W
Anchor (small boats, 0.75 mile west of entrance): 55°07.38' N, 132°11.91' W

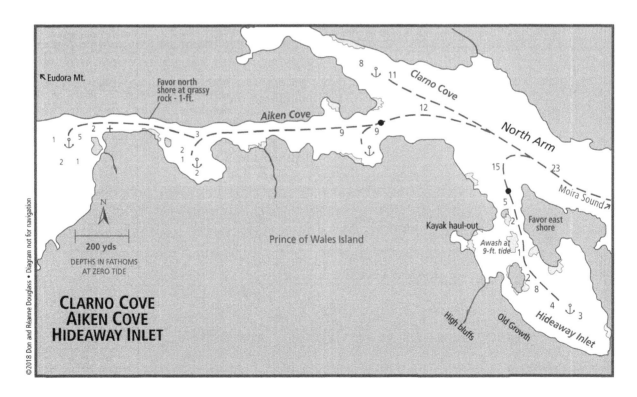

Aiken Cove is a narrow inlet with quiet anchorage for small craft. We have used all three anchor sites; choose the one that suits you best. Enjoy the views of the high peaks of Eudora Mountain.

Anchor in 8 fathoms in outer anchorage; 2 fathoms in inner anchor sites in sand with fair holding.

## Niblack Anchorage (Moira Sound)
Niblack Anchorage is 2.5 miles west of Moira Island.
Chart 17432
Entrance (south tip of Clare Island bearing 350°T at 0.08 Nm): 55°03.45' N, 132°06.25' W
Anchor: 55°03.93' N, 132°08.60' W

Good anchorage can be found northwest of Red Rock.

Anchor in 8 fathoms; sand and gravel with fair holding.

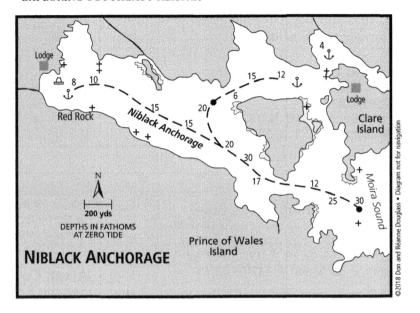

## Clare Island Cove (Niblack Anchorage)
Clare Island Cove is on the northeast shore of Niblack Anchorage.
Chart 17432
Entrance: 55°03.92' N, 132°07.31' W
Anchor (large boats): 55°04.00' N, 132°06.83' W
Anchor (small boats): 55°04.10' N, 132°06.48' W

Very good shelter can be found in what we call "Clare Island Cove." The north and west shores of Clare Island are very well protected. The inner basin has a mid-channel rock and reef and is suitable for small craft under fair conditions only.

Large boats anchor in 12 fathoms over mud bottom. Smaller boats anchor (inner basin) in 4 fathoms over sand.

*Eudora Mountain is your backdrop in Aiken Cove.*

*Private float at Niblack Anchorage*

*Use Red Rock as a landmark at Niblack Anchorage.*

## Kegan Cove (Moira Sound)
Kegan Cove is 5.5 miles southwest of Moira Island.
Chart 17432
Entrance: 55°00.95' N, 132°09.40' W
Anchor: 55°01.25' N, 132°09.97' W

Kegan Cove is a very small, intimate place and another of our favorites. It is suitable for smaller boats only when tide and currents

*Keep a careful bow watch as you enter Kegan Cove Narrows.*

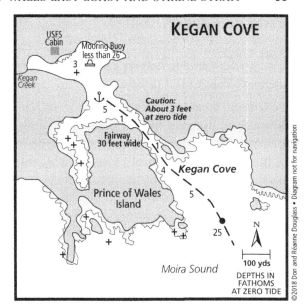

allow transiting the tiny narrows. If in doubt, check it out by dinghy first. There is a USFS cabin on the creek and a small USFS buoy at the head of the cove.

Anchor in 5 to 7 fathoms over brown mud, sand and shells with very good holding.

## Johnson Cove (Moira Sound)
Johnson Cove is 4 miles southwest of Moira Island.
Chart 17432
Entrance: 55°00.74' N, 132°05.92' W
Anchor: 54°58.37' N, 132°05.66' W

Anchor in 6 fathoms over brown mud and small rocks with fair holding.

## South Arm (Moira Sound)
South Arm is 6 miles southwest of Moira Island.
Chart 17432
Entrance: 54°59.61' N, 132°09.11' W
Anchor: 54°56.00' N, 132°12.25' W

Anchor in 7 fathoms over sand and gravel with fair holding.

## West Arm (Moira Sound)
West Arm is 7 miles southwest of Moira Island.
Chart 17432
Entrance: 55°00.27' N, 132°10.00' W

Pleasant temporary anchorage can be found among the islets on the south side of West Arm at the entrance to South Arm.

## Frederick Cove (West Arm)
Frederick Cove is 8.5 miles southwest of Moira Island.
Chart 17432
Entrance: 54°59.62' N, 132°13.64' W
Anchor: 54°58.85' N, 132°18.02' W

We have no local knowledge of Frederick Cove. However, it appears from a distance to have spectacular scenery with good anchorage at its head, favoring the north shore at the narrows, and to be pleasant temporary anchorage for small craft in two tiny coves northwest of the entrance point. Anchorage (head of bay) is reported in 6 to 8 fathoms over a soft bottom.

*Old wooden ferry boat hard aground in Johnson Cove*

## French Harbor (Dutch Harbor)
French Harbor is 4 miles north of Moira Rock.
Chart 17432
Entrance (French Harbor): 55°08.45' N, 132°00.66' W
Entrance (Dutch Harbor): 55°09.31' N, 131°59.70' W

## Bull Rails Instead of Cleats for Securing Dock Lines
### Linda Lewis and David Parker—M/V *Royal Sounder*

We all know how to use cleats to secure our lines to the dock. But cleats aren't what you find in Southeast Alaska. What you'll find are Bull Rails—long pieces of timber on the dock. The Bull Rails require you to get off the boat, lead your line under the rail, then over the rail to tie off or run back to the boat. OK most of the time. But it can be a real problem when the currents are running, the wind is blowing, or the helm is making mistakes—or all of the above.

There is help for those times. We call it "The Hook." It is a device (a line with a hook) that can be thrown from the boat onto the dock, then dragged back until it hooks the Bull Rail. Voila! You're attached to the dock long enough for you to get off and run secure dock lines. It's a life-saver in tough docking situations. We know of one line-handler who is disabled and uses the hook for every docking. It would also be useful if someone on your boat is injured or less nimble than usual. We highly recommend having it onboard.

*Bull rail with a line that has been there awhile*

*Unique way to secure lines to bull rails*

*"The Hook" is a big help getting a line to the dock*

Dutch Harbor is immediately north of French Harbor. Both harbors are really rock piles with many isolated rocks, reefs, kelp beds and channels that offer temporary anchorage in prevailing westerlies, but no serious protection or swinging room in southeast gales.

## Cholmondeley Sound (Prince of Wales Island)
Cholmondeley Sound is entered between Chasina Point and Skin Island.
Chart 17436
Entrance: 55°16.88' N, 132°03.88' W

Cholmondeley (pronounced "Chumly") Sound is another great sound on Prince of Wales Island. Like Moira Sound, it is a marvelous and remote place to explore and enjoy. Keep in mind that these small-scale charts may lack sufficient detail for safe navigation.

## Kitkun Bay (Cholmondeley Sound)
Kitkun Bay is 7 miles south of Skin Island Light.
Chart 17436 (inset)
Outer entrance: 55°12.76' N, 132°08.92' W
Inner entrance: 55°11.59' N, 132°08.77' W
Anchor (Inner Sanctum): 55°09.31' N, 132°11.54' W

This bay raises the definition of "landlocked" and "isolated" to a new and higher standard, and we have report of good anchorage at the south end of the bay.

## Dora Bay (Cholmondeley Sound)
Dora Bay is 7 miles southwest of Skin Island Light.
Chart 17436
Entrance: 55°13.85' N, 132°13.21' W

We have seen several inviting small coves along the shore of Dora Bay, but we have no local knowledge of them.

## Sunny Cove (Cholmondeley Sound)
Sunny Cove is 7 miles southwest of Skin Island Light.
Chart 17436
Entrance: 55°14.93' N, 132°14.79' W
Anchor: 55°15.44' N, 132°16.22' W

It is reported that rain never falls in Sunny Cove, and that anchorage can be found in about 10 fathoms over sand and gravel with fair holding.

*Exploring Cholmondeley Sound*

## West Arm (Cholmondeley Sound)
West Arm is 8 miles southwest of Skin Island Light.
Chart 17436
Entrance: 55°15.01' N, 132°17.92' W
Anchor (1.5 miles west of confluence): 55°14.95' N, 132°20.30' W
Anchor (behind islet): 55°15.04' N, 132°24.12' W
Anchor (head of arm): 55°15.42' N, 132°27.70' W
Anchor (1.5 miles west of confluence) in 4 to 8 fathoms.
Anchor (behind islet) in about 10 fathoms over a soft bottom.
Anchor (head of arm) in about 10 fathoms off steep-to drying mud flat over a soft bottom.

## Clover Bay (Prince of Wales Island)
Clover Bay, between Clover Point and Anderson Point, is 1.5 miles west of Skin Island.
Chart 17436
Entrance: 55°18.12' N, 132°07.52' W

The cove north and west of King Island appears to offer shelter to small craft, but it is inadequately surveyed at this time.

## Kasaan Bay
(Prince of Wales Island)

Kasaan Bay, 47 miles north of Cape Chacon, is entered between Island Point and Grindall Island.

**Charts 17426, 17436**
Entrance (High Island Light bearing 252°T at 1.1 Nm): 55°24.38′ N, 132°08.05′ W

Fair Winds *of Ketchikan visiting Prince of Wales Island*

With its many small inlets and coves and secure anchorages, Kasaan Bay is a prime example of the many wonderful cruising opportunities available along both coasts of Prince of Wales Island. The Prince of Wales Chamber of Commerce publishes an annual information guide which includes lists of tour operators, travel opportunities, and service providers across the island https://www.princeofwalescoc.org/ Have lots of fenders out and be alert for the wake of the daily round-trip ferry operated by Viking Travel which provides round-trip service between Hollis and Ketchikan. http://www.alaskaferry.com/FerrySchedules/InterIslandFerry or call 800-327-2571. There is an extensive network of dirt roads on Prince of Wales Island. Car rental or shuttle arrangements can be made in Hollis, as well as in several of the other villages if you want to visit other parts of the island.

## Trollers Cove (Kasaan Bay)
Trollers Cove, behind a chain of islands, is 1.4 miles west of Island Point.
**Chart 17426**

*Use the transient float at Kasaan Bay cautiously; avoid it in heavy weather.*

CHAPTER 3 — CLARENCE STRAIT, PRINCE OF WALES EAST COAST AND STIKINE STRAIT

Entrance: 55°22.52' N, 132°12.84' W
Anchor: 55°21.89' N, 132°11.94' W

Trollers Cove is charted at the small scale of 1:40,000, but it appears to offer good shelter in all weather.

### Spiral Cove (Kasaan Bay)
Spiral Cove is immediately west of Trollers Cove.
Chart 17426
Entrance: 55°22.52' N, 132°12.84' W

Spiral Cove appears to offer complete shelter inside the tiny basin. Like Trollers Bay, it needs a large-scale chart.

### Kluanil Island Cove (Kasaan Bay)
Kluanil Island is 0.7 mile north of Spiral Cove.
Chart 17426
Entrance: 55°23.07' N, 132°13.65' W

Kluanil Island Cove appears to provide very good shelter in its small basin, but it needs a large-scale chart.

### Skowl Arm (Kasaan Bay)
Skowl Arm is the southern arm of Kasaan Bay.
Charts 17426, 17436
Entrance: 55°26.13' N, 132°16.47' W
Position (Old Kasaan site): 55°25.93' N, 132°22.30' W

*An orca calf is escorted, probably by her mom and two aunts, on the south side of Kasaan Island.*

*Playful orcas on the south side of Kasaan Island*

*Scene of an abandoned Haida village at Skowl Arm*

This is a wonderful historical site worth a visit. Only the longhouse poles and some gravesites of the traditional Kasaan native site remain. The Haida totems were moved to a new park at Kassan, 6.5 miles northwest. Temporary anchorage can be found off the beach.

Anchor in 6 to 8 fathoms in sand and gravel with fair holding.

### Saltery Cove (Skowl Arm)
Saltery Cove is 2 miles southwest of Skowl Point.
Charts 17426, 17436
Entrance: 55°25.06' N, 132°19.62' W
Anchor: 55°24.21' N, 132°19.68' W

Saltery Cove has good southeast protection. There is a large sport-fishing lodge in the cove. Saltery Cove has an irregular bottom, so be sure that if you anchor here you are over sand or mud, not rocks.

Anchor in about 10 fathoms; sand, gravel, some rocks and kelp. Fair-to-good holding.

### McKenzie Inlet (Skowl Arm)
McKenzie Inlet is 3.7 miles west of Skowl Point.
Charts 17426, 17436
Entrance: 55°23.60' N, 132°22.54' W
Anchor: 55°19.92' N, 132°21.74' W

Anchor in 8 fathoms over sand and gravel with fair holding.

### Smith Cove (Skowl Arm)
Smith Cove is 2 miles west of Kasaan Point.
Charts 17426, 17436
Entrance: 55°26.01' N, 132°19.80' W

Isolated shoals and rocks in Smith Cove require careful piloting and suggest an irregular rocky bottom.

### Little Goose Bay (Skowl Arm)
Little Goose Bay is 1.5 miles northeast of Goose Bay.
Charts 17426, 17436
Entrance: 55°25.00' N, 132°27.73' W

The head of Little Goose Bay has anchorage for one vessel with limited swinging room.

### Polk Inlet (Skowl Arm)
Polk Inlet, the west arm of Skowl Arm, extends west and south for 9.3 miles.
Chart 17426
Entrance: 55°25.12' N, 132°28.08' W

The entrance to Polk Inlet is encumbered with unmarked shoals and rocks which make navigation dangerous when the current is flowing. Reconnoiter first before entering. Passage at slack water is advised. There are a series of small basins at the head of Polk Inlet, each with narrow, intricate entrances that appear to lead to good, sheltered anchorages at the bitter end.

### Goose Bay (Polk Inlet)
Goose Bay is 1.5 miles south of the entrance to Polk Inlet.
Chart 17426
Entrance: 55°23.74' N, 132°29.22' W

The head of Goose Bay appears to provide good shelter, but Polk Inlet entrance is notoriously difficult to navigate.

## Happy Harbor (Kasaan Island)

Happy Harbor is on the northeast side of Kasaan Island.

Chart 17426
Entrance: 55°29.94' N, 132°19.62' W
Anchor: 55°29.65' N, 132°20.08' W

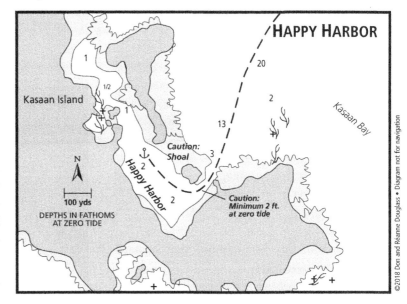

Happy Harbor requires careful navigation. However, we have found it worth the careful attention needed to enter it (two feet at zero tide) and welcome its secure shelter.

Anchor in 2 fathoms over sand and mud with fair holding.

## Kasaan (Kasaan Bay)

Kasaan, a village on the north shore of Kasaan Bay, is 10 miles northwest of Grindall Island.

Chart 17426

Entrance: 55°32.14' N, 132°23.91' W

The docks at Kasaan are being restored as we go to press (2018). You might consider anchoring in one of the nearby secure coves, and taking a dinghy to the village site.

The Whale House and totem park at the Organized Village of Kasaan on the north shore of Kasaan Bay were constructed between 1938 and 1940 by the Civilian Conservation Corps. The materials were taken from the historic Kasaan village on the north shore of Skowl Bay (see above). Tribal tours led by a knowledgeable and personable local guide are available

*The float at Kasaan is at the right in this picture.*

*A magical walk through the quiet forest at Kasaan brings you to totems like this.*

*Kasaan Bay totem*

907.617.3386; http://kasaan.org/visit-kasaan/totems-historic-district/

You may also take a self-guided walking tour along a trail that leads to the northwest from the top of the floats past a half-dozen homes. The meandering trail leads through a spruce, hemlock and cedar forest, passing totems which are attractively placed along the path. The longhouse was beautifully restored in 2016.

## Poor Man Bay (Kasaan Bay)
Poor Man Bay is 1.3 miles west of Kasaan Village.
Chart 17426
Position: 55°32.75' N, 132°26.02' W

Poor Man Bay is too shoal for shelter.

## Mills Bay, Lindeman Cove and Browns Bay (Kasaan Bay)
Mills Bay is 4 miles northwest of Kasaan Village; Lindeman Cove is 5.5 miles northwest of Kasaan Village; Browns Bay is 6 miles northwest of Kasaan Village.
Chart 17426
Entrance (Mills Bay): 55°33.66' N, 132°28.72' W
Position (Lindeman Cove): 55°36.00' N, 132°30.94' W
Position (Browns Bay): 55°35.76' N, 132°32.96' W

## Karta Bay (Kasaan Bay)
Karta Bay, at the head of Kasaan Bay, is 6 miles northwest of Kasaan Village.
Chart 17426
Entrance: 55°34.35' N, 132°33.68' W
Anchor: 55°34.03' N, 132°34.53' W

*The Haida longhouse and totem at Kasaan Bay*

Anchor in about 8 fathoms over a hard bottom with poor-to-fair holding.

## Little Coal Bay (Kasaan Bay)
Little Coal Bay is 1 mile east of Coal Bay.
Chart 17426
Entrance: 55°30.40' N, 132°27.97' W

Little Coal Bay is useful only for small boats in southerly weather. Coal Bay has more shelter and swinging room.

## Coal Bay (Kasaan Bay)
Coal Bay is 3.8 miles southwest of Kasaan.
Chart 17426
Entrance: 55°30.51' N, 132°28.99' W
Anchor: 55°29.87' N, 132°29.51' W

Anchor (head of bay) in about 6 fathoms.

### Kina Cove (Kasaan Bay)
Kina Cove is 0.5 mile west of Coal Bay.
Chart 17426
Entrance: 55°30.86' N, 132°30.54' W
Anchor: 55°29.60' N, 132°31.23' W

This cove offers good protection from southerly winds and makes a central location from which to explore Kasaan Bay.

Anchor in 8 fathoms over mud with good holding.

### Nanny Bay (Twelvemile Arm)
Nanny Bay is 2.7 miles west of Kina Cove.
Chart 17426
Entrance: 55°30.07' N, 132°35.12' W

Nanny Bay is useful for temporary anchorage in fair weather.

### Twelvemile Bay (Twelvemile Arm)
Twelvemile Bay is 3 miles southwest of Kina Cove.
Chart 17426
Entrance: 55°29.01' N, 132°34.34' W

Twelvemile Bay has a shallow entrance, but appears to offer shelter for small craft from southeast winds near the head of the bay.

### Clark Bay (Twelvemile Arm)
Clark Bay is about 0.4 mile northwest of the northeast point of Loy Island.
Chart 17426
Entrance: 55°29.49' N, 132°36.57' W

Clark Bay is the site of the Hollis ferry terminal. Roads from this terminal connect with Craig, Klawock and Hydaburg on the west side of Prince of Wales Island.

### Hollis Anchorage (Twelvemile Arm)
Hollis Anchorage is 10 miles west of Kasaan Island.
Chart 17426
Entrance: 55°28.44' N, 132°38.46' W
Anchor: 55°28.56' N, 132°40.04' W

The Hollis ferry dock shown on the NOAA chart is no longer operational; it has been converted to a launching ramp. The Inter-Island Ferry terminal is in Clark Bay, northeast of Hollis itself. Good holding may be found in

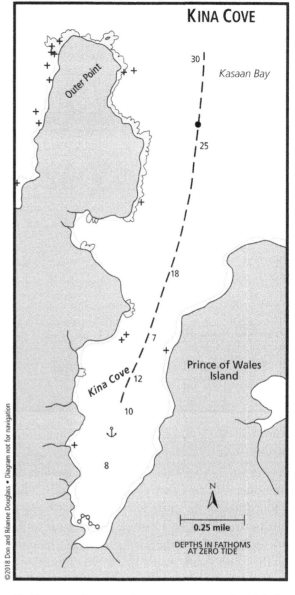

Hollis Anchorage, however entry should be carefully made. An area of shoal water clearly marked on the chart (55°28.65' N, 132°39.21' W) catches both visiting cruisers and some local boaters unaware every year.

### Lyman Anchorage (Prince of Wales Island)
Lyman Anchorage is 24.5 miles northwest of Ketchikan.
Chart 17426 (inset)
Outer entrance (0.5 mile northeast of Higgins Point): 55°32.88' N, 132°17.28' W
Inner entrance (0.1 mile northwest of Sawmill

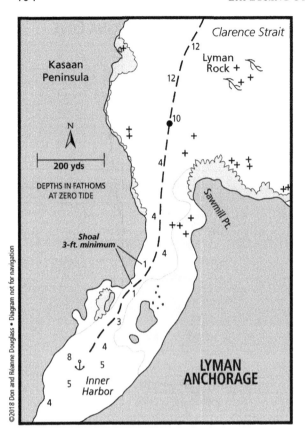

tom is irregular with kelp, sand and rocks and poor-to-marginal holding.

## Tolstoi Bay, West Cove (Prince of Wales Island)
Tolstoi Bay is 23 miles northwest of Guard Island.
Chart 17423 (inset)
Outer entrance (mid-channel between Tolstoi Point and Tolstoi Island):
55°41.01' N, 132°24.55' W
Inner entrance: 55°40.21' N, 132°25.70' W
Entrance (West Cove): 55°39.07' N, 132°26.45' W
Anchor (West Cove): 55°39.39' N, 132°26.81' W

Tolstoi Bay, West Cove, the second cove on the west side of the bay, is tucked behind a wooded peninsula. The cove is well protected from moderate southeasterly winds, with minor chop during gale winds. We anchored *Baidarka* here in a near gale and although we felt the wind gusts, we spent a comfortable night anchored in 9 fathoms north of the treed islet.

Point): 55°32.31' N, 132°17.75' W
Anchor: 55°31.94' N, 132°17.97' W

Lyman Anchorage is one of the most protected anchorages in this part of Clarence Strait. The 3-foot shoal at the entrance to the inner harbor can be traversed by most boats *only* on half-tide or more. Favor the west shore as indicated on the chart inset. Avoid Lyman Rock north of Sawmill Point, which is marked by extensive kelp.

Anchor in 6 fathoms over a soft bottom with fair-to-good holding.

## Windfall Harbor (Prince of Wales Island)
Windfall Harbor is 4 miles northwest of Lyman Anchorage.
Chart 17426
Entrance: 55°36.49' N, 132°20.39' W

Although Windfall Harbor is well protected from swells, wind and chop, we do not recommend it as an anchorage for cruising boats. Swinging room is quite restricted and the bot-

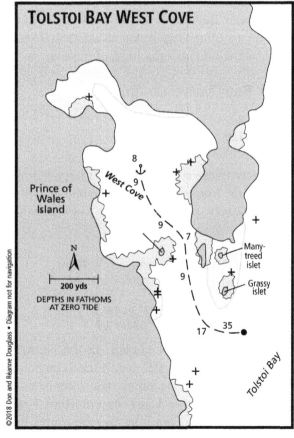

*Rig a fish-cleaning device for your boat.*

The entrance to the cove is somewhat restricted by rocks and the islet; favor the peninsula side. The entrance fairway carries adequate depths, from 10 to 12 fathoms throughout, and the inner cove has good swinging room over a wide flat bottom. Beware of several old cables tied to trees on the shore—they may lie on the bottom, as well.

Anchor (West Cove) in about 9 fathoms over dry gray mud with fair-to-good holding.

## Thorne Bay (Prince of Wales Island)
Thorne Bay is 8 miles southwest of Meyers Chuck.
Charts 17423 (inset), 17420
Outer entrance (mid-channel between Tolstoi Point and Island):
55°41.01′ N, 132°24.55′ W
Inner entrance (0.27 mile west of Thorne Head Light "2"):
55°40.77′ N, 132°27.93′ W
Thorne Bay (narrows, west entrance): 55°39.81′ N, 132°29.75′ W
Public floats: 55°40.92′ N, 132°31.44′ W
Anchor (south bight): 55°39.69′ N, 132°28.37′ W

Thorne Bay, once the largest logging camp in the U.S., is an attractive town with nice facilities for cruising boats. Incorporated in 1982 as the City of Thorne Bay, the town has convenient services that include groceries, hardware, marine supplies, liquor store, post office, and a medical clinic. Vehicles are available to rent for visits to other road-accessible villages on Prince of Wales Island, including Craig, Klawock, and Kasaan.

*The real world of Alaska—a one-man sawyering operation in Hollis*

*A true Alaska dog in Hollis*

The entrance to Thorne Bay is narrow and has strong currents. See the current *Coast Pilot* for detailed entrance instructions and study the inset on Chart 17423.

Thorne Bay Harbor has extensive floats for transients with fuel, power (30 amp), water and pay telephone, public restrooms, and showers available. To contact the harbor, call the City of Thorne Bay (907.828.3380). The city monitors Channel VHF 16. A smaller harbor, Davidson Landing, on the south side of town, was recently renovated and may also have transient mooring available.

McFarland's Floatel, located southwest of the city, offers basket weaving classes that are attended by people from all over the United States. They may have room at times for unregistered participants. Contact them for information or for dinner and B & B reservations (888.828.3335); Website: www.mcfarlandsfloatel.com.

Thorne Bay has a fairly flat bottom throughout its entire length. Cruising boats can anchor in 6 to 8 fathoms as desired; anchorage off McFarland's Floatel is also good.

Anchor in 7 fathoms in the southern arm of Thorne Bay over mud with very good holding.

*There is usually room for transients at the Thorne Bay floats.*

## Snug Anchorage (Prince of Wales Island)
Snug Anchorage is about 1 mile west of Tolstoi Island.
Charts 17423 (inset), 17420
Entrance (0.6 mile northeast of Thorne Head Light): 55°41.29' N, 132°27.13' W
Anchor (inner basin):
55°42.53' N, 132°28.88' W
Position (east cove): 55°42.38' N, 132°27.31' W

The entrance to Snug Anchorage, although tight and shallow, is well protected and secure in the north end of the anchorage.

Anchor in 3 to 16 fathoms at head of inner basin.

## Ratz Harbor (Prince of Wales Island)
Ratz Harbor is 14 miles northwest of Meyers Chuck.
Chart 17423 (inset)
Entrance (0.18 mile southwest of entrance light): 55°53.21' N, 132°35.58' W
Anchor (north): 55°53.23' N, 132°36.03' W
Anchor (south): 55°52.84' N, 132°35.78' W

Ratz Harbor, originally named "Gavan Rats" by Captain Tebenkov, then-Governor of the Russian-American colonies (1845–50), offers good pro-

*The popular McFarland's Floatel in Thorne Bay may be able to provide moorage; call ahead.*

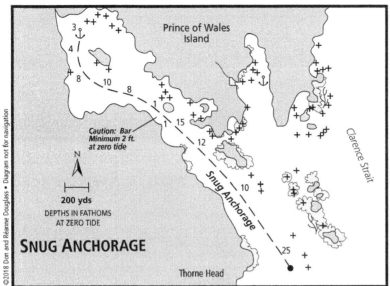

WSW on a distant mountain top.

The entrance to Ratz Harbor has easy access over a 3- to 5-fathom bar marked by a flashing 4-second light. There is plenty of swinging room for a number of boats.

If southerlies are expected, anchor on the south side. After the front has passed, move to the north end, as indicated on the diagram.

Anchor (north) in 6 fathoms in sticky mud with very good holding.

Anchor (south) in 9 fathoms over sticky mud bottom with good holding.

tection from southerlies and prevailing northwesterlies. It was used extensively in the past as a log staging and booming area but is now quiet. Cell phone reception is available just outside the bay from the tower visible to the

### Dewey Anchorage (Etolin Island)
Dewey Anchorage is on the south tip of Etolin Island just north of the entrance to Ernest Sound.
Chart 17423 (inset)
Entrance (0.6 mile west of Gull Point, Onslow Island): 55°54.11' N, 132°25.12' W
Anchor (0.14 mile east of Carlton Island): 55°54.71' N, 132°21.45' W

Dewey Anchorage provides temporary shelter when the chop of Clarence Strait kicks up. During southerly weather, a lee can be found on the northeast side of Carlton Island, using the inset on Chart 17423 as a guide.

Anchor in the lee of Carlton Island, as conditions warrant, in 6 fathoms over a bottom reported to be sand and shell; holding is unknown.

### McHenry Anchorage (Etolin Island)
McHenry Anchorage is 7.5 miles northeast of Ratz Harbor.
Chart 17360
Entrance (1.25 miles north of Double Island): 55°58.00' N, 132°27.92' W
Anchor: 55°57.94' N, 132°26.46' W

The inner basin of McHenry Anchorage is well sheltered in all but strong westerlies. Avoid rocks on the south side of fairway and anchor in south center of basin.

Anchor in 6 fathoms.

*A cruise ship in Clarence Strait passes the Ratz Harbor anchorage.*

## McHenry Inlet (Etolin Island)
McHenry Inlet is 2.5 miles north of McHenry Anchorage.
Chart 17382
Entrance: 56°00.42' N, 132°28.33' W
Anchor: 56°01.53' N, 132°23.04' W

Anchor in about 13 fathoms.

## Burnett Inlet (Etolin Island)
Burnett Inlet is 5 miles northeast of Point Stanhope.
Chart 17382 (inset)
Entrance (0.25 mile southeast of Fawn Island): 56°03.01' N, 132°29.25' W
Anchor (Cannery Point): 56°04.16' N, 132°28.87' W

Burnett Inlet has a very narrow entrance with high peaks on both sides. It is deep except for an area 4 miles north of Cannery Point where minimum depth is 1-1/2 feet. Avoid the shoal on the north side of Cannery Point, which extends 100 yards from shore. There is a large basin 4 to 8 fathoms deep, 5.7 miles above Cannery Point.

Anchor in 6 fathoms over a hard bottom with fair holding.

## Mosman Inlet (Etolin Island)
Mosman Inlet is 4 miles northeast of Point Stanhope.
Chart 17382
Entrance (mid-channel between Mosman Point and Fawn Island): 56°03.28' N, 132°31.16' W

The islands to the north of Mosman Island appear to offer a number of potential anchor sites in the 4- to 6-fathom range; however, the channels between the islands are only charted at 1:80,000. This area remains ripe for exploration.

## Rocky Bay, Cooney Cove (Etolin Island)
Rocky Bay, north of Point Stanhope, is 3 miles northeast of Point Stanhope Light.
Chart 17382
Entrance (1.3 miles southwest of Mosman Point): 56°02.46' N, 132°33.83' W
Entrance (Cooney Cove, 0.6 mile southwest of Mosman Point): 56°02.99' N, 132°32.97' W

There may be anchorage available for small craft in about 10 feet of water at the head of Cooney Cove; however, the approach is reported foul and the bay is open to the south.

# CHAPTER 3 — CLARENCE STRAIT, PRINCE OF WALES EAST COAST AND STIKINE STRAIT

*Endless vistas of beauty in Southeast Alaska offer opportunities for contemplation (Kasaan Bay).*

## Cove 2 Miles Southeast of Lincoln Rock (Etolin Island)
Cove 1.5 miles Southeast of Lincoln Rock is 6 miles east of Coffman Cove.
Entrance: 56°02.90' N, 132°39.22' W

This unnamed cove, which is suitable for temporary anchorage only, allows exploration, via its northernmost entrance, of the labyrinth of islets and rocks of the unnamed bay to the east.

## Lincoln Rock (Clarence Strait)
Lincoln Rock is 4 miles northwest of Point Stanhope.
Chart 17382
Light: 56°03.42' N, 132°41.85' W

Pass inside Lincoln Rock for a good look at the remains of a lighthouse that played an important role in earlier times but eventually succumbed to winter storms. If you look carefully you will also find the remains of a WWII bunker.

## Coffman Cove (Prince of Wales Island)
Coffman Cove is 26 miles northwest of Meyers Chuck.
Chart 17401
Entrance (1.7 miles southeast of Beck Island Light): 56°01.55' N, 132°49.80' W
Public float: 56°00.67' N, 132°49.95' W

Coffman Cove, formerly a logging camp, is now a small community with a general store that sells groceries and clothing. Coffman Cove Harbor underwent a major renovation and expansion in 2010/2011. There are now 60 moorage slips and 180 feet of transient moorage along the public float. Fresh water and shore power are available, as well as restrooms. Showers and laundry are available at the seasonally-open RV park nearby, and the public library offers wireless internet access. The transient moorage is generally occupied by commercial fishing boats and it can be

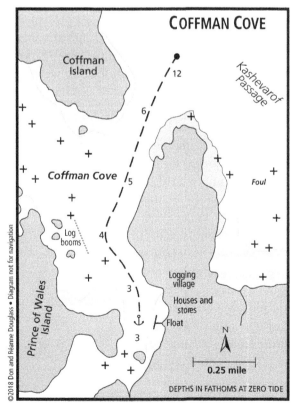

difficult for the recreational boater to find a spot. Lake Bay and Barnes Lake to the west are popular recreation areas for hunting, fishing, canoeing, and kayaking.

Although the cove offers good shelter, watch out for work boats that come and go at all hours. The entrance is clear and a mid-channel course is advised. Anchorage can also be found off the public float.

Anchor in 3 fathoms over a soft bottom with good holding.

## Kashevarof Passage (Clarence Strait)
Kashevarof Passage lies between the Kashevarof Islands and Stevenson, Thorne and Prince of Wales islands.
Chart 17382
Southeast entrance (0.9 mile south of The Triplets and 1 mile southeast of Beck Island Light): 56°02.65′ N, 132°49.85′ W
North entrance (0.5 mile north of Fire Island): 56°14.54′ N, 133°03.47′ W
North entrance (0.5 mile east of Colpoys Light): 56°20.17′ N, 133°10.78′ W

Kashevarof Passage is an alternate route to Snow Passage to the east. It is more protected and the velocity of its current is considerably less. This route also allows you to avoid the Snow Passage commercial traffic, as well as putting you within easy reach of good anchorage in Exchange Cove.

You can follow Kashevarof Passage all the way to Point Colpoys (on the northeast corner of Prince of Wales Island) by carefully hugging the Prince of Wales coast for a smooth-water route. Proceed carefully, watching your charts and the waters around you for hazards. If your initial plan was to transit Snow Passage, don't change your mind along the way and try to take a route through the Middle Islands group south of Shrubby Island; these passages can be choked with logs, in addition to the rocks and reefs.

## Lake Bay (Stevenson Island)
Lake Bay is 1 mile southwest of Beck Island Light.
Chart 17401
Entrance (0.3 mile southeast of Beck Island Light): 56°02.59′ N, 132°51.40′ W
Anchor (0.16 mile northwest of fishery float, 0.8 mile south of Keg Point): 56°01.25′ N, 132°55.70′ W

The entrance to Lake Bay is filled with rocks and shoals. Use Chart 17401 as your guide if you want to enter it. Anchorage can be found mid-channel off the outflow of Lake Bay Creek, about 300 yards northwest of the buildings. This site offers protection from southerlies, and is a good place to explore the lake and lagoons to the west. Watch for strong ebb currents and dangerous rapids south and west of Stevenson Island.

Anchor in about a 6-fathom hole over a bottom of sticky mud and shells with very good holding.

## Whale Passage
Whale Passage lies between Thorne Island and Prince of Wales Island.
Chart 17382
Southeast entrance (3.8 miles northwest of

*This black bear became uneasy as the photographer came nearer.*

# CHAPTER 3 — CLARENCE STRAIT, PRINCE OF WALES EAST COAST AND STIKINE STRAIT

*Anchor check; researching the character of the bottom.*

Beck Island Light): 56°03.89' N, 132°58.16' W
Anchor (northwest bay): 56°05.85' N, 133°07.14' W
Northeast entrance (2.7 miles southwest of Kashevarof Passage Light): 56°08.35' N, 133°03.40' W

## Blashke Islands

Blashke Islands lie between Clarence Strait and Kashevarof Passage; southwest entrance is 3.9 miles northwest of Beck Island Light.
Chart 17382
Southwest entrance: 56°06.32' N, 132°54.84' W
Anchor (first basin): 56°07.31' N, 132°54.86' W
Anchor (second basin): 56°07.56' N, 132°54.41' W

Blashke Islands — a complex of islands with unusual topography — can be appealing to cruising boats because they are located just a day's cruise north of Ketchikan. The islands are part of the Kashevarof Islands, which have endless cruising and fishing possibilities; exercise caution, as the area is not charted at large scale.

Numbering about 20 islands in all, the area is fun to explore by dinghy or kayak. The complex is shaped like a giant set of molars that have opened slightly to create intricate waterways. Landlocked and isolated, the anchor sites shown on the diagram offer shelter and solitude, which is otherwise seldom found near the Inside Passage route.

Small, old-growth trees line the shores, with few signs of modern visitors, though we've found several shell middens, an empty bottle filled with a mining claim notice, and hunting campsites. Sitka black-tailed deer, marten, and eagles are locals here. A trail leads across the neck to an aquaculture operation in the south-facing cove; boaters are asked to respect the privacy of the site and not to "drop in."

The entrance to the Blashke Islands is intricate and somewhat difficult. You must make a very slow approach, posting alert lookouts on your bow. Do not attempt to enter in foul weather, limited visibility or by radar. The first narrows is about 100 feet wide, and the entrance to the second basin is even narrower.

*Purse seiner bringing in its net, Clarence Strait*

There are many rocks and shoals outside the islets, as well as along the narrow inside route. The bottom is irregular and the patterns of current are complex, due to the many different openings.

The Blashke Islands themselves are poorly charted at 1:80,000 and the various electronic charts have large errors in this area. Do not be surprised if your chart plotter shows you cruising over land with errors as much as 200 feet in these narrow channels. Stay mid-channel, with an alert bow watch, and proceed slowly. Stop any time you are uncomfortable and do not continue until you are convinced it is safe to do so.

Pick your way carefully through the nar-

## GEORGE VANCOUVER

If there's one boater who looms larger than all the others in this part of the world, it's George Vancouver. The British mariner, who learned his trade with Captain Cook, arrived in the Pacific Northwest in April 1792 as captain of HMS *Discovery*, with orders to survey every inlet and outlet on the west coast between the Strait of Juan de Fuca, in northern Washington State, and Alaska. His subsequent charts—compiled primarily from surveys undertaken in small boats—were so detailed and accurate that they have continued to be used into modern times. Vancouver's legacy is also enshrined in place names up and down the northwest coast, including eponymous cities in British Columbia and Washington State, Vancouver Island, and numerous places named after friends, patrons, and members of his crew.

Vancouver was born in King's Lynn, an English seaport, in 1757. He joined the Royal Navy at the age of 13 and served as a midshipman on Captain Cook's second and third voyages to the Pacific (1772-75 and 1776-80, aboard HMS *Resolution* and *Discovery*, respectively). In 1780, Vancouver was commissioned as a lieutenant and spent the next decade aboard warships. In 1790, after the Spanish ceded their rights to Nootka Sound on what is now Vancouver Island (see sidebar on *The Spanish Claims to Alaska*), he was given command of *Discovery* to take formal British possession of the outpost at Nootka Sound and survey the adjacent coasts.

*Discovery* sailed from England via Cape Town, the southern tip of Western Australia, Tahiti, and Hawaii, arriving off the Oregon coast a year later. The ship entered the Strait of Juan de Fuca, between Vancouver Island and the Washington state mainland, on 29 April, 1792. In June, Vancouver surveyed the harbors and waters around what is now Vancouver, B.C., and encountered the Spanish explorers Galiano and Flores. He and the Spaniards surveyed Georgia Strait together for the next three weeks before Vancouver departed for the settlement on Nootka Sound. He was welcomed by the Spanish commander, Juan Francsico Bodego y Quadra, who was still awaiting instructions from Spain as to the terms of the handover of the outpost to the British, so Vancouver deferred taking possession. The two men got along well enough that they decided to name the newly-charted island on which Nootka Sound was located *Quadra and Vancouver Island*. (After the Spanish departed the region for good, in 1819, the first part of the name was dropped.)

From Nootka Sound, Vancouver sailed south along the west coast to what is now southern California. He spent the winter charting parts of the Sandwich Islands (Hawaii), then returned to the Pacific Northwest the following spring to continue his explorations. He circumnavigated Prince of Wales and Revillagigedo Islands, and charted parts of the surrounding coasts. As winter approached he sailed south, hoping to meet up with Bodega y Quadra and complete his political mission, but this did not happen. He and his crew spent a second winter in Hawaii, then returned to Alaska for a third summer (1794), visiting Cook Inlet and surveying Chichagof and Baranof Islands, Admiralty Island, Kupreanof Island, and the Lynn Canal. Vancouver's journals suggest that although several hostile incidents with natives, especially Tlingits, occurred towards the end of his final season, he had generally amicable relations with the indigenous people of the region, as well as with the Spanish.

*Discovery* returned to Great Britain, via Cape Horn, in September 1795. Exhausted from his years at sea, Vancouver retired to Petersham, west of London. He was vilified by several prominent former shipmates, including his sailing master and deputy surveyor Joseph Whidbey, and died in obscurity in 1798, aged 40, less than three years after the completion of his greatest voyage. He was buried in the graveyard of St Peter's Church, in Petersham. The Hudson's Bay Company placed a plaque in the church in 1841, and Vancouver's grave receives many visitors from Alaska and Canada to this day.

—AC

rows, using the diagram as a general guide only. *Beware: There may be some surprises!*

When approaching from Kashevarof Passage to the southwest, we have used a course of about 348° magnetic, crabbing as required by wind or current. Avoid the rock and reef marked by a kelp patch a mile south of the entrance. Once inside the first narrows, work your way carefully into the two basins as indicated in the diagram.

A small exterior passage to the south of Blashke Islands connects to Clarence Strait and hence to Wrangell. As you exit the Blashke Islands on a southbound trip, turn southeast 1/4 mile out and head for Rose Rock over a 9-fathom bottom. When you are halfway between the point on the south island and Rose Rock, turn east. From here, the bottom follows a 12- to 16-fathom curve, not the 39 fathoms as indicated on the chart.

Pass south of the rock located a half-mile southeast of the southernmost Blashke Island. This unnamed rock dries on about a 6-foot tide. As you approach this rock, depths are

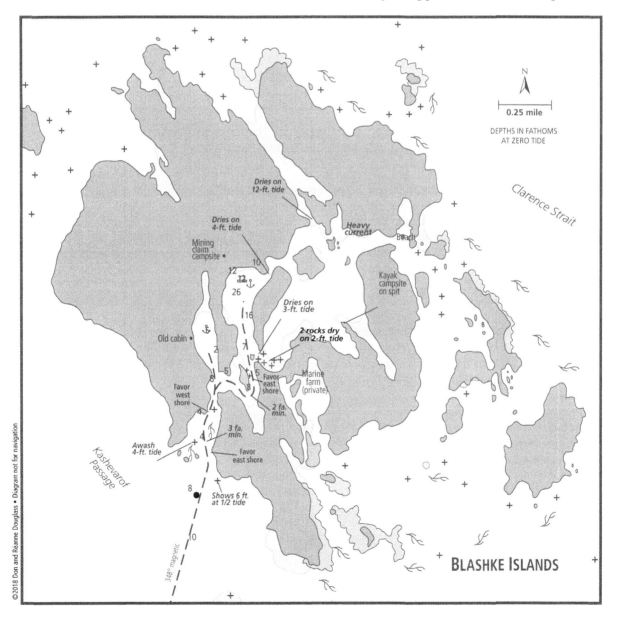

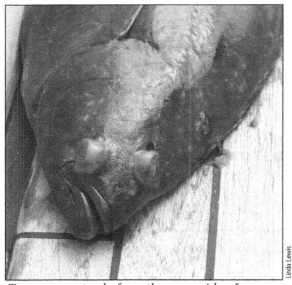
*Two eyes protrude from the same side of a halibut's head.*

37 fathoms for a short time before rising to an 8-fathom shoal southeast of the rock. East of here, you quickly re-enter an area of 100 fathoms or more.

Within the Blashkes there is a private buoy at the head of the second basin. You can use the buoy, as we have, or anchor nearby towards the drying passage to the east. Entry into the large central basin is restricted to small craft due to the foul area at the west opening; the east opening has strong currents and is unsurveyed.

Anchor (first basin) in 5 fathoms over mud with good holding.

Anchor (second basin) in 12 fathoms over an unrecorded bottom.

## The Eyes Have It: Up Close on the Inside Passage
### Roderick Frazier Nash—M/V *Forevergreen*

In the summer of 1990, Don Douglass and Réanne Hemingway-Douglass visited my wife, Honeydew, and me at our home in Crested Butte, Colorado, on the occasion of Don's induction into the Mountain Bike Hall of Fame. On our refrigerator, he noticed a snapshot of our then brand new Nordic Tug, *Forevergreen*. It was love at first sight, and we think the Douglass' first *Baidarka* was conceived that Colorado afternoon.

But before the birth of *Baidarka*, Don offered to crew for me on a southerly transit of the Inside Passage from Juneau to Anacortes in the fall of 1991. I was, of course, honored to have a seaman of Don's skill and vigilance on board, and his enthusiasm was worth at least two knots all the way!

The most memorable twenty-four hours of the trip began before we even reached the waters of Southeast Alaska, on September 3 in Graham Reach, south of Butedale, British Columbia. The Canoona River carries a substantial volume of water off Princess Royal Island, and its dramatic whitewater entrance into the ocean attracted our attention. I idled *Forevergreen* alongside a patch of kelp in forty feet of water and gave Don the wheel with a request to jog against the wind and current.

I tossed a three-inch, rubber-tailed jig with a light spinning outfit and twelve-pound-test line, hoping for a rockfish or ling cod for supper. I was disgusted when the line immediately snagged on the bottom, and I whipped the tip of the rod back and forth to free the lure.

But then I noticed a slow, steady pull of line from the reel. Impatiently, I called forward to Don to hold the boat in position. He replied, "Captain, we haven't moved a yard since you cast." And still the drag kept releasing line—no electricity, as with a big salmon—just pulse, pulse, pulse.

It finally dawned on me that something—a big something—was taking line into the deep water in the center of the channel. I couldn't turn the fish, so Don engaged the gears, and we went along for the ride. An hour later, we were a half-mile from the shoreside kelp bed, and I was exhausted from the pump-and-reel routine.

Finally, my second crew member, Scott, who was standing on the cabin roof shouted, "My God! You've hooked a Volkswagen!" Of course it was a halibut, normally the largest fish found in northern coastal waters. And this one was indeed huge.

Once the big fish surfaced, our problems began. The net—okay for salmon—looked like a tea strainer compared to the five-foot-long halibut. So we went to Plan B.

Don rigged a half-inch mooring line into a slipknot and waited like a cowboy with a lariat, while slowly

## Exchange Cove (Exchange Island)

Exchange Cove, on the northwest side of Kashevarof Passage, is entered 12.1 miles northwest of Beck Island Light.

Chart 17382
Entrance: 56°13.03' N, 133°03.46' W
Anchor: 56°12.27' N, 133°04.24' W

Exchange Cove offers convenient and well-protected anchorage with lots of swinging room for a number of boats. It makes an excellent base camp for exploring the islets of northern Clarence Strait. Aboard *Baidarka*, we entered the cove several times at night using radar and electronic charting with little difficulty. Some electronic charts seem to have horizontal datum errors, so pay attention and post an alert lookout on entering.

When entering the cove, use the north

*A tufted puffin glides serenely by.*

I led the fish on a course parallel to the swim deck. Somehow, Don managed to reach down, slip the noose around the halibut's tail and cleat the line off.

When she felt the pull (all halibut over 100 pounds are female), she dove for the bottom, actually towing *Forevergreen* backwards. But with a mooring line of 1,200-pound test, we were in control.

After a flurry of action, the fish lay limp, and Don and Scott managed to haul it out of the water over the swim deck and partially over the transom. A quick measurement showed a length of five and a half feet which—tables reveal—amounts to 157 pounds. I immediately understood the significance of this number. In sport angling there is a special distinction reserved for persons who have landed a fish ten times the test of their line or leader. For instance, a twenty-pound trout on a two-pound fly line tippet would qualify. And I was using twelve-pound test. "Heroics! National recognition!" I thought. "Take the fish into Klemtu for official weigh-in and eat halibut steak for two months!"

But as I knelt on the swim deck to unhook the tiny rubber jig, I looked directly into the two eyes on the topside of this flat bottomfish. They were yellow-green, flecked with brown, and about two inches wide, each. In them, I saw a wisdom acquired over perhaps fifty years of survival. Here was a microcosm of all the wildness that makes the thousand-mile coastline north of Puget Sound so wonderful. Here was a fellow traveller in the odyssey of evolution nearly as large and as old as I was.

So I unhooked the ridiculous orange lure from that huge lip, Don released the lasso, and the largest fish I have ever caught slipped back into the sea. She lay still a moment, then pumped her huge tail and slowly sank into her blue-green world of swaying kelp and scurrying baitfish. Don and I understood, without speaking, that this was a moment of planetary modesty—a small compensatory gesture against the massive environmental chaos our species is spreading over the earth.

Later that evening we anchored in Cougar Bay off Tolmie Channel and happily ate canned stew, instead of fresh halibut.

The next morning, fog obscured even the cruising boat anchored a hundred feet away from us. We navigated with radar out into Finlayson Channel, and by the time we reached Oscar Pass the fog had dissipated. Don, manning the helm at the time, noticed a dark head on our course. Maybe a seal or an otter? No, it was a bear! The animal was about a quarter-mile from shore, and swimming north across our bow. Why, we wondered? Marital stress, technological unemployment, bad bear day? Or simply to reach the other side? But there he was, an old male with silver hairs on his muzzle—just like Don and me. And again, the eyes had it: we saw the terror in them as we approached, and so we veered off and went our separate ways in peace.

Big halibut and nautical black bears—you don't encounter them every day on the Inside Passage—but the magic of this place is that you still can. Up here, you are moved by ancient currents. That's why we cruise the Northwest!

*Deep Bay offers a quiet anchorage toward the head of the bay.*

entrance, off Kashevarof Passage, avoiding the rocks close to the west shore of Exchange Island. Find an appropriate anchoring depth prior to reaching the southern extreme of the island. The fairway seems to have a flat bottom with few rocks. The window south of Exchange Island is foul and useful for kayaks and tenders only. Do not overshoot the ground on the large mud flat at the head of the cove.

Anchor in 6 fathoms over soft mud and sand with very good holding and lots of swinging room.

### Salmon Bay
Salmon Bay is 2.5 miles southeast of Point Colpoys.
Chart 17382
Entrance: 56°18.28' N, 133°08.81' W
Anchor: 56°18.16' N, 133°09.44' W

Anchor in 1 to 2 fathoms over sand and mud with fair holding, restricted swinging room.

### Snow Passage (Clarence Strait)
Snow Passage is between Bushy and Zarembo islands.
Chart 17382
South entrance (1.0 mile southeast of Bushy Island Light):
56°15.73' N, 132°56.57' W
North entrance (1.0 mile northwest of Bushy Island Light):
56°17.32' N, 132°58.64' W

Snow Passage is the narrow passage between the west shore of Zarembo Island and the many islands and islets found in the Kashevarof Islands to the west. The areas from Blashke Islands on the south to Scrubby and Bushy Islands on the north offer some fine exploring and kayaking.

The passage is narrow, with strong currents, and is used frequently by northbound cruise ships that follow a route through Sumner Strait and then Chatham Straits. The currents in Snow Passage can be deceptive, and they are not laminar flow. Several cruising boats and single-handed boats have grounded here by not paying enough attention to circular currents, which have set them ashore.

This is a very good place to watch whales and sea lions cavorting and feeding in the upwelling currents and eddies.

Steamer Bay is the only easily accessible anchorage at the junction of Clarence Strait and Stikine Strait. Locals have reported good anchorage deep in the bay.

## Stikine Strait
Stikine Strait lies between Etolin and Zarembo islands.
Chart 17382
South entrance: 56°13.33' N, 132°45.52' W
North entrance (Point Ancon light brg 115°T at 0.9 Nm): 56°24.70' N, 132°34.83' W

## Steamer Bay (Etolin Island)
Steamer Bay is 7.5 miles north of Lincoln Rock Light.
Chart 17382
Entrance (1 mile southeast of Mariposa Rock): 56°10.51' N, 132°42.55' W
Anchor: 56°09.04' N, 132°40.80' W

The bay 2 miles north of Steamer Bay—Kindergarten Bay—is strongly recommended for small craft.

## Kindergarten Bay (Etolin Island)
Kindergarten Bay is 2 miles north of Steamer Bay.
Chart 17382
Entrance: 56°12.23' N, 132°42.67' W
Anchor (southeast of wooded islet): 56°12.19' N, 132°41.15' W

Kindergarten Bay offers anchorage southeast of the wooded islet. Avoid the rock on the southwest side of the largest islet. The terrain at the head of the cove is very steep and may be subject to williwaws generated by easterly winds.

Anchor in 5 to 10 fathoms.

## Quiet Harbor (Etolin Island)
Quiet Harbor is 2 miles northeast of Kindergarten Bay.
Chart 17382
Entrance: 56°14.29' N, 132°39.86' W
Anchor: 56°13.96' N, 132°39.82' W

Quiet Harbor, true to its name, is out of the current that roars by outside, and offers good protection from all but north winds. However, depths are so great that unless you use a shore tie you won't have much scope.

Cruising boats can pass inside Molver Island, one mile to the east, where the water is half as deep and may offer very good anchoring opportunities, but the current is strong. Roosevelt Harbor, 9 miles to the north, is reported to offer protection from southerly winds.

Anchor as close to shore as practical in about 15 fathoms over an unrecorded bottom.

## Roosevelt Harbor (Zarembo Island)
Roosevelt Harbor is 0.7 mile northwest of South Craig Point.
Chart 17382
Entrance: 56°24.09' N, 132°37.50' W
Anchor: 56°23.75' N, 132°38.16' W

Locals report that Roosevelt Harbor offers very good protection from strong southeast winds. There are two USFS float cabins and a USFS dock at the head of the bay. This is a good staging point for timing your entry into Wrangell Narrows (allowing for the necessary time to transit Sumner Strait).

Anchor deep in the bay.

## Deep Bay (Zarembo Island)
Deep Bay is 1.1 miles north of South Craig Point Light.
Chart 17382
Entrance: 56°24.48' N, 132°37.68' W

A USFS float cabin is tied to the western shore. We spent an afternoon here rafted to M/V *Saccalaurie* (on her anchor) about 2/3 of the way toward the head of the bay without any problem.

## Chichagof Pass
Chichagof Pass, between Woronkofski and Etolin islands, connects Stikine Strait with the north part of Zimovia Strait.
Chart 17382
East entrance (0.8 mile north of Young Rock): 56°22.47' N, 132°23.55' W
West entrance (0.5 mile south of Drag Island): 56°20.60' N, 132°32.51' W

## Circle Bay (Woronkofski Island)
Circle Bay is 5.5 miles south of Wrangell.
Chart 17382
Entrance (0.4 mile northwest of Hat Island Light): 56°22.81' N, 132°25.93' W

Circle Bay, the bight behind Hat Island, provides temporary anchorage close to shore in fair weather only.

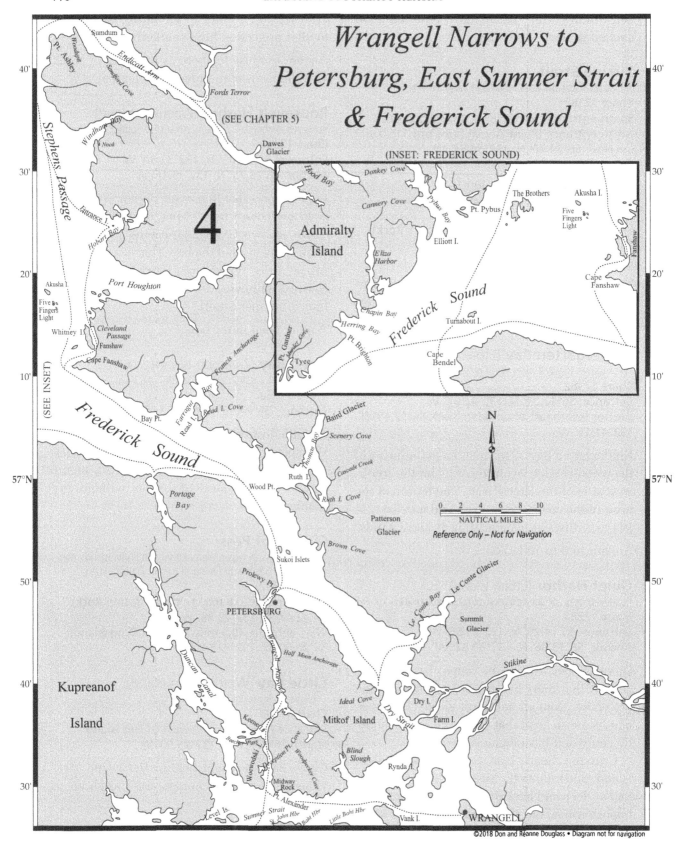

# 4

# SUMNER STRAIT AND FREDERICK SOUND VIA WRANGELL NARROWS AND PETERSBURG

## INTRODUCTION

Sumner Strait, the main outlet of the mighty Stikine River that flows from deep inside British Columbia, is one of the great inlets of Southeast Alaska. Running due west from Wrangell, Sumner Strait turns south at the northwestern tip of Prince of Wales Island and flows into the Gulf of Alaska. Kuiu, Kupreanof and Mitkof islands lie along the northern shore of Sumner Strait, separating it from Frederick Sound and Chatham Strait. The eastern part of Sumner Strait has generally calm waters unless a strong easterly is blowing. South of Point Baker, the strait is subject to strong southerlies which—combined with a typical 4-knot ebb current off Point Baker—kick up a nasty chop.

The standard northbound route from Wrangell or Clarence Strait leads through Wrangell Narrows to Petersburg. The alternatives are Keku Strait or Cape Decision to Chatham Strait, but almost all vessels choose Wrangell Narrows; it is longer but easier and usually faster. Dry Strait, north of Wrangell across the Stikine delta, is not recommended for cruising boats.

Chatham Strait via Cape Decision is the deep-water route used by large ships heading to Sitka and Juneau. It is 50 miles longer than the route through Wrangell Narrows and it is subject to nasty chop during moderate southerly weather.

Remote and beautiful, Keku Strait is a more viable alternative for pleasure craft thanks to the navigation aids in Rocky Pass—the centermost 20 miles of the strait. Keku is a considerably shorter route for boats travelling between Ketchikan and Sitka. However, it is not a "piece of cake," and traversing it requires careful plan-

*Whales—such as this pod of orcas—frequently can be spotted in Frederick Sound and Sumner Strait.*

ning and diligent execution. Please see Chapter 8 for more detailed information on Rocky Pass. Read our description and use your own judgment. The narrow 5-foot-deep dredged channel of the 1970s has slowly been filling in, and kelp abounds in some places. It was last dredged in 2008, and it is reported to be much shallower than the controlled depth. Any vessel larger than a runabout needs to give serious thought before committing to Keku Strait, and the transit of Rocky Pass should be considered at high tide only. But the rewards are more than just the saving in distance. This is pristine wilderness, almost completely protected by countless islands and islets. After a summer of experience with Alaskan tides, currents, narrows and other phenomena, using Keku Strait and Rocky Pass on a southbound passage can be a fitting conclusion to a world-class cruise.

Dry Strait crosses the Stikine delta to reach the northern fork of the Stikine River. This route largely dries into a rippled 5-mile-long mud flat at 6 feet above zero tide. For this reason it is seldom used and even then only by a few Wrangell locals who have intimate knowledge of the changing channels.

Wrangell Narrows, the recommended north-south route, is used extensively by the Alaska ferry, small-to-medium cruise ships, barges, log rafts, and fishing boats of all sizes and shapes. A transit of the narrows can be harrowing to pleasure craft because these vessels pass close alongside, and the large ones may force you to the shallow margins.

The route is completely marked by navigation aids, but it is essential to carry and refer to Chart 17375 to keep you from getting confused in places. Although a nighttime transit is relatively easy, there are so many blinking red and green lights that you must use radar or GPS to determine which marker is ahead of, or behind, another.

Transiting Wrangell Narrows requires the crew to be alert and the person at the helm to look aft frequently to avoid being surprised and overtaken by a large ship travelling at high speed. One of the big advantages to using the Narrows lies in the destination at its north end—Petersburg, a clean, friendly town of Norwegian heritage and ambience. In summer, it is a busy place; salmon derbies and other festivals draw large crowds. Petersburg is also a good place to launch your own expedition to see the floating ice from Le Conte Glacier or visit the glaciers in Tracy and Endicott arms.

The west end of Frederick Sound is renowned for its wildlife. In 10 cruises to Alaska, we have seen some of the best displays of whales here and witnessed the greatest number of grizzly bears along shore. The eastern shore of Admiralty Island, from Point Gardner to Gambier Bay, has several well-protected inlets and coves where you can watch for grizzlies and spend time exploring.

*A prime specimen brown bear dining on the grass*

# WRANGELL TO PETERSBURG VIA WRANGELL NARROWS

## Vank Island
Vank Island is 2.1 miles northeast of Zarembo Island and 7 miles west of Wrangell.
Chart 17382
Anchor north end: 56°29.25' N, 132°38.46' W

In fair weather, cruising boats can find temporary anchorage in the bight off the north end of the island. This bight may also provide some protection from southeast winds.

Anchor in 7 fathoms at the north end over an unrecorded bottom.

## Mud Bay (Vank Island)
Mud Bay is 0.3 miles northwest of Neal Point Light and 7.2 miles west of Wrangell Harbor.
Chart 17382
Entrance: 56°27.09' N, 132°36.46' W
Anchor: 56°27.22' N, 132°36.21' W

On the southeast side of Vank Island, the small indentation called Mud Bay offers some protection from easterly williwaws, known locally as Stikine winds. Woodpecker Cove would be a better choice in these conditions.

## Sokolof Island Cove (Sokolof Island)
Sokolof Island Cove is 0.9 mile northeast of Two Tree Island Light and 7.5 miles northwest of Wrangell Harbor.
Chart 17382
Entrance: 56°29.98' N, 132°36.94' W
Anchor: 56°29.95' N, 132°36.43' W

---

## SPANISH CLAIMS TO ALASKA

Spanish place names are ubiquitous in California and other southwestern states, but in Alaska they sometimes raise eyebrows. Revillagigedo Island and Valdez, Cordova and Malaspina Glacier, and the names of many other lesser-known places are Spanish. They have their origins in the 1513 claim by the Spanish explorer Vasco Nuñez de Balboa, on behalf of the Spanish Crown, to the entire west coast of North America.

Balboa was the first European to reach the Pacific Ocean. His claim of Spanish sovereignty was based on a papal bull of 1493 that granted to Spain all lands 100 leagues (approximately 345 miles) along a meridian to the west and south of the Azores or Cape Verde Islands (which were claimed by Portugal). Issued by Pope Alexander VI, who was friendly to Spain, the bull (the *Inter caetera*) was issued in the wake of Christopher Columbus's discoveries of the previous year, and was intended to forestall any potential Portugese claims to the Pacific. Spain and Portugal were competing major naval powers at that time, and each sought control of the Atlantic sea lanes between the Iberian Peninsula and the Antilles. They ignored the papal bull in favor of the mutually agreeable Treaty of Tordesillas of 1494, which moved the Spanish meridian to 370 leagues (1110 miles) west of the Cape Verde Islands. Balboa's subsequent claim of all Pacific territories for Spain was made under the terms of both the 1493 papal bull and the Treaty of Tordesillas.

Spain sought to colonize the Pacific Northwest only in the late 18th century, after moving northwards from Mexico into California. By this time British and Russian fur traders and other settlers had discovered Alaska (see sidebar on Russian Alaska). A series of eleven Spanish expeditions set forth between 1774 and 1793 to defend Spanish territorial claims. This is the period from which many of the Spanish place names in Southeast Alaska and elsewhere in the Pacific Northwest arise. Expedition commanders included Haro, Fidalgo, Malaspina, Galiano and Valdes.

In 1789, a Spanish settlement was established on Nootka Sound, on the west coast of Vancouver Island. This became the site of an international diplomatic dispute, after the Spanish seized several British fur trading ships and Britain threatened to send its superior naval forces against mainland Spain in retaliation. Spain backed down, surrendering territorial and trading claims to Britain and opening the proverbial door to British settlement of the Pacific coast of Canada.

Finding its North American possessions to be increasingly difficult to maintain, Spain withdrew entirely from the North Pacific in 1819, ceding its territories in the region to the United States as part of the Adams-Onis Treaty. This treaty settled border disputes between the two countries that had arisen since the American Revolution. It is better known for the acquisition by the United States of Florida and Spanish territories beyond the Rocky Mountains to the Pacific Ocean.

—AC

"Sokolof Island Cove," as we call it, provides good shelter for one or two boats in all but strong westerlies. Avoid the rock off the south entrance.

Anchor in 8 fathoms over a hard bottom with fair holding.

## Woodpecker Cove (Mitkof Island)
Woodpecker Cove is 4 miles east of Point Alexander.
Chart 17382
Entrance: 56°29.86' N, 132°49.69' W
Anchor: 56°29.97' N, 132°49.44' W

Woodpecker Cove offers good protection from easterlies, and is used by local fishing boats. The head of the cove has a landing beach with a kayakers' campsite.

Anchored deep in the cove, you can get out of strong ebb currents and obtain shelter from all but southwest winds. However, if a major low-pressure front with strong southeast winds approaches, the two Baht harbors on the north side of Zarembo Island might be better choices for less fetch.

Anchor in about 6 fathoms near the head of the cove over sand and gravel with fair-to-good holding.

## Baht Harbor (Zarembo Island)
Baht Harbor, on the north shore of Zarembo Island, is 6 miles east of St. John Harbor.
Chart 17382
Entrance: 56°27.11' N, 132°48.93' W
Anchor: 56°26.61' N, 132°48.69' W

Baht Harbor offers temporary protection from southerly storms but is exposed to other weather. St. John Harbor, 6 miles west, is a superior small-craft harbor.

Anchor in about 8 fathoms close to shore as swinging room allows.

## St. John Harbor
St. John Harbor, on the northwest corner of Zarembo Island, is 4.2 miles south of the south entrance to Wrangell Narrows.
Chart 17382
North entrance: 56°27.20' N, 132°57.70' W
Southwest entrance: 56°26.71' N, 132°59.79' W
Anchor: 56°26.39' N, 132°57.68' W

St. John Harbor is considered the best anchorage in the area; from inside the protected harbor, you can watch the current racing by outside at Vichnefski Rock. Entering is easiest from the west of Low Point. The southwest entrance requires careful piloting because of the narrow channel and irregular bottom. Some locals like to anchor deep in the harbor off the drying flat; we prefer the area farther north that offers more swinging room.

On one particular summer cruise, our daughter and son-in-law set out southbound in *Cosmos* from St. John. At Point St. John they encountered 30-knot winds and 6-foot seas. Conditions worsened as they reached Stikine Strait, so they turned around and headed back to St. John.

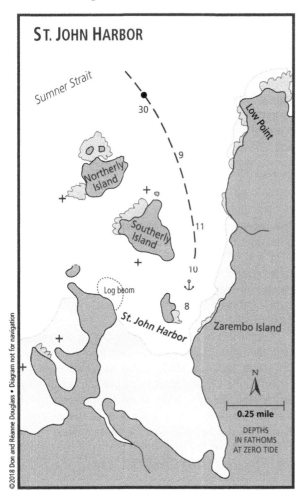

The harbor has an interesting natural feature—a carbonated artesian spring found on the mud flats in the southwest corner of the bay, about a quarter-mile past the house on the west side of the bay. The spring is visible only at low tide.

Anchor between Southerly Island and the islet at the head of the harbor in 7 fathoms over sand with good holding.

## SUMNER STRAIT, WEST OF ZAREMBO ISLAND

### Red Bay (Prince of Wales Island)

Red Bay, on the north side of Prince of Wales Island, is 10.6 miles east of Point Baker and 33 miles southwest of Wrangell.
Chart 17381
Entrance: 56°19.89' N, 133°18.23' W
Anchor (outside, 0.5 mile northwest of Dead Island): 56°19.60' N, 133°18.55' W
Anchor (Flat Island): 56°18.80' N, 133°19.38' W
Anchor (head of bay): 56°16.63' N, 133°19.87' W

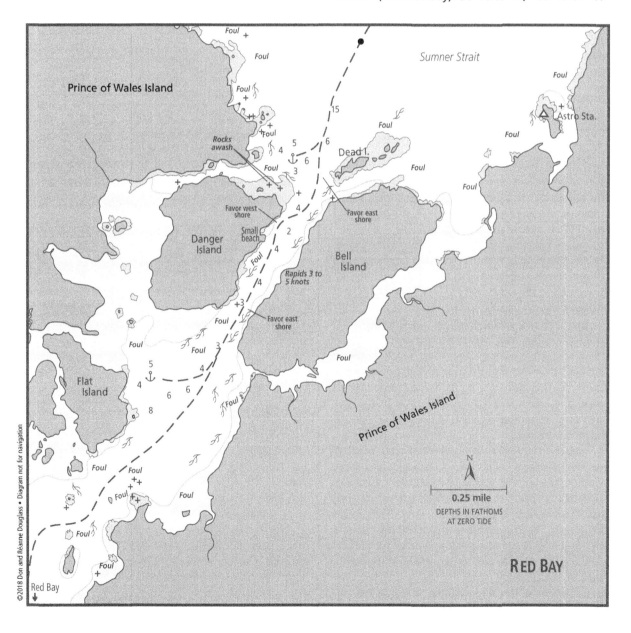

Red Bay, a large inlet with several choices for good protection in all kinds of weather, is a good place to head when you need to anchor in central Sumner Strait. Be sure you are using the large scale chart noted above. Anchorage is possible at the west side of the entrance, near Flat Island; however the movements of the current on the uneven bottom all around you may resemble a "simmering pot," which makes some boaters uneasy. You may be comfortable deep in the inlet at the head of the bay where the water is shallow over a large area. There are a number of landing beaches and campsites along the way. Avoid areas where the bottom has newspaper kelp; check that you set your anchor well.

The edges of the entrance channel are fouled with rocks and kelp, and large patches of kelp line the bottom. The current in the entrance channel reaches 3 to 5 knots, with the fastest water flowing through the deepest part of the narrow channel. Some cruisers consider this a favorite anchorage, but we suggest entering and exiting the bay when the water is quietest, 1-2 hours before or after slack. Entering in limited visibility or by radar is not advised.

Anchor (outside) in 4 fathoms over mud and shells with good holding.

Anchor (Flat Island) in 5 fathoms over a mud, gravel and kelp bottom with fair holding.

Anchor (head of bay) in 4 fathoms over gray mud with good holding.

## Whale Songs
### Excerpted from *Sea Stories of the Inside Passage*—Iain Lawrence

Every day we went a little farther south in Alaska, and every night we anchored somewhere new, in a different bay surrounded, like the last, by trees and rock. Kristin would settle under the skylight in the forward berth and say, "Put on a tape."

And I'd poke the cassette into its slot, start it going. I don't listen to a lot of music. In the last ten years, I've bought only one album, Judy Collins' Colors of the Day. So we played the same music in the same place, over and over and over again.

Then we ran into the whales. They were Orcas, going the same way we were, plowing in formation along a dead-straight line, rising together, falling together, steaming forward as purposefully as a naval task force. They passed us on each side, surrounded us ahead and astern and, for a moment, we might have been one of them, all heading south on a wonderful, mysterious voyage.

"Wow," said Kristin. We could hear them breathe, see the little flaps on their blowholes open and close. Without slowing, they pulled ahead and kept on going.

I don't know how it happened, but we decided that if we played music for them, the whales might stay around. So I went below and poked the cassette back in its slot. I turned up the volume and the music came blasting out, Farewell to Tarwathie, with its weird, haunting whale songs.

It thundered through the boat. It made the rigging vibrate like guitar strings; the cries of the whales screamed through inch-thick planks and blasted down into the sea twelve hundred feet deep. I twisted the knob until it wouldn't go any further.

I had to yell to Kristin over the music and the engine. "Is it working?"

She screamed back. "What?"

I said, "Is it working?" And the whales on the tape screeched and shrieked.

Kristin called through the hatch; I didn't have a clue what she said. I poked up my head, had a quick look around. I could almost see the music, shimmering like heat over the cockpit, the notes ricocheting in every direction. I said, "I can't hear you down there."

"What?" she said.

I yelled; I couldn't yell any louder than that. "I said I can't hear you."

"What?" She shook her head. "I can't hear a word you're saying."

"Oh, for God's sake," I said, and switched off the tape.

The Orcas were already half a mile away. Kristin said, "I think you scared them off."

We anchored that night in the same place again, right under the Dipper, just beside Cassiopeia. Kristin crawled into the berth, under the skylight. "Put on a tape," she said. "Anything but Judy Collins."

## Merrifield Bay (Prince of Wales Island)
Merrifield Bay is 1 mile east of Point Baker.
Chart 17378
Entrance: 56°21.46' N, 133°35.54' W
Anchor: 56°21.03' N, 133°35.33' W

Merrifield Bay has easy access and is little used. We have liked it during fair weather but would choose Point Baker in a storm.

## Point Baker (Prince of Wales Island)
Point Baker, on the northernmost tip of Prince of Wales Island, is 1.8 miles north of Port Protection.
Chart 17378
Entrance: 56°21.59' N, 133°37.26' W
Anchor: 56°21.16' N, 133°37.25' W

Point Baker is a fishing community in the small cove at the very northern tip of Prince of Wales Island. It affords very good shelter from all weather, and is a good place to wait to optimize your timing if you are considering a northbound transit of Rocky Pass.

The 440-foot long state owned public float can be busy, and you may have to raft. Consult your chart carefully before approaching the float's south end. The water shallows markedly there (nine feet at zero tide) and numerous rocks lie just beyond the end of the dock. The Point Baker Trading Post ( www.pointbaker.com ) was established in 1936. Their season runs mid-May to mid September. Operations include the Outpost, offering marine fuels, unleaded gas, diesel, and stove oil. Laundry and public showers are available. The Baywatch Café serves specials, and you can enjoy a drink in the Liar's Club, the last floating saloon in Southeast Alaska. There is a small convenience store, and lodging and fishing charters are also available. The dock supplies washdown water, but not drinking water. To fill your tanks or for additional services, visit nearby Port Protection (see Chapter 9). Temporary anchorage can be taken almost anywhere in the bay, except the south end; avoid existing floats and moorings.

Anchor off the public float in 3 fathoms over mud, gravel and some rocks with fair-to-good holding.

## SUMNER STRAIT, NORTH SHORE

### Duncan Canal (Kupreanof Island)
The entrance to Duncan Canal is 3 miles west of the entrance to Wrangell Narrows.
Chart 17360
Entrance (0.6 mile east of Lung Island):
56°30.52' N, 133°02.96' W
Anchor (0.3 mile northwest of south tip of Big Castle Island):
56°39.32' N, 133°10.70' W

Kupreanof Island is nearly cut in half by a low, marshy notch extending from Duncan Canal to Portage Bay on Frederick Sound.

There is no large-scale chart for entering Duncan Canal, so proceed slowly with an alert lookout.

Anchorage can be found in several sites; avoid rocky patches and shoals. Small craft may prefer the more intimate and shallow Little Duncan Bay.

Anchor (near Castle Island) in 5 fathoms over mud with good holding.

*The dock at Point Baker*

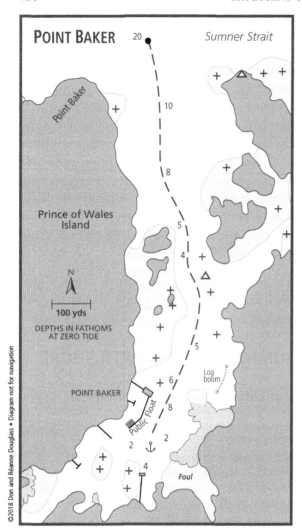

*The post office in the community building at Point Baker*

### Little Duncan Bay (Kupreanof Island)
Little Duncan Bay, on the west shore, is about 5 miles from the entrance to Duncan Canal.
Chart 17360
Entrance: 56°34.98' N, 133°06.12' W
Anchor: 56°36.03' N, 133°07.93' W

Little Duncan Bay is a narrow channel 6 to 10 feet deep at zero tide. Avoid rocks at the entrance and along the shore. Good shelter can be found west of Emily Islet.

Anchor in 6 to 10 fathoms over sand and mud with good holding.

### Kah Sheets Bay (Kupreanof Island)
Kah Sheets Bay is immediately west of the entrance to Duncan Canal.
Chart 17382
Entrance: 56°30.04' N, 133°05.52' W
Anchor: 56°30.72' N, 133°06.72' W

Kah Sheets Bay is a large, shallow mud flat filled with isolated islets and rocks. It is largely used for temporary anchorage by log tugs and fishing boats. The shallow 1-fathom bay west of the south island provides good anchorage in fair weather.

Anchor in 6 to 9 fathoms over mud with good holding.

### Douglas Bay (Kupreanof Island)
Douglas Bay, on the north side of Sumner Strait, is 4.7 miles north of Eye Opener Rock.
Charts 17382, 17360
Position: 56°27.67' N, 133°16.55' W

Small craft may find temporary anchorage in fair weather in about 2 fathoms at the head of the bay, 0.8 mile north northeast of Moss Island.

### Totem Bay (Kupreanof Island)
Totem Bay is 11.7 miles west of Duncan Canal and 10.5 miles northeast of Point Baker.
Chart 17360
Entrance: 56°26.39' N, 133°19.70' W
Anchor: 56°29.30' N, 133°24.02' W

Totem Bay is a south-facing shore popular with the locals. While not secure in south-

CHAPTER 4 — SUMNER STRAIT & FREDERICK SOUND VIA WRANGELL NARROWS & PETERSBURG 127

*A sure bet for seeing whales is found at Pt. Baker; remember to keep your distance.*

*Spotting marker R"58" means you are nearing the north end of Wrangell Narrows.*

erly weather, good protection from prevailing westerlies can be found at the head of the bay. Avoid all kelp, which hides rocks. This is a great place to explore.

Anchor in 5 to 10 fathoms over mud with good holding.

## Wrangell Narrows

Wrangell Narrows lies between Mitkof Island on the east and Woewodski and Kupreanof islands on the west.
Chart 17375
South entrance (Point Alexander Light brg 100°T at 0.50 Nm): 56°30.64' N, 132°57.91' W
North entrance: (100 yards west of Buoy "62"): 56°49.58' N,
132°56.17' W

Nearly all north- and south-bound traffic in South-east Alaska passes through Wrangell Narrows. Although it can be a busy, congested passage, it is the simplest and most convenient route compared to the alternatives, and it can be readily planned for and transited by prudent cruisers. If you're new to Southeast Alaska, you will find it very satisfying to include a passage

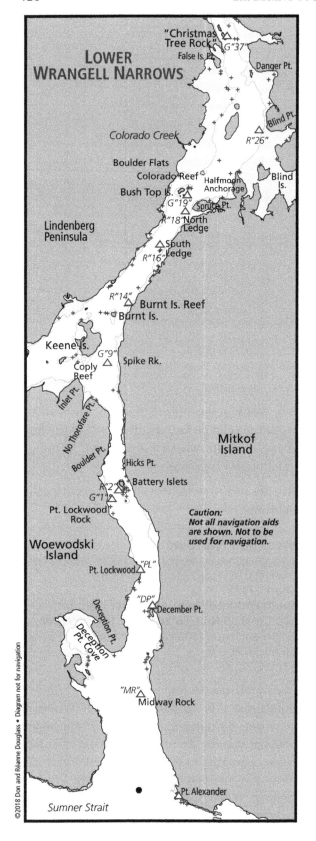
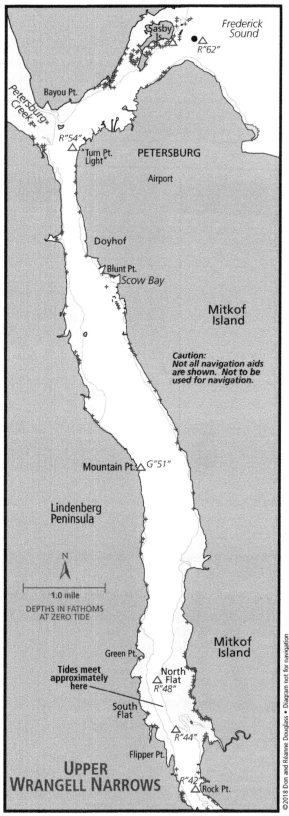

through the 21-mile Wrangell Narrows among your cruising accomplishments.

The Narrows can best be described as a "piloting" challenge—one in which looking out the window and navigating with landmarks and navigation aids (and your depth sounder) is paramount. You should study the charts well before you begin the actual passage. Then, as you make your transit, your eyes must be directed out the window most of the time. You need to be looking for the next navigation aids and for traffic.

We recommend reading and understanding the information in the most recent edition of the U.S. *Coast Pilot*. Please check the official website for updated information: https://nauticalcharts.noaa.gov/publications/coast-pilot/index.html

A helpful additional resource is the book *Wrangell Narrows at a Glance* (Boone Maritime Press, Oregon City, Oregon, 2012, www.WrangellNarrows.com), an easy-to-use guide to transiting the Narrows by Alaska State Ferry Master and Pilot, Louis Boone, Jr. The small volume is full of valuable information on ship handling in strong currents and narrow waterways, and includes hand-drawn sketches of the path from the helmsman's view, with headings, Aids to Navigation, and information about the many hazards.

Wrangell Narrows is well marked throughout, with over 60 numbered navigational aids, including five sets of range markers. In preparation for your transit, review the chart carefully. Note the placement, color and numbering of navigation aids, and identify and note the spots that are especially challenging. Some cruisers making their first transit through Wrangell Narrows create and print out their own list of the navigation aids (name, color, number) in order of approach. During transit, the crew gives information on the upcoming navigation aid, calling out the number of each aid as it is sighted, and checking it off (or noting the time) on the list as it is passed.

*Marker R"14" at the south end of Wrangell Narrows*

The first of the northbound navigational aids is situated at Point Lockwood Rock, at the south entrance to the Narrows. Here, where the dredged, 300-foot-wide channel begins, deep-draft vessels have little or no maneuvering room, and small craft must keep out of their way to avoid being run over! Shuffling for fairway position starts right here, in the stretch between Lockwood Rock and Battery

*A tug shortens tow cables in Wrangell Narrows.*

*Some of the 60 navigation aids to be found along Wrangell Narrows*

Islets. Small vessels heading north can use the narrow channel east of Battery Islets by keeping the green markers close to port.

Dealing with the large flow of traffic will be one of your primary concerns on this passage. Make notes on your chart of some of the other areas where traffic issues are especially important, for example Green Rocks/Christmas Tree Rock, which larger ships must pass by very closely. During your entire transit of the Narrows, keep an eye out, both ahead and behind—commercial traffic tends to pass quite close at high speed, creating large wakes.

Friends tell us that they have learned to carry the flood north past Green Point and anchor south of Scow Bay to await the end of the southbound flood. Then they up anchor and proceed to Petersburg to arrive at slack water before the ebb so they can maneuver in the docks.

Wrangell Narrows is a good place to use AIS since radar is useless because of the bends. AIS will let you look ahead to anticipate and avoid traffic by moving to the side. Tugs and tows need a lot of room, since a tow may sheer quite wide of its tug as it rounds a bend, especially in the strong tidal currents.

Make notations on your chart of the areas where you might expect the most turbulence. For example, when the current is running, areas of the fastest and most turbulent water occur at Spike Rock Light G"9," South Ledge Light R"16," and Turn Point Light R"54."

Indicate on your chart the place where the currents generally meet (approximately just above the halfway mark, between R"44" and R"48") so you can plan the timing for start of your trip. If you enter on the last half of the flood tide, you can pick up the first of the ebb on the other side and have favorable currents the entire trip.

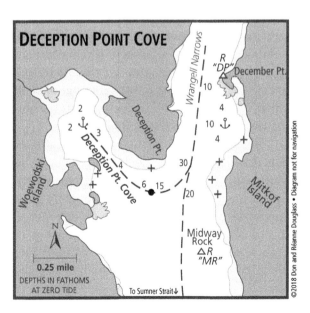

## Midway Rock (Wrangell Narrows)
Midway Rock, inside the south entrance to Wrangell Narrows, is 1.3 miles north of Point Alexander.
**Chart 17375**
**Midway Rock Light: 56°31.80' N, 132°57.91' W**

Midway Rock marks the beginning of the narrows and strong currents. From this point

*Lining up the range marks carefully will help to keep you on course in Wrangell Narrows.*

on, you need to monitor VHF closely for announcements of larger vessels and tugs with slow-moving tows that may be transiting the narrows.

Cruising boats needing a place to stay can tuck up deep in Deception Point Cove to avoid the area where commercial traffic sometimes waits for fog to clear, or where tugs usually adjust the length of their tow lines.

## Deception Point Cove (Woewodski Island)
Deception Point Cove, on the west side of Deception Point, is 2.3 miles northwest of Point Alexander.
Chart 17375
Entrance: 56°32.18' N, 132°58.77' W
Anchor: 56°32.55' N, 132°59.19' W

"Deception Point Cove" is the name we've given to the large, shallow cove northwest of Midway Rock. The cove offers good shelter from northerly winds as well as convenient anchorage in stable weather. Easy to access, it's a good place to wait for daylight, for the tide to change, or for fog to lift.

Although this area is sometimes used as temporary storage for log rafts or other commercial operations, it can still accommodate a number of boats.

Should southeast chop develop, you can move to the bight just south of December Point to escape it, or in case of a major storm, move into Keene Island Bay for more complete protection.

When entering Deception Point Cove, favor the Deception Point shore and avoid the reef, rocks and shoals off the south and west sides.

Anchor in 2 to 3 fathoms over sticky mud with very good holding.

## December Point Bight (Mitkof Island)
December Point Bight is 0.29 Nm south of December Point Light.
Chart 17375
Entrance: 56°32.62' N, 132°57.85' W
Anchor: 56°32.58' N, 132°57.57' W

This shallow bight has a conveniently located 4-fathom patch out of the traffic lane along the eastern shore that allows temporary anchorage with relatively good shelter from southeast chop.

Cruising boats can wait here for optimum timing to transit Wrangell Narrows. It isn't restful, however, due to the nearly constant traffic and feeling the wake of other vessels.

Anchor in 4 fathoms over a mud, shell and rock bottom with good holding if well set.

## Keene Island Bay (Keene Island)
Keene Island Bay is on the west side of Keene Island at the northeast end of Beecher Pass.
Chart 17375Southwest Entrance (No Thorofare Point brg 343°T at 0.20 Nm): 56°35.50' N, 132°58.74' W
Anchor: 56°36.12' N, 132°59.60' W

The eastern side of what we call "Keene Island Bay," north of Coply Reef, is out of the current and away from traffic. Cruising boats can find good shelter here. Notice on the chart that you will see your first set of range markers on your way towards the area of Keene Island.

*Caution:* The entrance to Keene Island Bay—north and east of Inlet Point on the south side of Coply Reef—is narrow and shallow with numerous foul areas and strong currents. Study Chart 17375, check tide levels, and stay alert while entering.

Anchor in 4 to 5 fathoms over a mixed bottom of mud and shells with good holding.

## Halfmoon Anchorage (Mitkof Island)
Halfmoon Anchorage is 7.5 miles north of Point Alexander.
Chart 17375
Entrance: 56°38.08' N, 132°56.32' W
Anchor: 56°38.05' N, 132°56.06' W

Halfmoon Anchorage is a bight on the eastern shore just above light R"18." If you want to get out of the traffic, this is a good place to do so.

Note the range markers that help guide you towards Bush Top Island, near Halfmoon Anchorage, then another set northeast of the anchorage. Also be alert to the possibility of a fishing opening in the adjacent Blind Slough area to the east; vessels intent on fishing may not be as courteous as you would like.

Anchor in 3 fathoms halfway between Spruce Point and Anchor Point, near the drying flat over a mud bottom with good holding.

## Green Rocks / Christmas Tree Rock (Wrangell Narrows)
Christmas Tree Rock is 9.4 miles north of Point Alexander.
Chart 17375
Position: 56°39.97' N, 132°55.93' W

The rock on which light G"37" is placed has a finely shaped, 30-foot tree on its summit, so we have called it "Christmas Tree Rock." Alaskan charts and maps call the group of rocks Green Rocks. Ferryboats and cruise ships must pass very close to this rock so give them plenty of room.

## Papkes Landing (Mitkof Island)
Papkes Landing, on the east side of the narrows, is 0.25 mile north of Red Buoy "42."
Chart 17375
Position: 56°40.63' N, 132°56.13' W

Papkes Landing has two public floats, 60 and 100 feet long, with no water or power. You may find temporary anchorage north of Papkes Landing, 0.70 mile north of Green Rocks / Christmas Tree Rock.

Anchor in 5 fathoms, north of the skiffs and log boom storage area.

## Green Point Bight (Kupreanof Island)
Green Point is 0.4 mile north of Green Point.
Chart 17375
Anchor (0.24 mile northwest of light R"50"): 56°42.39' N, 132°57.29' W

The currents generally meet just south of Green Point between lights R"44" and R"48." North of this point, Wrangell Narrows opens up for 5 miles before narrowing again a few miles south of the approach to Petersburg.

In severe fog, we have anchored overnight next to the west shore, north-northwest of light G"49," in 4 fathoms with good holding. Located on the north edge of South Flat, this site also makes a good lunch stop or a place to wait for the ebb to give you a free boost north.

Anchor in 4 fathoms over mud with good holding.

## Scow Bay (Mitkof Island)
Scow Bay, on the east side of Wrangell Narrows, is 3 miles south of Petersburg.
Chart 17375
Position: 56°46.55' N, 132°58.22' W

Watch for tugs and barges using the container terminal at Scow Bay.

## Petersburg Creek (Kupreanof Island)
Petersburg Creek enters the narrows from the west side opposite Turn Point.
Chart 17375
Entrance: 56°48.42' N, 132°59.27' W

Two sets of range markers near Petersburg

# Petersburg

## Don Douglass & Réanne Hemingway-Douglass

Named for its founder, Peter Buschmann, who built the first cannery and sawmill here in the late 1800s, clean, neatly laid-out Petersburg is famous for its Norwegian heritage. Because it lacks a deep-water port, large cruise ships do not call here, and the town has retained its friendly, unhurried atmosphere. Its popular Little Norway Festival, held the third weekend of May each year, draws locals and "outsiders" alike.

Known as the halibut capital of Alaska, Petersburg's economy depends on its fishing fleet and seafood processing plants—it is the major fish-processing center in Southeast Alaska. Plan to spend a few days here. Walk around the town and admire the brightly painted houses and the well-tended yards and gardens.

After you've done your marketing, take the trail that leads downhill to town from the U.S. Forest Service building. The trail passes through muskeg, stunted pines and 100-foot-tall cedars and hemlock to a "peak" where you have a view of the snow-capped mountains across Frederick Sound—this is a real "photo op" hike. (But don't forget to wear boots!)

For further diversion, rent a bicycle and head south on Mitkof Highway, checking out additional hiking trails along the way; visit the shops that carry Norwegian sweaters and crafts; or spend an afternoon in the Clausen Memorial Museum, which features local history.

About 15 miles south of Petersburg, an observation blind that overlooks Blind Slough allows you to view one of the wintering areas of trumpeter swans, and if you arrive in April, you may be lucky enough to catch sight of these magnificent birds. Excursions to nearby Le Conte Glacier by boat or floatplane also can be arranged.

For further information about the harbor and the town, check: https://www.petersburg.org/

*Petersburg is proud of its Norwegian heritage.*

*Petersburg's Norwegian Festival means parades and food and dancing.*

*The kids are a big part of the festivities.*

*Petersburg has an active commercial fishing fleet.*

*The Alaska Marine Highway (ferry) travelling south through Wrangell Narrows at R"42"*

*The Petersburg waterfront comes into sight after the last turn up Wrangell Narrows.*

Creek help guide you around this last corner before you arrive at the town of Petersburg.

## Petersburg (Mitkof Island)

Petersburg is 1 mile inside the north entrance of Wrangell Narrows on the east side.
Chart 17375
North Harbor entrance: 56°48.84' N, 132°57.79' W
South Harbor entrance: 56°48.68' N, 132°57.91' W

Petersburg (pop. about 3,500) is popular with recreational cruisers partly because the Wrangell Narrows passage is too constricted for large cruise ships to transit. Petersburg has three boat harbors, which have been upgraded in the past few years. The three municipal harbors have a total of 650 moorings. The harbormaster's office is located adjacent to North Harbor and is staffed 24 hours a day. Since the harbors are usually congested in summer months, the harbormaster suggests that you call on VHF Ch 16 at least 30 minutes before your arrival, then switch to Ch 9 to receive a mooring assignment. Despite crowded conditions, they do their best in Petersburg to find a place for pleasure boats, frequently by "hot berthing" (essentially, renting you the slip of a fisherman who is away). Current can be very heavy in the outer harbors, so plan your arrival and departure accordingly.

All standard amenities may be found in the three Petersburg harbors: water, power, telephone, garbage dumpster, waste oil disposal and showers. Propane can be purchased at Petersburg Bottled Gas (907.772.4270; 8:30 a.m.–5:00 p.m.) at 3rd and Haugen Drive. Full repair services are available in town. A small-boat (40 feet or less) tidal grid is located just beneath the harbormaster's office in North Harbor. A larger tidal grid is located at the south end of South Harbor. A rail haul-out and two cranes, located south of the fuel dock, are also available.

---

### Lessons from the Petersburg Birds
Linda Lewis—Journal Notes—
M/V *Royal Sounder*

I'm beginning to understand what the birds can teach me about the weather. The seagulls are thick on the roofs of the buildings here in Petersburg—all hunkered down, tucked in tight, solid and safe. They look like patches of tapioca pudding up there on the roofs. A big storm is coming and the birds are not flying. They're just waiting. Like us. I figure we must be doing the right thing.

Suddenly the winds come whistling through and I look back at the rooftops to see how the birds are reacting. What do I see? A gang of seagulls swirling and riding the wind. Dive-bombing. Doing wheelies. Rising on the gusts. (Just like some people I know.)

I realize that we are like these birds—living all out—tucking in and out of the winds. For me, that is the real lesson from the Petersburg birds.

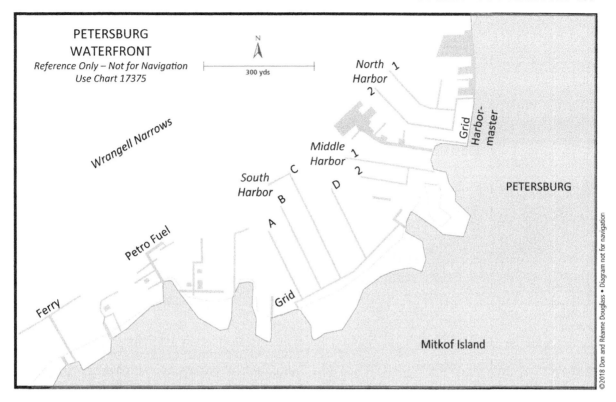

Other services include Glacier Laundry (self-service, open daily 8 a.m. 9 p.m.), located just a half-block from North Harbor; for groceries, The Trading Union IGA, a block east of North Harbor. Hammer & Wikan, 14 blocks south of town, has a larger selection. The Trading Union, across from the grocery store, and the NAPA auto parts store both carry marine and hardware supplies.

In case you need to make a crew change, both the Alaska State Ferry and Alaska Airlines serve the town. The FM public radio station at 91.1 MHz was named KFSK as a reminder of Petersburg's Norwegian heritage (Fisk is the Norwegian word for fish). They broadcast public service

*View from harbormaster's office—North Harbor at Petersburg; large building in upper left is a good landmark.*

## Haul-out Grids in Southeast Alaska
### Q & A with Don Douglass

Baidarka *and* Enetai *on the perpendicular grid in Pelican.*

*Petersburg's parallel grid*

While cruising in Southeast Alaska you may need to get your boat out of the water for compelling reasons such as inspection or repairs. In larger places like Ketchikan or Sitka you will find the familiar travel lift. But in selected smaller towns your only option is something called a Tidal Haul-out Grid. Here are a few tips from Don Douglass on the use of these grids.

**Q:** *I have heard that the most likely way to get my boat out of the water in Southeast Alaska is by using a "Grid." What is that?*

**Don:** It's a series of carefully placed wooden beams (approx 6 x 6s placed about 6 feet apart) in the protected area of a harbor. At low tide these beams become exposed. You drive your boat onto this grid of beams at high tide; when the tide goes down, these beams become bare and you can inspect the boat or work on it.

**Q:** *Where can I find a grid?*

**Don:** Petersburg, Wrangell, Craig, Pelican, Elfin Cove and many other small coves. Don't look for them as much in the major ports; expect them in smaller towns where there are fishing vessels.

**Q:** *Can any boat be placed on a grid?*

**Don:** No! Grids are best used by boats with a flat keel—up to about 60 feet long. (Think: fishing vessels.) Sailing vessels or boats with fin or rounded keels risk tipping or damage. It can be done, but with great caution by someone who knows what they're doing. If in doubt, make local inquiries. If you are only changing a prop, you are better off hiring a diver.

**Q:** *I wonder if my boat is right for a grid.*

**Don:** Take pictures of your boat's bottom during your annual haul-out ... and carry the pictures with you. You'll be especially glad you did as you consider your careful placement on the grid. You need to know exactly what your keel looks like and whether anything (like a rudder) projects below your keel. You don't want your vessel

*Prop work on the grid in Petersburg*

*These keel configurations are what the grids were designed for.*

resting on your rudder. The flatter the "foot" of your keel, the more stable you will be on the grid.

**Q:** *Sounds tricky. Is anyone available to help me when I must do this?*

**Don:** You're pretty much on your own. Whenever you see a grid in use, watch carefully. Find someone to talk to who knows this particular grid. Ask questions; Alaska fishermen are very friendly.

**Q:** *Do you have to pay to use a grid?*

**Don:** They are usually free; might carry a nominal fee.

**Q:** *When I want to arrange to use a grid who do I talk to?*

**Don:** The harbormaster. There is usually a sign-up schedule—first come, first served. One tide cycle is usually the polite duration of stay.

**Q:** *OK. Here's the hard part: When and how do I drive onto the grid?*

**Don:** Considering your draft, go in at high tide when you will have about a 6- to 12-inch clearance. Grids have tide gauges posted, against which you can measure water depth. (Remember we have mixed-pattern tides on the West Coast.)

Pick the high tide carefully. Consider issues of current, spring/neap tides, and whether you will be leaving the grid in the dark. Make sure the exit tide will be as high or higher than when you went on the grid. Local weather or atmospheric conditions can change tide levels somewhat.

**Q:** *Can you give me more detail about driving onto the grid and securing my boat to it?*

**Don:** If the grid is perpendicular to the shore, just drive up onto it bow first. If the grid is parallel to the shore, make sure you check which end is for the bow and which for the stern; on some grids the beams are lower at one end than the other.

Have your lines and fenders in place. (Use sacrificial lines as the creosote on the pilings is very messy.) Remember your bottom configuration and position yourself accordingly. Be sure to span as many beams as possible to spread the weight of your vessel. Drive onto the grid until your cleats are more or less opposite the pilings and run your lines directly across (horizontal), then tie up securely. (The lines don't have to be super tight.)

**Q:** *A few more details, please. Is power available? And can I stay on my boat?*

**Don:** Make local inquiries. Power is not usually available; however you might be able to work something out with someone nearby. Yes, you can live aboard it if you wish. Be careful using the very steep ladders (vertical and slippery). Rig a line and bucket to lower and raise things you need to carry.

**Q:** *Can you tell me anything else to allay my anxieties?*

**Don:** It sounds scarier than it is! Take any opportunity to watch someone else doing it. Look at the grid timbers at low water when they are exposed. Carry your boat-bottom pictures with you. As the tide goes out or lifts you off you will be surprised how smooth the whole procedure is.

*Petersburg: Notice the tide gauge at the distant right and the very steep, slippery ladders along the left side.*

announcements to Southeast Alaska.

Search for a WiFi connection with your laptop and an area-owned service provider's sign-up screen may appear. You can purchase packets of time on this secured connection. The library in town also has WiFi and computer time available via a sign-up process.

## FREDERICK SOUND, EAST TO WEST

Frederick Sound extends from the north outlet of the Stikine River west to Chatham Strait west of Kake.
Charts 17320, 17360
East entrance: Most vessels enter Frederick Sound via Wrangell Narrows.
West entrance (mid-channel between Kingsmill Point and Yasha Island): 56°53.95' N, 134°29.06' W

*South Harbor at Petersburg accommodates larger vessels.*

Frederick Sound and Stephens Passage, although less encumbered with logs and deadheads than the channels to the south, both have icebergs. Calved from glaciers, these come in all sizes and shapes, and like clouds, their shapes often resemble mammals, fish, birds, or ships. It's fun to observe them at close hand, but remember that since two-thirds of their mass lies below water, they are inherently unstable and subject to rolling without notice.

The cold waters of Frederick Sound also seem to attract humpback whales and orcas. We've seen them between Kake and Gambier Bay in sizes and numbers as great as those in Glacier Bay.

Le Conte Glacier, the southernmost tidewater glacier on the North American continent, is difficult to approach, and the bay is not recommended for cruising boats because its shallow and dangerous entrance bar typically is full of grounded and moving icebergs. However, if you're interested in visiting the glacier, guided tours are available from Petersburg or Wrangell. Le Conte Glacier is the source of floating ice in the southeast part of Frederick Sound, while Holkham Bay is the source of the ice floating in the central part of Stephens Passage. If you want to observe a non-tidal glacier, visit Thomas Bay and the flats off the face of Baird Glacier.

Between Petersburg and Juneau, with a few exceptions, you traverse an area that uses only small-scale Charts 17360 (1:217,828) and 17300 (1:209,978). You're on your own to explore the many intimate gunkholes from Frederick Sound all the way up Lynn Canal to Skagway. Don't forget the added challenge of reduced visibility through the opaque water.

## FREDERICK SOUND, EAST SECTION

### Stikine River

The Stikine River exits mainland Alaska via Dry Strait 13 miles northwest of Wrangell Harbor.
Chart 17360
Position: (See Dry Strait north entrance below.)

The Stikine River, which has its source deep in the interior of British Columbia, flows northwest and south for 330 miles, finally

*Cruise ship travelling west in Frederick Sound crosses the north entrance of Wrangell Narrows.*

entering the Pacific above Wrangell. Glacial effluent discolors the saltwater for many miles and creates strong ebb currents that mask much of the floods.

The river's name—a derivation of the Tlingit word meaning "Great River"—which it is!—has gone through many spelling adaptations, including that of John Muir's "Stickeen."

## Dry Strait
Dry Strait, between Mitkof Island and the mainland, connects Sumner Strait to Frederick Sound.
Chart 17360
North entrance (0.25 mile northeast of green light "5" west of Dry Island): 56°38.45' N, 132°36.63' W

Dry Strait largely dries into a rippled 5-mile-long mud flat at 6 feet above zero tide. It is seldom used and then only by a few Wrangell locals who have intimate knowledge of the changing channels. It is *not* recommended for cruising boats.

## Ideal Cove (Mitkof Island)
Ideal Cove, on the south side of Frederick Sound, is 1.7 miles south of Coney Island and 13.8 miles southeast of Petersburg Harbor.
Chart 17360
Entrance: 56°40.35' N, 132°38.03' W
Anchor: 56°39.77' N, 132°38.35' W

Ideal Cove is a wonderfully secluded anchorage far off the beaten path and an ideal place from which to explore Dry Strait (by dinghy) and Le Conte Bay.

Underwater visibility is limited due to glacial melt from the Stikine River.

Anchor in 6 fathoms over a mud bottom with good holding.

## Le Conte Bay

Le Conte Bay, on the north side of the head of Frederick Sound, is 15 miles southeast of Petersburg Harbor.
Chart 17377
Inner entrance (0.3 mile south of Indian Point): 56°44.66' N, 132°31.81' W
Outer entrance (3.3 mile west of Indian Point): 56°45.86' N, 132°37.12' W

*Hovercraft leaving Wrangell for a Stikine River trip*

Le Conte Bay and the Stikine River Delta are remote and rugged wilderness areas full of various kinds of water fowl: scoters, guillemots, mergansers, gulls, and eagles.

Home to the southern-most tidewater glacier in North America, Le Conte Bay attracts special interest. However, its remoteness, difficult entrance, and lack of nav-aids mean that it is seldom visited by cruising boats. The water is opaque, giving you no visual warning of depth or rocks. We do not recommend it, except for expeditionary-type excursions. Tracy Arm, 60 miles to the north, is much easier to enter and has become the route of choice for cruising boaters who want to experience Alaska glaciers first hand.

Disintegration of the face of the glacier makes the approach to Le Conte Bay potentially hazardous. If you do visit, you must favor the north shore to avoid the large drying mud flats that flow out of the Stikine River North

*These cruisers must have enjoyed the unusually calm waters they found in Frederick Sound.*

*Glacier fields can be seen high above Frederick Sound.*

Arm, while at the same time avoiding a line of rocks that extend from the north shore into the narrow, shallow channel for a few hundred yards about 1¾ miles west of Indian Point. It is important to identify and avoid this dike of rocks as well as any stationary icebergs, which pose major obstacles!

We have found that the best time to approach the entrance bar is just after low water so you can identify the dike and rocks and have a rising tide for several hours if you should ground. At low water the bar can be plugged with grounded bergs. At the same time, a strong 3- to 5-knot flood current can put both you and numerous small bergie bits on a direct collision course with temporarily stranded, house-sized ice chunks of ice, leaving you unsure of which side to pass. It is not unusual to see bergs 200 feet across, standing fast and several stories high while the small stuff crashes into them. You hear the bergs growling from all the contact and, needless to say, you should avoid getting caught in between. We have anchored here in the silt when we needed time to figure out exactly what to do.

We found the minimum depth in the fairway of the channel across the entrance bar to be between 3 and 4 fathoms just east of the south end of the rocky dike at about 56°44.70' N, 132°34.02' W. Once you reach deeper waters south of Indian Point, the current decreases and depths quickly drop to over 30 fathoms. Beware, the mud flats on the south side are ever-changing and steep-to.

## Brown Cove
Brown Cove, on the northeast side of Frederick Sound, is 7.1 miles northeast of Petersburg Harbor.
Chart 17360
Entrance: 56°53.23' N, 132°48.83' W

## Sukoi Islets (Frederick Sound)
Sukoi Islets are 3.8 miles north of the entrance to Wrangell Narrows.
Chart 17360
Position: Sukoi Islet Light (brg 090°T at 0.25Nm): 56°53.76' N, 132°57.12' W

## Thomas Bay
Thomas Bay, between Wood Point and Point Vandeput, is 12 miles north of Petersburg Harbor.
Charts 17367, 17360
Entrance (0.2 mile southwest of Buoy "2"): 56°59.09' N, 132°58.24' W

Thomas Bay, with Baird Glacier at its north end, is a classic example of an Alaskan fjord. Set at the foot of high snowy peaks, with glaciers towering above, this bay is well worth exploring. Like other fjords, as you proceed to its head the water changes from light green to a creamy, opaque color, with glacial silt that provides no through-water visibility. Ruth Island Cove, at the south end of the bay, offers the best shelter and is a good base camp from which to do your exploring.

The entrance to Thomas Bay is narrow

*The mighty Stikine drains snowfields and glaciers.*

but well marked with buoys. Minimum depth over its bar is 5 fathoms. The ebb current and turbulence can be strong for the first half-mile.

### Bock Bight (Thomas Bay)
Bock Bight is about 1.8 miles east of Wood Point.
Charts 17367, 17360
Position: 56°59.78' N,
132°53.75' W

Bock Bight brings a new meaning to the term "landlocked." (Perhaps "seaweed-locked" is a better term.) Although it might be worth fighting your way through the kelp for a bombproof anchorage, Ruth Island Cove is generally more convenient and easier to enter.

### Ruth Island Cove
(Thomas Bay)
Ruth Island Cove is 5 miles east of the Thomas Bay entrance bar.
Charts 17367, 17360
Entrance: 56°58.71' N, 132°48.73' W
Anchor (Ruth Island Cove): 56°58.82' N, 132°49.04' W
Anchor (southern part of bay): 56°58.21' N, 132°49.09' W

Ruth Island Cove is the well-sheltered cove facing the drying mud flat formed by the terminal river of Patterson Glacier. The cove has little fetch so you can stay here protected from all but small chop. At times, williwaws from Patterson Glacier may funnel through the

---

## Dry Strait—Good Judgment or Lack of Courage?
### Don Douglass & Réanne Hemingway-Douglass

After a pleasant night anchored in Ideal Cove, we started a southbound passage of Dry Strait, but soon discovered that we lacked the courage to continue. Or had we acquired good judgment? We anchored quickly in 6 feet of water on the west side of Dry Island and launched the dinghy. The outboard wouldn't start and the current, flowing north at 3 knots, immediately carried us away. We barely managed to row back to *Baidarka*. We made a hasty decision—to turn back immediately.

The river is so opaque that we couldn't see a quarter-inch below its seething surface. Everything "disappeared" in the murky water—an oar, a hand—as if it were plunged into cement. Our echo sounder went nuts, bouncing off all the turbulence and changing densities, sending confusing messages about the depth. We wondered what the mud was doing to our prop and cooling system. Then we remembered what an old-timer had told us years earlier in Wrangell: If you get caught on a bar, just work the engine in reverse and forward many times until you dig a cradle in which the hull can sit, high and dry; failing that, your boat will lay over (in the current) and—when the tide and river meet at your gunnels—it will fill with water.

The mighty Stikine is a serious challenge, with strong fresh-water currents on the surface pushing and pulling you ever backwards. If exploring the Stikine really tempts you, we suggest contacting Stickeen Wilderness Adventures in Wrangell. The outfit has been guiding this type of expedition in the area for nearly two decades.

# CHAPTER 4 — SUMNER STRAIT & FREDERICK SOUND VIA WRANGELL NARROWS & PETERSBURG 143

cove, but you can protect yourself from these to some extent by anchoring farther south in the narrow channel that serves the residents in the southernmost part of the bay. It may take a little longer to go around the east side of the island, but we find it easier and less congested with seaweed.

You must avoid a large drying rock just north of the cove off the easternmost tip of Ruth Island. Although this cove can be a popular anchorage, it does have enough room for several boats.

By kayak, we discovered that the main part of Patterson River now flows by the center islet, which has several small trees on it. Patterson Glacier has receded, and its snout cannot be seen from a boat.

Anchor in 7 fathoms over sand and mud with good holding.

## Cascade Creek Bight (Thomas Bay)
Spray Island Bight is 1.0 mile east of Ruth Island.
Charts 17367, 17360
North entrance: 57°00.32′ N, 132°47.80′ W

You can explore the east shore of Cascade Creek Bight by following the overgrown skid road at Delta Creek, or take the waterfall trail at Cascade Creek. Some boats find anchorage in the shallow bight off the cabin and beach at Cascade Creek.

The bottom is steep-to near shore, so a shore-tie may be a good idea when anchoring.

## Scenery Cove (Thomas Bay)
Scenery Cove is in the north part of Thomas Bay 7.5 miles from the entrance.
Charts 17367, 17360
Entrance: 57°04.63′ N, 132°49.24′ W
Anchor: 57°04.69′ N, 132°47.76′ W

This truly scenic cove is a good place to wait while a shore party explores the base of Baird Glacier. There is room for one boat to anchor at the head of the cove off the steep drying beach, with due regard for tide level and holding power. Maintain an anchor watch and remain in radio contact with any crew that go ashore.

*Approaching Le Conte Bay*

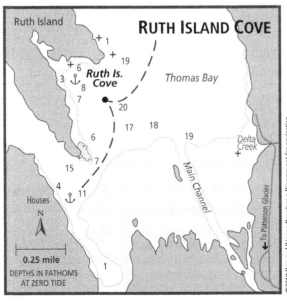

*Ice on the Le Conte Bay bar*

Anchor in 10 to 15 fathoms. Bottom not recorded.

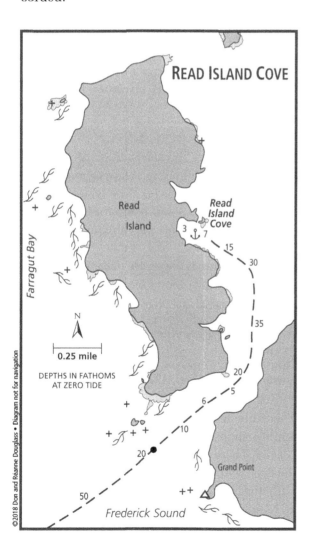

## Baird Glacier Mud Flats (Thomas Bay)
Baird Glacier mud flats are 8 miles from the entrance to Thomas Bay.
Charts 17367, 17360
Position: 57°05.50' N, 132°49.58' W

As the Baird Glacier continues to retreat, reaching the pool at its snout involves a good long hike, but a rewarding one. It can be dangerous traversing the ice cold and rapidly flowing river that shoots under the glacier snout and erupts from the pool like a geyser. It is best to have someone drop you off since there is no place to leave a dinghy.

## Farragut Bay
Farragut Bay is 20 miles northwest of Petersburg.
Charts 17367, 17360
Entrance: 57°05.95' N, 133°14.87' W

The third cove north on Read Island is said to offer the best protection; however, the bottom along the shoreline is rocky, so holding is variable and requires that you set your anchor well.

## Read Island Cove (Farragut Bay)
Read Island Cove is 1.3 miles north of Grand Point Light.
Charts 17367, 17360
South entrance: 57°05.64' N, 133°11.57' W
North entrance: 57°08.11' N, 133°10.38' W
Anchor: 57°06.76' N, 133°11.20' W

We have found the second cove on the east side of Read Island quite comfortable and its south entrance easily accessible.

Anchor in 4 fathoms over a mixed bottom of sand and rocks with fair holding.

## Francis Anchorage (Farragut Bay)
Francis Anchorage is north of Read Island.
Charts 17367, 17360
Entrance: 57°08.58' N, 133°11.08' W
Anchor: 57°08.65' N, 133°08.10' W

Francis Anchorage is too deep for cruising boats and may be subject to blasts of williwaws.

## Portage Bay (Kupreanof Island)
Portage Bay, on the north side of Kupreanof Island, is 7 miles west of Cape Strait, 13 miles southeast of Cape Fanshaw, and 17 miles northwest of Petersburg Harbor.

Charts 17367, 17360
Entrance: 57°01.11' N, 133°19.55' W
Anchor north (0.15 mile southeast of East Point): 57°00.15' N, 133°19.37' W
Anchor south (0.9 mile northwest of Stop Island): 56°58.09' N, 133°18.20' W

Portage Bay, located on the main route of the Inside Passage, makes a convenient stopover. The large bay has a feature that's hard to find as you go north—acres and acres of good, shallow holding ground with unlimited swinging room.

In stable weather, it's not necessary to go farther than 0.35 mile due south of East Point Light, where you can find good shelter from prevailing winds. At times, however, the wind may whistle through the large U-shaped valley at the head of Portage Bay, and if this happens, you can minimize fetch by anchoring deep in the bay as close to Harrington Rock and Stop Island, as safety allows.

The entrance to Portage Bay is restricted, with wide shoals on either side. We advise a

*This anchor check shows a mud bottom.*

mid-channel course. Minimum depth is about 3 fathoms. From outside, head due south for the East Point light, then pass midway between West Point and East Point navigational aids before turning south into the bay. Both sides of the bay dry, so stay near the center.

Anchor (East Point) in 6 fathoms over mud and rock with good holding.

Anchor (Stop Island) in 3 fathoms over mud and sand with good holding. Some boaters have reported difficulty anchoring in Portage Bay due to newspaper kelp.

## Cape Fanshaw

Cape Fanshaw, on the east side of the junction of Stephens Passage and Frederick Sound, is 30 miles northwest of Petersburg.
Charts 17365, 17360
Position: Cape Fanshaw Light (brg 090°T at 0.50 Nm): 57°11.12' N, 133°35.38' W

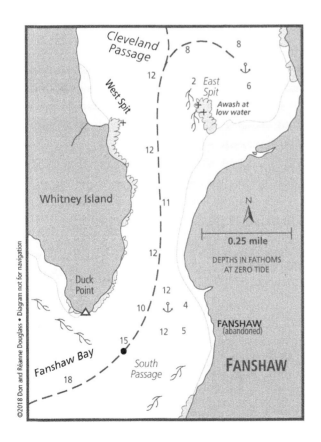

*Icebergs make good vantage points for eagles.*

Give Cape Fanshaw a wide berth—turbulent, shoal water extends over 600 yards off the light on the point.

## Cleveland Passage
Cleveland Passage separates Whitney Island from the mainland.
Chart 17365
South entrance: 57°12.49' N, 133°30.83' W
North entrance: 57°15.24' N, 133°32.03' W
Anchor (0.8 mile east of Duck Point Light): 57°12.69' N, 133°30.50' W
Anchor (East Spit): 57°13.39' N, 133°30.20' W

You can extend your smooth-water route a few additional miles by using Cleveland Passage. Pleasant and straightforward, it has two possible very nice anchor sites that afford fair-to-good protection depending on wind conditions.

Anchor off the abandoned Fanshaw site east of Duck Point for protection from southeast and northeast winds.

You can also anchor east of East Spit, 0.65 mile north of the Fanshaw site; this provides good protection in southeast weather and in prevailing weather. There will be some afternoon chop from the north. It is a short walk south to an old abandoned fox farm. Old machinery on Whitney Island and at Fanshaw is interesting (east of the East Spit anchorage).

Anchor (south bay) in 10 fathoms over a soft bottom with good holding.

Anchor (East Spit) in 6 fathoms over a hard bottom with fair holding.

## Steamboat Bay
Steamboat Bay is 1 mile northeast of Whitney Island and has Foot Island on its north side.
Chart 17365
South entrance: 57°16.12' N, 133°32.09' W
North entrance (0.1 mile southwest of Ford Point): 57°16.70' N, 133°31.71' W

Steamboat Bay is exposed to westerly chop; we recommend anchoring east of Foot Island. *Note:* Use the north entrance to avoid crossing the drying sandspit that connects to Foot Island.

Anchor in 7 fathoms over sand with good holding.

## Surprise Harbor (Admiralty Island)
Surprise Harbor, just east of Point Gardner, is on the southernmost extremity of Admiralty Island.
Chart 17336
Entrance: 57°00.30' N, 134°35.21' W

Surprise Harbor is open to the south. It has much kelp and is not a good anchorage. It is, however, a good lee when the wind is blowing strong down Chatham Strait.

We prefer Murder Cove (Tyee) when the winds are blowing.

## Murder Cove (Admiralty Island)

Murder Cove is 1.5 miles northeast of Surprise Harbor.
Chart 17336
Entrance: 57°00.70' N, 134°33.32' W
Anchor: 57°02.82' N, 134°32.69' W

We have found fair protection from all weather farther in off the abandoned cannery building in the cove at the head of the narrow channel. Avoid all kelp patches, as these mark rocks and reefs. Some users have commented on the abundant horseflies.

*Afternoon winds often bring chop.*

Anchor in about 5 fathoms over sand and mud with fair-to-good holding.

## Rod's Cove (Admiralty Island)

Chart 17320
Entrance: 57°01.99' N, 134°28.42' W
Anchor: 57°01.89' N, 134°29.27' W

> Carroll Island, on the N side of Frederick Sound is a small island 4.5 miles E of Point Gardner Light. The island is conspicuous, but appears as a point of the main shore. (CP)

Our friend Roderick Nash told us of this small, snug anchorage behind Carroll Island, so we call it "Rod's Cove." We have found Rod's Cove a very pleasant place—quiet and intimate—for a temporary or overnight stop in fair weather. It can also provide strategic shelter and a place to wait for better conditions at the confluence of Chatham Strait and Frederick Sound. In serious weather, swells may enter the cove from the southeast.

At a distance, from any direction, Carroll Island appears as a peninsula. However, there is a 100-foot-wide channel on the north side of Carroll Island that connects to the small cove to the northwest. A narrow, unnamed island to the south provides additional protection. Entry is from the east, north of Carroll Island.

It's a quiet anchorage and a good place to explore by dinghy.

Anchor in 3 fathoms over a sand bottom, shells with some kelp; good holding.

## Herring Bay (Admiralty Island)

Herring Bay is 10 miles northeast of Point Gardner Light.
Charts 17336, 17320
Entrance (0.50 mile east of Brightman Point):
57°05.91' N, 134°21.38' W
Anchor (200 yards off the drying mud flat): 57°06.52' N, 134°23.81' W

*A playful bear in Cannery Cove puts on a real show.*

Herring Bay provides easy-to-get-to

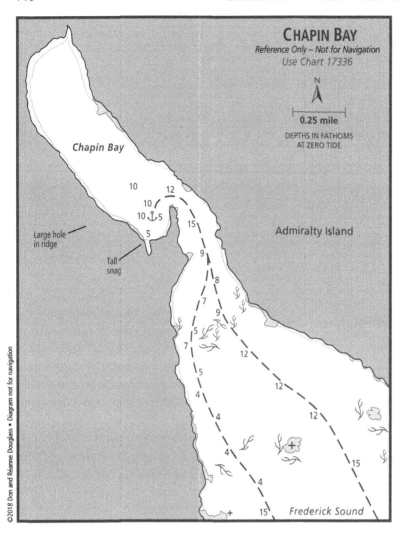

anchorage in fair weather. However, Chapin Bay offers better protection.

Anchor in 4 fathoms over mud and pebbles with good holding if the anchor is well set.

## Chapin Bay (Admiralty Island)
Chapin Bay is on the north side of Frederick Sound, 12.4 miles northeast of Point Gardner.
Charts 17336, 17320
Entrance: 57°07.75' N, 134°18.64' W
Anchor: 57°08.91' N, 134°20.41' W

Chapin Bay has been used in the past for log storage. Avoid the reefs at the entrance. Good protection is found in the lee of the narrows spit.

Anchor in 9 fathoms over sand with good holding.

## Woewodski Harbor
(Admiralty Island)
Woewodski Harbor lies between Liesnoi Island and Deepwater Point.
Chart 17365
Entrance: 57°09.99' N, 134°14.43' W
Anchor (shallow draft vessels 0.5 mile west of Jaw Point): 57°10.17' N, 134°15.90' W

Woewodski Harbor is not particularly well sheltered; however, we like to anchor on the large shallow shelf between Jaw and Log points on Liesnoi Island. This avoids the currents of South Passage in Eliza Harbor. When entering, avoid the rocky patches marked by kelp. North Passage is passable but has strong currents on spring tides.

Anchor in 2 fathoms over sand, mud, pebbles and isolated rocks with fair-to-good holding.

## Eliza Harbor
(Admiralty Island)
Eliza Harbor is 10 miles south of Pybus Bay.
Chart 17365
Entrance (0.4 mile south of Pin Point): 57°09.11' N, 134°15.81' W
Anchor (0.4 mile west of Saw Point): 57°09.51' N, 134°17.84' W

Eliza Harbor is calm beyond the shallow narrows off Saw Point. Strong currents flow through South Passage during spring tides; transit during slack water is advised. Avoid the mid-channel reef extending out from Saw Point in South Passage by favoring the north shore. Avoid a mid-channel reef south of Thumb Point shown on Chart 17365.

*Making friends with reclusive fishermen is an art.*

North Passage has about a 3-knot current on flood. Favor the north shore to avoid mid-channel shoals along the south shore.

Protection can be found from wind and chop 0.4 mile west of Saw Point; however, getting a good anchor set is problematic.

Anchor in about 7 fathoms over hard rocky bottom with newspaper kelp. Very poor holding unless your anchor is well set through the kelp.

### Little Pybus Bay
(Admiralty Island)
Little Pybus Bay is 3 miles south of Pybus Bay.
Chart 17363
Entrance: 57°12.74' N, 134°08.30' W

Little Pybus Bay is largely foul at its north end; however, small craft can find temporary an-

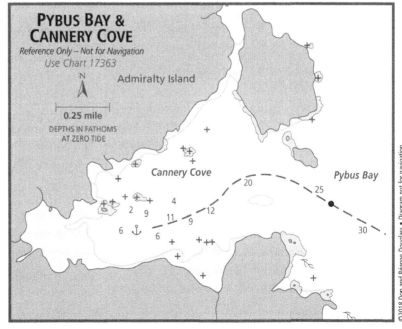

*Whale sounding close to the boat*

chorage in a narrow channel on its west shore. Pybus Bay offers better shelter.

## Pybus Bay (Admiralty Island)
Pybus Bay is 12 miles northeast of Chapin Bay and 12 miles southwest of Gambier Bay.
Chart 17363
South entrance (1 mile north of Spruce Island): 57°13.87' N, 134°05.00' W

Enter Pybus Bay through West Channel, between Grave Island Light and Elliott Island. Favor the western shore once you've cleared the reef extending 0.4 mile north of the light. Avoid the reef 0.74 mile due south of the light, and the rock and shoals one-half mile southeast of the south spit of Elliott Island.

Pybus Bay is well protected by all the islets at its entrance. You have three good coves to anchor in. The inner basin contains Sheldon Cove, one of our favorite coves.

## Cannery Cove (Pybus Bay)
Cannery Cove, on the west shore of Pybus Bay, is 3.5 miles northwest of Elliott Island.
Chart 17363
Entrance: 57°18.51' N, 134°07.38' W
Anchor: 57°18.34' N, 134°09.26' W

Cannery Cove, named after the cannery formerly located here, provides good protection from all weather and is one of the best anchorages in this part of Frederick Sound. Access is easy; however, avoid the 1/4-fathom rock on the south side of the entrance. Locals love to set their crab pots here, anchor, and let down a halibut line.

Chapin Bay, 12 miles to the southwest, is another well-protected anchorage in southerlies, as is Snug Cove 10 miles north.

Anchor in 8 fathoms over sticky mud with good holding.

## Donkey Bay (Pybus Bay)
Donkey Bay is on the west side of Pybus Bay and 1.8 miles north of Cannery Cove.
Chart 17363
Entrance: 57°20.41' N, 134°08.81' W

The southwest corner of Donkey Bay, called Sheldon Cove, is useful for small craft.

## Sheldon Cove (Donkey Bay)
Sheldon Cove is the southwest corner of Donkey Bay.
Chart 17363
Entrance: 57°20.08' N, 134°09.57' W
Anchor (inner basin): 57°19.98' N, 134°09.85' W

Sheldon Cove is the tiny 5-fathom anchor hole deep in Donkey Bay. It is suitable only for small craft (less than 40 feet). You can't beat this for a small intimate setting with lots of islets to explore.

Anchor in the corner off the 6-fathom hole.

## Henry's Arm
Henry's Arm is across Pybus Bay and opposite Donkey Bay.
Chart 17363
Entrance: 57°20.15' N, 134°07.23' W
Anchor: 57°20.78' N, 134°06.44' W

If Sheldon Cove is too small, try Henry's Arm, which is well sheltered with much more swinging room.

Anchor in 8 fathoms over mud and sand with good holding.

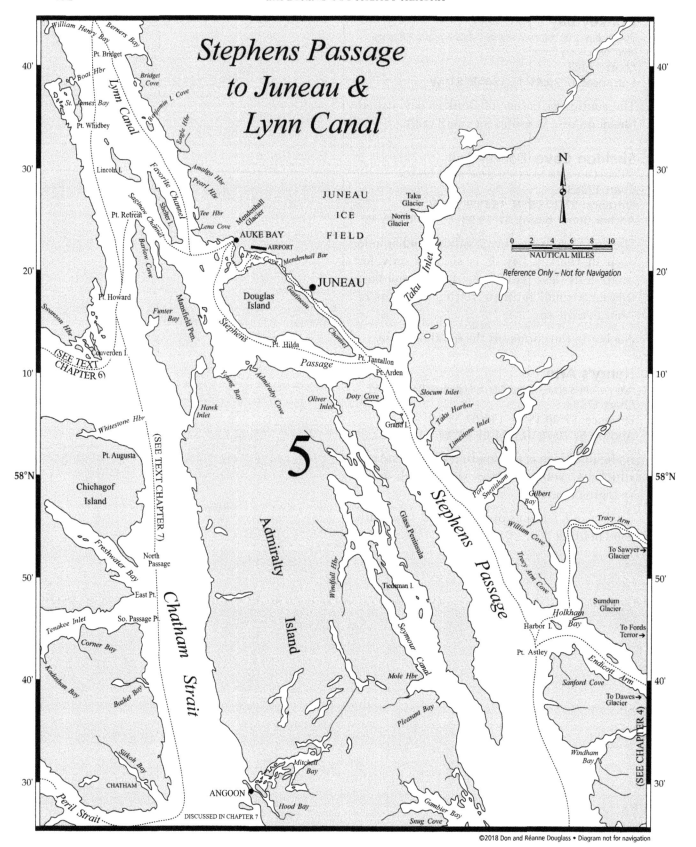

# 5

# STEPHENS PASSAGE, PORT HOUGHTON AND GAMBIER BAY TO JUNEAU AND LYNN CANAL SOUTH

## INTRODUCTION

The eastern portion of Stephens Passage gives you your first taste of the ABC islands (Admiralty, Baranof, Chichagof), where the great brown bear (grizzly) often appears along shore hunting for migrating salmon. These waters attract large numbers of humpback whales and orcas and, in summer, you can frequently catch some wonderful "exhibitions." Be aware, also, that in Stephens Passage you may encounter icebergs and "bergie bits," whose source is the glaciers in the Tracy Arm-Fords Terror Wilderness.

One of the more exciting experiences in Southeast is navigating ice-choked waters and watching tidewater glaciers calve. Tracy and Endicott Arms have outstanding tidewater glaciers that crack and split huge chunks of ice off their snouts into the saltwater; it's a thrill to see this. Holkham Bay and the narrow, deep-sided fjord at Fords Terror are also home to glaciers which are second-to-none for their beauty and ease of access. Some boaters prefer these glaciers to those of Glacier Bay National Park and Preserve, particularly as Tracy Arm and Endicott Arm have no restrictions for pleasure boaters regarding entry. However, because these areas are not patrolled and there is little radio reception, you're on your own here. Please navigate safely and cautiously so all boaters can continue to enjoy this freedom.

The massive Juneau Ice Field, at the north end of Stephens Passage, marks the beginning of Lynn Canal, one of the longest fjords on the North American continent. While this huge

*The* Maple Leaf *about to pass* Baidarka *in Stephen's Passage*

fjord has no tidewater glaciers, magnificent hanging glaciers adorn the passage to Skagway.

Juneau, Alaska's state capital, is tied with Fairbanks as the state's second largest city, with a population of about 32,750 people. It has one of the loveliest settings of any of the 50 state capitals. Built along a narrow strip of land at the foot of the stunning snow-capped Coast Range, it can be reached only by air and sea. The waterfront makes a lasting first impression after you've visited smaller ports of call. First-class art galleries, shops, restaurants, and an attractive downtown historic district are a real treat for the visitor. The city is also home to the State Legislature and hosts the Alaska State Museum, the six-story Capitol built in 1930, and the Governor's Mansion. Numerous attractive totem poles are scattered throughout this city. Some of the more notable are the Four-Story Totem on Seward Street outside the Juneau-Douglas City Museum; the Friendship Pole in the lobby of the Court Building; and the Governor's Totem Pole in front of the Governor's Mansion.

For boaters aboard pleasure craft, the downside to visiting Juneau is that you have to share the city with the more than a million other visitors who arrive by cruise ship during the summer season.

If you plan to moor in downtown Juneau, take Gastineau Channel to Harris or Aurora Harbors. Moorage is also available at the Douglas Harbor facilities south and west of town, and at the larger public floats located at Statter Harbor in Auke Bay, north of the city.

Cruising vessels making their way from Juneau to Auke Bay should head south to Stephens Passage, then north via the west side of Douglas Island. This route is recommended, because Mendenhall Bar, immediately north of Juneau, is a mud flat that extends essentially from Aurora Harbor northwest to Fritz Cove, below Auke Bay. Only small, shallow-draft vessels with expert local knowledge should attempt transit of the bar. We do not recommend its use by cruising boats.

Lynn Canal is a popular area for salmon fishing and its waters are frequently quite benign; however, the seas can quickly reach alarming proportions, particularly under certain winds and currents when a south wind opposes a strong ebb tide. The generally calm waters in all of the north-south trending fjords in this area can quickly reach alarming proportions under certain conditions, particularly when a south wind opposes a strong ebbing current. If these conditions develop, you should have an alternative plan ready and seek shelter quickly in a small cove en route.

## Stephens Passage

Stephens Passage extends 88 miles northward from Frederick Sound at Cape Fanshaw to Shelter Island, where it divides into Saginaw and Favorite channels and connects with Lynn Canal.
Charts 17360, 17300, 17311, 17313, 17314
South entrance (6.3 miles northwest of Cape Fanshaw): 57°13.24' N, 133°45.12' W

Stephens Passage is a wide channel that carries a lot of traffic. Since the winds generally follow the channel—north or south—it doesn't take much south wind opposing a strong ebb current to kick up a nasty chop. (Chatham Strait and Lynn Canal both have the same problem.) Early morning transits are usually calm, and when afternoon breezes pick up, you can duck into a side inlet until conditions settle down. Unfortunately, only a small-scale chart exists for Stephens Passage and Port Houghton, requiring extra caution along the shore and in some of the small anchorages. Fortunately, NOAA has issued a large-scale chart for the popular glacier-viewing destination of Tracy Arm (Chart 17311), as well as for the inlets and bays of Port Snettisham (17313) and Taku Harbor (17314).

Several good anchorages are available in Stephens Passage. The best ones are Cannery Cove in Pybus Bay, Snug Cove in Gambier Bay, Sandborn Canal in Port Houghton, Seymour Canal and Taku Harbor.

## Port Houghton

Port Houghton is 9 miles north of Cape Fanshaw.
Chart 17360
Entrance (1.5 mile northeast of Point Walpole): 57°19.98' N, 133°30.13' W

Port Houghton has two unusual features—the large tidal basin at the bitter end and beautiful Sandborn Canal.

## Sandborn Canal (Port Houghton)

Sandborn Canal is a long narrow arm southeast of Walter Island.
Chart 17360
Entrance: 57°17.75' N, 133°15.57' W
Anchor: 57°16.34' N, 133°14.70' W

*This finely etched wolf track looks like it was recently made.*

It is a pity that this area has not yet been charted at a large scale. Sandborn Canal is out of the way for most cruising boats, but it is well worth visiting as a well-sheltered anchorage and as a natural habitat area. We have seen more wildlife here, including bear and moose, than almost any place in Southeast Alaska. When our daughter and son-in-law anchored their boat *Cosmos* here, they launched their kayaks and paddled upstream about a mile, leaving the boat about an hour and a half before high tide. They recommend it as great fun!

When entering, watch for shoals on either side of the canal.

Anchor in about 5 fathoms over sand and mud with good holding.

## Hobart Bay (Entrance Island)

Hobart Bay, on the north side of Point Hobart, is 14 miles north of Cape Fanshaw.
Charts 17363, 17360
Entrance (0.5 mile southwest of Entrance Island): 57°24.42' N, 133°27.67' W
Entrance (Entrance Island cove): 57°24.68' N, 133°26.17' W
Entrance (inner bay): 57°25.30' N, 133°25.99' W
Northwest arm position: 57°26.58' N, 133°26.72' W
Salt Chuck entrance: 57°26.44' N, 133°21.32' W
Public float: 57°24.76' N, 133°26.40' W

Entrance Island is quite small, and the inlet on its south side is almost tiny. But because it offers good shelter, it attracts a lot of northbound cruising boats.

There is a public float (12 by 100 feet) in the west part of the bay, but it is in poor condition and should not be used. The pilings are reported to be well-set, but the float is waterlogged and unstable. The inner side of the float is appreciably shallower than the outer side of the float. Know your draft and check the tide tables. You may want to avoid the inside of the float during minus tides.

In calm weather, we have successfully an-

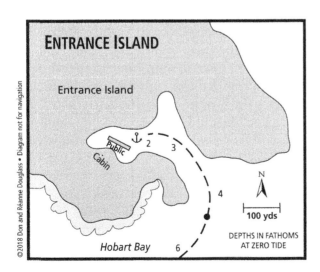

chored in the tiny cove on the north side of the inlet, but there's little swinging room or scope here. Snug Cove in Gambier Bay to the west, described below, is a better anchorage.

The inner basin at Hobart Bay has experienced recent-logging activity. The inner entrance is narrow with fast currents and encumbered with rocks. Secure anchorage can be found in its large northwest arm. The salt chuck at the east end is separated from the inner basin by tidal rapids.

## Gambier Bay—Snug Cove, North Cove, Good Island Nook, Good Island Inlet Basin, Last Chance Harbor
(Admiralty Island)

Gambier Bay, on the west side of Stephens Passage, is 8 miles north of The Brothers.
Charts 17362, 17360
Entrance (0.8 mile south of Gambier Island Light): 57°25.32' N, 133°50.77' W
Snug Cove entrance (Chock Island bearing 346°T at 0.5 Nm): 57°26.38' N, 133°57.59' W
Position (Last Chance Harbor): 57°28.16' N, 133°52.43' W
Anchor (Snug Cove): 57°25.37' N, 133°58.18' W
Anchor (Good Island Nook): 57°28.78' N, 133°53.39' W
Anchor (Good Island Inlet Basin): 57°31.93' N, 133°56.62' W
Anchor (unnamed cove 1.4 miles northwest of Gain Island): 57°28.84' N, 133°56.43' W

Gambier Bay is strategically located at the south end of Stephens Passage and the north end of Frederick Sound. You won't find such good protection from southeast winds again until you reach Taku Harbor, 20 miles north on the east side of the passage.

Many small coves among the islets and reefs guard the entrance to Gambier Bay. The tiny cove northwest of Last Chance Harbor to the east of Good Island offers good shelter for small craft and is easy to get to. However, if you're looking for shelter from south winds with lots of swinging room and good holding, consider anchoring in Snug Cove off the edge of its large drying mud flats. *Tintagel* reported

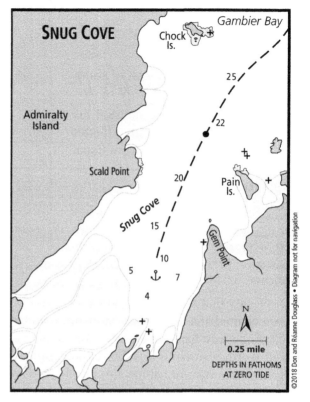

williwaws in Snug Cove, however, and added that when the wind died the mosquitoes swarmed in. They found what they considered a better site on the northwest shore of Snug Cove just beyond Chock Island, to the west of Hutchinson-Muse Island. They anchored in 6 to 9 fathoms with good holding.

We spent comfortable nights anchored in the unnamed cove bearing 325° true at 1.15 miles from the entrance light north of Gain Island. We also like the small basin at the head of Good Island Inlet.

If you're approaching from the north in limited visibility, the conservative approach to Snug Cove is to avoid the nasty shoal 2 miles northeast of Gambier Light on Gambier Island, then round the light, giving it a wide berth of 1/2 mile.

Head northwest 3 miles until you're almost due east of the entrance marker light on the reef northeast of Gain Island. Pass fairly close to this light (avoiding the small reef to the south), then head northwest and round by

300 yards the unnamed island mentioned in *Coast Pilot* before you head south, then southwest, into Snug Cove.

We have found that the passage between Church Point and Gain Island is fine for small craft; however, the current can be strong during spring tides. If in doubt, use the northwest entrance. When coming from the south we recommend the narrow passage west of Price and Chapel islands.

Anchor (Snug Cove) in 8 fathoms over soft mud with good holding.
Anchor (Good Island Nook) in 4 fathoms over mud and shells with good holding.
Anchor (Good Island Inlet Basin) in 6 fathoms over sand with good holding.
Anchor (unnamed cove) 1.4 miles northwest of Gain Island) in 4 fathoms over sand and mud with good holding.

## Windham Bay
Windham Bay, on the mainland side of Stephens Passage, is 7.5 miles north of The Twins and 17 miles north of Five Finger Light.
Charts 17363, 17360
Entrance (0.9 mile southeast of Point Windham): 57°33.17′ N, 133°32.76′ W
Entrance (nook, south side): 57°33.00′ N, 133°30.32′ W
Entrance (narrows): 57°35.15′ N, 133°27.11′ W
Anchor (entrance nook): 57°32.54′ N, 133°29.94′ W

The head of Windham Bay is landlocked, offering almost total isolation from Stephens Passage. We have not used the nook on the south side of the Windham Bay entrance, but we have friends who weathered a strong southeasterly here better than we did tucked in behind Point Astley (Holkham Bay), 11 miles north. If you need shelter from strong southerly winds, go deep into the cove.

Depths in the bay are even greater than those marked on the chart, and it tends to be a rather gloomy place. The bitter end of the bay at the delta of Chuck River is steep-to, and we have not found a good anchor site there.

## Seymour Canal (Admiralty Island)
Seymour Canal lies between Admiralty Island on the west and Glass Peninsula on the east.
Charts 17360, 17300
Entrance (2.3 miles south of Point Hugh): 57°31.98′ N, 133°49.89′ W

## Pleasant Bay (Seymour Canal)
Pleasant Bay, on the southwest side of Seymour Canal, is 7.1 miles northwest of Point Hugh.
Chart 17360
Entrance: 57°38.87′ N, 133°59.31′ W
Anchor: 57°38.57′ N, 133°59.49′ W

Pleasant Bay is the first cove inside Seymour Canal. Small craft can enter by finding the narrow channel on the north side of the entrance between a rocky ledge (which looks like a breakwater) that extends south from the point, and a reef extending northwest from the northernmost of the two entrance islets. Stay mid-channel with about 6 fathoms in the fairway approximately 100 feet off the rocky ledge on your starboard hand.

Pleasant Bay offers good shelter in all weather if your anchor is well set. However,

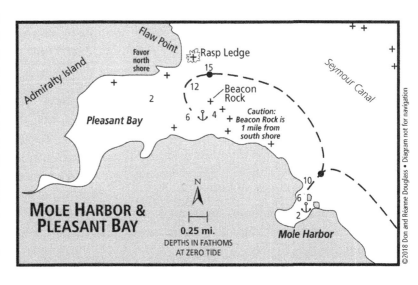

*Although they look serious, these two brown bear yearlings rough-housed like this for a long time.*

the shallow bay has only a thin layer of mud over a hard bottom and holding is poor-to-fair. Multi-anchors may be called for if strong winds are expected; otherwise move to Mole Harbor.

The head of the bay shoals to bare at low water. One or two small craft may be able to anchor in the backwater behind the shoal on the west shore.

Anchor in 4 fathoms over a thin mud layer with poor-to-fair holding.

## Mole Harbor (Seymour Canal)
Mole Harbor, on the southwest shore of Seymour Canal, is 9.5 miles northwest of Point Hugh.
Chart 17360
Entrance: 57°40.50' N, 134°02.00' W
Anchor: 57°39.88' N, 134°02.35' W

Mole Harbor is entered north of a chain of rocky reefs which extends nearly a mile from the south entrance point. Avoid Rasp Ledge off Flaw Point at the north entrance to the harbor. Beacon Rock, at the north end of the reefs, bares at low water. Small craft can anchor a couple hundred yards southwest of Beacon Rock.

Anchor in 3 to 10 fathoms over mud with good-to-very-good holding and lots of swinging room.

## Sore Finger Cove (Seymour Canal)
Sore Finger Cove, on the east shore of the canal, is 4.5 miles north of Mole Harbor and 11.2 miles northwest of Point Hugh.
Chart 17360
Position: 57°43.64' N, 134°00.13' W

Sore Finger Cove looks like an open bight on the small-scale chart, but it is reported to be useful in all winds except westerlies. *Note*: The S/V *Beltane* reported finding 14 fathoms with a sand and shell bottom. A shallower anchorage might be located on the east side, deep inside the cove, but this is uncomfirmed. Another boat reported having spent almost a month inside the cove without any problems.

Anchor in 1 to 14 fathoms over sand and shells with good holding; little swinging room.

## Short Finger Bay (Seymour Canal)
Short Finger Bay, directly east of Faust Island, is 16 miles north of Point Hugh.
Charts 17360, 17300
Entrance: 57°48.67' N, 134°02.45' W
Anchor: 57°48.22' N, 134°01.80' W

Short Finger Cove is entered north of a series of rocks and reefs extending northwest 0.3 mile from the small peninsula forming the west shore of the bay.

Anchor in about 5 fathoms over mud with good holding.

## Windfall Harbor (Seymour Canal)
Windfall Harbor, on the west side of Seymour Canal, is 23.5 miles north of Point Hugh.
Chart 17300
Entrance: 57°52.63' N, 134°14.91' W
Anchor: 57°50.25' N, 134°17.75' W

Windfall Harbor is known for the Pack Creek Bear Viewing Area at nearby Pack Creek (located at approximately 57°54.3' N, 134°17.0' W).

The observatory is controlled by the U.S. Forest Service and is intended to give visitors a safe opportunity to view wild brown bears. Rangers are present at the arrival location and at the viewing area, which is at the end of a one-mile trail. Visit the Forest Service

*Iceberg rolls in front of* Baidarka.

allowed per day. Permits are available from www.recreation.gov with a per-person fee.

*IMPORTANT NOTE*: For the protection of Pack Creek's bears and the safety of all visitors, the Pack Creek mud flats are closed to boat traffic at all tides. These flats flood at approximately +12' tide.

Good shelter can be found near the head of the harbor over an oozy bottom of sticky mud.

Anchor in about 12 fathoms over sticky mud with very good holding.

## Fool Inlet (Seymour Canal)

Fool Inlet, on the east side of Seymour Canal, is 9 miles north of Windfall Harbor.
Chart 17300
Entrance: 58°01.43' N, 134°14.89' W

website for information: https://www.fs.usda.gov/tongass/ and search for Pack Creek. This is reservations only area. Only 24 visitors are

## Pack Creek Brown Bears
### Steven Hannon—S/V *Beltane*

A visit to Pack Creek is well worth the 25-mile trip up Seymour Canal on Admiralty Island. Anchor immediately south of the dinghy haul-out lines that are marked by four florescent-orange buoys west of Windfall Island. The anchorage is tenuous on the little creek delta that drops off quickly into 15 fathoms. A more secure if exposed anchorage is south of Swan Island, a mile and a half east. The authorities do not want boats moored on the Pack Creek delta, which is north of the spit that separates the two creeks.

The weather report was benign for my visit so I perched on the delta at low tide. I was just getting my anchor sorted out when a brown bear came out of the woods and walked right along the waterline, not more than 40 yards away. She was very intent upon her clamming and paid me no apparent attention. A USFS ranger and an Alaska Fish and Game officer came right out to my boat to explain the procedure and collect the fee. I arranged to meet them the following morning.

Nine a.m. and I was on the beach being given a hand to haul my dinghy offshore on a continuous line. Leaving a dinghy on the beach would invite its being reduced to kindling or hypalon strips. Too many irresistible smells on a well used dinghy. The bears are habituated to people but great effort is made to avoid their getting any human food. All food must be left in a locker at the haul-out.

We walked around to the viewing area on the Pack Creek estuary. The ranger was carrying a spotting scope and a stainless steel .30/06. Immediately upon arrival we saw the same chocolate and cinnamon sow I had seen on the beach the evening before, but now in the company of a large male. It was mid-June and he had very obvious amorous intentions, but she was having none of it. She would sit down whenever he came very near. He had to be content with munching on sedges.

After watching her for a while the ranger said, "Watch this." The boar was not leaving her alone so she got up and ambled straight toward us. She was covering the 200 yards very quickly and was soon across the creek and heading up to our observation site.

The boar followed but was getting progressively more upset. He'd fall back and then tentatively catch up, all the while grunting and growling and making short, loud exhales that steadily increased in frequency. The ranger explained that the still-underage female had learned that she could get rid of him by getting near people!

About 40 to 50 yards away the boar could take no more. Proximity to people trumped his sex drive. He stood upright, whuffed loudly, then bolted for the far side of the sedge meadow. The female slowly made her way after him, and for the rest of our visit she didn't have to either sit down or come back to us. The whole episode was not unlike what one sees on a Friday night in the Hotel Alaska bar in Juneau.

Fool Inlet is the bitter end of Seymour Inlet. A canoe/kayak portage trail leads from the upper end of Fool Inlet to Oliver Inlet on a nearly level track. The inlet is a rock pile with fast-moving currents, and since no large-scale chart exists for this area, you are on your own—as the name implies.

## Holkham Bay

Holkham Bay, on the east side of Stephens Passage, has two extensive arms—Tracy Arm and Endicott Arm.
Chart 17311
Entrance (2 miles west of Harbor Island):
57°45.43' N, 133°42.37' W

Holkham Bay discharges large chunks of ice into Stephens Passage that originate from the calving tidewater glaciers in Tracy and Endicott Arms. While the average temperature of the water near the glaciers is 32°F, by the time it leaves Holkham Bay it has warmed to about 40°F.

Sumdum Glacier, high on the south side of Mt. Sumdum, is clearly visible from Stephens Passage. (According to John Muir, "sumdum" was the native word for the sound made by calving glaciers.) The entrances to both Tracy and Endicott arms contain turbulent water and fast-moving icebergs, so use caution in these vicinities.

Pack ice off the glaciers usually keeps small boats at least a half-mile away. Although kayaks and dinghies can approach the glaciers at closer range, calving ice (some pieces as large as buildings) can cause high waves that present extreme hazards to boats of that size. In addition, icebergs often roll over without warning and can swamp a cruising boat. Watch for blue ice that is barely breaking the surface, as it can be difficult to see in choppy water. Since it's difficult to avoid all ice when you're cruising near glaciers, carry a backup propeller if you intend to push deep into these areas.

Cruise ships and day-tour boats also enter Holkham Bay and its two scenic arms. Some skippers of small local boats complain that the propellers of the larger vessels chew up bergie bits, leaving numerous smaller chunks that are difficult to avoid. We have found floating summer ice in Stephens Passage as far north as Point Anmer, 12 miles north of Holkham Bay.

## Point Astley, Wood Spit

Point Astley is the south point at the entrance to Holkham Bay, and Wood Spit extends 0.8 mile in a north direction from the south entrance point of Endicott Arm.
Chart 17311
Anchor (Wood Spit): 57°43.23' N, 133°35.10' W

We anchored here once when the barometer had fallen a quarter-inch in 24 hours and Stephens Passage was kicking up a nasty southeast blow. We tucked into the bight just east of Point Astley, where we found good protection in 6 fathoms. We had a front row seat watching wild water blow out of Endicott Arm and up Stephens Passage. After the front passed, the wind backed to the northeast and screamed out of Tracy Arm. We spent the

---

### Meditations on Passing Sumdum Glacier
#### Don Douglass

We are passing Sumdum Glacier to starboard on an unusually clear, calm day. Sumdum is one of the closest glaciers along the ferry route south of Juneau. The tongue of Sumdum has receded to about 1000 feet above sea level.

It is so clear that I believe that, as pre-historic man watched the islands grow out of the water ahead and sink into the sea astern, it was obvious to him that the world was at least curved, if not round. At first we see only a small blip of land on the horizon—the high point of a distant ridge—that rises to a peak. The peak grows taller and wider as we approach until it overtakes the land. As we continue away, we see the shoreline and then this land dance reverse as the land falls slowly behind us to a mere point, then disappears.

The curvature of the earth is such that a paddling kayaker can't see a log floating ahead in the water until the log is within a mile or so ahead and then, quickly, the log dips below the horizon. Early man must have learned as much from observation as any modern day humans learn in school.

---

remainder of the night rolling and pitching uncomfortably off the rocky lee shore.

Boats anchored on the far east end of the bight, tucked next to Wood Spit, might escape some of the chop from the outflow of Tracy Arm. Although we consider Point Astley a marginal anchorage, we would use Wood Spit in stable conditions or in strong southerlies.

Anchor (Wood Spit) in 10 to 15 fathoms over hard sand and pebbles with fair-to-good holding, depending on how well you set your anchor.

### Harbor Island (Holkham Bay)
Harbor Island is in the middle of the entrance to Holkham Bay.
Chart 17311
Entrance (southwest): 57°44.92' N, 133°37.15' W
Anchor (0.15 mile west of Round Islet):
57°45.19' N, 133°36.74' W

We have never used this as an anchorage, but we have seen other boats anchored between Harbor Island and Round Islet. The anchor site looks a little exposed to us but it could be satisfactory in fair weather.

Anchor in 3 to 6 fathoms over hard clay and shells. Set anchor well since the area is subject to currents.

### Endicott Arm (Holkham Bay)
Endicott Arm is the south arm of Holkham Bay.
Chart 17311 (northwest end of Endicott Arm)
Chart 17360 (rest of Endicott Arm)
Entrance (mid-channel 0.48 mile north of Wood Spit Light): 57°44.74' N, 133°34.56' W

From Harbor Island, Endicott Arm extends southeast 30 miles to Dawes Glacier. Since this glacier calves great amounts of ice, it's often difficult to approach it closer than a couple of miles.

The small bay in front of North Dawes Glacier may give some shelter from prevailing winds and the massive ice in the main channel, but we have no details about any anchor sites.

There are no convenient anchorages in Endicott Arm. Cruising boats generally stay

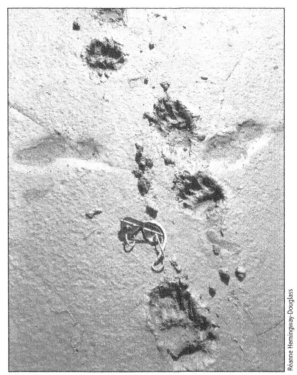

*Fresh bear tracks in the mud*

overnight behind Wood Spit, in Tracy Arm Cove ("No Name Cove"), or in Taku Harbor.

### Sanford Cove (Endicott Arm)
Sanford Cove is 5 miles inside the entrance to Endicott Arm, on the south shore.
Chart 17311
Entrance: 57°41.09' N, 133°29.62' W
Anchor: (approximate) 57°40.67' N, 133°29.47' W

Sanford Cove appears to offer good protection from southeast winds but depths are too great for convenient anchoring. We generally favor Fords Terror, which has more moderate depths.

### Fords Terror (Endicott Arm)
Fords Terror is 15 miles from the entrance to Endicott Arm.
Chart 17360
Entrance: 57°36.64' N, 133°11.15' W
Entrance (east arm): (approximate) 57°41.38' N, 133°08.71' W
Temporary anchor (outer basin): (approximate) 57°38.24' N, 133°10.23' W

Fords Terror shows up on the chart as an unsurveyed indentation on the north side

*Endicott Arm*

of Endicott Arm. It was reportedly named in 1889 for a crew member of the *Patterson* who entered the narrows, got caught inside and spent a terrifying six hours until the tide reversed.

Not much hard data exists on Fords Terror, and since it's extremely remote and there is negligible radio reception, cruising boats seldom visit—though skippers with a penchant for exploring may find it irresistible. VHF reception is poor, and in spite of giving Securite calls, we have been surprised by vessels traveling towards us.

We find the surroundings of Fords Terror spectacular—high granite mountains with snow bowls and hanging glaciers, vertical cliffs and, in the basin south of the rapids, a spectacular waterfall.

The outer bay is deep to the outlet of the rapids, where there are large shoals dotted with glacial erratics (rocks) on either side. The shoals dry near low water and present a hazard due to the opaqueness of the water.

A channel that begins just off the high waterfall on the east wall leads to a temporary anchor site north of the northernmost shoal (see diagram) where you can wait for proper slack water to transit the rapids. Navigate very cautiously here. The diagram of the outer bay and rapids in Fords Terror comes from a hand sketch in our logbook. Use it only as a rough guide, with the utmost caution and verification on your part.

The rapids in Fords Terror, which form a 2- to 3-foot waterfall during spring tides, have a straight length of about 100 feet. Where the narrows turn north, the whitewater quickly subsides. Passage can be made easily near high-water slack with 3 to 4 fathoms in the fairway. As noted below, we have also transited this passage several times at low water slack.

With the exception of a few hundred yards, the water on either side of the rapids is quite deep, and for the most part, the cliffs are steep-to and can be approached closely. Small icebergs from Dawes Glacier occasionally make their way into the mile-long outer bay, and sometimes even inside the rapids on flood tides.

We have not been able to locate the shoal with 1/4 fathom over it at zero tide mentioned in *Coast Pilot*. On one occasion—when the tide tables predicted a low tide of 1.5 feet for 0922 at Juneau—we waited 200 yards north of the rapids, anchored midstream in 3 knots of ebb current.

Joined by Ron Storro-Patterson, skipper of *Delphinus*, we plumbed the rapids for an hour and found the bottom quite level and the water adequate for passage. Long strings of kelp near our anchorage did not start to stream northward (indicating the start of the flood) until 1050 hours. We motored through the rapids at 1106 on the beginning flood at fast idle with good control, favoring the west side of the center channel, where we found a minimum depth of 12 feet. By the Rule of Twelfths, we estimate that Juneau tide at 1106 was 5 feet. Therefore, the minimum tide level behind the rapids in Fords Terror on that tide was about 5 feet, not 1.5 feet as listed for Juneau.

These findings indicate to us that the time of each slack water varies with the change in tide level on the south side of the rapids. The larger the tide, the later the slack, and it probably varies from one to a little over two hours behind that of Juneau. We surmise that the water behind the narrows has a much smaller dynamic tide range—perhaps as little as half the Juneau range (i.e., 7.5 feet when Juneau has 15 feet)—and that ebb currents are stronger, on an average, than floods.

We estimate that the fairway through Fords Terror Rapids carries 8 feet at zero tide (as measured in Juneau tide level), and shallow-draft boats do not have to limit their transit to high-water slack only.

## Forevergreen Nook (Fords Terror)
Forevergreen Nook is 4 miles northeast of Fords Terror.
Chart 17360 (small-scale chart) and 17311
Entrance (east arm): (approximate) 57°41.38' N, 133°08.71' W
Anchor: 57°41.47' N, 133°07.94' W

The eastern arm of Fords Terror has a shallow spit at its entrance that extends from its north side more than halfway to its south wall; you can enter it only on the upper half of the rising tide. Rocks and kelp are present from this spit

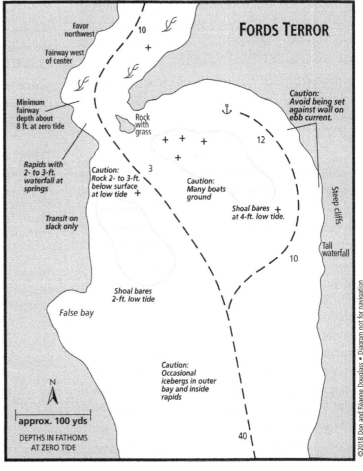

*Fords Terror*

### West Arm Anchorage (Fords Terror)
West Arm Anchorage is at the head of the west arm.
Chart 17360
Entrance: 57°41.42' N, 133°09.69' W
Anchor: (approximate) 57°41.90' N, 133°11.00' W

We found relatively safe anchorage at the head of the west arm, just off a steep shoal near the stream. A steep bank—with a bottom that rises from 12 fathoms to 2 fathoms within just 20 yards—lies off this shoal. If you choose this site, set your anchor well in case of williwaws.

Anchor northeast of the large waterfall just south of the river's outlet in 12 to 14 fathoms; bottom is sand, gravel and rock with fair holding. Move out into deeper water with more scope if an easterly picks up.

### Dawes Glacier (Endicott Arm)
Dawes Glacier, at the head of Endicott Arm, is 26 miles from the entrance to Endicott Arm.
Chart 17360
Position: 57°30.06' N, 132°53.99' W
Position (North Dawes Glacier): 57°32.08' N, 133°00.55' W

North Dawes Glacier is 4.3 miles northwest of Dawes Glacier in a small inlet walled by two mile-high peaks.

### Tracy Arm (Holkham Bay)
Tracy Arm, the north arm of Holkham Bay, extends north and east for 22 miles to its head and North Sawyer and South Sawyer glaciers.
Chart 17311
Entrance (start of mid-channel range):
57°46.59' N, 133°38.06' W

Tracy Arm is a beautiful fjord with deep water and impressive vertical granite walls. At the head of the arm, two scenic tidewater glaciers, North Sawyer and South Sawyer, generate the blue-and-white icebergs you encounter in the fjord. Magnificent glacier-polished peaks of up to 5,000 feet flank Tracy Arm, and classic U-shaped valleys run between the ridges. Because of its high, steep sides, you lose all radio reception and, from time to time, you lose GPS signals as well.

Large tour vessels and float planes from

to the south wall, with two rocks about 30 feet away from the latter. At normal low tides, there is a 100-foot channel of unknown bottom. It is largely filled with kelp and has a depth of about one fathom between the two rocks. It is possible that this bar nearly dries on minus tides.

According to Rod Nash, of M/V *Forevergreen*, you can find snug anchorage inside the eastern arm, just east of the gravel spit on the north side of a whale-shaped islet. To reach this site, circle around the south side of the islet and approach from the east. Near mid-tide, Rod found 15 feet minimum through the narrow entrance of the arm.

Anchor southeast of the gravel spit in 2 to 3 fathoms over mud with good holding.

Juneau visit Tracy Arm, decreasing the enjoyment for pleasure boaters. While no restrictions have been placed on the numbers and types of vessels that can enter Tracy Arm as yet, we predict that some sort of government regulation will eventually be imposed.

At the entrance bar to Tracy Arm, pass red buoy N"2" to starboard. Although this buoy is a helpful navigational aid, its position should not be relied upon—it is sometimes moved or carried away by icebergs! Green buoy C"1" is generally more dependable, but it is also subject to being moved out of position. As your best guides, use the range marks behind you on Harbor Island and the sector light located to the northeast.

*Maintain a bow watch when exiting Fords Terror at low water.*

## Fords Terror
### Mary Fox—M/V *Hannah Jane*

From our anchorage in Tracy Arm Cove, we left to explore Endicott Arm and Dawes Glacier at its end before returning to Fords Terror to await slack water. Basing our transit of the "rapids" in Fords Terror on the 3:02 P.M. Juneau tide, we arrived early, anchored near the waterfall outside the entrance, and watched the water rip around the rocks as it headed around the corner and into the rapids area. Here, slack water was about 40–45 minutes after high water in Juneau.

With binoculars, I could watch the rapids slow down and eventually flatten out as the white water subsided. Aligning the thin waterfall with our stern, we headed for the "flat" rapids. It was quite a thrill for us as this has been a long-held dream of ours. Six years ago we explored Alaska in our 27-foot Sea Ray but didn't have the cruising range to enter Fords Terror and Tracy Arm.

Gliding past Forevergreen Nook, we headed for the West Arm Anchorage and anchored in front of the waterfall in 22 feet of water. Since the Douglasses' book, *Exploring Southeast Alaska,* says there is a drop off, I was somewhat concerned about the 22-foot depth, thinking we might be over the shoal. My husband Al thought we were okay.

Once the boat was secured, we launched our dinghy and explored Forevergreen Nook on a falling tide. We scooted past the shallow spit as we hugged the south wall. We slowly motored past cascading waterfalls up to the head of the nook where there is another cascading waterfall and a good-size stream. As we cut between two grassy knolls, a raven swooped down over our heads, screeching at us and making dive bomb attacks until it finally flew away, confident it had scared off the intruders.

Returning to our boat, we were dismayed to clearly see the bottom off the stern! Though the depth sounder showed plenty of water, we had swung back over the shoal and the aft part of the keel was hitting bottom. I started the engine as Al headed forward to begin pulling in the chain anchor rode.

I put the engine in forward, but the boat wouldn't move as we are sitting on the mud. "More power," Al screamed. Slowly, I added more power fearing the boat would burst apart. Nothing. "MORE POWER," Al screamed again! Finally, I gave it the last thrust and I could feel the transom fishtailing off the mud. With a slight scrape, *Hannah Jane* was floating once again and we pulled in the rest of the anchor. This time we set the anchor in about 70 feet of water!

It is hard to adequately describe the beauty of Fords Terror with its majestic soaring granite mountains, waterfalls cascading everywhere, and such stillness. Because of the remoteness and isolation, few people come. We were the only people in all of Fords Terror for two days. It was like having Yosemite National Park in California all to ourselves!

*Authors' Note: Since this sidebar was written, we've received reports that mini-cruise ships have been anchoring in the outer section of the bay and ferrying their passengers into Fords Terror by tender, leaving little space for the smaller private cruising boats. Be aware that, in high season, you may find wall-to-wall boats.*

## Glacier Ice Cruising—Keeping it Safe and Enjoyable
Captain Richard M. Friedman - M/V *Explorer* & M/V *Alaskan Song*
Crewed Yacht Charters in Southeast Alaska

One of the most spectacular and beautiful places to visit in Southeast Alaska is the Sawyer Glacier complex in Tracy Arm. By taking some simple precautions, knowing the current patterns and making judicious choices of anchorage and timing, you can safely navigate what otherwise can be hazardous waters.

As one cruises through Stephens Passage, approaching the entrance to Holkham Bay, it is not uncommon to see larger ice bergs that have escaped over the two terminal moraines or bars of Tracy and Endicott Arms. That should signal the prudent mariner to keep a closer lookout for small "bergie bits" or pieces of ice that could damage a hull or a boat's running gear.

*Yacht charter vessel* Explorer *at North Sawyer Glacier*

Larger ice is occasionally seen as far as ten miles north or south of the entrance but the smaller bits are usually no more than a mile or two north or south.

The most hazardous pieces are the smaller, denser bits of ice, just a few feet in diameter that can be extremely difficult to see depending upon sea conditions and the angle of the sun. The denser ice that breaks off from the lower part of the glacier is heavier, floats lower on the surface, and, because any air content has been compressed out of it, is more transparent, making it much more difficult to spot. Wearing polarized sun glasses, even if it is cloudy, can greatly enhance the mariner's ability to see this low floating, clear ice.

From Holkham Bay into the arms, one must cross what is referred to as the Tracy Arm or Endicott Arm bar. These are actually the terminal moraines, the point of greatest advance of the glaciers during the last ice age, where the glaciers pushed a wall of scree, boulders and gravel, receding and leaving the "bar" behind. Both ebb and flood currents can run at up to six knots across the Tracy Arm bar but diminish quite quickly once you have crossed. The current ebbs down Tracy Arm at all times, even on a rising tide, however the velocity increases on the ebb. It only actually switches direction near the entry bar.

This author likes to anchor in "No Name Cove" just 1.5 nm NNW of the Tracy Arm Bar in time for dinner and then make an early morning departure up the arm. This helps to avoid the go-fast tour boats that run day trips out of Juneau. A 7 A.M. departure will allow you to make the 23 nm cruise up Tracy Arm, arriving at the head by the glacier with very few, if any, other boats to spoil your experience. An hour or two spent in the area and then the cruise back out the arm will have you passing the bulk of the day's traffic on its way in.

Moving up the arm, the ice will get thicker the closer you get to the glaciers. Just how much ice depends on the volume of recent calving activity, while the ice's distribution will depend on the wind and current. Typically, the ice is thicker on the wide side of the channel's turns. Again, this can vary given stronger winds but this is the general pattern with the influence of currents only. Ice can be more readily avoided by taking a "race-course" path, hugging the inside corner of each bend in the channel. As the ice thickens, you should slow down; use your binoculars to find your clearest path up to a half mile ahead and get one or two shipmates to keep a watch for ice as well.

An increasingly large number of cruise ships have been coming into Tracy Arm over the past few years. While they clearly detract from the experience of the place, they can offer some help to the yachtsman in clearing a path through the ice in what might have been a difficult or otherwise hazardous approach. They will leave small bits in their wake so proceed with caution.

There are times when the sheer volume of ice will force a prudent mariner to make the tough decision to turn back before the glaciers even come into view. There is no radio contact from inside the arm as the high granite cliffs of the canyon limit VHF radio propagation except with other boats in the immediate vicinity.

Should you be successful in getting up near the glacier, bear in mind that the currents move ice about quite vigorously near the glaciers in the two "armlets" that make the final approach to the North and South Sawyer glaciers. It is quite possible to easily find your way deep into the arm and be just ½ mile away from the glacier's face and then have the ice shift, effectively blocking you in until it clears back out. Be on the watch for this, looking behind you once in a while, as you are watching and listening to the glacier.

*Pushing the smaller bergie bits away in Tracy Arm*

This is a passage of a lifetime. It is akin to cruising up the Yosemite Valley in a boat. Knowing how to move through the ice, proceeding with caution and prudence and being willing to turn back, if necessary, are key to avoiding problems and being able to continue on your cruise without having to stop for costly repairs.

*Calving ice at South Sawyer Glacier*

It is possible to anchor temporarily in 8 fathoms off a stream frequently covered by a snow bridge on the south shore of Tracy Arm at about 133°20' W longitude, facing a major U-shaped valley and 50 yards from a waterfall.

## Tracy Arm Cove (Tracy Arm)
Tracy Arm Cove is 2.5 miles from Harbor Island.
Chart 17311
Entrance: 57°47.64' N, 133°37.09' W
Anchor (west shore): 57°48.50' N, 133°38.11' W
Anchor (north shore): 57°48.61' N, 133°37.98' W

The cove we call "Tracy Arm Cove" is unnamed on the nautical chart. Some locals call it "No Name Cove." Whatever name you choose, it is the best anchorage in Holkham Bay and makes a good base camp from which to explore Tracy Arm and Endicott Arm.

Caution: Before entering the cove, study your chart for the location of the 2-fathom bar (actually a lateral moraine from the glacier) that extends from the cove opening's west side in a generally northeast direction. Note that the schematic route on our diagram for entering the cove crosses this bar, which is 2-fathoms at mean low water. Be sure you know the stage of the tide and adjust your course to the east (i.e., closer to the "60-ft. between rocks" notation on

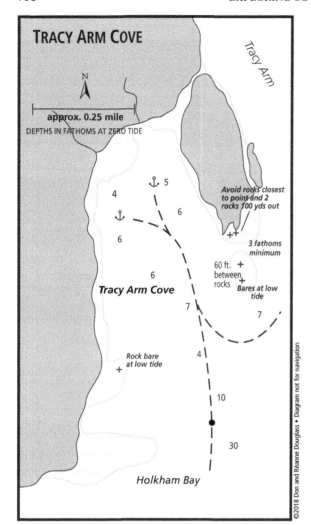

the diagram) when you are transiting the cove at lower tides, especially on Spring Tides.

The cove is relatively flat, but holding varies due to its mixed bottom. Although well protected from northerly winds, it is open to the south. In anything stronger than light southerlies, it receives quite a chop, and icebergs enter it on flood tide with gusto. Cruise ships anchor here to drop passengers for tours in smaller boats.

To avoid some of the chop and ice, old-timers anchor near the west shore, as indicated on the diagram. We have spent several comfortable nights here. (The exception was a night when a large berg entered the cove, broke in two, and the pieces circled around our boat.) The shallower you can anchor, the more chance the bigger bergs will ground before hitting you. However, the 2-4-fathom bar and shoals at the entrance do a pretty good job of keeping out house-sized monsters.

When leaving the cove for Sawyer glaciers, avoid the submerged rocks extending a quarter-mile or more from the south tip of the east island. It is recommended to pass well south of this reef with its two drying rocks. A small channel inside this major reef and two smaller rocks close to the point has 3 fathoms in the fairway. However, boats have had trouble staying in the narrow fairway and have lost props in the process. The north shore of Tracy Arm entrance is riddled with sea caves.

Anchor in about 4 fathoms over a mixed bottom with good holding if your anchor is well set.

### William Cove (Tracy Arm)
William Cove, on the west side of the arm, is 6 miles north of the entrance to the arm.
**Charts 17311, 17300**
Entrance: 57°50.86' N, 133°36.89' W

*The North Sawyer Glacier appears off your port as you are approaching South Sawyer Glacier.*

*William Cove [is] a deepwater anchorage with constricted swinging room and hard bottom with patches of mud... An anchorage for small boats in 5 fathoms, rocky bottom, is reported available in the small bight on the W side of the arm, about 2 miles above the entrance... (CP)*

We haven't found a good place to anchor in William Cove yet. The clay bottom is hard, and bergs fill the bay on southerly winds. However in 2004, Non-Pareil reported finding good anchorage in 2 fathoms off the small creek in William Cove. Swinging room within the cove is restricted.

*South Sawyer Glacier—Look for the clearest path through the pack ice and proceed very slowly.*

## North Sawyer and South Sawyer Glaciers (Tracy Arm)

North and South Sawyer glaciers are at the head of Tracy Arm.

Charts 17311, 17300
North Sawyer Glacier arm entrance: (approximate) 57°53.39' N, 133°11.20' W
South Sawyer Glacier dog-leg position: (approximate) 57°51.72' N, 133°08.11' W

North Sawyer Glacier has receded remarkably in recent decades and is now mostly land-bound. In fact, it is no longer visible from Sawyer Island. Approach it carefully, avoiding the large icebergs in the main channel.

To reach South Sawyer Glacier, the much bigger tongue, you must make a dogleg for about two miles to the north and east. However, icebergs make it difficult to approach much further.

Calving glaciers may create 25-foot-high waves, and although they quickly die down, they can be dangerous to within a half-mile. Local excursion boats from Juneau arrive just after noon; study the path they take through the ice. We have found the pack ice so thick at South Sawyer, and the channels along either shore so changeable, that we couldn't get to where we could see the glacier. Once, when the wind changed, we were surrounded by chunks of ice, and the channel behind us closed. At such times, it helps to keep a boat hook handy to push away chair-sized bergs. In addition to admiring the bergs, you can

*Navigate gently around seal pups in Fords Terror and Tracy Arm.*

*Dawes Glacier, in Endicott Arm*

watch hundreds of seals floating on slabs of ice near the glacier.

For the trip of a lifetime, consider hiring a floatplane from Juneau take you for a spin. From the air you can view the indescribable raw beauty of the huge ice fields, with giant seracs and frozen lakes stretching to the Canadian border and beyond. The coloration of the different glacier arms, the crevasses and overfalls are spectacular. On one flight, we saw mountain goats working their way along rocky ridges that seemed encased in a sea of ice.

## Port Snettisham
Port Snettisham, on the east side of Stephens Passage and 13 miles north of Holkham Bay, has two arms—Speel Arm and Gilbert Bay.

Charts 17313, 17300
Entrance: 57°57.46' N, 133°52.73' W

Port Snettisham is a classic fjord with high steep sides and deep water throughout. The port itself is at the head of Speel Arm where a large hydroelectric plant that supplies much of the Juneau area is located. The channel leading to the power plant and its private float is very narrow and shallow and is not much use except in an emergency. *Note*: Extreme magnetic disturbances of 78° or more have been observed at the entrance to Port Snettisham. Mallard Cove, 0.5 mile west of Fannie Island, is a fair-weather anchorage only.

### Southeast Cove (Port Snettisham)
Southeast Cove is 1.7 miles inside Port Snettisham.
Charts 17313, 17300
Position: 57°58.24' N, 133°49.24' W

The small cove just inside Port Snettisham, which we call "Southeast Cove," can be a useful place to hide when a nasty southerly chop occurs in Stephens Passage; however, Gilbert Bay has more swinging room.

### Gilbert Bay (Port Snettisham)
Gilbert Bay is the south arm of Port Snettisham.
Charts 17313, 17300
Entrance: 58°00.06' N, 133°44.50' W
Anchor: 57°56.73' N, 133°42.25' W

Anchorage can be found at the head of Gilbert Bay off the drying mud flat at the mouth of Sweetheart Creek. The bay is useful in fair-to-moderate weather, but it is exposed to weather that spills over a shallow divide from Tracy Arm, and may be blasted by williwaws.

Anchor in about 8 fathoms over mud (the bottom is steep-to) with fair-to-good holding.

## Limestone Inlet

Limestone Inlet, on the east side of Stephens Passage, is 2 miles southeast of Taku Harbor.
Charts 17314, 17300
Entrance: 58°01.82' N, 133°59.84' W
Anchor: 58°02.14' N, 133°58.25' W

Anchorage may be found off the large grassy meadow in 10 fathoms or less over a gravel bottom. A small private float and buoy lie near the head of the bay.

## Taku Harbor

Taku Harbor, on the east shore of Stephens Passage, is 19 miles southeast of Juneau.
Charts 17314, 17300
Entrance: (Grave Point Light bearing 305°T at 0.48 Nm): 58°03.45' N, 134°02.32' W
Public float: 58°04.11' N, 134°00.80' W
Anchor (south end of harbor): 58°03.82' N, 134°01.05' W

Taku Harbor is a popular and well-placed anchorage that offers some of the best protection between Juneau and the south end of Stephens Passage. It has easy access and can be entered without trouble using radar. A short boardwalk trail that wraps around the shore off

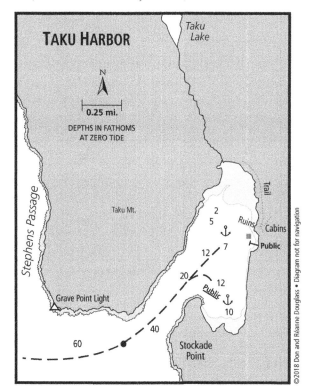

the float is a good place to stretch your legs. An additional detached 200-foot public float is located in the south end of the harbor.

Taku is named for a sub-division of the

---

## Hypnotic Icebergs!
### Réanne Hemingway-Douglass

"Move in closer," I shouted to Don over the noise of the engine. "I want to get a close-up photo of the ice dripping down."

Our two crew members had just taken off in Don Kyte's amphibious, Seabee, for a flight over Tracy Arm and the glaciers, and we were motoring slowly near the head of the arm, admiring the various shapes of the icebergs. A berg the size of a two-story house, but much wider, caught my eye. Its shape reminded me of a dolmen perched on four huge, squat legs, and its translucent blue captivated me.

"Closer!" I yelled again. The shades of turquoise were stunning and I had lost all sense of the boat and its safety. All I wanted was to get more shots of this beautiful creature. "That's perfect!" I shouted. I could almost touch the overhanging lip, and I snapped shot after shot.

Suddenly, water started streaming down the side of the berg. "Back up. Back up!" I yelled. "It's rising!"

Don stared at the iceberg, seemingly hypnotized, without paying attention to me.

"REVERSE!" I screamed.

He suddenly came to his senses and jammed the throttle into full reverse. The prop cavitated wildly, and we quickly drew back 100 yards. The iceberg rose from the water then fell, time and time again, sending swells in all directions—a giant sea monster teeter-tottering, cracking and growling. It continued to rise slowly until the lip and legs towered more than 25 feet above the water. It rocked back and forth for twenty minutes, then slowly stabilized.

We looked at one another and rolled our eyes, sighing almost simultaneously, "That was close! We'd better not try that again."

*M/V Homeshore cruises close to the face of South Sawyer Glacier.*

*The crew of S/V Mahina Tiare choose to do their glacier-viewing under full sail.*

Tlingit tribe who once lived in the vicinity. In 1840, a Hudson's Bay trading post was established here; in the 1900s it was the site of a commercial cannery that is now in decay. Remains of piers, boilers, bunkhouses, and electrical generators are being overtaken by dense brush. Bear fish for salmon in the stream north of the old cannery, so remain alert if you explore the area when the salmon are running. If you moor to the float, do not leave any food or garbage outside on your deck—you may be boarded by a black bear! River otters roam the dock area at all hours. The dock is also a Seaplane Base.

You can anchor along the east shore in shallow water off the stream outlet to watch for bears. However, as you maneuver here don't stray north beyond our indicated anchorage, as this area quickly shallows. In southeast weather, anchor on the south side for best protection. Most people anchor in the southeast bight in shallow water, as there are frequently crab pots in the northern part of the harbor. A heavy southeast wind can whip across the westerly point with violent force.

Anchor (south end) in 8 to 10 fathoms over hard gravel and soft sand with good holding if well set.

## Doty Cove (Admiralty Island)

Doty Cove, on the west side of Stephens Passage, is 13.5 miles south of Juneau.

*An iceberg corridor in Tracy Arm beckons; resist the temptation to get too close to these unstable bergs.*

Chart 17300
Entrance: 58°06.82' N, 134°10.86' W
Anchor: 58°07.21' N, 134°12.69' W

Favored by local fishermen, Doty Cove offers good protection in fair weather only. There is a 4-fathom shoal near its head which makes a reasonable anchor site.

## Suicide Cove
Suicide Cove is 1 mile south of Slocum Inlet.
Charts 17314, 17300
Entrance: 58°06.89' N, 134°04.33' W
Anchor: 58°07.00' N, 134°04.15' W

Particularly in the winter, Taku Inlet can be subject to violent storms, known locally as "Taku winds." Protection from these is available in Suicide Cove, a shallow tiny bight just south of 1,060-foot Butler Peak. Although open to the south, it is protected from the winds that blast down the inlet. It is rocky, however, and confused seas caused by conflicting currents can make it extremely treacherous.

Temporary anchorage can be found in 5 fathoms over a rocky bottom.

## Slocum Inlet
Slocum Inlet, on the east shore of Stephens Passage, is 15 miles southeast of Juneau.
Charts 17314, 17300
Entrance: 58°08.10' N, 134°04.58' W
Anchor: 58°07.86' N, 134°04.02' W

Slocum Inlet will give protection from southerlies behind Circle Point if you get a good bite with your anchor. However, we suggest heading for Taku Harbor or making the run to Juneau.

Anchor close to the steep-to mud flat in the southeast corner over sand with fair holding if well set.

## Taku Inlet
Taku Inlet, on the northeast side of Stephens Passage, extends about 15 miles to Taku Glacier at its head.
Chart 17315
Entrance: (Bishop Point bearing 303°T at 1.08 Nm): 58°11.47' N, 134°07.29' W

Taku Inlet is a large impressive waterway

*A plaintive face; do not disturb harbor seal pups.*

which drains the Juneau Ice Field and upper British Columbia.

On one trip, we headed up Taku Inlet for a view of the glacier. We got as far as the anchorage east of Jaw Point, but instead of being rewarded with a view of the glacier, we were greeted by nasty, opaque chop.

Taku Inlet is famous for its dangerous winds and breaking seas that start at Greely Point northward or from southward if a downslope Taku wind is blowing. Opaque glacier water makes for spooky navigation. For a faster way to see it, take a short airplane ride from Juneau.

## Gastineau Channel
Gastineau Channel separates Douglas Island from the mainland.
Chart 17315
Entrance (south): 58°12.05' N, 134°14.24' W

Gastineau Channel has easy access from the south, but it is extremely busy: keep a sharp eye at all times for cruise ships, floatplanes taking off and landing, and kayakers. To reach Harris Harbor or Aurora Harbor, you pass under Douglas Bridge, which has a minimum height of 50 feet. The float south of the bridge is reserved for cruise ship tenders and tour boats and is off limits to pleasure craft. Moorage in all Juneau harbors is assigned by the harbormaster's office, which monitors Ch 16 and 73. If you plan to remain in Juneau for any length of time, make prior arrangements with the Harbor authorities.

Harris and Aurora harbors in downtown Juneau have transient moorage, as does Douglas Harbor, south of the Douglas Bridge on the west side of Gastineau Channel. Statter Harbor, in Auke Bay, 12 miles north of Juneau, is a transient-only harbor and the largest of the facilities in the greater Juneau area.

One of the many cruise ships you may see approaching Juneau

## Juneau (Gastineau Channel)
Juneau, on the northeast side of Gastineau Channel, is 8 miles north of Stephens Passage.
Chart 17315
Entrance (Harris Harbor): 58°18.01' N, 134°25.76' W
Entrance (Aurora Harbor): 58°18.20' N, 134°26.04' W

Juneau is Southeast's largest city, Alaska's state capital, and the most cosmopolitan of the cities along the Inside Passage. It's a friendly community where you can see people in slickers and rubber boots (called Juneau sneakers by locals) meeting with friends dressed in business suits. An estimated half of the 32,000 residents are involved in government; the rest work in tourism, fishing, mining, transportation, consulting, and construction.

The city sits along a narrow strip of land, flanked on either side of Gastineau Channel by magnificent snow-clad mountains. In addition to its lovely setting, the city offers wonderful gift shops, espresso bars, and supermarkets. If you're interested in history, the Alaska State Museum and the Alaska State Library are musts. Pick up the Juneau Walking Tour brochure from the Visitor's Bureau for ideas on other things to see. Tours are available to Mendenhall Glacier. Rent kayaks to tour the harbor or nearby areas or rent a car at the airport and do your own touring. If you moor in Auke Bay, bus service to the city center is frequent and there are shopping centers in between.

The area around Juneau has hundreds of trails, ranging from beach walks to mountain trails and boardwalks. Point Bridget Trail is one of our favorite hikes. The easy 7-mile

Juneau's Gastineau Channel; Harris and Aurora Harbors are on the northeast side of the bridge (lower center part of the photo).

trail begins at milepost 39 north of Juneau on Glacier Highway and leads through a variety of ecosystems—muskeg, beaver ponds, wet meadows and spongy tundra with stunted forest—on its way to Point Bridget beach.

Transient moorage in the Juneau area is available at Harris Harbor, Aurora Harbor, and Douglas Harbor, with additional moorage at Statter Harbor which is 12 miles by road and 35 miles by water to the north in Auke Bay.

A great deal of information about the various harbor facilities is available on the Ju-

## Juneau
### Don Douglass & Réanne Hemingway-Douglass

Juneau is a place of glaciers, gold and government. Conifer-covered hills provide a green backdrop to Alaska's bustling capital city. Although gold mining was Juneau's first industry, it has slipped in importance since World War II. Now, government accounts for the most jobs, followed by tourism, fishing, retail, and mining. Juneau's population is over 32,000 people, but when as many as five cruise ships tie up, it can swell by more than 13,000. Happily, most sail away in the evening.

### Around town
Tourists from cruise ships flock to souvenir and jewelry stores on Franklin Street and eat lunch at the Red Dog Saloon. Near the docks, the streets are filled with tour buses and yellow minivan taxis. But traffic fumes and crowds thin out as you stroll in residential areas. You'll see Victorian homes as well as quirky cottages in pastel colors, flower gardens, streets so steep that some of them have metal or wooden stairways, and an atmosphere that says artists and rugged individualists live here.

See the Governor's House at 716 Calhoun Avenue and the 1894 St. Nicholas Russian Orthodox Church on 5th St. Walk to the end of 6th St. and step from the city into the forest at the Mt. Roberts Trailhead. If prepared for a hike, keep going five more miles to Roberts Peak.

Learn about Juneau by touring the Alaska State Capitol, the Juneau-Douglas City Museum and the Alaska State Museum.

### What to do
Kiosks lining the dock offer a variety of day and half-day tours. Salmon bakes, helicopter and float plane rides can be arranged, as well as fishing or hiking excursions. Or book a boat trip to see waterfalls, wildlife and the twin Sawyer Glaciers in Tracy Arm Fiord.

The spectacular Mendenhall Glacier is only 13 miles from downtown along the Gastineau Channel. Buses and taxis will take you there, or you can rent a car. Or visit the glacier via a short but dramatic helicopter ride through the "Back Door of Suicide," looking down at the Suicide Ice Fall. You can do a quick turnaround, stay for a 2-hour hike or ride a dogsled.

The Mt. Roberts Tramway, located at the dock, offers a five-minute ride to the top of Mt. Roberts, where you can take in the views, shop and eat. Watch artists carving, beading or creating totems before you ride back down.

You can tour the Alaska-Juneau Mine to learn about mining and its role in Juneau's history or pan for gold in Gold Creek.

Juneau is home to places of more specialized interests, including the Mendenhall Golf Course, the Perseverance Theater, the Macaulay Salmon Hatchery, and the Alaskan Brewing Company (tour and tasting: https://alaskanbeer.com/visit/).

### Museums
The Juneau-Douglas City Museum is small but interesting. On display are recently-recovered photos of mining operations and a large fish trap as well as exhibits that recall mining and pioneer days.

Spending time at the Alaska State Museum at 395 Whittier St. will give you a good working knowledge of the state's history, art and natural resources. Its galleries house contemporary artwork and objects from the Haida, Tlingit, Tsimshian as well as Aleut and Athabascan cultures. You'll see clothing, baskets, ivory billikens, totems, and maritime and Russian artifacts.

Before you leave Juneau, pet Patsy Ann. She was a well-loved bull terrier who used to frequent the docks whenever a ship would arrive and now her bronze effigy sits on the waterfront.

Two interesting shops are Hearthside Books and Toys for Alaskan items (245 Front St.) and Observatory for rare books (200 N. Franklin St.).

For visitor information visit the Juneau Convention & Visitors Bureau at Centennial Hall Convention Center, 101 Egan Dr. (tel. 888.586-2201; www.traveljuneau.com ).

*The bronze effigy of Patsy Ann greets Juneau tourists.*

neau Harbor website: http://www.juneau.org/harbors/explore_harbors.php Visiting vessels should call the harbormaster on VHF Ch 73 for assignment to slips and transient floats. Water and power are available at most spaces. A 14-day limit is enforced on the transient floats. The harbormaster is available from 0700 to 2330 during summer months.

Harris Harbor is the closest marina to downtown Juneau, with 204 slips. Most slips have power. A shower and self-service laundry are just across the road from the harbor, and grocery, liquor, and other shopping are nearby.

Aurora Harbor is the largest of the Juneau harbors, with 449 slips. Docks are in good shape, with much refurbishment in 2012. Most slips have power. Showers and laundry are ½ mile from the harbor office. City Center is ½ mile to the south, but quite walkable.

Fuel can be obtained at Taku Fuels, on the southeast corner of the Juneau Harbor Basin, or at Petro Marine, on the west side of Gastineau Channel, just north of the Juneau-Douglas bridge.

### Douglas (Douglas Island)
Douglas Harbor, on the southwest side of Gastineau Channel, is 1.9 miles south of the Juneau-Douglas Bridge.
Chart 17315
Entrance (small-craft harbor): 58°16.57' N, 134°23.30' W

Douglas Harbor facilities have been upgraded with new floats and electricity. The basin has a double-lane boat launching ramp and a new pump-out station. There are 190 slips, with power and water available on the floats and at many, but not all, slips. The harbor is dredged to 12 feet, with adequate maneuvering room in the new section

For availability of pleasure craft moorage, check with the Juneau harbormaster, VHF Ch 73 (907.586.5255). There are no showers or other services in the harbor. For easy access to downtown Juneau, the City Transit System runs along Savikko Road, adjacent to the harbor.

*Bagpipes and drums celebrate the* Veendam's *arrival in Juneau.*

CHAPTER 5 — STEPHENS PASSAGE, PORT HOUGHTON, GAMBIER BAY TO JUNEAU, LYNN CANAL 177

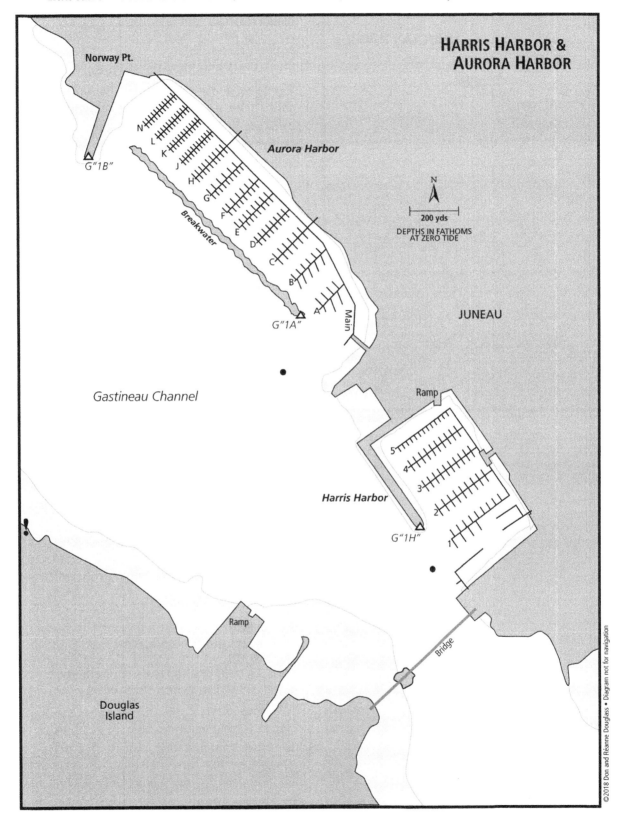

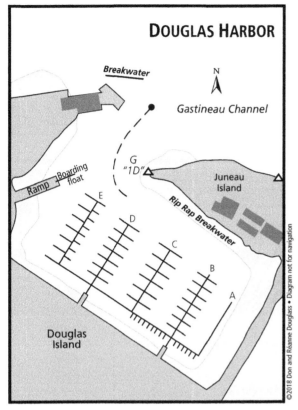

## Mendenhall Bar
Mendenhall Bar is the drying mud flat between Juneau and Fritz Cove and Auke Bay.
**Chart 17315 and USCG diagram**

The route across Mendenhall Bar appears as a shortcut to Auke Bay and is sometimes used by small, shallow-draft boats with expert local knowledge. Vessels with a draft of 3 feet or less can cross on a 15-foot tide; however, the center of the bar dries at 10 feet above MLLW. Many boats that attempt it run aground, to the amusement of locals. It is a tricky passage with poor underwater visibility and is not advised for visiting cruising boats, which should use Stephens Passage along the west of Douglas Island to reach Auke Bay.

If you insist on trying it with your dinghy or a skiff, check with the harbormaster first. It's a good idea to follow a local small boat that has first-hand knowledge. The narrow channel changes from year to year and is full of silt. Because of the silting, it's easy to get off course. The approach from the northwest through Fritz Cove and Mendenhall Bar is narrow, shallow and seasonally marked. It is not recommended for navigation without local knowledge.

Tide gauges at either end of the channel indicate the present amount of water over the shallowest part of the bar. Remember that tide tables are only approximate and can be influenced by wind and barometric pressure. Actual high tide levels are frequently lower than the predicted levels.

## Auke Bay
Auke Bay is 3.5 miles north of Fritz Cove.
**Chart 17315**
**Entrance (mid-channel between Battleship Island and Indian Point): 58°22.00' N, 134°40.77' W**

Statter Harbor in Auke Bay, 12 road miles or 35 water miles north of Juneau, has space for more than 300 transient boats. Reservations are accepted for vessels larger than 60 feet in length overall on the floating concrete breakwater. Contact the Juneau harbormaster

*The road north from Juneau leads to a dead end.*

for assignment on VHF 73. All other moorage space is on a first-come, first-served basis and there is room for approximately 324 vessels to tie up. There are no slips, but power and water are available at the heads of the fingers. It can be challenging to find a spot, and the outside ties can be very rolly due to constant boat traffic.

The harbor, which is very busy during summer months, has a 10-day transient vessel limit, after which the vessel must depart for a minimum of six hours before returning. (This limit does not apply to vessels requesting reserved moorage.) Be sure that you leave the dock by 1100 on your check-out date or you will be charged for another day's moorage.

The harbormaster's office, located at the head of the dock, has restrooms, showers, pay telephones and a weather service squawk box. A seasonal snack bar located in the parking lot has great sandwiches and fries and is a popular place with visitors and boaters. Kayaks can be rented at a kiosk in the harbor parking lot. A convenience store with wine and beer is located just uphill from the harbor office; a self-serve laundromat is a block uphill, and the Auke Bay post office is nearby. Buses to Juneau city center run frequently.

*This sign points out the seriousness of driving the road to nowhere.*

Auke Bay has two fuel docks: Petro Marine at DeHart's Marina and Tesoro Fuel at Fisherman's Bend.

For major provisioning and marine supplies, you must go to Juneau. Although there is bus or taxi service to town, we find it more convenient to rent a car for a day or two. The drawback to having your own vehicle is that parking space at Statter is limited and the hourly limits are strictly monitored.

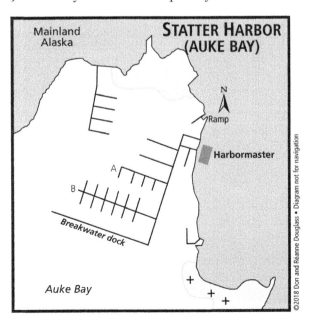

## White Knuckles
### Réanne Hemingway-Douglass

The captain, with tongue in cheek, tells me he considers the Mendenhall Bar a pre-requisite to attempting either Dry Strait or Dry Pass. While we've tried all three, we've had varying degrees of success.

Years ago, we made the transit across Mendenhall Bar in our first *Baidarka*, bumping our keel twice on the sandy, muddy bottom—a high-adrenaline experience! We navigated Dry Pass (Chichagof Island) successfully in our 32-foot Nordic Tug (west to east), but the two attempts we've made to transit Dry Strait from either end turned our knuckles white and we reversed course each time.

Now, after years of too much excitement, we heed our own printed recommendations and can attest to the fact that Dry Strait is definitely for a few knowledgable locals! (See Chapter 4 for Dry Strait details.)

The harbormaster monitors VHF Ch 73. The telephone for the Auke Bay office is 907.789.0819. Boaters can register at either Auke Bay or Harris Harbor.

## NORTHERN STEPHENS PASSAGE
(See the following chapter for Lynn Canal north of Benjamin Island.)

### Oliver Inlet (Admiralty Island)
Oliver Inlet, on the south side of Stephens Passage, indents the north end of Admiralty Island.
Chart 17300
Entrance: 58°08.96' N, 134°19.94' W
Anchor: 58°06.54' N, 134°18.37' W

Oliver Inlet is a quiet and peaceful anchorage surrounded by moss-covered trees. Narrow and 3 miles long, it never seems to be disturbed by wind and chop. Time stands still here; a breaking twig seemingly reverberates for minutes. To us, Oliver Inlet has an almost

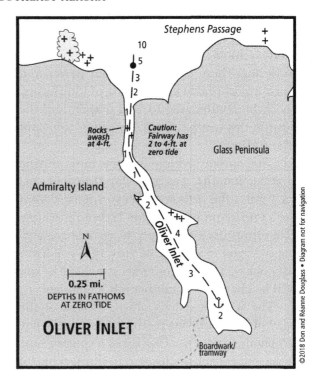

*Approaching Auke Bay; Mendenhall Glacier in sight*

spooky quality.

Entering it takes some planning, however. Traverse it near slack water with an adequate tide level. On a 13.2-foot slack tide we found a minimum of 8 feet under the keel. For small craft, entering is fairly easy during neap tides; however, during spring tides the currents are dangerous.

Anchor anywhere in the inlet once you pass south of the narrows. The bottom is

*Auke Bay's Statter Harbor at sunrise*

*Larger vessels can moor at Statter Harbor's concrete breakwater.*

quite flat and composed of sand, mud and decaying matter with good sticky holding.

The tramway/boardwalk on the west shore leads to Seymour Inlet and a State Parks cabin, a mile to the south. Do not plan on packing a skiff to the other side. This short, narrow and level land mass is all that connects Glass Peninsula to Admiralty Island. Brown and black bears swim across what's called "The Very Berry Zone." On the Seymour Canal side, a 15-foot tide is needed to launch a kayak or skiff.

Anchor in 2 to 3 fathoms over sand and mud with very good holding.

## Admiralty Cove (Admiralty Island)
Admiralty Cove, on the south side of Stephens Passage, is just east of Young Bay and 7.8 miles west of Oliver Inlet.
Charts 17315, 17300
Entrance: 58°10.84' N, 134°36.32' W
Anchor (south of island): 58°10.70' N, 134°35.70' W
Anchor (east of island): 58°11.16' N, 134°34.90' W

The cove marked on Chart 17300 is largely filled with a mud flat, but a smaller cove south of the island connected to shore offers good protection in all but westerly winds. We have

*You can rent a kayak right from Statter's parking lot!*

anchored about 50 yards east of the north tip of this island in a small 4-fathom hole. The cabin on shore is one of many maintained by the USFS for use under permit.

Anchor (south of island) in 3 to 6 fathoms over mud with good holding.

Anchor (east of island) in 4 fathoms over mud and sand with good holding.

**Young Bay** (Admiralty Island)
Young Bay is 11 miles west of Oliver Inlet.
Chart 17315
Position: 58°10.41' N, 134°40.71' W

Young Bay is rather deep and exposed to make a convenient anchorage for small craft. A private dock in the southwest corner of Young Bay is used by a ferry that makes daily round trips to Juneau, bringing personnel who work at the Greens Creek Mine in Hawk Inlet.

**Saginaw Channel**
Saginaw Channel, between Mansfield Peninsula and Shelter Island, joins Stephens Passage with Lynn Canal.
Chart 17316
South entrance (Strauss Rock buoy bearing 053°T at 0.76 Nm): 58°21.22' N, 134°49.40' W
North entrance: (Point Retreat Light bearing 158°T at 1.2 Nm): 58°25.82' N, 134°58.18' W

Some small vessels coming out of Auke Bay pass north of Strauss Rock over a 1- to 2-fathom shoal to avoid the many sport fishing boats frequenting here.

**Adams Anchorage** (Shelter Island)
Adams Anchorage is off the south end of Shelter Island and 5 miles west of Auke Bay.
Chart 17316
Position: 58°22.16' N, 134°49.25' W

Adams Anchorage is a favorite for sport fishing boats during fishery openings. It makes a fair-weather anchor site, but receives a lot of wake from passing boats.

**Barlow Cove** (Mansfield Peninsula)
Barlow Cove is on the northeast side of the north tip of Mansfield Peninsula.
Chart 17316
Entrance: 58.24.11' N, 134°55.42' W

According to locals, small craft can anchor at the southeast head of the cove in less than 10 fathoms; mud bottom with good holding.

**Favorite Channel**
Favorite Channel, between Shelter Island and the mainland, joins Stephens Passage with Lynn Canal.
Chart 17316
South entrance: 58°22.27' N, 134°46.60' W
North entrance (Little Island Light bearing 250°T at 1.65 Nm): 58°33.00' N, 135°00.85' W

Favorite Channel contains Lena, Tee, Pearl, Amalga and Eagle Harbors on its east shore.

**Tee Harbor** (Favorite Channel)
Tee Harbor is 4.2 miles northwest of Auke Bay.
Chart 17316
Entrance: 58°25.46' N, 134°46.19' W
Anchor (south): 58°24.75' N, 134°45.63' W
Anchor (north): 58°25.79' N, 134°45.83' W

The private marina in Tee Harbor is used mainly by sport-fishing boats. A parking area several hundred yards up from the dock has space for boat trailers. The water in the harbor is partially discolored due to the glacier-fed creeks entering the harbor; visibility through the water is limited to 3–4 feet. Fuel and limited supplies are available at the float. If you enter the harbor, avoid the rock marked by buoy R"2."

*Fuel is available at Tee Harbor's sports-fishing floats*

## Pearl Harbor (Favorite Channel)
Pearl Harbor is 7.4 miles northwest of Auke Bay.
Chart 17316
Entrance: 58°28.60' N, 134°47.40' W

Pearl Harbor is a small indentation where some temporary shelter can be found from south winds in the lee of the south islet. Avoid the shoal on the north side of the islet when entering.

## Amalga Harbor (Favorite Channel)
Amalga Harbor is 0.8 miles north of Pearl Harbor.
Chart 17316
Entrance: 58°29.26' N, 134°47.58' W

Amalga Harbor is a tiny coastal opening sheltered by several islands on its north and west sides.

## Eagle Harbor (Favorite Channel)
Eagle Harbor is 8.5 miles northwest of Auke Bay.
Chart 17316
Entrance: 58°29.73' N, 134°48.10' W

Locals report temporary anchorages, close in, over 5 to 7 fathoms and good holding. Watch

---

## Treacherous Waters
### Don Douglass & Réanne Hemingway-Douglass

Lynn Canal extends from Chatham and Icy Straits in the south to Skagway, 84 miles to the north. The deep fiord has steep shores that reach to bare alpine summits, and hanging glaciers in canyons along the route are visible from the canal on a clear day.

Due to its north-south orientation, and because so many large rivers feed into it from the interior, strong winds are a common occurrence in Lynn Canal. Southerly winds are particularly dangerous because the canal gradually narrows toward the north, intensifying the winds. The length of the canal provides a long fetch where seas can build quickly to alarming heights. Williwaw winds (katabatic winds dropping from the hanging glaciers), of an intensity that covers the canal with spray, create poor visibility and make navigation difficult.

Considered an iron-bound coast, the steep rocky shores of Lynn Canal offer little if any protection from the elements. Small craft transiting the area are left to find what shelter they can in small indentations along the mainland shore or in the lee of small islands.

Approximately 3 miles northwest of Benjamin Island lurks Vanderbilt Reef (58°35.45' N, 135°01.13' W), awash on a 12-foot tide. Since tides in the area frequently reach 20 feet on springs (twice each month), the reef lies below the surface about half the time.

This reef marks Alaska's greatest maritime tragedy. On a stormy night in October 1918, the Canadian Pacific steamer, *Princess Sophia*, on its last southbound voyage of the year, ran aground on the reef at near full-speed. The ship, which was carrying 350 miners, businessmen, civil servants, their families and crew, did not sink at the time. In fact it appeared to have only minor damage. Rescue vessels, dispatched from Juneau the next day, waited for an opportunity to remove the passengers and crew, but by late afternoon the storm had worsened and the rescue vessels were forced to seek shelter behind Sentinel and Benjamin islands and in Bridget Cove. When they were able to return the following morning, all they found of the *Princess Sophia* was 20 feet of her mast extending above the water. The only survivor was a dog that managed to swim to the mainland and was found in Tee Harbor several days later. For a good account of the accident and its effect on post-gold rush Alaska, read *The Final Voyage of the Princess Sophia* by Betty O'Keefe and Ian Macdonald.

*Ships are the transport life-line in Southeast Alaska, bearing all kinds of goods.*

for the charted mid-channel rock north of the island northwest of Amalga Harbor.

## Lynn Canal
Lynn Canal extends northward from the junction of Chatham Strait and Icy Strait for about 58 miles to Seduction Point, where it divides into Chilkat and Chilkoot inlets.
Charts 17300, 17317
South entrance (Point Couverden bearing 270°T at 2.5 Nm): 58°11.50' N, 134°58.67' W

Lynn Canal—named by George Vancouver for King's Lynn, his birthplace in England—leads north to Haines and picturesque Skagway along a route of alpine splendor. The high, jagged peaks, snowfields and hanging glaciers along the canal are magnificent.

Winds kick up a nasty chop in this long fjord, so plan for alternative shelter should you need it. It is not always rough, however—the entire 85-mile trip from Juneau to Haines has been made in fair weather by jet skis.

## Howard Bay (Lynn Canal)
Howard Bay is northwest of Howard Point.
Chart 17316
Entrance: 58°16.40' N, 135°03.49' W
Anchor: 58°17.68' N, 135°04.49' W

Howard Bay provides shelter from westerlies and outflow winds but it is open to southeast gales.

Anchor in 10 fathoms over hard mud with fair holding.

## St. James Bay (Lynn Canal)
St. James Bay, on the west shore of Lynn Canal, is 11 miles northwest of Point Retreat.
Chart 17316
Entrance (Point Whidbey bearing 016°T at 0.7 Nm): 58°34.02' N, 135°08.76' W
Anchor: 58°37.37' N, 135°10.58' W

St. James Bay, adjacent Boat Harbor, and the surrounding shorelines comprise St. James Bay State Marine Park. The anchorage shown in the diagram is located in the northeast corner of the bay. Crab pots tend to be set in this area during summer, so you may need to anchor in deeper water.

Avoid the rocks and foul ground south of Point Whidbey. Steer east of the reef and rock that extend approximately ½ mile southeast from the island in the northeast corner of the bay.

Anchor approximately opposite the small islet in 3 to 7 fathoms; good holding.

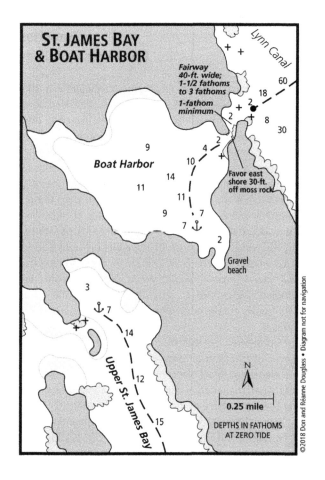

*Boat Harbor's entrance, viewed from inside*

## Boat Harbor (Lynn Canal)

Boat Harbor, on the west side of Lynn Canal, is 3.5 miles north of Point Whidbey.
Chart 17316
Entrance: 58°38.24' N, 135°09.33' W
Anchor: 58°37.78' N, 135°09.96' W

Boat Harbor is very inviting, but it should be used with great care. The entrance is almost invisible from the south, and you can completely miss it when you're only a quarter-mile from shore. Strong currents make steering difficult, so boats without local knowledge should reconnoiter by dinghy before entering. However, once you're inside, Boat Harbor provides an excellent anchorage for cruising boats. The harbor is totally landlocked, and lack of driftwood along shore indicates a calm anchorage. There are landing beaches and potential campsites along the sand and gravel shore, and a few crab pot floats on the west side of the harbor. Midsummer water temperatures frequently reach 62°F.

The tiny, somewhat difficult entrance is the price you pay for this near-perfect shelter.

We estimate the fairway to have a width of about 40 feet and a minimum depth of from 1 to 1.5 fathoms at zero tide. It is safest to enter at high-water slack. The fairway has an irregular bottom with reefs that extend from either side. Favor the east shore once you're inside the narrows.

Anchor in 7 fathoms over hard sand and gravel with fair-to-good holding.

## Benjamin Island Cove and Benjamin Island Bight (Benjamin Island)

Benjamin Island is 14 miles north of Auke Bay.
Chart 17316
Entrance (Benjamin Island): 58°34.17' N, 134°54.69' W
Anchor (Benjamin Island Cove): 58°33.93' N, 134°54.60' W
Anchor (Benjamin Island Bight): 58°33.21' N, 134°54.28' W

From the south, vessels can travel up Favorite Channel, Saginaw Channel, and through North Pass between Shelter and Lincoln islands, or up the main trunk of Lynn Canal until north of Little Island.

The bight on the south end of Benjamin Island is reported to offer some shelter from strong outflow winds whistling down Lynn Canal.

The cove on the north end of Benjamin Island provides shelter from southeast gales and is entered from the channel between the island and the mainland. Although the channel between Benjamin and North islands is suitable for kayaks and skiffs, cruising boats should probably not attempt the passage. You can enter the cove under radar in limited visibility, al-

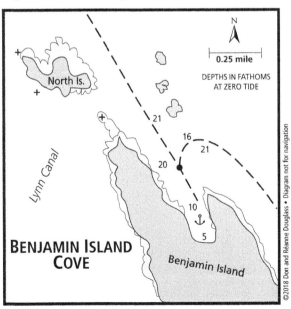

though you should post a crew member to look out for the small rocky islets northeast of the cove. Enter the cove in mid-channel and move close to the head where suitable depths for anchoring can be found. The head of the cove has a cobble beach and a campsite.

Anchor at the head of the cove in 6 to 8 fathoms.

## Vanderbilt Reef (Lynn Canal)
Vanderbilt Reef is 3.2 miles northwest of Benjamin Island.
Chart 17316
Position (Vanderbilt Reef Light): 58°35.42' N, 135°01.15' W

Vanderbilt Reef is the site of Alaska's own *Titanic* story: the tragic grounding and sinking of the Canadian Pacific steamship *Princess Sophia* during a storm in 1918; 350 people lost their lives, making it the worst maritime disaster in Inside Passage history.

If you drive the highway, there's a pull-out above the water where you have a good view of the reef.

A series of north-south islets occur along the eastern shore of Vanderbilt Reef. There is also a half-moon stony beach at the head of the eastern shore; this has few, if any, storm drift logs, indicating that may offer a temporary anchor site.

## Bridget Cove (Lynn Canal)
Bridget Cove is 3.2 miles northeast of Vanderbilt Reef and 18 miles north of Auke Bay.
Chart 17316
South entrance: 58°37.53' N, 134°57.22' W
North entrance: 58°38.56' N, 134°57.97' W
Anchor: 58°38.47' N, 134°57.38' W

Bridget Cove, within the 2,800-acre Point Bridget State Park, provides reasonable shelter. The highway north from Juneau lies a short distance inland to the east. The cove can be entered by the passages north or south of Mab Island. If you enter from the south, favor the Mab Island side, watching for rocks and a reef that extend south from the south point of the island. A reef parallel to the mainland shore extends north from the outer south point of Bridget Cove.

If you enter from the north end of Mab Island, avoid the rocky reefs that extend short distances from either shore.

We have observed vessels of up to 60 feet (seiner tenders) anchored in the channel between the island and the mainland. Except for the cobbled shores in the southeast and northeast bights, the shorelines of the cove are rocky. You can land a dinghy at the head of the northeast bight. If you rent a car and drive north from Juneau, Point Bridget State Park has a trail that leads from the road southwest to the cove. There is a well-defined trail across the Pt. Bridget peninsula to the river mouth.

Anchor in the northeast bight in 5 to 7 fathoms over mud with good holding.

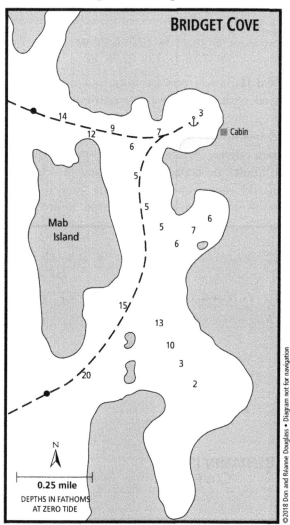

## Berners Bay (Lynn Canal)
Berners Bay is 23 miles north of Auke Bay.
Chart 17316
Entrance: 58°42.43' N, 135°00.44' W

Berners Bay is rather deep and exposed for small craft, though it offers some relief from downslope winds. Small craft will find more secure anchorage in Echo Cove on the southeast side of the bay.

## Echo Cove (Berners Bay)
Echo Cove is the second bight 2 miles east of Pt. Bridget.
Chart 17316
Entrance (1.8 miles northeast of Pt. Bridget): 58°41.28' N, 134°56.06' W
Anchor: 58°39.86' N, 134°54.80' W

*Réanne and Don admiring a massive piece of driftwood on the beach.*

The entrance to Echo Cove is narrow and shallow, but the cove is well protected from all weather and is a favorite of local fishing boats.

Primitive campsites can be found on shore. The absence of drift logs indicates good protection. Above the cove, there is a parking lot and a boat launch ramp.

Anchor in 4 to 8 fathoms over a soft bottom.

## William Henry Bay (Lynn Canal)
William Henry Bay is 9 miles north of Point Whidbey.
Chart 17316
Entrance: 58°43.44' N, 135°13.81' W
Anchor: 58°42.66' N, 135°14.40' W

William Henry Bay provides easy access and excellent protection from southerlies; when southeast storms are raging outside, it is dead calm inside the bay. The entire bottom is flat, and there is swinging room for several boats. The best anchorage is off the Beardsley River outlet. The beach, which can be approached by dinghy, is mostly gravel. The bay offers good views of snowfields to the south and a verdant valley to the west.

Entrance can be made easily in limited visibility with radar. Avoid the rocky, kelp-covered reef that extends from Lancer Point; it dries at 3 feet.

Anchor in 12 fathoms over sand and mud with good holding.

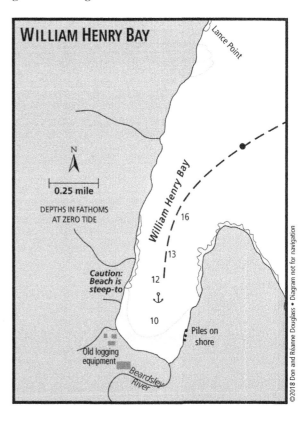

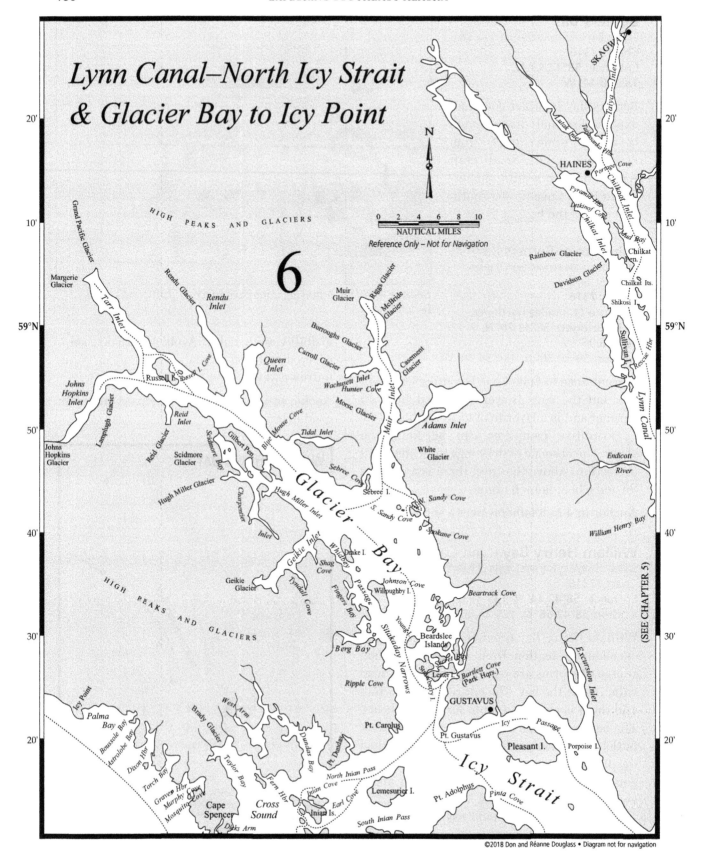

# 6

# LYNN CANAL NORTH, ICY STRAIT AND GLACIER BAY, CROSS SOUND TO ICY POINT

## INTRODUCTION

Mountains covered with massive icefields, hanging glaciers, stunning scenery—you find all of this and more as you proceed north in Lynn Canal and then south and west into Icy Strait and Glacier Bay National Park. This is also a remote region of high-latitude, frigid waters, limited radio reception and extreme tides, so be well prepared!

From Point Retreat at the northern tip of Admiralty Island (28 miles northwest of Juneau), Lynn Canal continues north for 60 miles, where it breaks into three inlets: Chilkat, Chilkoot and Taiya. The landscape along the canal becomes increasingly dramatic; the mountainsides that rise steeply from the water's edge are filled with snow bowls and hanging glaciers.

In Chilkoot Inlet, the craggy Cathedral Peaks provide a spectacular and classic Alaskan backdrop for the town of Haines. The Alaska State Ferry calls here and drops off passengers who drive north on the Haines Highway to connect with the Alaska Highway. Haines itself is worth a visit; cruising boaters will find it a friendly community, with an excellent museum, totem poles, and art galleries. Many events are put on for summer visitors, including performances by the Chilkat

*Glacier Bay in all its magnificence*

Dancers. Haines is also the site of the popular Southeast Alaska State Fair, held each August. Twenty miles north of Haines is the Chilkat Bald Eagle Preserve, where over 3,000 eagles make their winter home.

*A perfect bird ice sculpture in Glacier Bay*

Skagway nestles at the bitter north end of Taiya Inlet, in the beautiful Skagway River delta. Famous for its gold rush history, the main part of the town now comprises the Klondike Gold Rush National Historical Park. The Chilkoot Trail, originally an Indian trail over the 3,500-foot Chilkoot Pass, became famous in the late 1800s as thousands of prospectors hiked it to reach the Klondike gold fields, in the Canadian Yukon Territory. Photos of the gold rush period can be seen in many local establishments.

West of the southern end of Lynn Canal lies Glacier Bay National Park and Preserve. This is a gem covering 3.3 million acres of wilderness. Famous for its concentration of tidewater glaciers, the park contains many square miles of austere land recently revealed by receding ice. When Captain George Vancouver and his men explored the area in 1794, they found Icy Strait choked with "solid mountains of ice." By the time John Muir visited Glacier Bay from Wrangell by canoe 85 years later (in 1879), the ice had retreated 48 miles up the bay. Muir was the first to document the topography of Glacier Bay, and his writings are classics in the literature of glacial studies.

In addition to changes in the position of glacier fronts, the effects of ongoing glacial retreat are also visible in the succession of different flora, from mature (200-year-old) rainforest species in Bartlett Cove, to successively younger vegetation as you proceed northward in Glacier Bay. The land in the upper reaches is still raw, the rock scraped and ground to smooth surfaces where small plants and lichens are just beginning to establish themselves.

Along with its magnificent glaciers, the park is also renowned for its wildlife—nearly 200 species of birds have been sighted here. Whales, orcas and seals frequent the waters and bears can sometimes be spotted along shore.

The park boundaries encompass not only Glacier Bay proper, but also the area west of Icy Strait in Cross Sound, all the way along the outer coast to Dry Bay, 90 miles north of Cape Spencer. Between June 1 and August 31, boaters require a permit to enter Glacier Bay National Park north of a line between Points Gustavus and Carolus. Please see our sidebar on permitting procedures, which changed significantly in 2017. The number of boats allowed within the permit area is limited to 25 a day—which means just three or four new vessels per day may enter.

The remote and beautiful park areas to the west of Glacier Bay proper have no permit requirements for private use. You can easily spend a week exploring Dundas Bay, Fern Harbor, Dicks Arm and Graves Harbor.

The National Park Service website for Glacier Bay has many pages devoted to helpful information on visiting the park. https://www.nps.gov/glba/index.htm

## LYNN CANAL NORTH

### Rescue Harbor (Sullivan Island)
Rescue Harbor, on the southeast side of Sullivan Island, is 2.2 miles north of Sullivan Rock. Sullivan Island, on the W side of Lynn Canal, is about 6 miles NW of Point Sherman.
**Chart 17317**
**Entrance:** 58°56.09' N, 135°17.95' W
**Anchor:** 58°56.43' N, 135°18.47' W

Rescue Harbor, the second bight on the southeast side of Sullivan Island, provides very good shelter from winds from southwest through north to northeast. Its beach, gray sand with gravel, becomes steep-to about 100 yards offshore.

You can enter Rescue Harbor by radar in

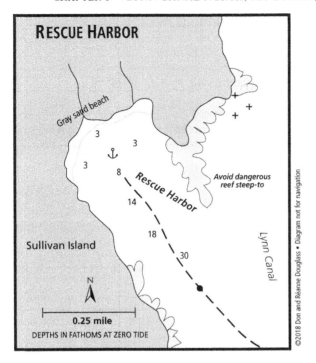

tion of hauled out seals or sea lions, and vessel speed must be less than 10 kts. Moderate protection from southerlies can be obtained here.

The entrance to the bight requires caution due to an irregular bottom, numerous rocks and a foul area. Pay attention to the *Coast Pilot #8* directions, as the small-scale chart is inadequate for navigation.

Anchor in about 2 fathoms over gravel and rocks with poor-to-fair holding.

### Sullivan West Bight
Sullivan West Bight is 1 mile west of Sullivan Island and 2.6 miles northwest of Sullivan Rock.
Chart 17317
Entrance (south): 58°54.10' N, 135°18.78' W
Anchor: 58°55.57' N, 135°22.06' W

"Sullivan West Bight" is our name for the bight 2.6 miles northwest of Sullivan Rock. This site is tucked below the snowfields and glaciers on the west side of Lynn Canal and offers some protection in the lee of Sullivan Island off the drying mud flat in sticky mud. Pass south of Sullivan Rock and avoid both the foul area

limited visibility, but be careful to avoid the reef on the east side, which is steep-to with depths of 30 fathoms 150 feet off its south edge. This reef extends over 400 yards offshore.

Do not confuse Rescue Harbor with the first bight north of Sullivan Rock.

Rescue Harbor is exposed to the southeast. For protection from southerlies, see Sullivan West Bight below.

Anchor in 3 to 5 fathoms over sand and mud with excellent holding.

### Shikosi Island Bight (Shikosi Island)
Shikosi Island Bight is on the north side of Shikosi Island, one of the four islands in the Chilkat Islands chain.
Chart 17317
Entrance: 59°02.31' N, 135°16.36' W
Anchor: 59°02.08' N, 135°16.32' W

Shikosi Island Bight, small and picturesque, offers fair-weather anchorage with great views of the snowy massifs bordering Lynn Canal. At times, the rocks scattered around Shikosi and Kataguni islands are covered with seals. Remember that federal regulations require all vessels, including kayaks, to remain a minimum distance of ¼ mile from any concentra-

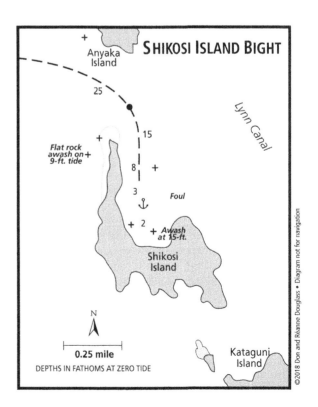

at the tip of Sullivan Island and the rock 400 yards offshore, 0.6 mile north of the bight.

Anchor in 12 fathoms over sticky mud with very good holding.

## Chilkat Inlet (Lynn Canal)
Chilkat Inlet, at the head of Lynn Canal, lies west of Chilkat Peninsula.
Chart 17317
Entrance (Seduction Point bearing 083°T at 0.83 Nm): 59°04.74' N, 135°20.12' W

Chilkat Inlet is 9 miles long and largely shoal with opaque water. Small craft can find shelter in Letnikof Cove, but most boats that visit Haines use the harbor in Portage Bay.

## Kalhagu Cove (Chilkat Inlet)
Kalhagu Cove, on the southwest side of Chilkat Peninsula, is 7.8 miles southeast of Haines.
Chart 17317
Position: 59°06.42' N, 135°21.34' W

## Letnikof Cove (Chilkat Inlet)
Letnikof Cove, on the east shore of Chilkat Inlet, is 4 miles southeast of Haines.
Chart 17317
Entrance: 59°10.59' N, 135°24.21' W
Anchor: 59°10.33' N, 135°23.26' W

Letnikof Cove is popular with locals in summer. It offers shelter from southeast gales, but is open to downslope winds.

This location has small craft floats but no electricity, water or fuel.

## ELDRED ROCK LIGHTHOUSE

This historic octagonal building is a notable landmark to boaters traversing the Lynn Canal between Juneau and Haines or Skagway. Built in 1906, it is the oldest remaining lighthouse in Alaska, and has been listed on the National Register of Historical Places since 1975. It was one of four manned lighthouses that were constructed in Lynn Canal between the years 1902 and 1906 in response to a series of shipwrecks that occurred during the bustling Gold Rush era of the late 1890s. The most notorious incident involved the steamship *Clara Nevada*, which came to grief near Eldred Rock on February 5, 1898, on a voyage from Skagway to Seattle. Four of the eighty-odd people on board survived, and 850 pounds of gold was lost. The remains of the steamer resurfaced briefly during a storm ten years later, to the astonishment of the lighthouse keepers at the time, but whether the original sinking was an accident or an act of sabotage remains a mystery to this day—and the gold has never been found!

The Eldred Rock lighthouse was commissioned by Congress in the aftermath of the *Clara Nevada* tragedy. As with other lighthouses of the time, it was built to an octagonal design, but with a unique solid lower story which still stands today—unlike the all-wood structures of other Alaskan lighthouses. The main building on Eldred Rock was comparatively roomy, with ample living space for three keepers. This was doubtless appreciated by the various men who served in that capacity, as winter storms could be so severe that venturing out of doors was sometimes impossible. In fairer weather, the Eldred Rock lightkeepers were regularly supplied by vessels from Haines that brought them provisions, fuel, fresh water and—in later decades—movies.

The original light was a kerosene-fueled 2100 candle power lamp with a French-made Fresnel lens. Situated at 91 feet above sea level, it had a range of 15 miles and operated in conjunction with a compressed-air fog horn. The lens consisted of two opposing bulls-eye panels, four feet and fourteen inches in diameter, respectively. A sheet of red glass between the larger panel and the light source produced alternating red and white flashes from the revolving lens.

The Eldred Rock lighthouse was decommissioned as a manned facility in 1973, and the light was replaced with an automatic beacon. The original Fresnel lens was acquired from the Coast Guard by the Alaska State Museum in 1976, and is on permanent loan to the Sheldon Museum and Cultural Center in Haines.

The Coast Guard continues to operate the beacon on Eldred Rock as a "minor light," but the lighthouse buildings have fallen into various states of disrepair. In 2014, the non-profit Eldred Rock Lighthouse Preservation Association was formed, under the auspices of the Sheldon Museum, with the mission of restoring, maintaining and operating the lighthouse as a historic site. For further information, or to send a donation to support the preservation efforts, visit http://www.eldredrocklighthouse.org

—AC

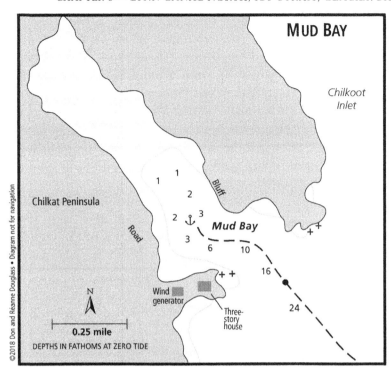

## Mud Bay (Chilkoot Inlet)
Mud Bay is about 4 miles northwest of Seduction Point.
Chart 17317
Entrance: 59°08.73' N, 135°19.99' W
Anchor: 59°09.05' N, 135°20.67' W

Mud Bay offers excellent protection from all but southeast winds. There are several cabins and houses around the bay. To the west, the bay offers good views of rugged peaks and Rainbow Hanging Glacier.

Avoid the rocks off the south point and the numerous crab pot floats spread over the large, shallow inner bay. The water has a milky appearance due to the outflow of Katzehin River.

Anchor in 2 to 3 fathoms over soft mud with good holding.

## Chilkoot Inlet (Lynn Canal)
Chilkoot Inlet, the east arm of Lynn Canal, extends northward 12.6 miles, where it divides. The east arm of Chilkoot—Taiya Inlet—terminates at Skagway.
Chart 17317
South entrance (Seduction Point bearing 270°T at 1.7 Nm): 59°04.86' N, 135°15.11' W

## Kelgaya Bay (Chilkoot Inlet)
Kelgaya Bay is 2.5 miles southeast of Haines Harbor.
Chart 17317
Position: 59°12.75' N, 135°22.20' W

## Portage Cove (Chilkoot Inlet)
Portage Cove is about 2.5 miles northwest of Battery Point.
Chart 17317 (inset)
Entrance: 59°14.04' N, 135°24.82' W
Anchor: 59°13.83' N, 135°26.29' W

Open anchorage can be found between the small-craft basin and the first pier south. This can be a bouncy anchorage due to chop from both north and south and traffic in the basin. Most skippers prefer to anchor southeast of the second pier, just west of the point.

Anchor in 6 fathoms over soft mud with good holding.

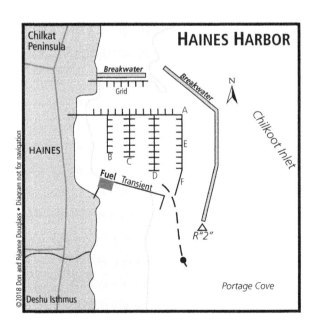

## Haines (Chilkoot Inlet)
Haines, at the outlet of the Chilkat River, lies on the west side of Portage Cove, 59 miles north of Auke Bay.
Chart 17317
Entrance (small-craft basin): 59°13.94' N, 135°26.32' W

*Small-boat harbor at Haines*

Haines is a borough of about 2,300 inhabitants. It is surrounded by ice-capped mountains, from which glaciers spill down sheer granite walls into Lynn Canal and Chilkat Inlet. The paved Haines Highway, originally built during World War II, roughly follows the old trading trail used by native Alaskans to reach the interior and it connects with the Alaska Highway at Haines Junction, 150 miles to the north.

The 48,000-acre Alaska Chilkat Bald Eagle Preserve along the Chilkat River hosts the largest gathering of bald eagles in the world.

# Haines
## Don Douglass & Réanne Hemingway-Douglass

Approaching Haines via Lynn Canal, you'll notice how the white, pitched-roof buildings of Fort William H. Seward echo the snowy mountain peaks in the background. Built in 1902 as a response to border disputes with Canada, the fort was decommissioned in 1947 and now houses galleries, restaurants and the Hotel Hälsingland.

Haines, named for Presbyterian missionary Francina Haines, is located on a peninsula between the Inside Passage and the Chilkat River. The Haines Highway connects to the Alaska Highway at Haines Junction, Yukon, 155 miles north of Haines.

More than 2,500 residents live in this pocket of civilization in the wilderness. It's a haven for artists who create ceramics, woodcarvings, jewelry, sculptures and paintings and display their handiwork in galleries and shops.

In winter, the 48,000-acre Chilkat Bald Eagle Preserve is home to the greatest concentration of bald eagles anywhere. Plenty stick around in summer, too. To watch them, book a float trip on the Chilkat River, take a guided tour of the preserve, or rent a car and drive up the Haines Highway where you can view the birds from pullouts.

Haines residents party all summer long, starting in May with Fort Seward Days and the King Salmon Derby. The Summer Solstice Celebration is held in June, and in July there's the Independence Day Celebration, the Southeast Alaska State Fair, and the Bald Eagle Music Festival.

Opportunities for hiking, birding, photography, hunting, fishing, mountain biking and other outdoor activities mean you won't get bored while you're in port.

### Places of Interest
Sample the local beers at the Haines Brewing Company, 327 Main St, Haines (907.766.3823).

You can visit Dalton City at the Southeast Alaska Fairgrounds. This was the movie set for *White Fang*. A two-day brew-fest is held here in May.

The Hammer Museum, 108 Main St. is a unique museum that tells the story of man's most basic tool, the hammer. You can see a collection of 1,400 hammers (907.766.2374, www.hammermuseum.org).

At the Tsirku Canning Company, located at Fifth and Main, you can see an antique salmon canning line in action (907.766.3474, www.cannerytour.com).

The Sheldon Museum and Cultural Center, 11 Main St., houses displays about pioneer history, as well as Tlingit art and cultural practices such as the potlatch (907.766.2366, www.sheldonmuseum.org).

For more information, contact the Haines Convention and Visitors Bureau, 122 Second Ave. (907.766.2234 or 800.458.3579, www.haines.ak.us).

### Moving On
It would be a shame to be so close to Skagway and not visit. One option is to rent a car and drive the 350 road miles via the Golden Circle route (see: www.goldencircleroute.com).

Or go by water, which is much shorter. If you want to take a break from navigating your own vessel, hop on the Fairweather Express for a 35-minute ride to Skagway. For tickets and reservations (907.766.2100 or 888.766.2103; www.chilkatcruises.com).

Warm water upwelling from geothermal activity keep some stretches of the Chilkat ice-free late into fall. Chum and coho salmon spawn here much later than in other areas, attracting between 2,000 and 4,000 eagles for a two to three week period. The National Bald Eagle festival—held every November—hosts numerous activities, including photography workshops and Native cultural performances. www.baldeagles.org.

Sport fishing, camping, and hiking are popular among visitors and residents here, and native crafts and dancing can be viewed during summer months.

The town has a laundromat, showers, several hotels, and a well-stocked market. Haines Brewing on Main Street offers local brews, although no food service at this writing. Other food and drink options include a distillery and a variety of bakeries and small restaurants. Visitors enjoy the Sheldon Museum and Cultural Center, the Jilkaat Kwaan Native Heritage Center, and the quirky Hammer museum. Fuel and water can be obtained in the harbor. The Alaska ferry terminal is located in Lutak Inlet, 3 miles north of town. The only air service is via Alaska Seaplanes, flying to and from Juneau several times a day, weather permitting.

Haines Harbor is undergoing a renovation at this writing, which should be complete in 2018. At present, there is a small, compact boat basin. The harbormaster says they "try to find a hole for cruising boats." Somehow they almost always manage to do it. If they can't find a place for you, you can also anchor in Portage Cove (see above) between the basin entrance and the first wharf south. Telephone the harbormaster at 907.776.2448

*Some cruisers avoid the time-consuming Lynn Canal passage by taking the Fast Ferry from Juneau to Skagway.*

or 907.766.2231. Some visitors recommend keeping your boat in Haines while visiting Skagway via the Haines-Skagway Fast Ferry, a passenger-only ferry with daily service during the summer season.

Be sure to check your chart and follow the dredged channel into the boat basin, staying well clear of the shoaling area from the west that extends to the south side of the transient dock.

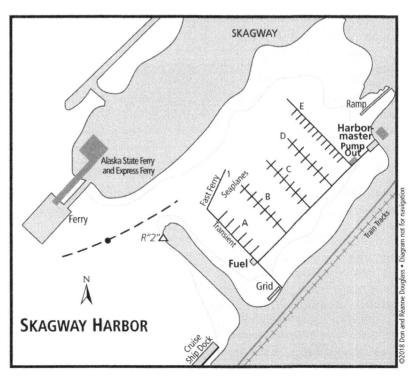

## Lutak Inlet (Chilkoot Inlet)
Lutak Inlet is the west arm of Chilkoot Inlet.
Chart 17317
Entrance: 59°16.91' N, 135°25.50' W

The half-mile-wide Chilkoot River drains Chilkoot Lake at the head of the inlet. An Alaska State Ferry terminal is located in Lutak Inlet at approximately 59°16.92' N, 135°27.72' W.

## Taiyasanka Harbor
Taiyasanka Harbor, at the foot of the Ferebee River valley, is 4 miles north of Haines.
Chart 17317
Entrance: 59°17.72' N, 135°26.03' W

Taiyasanka Harbor can provide welcome shelter from southerly weather.

## Taiya Inlet (Chilkoot Inlet)
Taiya Inlet is the north arm of Chilkoot Inlet.
Chart 17317
Entrance (Taiya Point bearing 270°T at 0.5 Nm): 59°17.23' N, 135°23.03' W

## WHITE PASS & YUKON ROUTE

Skagway has plenty to see and do, but if you have time and money to spare, and are keen to travel beyond the town—take the train! The 67-mile White Pass & Yukon Route is an authentic relic of the gold rush era, and offers spectacular day-trips in summer to Bennett, BC, and Carcross, YT, and back. The narrow-gauge tracks climb 3000 feet in 20 miles, with steep (3.9%) grades, tight turns, tunnels, bridges and trestles—and outstanding views almost all the way.

The WP&YR railroad is an International Historic Civil Engineering Landmark, an honor it shares with the Statue of Liberty and Eiffel Tower. It was first conceived of in 1898, two years after gold was discovered at Bonanza Creek, a tributary of the Klondike River 600 miles to the north. Tens of thousands of would-be miners who arrived by steamship in Skagway from 1897 onwards faced the prospect of making their way overland on foot or by horse or mule to the goldfields. Both the White Pass Trail out of Skagway and the Chilkoot Trail from nearby Dyea were steep and posed numerous geographical and climatic hazards. The Canadian government required, in addition, that each person carry at least a ton of supplies into the Yukon. In 1899, an enterprising engineer constructed a 12-mile toll road out of Skagway, but the toll gates were largely circumvented and the venture went bust. Various railroad proposals were put forth in the meantime, including a successful pitch by Michael J. Heney, an American railroad contractor, to Sir Thomas Tancrede, a London investor. The two men met by chance in Skagway. "Give me enough dynamite and snoose," Heney is alleged to have said, "and I'll build a railroad to Hell."

The White Pass & Yukon Railroad Company was duly formed, in April 1989, and represented an amalgam of American engineering, British financing, and Canadian labor. The first four miles of track were laid within the first two months along the defunct toll road. The next 106 miles, to Whitehorse, YT, were infinitely more challenging, requiring the construction of tunnels, bridges and trestles, and the use of some 450 tons of explosives to blast through the almost-solid rock of the Coastal Mountains between Skagway and White Pass. The work continued through the winter months, in temperatures as low as 60-below. Thirty-five thousand men worked on the railroad overall, though some of them stuck at it for only a day. On the steepest slopes, they relied on rope lifelines to prevent them from falling. The project ultimately cost $10 million and 35 lives.

Construction of the railroad was completed on July 29, 1900, when the tracks of northern and south track-laying crews were joined with a golden spike at Carcross, midway along the route. By that time the gold rush had begun to ebb. However, the WP&YR railroad provided a much-needed transportation service to the interior of the Yukon, and the company carried passengers, freight, and mine products for the next 80 years— until 1982, when operations were suspended as the mining industries in the Yukon went into recession.

In 1988, the WP&YR railroad was re-opened as a heritage railway, operating between Skagway and Carcross. Today, it carries as many as 400,000 sightseers every summer, and is the Alaska cruise ship industry's most popular shore excursion. We recommend it for small boat cruisers, also. The trains consist of vintage parlor cars pulled by diesel locomotives, although the company still operates a steam engine also. Visit wpyr.com for further information and to make reservations. If you end up riding the WP&YR rails, remember to take your passport!

—AC

Taiya Inlet has the Taiya River on its north shore, and the town of Skagway and Skagway River on its northeast shore.

## Skagway (Taiya Inlet)
Skagway is 13.5 miles north of Haines.
Chart 17317 (inset)
Entrance (small-boat basin):
59°26.91' N, 135°19.43' W

The historic town of Skagway is nestled in the V-shaped Skagway River Valley, between majestic mountain ranges. The town's population of about a thousand people swells dramatically in

*The entrance to Skagway's small-boat basin is at the top left.*

## Skagway
### Don Douglass & Réanne Hemingway-Douglass

Skagway comes from the Tlingit word "skagua," meaning "home of the north wind." In 2000 the population was 862, but a century earlier thousands of men passed through on their quest for gold. That's why the town is called "Gateway to the Gold Rush of '98." It's the northernmost port of the Inside Passage, and Alaska's largest town in area, covering 453 square miles.

You can learn about local history at the Klondike Gold Rush National Historical Park. Rangers lead tours of the Skagway Historic District, a collection of 15 restored buildings, including a cigar store, bakery and dry goods store. See www.nps.gov/klgo for details. The Trail Center will give you information on the many hiking trails nearby, including the 33-mile Chilkoot Trail. If you're up for a strenuous, multi-day hike you can recreate the miners' trek to gold country.

The waning years of the nineteenth century were wild times. Outlaw Jefferson "Soapy" Smith and his gang prevailed until Frank Reid, fed-up citizen, shot him in 1898. Reid was wounded in the fray and died 12 days later. Both men are buried in Gold Rush Cemetery.

Nowadays, the stampede of visitors is from cruise ships. Tourists shop in Skagway's many gift shops and explore the area via tours that include flights over glacier country, hiking trips, bus trips to Carcross (short for Caribou Crossing) in the Yukon Territory and Dyea at the head of Taiya Inlet, trailhead for the Chilkoot Trail. You can pan for gold at the Liarsville Trail Camp. Other activities include Jeep tours and sled dog rides, rock climbing and canoeing.

Skagway offers a range of lodging from cabins and hostels to bed & breakfast inns and motels. Downtown is the Skagway Inn, established in 1897 as a brothel. It's more respectable now and houses Olivia's Restaurant. There are also pubs, cafes and saloons.

### Attractions
The Skagway Museum outlines local history and is located at Seventh and Spring in the McCabe College Building (tel.: 907.983.2420; Website: www.skagway museum.org).

At Jewell Gardens, mile 1.1 on the Klondike Highway, you can see the flowers of Alaska and sip afternoon tea in the conservatory (tel.: 907.983.2111; Website: www. jewellgardens.com).

The White Pass and Yukon Route Railroad, completed in 1900, runs sightseeing tours on vintage trains. You can chug up to the summit of White Pass via tunnels and trestles, seeing spectacular scenery on the way. The office is at Second Ave. and Spring St. (tel.: 907.983.2217 or 800.343.7373; Website: www.whitepass railroad.com).

For further information, contact the Skagway Convention & Visitors Bureau, P.O. Box 1029, Skagway, AK 99840 (tel.: 907.983.2854 or 888.762.1898; Website: www.skagway.com).

*Start exploring Skagway's rich history here in the historic district.*

summer as thousands of tourists descend from cruise ships.

In the late 1890s, the town was home to over 20,000 people as thousands of miners trudged north over the White Pass or Chilkoot trails during the Klondike gold rush. During its heyday, Skagway supported more than 80 saloons, as well as numerous other businesses. Nowadays, you can tour the boardwalks of the restored historic district, browse its shops, galleries and saloons, visit its museums, take in its daily shows, and ride the famous White Pass and Yukon Railroad (twice-daily runs in summer season).

If you like to stretch your hiking muscles

*Boat names and a skull "decorate" Skagway's rock wall.*

and want to take in the views from above the town, trails lead out and around Skagway. Or—if you're so inclined and can spare the time—you can hike for several days along the Chilkoot Pass Trail. Advance permits are required from the Klondike Goldrush National Historic Park. ( https://www.nps.gov/klgo/planyourvisit/permits.htm )

The Skagway small-boat basin has about 14 feet of water (at zero tide) at its entrance and a capacity for about 165 boats. The harbor monitors Ch 16, or you can telephone 907.983.2628. The electrical system includes 30- and 50-amp power. There is a 60-foot, small-craft grid in the southeast corner of the basin; a pump-out is located at the foot of the gangway that leads to the harbormaster's office. Transient moorage is on a first-come, first-served basis. Call ahead to alert the harbormaster, and they may be ready to accommodate you when you arrive.

Nearby facilities include a large market, laundromat, liquor store, medical clinic, bank and a variety of restaurants. Seasonal showers and bathrooms are located at the harbormaster's building at the head of the dock. Ice can be purchased at the seafood company above the dock. The town is serviced by air from Juneau, by motor vehicle along the Klondike Highway, and by the Alaska ferry.

Pleasure boaters who do not want to make the long slog up Lynn Canal can leave their boats in Juneau and take the Alaska Marine Highway's "Express Ferry" for overnight trips to Haines or Skagway.

### Nahku Bay (Taiya Inlet)
Nahku Bay is 2 miles northwest of Skagway at the head of Taiya Inlet.
**Chart 17317 (inset)**
Entrance: 59°27.72' N, 135°20.45' W

The Taiya River flows into Nahku Bay.

*A humpback breaches near a favorite whale-watching location in Icy Strait: Pt. Adolphus, on the northern tip of Chichagof Island.*

## Long Bay and Taiya River
Long Bay is 1 mile northwest of Skagway.
Chart 17317 (inset)
Long Bay (entrance): 59°27.79' N, 135°21.42' W

Long Bay is deep and exposed to southerlies. Protection from northwesterlies can be found at its head in 10 to 15 fathoms.

## ICY STRAIT TO CROSS SOUND
### Icy Strait
Icy Strait extends northwest 27 miles from Chatham Strait to Point Adolphus, then west 16 miles to the Inian Islands.
Charts 17300, 17302
East entrance (Hanus Reef Light bearing 090°T at 1.8 Nm): 58°07.84' N, 135°03.43' W
West entrance: (North Inian Pass Light bearing 142°T at 0.9 Nm): 58°16.94' N, 136°25.11' W

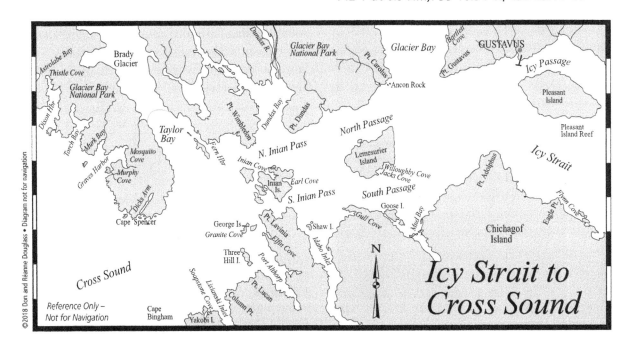

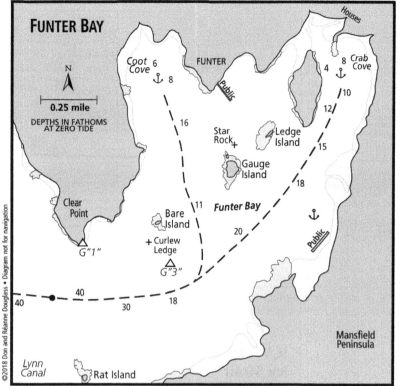

Icy Strait is the main east-west route connecting Chatham Strait and Cross Sound to Glacier Bay and the Gulf of Alaska.

Upper Chatham Strait, between Admiralty and Chichagof islands, extends southward from Icy Strait and Lynn Canal to Peril Strait.

## Funter Bay (Mansfield Peninsula)

Funter Bay is on the east side of Chatham Strait at its junction with Lynn Canal.
Charts 17316 (inset), 17300
Entrance: 58°14.29' N, 134°55.77' W
Public float: 58°14.64' N, 134°53.05' W
Anchor (Coot Cove): 58°15.32' N, 134°54.32' W
Anchor (Crab Cove): 58°15.32' N, 134°52.87' W

Funter Bay, like Swanson Harbor, provides good protection at the southern end of Lynn Canal. Space at the public float on the southeast corner of the bay is often taken. The float is in poor condition and bears have been reported, but good anchorage can be found in either Coot Cove or Crab Cove. There is an Aleut Russian Orthodox cemetery in Crab Cove.

This is a low point across Admiralty Island, so east and west winds whistle across here and in Hawk Inlet to the south.

Anchor (Crab Cove) in 8 to 10 fathoms over soft mud with good holding.

Anchor (Coot Cove) in 6 to 10 fathoms over sticky mud with very good holding.

## Swanson Harbor

Swanson Harbor is 18 miles southwest of Auke Bay and 30 miles southeast of Glacier Bay.
Chart 17316
Entrance (Swanson Harbor Entrance Light "2" bearing 340°T at 0.35 Nm) 58°11.27' N, 135°04.48' W
Public float: 58°12.79' N, 135°06.59' W
Anchor (harbor): 58°12.85' N, 135°07.47' W

*Two public floats are available in Swanson Harbor.*

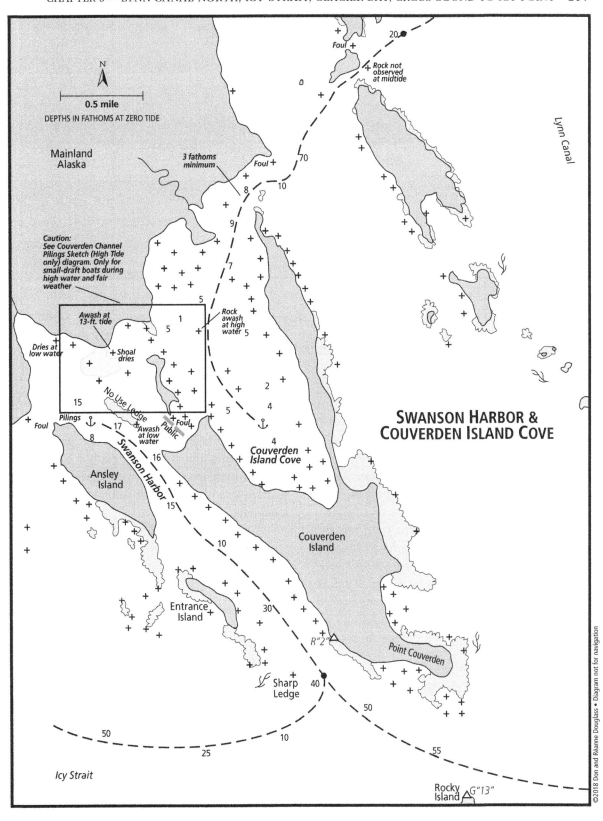

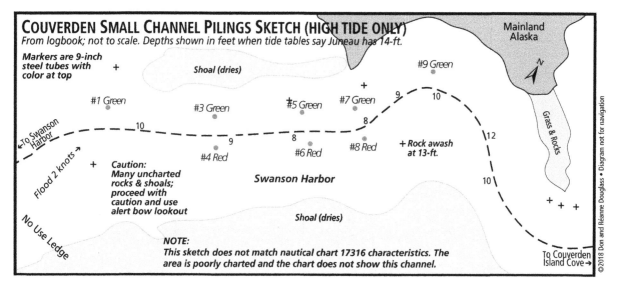

Swanson Harbor is strategically located at the intersection of Icy Strait, Chatham Strait and Lynn Canal, and provides good shelter for cruising and fishing boats. Two detached concrete public floats in the east side of the bay are used by sport fishing boats and for vessels preparing to enter Glacier Bay. A fish-cleaning station is located on one of the floats. VHF and cell phone coverage can be very spotty in this area.

Enter Swanson Harbor from the south via the channel west of Point Couverden. Avoid Sharp Ledge, which extends a half-mile or more southeast of Entrance Island. Watch carefully for submerged rocks along both shores. As you proceed deeper into the channel watch for No Use Ledge on the east; some of this area is marked by kelp. There is a rock awash at low water about 150 yards SSE of the obvious No Use Ledge shoal area. The best anchorage for small craft is in the bight on the northeast end of Ansley Island.

## Couverden Island Cove (Couverden Island)

"Couverden Island Cove" is what we call the indentation on the north side of Couverden Island.
Chart 17316
Northeast entrance: 58°14.28' N, 135°05.24' W
Anchor: 58°12.77' N, 135°05.43' W

Couverden Island Cove is a favorite of local fishermen and other boaters who want solid protection from all weather. Extra caution is required in this area, as it is poorly charted and shoal with many rocks. The entrance route to Couverden Island Cove is made from the northeast tip of the island's long, thin eastern peninsula, with about 3 fathoms minimum in the narrow fairway. Some professional skippers caution against using this anchorage and advise using the Swanson Harbor anchorage (above) instead. Consider your abilities carefully before choosing this anchorage, and proceed cautiously.

Avoid the shoals and rocks in the center of Couverden Island Cove. A dangerous charted rock, awash at high water, lies at 58°13.35'N, 135°06.20'W.

Anchor in 4 fathoms over sand and mud with very good holding.

## Couverden Channel
Chart 71316

Couverden Channel is a small, very narrow channel between mainland Alaska and an unnamed island northeast of Couverden Island. Shallow-draft boats *only* can transit it via a shallow bar that is not shown on Chart 17316. Transit should be made *only on high water slack* and only in fair weather. Note that C on

Chart 17316 states: "The highwater channel between Swanson Harbor and the cove behind Couverden Island is marked by pilings. Tide boards at each end show least channel depth."

For a suggested pathway through this channel, see our Couverden Channel Pilings Sketch (High Tide Only). Tide boards show depths in feet when Juneau tide tables show 14 feet, as derived from notes in our logbook. *Use the channel at your own risk.*

On June 25, 2004, the S/V *Merlin* of Southampton, England, a 40-foot centerboard sailboat drawing 3½ feet with the centerboard up, transited this channel using our sketch and verified that the depth in the channel was the predicted tide level in Juneau minus 6 feet.

The channel has a flat, sandy bottom that requires an alert bow watch, careful monitoring of a depth sounder and a visual approach to ensure safe passage. We advise reconnoitering this channel by dinghy before attempting a passage.

**Spasski Bay** (Chichagof Island)
Spasski Bay is 9 miles southwest of Swanson Harbor.
Chart 17316
Entrance (Neck Point bearing 305°T at 0.6 Nm): 58°06.71' N, 135°18.31' W
Anchor: 58°06.95' N, 135°19.97' W

Spasski Bay entrance is surrounded by rocks and shoal, and currents here cause turbulence. A good calm anchor site in prevailing northwest winds can be found at the head of the bay. Most southeast winds appear to pass up Icy Strait with little effect on Spasski Bay.

Anchor in 4 fathoms over mud, sand and gravel with fair holding.

**Port Frederick** (Chichagof Island)
Port Frederick is on the south side of Icy Strait between Crist Point and Point Sophia.
Chart 17302
Entrance (Pinta Rock buoy bearing 000°T at 0.6 Nm): 58°09.38' N, 135°27.28' W

Port Frederick extends 15 miles southeast from Pinta Rock. Hoonah lies along its north-

*Boots are a necessity on the rainforest trails.*

eastern shore, and there are intriguing bights and lagoons at its head. This is a good place to anchor if you are waiting to enter Glacier Bay.

**Hoonah** (Port Frederick)
Hoonah, inside the east entrance to Port Frederick, is 25 miles southeast of Bartlett Cove in Glacier Bay.
Chart 17302
Entrance: 58°06.72' N, 135°27.24' W
Float: 58°06.42' N, 135°26.85' W

As you enter Port Frederick on your way to Hoonah Harbor keep a careful look out for large ship traffic, including cruise ships, high speed tourist ferries, and the Alaska State Ferry. The ferry terminal is located northwest of the breakwater entrance to the harbor at approximately 58°06.95' N, 135°27.40' W.

Exercise caution in the waters surrounding Hoonah Harbor, paying close attention to the information in the most recent *Coast Pilot*. Some charted depths may be off by a fathom or more due to a 1958 earthquake in Southeast Alaska, and a datum discrepancy may still exist between latitude and longitude on some charts. Numerous shoals, rocks, and tricky passes are in the immediate vicinity of the harbor.

Hoonah is the largest Tlingit settlement in Southeast Alaska. It is a popular spot for cruising boats waiting for entry to Glacier Bay. In 2016, an Alaska Native-owned cruise ship destination opened at Icy Strait Point, with a 400-foot long cruise ship dock. The privately-owned facility welcomes more than 75 cruise ship calls between May and September, with visitor numbers exceeding 160,000. Additional visitors arrive on day trips from Juneau via high speed catamaran.

*Hoonah's transient dock*

The facility has several restaurants as well as an adventure center with the world's largest zipline ride. The former Icy Point cannery has been renovated and is now a cultural center where local artisans sell their crafts and Tlingit dancers perform.

Despite the huge increase in visitors, cruising boaters are still welcomed in Hoonah, and the harbormaster does his best to accommodate pleasure craft. Moorage can be found inside the harbor breakwater beyond Hoonah Cold Storage dock by calling the harbormaster on Ch 16 to arrange for a slip; change to 09 or 14. In 2007, the harbor added additional floats to accommodate 40-foot vessels.

Some cruisers choose Hoonah Harbor as a winter storage site, in part because Hoonah's proximity to the Pacific Ocean results in relatively temperate winter weather compared to ports farther inland.

Laundry, showers, power and water are available within

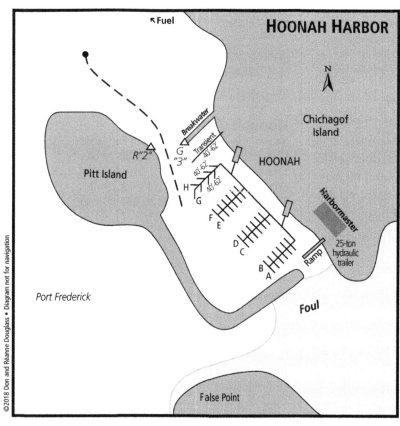

the harbor, as well as a travel lift; there is no pump-out station. Telephone the harbormaster at 907.945.3670.

Hoonah Trading Company (monitors Ch 11), in the outer harbor, sells groceries, hardware, and fuel (gasoline, diesel and propane).

You can stretch your legs along the road between the cultural center and the end of the road to the south.

The outer harbor (city) floats include a drive-down ramp. There is no power

*Hoonah Harbor—some cruisers store their boats here over the winter.*

## Fourth of July at Hoonah

At 11 o'clock on Fourth of July morning, we stood with a small group of boaters on Hoonah's main street, waiting for the parade to start. Crowds were gathering along the parade route, milling around a totem pole and sitting on the curb. Young men had perched themselves on rooftops of nearby buildings. Red, white and blue pennants flapped in the breeze.

The parade started with sirens and horns. A police car led the way, followed by a string of tour vans, cars, veterans carrying flags, a pickup truck decorated with paper fish, and a US Forest Service truck carrying Smokey the Bear. From each vehicle people threw handfuls of candy into the street. Swarms of children rushed to gather up packages of M&Ms, lollipops and taffy.

The parade was over in a few minutes. It turned the corner, heading for the picnic grounds just out of town, the crowd behind it. We followed, stopping briefly on the waterfront to watch a logger practicing for the log-rolling competition.

The aroma of barbecue wafted across the picnic grounds where people stood in line at concession stands to buy hamburgers, Indian fry bread, and watermelon. Clouds had crept in during the parade and a fine mist was falling. No one paid it any attention.

The crowd drifted toward a grassy area. A man standing on top of a van with a loudspeaker announced a foot race for girls 2–3 years old. Little boys raced next and on they went through to the 17–21-year-olds.

After the races, a man unloaded a flat of eggs from the van and the announcer called, "Egg toss! Granddaughters and grandmothers." Middle-aged to elderly women stepped onto the field, facing young women and girls. Each grandmother took an egg and stood a few feet from her granddaughter. On the announcer's, "Throw!" the grandmothers tossed their eggs gingerly to granddaughters, who then tossed them back. With each throw, granddaughters and grandmothers stepped farther apart. When someone missed a catch, that pair dropped out.

"Last pair to throw wins!" cried the announcer.

Grandsons and grandfathers came next, followed by mothers and daughters, fathers and sons, mothers and sons, and every possible combination of family relationship, finally ending with husbands and wives. The field grew speckled with white and yellow splotches and contestants wiped sticky egg from hands, clothes, and faces. People took multiple turns and the inevitable splats became more dramatic as the pairs got better and better at throwing eggs. With each contest, the number of contestants grew, as did the laughter. I watched adult brothers and sisters throwing eggs and laughing. I was amazed. I couldn't imagine this many adult siblings in one place in Seattle.

Hoonah might be just a small town, but its Fourth of July was surely one of the most fun we'd ever experienced.

Adapted from *Glaciers, Bears and Totems: Sailing in Search of the Real Southeast Alaska* by Elsie Hulsizer. Harbour Publishing, 2010.

or water at this site and the area is subject to strong northwesterlies; a fee is charged for moorage.

The harbor has a 5-knot, no-wake zone that begins off the ferry terminal. Boaters are asked to respect this limit.

For a quieter anchorage, consider Neka Bay, 7.5 miles southwest.

### Neka Bay (Port Frederick)
Neka Bay, on the west side of Port Frederick, is 9 miles from the entrance.
Chart 17302
Neka Bay (Entrance, Neka Island bearing 213°T at 0.5 Nm): 58°02.51' N, 135°37.71' W
Anchor (Neka Bay): 58°03.08' N, 135°40.01' W
Entrance (North and South Bight, Neka Island bearing 300°T at 0.4 Nm): 58°01.79' N, 135°37.59' W
Anchor (North Bight) 58°02.35' N, 135°40.94' W

The north arm of Neka Bay has good shelter for cruising boats although southeast or eastern winds can funnel in, leading to rolly conditions. Anchor west of the tugboat buoys on the north side of the small islet. You can also find protection in North Bight. From here we've explored the drying reef by dinghy and watched humpback whales surface, spout and breach nearby. Bears are frequently seen in the area west of the North Bight anchorage. Avoid the charted rocks off the entrance to North Bight. South Bight has a 4-fathom hole and is very well protected, but its entrance is shallow and constricted.

Anchor (Neka Bay) in about 4 fathoms over mud with excellent holding.

Anchor (North Bight) in 6 fathoms over green mud with good holding.

### Southwest Arm at Head of Port Frederick (Port Frederick)
The southwest arm at the head of Port Frederick is 2 miles southwest of Eight Fathom Bight.
Chart 17302
Entrance: 57°59.58' N, 135°45.96' W
Anchor: 57°59.31' N, 135°48.30' W

The head of Southwest Arm appears to be a remote getaway with excellent shelter over a grassy, sticky bottom. Tenakee Inlet is only a few hundred yards to the southwest over land, but many miles by water!

### Flynn Cove (Chichagof Island)
Flynn Cove is 7 miles southeast of Point Adolphus and 15 miles from the entrance to Glacier Bay.
Chart 17302
Entrance: 58°13.10' N, 135°37.03' W
Anchor: 58°12.34' N, 135°35.20' W

Flynn Cove is a great anchor site if you're waiting to enter Glacier Bay. It's large and has

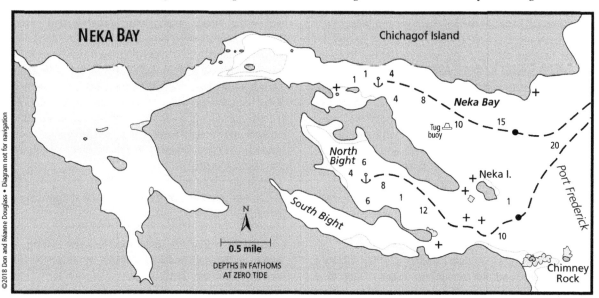

*The large Trading Company store in Hoonah surprises many cruisers.*

a fairly consistent bottom with grassy shores where you can stretch your legs. When entering the cove, stay well north of Harry Island and the rocks and shoals on its west side before turning south. Pass a grassy islet and a 200-yard-long reef awash on a 12-foot tide. Once past the reef, favor the northeast shore, avoiding a ledge awash on a 15-foot tide. Anchor toward the head of the bay, monitoring your depth sounder as you approach.

Anchor in about 9 fathoms over sticky mud with good holding.

### Excursion Inlet (Sawmill Bay)
Excursion Inlet is 16 miles east of the entrance to Glacier Bay.
Charts 17316, 17318
Entrance: 58°22.04' N, 135°27.03' W
Anchor (Sawmill Bay): 58°28.31' N, 135°29.78' W

Excursion Inlet was cut out of the towering peaks by glaciers long ago, and is too deep for convenient anchoring. The western arm of the inlet is called Sawmill Bay. However, fair shelter at reasonable depths can be found in the eastern bight near the head of Sawmill Bay. The areas around the dock and cannery were used as a camp for German prisoners-of-war camp during World War II and there is a small museum. Cruisers have reported that it is still possible to moor a dinghy temporarily at the Cannery Town docks, but they are in poor repair and unsuited for larger craft.

Anchor in Sawmill Bay in about 10 fathoms.

### Icy Passage and Pleasant Island Cove
Icy Passage lies 8 miles east of the entrance to Glacier Bay, between Pleasant Island and the mainland.
Chart 17302
Anchor (Pleasant Island Cove): 58°23.02' N, 135°37.16' W
Anchor (south of Gustavus): 58°22.80' N, 135°42.30' W

The north shore of Icy Passage includes the village of Gustavus (pronounced Gus-TAY-vus). Temporary anchorage can be found in shallow water along either the north or south shore, but beware of strong winds and tidal currents. Pleasant Island Cove is a convenient anchorage with easy access by radar. The large, flat 1½ to 2 fathom area east of the Icy Passage spit is well protected from most summer winds, and is out of the westerly chop sometimes found off Gustavus. This is one of the closest anchorages to Bartlett Cove if you are waiting for your date

*Baidarka anchored in Flynn Cove*

to enter Glacier Bay National Park. There is room here for quite a few boats, and many charter fishing boats anchor here. We recommend anchoring immediately east of the lone tree on the spit, avoiding the numerous crab pot floats. We have found the bottom to be hard blue-gray clay packed with clam shells, not the mud mentioned in the *Coast Pilot*. This makes setting your anchor difficult—you must set it slowly or it will break out before burying itself. The last of the flood tide flows west; we have measured currents to 2 knots on spring tides.

In a serious southeast blow, consider anchoring on the west side of the spit. Alternatively, you can anchor on a shoal on Pleasant Island, south of Gustavus pier and 2.5 miles west of Icy Passage Light over a steep-to, rocky bottom.

Anchor in 2 fathoms over hard blue-gray clay, sea grass and clamshells with poor-to-fair holding. Holding is good if your anchor is well dug in.

## Gustavus (Icy Passage)
Gustavus is on the north side of Icy Passage.
Chart 17302
Float: 58°23.23' N, 135°43.77' W

Gustavus is the village that serves Glacier Bay National Park. The airport, located 2 miles north of the public float, is served by regular Alaska Airlines flights, and the town is a busy transportation hub in the summer. The float is frequently crowded in tourist season. Local or visiting boats anchor or tie to moorings on either side of the float. No overnight ties are allowed and conditions here are too exposed for overnight anchoring.

## Glacier Bay National Park and Preserve
The entrance to Glacier Bay, between Point Gustavus and Point Carolus, is 16 miles northeast of Elfin Cove and 23 miles northwest of Hoonah.
Chart 17318
Entrance: 58°22.73' N, 135°58.84' W

The *U.S. Coast Pilot* for Glacier Bay contains a long series of warnings:

> [Glacier Bay] is about 50 miles long to the head of Muir Inlet, 54 miles to the head of John Hopkins Inlet, and 62 miles to the head of Tarr Inlet.... above Willoughby Island both shores of the bay are steep and foul, and should be avoided.
>
> Glacier Bay National Park and Preserve, 4,400 square miles in area, comprises all of Glacier Bay. It has over 20 tremendous glaciers and many others almost equally impressive. They illustrate all stages, from actively moving ice masses to those that are nearly stagnant and slowly dying.
>
> Humpback whales frequent Glacier Bay.... All motor vessels are prohibited from pursuing or approaching within 0.25 mile of humpback whales.
>
> Currents. The tidal currents from Point Gustavus to Willoughby Island at times attain a velocity of 6 knots or more. Heavy tide rips and swirls occur abreast Beardslee Islands....
>
> Ice. Numerous discharging glaciers enter the bay, and glacial ice is always present, sometimes in enormous quantities in Muir Inlet, Tarr Inlet, and Johns Hopkins Inlet.... When the ice falls from the faces of the glaciers, it may create waves 30 feet high. Therefore, small boats should not approach closer than 0.5 mile to active glaciers. Icebergs are unstable and should

*A cruise ship appears out of the fog in Icy Strait.*

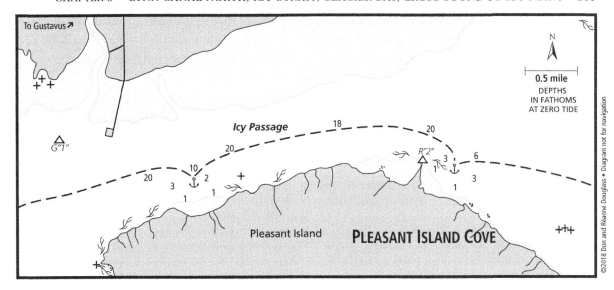

*not be approached closely because, if disturbed by swell from the small boat passing, they may roll over or break apart at any time . . .*

*Vessels are advised to carry extra propellers aboard when navigating Glacier Bay, and single-screw vessels should not attempt to navigate the bay at all. (CP)*

The prudent mariner will remain aware of this advice. Regardless, a cruise through Glacier Bay in one's own boat is the ultimate aspiration of many cruisers. Please see the sidebar detailing the permitting process and regulations for Glacier Bay and then enjoy planning your cruise with the help of the individual entries which follow.

Weather in Glacier Bay during summer is usually cool and rainy with temperatures that average about 50°F, although clear, windless days that cause short-term heat waves do occur.

## Orcas Finish Moose
### Don Douglass

In June '92, while *Baidarka* was in Icy Passage, a moose was killed by orcas off Pleasant Island.

Two moose were swimming Icy Passage when they were attacked by a pod of orcas. One moose was killed outright; the other died when he swam into a kelp bed, apparently got tangled up, exhausted himself and drowned.

Glacier Bay has wide tidal ranges (up to approximately 20 feet), with floating ice of different sizes moving at varying drift rates. Williwaws sometimes blow off the glaciers bringing threatening ice or making an anchorage insecure. Cautious, prudent navigation is essential, especially around floating ice or in opaque waters. Although the entire park has been resurveyed within the last 20 years, continued glacial retreat and isostatic rebound continue to dramatically alter depths, especially in the shallower coves and inlets. Use caution.

Anchor sites in Glacier Bay are relatively few for the hundreds of miles of shoreline. They tend to be deep, with hard bottoms and poor-to-fair holding. The channels are steep-to, and the shoals along shore provide inadequate swinging room. It is also almost impossible to get an anchor to bite well—which is understandable when you consider that glaciers carved these fjords out of solid rock. The thin layers of mud and silt on the bottom are swept by strong tidal currents, adding to the difficulty of anchoring.

For updated park information, visit https://www.nps.gov/glba/index.htm. Vessel course and speed restrictions apply in the Whale Waters regulatory area in the mouth of Glacier Bay from May 15 through September 30. Note that the dates during which only non-motorized access is permitted for certain waters vary from place to place around the park. As a courtesy to kayakers and other self-propelled travelers, please watch your wake!

No pets are permitted ashore anywhere in Glacier Bay National Park and Preserve with the exception of the Bartlett Cove Public Use

## Glacier Bay National Park and Preserve Permits

Vessel use in Glacier Bay is regulated by the National Park Service to protect park wildlife and other resources while providing a range of recreational opportunities to park visitors. Glacier Bay National Park and Preserve collects no entrance fees from private visitors. https://www.nps.gov/glba/index.htm

All motorized pleasure boat operators are required to obtain a non-fee permit prior to entering Glacier Bay north of a line between Point Gustavus and Point Carolus anytime between June 1 and August 31. This area includes Bartlett Cove, the site of Glacier Bay Lodge and the park's visitor center, because Bartlett Cove is one of the most heavily used whale feeding areas. Vessels entering without a permit may be denied access to the bay, asked to leave, and issued a citation.

All boaters are required to call on VHF Ch 16 and then switch to Ch 12 immediately upon entering the bay. Proceed directly to the Visitor Information Station in Bartlett Cove for a required boater orientation prior to continuing in the bay.

There are still many places within park boundaries where you can enter without a permit and find beautiful and remote anchor sites—for example, to the east in Excursion Inlet and to the west in Dundas Bay, as well as north of Cape Spencer. Note that you may enter Glacier Bay National Park before June 1 and after August 31 without a permit. However, park authorities ask that you call them on VHF Ch 16 to inform them of your entrance and exit. All park regulations are still in effect during the non-permit period.

Vessel operators may apply for private vessel permits by fax, phone, radio, email, in person at the Bartlett Cove Visitor Information Station, or by USPS mail. In addition, vessel operators may apply for private vessel permits at the Hoonah office during normal business hours M-F. Please note that this office is staffed only intermittently.

Applications are time-stamped and handled in the order received at or after 7a.m. However, applications received in person are given priority over all other applications. Applications with the same date/time stamp are prioritized by 1) fax and email; 2) radio and phone; 3) USPS letter.

Applications will be reviewed upon receipt and a response form will be sent to the applicant.

Permits are issued to the vessel operator and an operator may hold up to 2 permits at any one time. Each permit may be for up to 7 days, for a maximum of 14 days out of any 21 days.

Regulations provide that no more than 25 private vessels may be permitted each day from June 1 through August 31. The twenty-five permits are divided into twelve Advanced Notice Permits and thirteen Short Notice Permits.

Advance Notice permits may be issued to boaters applying no more than 60 days in advance of the entry date. Advance application is strongly advised, particularly from June 11 through August 2. You may reserve up to seven consecutive days. At the peak of the summer season, permits may be difficult to get. If you are denied an advanced notice permit because the allotted permits have all been distributed, you may wish to apply for a short notice permit later. Holders of Advance Permits are requested to confirm their arrival at least 48 hours prior to the beginning of their permit entry date.

Short Notice Permits may be issued to boaters applying no more than 48 hours in advance of the requested entry date. It is possible that all the permits may have been issued when you apply for a Short Notice Permit. If that happens make sure you ask to be put on the "Short Notice Waitlist." Every morning at 7:00 a.m., a new waitlist is started. Be sure to give accurate contact information and be available to be contacted. If an attempt is made to contact you and you don't answer, you will be taken off the list until you ask to be put back on. If you don't hear from anyone by 7:00 p.m. you will need to ask the following day to be put back on the Waitlist.

All campers and kayakers in the park are also required to attend an orientation program at the Visitor's Center before receiving their camping permits and bear-resistant food containers. Permits are free and required from May 1st through September 30th. The campground located at Bartlett Cove has bear-resistant food caches, firewood, and a warming hut. If desired, campers may be dropped off in the backcountry by the Park's concession-operated tour boat.

—LW

Dock, the beach between the Bartlett Cove Public Use Dock and the National Park Service Administrative Dock, and within 100 feet of Bartlett Cove Developed Area park roads or parking areas.

Since few anchor sites are located near glaciers, you may consume more fuel than expected as you sightsee, so it's a good idea to check your fuel levels, both at entry and upon exit of Glacier Bay.

The area west of Glacier Bay to Cape Spencer, then north 90 miles to Dry Bay—although within the Park boundaries—lies outside the mandatory permit area. Later in this chapter, we describe anchor sites on both sides of Cape Spencer for boaters who want to experience some of the rugged backcountry to the south and west of the Fairweather Range.

*Glorious Glacier Bay National Park*

### Bartlett Cove (Glacier Bay)
Bartlett Cove, on the east side of Glacier Bay, is 4 miles north of Point Gustavus.
Chart 17318 (inset)
Entrance: 58°26.44' N, 135°55.25' W
Public float: 58°27.31' N, 135°53.30' W
Anchor: 58°27.47' N, 135°53.18' W

Bartlett Cove is the headquarters of Glacier Bay National Park. It is connected by road to Gustavus and represents the last outpost of civilization before you head deeper into the fjords. Pleasure boaters are required to check in here and receive an orientation; you must also have a park permit for your boat or be subject to a fine. The park has programs that include slide presentations and nature walks. Please do your part to keep this special environment pristine by observing all park regulations.

Glacier Bay Lodge is a short distance east of park headquarters. It has internet, showers and laundry facilities for campers and boaters, as well as comfortable lodging, a restaurant, gift shop and interpretive center. Gas and diesel are sold at the fuel dock (operated by Glacier Bay Lodge) from approximately May 20 to September 10. Call the lodge ahead of time on Ch 16 to arrange for fuel.

An interesting nature trail circles around a small lake to the west of the lodge.

Space on the docks at Bartlett Cove is limited and use is strictly limited to 3 hours. Read the signs carefully and park only in a designated space. Water is available on

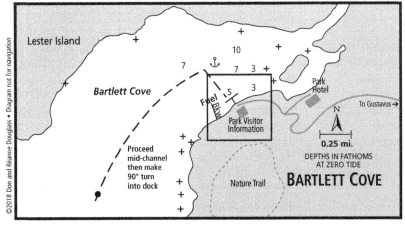

*Approach the Bartlett Cove dock after a 90-degree turn from mid-channel.*

the dock. Cruising boats may anchor outside the no-anchoring area to the north and take a dinghy to the dock.

As you enter at a speed of no more than 20 knots (this may be reduced to 13 kts by Park authorities depending on whale abundance), take a mid-channel course, 1 mile offshore and, upon approaching the docks, turn 90 degrees toward the floats. Watch for the wake of high-speed charter boats that may pass close by you inside the bay. You can tie up at the dock for no more than 3 hours and you must have a park entrance permit before doing so.

Anchor in 6 fathoms, 200 yards north of the dock, over mud with good holding.

## Ripple Cove (Glacier Bay)
Ripple Cove, on the west side of Glacier Bay, is 6.2 miles west of Bartlett Cove.
Chart 17318
Entrance: 58°27.06′ N, 136°04.19′ W
Anchor: 58°27.17′ N, 136°05.08′ W

Ripple Cove is a good temporary anchorage in fair weather. We have used it as a lunch stop, or a place to wait for favorable currents or to get organized before heading up into Glacier Bay. The approach is simple and it is out of nearly all the current of Sitakaday Narrows.

Anchor in 2 to 3 fathoms over sand and mud with good holding.

## Beardslee Islands (Glacier Bay)
Beardslee Entrance, the approach to Beardslee Islands is 4.9 miles northwest of Bartlett Cove.
Chart 17318
Entrance (George Point bearing 000°T at 0.7 Nm): 58°29.63′ N, 136°00.45′ W

---

## A High-Latitude Emergency
### Lachlan and Becky McGuigan, S/V *Xephyr*

It was getting dark, which in Glacier Bay, Alaska is almost tomorrow. Crab pots littered the anchorage. The engine gave a strangled cough and died. The pots were catching more than crabs tonight. A morning dive was a chilling prospect.

Making do with what I had, I donned a thin wet suit (1/8 of an inch is not enough), a light jacket, quilted hood, boots, and sailing gloves. My accessories included mask, snorkel and a fanny-pack of zinc weights.

We rigged a guide-line under the boat, rafted the dinghy as a work float, taped a hose to the snorkel, and went in. The water was the temperature of a martini with visibility like milk. Scary stuff. The snorkel kinked. No air. Straighten the snorkel and try again. No air. Shorten the hose. Still can't get air below 2 feet. Bag the snorkel.

The guide-line curves into the darkness. No prop here. We move the line three times before a shadowy prop materializes. Dive, search the murk for the rope end, unwrap a loop. One dive per wrap. After each dive the crew dumps very hot water (feels lukewarm) inside my wetsuit. Finally there is enough line free to bring the end to the surface. Heavy duty, expensive stuff; just like on our boat. Funny they would use it for crabbing. Hello??!! This isn't a crab pot float line. We ran over our own jib sheet. Crab fishermen aren't so bad after all. More hot water. Back down. I fantasize about hot showers. Only icebergs are comfortable here. My average dive lasts 10 seconds. Up on the dinghy, hot water down the wetsuit, drag myself down the guide-line. My lungs tell me to stop. Back to the dinghy for more blessed water. Only six more wraps to go. Last wrap. Warm up the champagne. Let's celebrate!

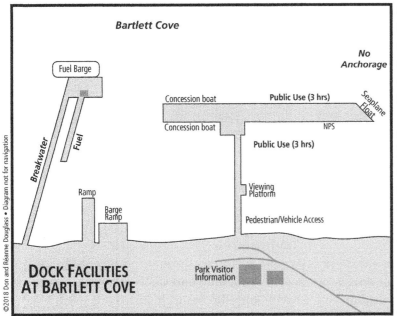

Dock Facilities at Bartlett Cove

The Beardslee Islands are a labyrinth of islands and islets connected by tiny channels with many rocks and foul bottoms. They are an exciting place to explore by kayak. This area is closed to motorized travel from May 1 to September 15, and some critical wildlife areas are permanently closed.

### Berg Bay (Glacier Bay)

Berg Bay is 8.9 miles northwest of Bartlett Cove.
Chart 17318
South entrance: 58°31.89' N, 136°07.74' W
Anchor (west arm): 58°31.08' N, 136°13.55' W
Anchor (Nifty Nook): 58°32.75' N, 136°10.25' W

Berg Bay is where John Muir first camped during his 1879 exploration of Glacier Bay. We find it interesting and well sheltered. However, entering is difficult due to rocky bars and poor charting. The bottom is generally irregular and an alert bow watch is required. The small entrance north of Netland Island is choked with kelp and has a large mid-channel rock awash on an 8-foot tide. The main entrance is south of Netland Island by way of a shallow rocky bar; this has a broken area near mid-channel that dries on about zero tide.

We suggest following an entrance track close to Netland Island and south of the rock pile; avoid detached rocks off the south coast of the island. Current can be quite strong across the bar and passage near high-water slack is recommended.

An intimate anchor site that we call "Nifty Nook" can be found behind the small unnamed island in the far northwest corner of the bay. Once you have successfully crossed the Berg Bay entrance bar, turn north to find the nook by carefully crossing a small bar with about 9 feet of water. The anchor site then opens into a very well protected hole of about five fathoms.

The main bay has a well-sheltered anchorage at its western head, with room for many boats. The two west ends of this bay are interesting to explore, as is the lagoon entered 0.5 mile south of Netland Island and southwest of Lars Island.

The entrance to the lagoon is a raging torrent on a spring tide, but entry can be made by

*Bartlett Cove's transient dock*

*The fuel dock at Bartlett Cove, as viewed looking west from the vehicle ramp*

*For those who choose to anchor at Bartlett Cove, there is an excellent dinghy dock.*

a small, shallow-draft vessel, skiff, or dinghy at high-water slack. The lagoon, which harbors extensive bird life, is a special place to investigate. Very well sheltered anchorage can be found inside it in about two fathoms. The bottom of the lagoon is very irregular and should be reconnoitered by dinghy before entry. Avoid the shallow rock pile in the center of the "fairway" just inside the entrance channel to the lagoon

Anchor in the far west corner of the main bay in 10 fathoms over sand, mud and shale with fair-to-good holding.

Anchor in Nifty Nook in about 1 to 2 fathoms over sand, mud and shale; fair-to-good holding with very limited swinging room.

### Fingers Bay—North Arm (Whidbey Passage)
Fingers Bay, on the west side of Whidbey Passage, is 12.3 miles north of Bartlett Cove and approximately 1 mile west of Willoughby Island.
Chart 17318
North entrance: 58°35.19' N, 136°11.14' W
Anchor (North Arm, South Bight): 58°34.95' N, 136°12.91' W

We have found good shelter in the South Bight of the North Arm of Fingers Bay. The entrance to both the north and south arms are shallow with an irregular bottom, so keep a sharp bow watch as you approach.

Anchor in the South Bight in 6 to 10 fathoms over sand and mud with fair-to-good holding.

### Fingers Bay—South Arm
The south arm of Fingers Bay is approximately 1 mile west of Willoughby Island.
Chart 17318
Entrance: 58°34.62' N, 136°11.02' W
Anchor (Northwest Bight): 58°34.78' N, 136°12.28' W
Anchor (Southwest Bight): 58°34.21' N, 136°12.10' W
Anchor (Southeast Bight): 58°33.66' N, 136°10.79' W

*Berg Bay Lagoon is especially attractive for its bird-watching opportunities.*

*The entrance to Berg Bay is over a shallow, rocky bar seen here at low tide.*

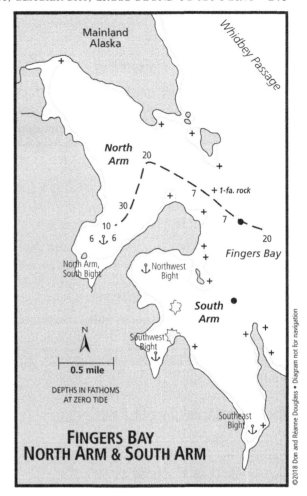

**FINGERS BAY NORTH ARM & SOUTH ARM**

The south arm of Fingers Bay, which is smaller than the north arm, has three sheltered anchor sites. Its entrance is narrow and requires careful studying of the chart to avoid the hazards. Caution: the bottom is somewhat irregular and is poorly charted.

When entering the bay, avoid the unnamed center reef awash on an 11-foot tide.

The first anchor site can be found in the Northwest Bight. The second anchor site, in Southwest Bight, has a shallow bar at its entrance and you must once again maneuver around the center reef (awash on an 11-foot tide), and avoid rocks that extend halfway out from the eastern shore. The third anchor site is found in the Southeast Bight.

Remember that to enter and exit the south arm of Fingers Bay, you must avoid the center reef and rocks.

Anchor (Northwest Bight) in 7 fathoms over a bottom of silt over gravel; fair-to-good holding.

Anchor (Southwest Bight) in 8 to 11 fathoms over an irregular bottom with silt over gravel; fair holding.

Anchor (Southeast Bight) in 10 fathoms over a bottom of silt and gravel; fair-to-good holding.

## Beartrack Cove

Beartrack Cove, on the east side of Glacier Bay, is 7.6 miles north of Bartlett Cove.
Chart 17318
Entrance: 58°37.24' N, 135°57.06' W
Anchor: 58°35.17' N, 135°52.30' W

A shallow bight one mile south of Beartrack Island affords fair anchorage, subject to northwest chop, on the south shore close to the Beardslee Islands Wilderness non-motorized area. It can be used in fair weather as a kayak home base. For better shelter, choose Beartrack Island.

## Beartrack Island
Beartrack Island is 8.6 miles north of Bartlett Cove.
Chart 17318
Anchor: 58°36.15' N, 135°52.07' W

The tiny cove on the north side of Beartrack Island provides very good shelter. Swinging room is limited so a stern-tie is recommended.

## Johnson Cove (Willoughby Island)
Johnson Cove is 11.3 miles northwest of Bartlett Cove.
Chart 17318
Entrance: 58°36.25' N, 136°06.30' W
Anchor: 58°36.35' N, 136°06.90' W

Tiny Johnson Cove can provide welcome shelter in blowing northerlies. This is a perfect lunch stop during prevailing northwest winds. It is open to southeast chop and is not recommended as an anchorage in gales. Swinging room is limited in the cove.

Anchor in 2 to 4 fathoms over sand with fair holding.

## Spokane Cove (Glacier Bay)
Spokane Cove is 14.5 miles north of Bartlett Cove.
Chart 17318
Entrance: 58°41.03' N, 135°58.42' W
Anchor: 58°41.88' N, 135°57.45' W

Spokane Cove provides fair shelter deep in the cove off the bluff on its south shore.

Anchor in about 6 fathoms over sand with fair holding.

## South Sandy Cove (Glacier Bay)
South Sandy Cove is 15.4 miles north of Bartlett Cove.
Chart 17318
Entrance: 58°42.05' N, 135°59.82' W
Anchor (west): 58°42.63' N, 135°59.76' W
Anchor (east): 58°42.49' N, 135°58.59' W

Sandy Cove is one of the more popular anchorages in Glacier Bay and offers easy access. South Sandy Cove is not as good an anchorage as North Sandy Cove, but it provides two anchor sites. Of these, the west site is usually preferred over the east site, because it is more protected from northerly chop and the bottom gives a better anchor bite. If a strong southerly is expected, North Sandy Cove provides better shelter.

The Park Service maintains a seasonal float cabin here for back country rangers who serve the more remote areas of the park. It's interesting to note that, as late as 1855, the terminus of the glacier later named after John Muir covered 15-mile-wide Glacier Bay north of Sandy Cove from east to west.

Anchor (west) in 6 fathoms over a mixed bottom of sand and mud with good holding.
Anchor (east) in 5 fathoms over a hard rocky bottom with poor-to-fair holding.

## North Sandy Cove (Glacier Bay)
North Sandy Cove is 16.2 miles north of Bartlett Cove.
Chart 17318
Entrance (west of Puffin Island): 58°43.58' N, 136°01.03' W
Entrance (east of Puffin Island): 58°44.01' N, 136°00.16' W
Anchor: 58°43.14' N, 135°59.19' W

*Cascades tumble down Shag Cove's walls.*

North Sandy Cove is our choice for easy anchoring with good protection and holding. It is safe to enter the cove from either the west or the north, and possible anchor sites are available over a relatively large area. Note that this is a noise restricted area: generators are prohibited from operating between 10 p.m. and 6 a.m. from June 1 through August 31. This is a good place to view wildlife as you relax on grassy meadows.

Anchor in 5 fathoms in the south corner, or further north in 10 fathoms over sand with good holding.

## Shag Cove (Geikie Inlet)

Shag Cove is 1 mile inside the entrance to Geikie Inlet on the south shore.
Chart 17318
Entrance: 58°39.44' N, 136°20.09' W
Anchor: 58°37.46' N, 136°18.74' W

Shag Cove is a classic U-shaped glacial valley. Polished granite walls rise 1,000 feet; numerous waterfalls tumble down these walls; small bowls that hold year-round snow nestle here and there. The water throughout the cove is turquoise blue with rock flour.

Shag Cove offers good shelter in all weather. It also provides a good home base from which you can explore wildlife and nature's

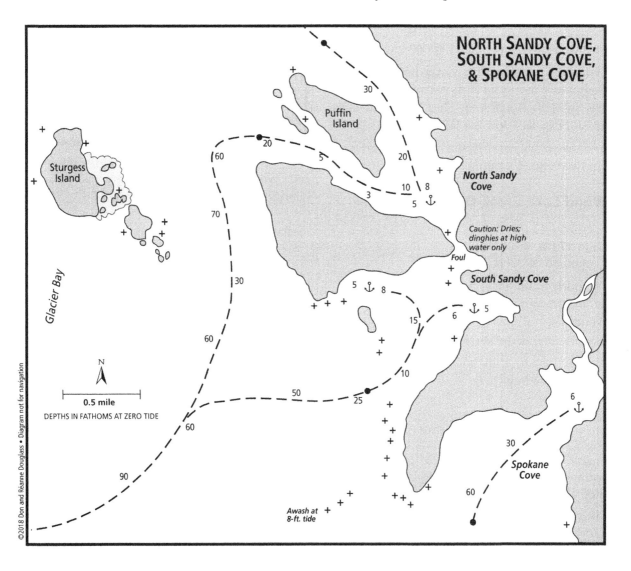

beauty away from the main route. You may spot a bear or two along the beach, flipping over rocks in search of shellfish.

Marble Mountain, on the north side of the cove, rises 3,366 feet above the water and is less than a half-mile away. This mountain has one of the sharpest vertical rock walls within the park.

Anchor near the head of the bay in about 13 fathoms where there is good, almost land-locked protection, over a bottom of a thin layer of mud over sand and gravel; good holding.

## Tyndall Cove (Geikie Inlet)
Tyndall Cove is 2 miles southwest of Shag Cove.
Chart 17318
Entrance: 58°37.65' N, 136°23.80' W
Anchor: 58°35.69' N, 136°21.52' W

Tyndall Cove, like Shag Cove, provides good shelter and more sun at its narrow head. It has less swinging room than Shag Cove and feels more intimate below the towering peaks.

Anchor in about 10 fathoms over sand and mud with good holding.

## Wood Lake Creek Outlet (Geikie Inlet)
Wood Lake Creek Outlet is 8 miles southwest of the entrance to Geike Inlet.
Chart 17318
Anchor: 58°35.32' N, 136°28.31' W

Temporary anchorage surrounded by spectacular scenery can be found off the outlet to Wood Lake. This is a good base from which to explore the nearby streams and mud flats.

Anchor in 5 to 10 fathoms over sandy gravel with fair holding.

## Muir Inlet (Glacier Bay)
Muir Inlet extends north and then west for over 24 miles from Glacier Bay.
Charts 17318
Entrance (Caroline Shoal bearing 270°T at 0.75 Nm): 58°46.45' N, 136°05.90' W

Muir Inlet has two accessible glaciers—Muir and Riggs. Although neither of these glaciers reach tidewater any more, both are worth a

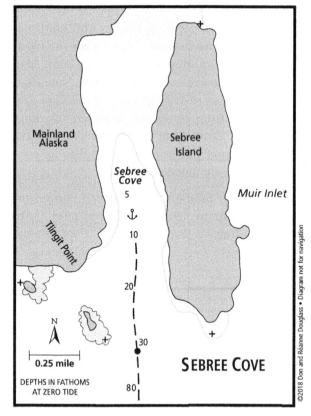

visit by kayak, or by motor vessel during periods when entry restrictions are not in force. Check the regulations when you visit.

## Sebree Cove (Muir Inlet)
Sebree Cove is 10.1 miles north of Bartlett Cove and 10 miles southeast of Blue Mouse Cove.
Chart 17318
Entrance: 58°44.79' N, 136°10.07' W
Anchor: 58°45.56' N, 136°10.20' W

Sebree Cove, located at the south end of Muir Inlet, provides excellent protection during

*Seen in Wachusett Inlet; "Hey Skipper, did you check the tide tables last night?"*

westerlies. Since it is open to the south, however, it is a fair-weather anchorage only. The wind frequently changes direction to the northeast in early morning.

Anchor in 5 fathoms over a good sand/mud bottom with fair-to-good holding.

### Adams Inlet (Muir Inlet)
Adams Inlet is 24.1 miles north of Bartlett Cove.
Chart 17318
Wilderness entrance: 58°50.70' N, 136°03.47' W

Adams Inlet, like the Beardslee Islands, cries out for exploration but it is restricted to non-motorized boats.

### Maquinna Cove (Muir Inlet)
Maquinna Cove is 25 miles north of Bartlett Cove.
Chart 17318
Position: 58°51.71' N, 136°03.34' W

Maquinna Cove is the small bight on the north side of the entrance to Adams Inlet. It is exposed to all weather and is useful only as a temporary stop in fair weather.

### Hunter Cove (Muir Inlet)
Hunter Cove is 28 miles north of Bartlett Cove.
Chart 17318
Entrance: 58°54.21' N, 136°06.96' W
Anchor: 58°54.62' N, 136°07.54' W

Hunter Cove, though exposed to the southeast, provides good downslope protection if you tuck in close to shore.

Anchor in less than 10 fathoms over sand and mud with fair holding.

### Wachusett Inlet (Muir Inlet)
Wachusett Inlet is 28 miles north of Bartlett Cove.
Chart 17318
Entrance: 58°56.54' N, 136°07.70' W

Wachusett Inlet has a stunning hanging glacier. The head of the inlet is a restricted entry area from May 16 through August 31. We have taken overnight anchorage east of the two rocks, but the sand is very thin over a hard rocky bottom with poor holding. The photo gives you an idea of tidal swing and the care needed in transiting and anchoring in Glacier Bay.

*Don't forget to scoop up some of the longest-lasting cocktail ice you'll ever get.*

### Riggs Glacier (Muir Inlet)
Riggs Glacier is 37.9 miles north of Bartlett Cove.
Chart 17318
Position: 59°04.14' N, 136°11.04' W

Riggs Glacier, which has restricted entry, is a good area to explore by kayak. We have found temporary anchorage in fair weather along the north shore off the glacier in about 10 fathoms.

### Muir Glacier (Muir Inlet)
Muir Glacier is 41 miles north of Bartlett Cove.
Chart 17318
Position: 59°05.42' N, 136°22.47' W

Muir Glaicer is a fair hike from the water.

### Hugh Miller Inlet (Glacier Bay)
Hugh Miller Inlet is one mile southwest of Blue Mouse Cove.
Chart 17318
Wilderness entrance: 58°45.18' N, 136°28.79' W

Hugh Miller Inlet is a Wilderness Area with entry restricted to non-motorized boats from

May 1 through August 31. By anchoring in Blue Mouse Cove, you can easily take a kayak or row your dinghy (with no engine attached) into the inlet.

## Blue Mouse Cove (Gilbert Peninsula)
Blue Mouse Cove is 27.3 miles northwest of Bartlett Cove.
Chart 17318
Entrance: 58°47.30' N, 136°28.95' W
Anchor (southeast): 58°46.69' N, 136°29.13' W
Anchor (southwest): 58°47.00' N, 136°30.41' W

Blue Mouse Cove is perhaps the most popular anchorage in Glacier Bay proper, due to its location as a jumping-off point for the kayak exploration of Hugh Miller Inlet. We have found holding ability to be somewhat marginal. Protection from both north and south winds is good, and there is generally little concern about drifting ice. The south side of the cove offers satisfactory anchorage. You may sight wolves and bear along shore and, occasionally, humpback whales visit the cove. The bottom is irregular with a mixture of silt, mud, gravel and rocks. This anchorage is a noise-restricted area, with generators prohibited between 10 p.m. and 6 a.m.

Anchor (southeast) in 6 to 10 fathoms over a thin layer of silt on top of a hard rocky bottom with poor-to-fair holding. Be sure to test the set of your anchor.

## Tidal Inlet (Glacier Bay)
Tidal Inlet is 3.5 miles northeast of Blue Mouse Cove.
Chart 17318
Entrance: 58°48.90' N, 136°24.37' W
Anchor: (cove northwest of entrance): 58°49.40' N, 136°26.00' W

We recommend anchoring in the small cove 1 mile northwest of the entrance to Tidal Inlet. This a fair-weather site only but with good views to the west.

Anchor in about 8 fathoms over a rocky bottom with poor-to-fair holding.

## Rendu Inlet (Glacier Bay)
Rendu Inlet is 35 miles northwest of Bartlett Cove.
Chart 17318
Wilderness Entrance: 58°53.91' N, 136°36.45' W

Rendu Inlet is a Wilderness Area restricted to non-motorized access.

## Reid Inlet (Glacier Bay)
Reid Inlet is 11 miles northwest of Blue Mouse Cove.
Chart 17318 (inset)
Entrance: 58°52.37' N, 136°48.92' W
Anchor (west): 58°51.70' N, 136°49.24' W

Reid Inlet is a good cruising boat destination because it's free of large cruise ships. The inlet is not as overwhelming as other nearby fjords, and its proximity to Johns Hopkins Inlet and the glacier in Tarr Inlet make it a convenient overnight anchorage. You can approach Reid Glacier, land a dinghy on either side, and explore the glacier's snout, which no longer reaches tidal water. Use caution if you do this, however.

The entrance to Reid Inlet is somewhat narrow and shallow, but you can usually find 3 to 6 fathoms across the bar. We have anchored overnight in the inlet when icebergs

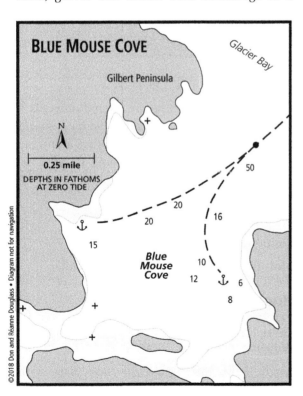

*Approaching the Reid Inlet anchorage; Reid Glacier*

have not been threatening. You can anchor on either the west or east shore, the eastern being significantly deeper. Reid Inlet is a noise-restricted area, with generators prohibited between 10 p.m. and 6 a.m.

The area near the west shore, inside the entrance, is the most commonly-used anchor site. It is also a good place to get ashore. You can walk all the way from the north point, where you can explore an old miners' site. Be aware that winds can blow off the glacier at night, making the anchor site marginal.

Anchor (west) in 3 to 10 fathoms over silt and sand with fair holding.

### Lamplugh Glacier (Johns Hopkins Inlet)
Lamplugh Glacier is 15.5 miles northwest of Blue Mouse Cove and 42.5 miles northwest of Bartlett Cove.
Chart 17318 (inset)
Position: 58°53.81' N, 136°56.29' W

Lamplugh Glacier is a tidewater glacier and a great spot for photos. It's also a good place to fill your ice chest with long-lasting glacial ice.

Kayakers frequently camp on the east side of the glacier snout.

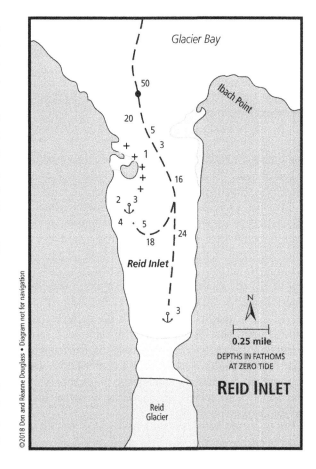

## Johns Hopkins Inlet (Glacier Bay)

Johns Hopkins Inlet is 44.7 miles northwest of Bartlett Cove.
Chart 17318 (inset)
Entrance (north of Lamplugh Glacier): 58°54.48' N, 136°55.71' W

North-facing Johns Hopkins Inlet is frequently choked with several square miles of floating ice with pack ice near its head. Entry to the inlet is prohibited due to the presence of seal pups from May 1 through June 30, with size and speed restrictions after that. It is interesting to note that Johns Hopkins Glacier extended nearly to the entrance to Reid Inlet as recently as 1892.

## Russell Island Passage (Russell Island)

Russell Island Passage is 40.3 miles northwest of Bartlett Cove.
Chart 17318 (inset)
South entrance: 58°54.59' N, 136°46.08' W
North entrance: 58°57.33' N, 136°52.00' W
Anchor: 58°55.48' N, 136°48.36' W

We delighted in watching the orcas cruise though the passage; however, our experience

---

### Reid Inlet: A Matter of Perspective.

Our first sight when we entered Reid Inlet was the wrinkled white tongue of Reid Glacier flowing down from the mountains. It dominated the view and I couldn't take my eyes off it.

We anchored *Osprey* on the west side of the inlet off a spit and prepared to go ashore. As we were putting the outboard on the dinghy, one of our two visiting crewmembers pointed to a small beige tent on the beach and laughed, "Look at that tiny tent!"

"It's probably a one-person tent," I told her.

"No, it's too small for anybody to sleep in."

Later I realized she must not have understood how far we were from shore.

As we headed up inlet, we seemed to be taking forever to get to the glacier. Was something wrong with the outboard? Finally, Steve beached the dinghy next to a pile of rocks. "It shouldn't take us long to walk from here."

We had been hiking for about 15 minutes when I suspected that we were not as close to the glacier as we had supposed. Piles of gravel became mounds of rocks. There was nothing that our eyes could use to set a scale: no trees, no houses; only rocks and ice that could be any size at all, and invariably turned out to be bigger than we first thought.

Finally, we reached the face of the glacier. An irregular wall cut by blue ice caves and white battlements confronted us. The glacier's size astounded me: much larger than I had guessed when looking at it from the boat. We touched the cold blue ice and listened to the sounds of the glacier creaking and cracking. Finally, we turned and headed back to the dinghy.

A trip to Glacier Bay has been described as "traveling back in time," meaning the closer you are to a retreating glacier, the newer the land is. We're talking not of geological time measured in eons or human time measured in generations, but botanical time measured in species established and plant sizes attained.

An 1892 map of this area shows solid ice where Reid Inlet is today. Photos from the 1940s show the glacier's snout just off the spit—roughly where we had anchored.

As the others walked along the water's edge, I moved inland, still keeping parallel to shore. Close to the glacier, the gravel was bare, but farther on I saw yellow lichens clinging to rocks, then the first green plants—small pink fireweed scattered in barren glacial soil. Still farther, green mats of Dryas plants spread across the gravel, their size and number increasing with the distance from the glacier.

When a glacier retreats, it leaves barren rock scoured of soil and piles of gravel that lack nutrients. As wind or animals carry in seeds, plants recolonize the land in successive stages, each one preparing habitat for the next. Lichens come first, anchoring themselves on the rocks. As they grow, lichens secrete acids that break up the rocks and create soil for the next settlers: fireweed, Dryas, moss and rush. Willows and alder follow a couple of decades later. Alders stabilize the soil, pulling nitrogen from the air. When alder thickets become so dense their own progeny can't survive, young spruce trees crowd in. We saw alder and willow near the entrance to the inlet where we had anchored *Osprey*.

When we got back to the dinghy, I looked at the sparse vegetation on the land above it and realized we had about 60 years to travel to get back to *Osprey*.

Adapted from *Glaciers, Bears and Totems: Sailing in Search of the Real Southeast Alaska* by Elsie Hulsizer. Harbour Publishing, 2010.

*Wandering among the ice boulders at Reid Glacier*

*Lamplugh Glacier*

anchoring at the north corner of Russell Island was somewhat marginal. Our friend, Rod Nash, found a more secure anchorage just west of the small islets on the northeast-central part of Russell Island, as indicated in the diagram. This is one of the better up-bay anchorages, but it is a whale-restricted area.

Anchor in 6 to 10 fathoms over sand and mud with fair holding.

**Tarr Inlet** (Glacier Bay)
Tarr Inlet is 43 miles northwest of Bartlett Cove.
Chart 17318 (inset)
Entrance (Russell Island bearing 090°T at 1.0 Nm): 58°56.33' N, 136°53.62' W
Anchor (cove): 59°01.04' N, 137°01.78' W

The cove in Tarr Inlet provides temporary anchorage with shelter from southerly winds. It is exposed to ice calving from the nearby glaciers and you must guard against moving icebergs at all times. The cove is also used by kayak mother-ships that can generate uncomfortable wakes for small craft.

Anchor in 5 to 10 fathoms over silt with fair holding.

**Margerie Glacier**
(Tarr Inlet)
Margerie Glacier is 23 miles northwest of Blue Mouse Cove and 50.5 miles northwest of Bartlett Cove.
Chart 17318 (inset)
Position: 59°02.48' N, 137°03.54' W

Margerie Glacier offers the quintessential tidewater glacier experience. 200-foot-high cliffs of ice calve into the deep bay, creating large waves that may pose danger for small craft. To prevent prop damage, watch out for the build-up of ice as the wind changes direction.

This is one of two destination glaciers for many large cruise ships in Glacier Bay. (The other is Grand Pacific Glacier.) Be alert for traffic.

**Grand Pacific Glacier** (Tarr Inlet)
Grand Pacific Glacier is 24 miles northwest of Blue Mouse Cove and 51.1 miles northwest of Bartlett Cove.
Chart 17318 (inset)
Position: 59°03.32' N, 137°03.33' W

Grand Pacific Glacier is at the far north end of Glacier Bay, at the head of Tarr Inlet. It is a wall of ice a mile and a half wide and has its source deep in the Saint Elias Mountains. It is difficult to approach the snout of the Grand

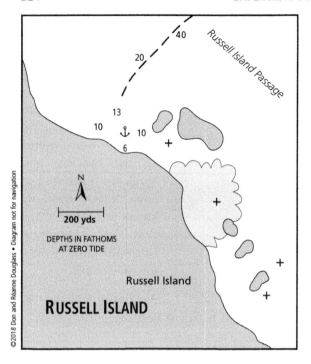

Pacific because the inlet is so chock-full of ice; careful navigation is necessary to prevent prop damage. Watch out for the build-up of ice as the wind changes direction, and stay well clear of cruise ships whose turning radius may be greater than you imagine.

## Lemesurier Island—East Coast
(Icy Strait)

Lemesurier Island is in the middle of Icy Strait, 4 miles east of the Inian Islands and 5 miles southwest of the entrance to Glacier Bay.

**Chart 17302**
**Anchor: 58°17.51′ N, 136°01.52′ W**

Fair anchorage can be found on the east side of Lemesurier Island over a large, shallow area sheltered from west wind and chop, although ebb current may be very strong. This is the closest place to anchor temporarily when you are waiting for clearance to enter Glacier

*Margerie Glacier—the sounds of cracking ice combined with its stunning beauty make this a favorite for many cruisers.*

Bay. We have sighted as many whales around this island as inside the park.

Anchor in 7 fathoms over sand with fair holding.

## Willoughby Cove and Jacks Cove (Lemesurier Island)

Willoughby Cove is on the southeast side of Lemesurier Island.
Chart 17302
Position: 58°16.03' N, 136°03.60' W

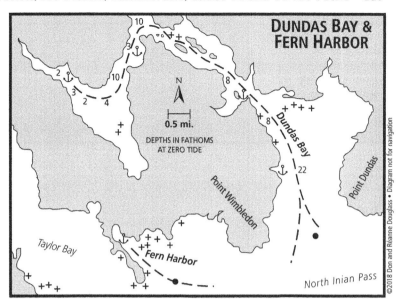

The bight east of Iceberg Point on Lemesurier Island is known as both Willoughby Cove and Jacks Cove. It provides temporary anchorage over a sand and pebble bottom in 5 to 10 fathoms. Avoid the rocks along the shore.

## Mud Bay (Chichagof Island)

Mud Bay, on the southeast side of South Passage, is 10 miles south of the entrance to Glacier Bay.
Chart 17302
Entrance: 58°13.64' N, 135°59.95' W
Anchor: 58°12.09' N, 135°59.40' W

Mud Bay is a large open roadstead filled with mud along its shore. It is somewhat sheltered from southerlies and has easy entry. It is a good place to wait for favorable currents in passages to the west. Mud Bay is shallow throughout; anchor in variable depths off the drying mud flats.

Anchor temporarily in about 6 fathoms over mud with fair holding.

## Idaho Inlet (Chichagof Island)

Idaho Inlet, southeast of the Inian Islands, is 5 miles northeast of Elfin Cove.
Chart 17302
Entrance (South Inian Pass Light R"6" bear-

---

### When Big Brother Can't Do the Job
(From the First Mate's Diary)
Réanne Hemingway-Douglass

A voice came over Ch 16, low and deliberate, without identifying itself. "Does anyone know what conditions are off Yakobi Island?"

We had been trying to rouse Juneau Coast Guard ourselves to ask the same question, but there was no contact in Cross Sound.

Another voice came on: "S'posed to be winds west 26 knots."

A pause, then a third voice: "Winds southwest, 17 knots, seas 6 feet."

Ten minutes later a woman's voice announced, Okay, for those of you who haven't heard the weather, go to Channel 67. . . . Here it is. From Yakutat: winds east 20, seas 6 feet. Outlook: winds southeast 15, seas 7 feet."

The voice went off without identifying itself, without signing off, and one by one male voices came on. "Thank you . . . " "Thank you . . ." "Thank you . . ."

*Baidarka*'s first mate picked up the microphone and added a feminine thank you.

"That's Alaska for you," said the skipper. "When Big Brother can't do the job, the fishermen take care of one another."

ing 278°T at 1.5 Nm): 58°13.64' N, 136°12.73' W
Anchor (head of inlet): 58°04.86' N, 136°08.31' W

Some cruisers have reported wonderful halibut fishing in this inlet.

## Dundas Bay, Horsefly Bay and Mickey's Arm

Dundas Bay, on the northwest side of Icy Strait, is north of the Inian Islands.
Chart 17302
Entrance: 58°18.63' N, 136°19.92' W
Anchor (cannery site): 58°20.18' N, 136°21.72' W
Anchor (SE gale): 58°21.04' N, 136°29.68' W
Anchor (Horsefly Bay): 58°22.15' N, 136°23.74' W
Anchor (Mickey's Arm): 58°22.86' N, 136°32.81' W
Anchor (southwest arm): 58°23.34' N, 136°29.11' W

*Lamplugh Glacier cave spewing water and ice*

Dundas Bay lies outside the required permit area of Glacier Bay National Park. Designated as a Wilderness Area, it allows explorers to avoid the "madding crowd" of large cruise ships although smaller tour boats visit almost daily.

Exercise extreme caution when entering. The outer bay is deep, with strong currents. As you head into the west arm, west of Dun-

---

### John Muir's *Stickeen*
#### Don Douglass & Réanne Hemingway-Douglass

In the summer of 1880, John Muir set out from Fort Wrangell in a canoe to continue his exploration of Southeast Alaska. He was joined by a native American crew and by his friend and companion, the Reverend S.H. Young with his little black mongrel, Stickeen. Although Muir had tried to dissuade his friend from taking the dog, Stickeen soon became a fixture of the group, taking part not only in the exploration, but in the hunting as well.

Near the head of Taylor Bay at the foot of Brady Glacier, the group made camp in a grove of spruce. The next morning, in a raging storm, Muir set off from camp. "I made haste to join [the storm]; for many of Nature's finest lessons are to be found in her storms, and if careful to keep in right relations with them, we may go safely abroad with them, rejoicing in the grandeur and beauty of their works and ways . . . "

Mr. Young and the crew were still asleep, but not Stickeen who, despite numerous scoldings from Muir, refused to return to camp.

". . . The pitiful little wanderer just stood there in the wind, drenched and blinking, saying doggedly, 'Where thou goest I will go.' So at last I told him to come on if he must, and gave him a piece of the bread I had in my pocket; then we struggled on together, and thus began the most memorable of all my wild days."

For the full and humorous story, see *Stickeen,* by John Muir, first published in 1897. [Quotes are taken from the Heyday Books illustrated edition, ISBN 9780930588489.]

das River, keep a mid-channel course, favoring the south shore. Temporary anchorage can be found in the drying bight on the south shore, south of the small island. (We named this site "Horsefly Bay" because of the large horseflies that appeared after the wind died down.) The entrance to this shallow cove is on the south side of the island; the areas west and north of the island are foul.

The upper part of this west arm is filled with a number of small islands and islets. The fairway lies between the two major islands, then favors the north shore until the division occurs between the northwest and southwest arms. Good anchorage, with fair protection from southeast winds, can be found in the first part of the southwest arm; favor the east shore in about 7 fathoms. Anchorage can also be found at the head of the northwest arm; avoid the dangerous mid-channel rock near the head of the arm by favoring the west shore.

Our favorite Dundas Bay anchor site lies in the far west end of the southwest arm. Once past the small islets and rocks west of the anchor site noted above, follow the north shore around the point to just below a terminal moraine from a chute of the Brady Glacier, two miles away. We call this site, "Mickey's Arm" in honor of Frenchwoman Michèle Demai, skipper of *Nuage*—a cutter-rigged, steel-hulled sailboat—who first told us about this place. (Mickey and a companion spent the winter of 1996–97 in *Nuage*, ice-bound in Gut Bay.)

We recommend anchoring off the small islet off a small bight with a drying mud flat. There is some fetch at this site in southeast

*Dundas Bay is a wonderful alternative for cruisers who do not have a park permit.*

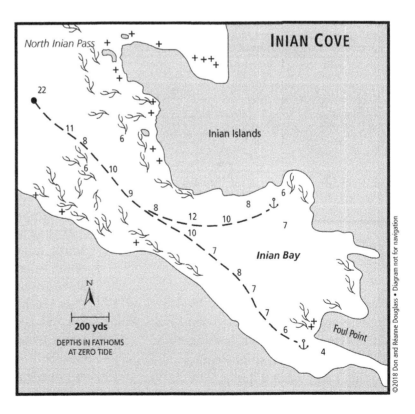

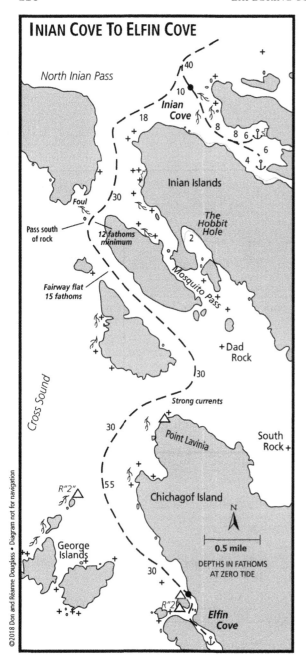

### Fern Harbor (Taylor Island)
Fern Harbor is on the east side of Taylor Island.
Chart 17302
Entrance: 58°17.36' N, 136°28.29' W
Anchor: 58°18.37' N, 136°30.16' W

Fern Harbor can be a safe haven when strong current and nasty chop occur at the east end of Icy Strait; however, in a southeast gale more shelter can be found in Inian Cove. We like Fern Harbor and so do large numbers of sea otters.

Anchor in 5 to 7 fathoms in sand, mud and silt with fair-to-good holding.

### Taylor Bay (Cross Sound)
Taylor Bay, on the northwest side of Cross Sound, is 6 miles northeast of Cape Spencer.
Chart 17302
Entrance: 58°16.45' N, 136°30.70' W

Taylor Bay lies at the base of large Brady Glacier. It is the setting for John Muir's story, *Stickeen*, which is one of our all-time read-aloud favorites.

An interesting small cove lies 0.5 mile northwest of Taylor Island; however, Taylor Bay is charted at the small scale of 1:80,000, so use caution. Fern Harbor is the best place from which to explore the area.

### North Inian Pass
North Inian Pass lies between the Inian Islands and Point Wimbledon.
Chart 17302
East entrance (Point Dundas bearing 008°T at 1.4 Nm): 58°17.56' N, 136°17.30' W
West entrance (Taylor Island bearing 311°T at 1.25 Nm): 58°16.22' N, 136°27.06' W

North Inian Pass is generally preferred over South Inian Pass. Time your passage carefully, since strong current runs through North Inian Pass, reaching 8 to 10 knots on spring ebbs, and large waves, dangerous to small craft, develop when winds oppose the currents. Inian Cove (see below) offers good, convenient shelter, out of the current, and is well protected from southeast gales.

weather; in a southeast gale, anchor southeast of the small island, in the shallow southern part of the bay to minimize fetch.

Anchor temporarily (Horsefly Bay) in 1 to 2 fathoms south of the island in sand and gravel off a drying mud flat; fair holding.

Anchor (Mickey's Arm) in 2 fathoms over sand and mud with good holding.

## Inian Islands

The Inian Islands, 4 miles north of Elfin Cove, separate Icy Strait from Cross Sound.
Chart 17302 (inset)

The Inian Islands have frequent summer fog, which can conceal the huge cruise ships that transit the area; encountering them in these conditions can be a spooky experience! Monitor your VHF for pan-pan calls, and pay attention to your AIS. The current is very strong on either side of the islands. Excellent shelter can be found in Inian Cove (see below).

## Inian Cove (Inian Islands)

Inian Cove is 4 miles north of Elfin Cove.
Chart 17302 (inset)
Entrance: 58°16.15' N, 136°21.01' W
Anchor (southeast): 58°15.50' N, 136°19.64' W
Anchor (northeast): 58°15.89' N, 136°19.80' W

Deep within Inian Cove, cruising boats can find excellent shelter in two places, as indicated on the diagram. Extensive kelp patches at the entrance reduce summer chop and swell to a minor surge; entering does not present a problem as long as you avoid these kelp patches. Depths are moderate, but the bottom is irregular. Be alert for uncharted rocks in the area.

Anchor (southeast) in 4 to 6 fathoms over sand, mud, pebbles and some kelp, with very good holding.

Anchor (northeast) in 6 to 8 fathoms over mud and pebbles with good holding.

## Earl Cove (Inian Islands)

Earl Cove is 1 mile southeast of Inian Cove.
Chart 17302
Entrance: 58°15.34' N, 136°17.25' W
Anchor: 58°15.44' N, 136°18.13' W

*Elfin Cove's transient dock (at right)*

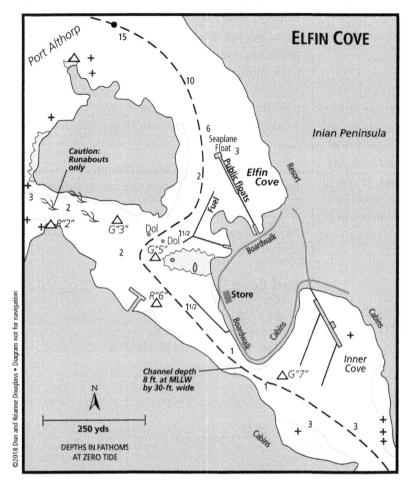

Ice in Earl Cove is not generally a problem in summer. The cove offers good shelter from northwest winds and current.

Anchor in about 4 fathoms at the head of the cove over mud with fair holding.

## South Inian Pass

South Inian Pass, south of the Inian Islands, connects Cross Sound and Icy Strait.
Chart 17302
East entrance (Idaho Inlet Light bearing 180°T at 0.5 Nm): 58°14.38' N, 136°15.45' W
West entrance (Point Lavinia Light bearing 112°T at 0.5 Nm): 58°13.48' N, 136°22.16' W

South Inian Pass has strong currents with dangerous turbulence, especially during spring tide and gale winds. Both North and South Inian Pass are very picturesque, with a steep-sided, ironbound coast that houses many sea caves.

Note that the tide in South Inian Pass turns to ebb about 1.5 hours before the tide table.

## Cross Sound

Cross Sound, southwest of the Inian Islands, separates Chichagof and Yakobi islands from the mainland.
Charts 17302, 17301, 17300
West entrance (Cape Spencer Light bearing 000°T at 3.8 Nm): 58°08.11' N, 136°38.48' W

During summer, southwest swells in Cross Sound can heap up to dangerous proportions when strong ebbs meet

*The inner cove at Elfin Cove*

## Elfin Cove (Chichagof Island)

Elfin Cove is east of the George Islands at the entrance of Port Althorp.
Chart 17302 (inset)
Entrance (entrance light bearing 200°T at 0.75 Nm): 58°11.88' N, 136°21.03' W
Fuel float: 58°11.71' N, 136°20.85' W

Elfin Cove is a quaint community perched along the sides of the harbor, and a favorite stop among cruising boaters. A 200-foot-long float in the outer harbor has limited space for transient vessels with moorage on either side of the float. The fuel dock, south of the float, sells gasoline, diesel and propane (907.239.2208; monitors VHF Ch 16). Drinking water is available at the fuel dock and the inner harbor floats.

*Elfin Cove*

A boardwalk that begins at the head of the transient dock and encircles the community (see diagram) leads to the village where seasonal businesses include a general store, laundromat and showers, postal service, and café. Weak cell signal may be found on the south side of the boardwalk facing Mt. Althorp.

## Elfin Cove
### Linda Lewis—Journal Notes—M/V *Royal Sounder*

So often when you have heard about a place for years it can be less than you expected once you arrive. Not so Elfin Cove. It is enchanting. What is it about a tiny, wandering-fairways, many-coves place that I find so endearing? I wonder if it is about being womb-snug in full beauty.

This is a place of meandering boardwalks going in multiple directions, lined by homes, a few shops and friendly people. A bird is scolding in my ear as I sit here writing this, kids across the water play and splash. This is a rare chance among our stops to walk and walk and walk. This tiny village nearly sings out the attention and love and care it has been given. The word "charming" really means something when you gaze around in Elfin Cove.

*A wooden sentry along the boardwalk at Elfin Cove*

*Elfin Cove's boardwalk magic*

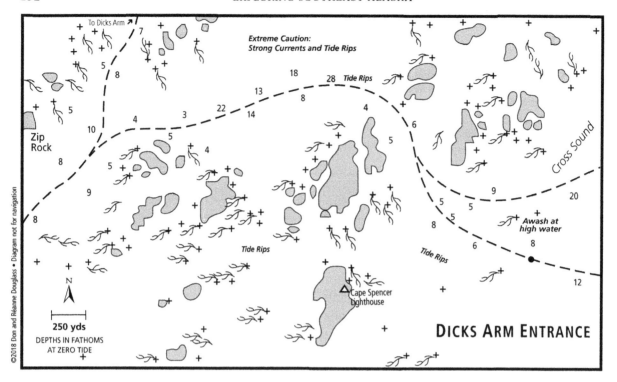

The inner cove (south) is reached by a narrow passage; the fairway at low tide has a maximum width of about 30 feet and a minimum depth of about 8 feet. The two floats in the inner cove are used mainly by locals. Under-powered boats should enter the south cove on a flood and exit on an ebb. A tidal grid is located in the inner cove. In the past, cruis-

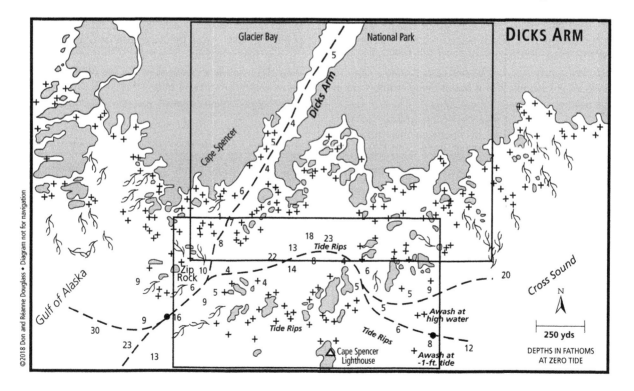

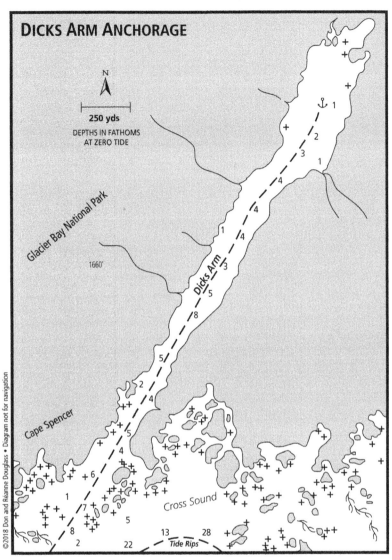

Granite Cove is used by fishermen wanting convenient shelter during fair weather.

## Port Althorp (Chichagof Island)
Port Althorp, on the southeast side of Cross Sound, lies between Point Lucan and Point Lavinia.
Chart 17302
Entrance (Althorp Rock Light bearing 175°T at 0.75 Nm): 58°10.70' N, 136°21.69' W
Entrance (cove): 58°08.68' N, 136°17.58' W
Anchor: 58°06.27' N, 136°17.00' W

Port Althorp Cove is 2.5 miles southeast of Althorp Rock. It is a tiny, landlocked cove suitable for shallow-draft small craft. Good shelter can also be found at the southern end of Port Althorp.

Anchor in 5 fathoms over soft mud with good holding.

## Cape Spencer
Cape Spencer Light, the northwest entrance point to Cross Sound, is 9.3 miles west of Elfin Cove.
Charts 17301, 17302
Cape Spencer Light position: 58°11.94' N, 136°38.43' W

Cape Spencer marks the passage from the sheltered inside waters to the open Pacific Ocean and Gulf of Alaska. Glacier Bay National Park extends 55 miles to the northwest, past Lituya Bay and Cape Fairweather to Dry Bay. Good shelter for small craft can be found in Dicks Arm.

ing vessels have entered and anchored in the inner cove, however locals prefer that visitors do not do this.

From Elfin Cove to Lisianski Inlet, high cliffs with crevices and craggy towers line the way. Along the waterline, there are wind-sculpted caves.

## Granite Cove (George Island)
Granite Cove, on the south side of George Island, is 1.4 miles west of Elfin Cove.
Chart 17302
Position: 58°11.74' N, 136°23.61' W

## Dicks Arm (Cross Sound)
Dicks Arm anchor site is 2.3 miles north of Cape Spencer Light.
Charts 17301, 17302
Main entrance: 58°12.04' N, 136°40.04' W
Alternative entrance (east of Cape Spencer Light: 58°12.01' N, 136°37.42' W
Anchor: 58°14.04' N, 136°37.36' W

*Feast on the magnitude of the landscape in Icy Strait.*

Dicks Arm provides good shelter for small craft when the Sound is heaping up off Cape Spencer. The entrance to the inlet, which is somewhat daunting, requires careful piloting. It is essential to give this place a wide berth in stormy weather. The numerous rocks off the entrance give remarkable protection to the narrow inlet, and the head of the arm is snug and quiet.

## Graves Harbor

Graves Harbor, entered between Graves Rocks and Libby Island Light, is 5 miles northwest of Cape Spencer.
Charts 17301, 17302
Entrance: 58°15.52' N, 136°46.50' W
Anchor (south arm): 58°16.60' N, 136°41.24' W

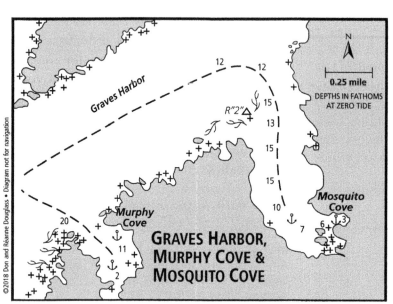

Protected anchorage can be found at the head of Graves

Harbor. However, for a more intimate setting, you might want to anchor in what is known locally as Mosquito Cove, in the southeast corner of the south arm of the harbor. From Graves Rocks you can begin to see the edge of La Pérouse Glacier behind Icy Point.

Graves Rocks are a major haul-out spot for sea lions; please don't disturb them. You can transit inside Graves Rocks with a minimum of 8 fathoms in the fairway.

Anchor (south arm) in 7 to 12 fathoms over mud with good holding; good swinging room.

## Murphy Cove (Graves Harbor)
Murphy Cove is on the southeast side of Graves Harbor, about 1.7 miles above Graves Rocks.
Charts 17301, 17302
Entrance: 58°16.55' N, 136°43.57' W
Anchor: 58°16.27' N, 136°43.11' W

Murphy Cove, inside Graves Harbor, is a popular anchorage for fishing boats and boats heading north. The site provides fairly comfortable anchorage in stable weather and is a good place to watch the weather of the outer waters. For a landlocked anchorage during stormy weather, Mosquito Cove at the southeast head of Graves Harbor offers bombproof protection; however, weather conditions in

*Natural arch at Boussole Bay*

the Gulf cannot be determined from this site.

Anchor (off the lagoon entrance) in 4 to 6 fathoms over sand and mud with good holding.

## Mosquito Cove (Graves Harbor)
Mosquito Cove is at the southeast corner of the south arm of Graves Harbor.
Chart 17301
Anchor: 58°16.53' N, 136°40.63' W

Mosquito Cove is a wonderful land-locked cove, but, yes, it has mosquitoes. However, for such shelter and stillness so close to the Gulf of Alaska, these are a small price to pay. You can find steep-to anchorage northwest of the islets, or in the cove south of the islets in shallower water. Swinging room is limited at both sites.

Anchor in 3 fathoms over brown mud and shells with good holding.

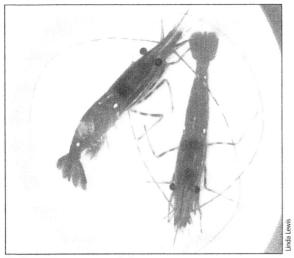

*Delicate creatures of the sea*

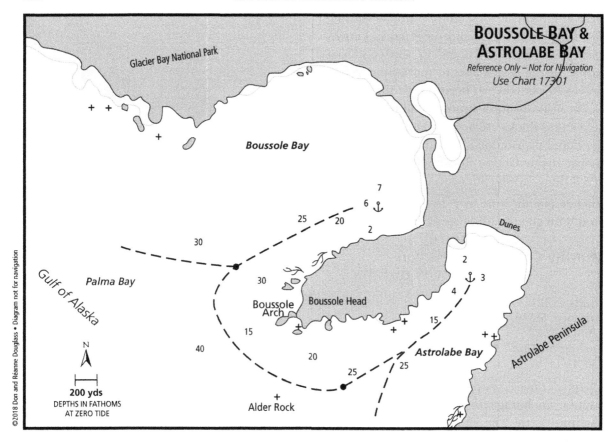

## Torch Bay
Torch Bay is 7 miles northwest of Cape Spencer.
Chart 17301
Entrance (Venisa Point bearing 112°T at 0.7 Nm): 58°17.89' N, 136°48.88' W
Anchor (east cove): 58°19.37' N, 136°46.50' W

When you approach Torch Bay, avoid the outlying shoals. Reasonable shelter can be found in the small cove on the east shore near the head of the bay. The bottom of the cove is somewhat irregular, indicating many rocks, so be careful to check the set of your anchor. This bay is a favorite of sea otters.

Anchor (east cove) in 4 to 6 fathoms over a hard bottom with poor-to-fair holding.

## Dixon Harbor, Hankinson Cove
Dixon Harbor, 11 miles northwest of Cape Spencer, is entered between Sugarloaf Island and Astrolabe Point.
Chart 17301
Entrance: 58°19.52' N, 136°53.37' W
Anchor: 58°19.91' N, 136°50.90' W

Dixon Harbor, the large bay 1.1 miles northeast of Sugarloaf Island, is wide and deep, with turquoise water originating from Brady Glacier.

On the south side of Dixon Harbor, there is a small cove inside a hook on the southwest side of Hankinson Peninsula. We call this site "Hankinson Cove" and have found it to provide good anchorage in stable weather. Depths along a mainly flat bottom range from 6 to 10 fathoms, making anchoring reasonable. The cove is surrounded by granite formations striated throughout with white. There is a small but rocky landing beach at the head of the cove. Logs along shore indicate that winter storms curve around into the bay at this site, but during stable summer weather the cove offers very good protection from the southwest to the southeast and fair-to-good from prevailing northwesterlies; no swell is felt in these conditions.

*Jim Kyle measures the 6'4" Bob Duke who is hugging his prize halibut, caught in Lituya Bay.*

Several dangerous rocks lie along the east side of the cove. Stay mid-channel as you choose your anchor site.

Anchor in 5 to 10 fathoms over sand, rocks and kelp; fair-to-good holding.

### Palma Bay
Palma Bay, between Astrolabe and Icy points, is 16 miles northwest of Cape Spencer.
Chart 17301
Entrance: 58°22.01' N, 136°59.59' W
Anchor (off Kaknau Creek 1.0 mile northeast of Icy Point): 58°23.73' N, 137°04.21' W

Palma Bay is a large, open bay with a lovely 3-mile-long sandy shore that looks inviting until you see the huge swells breaking heavily onto the beach. The wreckage of several fishing boats can be seen along the beach, a further sign of its exposure. Boussole and Astrolabe bays are moderately more sheltered in fair weather. Some temporary protection from westerlies can be found off Kaknau Creek 1.0 mile northeast of Icy Point. Avoid the rocks 200 yards or more from the west shore.

Anchor (Kaknau Creek) in 6 to 10 fathoms over sand with fair holding.

### Boussole Bay (Palma Bay)
Boussole Head is in the east part of Palma Bay, between Astrolabe and Boussole bays.
Chart 17301
Entrance: 58°23.12' N, 136°56.21' W
Anchor (Boussole Head): 58°23.30' N, 136°54.89' W

Boussole Head is remarkable for its magnificent arch, which was remarked upon by French explorer La Pérouse when he explored this coast in the late 1700s. Both Boussole and Astrolabe bays were later named for La Pérouse's two ships.

Temporary anchorage can be found along Boussole Head in fair weather.

Anchor in 8 fathoms over sand with fair holding.

## Astrolabe Bay (Palma Bay)
Astrolabe Bay is southeast of Boussole Head.
**Chart** 17301
**Entrance** (Alder Rock bearing 292°T at 0.38 Nm): 58°22.26' N, 136°55.15' W
**Anchor** (bay): 58°22.97' N, 136°54.08' W

Astrolabe Bay is ringed by grassy dunes above a light sandy beach, giving it the appearance of a well-manicured golf course. In good weather, it's fairly easy to land a dinghy at the northwestern end of the beach and, from there, hike to the dunes and a lagoon in Boussole Bay, 0.25 mile to the north. Be aware, though, that this is bear country and use caution when you go ashore. Remember to leave a responsible crew member aboard while a shore party goes exploring. It's a good idea always to carry a hand-held VHF with you in this territory.

Astrolabe Bay is a fair-weather anchorage only, and even in good weather swells may enter, causing uncomfortable rolling at night. During heavy southwesterly weather, swells create a dangerous lee shore.

Anchor in 3 fathoms over sand with fair-to-good holding.

## LA PÉROUSE

Despite its remoteness from anywhere civilized, late-eighteenth-century Alaska was a remarkably cosmopolitan place. Maritime explorers from Russia, Spain, Britain, and France all visited parts of the region in support of territorial claims made by their home countries, to investigate economic and settlement opportunities, and on voyages of scientific discovery. The French were represented by Jean François de Galaup, a heroic naval officer better known to history by his title, Comte de La Pérouse (1741-1788?).

A graduate of the naval college in Brest, La Pérouse rose through the ranks aboard French warships, distinguishing himself in several battles against the Royal Navy off the American coast and in the Caribbean. In 1782, he famously captured two English forts on Hudson Bay, allowing the survivors to sail to England on the promise that French prisoners would be released in return. In 1785, La Pérouse was appointed by the naval secretary to Louis XVI to lead a round-the-world scientific expedition. With two ships, *L'Astrolabe* and *La Boussole*, the expedition's aims were to add to the explorations and charts of the Pacific made by Captain Cook; develop maritime routes and colonization and trading opportunities; and add to the French store of scientific knowledge. Ten scientists were among the 220-men who set forth.

After rounding Cape Horn, calling into the Spanish colony in Chile, and visiting Easter Island and Hawaii, the expedition arrived in Alaska, landing near Mount St. Elias in June 1786. On 13 July, 21 men were lost in longboats as they attempted to cross the bar of Port de Français—now known as Lituya Bay. Though hampered by fog, La Pérouse pressed on after this tragedy to fill in some of the missing parts of Cook's charts of the Alaska and Pacific Northwest coasts, before heading south for Spanish *Las Californias* (California), then west across the Pacific to the coasts of NW Asia and Kamchatka.

In late 1787 and early 1788, the two ships were in the Southwestern Pacific, visiting Samoa, Tonga (where 12 men were killed by islanders), and SE Australia, where they spent six weeks at the fledgling British convict colony at Botany Bay. La Pérouse arranged with the British to have his charts and journals sent home to France, then set forth to conduct further explorations in the South Pacific before the expedition's proposed return to France in mid-1789. However, neither La Pérouse nor any of his men were ever seen again. Wreckage first found in 1826 off coral reefs in the Solomon Islands was confirmed in 2005 to have come from *La Boussole*. Crews of both ships are presumed to have been massacred by local islanders. A few survivors were said to have built a boat from the wreckage of *L'Astrolabe*, but they disappeared without trace. La Pérouse's journals were published in Paris in 1797 as *Voyage de La Pérouse*.

The names of La Pérouse Glacier, Boussole Head, and Astrolabe Bay, all south of Lituya Bay, are present-day memorials to his expedition.

—AC

*Most cruisers use electronic charting these days, but don't forget to always have your paper charts out and open—ready for the day's travel.*

## Icy Point

Icy Point, on the west side of Palma Bay, is 17 miles northwest of Cape Spencer.
**Chart 17301**
**Position (Icy Point bearing 052°T at 0.5 mile):**
**58°22.63' N, 137°06.26' W**

Rocks extend nearly a half-mile south from the tree line on Icy Point. Entering or exiting Palma Bay, give wide clearance to the point.

Lituya Bay, part of Glacier Bay National Park, lies 22.5 miles northwest of Icy Point.

For more information on Glacier Bay National Park north of Icy Point, including Lituya Bay, go to www.nps.gov/glba.

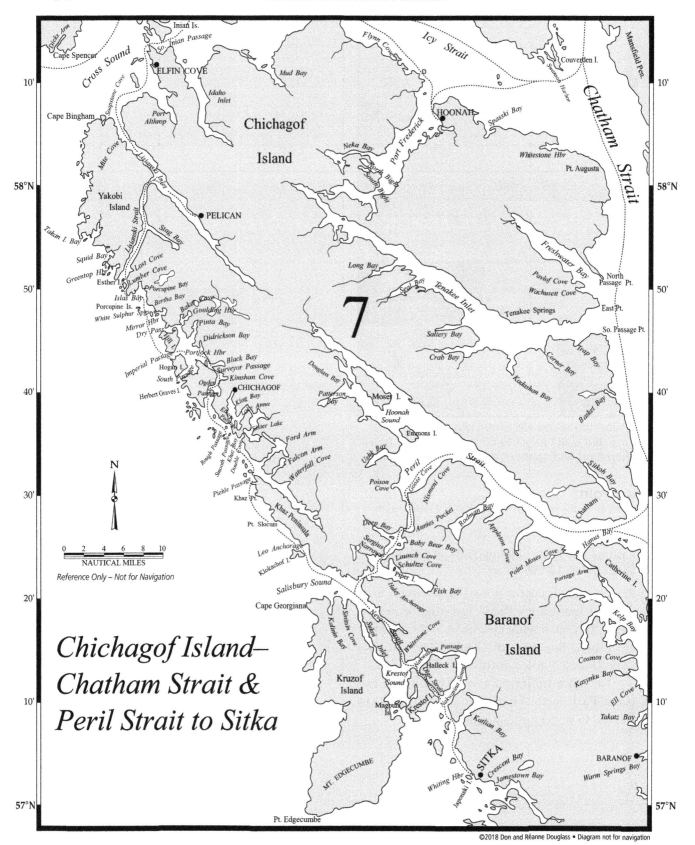

# 7

# CHICHAGOF ISLAND, CHATHAM STRAIT AND PERIL STRAIT TO SITKA

## INTRODUCTION

Chichagof Island is the "C" of the ABC islands (the others being Admiralty and Baranof). Home to the coast brown bear (grizzly), it lies south of Glacier Bay across Icy Strait. The northwestern part of Chichagof, as well as Yakobi Island and the southern part of Baranof and Pleasant, Lemesurier and Inian islands, are designated Wilderness Areas. The rugged west coasts of Chichagof and Yakobi are indented with many coves and gunkholes that show few signs of human intrusion. Except for a handful of navigation aids, a ruin here and there, and a trail and a cabin or two, the area remains unspoiled. In our experience, it offers some of the finest wilderness cruising available.

*Column Pt. at the west end of Lisianski Inlet, looking north towards the Fairweather Mountain range*

The western edge of Chichagof faces the open waters of the Gulf of Alaska. However, hundreds of small, unnamed islands, islets and rocks lie just offshore and provide semi-protected waters for boaters interested in cruising the "Outside Passage" route between Glacier Bay and Sitka. The more popular "inside" route, via Chatham and Peril Straits, is generally less exposed and requires less demanding navigation. However, the "Outer Passage," which leads south from Glacier Bay via Lisianski Inlet and Lisianski Strait to Sitka, is both shorter and more interesting. As it snakes along the west coast of Chichagof Island, this route keeps a number of islands and rocks to windward, and during fair weather the waters are reasonably smooth.

We like the Outer Passage for its scenic charm and solitude, and for its intricate passages and coves with complex entrances that challenge navigational skills. Although this route is shorter in terms of mileage than the

*Jock Sutherland and Ling Cod—an awesome pair!*

Inside Passage, it is so much more picturesque and wild that we have always found ourselves lingering, exploring the little coves and inlets along the way to Sitka. If you have large-scale charts of the area, and are in no particular hurry, consider using this Outer Passage. When the weather is fair—and when you have time to ride out any heavy weather that comes along—this is an exquisite route!

Set among countless islands on the west side of Baranof Island, Sitka—one of the jewels of Southeast Alaska—looks out toward the southern tip of Kruzof Island and the striking volcanic cone, Mt. Edgecumbe (3,271 feet). Once the proud capital of Russian Alaska, Sitka has a long and interesting history. The Russian influence is still seen in the Orthodox Church and Bishop's House, open daily for tours. Sheldon Jackson Museum houses one of the finest collections of Alaskan native art in North America. The local economy is supported by commercial fishing, sport fishing, tourism and a campus of the University of Alaska-Southeast. The town accommodates visiting yachts with extensive, newly renovated port facilities (breakwaters and floats) and a responsive staff in the harbormaster's office. Convenient air and ferry connections make it easy to arrange for pick-up of guests or crew. Full outfitting services and repair experts are available here.

Peril Strait, which separates Chichagof and Baranof islands, connects Sitka to Chatham Strait. This is the "inside" route taken by the Alaska ferry, as well as most commercial and recreational vessels. Sergius Narrows, at the west end of Peril Strait, is a narrow "rapids" that must be transited at, or near, slack water. There are several good anchor sites on either side of the narrows where vessels can wait to time the currents.

Tenakee Springs, on Chatham Strait, is a quaint settlement lining the shores of Tenakee Inlet. Its hot sulfur springs draw scores of Juneau boaters or visitors who arrive by ferry to partake of the waters, and to see a community that has remained "Alaska rustic."

*Note:* A difference in charted positions

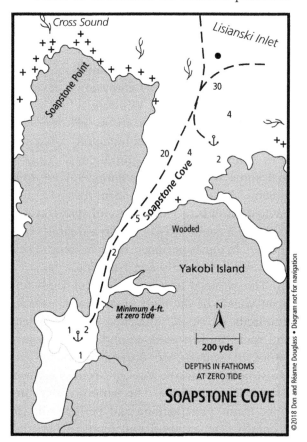

between Charts 17302 and 17303 is approximately 300 feet. Use caution in accepting waypoints along this coast, and visually check all critical positions.

### Lisianski Inlet (Chichagof Island)
Lisianski Inlet, on the northwest side of Chichagof Island and south of Cross Sound, is about 21.5 miles long.
Chart 17303 (inset)
Entrance (buoy G"1" bearing 087°T at 0.5 Nm): 58°06.91' N, 136°28.44' W

Lisianski Inlet is the north entrance to the smooth-water "outside" route to Sitka, which uses Lisianski Strait to reach the Gulf of Alaska. Both the inlet and strait were named after Russian Captain Urey Theodorovich Lisianski, who explored the area in 1804 aboard the *Neva*. The northern entrance to Lisianski Strait leads south about a third of the way down the inlet. Lisianski Inlet continues southeast to its head, beyond the village of Pelican.

### Soapstone Cove (Lisianski Inlet)
Soapstone Cove, on the west side of the entrance to Lisianski Inlet, is 7 miles southwest of Elfin Cove.
Chart 17303
Entrance: 58°06.27' N, 136°29.21' W
Anchor (outside): 58°06.14' N, 136°29.14' W
Anchor (inside): 58°05.65' N, 136°29.84' W

Small boats of 40 feet or less can pass in or out of the inner part of Soapstone Cove at half-tide or more, with a minimum depth of 4 feet at zero tide. Be careful to avoid a rock near the center of the narrow channel. Look for brown bear along the shore.

During World War II, this cove was the site of a secret naval operation. A piling located on the west side of the entrance to the inner cove and a bomb-shelter serve as reminders of that era.

Anchor in a 1½-fathom hole on the east side of the inner cove over mud with good holding.

### Mite Cove (Lisianski Inlet)
Mite Cove, 2.5 miles inside the entrance to Lisianski Inlet, is 8 miles south of Elfin Cove.
Charts 17303, 17302 (inset)
Entrance: 58°04.39' N, 136°26.21' W
Anchor: 58°04.09' N, 136°26.55' W

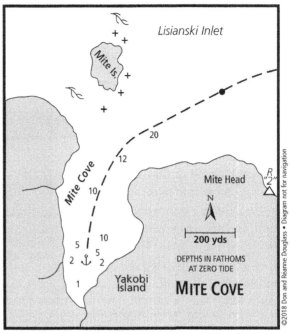

Mite Cove offers protection from most winds for several boats over a flat bottom. Old-growth trees line the shore, and there is a gravel beach near a stream at the head of the cove where you can land a dinghy. Newspaper kelp along the bottom of the cove may make setting your anchor a little difficult. If you have trouble, pull up your anchor, remove the kelp, and try again. Once your anchor is set, it should hold well.

Anchor in 6 fathoms over gravel and kelp with poor holding unless your anchor is well set.

### Pelican (Lisianski Inlet)
Pelican is 15 miles south of Elfin Cove.
Chart 17303 (inset)
Entrance: 57°57.51' N, 136°14.05' W
Float: 57°57.55' N, 136°13.70' W

Located midway down Lisianski Inlet's east shore, Pelican profits from a beautiful setting. To the west, across the inlet, precipitous, snow-covered peaks discharge melting snow that cascades down granite flanks into the inlet across from the boardwalk village.

Pelican Harbor has undergone many upgrades and improvements in the last ten years and Pelican has become a cruising destination not only for boaters from Juneau and Sitka but for "outsiders" as well. Village activities include a Chinook Salmon Derby in early June and a Fourth of July parade and fireworks show. The village of Pelican encourages tourism, although in a small way. There are no corporate lodge operations, or cruise ship calls.

The harbormaster's office does a masterful job of finding space for visiting boats and making everyone feel welcome. The town's floats have room for cruising vessels along with local fishing vessels. There are two tidal grids on the north side of the harbor gangway and another at the south side of the harbor. The town has only one authorized motor vehicle—the garbage truck. Quads are the only other motorized vehicles permitted along the boardwalk.

Businesses geared to tourism include the Highliner Lodge at the top of the harbor gangway, which has showers, laundry, liquor store, the latest in fish-cleaning and freezing facilities, B & B accommodations, Internet access and custom fishing packages. Lisianski Inlet Café is well-known for great breakfasts and fish and chips lunches.

A library where you can get Internet access, a post office, pay telephones (above the docks and at the post office) and two cafés—that include the infamous Rosie's Bar—round out the town's other amenities. For a fee of around $50, large grocery orders can be shipped by floatplane from Costco in Juneau. (There is almost daily service by floatplane.)

Kayaking along the inlet from Pelican is pleasant and there are several short hikes along the shore. Bear share Lisianski Inlet with people here, as well as in many other areas of Chichagof Island, so be cautious if you wander!

*Low tide in Pelican*

*Approaching the harbor at Pelican*

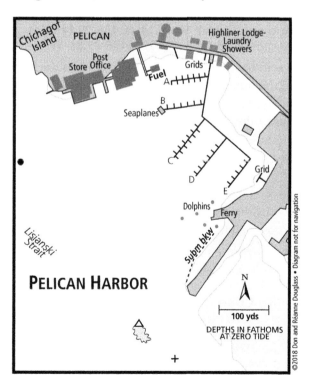

The harbormaster monitors VHF Ch 16 and 09. During busy summer holidays, it's best to call ahead to inquire about space at the floats. City Office (907.735.2202).

## Lisianski Strait

Lisianski Strait, 4.5 miles northwest of Pelican, connects Lisianski Inlet with the Gulf of Alaska.
Chart 17303
North entrance (Rock Point Light bearing 238°T at 0.3 Nm): 58°00.31' N, 136°20.74' W
South entrance (bell buoy GR bearing 306°T at 0.38 Nm): 57°49.56' N, 136°27.54' W

Lisianski Strait marks the entrance to West Chichagof-Yakobi Wilderness area. The area from Soapstone Cove on the north end of Yakobi Island to Sergius Narrows in Peril Strait is dedicated wilderness supervised by the Sitka Ranger District of the Tongass National Forest (907.747.6671). This wilderness has some of the most spectacular terrain and rainforest of the Inside Passage, with little evidence of human visitation. Hazards to navigation are poorly marked, and general nav-aids are few and far between.

Lisianski Strait's south entrance and the west coast of Yakobi Island have countless islets, rocks and reefs up to a mile or more offshore. Navigation in this area is recommended only in fair weather with good visibility.

Except for a small shoal northwest of the entrance to Stag Bay, Lisianski Strait is deep.

*Pelican is an all-boardwalk town; this is "Main Street."*

*This is the only form of motorized-transportation allowed on the boardwalk.*

### WHO WAS LISIANSKI?

Lisianski Strait and Lisiankski Inlet, on Chichagof Island, are named after Yuri Fyodorovich Lisianski (1773-1837), a Ukrainian-born naval officer and explorer. He trained as a Russian naval cadet and served in the Russo-Swedish War of 1788-90 and in Russia's post-war Baltic fleet, before sailing aboard a series of British ships. From 1803-06, Lisianski commanded the Russian-American Company merchant ship *Neva*, which took a decisive part in the 1804 Battle of Sitka, against Tlingit natives. He sailed extensively within the greater Pacific Ocean, visiting Easter Island and Hawaii, and was decorated by the Tsarist Russian government for his achievements.

—AC

In fair weather, some local boats avoid the chop off the strait's south entrance and most of the swell from the Gulf of Alaska by taking what is called the "Inside Passage" east of Esther Island and Urey and Threenob Rocks. This is a challenging route, and assistance will be difficult to obtain should you need help.

**Stag Bay** (Lisianski Strait)
Stag Bay, on the east side of Lisianski Strait, is 4 miles southwest of Pelican.
Chart 17303
Entrance: 57°55.76' N, 136°21.56' W

Stag Bay is steep-sided and picturesque with snow patches on its sides. A triangular island sits as a sentinel on the east side of the en-

## BERING AND CHIRIKOV

Among the great maritime explorers of Southeast Alaska, the name of George Vancouver generally looms largest (see sidebar: George Vancouver, Chapter 3). However, the region was first explored some fifty years earlier by a pair of intrepid Russians naval officers, Vitus Bering and Aleksei Chirikov. These two men and their crews set out in June 1741 from Petropavlovsk, on the Siberian peninsula of Kamchatka, in twin ships, the *St. Peter* and the *St. Paul*, to became the first Europeans to reach the northwest coast of North America.

Bering was a Danish-born officer in the Russian navy who led two expeditions from Kamchatka to explore the northeast coast of Asia and the west coast of North America. Chirikov was his deputy in both instances, and though his name has been less favored by map-makers, his achievements as an explorer and cartographer were at least as great as those of his boss.

The First Kamchatka expedition was conceived of by Tsar Peter the Great to determine whether the Asian reaches of the Russian empire were joined by land to America. This was of scientific as well as economic and political interest, and a great deal of Russian money was expended to determine the answer. Several early expeditions failed, but in 1728 Bering and Chirikov successfully sailed north from Kamchatka through what is now the Bering Strait. They ventured as far as 67°N, by which point the Russian coast receded away to the west. No land was sighted to the east due to adverse weather, but Bering was satisfied that Asia and North America were separated by open water. This conclusion was debated back in St. Petersburg however, and a second Kamchatka expedition was undertaken to fully settle the matter. This became known afterwards as the Great Northern Expedition, with Bering once again in command.

On June 20, 1741, six days out of Petropavlovsk, Bering and Chirikov lost sight of one another's ships in a storm. Each continued to sail east, but they never met up again. On July 16, Bering, aboard the *St. Peter*, sighted Mount St Elias on the Alaskan mainland. Several days later a landing party, including the German naturalist Georg Steller, was sent ashore on Kayak Island. Plagued by storms and fog, and possibly suffering from scurvy, Bering and his crew turned back for Russia but their ship foundered in November on an island at the far end of the Aleutian chain. Bering fell ill shortly afterwards and died, as did 28 of his crew over the ensuing winter. The 46 survivors built a boat from the wreckage of the *St. Peter* and returned to Kamchatka with news of their expedition—along with a stack of high quality otter pelts, which prompted the beginnings of the Russian fur trade in Alaska (see sidebar: Russians in Alaska, Chapter 1).

Chirikov and the crew of the *St. Paul*, meanwhile, had sighted Baker Island, west of Prince of Wales Island on July 15. Hoping to find a harbor in which to go ashore and replenish their stocks of fresh water, they followed the coast north to Baranov Island, beyond what is now Sitka. Chirikov sent out one of his two longboats to search for an anchorage, but it failed to return. A week later, the second boat was dispatched, but it, too, was lost. Unable to search for them, with no means of going ashore, and with his expedition hampered by fog, scurvy and (one imagines) low morale among the crew after the loss of their shipmates, Chirikov decided on July 27 to set sail for Russia. After sighting the Kenai Peninsula, Kodiak Island and the western Aleutians, and all but running out of water, the *St. Paul* reached Petropavlovsk on 12 October, 1741.

With the fate of Bering and his crew still unknown, Chirikov set forth the following spring to search for them. He passed close to Bering Island, where the *St. Peter* had been wrecked, but Chirikov was unaware of this. He explored nearby Attu Island before being forced to turn back by bad weather. Meanwhile, the survivors of the *St. Peter* had made their way to Petropavlovsk. Chirikov spent the remainder of his naval career in St. Petersburg compiling a map of the Russian explorations of Kamchatka and Alaska.

—AC

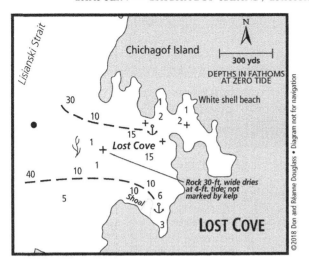

trance. Note that the head of the bay shallows very quickly. Bear sightings have been reported here by other cruisers.

## Lost Cove (Lisianski Strait)
Lost Cove is 2.5 miles northeast of the south entrance buoy of Lisianski Strait.
Chart 17303
Entrance: 57°51.70' N, 136°25.13' W
Anchor (northeast): 57°51.73' N, 136°24.53' W
Anchor (southeast): 57°51.55' N, 136°24.59' W

The several small back bays that form Lost Cove provide good shelter in fair weather. In foul weather, however, the north coves are open to southwest chop. In stable weather, boats of less than 30 feet can anchor in either the northwest or northeast cove in 2 fathoms; one vessel can anchor in 4 fathoms at the north entrance to the inner coves. Since swinging room is limited, we suggest using a shore tie. Be on the lookout for sea otters!

When entering the outer cove, beware of a 30-foot-wide rock mid-bay that dries on a 4-foot tide; it is not well marked by kelp. We do not advise a radar approach. Visibility of the water is about 10 feet. In summer, you may see small moon jellyfish and huge orange sea nettles wafting their way across the cove.

The southeast corner of the outer cove is protected from southerlies, allowing more swinging room for longer vessels.

Anchor (northeast) in 4 fathoms over mud, shells, and gravel with heavy kelp; good holding with a well-set anchor.

Anchor (southeast) in 6 fathoms over a mixed bottom with kelp; good holding if your anchor is well set.

## Yakobi Island's West Coast
Yakobi Island's west coast extends 10 miles southward from Cross Sound to Lisianski Strait.
Chart 17303

Yakobi's West Coast is rugged and wild. Numerous bays and bights offer shelter to small craft, but these are largely hidden by a labyrinth of rocks and islets that require very careful navigation. We recommend following the route only in fair weather and good visibility—approaching closer than one mile in foul weather and in depths less than 10 to 15 fathoms can subject a boat to breaking seas. We find Greentop Harbor to offer the best shelter from heavy weather along Yakobi's west coast, but entering it is a navigational challenge. (See below.)

## Bingham Cove (Yakobi Island)
Bingham Cove is on the south side of Cape Bingham.
Chart 17303
Entrance: 58°05.48' N, 136°32.92' W
Anchor: 58°04.89' N, 136°32.74' W

Bingham Cove has its south arm fairway constricted by rocks and a

*An island marks the junction of Lisianski Inlet and Lisianski Strait.*

*Exploring the many inlets along Chichagof Island*

shoal. If you want to use the cove, either follow a local fishing boat or contact one on Ch 16 for local knowledge. Our designated anchor site is suitable for shallow-draft boats only.

Anchor in 9 feet.

## Hoktaheen Cove (Yakobi Island)
Hoktaheen Cove is about 1.2 miles south of Cape Bingham.
Chart 17303
Entrance (Yakobi Rock bearing 030°T at 0.98 Nm): 58°04.32' N, 136°34.74' W
Anchor: 58°04.30' N, 136°32.93' W

Chart 17303 is the best guide to entering Hoktaheen Cove. The entrance requires a circuitous route avoiding the rocks and kelp. Entry is not advised in foul weather or during poor visibility.

Anchor in about 2 fathoms near the head of the cove.

## Surge Bay (Yakobi Island)
Surge Bay is 4.1 miles north of Cape Cross.
Chart 17303
Entrance (high rocky islet bearing 053°T at 0.50 Nm): 57°58.89' N, 136°34.35' W

The recommended entrance to Surge Bay passes close to three tiny islets to avoid the rocks that cover at high water 0.28 Nm southwest of these islets.

This part of the coast is subject to breaking waves any time depths are less than 10 to 15 fathoms. Once inside the numerous rocks and reefs, swells flatten out. However, surge may be felt anywhere in the bay.

Good shelter is reported at the north end of the bay in the lee of the small islands, by avoiding numerous rocks en route.

## Deer Harbor (Yakobi Island)
Deer Harbor is 1.7 miles northwest of Cape Cross and 7.7 miles northwest of the entrance to Lisianski Strait.
Chart 17303
Entrance (buoy G"1" bearing 133°T at 0.1 Nm): 57°56.23' N, 136°34.75' W
Anchor: 57°56.46 N, 136°33.13' W

The entrance to Deer Harbor is narrow and shallow and should not be attempted on the lower half of the tide or during foul seas when seas break or limit steering control. Once you are inside, you may not be able to get back across the bar if the weather worsens. Inside the landlocked harbor, the shelter is good; however, when heavy seas are running outside, surge can be felt inside. *Black Tie*, a 112-foot vessel, with a 6-foot draft, reported anchoring inside Deer Harbor and using a stern-tie to limit swinging room. The harbor is known locally as "The Fishmarket" because of its excellent king salmon fishing. We have spent several days at a time anchored here with several other boats enjoying good fishing and calm waters.

Anchor in 5 to 6 fathoms over sand and gravel with some kelp; fair to good holding.

## Takanis Bay (Yakobi Island)
Takanis Bay is 1.4 miles southeast of Cape Cross and 5 miles northwest of Lisianski Strait.
Chart 17303
Entrance (Cape Cross bearing 325°T at 1.4 Nm): 57°53.50' N, 136°32.11' W
Anchor (northwest branch): 57°55.47' N, 136°31.40' W

Takanis Bay, although open to the south, offers fairly good protection in its northwest arm. On a southbound route, you must clear a number of rocks, reefs, and islets south of Cape Cross

*Rough seas off the west coast of Yakobi Island*

before rounding up into Takanis Bay. Carefully work northward to the northwest arm of the bay, using your depth sounder and a bow watch. Despite its small scale, Chart 17303 can be of assistance in helping you thread your way. Numerous rocks and reefs lie at the entrance to the northwest arm, giving it protection from southerly weather. For maximum shelter, anchor north of the islet at the head the arm. Enter east of the islet; west of the islet two large rocks extend half way from the shore to the islet. Depths surrounding the islet in the cove vary from 6 to about 3 fathoms. Boats over 40 feet can anchor south of the islet. Swinging room is more limited north of the islet, so a shore tie may be useful.

The lack of drift logs on shore at this site indicates a fair amount of protection.

Anchor (northwest branch) in about 6 fathoms, brown sand, rocks and kelp with fair-to-good holding.

### Squid Bay (Yakobi Island)
Squid Bay is 3 miles northwest of Lisianski Strait.
Chart 17303
Entrance: 57°52.55' N, 136°30.25' W
Anchor: 57°53.13' N, 136°27.98' W

We have anchored temporarily in Squid Bay but did not care for it. Temporary relief can be obtained from southeast and southwest weather, but there are uncharted rocks and foam blows into the inner bay from the northwest.

Anchor (if you wish) in 7 fathoms over a soft bottom with kelp; poor-to-fair holding.

### Greentop Harbor (Yakobi Island)
Greentop Harbor entrance is 1.7 miles northwest of the Lisianski Strait entrance buoy.
Chart 17303
Entrance (entrance light bearing 097°T at 0.2 Nm): 57°51.33' N, 136°29.46' W
Anchor: 57°52.01' N, 136°27.01' W

Greentop Harbor is one of our favorite harbors for kayaking. It has lovely scenery and the shelter at the bitter end of the harbor is bombproof. Entering Greentop with a larger boat is difficult, however, and we do not recommend attempting it during heavy seas. The entire west coast of Yakobi Island is irregular, with many uncharted rocks, and Greentop is no exception. Its entrance is very narrow and intricate, and both sides of the fairway are choked with kelp. On our fourth visit, *Baidarka* hit a charted rock at the north end of Elbow Island; at much the same time, another boat, *Enetai*, hit an uncharted rock close ashore off the southwest corner. Fortunately, both vessels suffered minimal damage, as confirmed during grid haul-outs in Pelican.

If you want to risk entering Greentop, be sure to identify Greentop Island correctly in advance; it is 70 feet high, has a grassy top and a navigation light on its summit. The M/V *Royal Sounder* entered Greentop in June 2005 and stated that it was one of the worst entrances they had experienced in years.

*Baidarka approaching Greentop Island*

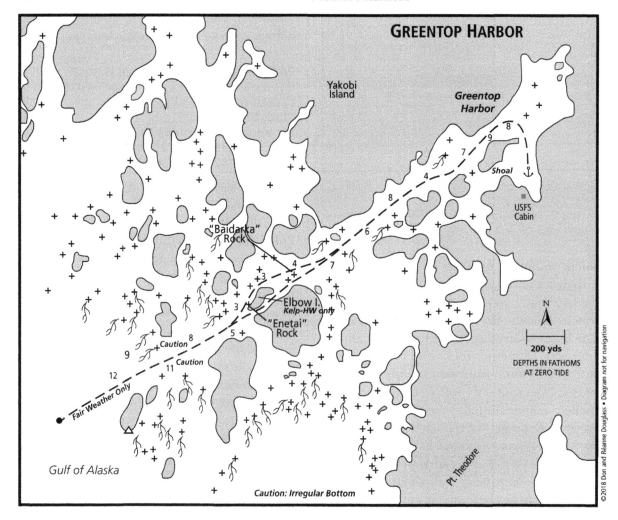

*The author stands on Baidarka Rock at a minus tide—north of Elbow Island*

There are several homesites and a U.S. Forest Service cabin on the east shore at the far end of the bay. The cabin was built on land homesteaded by Joe Scott, who lived there until 1985. It is a favorite stop for hardcore kayakers, whose comments you may read in the Forest Service guest book inside the cabin. You can anchor in several places, but we prefer the small cove off the USFS cabin where the water is perfectly smooth and the setting pristine.

Anchor in 4 fathoms over sand and mud with good holding.

## CHICHAGOF ISLAND'S WEST COAST
Chichagof Island's west coast extends 38 miles from Cape Cross to the west end of Klokachef Island.
Chart 17320

### Lisianski Inside Passage
Charts 17303, 17321
North entrance: 57°50.93' N, 136°25.88' W
South entrance: (Point Urey bearing 015°T at 0.64 Nm) 57°48.55' N, 136°25.32' W

The Lisianski "Inside Passage"—the smooth-water route between Lisianski Strait and Islas Bay (at the southern end of Lisianski Strait)—provides welcome shelter from the open Pacific but requires skillful and vigilant navigation. The entire coast of Yakobi and Chichagof islands has an irregular seabed with patches of rocks that extend two miles or more offshore. The south entrance to Lisianski Strait is full of rocks and reefs where seas heap up and break during spring ebb tides, as well as in areas of less than 10 to 15 fathoms exposed to the Gulf of Alaska. Such conditions are hazardous to cruising boats, and navigating along this coast or entering Lisianski Strait from the south is not recommended in foul weather or limited visibility.

Cruising boats travelling down Lisianski Strait can avoid much of the Gulf of Alaska swell that occurs at the southern entrance of the strait by taking the 3.5-mile, smooth-water Inside Passage. Swells are cut to a minimum, and rocks are well marked by kelp or turbulent water. However, this route is intricate, threading through many islets, rocks and reefs, and should be attempted in fair weather only.

Follow the Inside Passage south, first by staying close to the east shore of Esther Island, then favoring the west shore of the large island located west of Lumber Cove. Avoid kelp and surging water. From a point off the entrance to Lumber Cove, follow the deep channel south, heading roughly for Threenob Rock (avoiding rocks on your port hand). Pass east of Urey Rocks, then turn southeast to pass close north of Threenob Rock. Continue southeast, avoiding the rocks to the west and the shoals to the east. If you're heading for Porcupine Bay, turn east at about 57°48.55' N, and pass close north of the unnamed islets. If you're headed for Bertha Bay and Mirror Harbor, turn east-southeast and pass north of Beric and Winfred islands.

Along the Inside Passage, you can expect minimum depths to run 3 to 4 fathoms along Esther Island, and 4 to 5 fathoms 0.3 mile south of Esther Island. Otherwise, the depths are irregular and range from 8 to 15 fathoms minimum.

Fishing boats, with stabilizer poles extended, anchor close east of Esther Island in 3 to 4 fathoms.

### Canoe Cove (Lisianski Strait)
Canoe Cove is one mile southwest of Lost Cove and 1.4 miles north of Point Urey.
Chart 17303
Position: 57°50.61' N, 136°25.53' W

Canoe Cove hides its charms behind a fortress of rocks, shoals and a reef. Until a large-scale

---

## WHO WAS CHICHAGOF?

Many of the place names in Southeast Alaska are named for people—mariners, officials, and crew members of exploration ships—who actually visited the region at some point in its history. Others are named in honor of dignitaries of the time or friends of the namers. Chichagof Island, the "C" of the so-called ABC Islands, falls into the latter group. It was named by the Russian Admiral Lisianski in 1805 after his illustrious fellow countryman, the naval officer and Arctic explorer, Admiral Vasili Chichagof (1726-1809). In 1766, Chichagof commanded a three-ship expedition from Russia's northern port of Archangel to find a northeast passage. He failed to find a route but sailed as far north as 80°30'N. Chichagof also served as an administrator of several Russian ports, including Archangel, and was the victorious Commander-in-Chief of Russia's Baltic Fleet during the Russo-Swedish War of 1788-90. Schooled in Great Britain, Chichagof married an Englishwoman and spent his retirement years in that country.

National Geographic magazine refers to Chichagof Island as "Bear Island," because of its high concentration of brown bears—at 1-2 animals per square mile, the highest in the world.  —AC

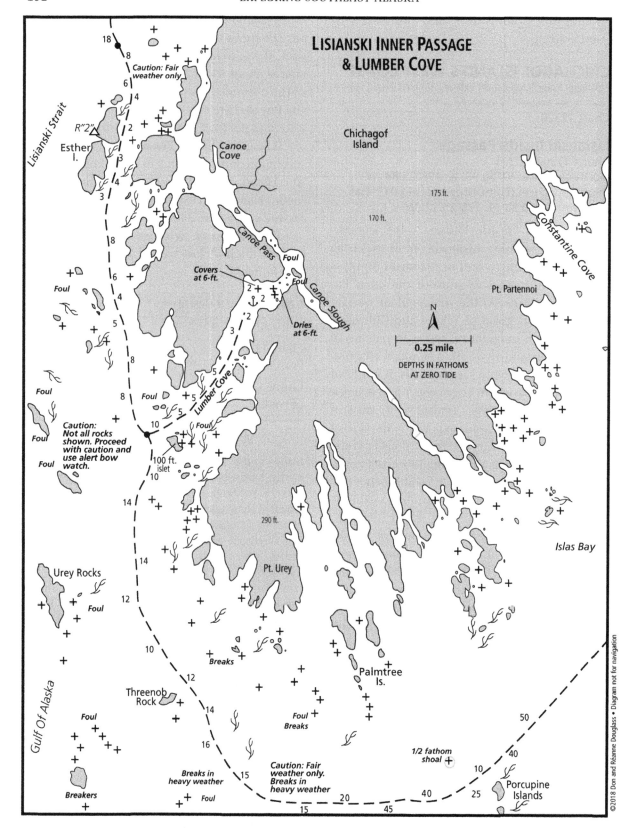

chart becomes available, visit only with a canoe or kayak.

## Lumber Cove (Chichagof Island)
Lumber Cove is 0.7 mile northwest of Point Urey and 2 miles south of Lost Cove.
Chart 17303
Entrance: 57°49.75' N, 136°25.85' W
Anchor: 57°50.15' N, 136°25.17' W

Lumber Cove offers surprisingly good protection in all but the foulest weather. Enter it from the Inside Passage, 0.5 mile northwest of Point Urey. A peninsula to the southeast and south, islets and large kelp beds to the southwest keep the north basin essentially landlocked. The basin has a wide, flat bottom of 2 to 3 fathoms with room for several boats.

Enter northwest of the 100-foot islet covered with trees and proceed northeast with a clear mid-channel. Depths decrease slowly from 10 fathoms to 2 fathoms as you enter. The inner basin has a flat bottom, and visibility through the water is about 6 feet.

This is an attractive anchorage where you can watch seals and sea otters. The entrance to Canoe Pass is foul but it is passable by kayak at high water.

Anchor in 2 to 3 fathoms over mud and clamshells with good holding.

## Islas Bay (Chichagof Island)
Islas Bay is 2.2 miles southeast of Lisianski Strait and 7 miles northwest of Portlock Harbor.
Charts 17321, 17303
West Entrance: (Beric Island bearing 160°T at 0.40 mi) 57°48.59' N, 136°24.04' W

Islas Bay, in the lee of Porcupine Islands, is part of the smooth-water route south. Watch for

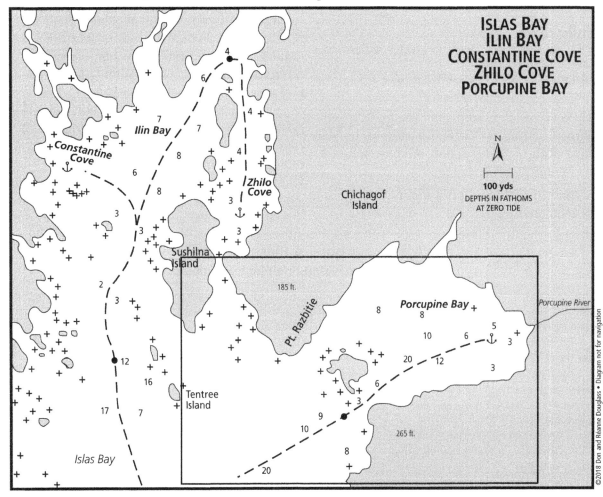

unmarked rocks and shoals north of Porcupine Islands and along the shore. The bay has several well-sheltered coves along its northern and eastern shore.

## Ilin Bay and Constantine Cove (Islas Bay)
Ilin Bay is the north part of Islas Bay.
Charts 17321, 17303
Entrance (Tentree Island bearing 115°T at 0.14 Nm): 57°49.84' N, 136°23.09' W
Position (Constantine Cove): 57°50.35' N, 136°23.34' W

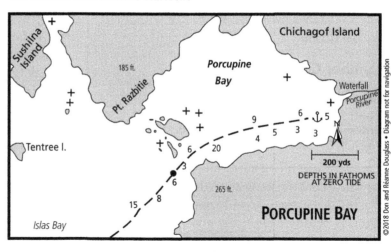

Large yachts may find anchorage in the middle of Ilin Bay or in Porcupine Bay 0.8 mile to the southeast. Constantine Cove, on the west shore looks interesting, but we have no local knowledge to offer.

## Zhilo Cove (Ilin Bay)
Zhilo Cove, in Ilin Bay, is 0.5 mile northwest of Porcupine Bay.
Charts 17321, 17303
Entrance: 57°50.57' N, 136°22.55' W
Anchor: 57°50.25' N, 136°22.44' W

Zhilo Cove offers very good shelter in a wilderness setting. Its foul south entrance breaks most of the southerly chop. We have found it very comfortable and quiet.

Anchor in 4 fathoms, sand and mud with fair-to-good holding.

## Porcupine Bay (Islas Bay)
Porcupine Bay is 2 miles northeast of Porcupine Islands and 2 miles east of Point Urey.
Charts 17321, 17303
Entrance: 57°49.71' N, 136°22.05' W
Anchor: 57°49.87' N, 136°21.37' W

Porcupine Bay is a well-sheltered anchorage with lots of swinging room. It is lovely and quiet, with steep green peaks towering above. Both Porcupine Bay and Zhilo Cove are good places to wait for better weather.

To enter, use the south entrance. From the islets north of Porcupine Islands, head for 2,215-foot Pinnacle Mountain. We found a minimum of 3 fathoms in the fairway, not the 6½ fathoms shown on the chart. The bottom of the bay is somewhat irregular; however, there is a fine 3- to 6-fathom shoal in the southeast corner where

---

## Mirror Harbor—A Piece of Cake?
### Don Douglass & Réanne Hemingway-Douglass

The skipper was confident. He'd been into Mirror Harbor several times. "Piece a cake," he told our crew. "But we need all of you at the bow to help negotiate the dogleg."

The three of us headed forward on deck. (One of us, like the skipper, had previous experience in the area.)

The tide was exceptionally low. "No way," I muttered to the others. "There's not enough room to maneuver.... Look! You can see the bottom right under the bow."

"I don't think it'll go, Don," Herb shouted.

"We'll give it a try," came the answer as we idled slowly forward.

"Reverse! Reverse! Rock! Rock!" we screamed in unison, gesturing excitedly so the skipper would understand.

We came to a slow halt, just a foot or two away from the rock.

The skipper came out of the pilothouse and looked over the bow pulpit. "Oooh, I see what you mean," he said, unperturbed. "Yeah, we might be able to make the turn if we had a bow thruster. Maybe we'd better anchor over there," he motioned with his head toward West Arm, ... "'til the tide comes up."

you have a good view of the waterfall. The bottom is very soft over a hard bottom, and it takes a light hand on the rode to set your anchor.

Anchor in 3 to 4 fathoms over a hard bottom covered with a thin layer of soft sand and coarse, broken shells. Holding is poor unless you set your anchor well; then it is fair.

## Bertha Bay (Chichagof Island)
Bertha Bay is 2 miles southeast of Porcupine Bay.
Chart 17321
Position: 57°47.93' N, 136°20.78' W

The north shore of Bertha Bay is home to the beautiful White Sulphur Hot Springs. However, Bertha Bay itself is foul and you should not attempt to anchor here.

After crossing the rolly Bertha Bay and the foul area west of Skinner Island, you can enter the perfectly smooth waters of Mirror Harbor by following a very narrow, intricate channel southeast of Post Island.

## White Sulphur Springs, West Arm, and Mirror Harbor (Bertha Bay)
White Sulphur Springs, 1 mile northwest of Mirror Harbor, is 55 miles northwest of Sitka.
Chart 17321; 55 miles NW of Sitka; 2.5 miles SE of Porcupine Bay
Position (hot springs): 57°48.33' N, 136°20.70' W
Entrance Mirror Harbor (Fairway Reef bearing 000°T at 0.12 Nm): 57°47.03' N, 136°19.85' W
Anchor (Mirror Harbor): 57°47.73' N, 136°19.09' W
Anchor (West Arm): 57°47.65' N, 136°19.53' W
Position (West Arm trailhead): 57°47.86' N, 136°19.97' W

Mirror Harbor is one of the most isolated and intricate places imaginable. It offers excellent protection from all weather and seas, but is also one of the most difficult harbors to enter. The challenge of entering is offset, however, by the nearby White Sulphur Hot Springs, where you can soak in perfect quiet. We recommend anchoring in Mirror Harbor and taking a dinghy to the trailhead in West Arm for the 15-minute walk to White Sulphur Hot Springs. The boardwalk trail passes through rainforest

*View of Bertha Bay from White Sulphur Hot Springs*

where Sitka spruce and skunk cabbage thrive and water lilies bloom in small ponds. Be bear aware as you walk.

The springs fill a comfortable, covered pool that looks out over Bertha Bay. There are changing rooms and an area to rinse your clothes; swimsuits are optional. There is also a very nice natural pool outside under a tree to the southeast. A USFS cabin is located next to this outside pool with primitive campsites to the east. During the summer, the cabin is often occupied by local vacationers or kayakers.

Entering Mirror Harbor should be attempted only at high-water slack. Boats over 30 feet will have trouble making the dogleg without a bow-thruster. We took our 40-foot *Baidarka* inside the harbor at both low tide and high

*South entrance to the Mirror Harbor complex*

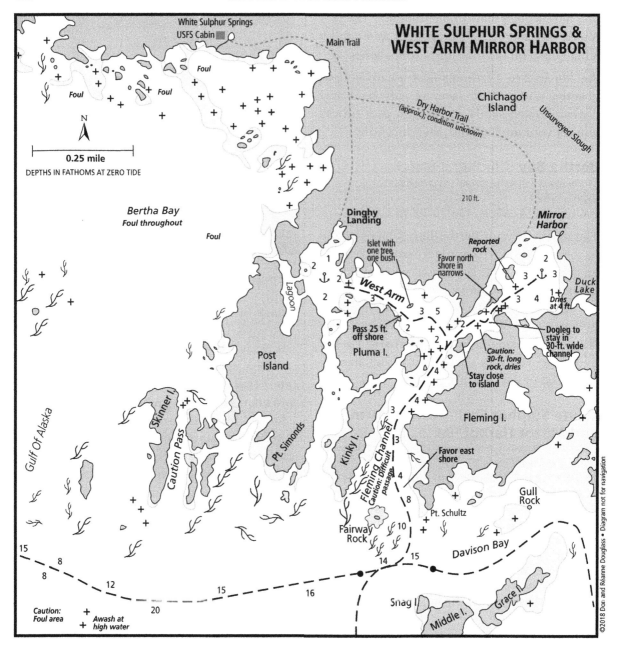

tide. At low tide, we were unable to make the dogleg despite using our bow-thruster. At high tide, we had no problem.

On earlier visits in our single-screw, 32-foot Nordic Tug (no bow-thruster), we were unable to make the dogleg on a minus one-foot tide, although we could maneuver fairly easily on an 8-foot tide. We have talked to skippers on sailboats with drafts varying from 6 to 8 feet and lengths up to 50 feet who made the dogleg successfully at high tide.

Chart 17321 is inadequate for entering Mirror Harbor, so we have used local knowledge resources, as well as our own experience, to try to create a meaningful diagram and route instructions. Use them at your own risk! Be sure to post a bow watch so you don't ground. You should enter Mirror Harbor just before high-water slack.

This is our suggested route:

Carefully locate Fairway Rock at the entrance and pass well to its south. Turn north when you're abeam Snag Island, and favor the east shore where the water is deeper along Point Schultz. Once you are inside Fleming Channel along Kinky Island, the swell dies off.

Avoid the kelp and shoal to your port side. Keep a mid-channel course until you have passed the several rocks on your port side that mark the entrance to the West Arm. At this point, stay close to the unnamed island with gnarled trees on the northwest side of Fleming Island.

Continue northeast, heading straight for a small islet that has a dangerous, mid-channel, submerged rock immediately to the east. You must make a very definite dogleg to the east just before you reach the steep-to islet (a few feet off!) to avoid a 30-foot-wide submerged rock (its tip dries on a 6-foot tide) on your starboard. This submerged rock defines the south side of the narrow channel. On this dogleg

*Critical dogleg with Mirror Harbor in the background*

you are pointed toward a shallow cove on the north end of Fleming Island.

Once clear of the large submerged rock to starboard (and islet to port), turn left (northeast) again and enter Mirror Harbor over a shallow bar. We found this bar to have approximately 3 feet over it at low water. Avoid the rocks on the east side of the bar by favoring the west shore.

Once you've crossed the bar, proceed to anchor as desired. Avoid two rocks close to the east shore of Mirror Harbor that dry at 4 feet, avoid also the northwest end of the bay, which shoals and has small rocks. The rock in the west center of the bay was reported as submerged, and we have not located it. When you're figuring tides, remember that Sitka reports tides as low as minus 3 feet.

The West Arm, in some ways, is more difficult to enter since you cannot pinpoint certain of the submerged hazards. Visibility is also decreased by eel grass and primeval-looking scum that floats along the top of the stagnant waters. Before you enter or anchor in this arm, it's a good idea to check it out first by dinghy.

Continuing south from Mirror Harbor you must pass outside Hill Island and re-enter the smooth water at Imperial Passage 4.5 miles to the south. If you're up for another challenge and have a shallow-draft boat less than 32 feet in length, and the tide conditions are right, you could try Dry Pass, 1.5 miles southeast.

*Wendy and Herb enjoy White Sulphur Hot Springs.*

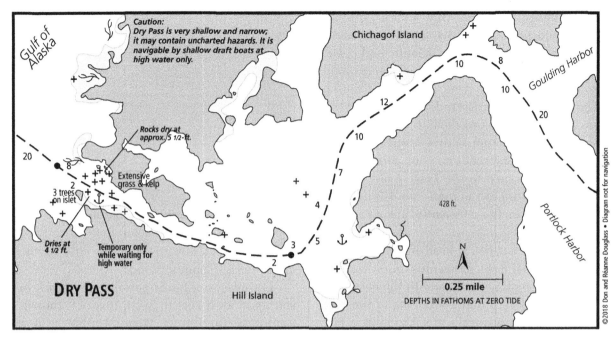

## Davison Bay (Chichagof Island)
Davison Bay is east of Mirror Harbor entrance and 1.2 miles northwest of Dry Pass.
Chart 17321
West entrance: 57°47.05' N, 136°19.52' W
East entrance: 57°46.94' N, 136°18.95' W

Davison Bay is a smooth-water route that leads from Mirror Harbor, around several small islands, to Little Bay and Dry Pass. The bay can be used for temporary anchorage while you wait for high water to enter either Mirror Harbor or Dry Pass. The shallow bar in the center of the bay requires a careful transit.

*Pond along trail to White Sulphur Hot Springs*

## Little Bay (Chichagof Island)
Little Bay is 1.5 miles northeast of Cape Dearborn.
Chart 17321
Entrance: 57°46.52' N, 136°18.22' W
Anchor: 57°46.80' N, 136°17.83' W

Calm and quiet anchorage can be found deep in the head of this narrow inlet.

Anchor in 2 to 4 fathoms over sand and gravel with fair holding.

## Dry Pass
Dry Pass, 1.5 miles south of the entrance to Mirror Harbor, separates Hill and Chichagof islands.
Chart 17321
West entrance: 57°45.96' N, 136°18.42' W
East entrance: 57°45.69' N, 136°17.10' W
Anchor (east entrance): 57°45.72' N, 136°16.87' W

Dry Pass is just that at low water—dry. This can give boaters an adrenaline rush, but Dry Pass is also chock-full of eel grass and a few patches of kelp, which confuses depth sounders and adds to the general excitement. The pass should be attempted only by smaller boats under proper conditions, and during the last few hours of a sufficiently-high flooding tide. Most cruisers find it more convenient to pass west of Hill Island and re-enter the sheltered waters of the

Outer Passage using Imperial Pass. We recommend Dry Pass only if you truly want to explore off-the-beaten path.

The northwest entrance to Dry Pass is tiny and encumbered with rocks, but once you've passed the first grass-covered bar, there is no ocean swell. Do not approach this northwest entrance from sea during heavy weather, when this shore becomes a dangerous lee. The sea bottom for two miles west of Dry Pass is irregular with rocky patches where the sea breaks during heavy swells—the same is true for much of the coast.

The narrows of Dry Pass are a good half-mile long, requiring that you find a suitable route between and around the shoals, avoiding grass, kelp, and . . . who knows what else!

The bottom throughout the pass is flat sand for the most part and, where the eel grass does not obscure visibility, the water is quite clear. (We have made it through in our 32-foot Nordic Tug, which draws 4 feet, with 2 or 3 feet to spare, on approximately a 6-foot Sitka tide.) We favor the south shore in the narrows, south of the islets, three-quarters of the way through. This is one of the shallowest parts and has considerably less water than that shown on Chart 17321.

When we first tackled Dry Pass on a southbound route, we anchored temporarily just inside the entrance in 6 feet (on a 4.5-foot flooding tide in Sitka), where the eel grass begins, so that we could reconnoiter by dinghy (a good idea!). The anchor site we used lies just off a small, rocky cave on the south shore fronted by a pin-shaped rock that—we calculate—covers at a 6.5-foot Sitka tide. (A 4-foot draft boat should wait until Pin Rock is awash before proceeding.) We took our dinghy into the narrows to probe the bottom and waited an hour for another foot of water.

Past the narrows, the bay opens up into a large, well-sheltered basin. Our friend Rod Nash once sighted 30 to 40 humpback whales here while transiting Dry Pass from south to north on *Forevergreen*.

On a northbound passage, transiting Dry Pass from the east end is easier. There are more anchoring options at low water, and you don't have the winds and swells at your back, as you do off the west entrance.

The scenery is rugged and untouched, just as it must have appeared to the early Russian explorers who visited this coast. You can safely anchor anywhere in the bay once you've passed through the narrows. It's probably faster to go around Hill Island and re-enter smooth water at Imperial Passage, but much less exciting!

Once you are anchored, enjoy the great kayaking in this bay. Also note that you are only a short dinghy ride away from White Sulphur Hot Springs in West Arm.

Secure anchorage can be found east of the east entrance to Dry Pass with lots of swinging room. A professional skipper told us he likes to anchor between the feet of the rabbit-shaped island in the bay in about 40 feet of water.

Anchor at the east entrance site in 4 fathoms over sand and mud with fair-to-good holding.

## Imperial Passage

Imperial Passage, the main entrance into Portlock Harbor, lies between Hill and Hogan islands, giving access to another part of the smooth-water Outer Passage.
Chart 17321
West entrance: 57°43.61' N, 136°17.89' W
East entrance: 57°43.91' N, 136°15.33' W

Imperial Passage is easy to enter, with good protection from swells. It is also the beginning of the smooth water route.

## Portlock Harbor (Chichagof Island)

Portlock Harbor is surrounded by Hill, Hogan, Herbert Graves, and Chichagof islands.
Chart 17321
North entrance (Dry Pass): 57°46.20' N, 136°15.79' W

Portlock Harbor is a large harbor with calm waters and many heavily wooded islets where limbs hang low to the water's edge. At this point you should begin to pick up the Coast Guard on Ch 16 and Ch 22A, after having poor-to-no reception since Icy Strait. Some of these radio dead-spots are slowly being improved by added repeater stations. Call Juneau Coast Guard for more information.

The harbor was named for Captain Nathaniel Portlock, the leader of a two-ship expedition to Alaska in 1787. After anchoring here for several weeks, he later published a sketch of the harbor. The captain of his second vessel was George Dixon, whose name appears on many geographic locations in Alaska, the most famous of which is Dixon Entrance. Both men had previously served as officers with Captain James Cook.

## Goulding Harbor (Portlock Harbor)
Goulding Harbor is at the northwest end of Portlock Harbor and has two branches.
Chart 17321
Entrance: 57°46.23' N, 136°15.48' W

The northeast branch of Goulding Harbor needs more exploration since good shelter may be available there. Goulding Harbor is poorly charted, so caution is required.

## Baker Cove (Goulding Harbor)
Baker Cove is the north arm of Goulding Harbor.
Chart 17321
Entrance: 57°47.11' N, 136°15.12' W
Anchor: 57°47.42' N, 136°14.96' W

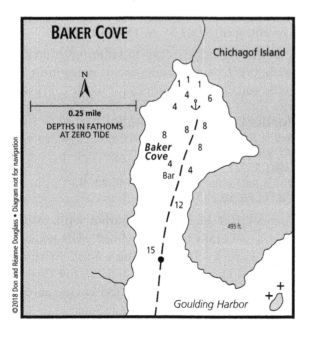

Baker Cove is the easiest place to anchor in lovely Goulding Harbor; the lack of driftwood along the grassy shore indicates excellent shelter. At low water, the east side at the head of the bay becomes landlocked.

Entrance can be made by radar if needed. An uncharted 4-fathom bar lies across the middle. The basin off the head of the cove is deeper and the shore steep-to.

Anchor in 8 fathoms over dark mud, shells and wood debris with good holding.

## Pinta Bay (Portlock Harbor)
Pinta Bay extends 2.1 miles north from Portlock Harbor)
Chart 17321
Entrance: 57°45.04' N, 136°12.88' W
Anchor: 57°46.79' N, 136°12.31' W

Anchorage can be found in about 6 fathoms at the head of the bay. The bottom is unknown.

## Didrickson Bay (Portlock Harbor)
Didrickson Bay is on the east side of Portlock Harbor.
Chart 17321
Entrance: 57°43.98' N, 136°11.39' W
Anchor (west shore): 57°44.54' N, 136°11.57' W
Anchor (head of bay): 57°44.77' N, 136°11.38' W

Didrickson Bay is well sheltered and easy to enter by favoring its east side. The head and sides of the bay are steep-to. The grassy shores here show no signs of driftwood. Sea otters play in the bay and, in late summer, salmon can be seen trying to head up creek.

Anchor off the waterfall at the head of the bay, or off to the side as indicated in the diagram; this is a favorite spot of local fishing boats.

Anchor in about 8 fathoms along the west shore, or at the head of the bay over soft mud and hard bottom. Holding is good if you set your anchor well.

## Troller Anchorage (Lydonia Island)
Troller Anchorage is on the north side of Lydonia Island.
Chart 17321
Anchor: 57°42.91' N, 136°10.60' W

"Troller Anchorage," is our name for the cove on the northwest corner of Lydonia Island, as it seems to be a favorite of local troller fishermen. Some protection from southerlies is reported.

Anchor in 6 fathoms over a mixed bottom.

## South Passage
South Passage lies between Hogan and Herbert Graves islands.
Chart 17321
West entrance: 57°40.98' N, 136°16.44' W
Northeast entrance: 57°42.02' N, 136°13.58' W

## Surveyor Passage
Surveyor Passage extends from Portlock Harbor to Ogden Passage.
Chart 17321
North entrance: 57°43.22' N, 136°10.28' W
South entrance: 57°41.83' N, 136°08.18' W

Narrow Surveyor Passage is bordered by high, snowy peaks that form the south flanks of Mt. Lydonia. Small slab avalanches are evident along the north wall of the passage. The waters throughout this short passage are calm, without any swell. The fairway through the passage is about 20 yards wide. Daybeacons mark a reef; on a southbound passage, take the green daybeacons to starboard, the red to port. Anchorage can be found along the shoals in a number of places. Watch for submerged rocks.

## Black Bay (Chichagof Island)
Black Bay extends east from Surveyor Passage for 1.2 miles.
Chart 17321
Entrance: 57°42.55' N, 136°09.46' W

Black Bay is truly landlocked. In most places the depths are too great for convenient small-craft anchorage; however, larger, deep-draft vessels can find moderate depths off the grassy margins at the head of the bay.

South of Point Lydonia, along the east side of Surveyor Passage, two islets partially block the entrance to Black Bay. On entering the bay, stay close under Point Lydonia, but favoring the northern islet, to avoid a ridge that extends about 50 feet off the point.

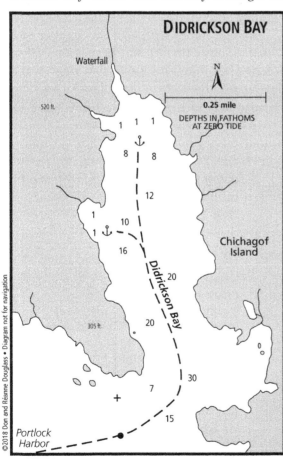

## Lessons from Adverse Experiences
### Don Douglass

Alaska-bound cruisers can learn important lessons from the adverse experiences of others. Keep these things in mind:

1. High-tech doesn't mean immunity from disasters or the ability to be able to communicate directly with authorities during emergencies.
2. Charts—especially in Alaska—are old, mostly small-scale and are replete with various errors or omissions. Even new charts and guidebooks must be used with skepticism and caution.
3. Be seriously prepared and self-sufficient when cruising in wilderness waters.
4. There are many radio blackout areas along the Pacific Coast and within fiords.
5. It's always good policy to keep an alert bow watch in any tight quarters or when the bottom is uneven.
6. Reduce speed to slow or dead-slow if you don't know that it is safe to proceed.
7. Cruising boaters are a friendly lot and are willing to lend a hand in emergencies. You can do the same when you're privileged to travel in these beautiful and remote areas.

## Kimshan Cove (Chichagof Island)

Kimshan Cove is east of Fitz Island at the junction of Ogden and Surveyor passages.
Chart 17321
Entrance: 57°41.46' N, 136°07.29' W
Anchor: 57°41.27' N, 136°07.17' W

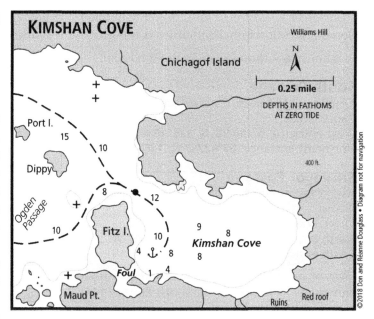

Landlocked Kimshan Cove provides excellent shelter and calm waters. Seals and sea otters like these waters; in fall, you see salmon jumping constantly here. Kimshan is said to be Chinese for "gold mountain;" there are old gold mines and interesting relics in the vicinity.

Although the shoreline is flat, the underwater contour is steep-to—8 fathoms just 200 feet from the beach.

Anchor in 6 to 8 fathoms over mud and grass with very good holding.

## Ogden Passage

Ogden Passage extends southward from Surveyor Passage to Khaz Bay.
Chart 17322
North entrance: 57°41.53' N, 136°07.51' W
South entrance at Smooth Channel:
57°36.81' N, 136°07.82' W

Ogden Passage is calm, smooth, and quiet, an untouched place that has a timeless feel to it. Inquisitive sea otters pass close by your boat, as if to say, "Who are you and what are you doing here?" Reduce your rpms and enjoy the beautiful, natural environment—though, as always, maintain your vigilance for uncharted hazards.

*Caution:* Some years ago the skipper of a 77-foot, state-of-the-art sailing vessel with a 14-foot draft found an uncharted rock in the narrow, middle section of Ogden Passage, on the west side of the channel at 57°39.329' N, 136°10.281' W. Several people were seriously injured; nearby boaters and the USCG came to their rescue. Be sure you are using up-to-date, corrected charts as this rock is now indicated and noted on the chart as "Rep (2003)."

*Lining up these two markers helps keep you in The Gate's channel; then make the turn to starboard into Elbow Passage.*

## Kukkan Passage

Kukkan Passage is on the southwest side of Herbert Graves Island.
Chart 17322
North entrance (Pole Point bearing 058°T at 0.7 Nm): 57°39.28' N, 136°14.97' W
South entrance (Snipe Rock G"1" bearing 170°T at 0.08 Nm):
57°38.33' N, 136°10.73' W

Kukkan Passage is a shortcut for cruisers who want to enter the south end of Ogden Passage from the outer waters.

## Tawak Passage and Gig Pass
Tawak Passage and Gig Pass are 4 miles north of Khaz Bay.
Chart 17322
South entrance (Tawak Passage): 57°37.19' N, 136°11.61' W
Position (Gig Pass): 57°37.11' N, 136°11.40' W

Gig Pass is a narrow passage that connects the south part of Ogden Passage to Tawak Passage.

## Elbow Passage
Elbow Passage is the west entrance to Klag Bay.
Chart 17322
Entrance: 57°37.08' N, 136°07.74' W

## The Gate
The Gate is the main entrance to Klag Bay.
Chart 17322
South entrance: 57°36.51' N, 136°06.20' W
North entrance: 57°36.82' N, 136°06.01' W

Most cruisers headed for Klag Bay use the Smooth Channel route, then turn northward to pass through The Gate. Note in the accompanying picture the markers (GW Bn "A" and RW Bn "B") used for making your way through channel safely. After transiting The Gate, make a starboard turn toward the eastern end of Elbow Passage, while staying alert to the effects of the current. Then easily follow Elbow Passage as it turns northward into Klag Bay—still minding the current.

## Klag Bay, Chichagof Village Site
(Chichagof Island)
Klag Bay is at the head of Khaz Bay.
Chart 17322 (inset)
South entrance (Rose Point bearing 200°T at 0.13 Nm): 57°37.74' N, 136°05.36' W
Anchor (Chichagof site): 57°39.73' N, 136°05.52' W

Klag Bay can be perfectly still inside, while boaters outside complain via VHF of 5-foot southeast seas and a rough ride.

Chichagof, at the head of the Klag Bay, was the site of a gold and silver mining village during the first half of the twentieth century. More than $13,000,000 in gold was brought out of area mines between 1905 and the late 1930s. On a nearby small island ("Radioville"), a re-

*Radio Transmitter license found in an abandoned building at Klag Bay*

tired signal corps operator ran a radio station, delivering messages from the outside world to the village site.

The abandoned mining site of Chichagof is fun to explore, although most of the buildings have collapsed in recent years. Equipment lies rusting along shore, sprouting moss or colorful wild flowers or young shoots of hemlock. One cruiser told us of finding a note at the kitchen table inviting them to make an entry in the diary; a picture of the original mining camp was placed nearby. For many cruisers, Klag Bay is a highlight of their Chichagof Island trip.

The bay is fairly flat at 4 fathoms over a long stretch and anchorage can be taken toward the head, avoiding rocks and a foul area from the islet to the eastern shore. This area is awash on low water and almost forms a breakwater.

Anchor in 4 fathoms over gray, sticky mud, clam shells and sand, with very good holding.

## Lake Anna and Sister Lake (Klag Bay)
Lake Anna is entered through a narrow channel on the east side of the north end of Elbow Passage. Sister Lake is joined to the northeast end of Lake Anna by a narrow, foul passage.
Chart 17322
Entrance (Lake Anna): 57°37.45' N, 136°05.00' W
Entrance (Sister Lake): 57°38.34' N, 136°02.46' W
Anchor (Lake Anna): 57°38.79' N, 136°02.76' W

Lake Anna and Sister Lake are remote and mapped at small scale, but are worth entering at the proper tide. We entered and spent the

*The story of the mining camp tells itself with sights like this.*

Chart 17322
North entrance: 57°36.82' N, 136°08.06' W
South entrance: 57°35.00' N, 136°07.62' W

## Smooth Channel

Smooth Channel connects Ogden Passage to Khaz Bay.
Chart 17322
North entrance: 57°36.81' N, 136°07.82' W
South entrance: 57°35.59' N, 136°05.73' W

As its name implies, Smooth Channel is more protected than Rough Channel to the west.

night at the north end of Lake Anna, off a creek. The depths inside the lake are substantial until toward the head, where they shallow to about 5 or 6 fathoms.

The passage joining Sister Lake to Lake Anna has extremely dangerous currents on ebb tides. There is a 0.25-mile portage trail from the southeast end of Sister Lake to Ford Arm.

Anchor in about 5 fathoms over mud and sand with good holding.

## Rough Channel

Rough Channel, west of Quit Point and Gray Rock, connects Ogden Passage to Khaz Bay.

## Khaz Bay (Chichagof Island)

Khaz Bay is the entrance to Slocum Inlet and Klag Bay.
Chart 17322
Entrance (Ninefoot Shoal buoy bearing 034°T at 1.9 Nm): 57°33.31' N, 136°07.72' W

Some guidebooks suggest using Khaz Bay to

*This Alaska State Library photograph shows what the mining camp looked like in its working prime.*

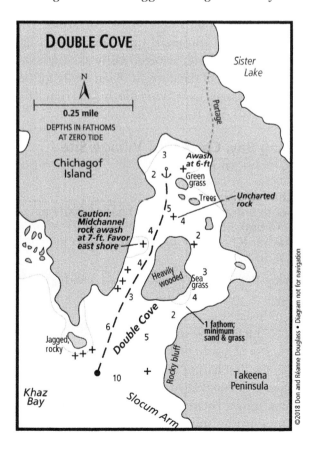

*The rusted remains of mining equipment*

once you're abeam the island; inside, it is perfectly calm.

A beach of small shale and grass that is free of driftwood lies at the head of the cove. The water is somewhat stagnant, with just 6-foot visibility; summer water temperature averages about 60°F.

Anchor in 3 fathoms over black mud with clam-shells and pieces of shale; excellent holding.

enter the Gulf of Alaska, then passing west of the buoy at Khaz Breakers, 4 miles offshore; however, we like to prolong the smooth-water route of the Outer Passage and have some fun making our way into the Gulf of Alaska at Khaz Point via Piehle Passage.

## Double Cove, Khaz Bay (Chichagof Island)
Double Cove is at the northeast end of Khaz Bay.
Chart 17322
Entrance: 57°35.50′ N, 136°03.90′ W
Anchor: 57°35.96′ N, 136°03.62′ W

Double Cove provides excellent shelter and is a good base from which to explore Khaz Bay and Klag Bay by inflatable. The area offers outstanding sport fishing and an unspoiled environment.

You can anchor with landlocked protection behind the point in the northwest corner or east of the heavily wooded island. Avoid the dangerous rock awash on a 7-foot tide in mid-channel on the west entrance; this rock, which is poorly charted, extends almost to the center of the channel with a shoal on its west side. You may want to consider using a stern-tie in this small anchorage. Prevailing swell dies

*A walk up the hill brings you to the mine shaft; you can do your own panning for gold in the nearby stream.*

*A homesteader's fireplace with name engraved—Chichagof Island*

## Slocum Arm (Chichagof Island)
Slocum Arm extends southeast from Khaz Bay.
Chart 17322
Entrance: 57°34.77' N, 136°04.11' W

Slocum Arm was named after one of the naval officers in the original nineteenth-century survey party.

## Ford Arm (Chichagof Island)
Ford Arm is northeast of Khaz Head and Slocum Arm.
Chart 17322
Entrance: 57°33.04' N, 136°00.43' W
Anchor (northwest arm): 57°36.04' N, 136°00.17' W
Anchor (southeast arm): 57°34.14' N, 135°55.62' W
Position (Rocky Bay): 57°34.01' N, 135°58.53' W

Anchorage can be found in Elf Cove or at the head of either the southeast or northwest arm of Ford Arm.

## Elf Cove (Ford Arm)
Elf Cove is 2.9 miles inside Ford Arm.
Chart 17322
Anchor: 57°35.45' N, 135°57.41' W

Anchor in about 6 fathoms with some exposure to southeast winds. Swinging room is limited.

## Falcon Arm (Slocum Arm)
Falcon Arm is 1.4 miles southeast of Ford Arm.
Chart 17322
Entrance: 57°32.04' N, 135°58.32' W
Anchor: 57°33.42' N, 135°55.96' W

*Inside an abandoned cabin on Chichagof Island*

> *A rock with 1 foot over it is 0.4 mile inside the bay, in the middle. Favor the NW shore for 0.5 mile from the entrance to avoid this rock and then keep in midchannel ... A good anchorage is in an expansion above a point on the NW side 1.5 miles from the entrance in 11 to 14 fathoms, soft bottom. (CP)*

You may find that the rock location (noted in the *Coast Pilot* text above) is reported differently on electronic charts and paper charts. This is common along the coast and skippers need to be cautious in this area. They must also be sure to keep their electronic charts updated. It has been reported that in one major vendor's electronic charting program, the rock is indicated in the vector view, but is not seen at all in the raster view. (Even though the raster chart properties dialog indicates a 1:40,000 scale, the raster chart does not display at this scale.) Electronic charting has become standard on cruising boats but it does have its problems. Paper charts should always be simultaneously in use.

Small craft can find good anchorage at the head of the bay in 6 fathoms over a soft bottom.

## Waterfall Cove (Slocum Arm)
Waterfall Cove is 1.8 miles southeast of Falcon Arm.
Chart 17322
Entrance: 57°31.15′ N, 135°55.92′ W
Anchor: 57°31.49′ N, 135°55.30′ W

> Waterfall Cove . . . is identified by a large waterfall about 1 mile above its head. Two bights are at the head; the E one dries and the W one, which has 4 to 11 fathoms, affords anchorage for small craft. (CP)

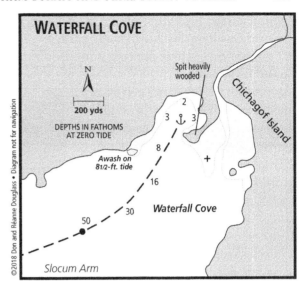

Waterfall Cove is an attractive anchorage offering good shelter behind the heavily wooded spit formed by the outlet of the river. It is protected from most winds and chop. Here, leaping salmon, soaring eagles and squawking ravens greet your arrival. The water is 60°F with visibility of 10 feet. A 500-foot vertical waterfall, about one mile inland, falls from a saddle, and the rugged granite outcropping of 2,700-foot Khaz Peak is topped with a green velvet crown. Deer and grizzlies may be sighted along the river's outlet.

Anchor in 4 fathoms over black mud, clamshell and shale chip with some kelp; good holding.

## Island Cove and Wooded Knoll Cove (Slocum Arm)
Island Cove is 4.5 miles southeast of Falcon Arm.
Chart 17322
Entrance (Island Cove): 57°28.95′ N, 135°52.01′ W
Anchor (Island Cove): 57°28.89′ N, 135°51.58′ W
Anchor (Wooded Knoll Cove): 57°28.73′ N, 135°53.41′ W

Island Cove is somewhat open to prevailing upslope winds; however, larger boats can get good protection from downslope winds here. Smaller boats may find what we call "Wooded Knoll Cove" more intimate, less open to chop, with more moderate depths.

Anchor (Island Cove) in about 15 fathoms over sticky mud with good holding. There is plenty of swinging room in this area.

Anchor (Wooded Knoll Cove) in 6 to 10 fathoms over mud and gravel with fair-to-good holding.

## Flat Cove (Slocum Arm)
Flat Cove, on the northeast side of Slocum Arm, is 6 miles southeast of Falcon Arm.
Chart 17322
Entrance: 57°28.30′ N, 135°50.23′ W

Flat Cove is steep-to and open to westerlies. Hidden Cove is preferable as an anchorage.

## Hidden Cove (Slocum Arm)
Hidden Cove is 1 mile north of the head of Slocum Arm.
Chart 17322
Entrance: 57°27.64′ N, 135°49.12′ W
Anchor: 57°27.93′ N, 135°49.07′ W

Hidden Cove is reported to offer secluded, well-sheltered anchorage. However, it may be subject to williwaws.

Anchor in 5 fathoms over an unrecorded bottom.

## Piehle Passage
Piehle Passage leads from Slocum Arm to west of Khaz Point.
Chart 17322
North entrance: 57°32.13′ N, 136°01.08′ W
South entrance: 57°30.06′ N, 136°01.67′ W
Entrance (alternative N entry): 57°32.94′ N, 136°02.25′ W

Piehle Passage is another of our favorite areas along the Outer Passage, but it requires careful piloting and should be attempted in good visibility and fair weather only. It is not recommended for larger vessels or those with limited maneuverability. But, if you feel confident using Piehle Passage, you can avoid about 6 miles of open water and have a good time doing it. We believe our diagram, in conjunction with Chart 17322, shows the correct route, and it checks with the ubiquitous white paint splashed on rocks by locals at critical turning points—but we offer you no guarantees!

*Piehle Passage—a smooth-water transit that avoids six miles of open ocean.* Caution: *careful piloting is required.*

If you have a small-to-moderate-sized cruising boat, you can use Piehle Passage without problems in good visibility, as long as you're cautious. It's best to go through at low tide when hazards are easier to spot and, of course, always post lookouts on your bow. Remember that—like all explorers—if you give this passage a try, you alone are responsible for your own decisions and safety. You can always turn around and retrace your steps if you get confused.

On a southward transit, head west from Slocum Arm, north of Khaz Head and south of island (215). Follow the deep-water channel until you have passed the small islet on your port side, southwest of island (215). At this point, turn south-southeast and pass close starboard to another islet (5 fathoms minimum). Continue deep into the cove in Khaz Head until you are almost to the westernmost peninsula of the head. The cove below Khaz Head provides good shelter in 8 to 9 fathoms. After passing two islets to starboard, turn west around these two islets and head for three small islands covered with trees 0.5 mile offshore—the northernmost of which is marked (120). Depths in this vicinity are 6 fathoms minimum.

Just past a 25-foot-high islet off the peninsula to port (identified by two light-colored knobs), turn southeast and remain close to the peninsula, east of the rocks and kelp patches. Stay about 60 feet from the bluff and 30 feet from the kelp to starboard.

When you are able to see the faded white paint on the peninsula to your port (minimum 4 fathoms—do not overshoot into the 2-fathom kelp patch north of the islet ahead), turn to the southwest, working your way in clear channels between the kelp patches and covered rocks (minimum 5 fathoms in the fairway). This is the trickiest part of the passage. Once you have cleared the kelp and rocks, turn southeast, passing to port the islet which is about 0.35 mile south of the white spot on the bluff; the islet has a white triangle on its south side. There are several more islets and kelp patches to pass on the port hand before you approach the northeast corner of Khaz Point.

About 400 yards off the peninsula at Khaz Point, the channel opens to the south-southwest. When you have passed the bare, jagged, 35-foot-high islet to starboard, turn south-southwest and pass west of Khaz Point, avoiding the breaking rocks to starboard. At what we judge to be the south entrance point (57°30.06' N, 136°01.67' W), depths in the fairway are 6 fathoms minimum. From this entrance point, turn south until you reach the 12- to 15-fathom curve, then turn southeast and parallel the coast, giving Point Slocum rock pile a wide berth of at least a mile.

As an alternative North Entrance to Piehle Passage when transiting southbound, you can enter further north in Slocum Arm, near the center point of Baird Island's eastern shore. Pass carefully the easternmost points of the southern portion of Baird Island, favoring the west side of this passage and avoiding the

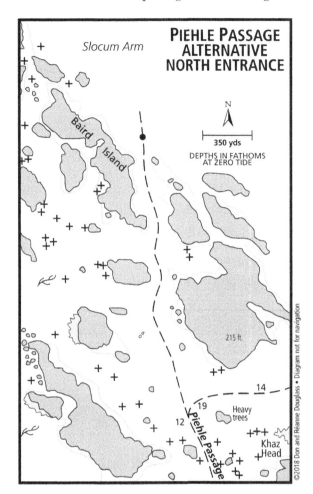

*Consider making your transit through Piehle Passage at low water when the rocks throughout are more visible to your bow watch*

*Khaz Point and south entrance to Piehle Passage*

charted 1-fathom shoal that extends west from the large unnamed island north of Khaz Head.

On a northbound passage, head for the entrance point west of Khaz Point before turning north-northeast into Piehle Passage. Then reverse the procedure described above.

---

### Piehle Passage—A Real Challenge for Experienced Mariners
Linda Lewis & Dave Parker
M/V *Royal Sounder*

We made it through Chichagof's Piehle Passage with the help of your diagram (very slowly with a very vigilant bow watch [Dave] —at low water and in good visibility as you advised), Don and Réanne. And you were so right about the tricky part. It was very confusing when the chart and the world outside the window didn't match. We saw no rocks or kelp dead ahead where you made the point that we were *not* supposed to go, but *lots* of rocks and kelp on our starboard where you referred to the white spot on the peninsula and said to turn to the Southwest (to our starboard).

Based on what we were both seeing outside the boat, I decided that instead of turning to starboard at that moment, I would proceed *very slowly* ahead a few feet. That quickly didn't feel right based on what Dave could now see. Stop the boat. Assess. I reminded myself of the point you had made to not overshoot past the white spot painted on the bluff. So we carefully backed up a bit, and when I was abeam the white spot, we made the right angle turn to starboard, staying with the course as I had laid it out from your notes. That did the trick! Just like you said.

---

*Note:* The white spot on the bluff and the white triangle mentioned above have faded in recent years.

From Khaz Point southward for about 6.5 miles, you are subject to the prevailing northwest swells of the Gulf of Alaska until you enter Fortuna Strait and the calmer waters of Salisbury Sound.

### Khaz Head Anchorage
Chart 17332
Anchor: 57°31.30' N, 136°00.95' W

We have anchored inside Khaz Head several times and found the site to offer protection from northwest swells. During southeast weather conditions we experienced some gusts at this site, but no swell. Fish and Game vessels frequently use this site as a refuge.

Anchor in 6 to 9 fathoms over brown mud and shell with very good holding.

### Fortuna Strait
Fortuna Strait lies between Chichagof and Klokachef islands.
Chart 17323
North entrance: 57°25.71' N, 135°54.85' W
South entrance: 57°23.84' N, 135°51.70' W

Leo Anchorage on the north shore of Fortuna Strait makes a good lunch stop.

### Leo Anchorage (Chichagof Island)
Leo Anchorage, on the northeast side of Fortuna Strait, is 5.5 miles northwest of Kalinin Bay.
Chart 17323
Anchor: 57°25.50' N, 135°51.67' W

Leo Anchorage provides good shelter in stable conditions and a welcome relief from the swell encountered a few miles to the north. The head of the bay has old-growth trees along its shore and a gray stone beach. In the fall, salmon swarm off the outlet to the stream, waiting for rains to swell the flow so they can reach their spawning grounds. Seals feed off the salmon and, farther off the beach, huge white and orange sea nettles float by. The bottom is steep-to and hard. Set your anchor well and test it.

CHAPTER 7 — CHICHAGOF ISLAND, CHATHAM STRAIT AND PERIL STRAIT TO SITKA        271

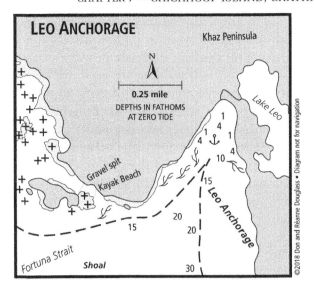

On the west point of the bay, just east of the wooded islet, there is a gravel spit, kayak beach and a 1-fathom anchor site surrounded by kelp. You can wait here temporarily and watch conditions to the northwest if you're heading northward. For shelter in southeast gales, we recommend Kalinin Bay.

Anchor in 4 to 10 fathoms over a hard bottom with kelp; good holding only if well set.

## Salisbury Sound
Salisbury Sound, bounded by Chichagof, Kruzof and Baranof islands, leads to the west entrance to Peril Strait and the northwest entrance to Neva Strait.
Chart 17323
West entrance (Point Kruzof bearing 183°T at 1.4 Nm): 57°21.70' N, 135°50.57' W
East entrance (Kakul Rock Light bearing 033°T at 0.55 Nm): 57°21.27' N, 135°42.45' W

The Gulf of Alaska swells gradually subside as you approach the east end of Salisbury Sound and fall into the lee of Kruzof Island.

Salisbury Sound was named by Captain Portlock in honor of the Bishop of Salisbury, superseding the name Bay of Islands bestowed nine years earlier by Captain James Cook.

## SALISBURY SOUND TO SITKA— EAST SIDE OF KRUZOF ISLAND
### Kalinin Bay (Kruzof Island)
Kalinin Bay, on the north side of Kruzof Island, is 2.5 miles inside the west entrance to Salisbury Sound.
Chart 17323
Entrance: 57°20.37' N, 135°47.00' W
Anchor: 57°19.15' N, 135°47.28' W

> Kalinin Bay . . . has anchorage near its head that is used by fishing craft, but its narrow entrance is obstructed by rocks.
>
> Large craft should favor the SW shore in approaching the entrance in order to avoid a 3¼-fathom kelp-marked shoal off the entrance. Favor the W shore in entering until up to the first bend, then steer midchannel courses. A large rock awash is about 100 yards off the E shore at the narrowest part of the channel, just before the bay widens to form the main anchorage. Another rock awash is close E.
>
> A submerged rock with 1 fathom over it, and usually marked by a halibut float during the summer, is 100 yards off the W shore and about 100 yards NW of the large rock awash. Also marking this site is the ruins of a building with stub piling that extends 10 yards offshore. Strangers should enter at half tide or low water, passing about 30 yards W of the large rock.
>
> Well-protected anchorage . . . can be found near the head of the bay in 4 to 5 fathoms, soft mud bottom. (CP)

Kalinin Bay, on the south side of Salisbury Sound, is one of the best anchorages in the area. Its proximity to the rich fishing grounds in Salisbury Sound, as well as to Peril Strait—the usual pleasure boater's route south to Sitka—make it popular with both sport fishing and cruising boats. Though not particularly secluded, it is convenient place to wait for proper tides or weather conditions.

*Salisbury Sound sea otters*

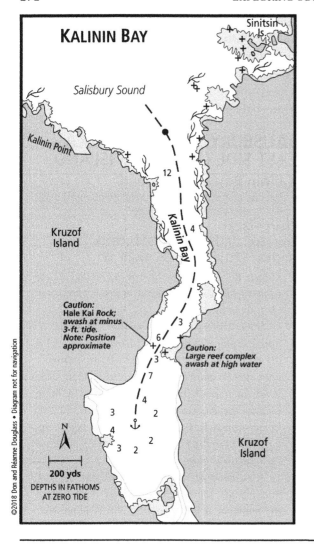

The entrance channel is a mile long, and care should be taken to remain mid-channel to avoid rocks along either shore. A large rock is awash at high water at the narrowest part of the entrance channel; this rock is part of a reef complex charted as extending from the eastern shore to near mid-channel.

Caution: About 100 yards to the northwest of the western edge of the reef complex, and 100 yards off the west shore, there is a large rock awash on a minus 3-foot tide which we call "Hale Kai (pronounced hah-lay-kie) Rock" after the vessel that grounded here, in 2005. The 2017 edition of *Coast Pilot* suggests that the preferred entrance route is about 30 yards west of the large rock awash at high water (see *Coast Pilot* quote above).

Aboard *Baidarka*, we have always followed a route close to the far western shore in about 1 fathom. However, several boaters have told us they prefer to pass between the large rock at the western end of the reef and the sometimes-marked (with a small float) Hale Kai Rock. A professional charter skipper advises hugging the reef complex on the east side as closely as you safely can in order to stay well clear of the rock. This route, between the Hale Kai Rock and the reef complex, appears to follow a deeper channel than the *Coast Pilot* route. The accompany-

## A Whale's Tale
*(From the First Mate's Diary, July 1997)*
### Réanne Hemingway-Douglass

We were snuggly anchored in Kalinin Bay after a choppy four-hour passage down the coast. Earlier in the day, we had heard a broadcast over Ch 16 asking anyone who had sighted a whale trailing a line to contact the USCG. There were no other details, and it wasn't until our arrival in Sitka that we heard the full story:

Two Sitka men were out fishing in Icy Strait in a 17-foot Boston whaler when they sighted a whale with a crab pot line and buoy wrapped around its tail. Thinking they could just cut the rope and free the whale, they decided to go to its rescue. But as they approached, the line snagged and caught on their prop.

The whale sounded, pulling the boat stern-under and dumping the two men into the icy waters. As the men struggled to stay afloat, the whale and the boat disappeared completely under water.

Suddenly the boat shot up again out of the water, intact, without the whale, without the line.

Fortunately, another boat witnessed the scene and sped to the rescue of the two men. "They were more astonished than anything," we were told. "They might have lost their lives, but that didn't seem to cross their minds."

Whatever happened to the whale, no one knows. Perhaps the poor creature is still out there in the Gulf of Alaska trailing a line behind its tail.

ing diagram shows a suggested path and the approximate position of the dangerous rock. In any case, you should approach this narrowest part of the entrance channel very carefully, paying attention to avoid the uncharted rock

Once you have passed south of these hazards, you enter a wide basin that has ample swinging room for a number of boats over a flat bottom.

An interesting hiking trail leads from the southwest end of the bay and heads west to Sea Lion Cove on the outer shore of Kruzof Island, via some rugged grizzly country. We have heard varying reports of the trail's difficulty.

Anchor in 4 fathoms over soft black mud and shells with very good holding. *Note:* the south half of the bay shoals to bare.

## Sinitsin Cove (Kruzof Island)
Sinitsin Cove, on the north shore of Kruzof Island, is 1.5 miles east of Kalinin Bay.
Chart 17323
Entrance: 57°20.43' N, 135°44.50' W

Sinitsin is used by commercial fishing vessels wanting a deep-water anchorage.

## Sukoi Inlet (Kruzof and Partofshikof islands)
Sukoi Inlet's north entrance is about 0.8 mile west of Kane Islands.
Chart 17324
North entrance: 57°19.47' N, 135°41.42' W
Anchor: 57°16.60' N, 135°40.50' W

Sukoi Inlet, like Kalinin Bay to the west, is another bombproof anchorage for cruising boats; however, it is 3.5 miles to shallow water, which some boaters find inconvenient.

Anchor in 6 fathoms over a thin layer of sand and mud over a hard bottom; good holding if your anchor is well set.

## Neva Strait
Neva Strait, between Baranof and Partofshikof islands, with Olga Strait, connects Salisbury Sound with Sitka Sound.
Chart 17324 (inset)
Northwest entrance (Scraggy Islands bearing 232°T at 0.34 Nm): 57°20.67' N, 135°41.82' W
South entrance (Neva Point Light bearing 081°T at 0.2 Nm): 57°14.02' N, 135°33.49' W

Neva Strait, a scenic and busy passage, is the route to Sitka. Be on the lookout for fast-moving vessels, especially ferries, since the narrowness of the strait makes passing difficult, particularly in foul weather or poor visibility. The buoy colors read from south to north, so keep the red markers to port on a southbound transit, and to starboard on a northbound transit. *Note:* Our flux-gate compass registered a 3-degree or more shift in Neva Strait off Zeal Point, requiring a correction of about 5 degrees.

## Gilmer Cove (Neva Strait)
Gilmer Cove is 1.2 miles northwest of Entrance Island.
Chart 17324
Entrance: 57°18.19' N, 135°38.28' W
Anchor: 57°18.06' N, 135°38.22' W

Gilmer Cove is a tiny cove on the west shore of Neva Strait, 1.5 miles southeast of Kane Islands Light. Although just large enough for one or two boats, with limited swinging room, the cove provides shelter from southeast winds and chop. The bottom of the cove is steep-to until near its head, where it begins to shallow. We have used Gilmer as a good temporary lunch stop.

Anchor in 6 fathoms over sand, gravel and newspaper kelp; fair holding with a well-set anchor.

*The fast ferry* Fairweather *pops out of the north end of Neva Strait.*

## St. John Baptist Bay (Baranof Island)

St. John Baptist Bay is east of Zeal Point and 2.5 miles southeast of Kane Islands.
Chart 17324
Entrance: 57°17.79' N, 135°36.25' W
Anchor: 57°17.16' N, 135°33.68' W

St. John Baptist Bay, strategically located at the north end of Neva Strait, provides good swinging room for larger boats.

Anchor in 10 fathoms over a soft bottom.

## Whitestone Cove (Baranof Island)

Whitestone Cove is on the east side of Neva Strait, near the south entrance.
Chart 17324 (inset)
Entrance: 57°14.95' N, 135°33.86' W
Anchor: 57°14.76' N, 135°33.64' W

Whitestone Cove is a small bight that provides temporary anchorage at its head. Although it is partially out of the current and the wake of passing vessels, it can hold just one or two small vessels. The cove gives good protection from southeast winds. Water temperatures range in the high forties here. We have found the cove filled with sea nettles in summer.

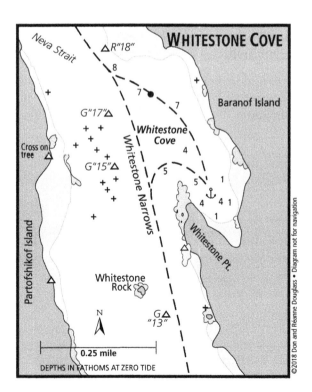

Anchor deep in the cove in 4 fathoms over mud, shells and grass with good holding.

## Nakwasina Passage

Nakwasina Passage separates the north side of Halleck Island from Baranof Island.
Chart 17324
West entrance: 57°14.14' N, 135°31.30' W
East entrance: 57°14.70' N, 135°22.80' W

## Olga Strait

Olga Strait separates Halleck and Krestof islands.
Chart 17324
Northwest entrance (Olga Point Light bearing 217°T at 0.31 Nm): 57°13.96' N, 135°31.83' W
Southeast entrance: 57°10.76' N, 135°26.83' W

Navigational aids mark Middle Shoal in the center of Olga Strait.

## Nakwasina Sound, Beehive Island Cove

Nakwasina Sound extends from the south entrance of Olga Strait and connects with Nakwasina Passage.
Chart 17324
South entrance (Nakwasina Sound): 57°10.45' N, 135°25.40' W
Entrance (Beehive Island Cove): 57°10.97' N, 135°26.26' W
Anchor (Beehive Island Cove): 57°11.17' N, 135°26.30' W

Beehive Island Cove is tiny and landlocked, just large enough for one or two small craft to anchor north of Krugloi Point.

Anchor in 6 fathoms with limited swinging room.

## Krestof Sound

Krestof Sound connects Neva Strait, through Hayward Strait, with Sitka Sound.
Chart 17324
North entrance (Partof Point bearing 282°T at 0.24 Nm): 57°13.61' N, 135°33.70' W
Northwest entrance (Sukoi Inlet): 57°14.74' N, 135°38.66' W
South entrance (meets Hayward Strait, West and East channels): 57°09.25' N, 135°33.80' W

Krestof Sound is a small inland "sea," bounded by Kruzof Island on the west, Partofshikof Island on the north and Krestof Island on the east. It is entirely landlocked, offering very good shelter. It is an interesting place to explore by small craft. The shore is free of signs of stress or logs. While most of the sound is unobstructed, the shores on the south end have numerous rocks and shoals that create navigational challenges, so proceed slowly. DeGroff Bay and Magoun Islands are our favorites for secluded anchorages.

## Mud Bay (Krestof Sound)
Mud Bay is west of the Magoun Islands.
Chart 17324
Position: 57°10.68' N, 135°36.72' W

Good protection from southerly weather can be found in Mud Bay near the southern buoy against the west shore, or off the cabin on the north shore near the trailhead to Shelikof Bay. The trail, which is about 5 miles long, heads due west to the north side of Shelikof Bay.

## Port Krestof (Krestof Sound)
Port Krestof is on the south side of West Channel.
Chart 17324
Anchor: 57°09.14' N, 135°35.30' W

We have found satisfactory anchorage in Port Krestof off the extensive drying mud flat. The current here is moderate and the pleasant, well-protected area is fun to explore by kayak.

A more sheltered anchorage with little or no current can be found in De Groff Bay.

Anchor in 4 to 6 fathoms over sand and mud with shells and fair-to-good holding. (A professional skipper who anchors here told us of finding numerous areas that have a rocky bottom.)

## West Channel (Krestof Sound)
West Channel is between Kruzof Island and the Magoun Islands.
Chart 17324
East entrance: 57°09.25' N, 135°33.80' W
North entrance: 57°09.61' N, 135°35.44' W

Southwest swell quickly dies down in West Channel north of Brown Point. In this area, numerous, small coves provide anchor sites. Although *Coast Pilot* says "West Channel should not be attempted except by small craft," we have easily transited West Channel by staying mid-channel in about a 4- to 13-fathom fairway, avoiding rocks along both shores.

## East Channel (Krestof Sound)
East Channel is between Krestof Island and the Magoun Islands.
Chart 17324
North entrance (mid-channel between Brady and Mills islands): 57°11.12' N, 135°33.76' W
South entrance: 57°09.25' N, 135°33.80' W

East Channel, which leads into DeGroff Bay, is the shortest route between Krestof Sound and Sitka Sound. Good anchorage can be found on the southeast side of the Magoun Island complex or in the central bay.

Avoid the charted shoals, especially during spring tides when strong currents are flowing.

## De Groff Bay (Krestof Island)
De Groff Bay is northeast of Magoun Islands.
Chart 17324
Entrance: 57°10.42' N, 135°32.66' W
Anchor: 57°11.05' N, 135°31.33' W

De Groff Bay is a special place where you can find solitude and lots of wildlife. The entrance is narrow and intricate, requiring skillful navigation near slack water. Favor the west shore at the inner narrows. Inside, the bay is totally landlocked and protected from all weather. There is plenty of swinging room for many boats, although we never saw another vessel here. Avoid the kelp patches, which may hide

*These Pigeon Guillemots have bright red-orange feet.*

rocks. Temporary anchorage might be found in the basin between the narrows, but the bottom may be rocky there.

Anchor in 3 to 5 fathoms over soft mud with good holding.

## Hayward Strait
Hayward Strait, at the south end of Krestof Sound, separates Krestof and Kruzof islands.
Chart 17324
South entrance: 57°08.31' N, 135°32.25' W
North entrance: 57°09.25' N, 135°33.80' W

Hayward Strait connects Sitka Sound to Krestof Sound. Freds Creek is the site of a U.S. Forest Service cabin, located 0.5 mile south of Point Brown.

## Promisla Bay (Krestof Island)
Promisla Bay is 7.3 miles northwest of Sitka.
Chart 17324
Position: 57°09.28' N, 135°31.22' W

## Eastern Bay (Krestof Island)
Eastern Bay is 7 miles northwest of Sitka.
Chart 17324
Position: 57°09.80' N, 135°28.30' W

Eastern Bay is sheltered by Siginaka Islands, which can be explored by kayak. Anchorage can be found in shallow water close to shore.

## Starrigavan Bay (Baranof Island)
Starrigavan Bay is 4.5 miles north of Sitka.
Chart 17324
Position: 57°08.04' N, 135°22.52' W

The Alaska State Ferry terminal is located on the south shore of Starrigavan Bay.

## Whiting Harbor (Japonski Island)
Whiting Harbor is 0.5 mile west of Sitka Harbor.
Chart 17327
North entrance: 57°03.47' N, 135°22.49' W
West entrance: 57°03.21' N, 135°23.07' W
Anchor (southeast corner): 57°02.75' N, 135°22.08' W

The Sitka harbormaster is encouraging recreational boaters to use the renovated transient dock. However, Whiting Harbor is a good choice for anchoring if necessary. Select your site according to the chop and depth. The site shown in the diagram is good for southerly winds.

Anchor in about 8 fathoms over a mixed bottom with fair-to-good holding. Be sure to check that your anchor is well set, since parts of the bottom are rocky.

## Sitka (Baranof Island)
Sitka is on the east side of Sitka Sound.
Chart 17327
West entrance (at breakwaters): 57°03.74' N, 135°21.96' W

Sitka (Tlingit for "by the sea") is perhaps the most popular of Southeast Alaska destinations. Its lovely setting, native culture, Russian history, museums and shops draw thousands of tourists who arrive by air, small cruise ships, ferry, or pleasure craft. Tourism and commercial fishing have been the mainstay of the local economy in the two decades since the closing of the town's large pulp mill in 1997.

Many cruise ships visit Sitka during the summer months. The cruise ships approach Sitka through Middle Channel, just south of

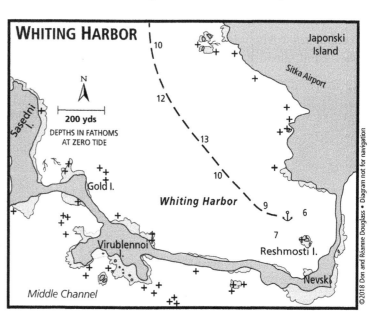

Sitka. There are frequently three large ships calling at Sitka at one time, but there are only two cruise ship docks, so the third ship will anchor in the eastern anchorage area off Crescent Bay. Passengers and cargo are transferred to shore at the lightering floats in Crescent Harbor and near the bridge. These floats are strictly reserved for use by cruise ships.

Sitka is an extremely popular destination for pleasure craft and moorage can be tight, particularly the week before and the week following the Fourth of July. Plan accordingly!

All berths are assigned by the Harbormaster, and mooring regulations are strictly enforced. Be forewarned that you may have to move your vessel if your assignment changes. Transient vessels are required to register with the Harbormaster within 8 hours of arrival. For your assignment, contact the Harbormaster's office on VHF Ch 16, and switch to Ch 14 as directed. Vessels of 100 feet or more are asked to call ahead (907.747.3439). The office is open year round from 7 a.m. to 11:30 pm, seven days a week.

## Unexpected Creatures
### Linda Lewis—Journal Notes—M/V *Royal Sounder*

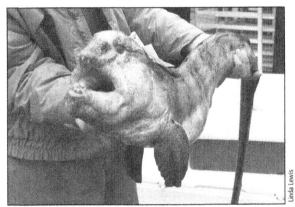
*Wolf eel caught in Sitka waters*

*Halibut caught in crab trap*

The most unexpected creature sightings can happen when you're cruising in Southeast Alaska.

This wolf eel was caught in the waters near Sitka. About six feet long, this creature is my idea of a nightmare in the flesh. However, in Sitka the wolf eel is considered a prize catch and this one was destined for someone's fireplace wall. Another unexpected creature sighting occurred in Glacier Bay when I pulled the crab trap up and saw two eyes on the same side of a head staring up at me. Now how did that halibut manage to get into my crab trap?

On one of our hikes I looked down into the crystal clear streams and saw a carpet of salmon literally at arm's length. And somewhere during our trip we spotted a hapless deer in the water frantically trying to avoid the wakes of not just one, but two boats. The deer went in circles for a while, then he managed to swim back the way he had come and find land safely.

Seeing the unexpected is part of the gift of cruising in these waters.

*Deer trying to avoid wakes of two boats. A near miss.*

Sitka has five main harbors (see descriptions below). The four non-transient harbors are Thomsen, Crescent, ANB, and Sealing Cove, as well as the City Wall moorage at the Port Facility, which can handle up to a 300' vessel. The primary transient harbors are Eliason Harbor (formerly called New Thomsen Harbor) and Thomsen Harbor.

All marine services and supplies are available for pleasure craft. The harbor has work floats and two tidal grids, and a private 60-ton travel lift can be made available in emergencies (Allen Marine, 907.747.8100). Diesel, gasoline and propane are available at the Sitka Petro Dock near Eliason Harbor (907.747.8460); diesel and gasoline at Sitka Petro Marine, near the bridge (907.747.3414). For repair service call Halibut Point Marine (907.344.4999), located at the north end of Sitka, opposite Old Sitka Rocks.

Lakeside Grocery (907.747.3317) is a block above the harbormaster's office, and Sea Mart (907.747.6266) about two miles north of the harbor. (Sea Mart will discount your taxi fare when you buy groceries.) In summer, Chelan Produce Company brings a truck to town several times a month stocked with fresh produce. They station their truck a block above the harbormaster's office—plan to arrive early for the best choices.

A self-serve and wash-and-fold laundry is located at 906 Halibut Point Road, just a block

*The Sitka Pioneers' Home*

uphill from Eliason Harbor. Sitka's general delivery U.S. Mail is handled at the postal substation on Lincoln, a block east of St. Michael's Cathedral.

The center of town is just a 10- to 15- minute walk from Eliason Harbor. Other businesses of interest to cruising boaters include Murray Pacific for nautical supplies, books and charts, on Katlian Street two blocks south of the harbor (907.747.3171); Sitka electronics, 232 Katlian (907.747.6570); Old Harbor Books, 201 Lincoln (907.747.8808), which has one of the largest selections of books on Alaska! Sitka Rose Gallery, which has a lovely variety of gifts, is for sale as we go to press.

We'll leave it to you to find your favorite restaurant. Ask around, since quality varies from year to year and from owner to owner. However, there's everything from continental to Japanese and Chinese and dynamite hamburgers.

*Sitka Harbor looking north*

# Sitka
## Don Douglass & Réanne Hemingway-Douglass

Sitka's natural beauty will captivate you even before you arrive. You'll take in views of jagged peaks topped with snow, forested islands, many with homes and docks, and fishing boats going to and fro in Sitka Sound.

When you dock you'll notice Sitka's Russian influence. Sitka was the center of the fur trade and home base to the Russian-American Company in the nineteenth century. It was the first capital of territorial Alaska until the honor was ceded to Juneau in 1906. Its current population is just under 8,900 people.

A walk around downtown gives you shopping opportunities galore, plus a view of important historical sites. Most prominent is St. Michael's Cathedral with its wealth of icons, many of which were saved from a 1966 fire that destroyed the original structure built in the 1840s. It's still an active Russian Orthodox Church. At the corner of Lincoln and Katlian Streets, you'll find the stately Pioneers' Home, and nearby is the Russian Cemetery and Block House. Walking the opposite direction on Lincoln, you'll soon arrive at the restored 1843 Russian Bishop's House, a National Historic Landmark.

Further out is the 100-acre Sitka National Historical Park on the site of the 1804 battle between Russians and Kiksadi. Now it provides a tranquil path through towering trees and past Tlingit and Haida totems, with views of the bay peeking through the foliage. Inside you can talk to local artists as they carve wooden masks or craft silver jewelry.

Walking back to town, stop in the Sheldon Jackson Museum, an absolute gem. It is named for its founder, a Presbyterian missionary who came to Sitka in 1877. He collected artifacts from many Alaskan cultures and built the concrete octagonal building to house them in 1885-87. You'll see well-lit displays of masks, watercraft and clothing, as well as argillite and ivory carvings. Allow plenty of time to slide open all of the exhibit drawers, where you'll find hundreds more tiny treasures.

Learn more about Sitka's history at the Isabel Miller Museum in Harrigan Centennial Hall at Crescent Harbor.

Cultural opportunities include the New Archangel Dancers who perform Russian folk dances at Harrigan Centennial Hall and native Naa Kahidi dancers appearing at the Sheet'ka Kwaan Naa Kahidi Community House. The annual Sitka Music Festival, featuring classical performers from around the world, is held each June.

In the surrounding forests and waters, you can bike, hike, kayak, snorkel and fish. If up-close wildlife

*St. Michael's Cathedral, Russian Orthodox Church, Sitka*

interests you, visit the Alaska Raptor Center, which cares for injured eagles, hawks, owls and other birds. Learn about marine life at the Sheldon Jackson Aquarium. Or, even better, take an excursion boat to the offshore St. Lazaria Island NWR, whose twisted volcanic cliffs harbor hundreds of puffins, murres and petrels. About seven miles north of Sitka, you will find the U.S.F.S. Starrigavan Recreation Area with its estuary bird viewing shelter and the Estuary Life nature trail.

Before you leave Sitka, climb to the top of Castle Hill to enjoy the views of the harbor and city. Think about how different Alaska, the U.S. and world history would have been if Russia had not decided to sell this chunk of land. You are standing right where the transfer took place in a ceremony on October 18, 1867.

The Sitka Convention & Visitors Bureau's website has valuable links https://visitsitka.org/ and the online harbor guide is full of information http://sitkaharborguide.com/ The harbormaster office is available at 907.747.3439 or VHF Ch 16.

## Eliason and Thomsen Harbors (Sitka)

Eliason and Thomsen Harbors are located on the northwest side of Sitka, inside the Sitka Sound breakwater.

**Chart 17327**
**Eliason Harbor: 57°3.544'N, 135°21.246'W**

Eliason Harbor is on the northern side of the facility, and Thomsen Harbor adjoins it to the south. Eliason and Thomsen Harbors are usually the designated harbors for transient pleasure craft, although visiting pleasure craft may be assigned a spot in one of the other harbors. The recently renovated south breakwater floats have water and power, and boast over 1,900 feet of moorage. Showers are available. You may be assigned to a slip that is normally occupied by a fishing boat, in which case be prepared to move your boat at the Harbormaster's direction, when the owner returns.

*Sitka Harbor with airport bridge in background*

## Crescent Harbor

**Chart 17327**
**Entrance: 57°02.92' N, 135°17.14' W**

Crescent Bay has no moorage for transient vessels and the harbormaster's office tightly controls these restrictions. Use of the lightering floats is strictly reserved for cruise ship tenders. At this writing (2018), planned renovation awaits funding.

## ANB Harbor

This facility was rebuilt in 2014 for the commercial fishing fleet. There are no showers available.

## Sealing Cove (Japonski Island)

Sealing Cove is 0.5 mile west of the bridge.
Chart 17327
Entrance: 57°02.68′ N, 135°20.59′ W

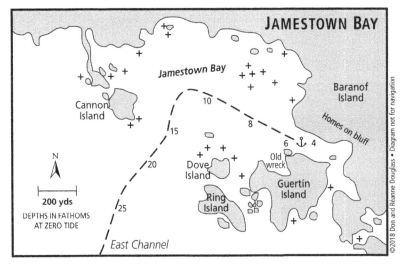

Berthage in Sealing Cove is strictly regulated by the harbormaster. Moorage in Sealing Cove is limited to boats less than 40 feet in length, and at present the harbor is filled mostly with local vessels.

## Jamestown Bay (Baranof Island)

Jamestown Bay is 1.5 miles east of Sitka.
Chart 17327
Entrance: 57°02.49′ N, 135°17.87′ W
Anchor (southeast): 57°02.48′ N, 135°17.14′ W

Some boats anchor in Jamestown Bay and commute the 2 miles to Sitka. The bay offers good protection from southerly storms in several of its small coves.

Anchor in about 4 fathoms over mud and sand with fair-to-good holding.

## OUTER PASSAGE SOUTH OF SITKA

*Note:* Due to potential exposure to the Gulf of Alaska weather and the lack of well-documented cruising-boat anchorages, the coastline south of Sitka along the west coast of Baranof is lightly used by cruisers. Most pleasure craft departing Sitka use Peril Strait for destinations east or south. In settled weather, however, the Outer Passage south of Sitka offers great exploring and a lot of wonderful surprises! This section of the coast is documented in Chapter 8.

## WEST COAST OF KRUZOF ISLAND

Charts 17325, 17320

## Sealion Cove (Kruzof Island)

Sealion Cove is 2 miles southeast of Cape Georgiana.
Chart 17325
Entrance: 57°18.26′ N, 135°51.49′ W

*Editor of our second edition, Linda Lewis, brings the* Royal Sounder *to the dock at Eliason Harbor in Sitka.*

*Propeller work in Sitka*

Sealion Cove has one of the most beautiful sandy beaches along the outer coast. It is exposed to northwest swells that crash onto its long, shallow beach, but in calm weather it's worth making a daytime stop here. Watch the tide level, otherwise; if you take a dinghy to shore, you may find yourself stranded for hours. We do not recommend anchoring overnight in Sealion Cove. As its name suggests, sea lions like this cove as they commute back and forth from the nearby Sealion Islands.

A fairly strenuous trail leads east from the cove to Kalinan Bay. Most hikers make a round-trip from the east side of Kruzof in order to leave their vessel in sheltered water. Be prepared for bear encounters if you attempt the trail.

### Gilmer Bay (Kruzof Island)
Gilmer Bay is 13 miles north of Cape Edgecumbe.
Chart 17325
Entrance: 57°12.91' N, 135°50.35' W
Anchor (Reef Cove): 57°13.83' N, 135°48.72' W
Anchor (NE of Reef Cove): 57°14.15' N, 135°48.31' W
Anchor (upper inlet): 57°15.17' N, 135°48.27' W
Anchor (Gilmer Cove): 57°18.06' N, 135°38.22' W

The shoreline of Gilmer Bay is surrounded by peaks that rise to over 2,300 feet, with flanks consisting of steep-sided granite cliffs and ledges and many avalanche areas. Several sites in the bay can be used for anchoring, depending on the weather.

The site we call "Reef Cove" is open to northwest chop and whitecaps that blow into the cove, but it is protected from the southeast. Beware of a pinnacle rock, located at 57°12.05'N, 135°49.98'W.

The site northeast of Reef Cove does not receive chop from the northwest and is preferable in northwesterlies. Although it may also be acceptable in southeast weather, it is open to the southwest and should be avoided in weather from that quadrant.

The upper inlet appears not to be subject to northerly winds; the prevailing northwest winds curl into the inlet, but die out at its head. Shore landing can be made on a small beach south of the stream that flows into the northernmost part of the inlet.

The last site, Gilmer Cove, is good in southeasterly weather. The cove is steep-to, but anchorage can be found in the middle in about 6 fathoms, slightly favoring the west shore.

*These eagles are in a feeding frenzy near a fish-cleaning station where the waste is being cast onto the beach.*

*Don't try to tie up your dinghy here! This dock at Crescent Harbor is only for use by cruise ship tenders.*

Visibility through the water is good at all sites.

Anchor (Reef Cove) in about 4 fathoms over hard sand and some kelp; fair-to-good holding.

Anchor (NE of Reef Cove) in 4 fathoms over hard sand with stone and some kelp; fair-to-good holding.

Anchor (upper inlet) in 7 fathoms over brown sand and mud; good holding.

Anchor (Gilmer Cove) in 6-8 fathoms over thin sand, gravel and newspaper kelp; fair holding with a well-set anchor.

### Shelikof Bay (Kruzof Island)
Shelikof Bay is 8.5 miles north of Cape Edgecumbe.
Chart 17325
Entrance: 57°08.54' N, 135°49.74' W

Shelikof Bay offers good anchoring in Goleta and Cuvacan coves. Goleta is popular with local fishing boats. Cruising boats without local knowledge should reconnoiter by dinghy before attempting to enter either cove.

### Goleta Cove (Shelikof Bay)
Goleta Cove, on the north side of Shelikof Bay, is 1.1 miles east of Point Mary.
Chart 17325
Entrance: 57°10.11' N, 135°47.82' W
Anchor: 57°10.32' N, 135°47.76' W

Goleta Cove has a very narrow, shallow entrance. Entry should be made to the west of the islet and east of a rock that is awash on a 6-foot tide. Once past the hazards, the cove opens to a flat sandy bottom with room for more than half a dozen vessels.

Anchor in about 3 fathoms near the center of the cove over sand with fair-to-good holding.

### Cuvacan Cove (Shelikof Bay)
Cuvacan Cove, on the north side of Shelikof Bay, is 1.6 miles east of Point Mary.
Chart 17325
Entrance: 57°09.68' N, 135°46.70' W
Anchor: 57°10.16' N, 135°46.88' W

Cuvacan Cove offers good protection inside the northernmost islet of a series of islets and reefs. However, it has a very tricky entrance and should be entered only with local knowledge or by reconnoitering by dinghy first.

*The Outer Passage continues south from Sitka.*

*Goleta Cove*

Anchor in 3 fathoms over sand with fair holding.

## Port Mary (Shelikof Bay)
Port Mary is at the head of Shelikof Bay.
Chart 17325
Entrance: 57°08.81' N, 135°45.70' W
Anchor: 57°08.78' N, 135°44.53' W

Port Mary is open to the west and southwest, but can be used as an anchorage in winds with an easterly component. A series of islets on the northwest side of the cove offer some protection from northwesterly swells. The coastline along this stretch is full of rocky outcroppings and sea caves, but the anchorage has a fairly flat, wide bottom.

Anchor in about 5 fathoms over a hard bottom; fair-to-good holding with a well-set anchor.

## Cape Edgecumbe Light (Kruzof Island)
Cape Edgecumbe is the southwest tip of Kruzof Island.
Chart 17325
Position (Light bearing 050°T at 0.50 Nm): 56°59.57' N, 135°52.16' W

> Mount Edgecumbe... is the prominent landmark for Sitka Sound. From any point seaward, it is easily distinguished by its isolated position, its flat top, its peculiar streaked appearance, and its reddishness. The upper part is a bare volcanic cone, usually snow-covered. (CP)

Mount Edgecumbe is 4.7 miles northeast of Cape Edgecumbe Light at the northwest corner of Sitka Sound.

## PERIL STRAIT (West to East)
Peril Strait, which connects Salisbury Sound to Chatham Strait, separates Chichagof Island from Baranof Island.
Chart 17320
West entrance (Kakul Rock Light bearing 127°T at 0.23 Nm): 57°21.85' N, 135°42.22' W
East entrance (Morris Reef Buoy bearing 036°T at 0.9 Nm): 57°27.02' N, 134°49.47' W

Peril Strait is used by almost all vessels that navigate to and from Sitka, so careful piloting is essential at all times. Strong current reacting with the wind creates large "square" waves, especially during southeast gales that blow through Peril Strait from east to west. Several coves along the south side of the strait afford good shelter.

## Kakul Narrows (Peril Strait)
Kakul Narrows forms the entrance to Peril Strait from Salisbury Sound.
Chart 17323
South entrance (Kakul Rock Light bearing 127°T at 0.23 Nm): 57°21.85' N, 135°42.22' W
North entrance (Channel Rocks Light bearing 152°T at 0.11 Nm): 57°22.52' N, 135°41.09' W

## Salmonberry Cove (Chichagof Island)
Salmonberry Cove is on the northwest side of Kakul Narrows.
Chart 17323
Position: 57°22.36' N, 135°42.04' W

Salmonberry Cove is exposed to traffic wake and southerly chop.

## Louise Cove (Baranof Island)
Louise Cove is east of Kakul Narrows.
Chart 17323
Entrance: 57°22.14' N, 135°40.06' W

Louise Cove is an open bight too deep for convenient anchorage.

## Bradshaw Cove (Chichagof Island)

Bradshaw Cove is 0.5 mile north of Channel Rock Light.

Chart 17323
Entrance: 57°22.98' N, 135°40.62' W

Bradshaw Cove, on the north side of Struya Narrows, provides good shelter from north winds, but the cove is not shallow enough to offer convenient anchorage. We suggest you travel 2.5 miles northeast to Schulze Cove, which offers more swinging room.

*Geologic formations on the west side of the Kruzof Islands*

## Fish Bay (Baranof Island)

Fish Bay is south of Sergius Narrows and extends eastward into Baranof Island.

Chart 17323
Entrance (Haley Rocks bearing 202°T at 0.27 Nm): 57°22.92' N, 135°37.92' W

Fish Bay has been used for log storage, resulting in locally difficult anchoring conditions. We prefer the shelter of Schulze Cove (see below).

## Haley Anchorage (Fish Bay)

Haley Anchorage is 1.2 miles southeast of Fish Point.

Chart 17323
Anchor: 57°22.31' N, 135°36.74' W

Haley Anchorage is somewhat protected from south winds and is frequently used by cruising boats to time their transit of Sergius Narrows. Since the anchorage is an open roadstead, we prefer the more protected Schulze Cove on the west side of Piper Island. Avoid Haley Rocks and anchor about 0.25 mile west of Haley Point.

Anchor in 10 fathoms over sand and gravel with poor-to-fair holding.

## Schulze Cove, Piper Island (Fish Bay)

Schulze Cove, with Piper Island in its entrance, is on the north side of Fish Bay.

Chart 17323
Entrance: 57°23.07' N, 135°35.80' W
Anchor: 57°23.61' N, 135°35.30' W

Our preferred anchorage in Schulze Cove is at the northeast side of Piper Island where there is very good protection in shallow water with a flat bottom and good swinging room. The channel at the north end of Piper Island is narrow with 2 to 3 fathoms in the fairway. While the site can be subject to heavy

*Mount Edgecumbe on Kruzof Island*

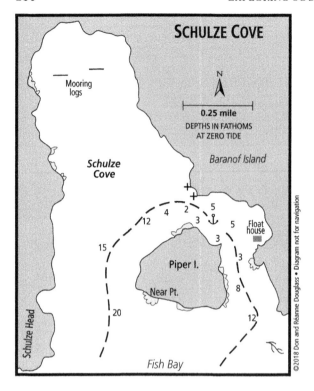

*Orcas charge through Peril Strait near Sergius Narrows.*

northerly winds, it is otherwise quite comfortable and conveniently located close to Sergius Narrows.

Anchor in 4 fathoms over mud and sand with good holding.

### Suloia Bay (Chichagof Island)
Suloia Bay is west of the south entrance to Sergius Narrows.
Chart 17323
Entrance: 57°24.31' N, 135°40.37' W
Suloia Bay is too deep, exposed and filled with gravel and kelp for convenient anchorage.

### Sergius Narrows (Peril Strait)
Sergius Narrows has a channel 450 feet wide, dredged to a depth of 21 feet.
Chart 17323 (inset)
West entrance: 57°24.29' N, 135°38.60' W
East entrance: 57°24.49' N, 135°37.34' W

See Current Tables for predictions since slack in Sergius Narrows does not coincide with Sitka high and low water. At ebb tide, Sergius Narrows is dangerous, with tide rips and turbulence, except near slack water—which is when you should plan your transit.

The tilt of the channel buoys is an excellent measure of the strength and direction of the current. Avoid transiting the Narrows when a large vessel has given a Sécurité announcement. You may wish to make a Sécurité call yourself on Ch 16 when there is limited visibility or heavy traffic or strong current that might impede steerage. This is especially important at the most restricted part of the channel, which is approximately

*The St. Lazaria Islands are west of Sitka—just off the south end of Kruzof Island.*

145 yards wide for a length of approximately 0.3 nm. Commercial vessels have priority, so you may have to wait your turn. Be mindful of the effect of your wake on other boats.

Small boats frequently use Canoe Pass; however, while the current is less than in Sergius Narrows, it can still be very strong—with tide rips. These conditions can be especially troublesome at the center of Canoe Pass (center: 57°24.12' N, 135°37.92' W), where a sharp turn is required. A Sécurité call on Ch 16 is advised. Avoid East Francis Rock.

## Launch Cove (Baranof Island)
Launch Cove lies immediately southeast of Sergius Narrows.
Chart 17323
Anchor: 57°23.93' N, 135°37.37' W

Small craft waiting for slack water can find temporary anchorage in the far west corner of Launch Cove. Strong back eddies sometimes enter the cove.

## Bear Bay and Baby Bear Bay (Baranof Island)
Bear and Baby Bear bays are northeast of Point Siroi Light.
Chart 17323
Entrance (Bear Bay): 57°25.25' N, 135°34.93' W
Anchor (Bear Bay): 57°25.13' N, 135°34.56' W
Entrance (Baby Bear Bay): 57°25.87' N, 135°34.26' W
Anchor (Baby Bear Bay): 57°26.28' N, 135°33.50' W

Baby Bear Bay, one of the best anchorages in this entire area, is sheltered from all weather and chop. Its shores are lined with beautiful, old, silvery cedar snags. However, its entrance channel is intricate and requires careful navigation. It is not recommended in foul weather or poor visibility.

The entrance to Baby Bear Bay is narrow and circuitous and full of rocks. Pass about 75 feet east of the islet on the north side of Bear Bay Island to avoid the dangerous "shark teeth" rocks to the northeast which appear to dry on a 6-foot tide in Sitka. Once you are clear of these rocks, turn north-northeast and pass through the narrow, shallow channel between Baranof Island and the unnamed island to port. Stay mid-channel, then favor the west shore as the narrows open up.

Continue to the northeast, and circle into the northwest corner of the small landlocked bay. Nothing man-made is visible from inside, and traffic passes by outside without disturbing Baby Bear's waters—it's completely calm here!

Deep Bay, across the channel, is easier to enter and has more swinging room.

Anchor in 4 fathoms over gravel with fair holding.

## Deep Bay (Chichagof Island)
Deep Bay is 2.5 miles n. of Sergius Narrows.
Chart 17323
Entrance: 57°25.78' N, 135°35.17' W
Anchor: 57°26.76' N, 135°38.04' W

Deep Bay is much easier to enter than Baby Bear Bay but it has more fetch in southeast weather.

Anchor in 8 fathoms over a soft bottom with good holding.

## Annie's Pocket (Baranof Island)
Annie's Pocket is 3.5 miles northeast of Sergius Narrows.
Chart 17323
Entrance: 57°26.89' N, 135°32.95' W
Anchor: 57°26.79' N, 135°33.01' W

"Annie's Pocket," named for *Baidarka's* first mate, is a small bight out of the traffic and current at the south end of Adams Channel. It is an excellent place to wait for proper conditions at Sergius Narrows, and it is sheltered from all winds except northerlies. When there is no wind, you can slowly drift in circles if you don't want to drop your hook while waiting. Annie's Pocket also makes a good overnight anchorage in stable conditions.

Avoid the large shallow sandbar to the east, off the outlet of Range Creek, and anchor off the gray pebble beach.

*This is the size of the shrimp you can catch in these waters.*

Anchor in 3 fathoms over sand and shells with good holding.

## Goose Cove (Baranof Island)
Goose Cove is 6.5 miles northeast of Sergius Narrows.
Chart 17323
Anchor: 57°30.56' N, 135°32.64' W

Goose Cove, an open bight subject to some chop but out of the strong current of Sergius Narrows, is protected from southerlies. It is a good place to wait for the proper timing of the narrows if you're westbound. To enter Goose Cove from the west, you can pass southeast of Povorotni Island; the passage has 2 to 3 fathoms with a sandy bottom.

Anchor in 10 fathoms over a soft bottom; fair holding.

## Ushk Bay (Chichagof Island)
Ushk Bay is 2.5 miles southwest of Emmons Island.
Chart 17323
Entrance: 57°33.73' N, 135°34.38' W

Deep anchorage may be found behind the peninsula near the head of the bay.

## Hoonah Sound (Chichagof Island)
Hoonah Sound is northwest of Peril Strait.
Chart 17323
Position: 57°37.98' N, 135°32.31' W
East entrance (North Arm, Pedersen Point Light bearing 251°T at 0.6

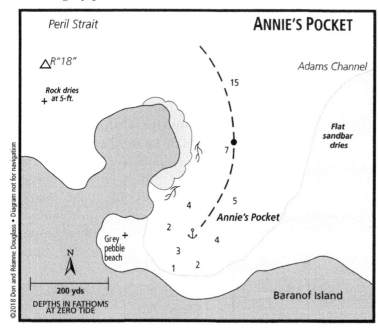

Nm): 57°39.77' N, 135°34.38' W
East entrance (South Arm, White Cliff Point bearing 023°T at 0.52 Nm): 57°37.83' N, 135°37.59' W

## Douglass Bay (Patterson Bay)

Douglass Bay is on the north shore of Patterson Bay west of Point Reynard.
Chart 17323
Entrance: 57°40.68' N, 135°43.68' W
Anchor: 57°41.10' N, 135°43.92' W

Douglass Bay has a reef that extends to mid-channel from its south shore.

Anchor in 6 fathoms off the drying mud flat over sand, gravel and green mud with fair-to-good holding.

## Nismeni Cove (Baranof Island)

Nismeni Cove lies on the east side of Nismeni Point.
Chart 17338
Entrance: 57°33.76' N, 135°23.66' W
Anchor: 57°33.59' N, 135°24.78' W

Nismeni Cove offers good protection from westerlies, but it is somewhat exposed to easterlies. You can enter from the west by using the channel south of Otstoia Island, staying 0.3 mile east of Nismeni Point before you turn

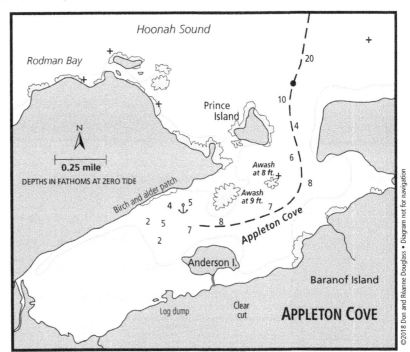

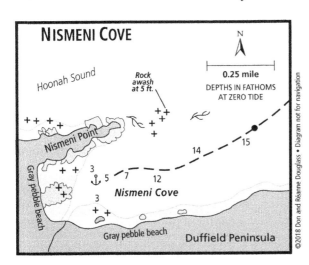

south into the cove. The reef mentioned in *Coast Pilot* is awash on about a 5-foot tide and is very dangerous. Chop from southeast winds may enter the cove.

Anchor in 4 fathoms over a mixed sand bottom with good holding.

## Rodman Bay (Baranof Island)

Rodman Bay is 6 miles southeast of Nismeni Point.
Chart 17338
Entrance (Rodman buoy G"1" bearing 105°T at 0.39 Nm): 57°29.87' N, 135°15.08' W
Anchor: 57°26.91' N, 135°23.76' W

Anchorage can be found in Rodman Bay south of Lauf Islands in about 10 fathoms over a soft bottom.

## Appleton Cove (Rodman Bay)

Appleton Cove is 1.5 miles inside Rodman Bay on the south shore.
Chart 17338
Entrance: 57°28.88' N, 135°16.28' W
Anchor: 57°28.25' N, 135°17.33' W

Appleton Cove offers very good shelter behind the western reef, north of what was once a busy logging operation located on the south shore. The cove is one of the most protected

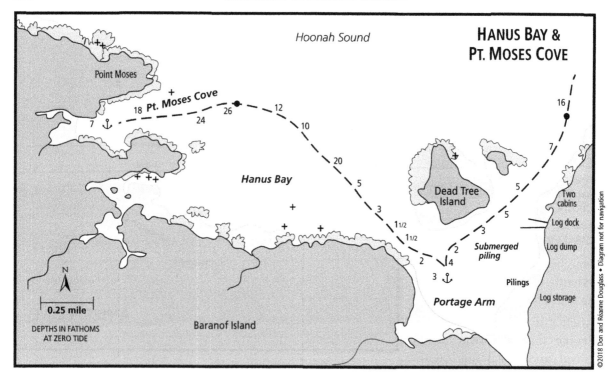

*Hanus Bay & Pt. Moses Cove*

anchorages in Peril Strait. Favor the east side of the entrance channel about 200 yards off the east shore. Avoid the reef in the center of the entrance, which is awash at 8 feet, as well as the reef north of Andersen Island. A professional skipper told us that the small cove to the east of the reefs also affords good anchorage, but to stay alert to the shoaling bottom.

Anchor in 5 fathoms over a soft bottom with good holding.

## Saook Bay (Baranof Island)
Saook Bay, on the south side of Peril Strait, is 4 miles southeast of Rodman Bay.
Chart 17338
Entrance: 57°27.17′ N, 135°08.99′ W

Saook Bay is too deep to be a convenient small-craft anchorage except along its steep-to shore, but it does provide shelter from all winds.

## Hanus Bay and Point Moses Cove
(Baranof Island)
Hanus Bay is on the south side of Peril Strait.
Chart 17338
East entrance (Hanus Bay): 57°25.06′ N, 135°00.28′ W
West entrance: (Hanus Bay): 57°25.18′ N, 135°03.12′ W
Anchor (Hanus Bay): 57°24.25′ N, 135°01.06′ W
Anchor (Pt. Moses Cove): 57°25.04′ N, 135°04.09′ W

Cruising boats can find protection from southerly weather in Hanus Bay, south of Dead Tree Island. Depths are quite shallow.

Avoid the temptation to make your entrance through the center of this east entrance to Hanus Bay as there is an area of shoal/drying sandbar in the middle, at about the area we note on the diagram as "submerged piling." Consult your charts carefully; you may find that you want to transit the more easterly, deeper 4- and 3- fathom areas to make your way to the anchorage. There are old submerged pilings or submerged logs in the vicinity, so enter cautiously, paying attention to Chart 17338 and your depth sounder.

Although easterly winds can howl through the opening to the southeast, fetch is relatively short, and there is enough swinging room to allow good scope. The creek outlet located at the lower center of the diagram is a good place to see brown bears.

You can also tuck in behind Point Moses immediately west to find good protection from westerlies.

Anchor (Hanus Bay) in 3 fathoms over mud with good holding.

Anchor (Pt. Moses Cove) in 8 fathoms over a mixed bottom with unrecorded holding.

## Lindenberg Harbor
Lindenberg Harbor is on the west side of Lindenberg Head, 3 miles north of Hanus Bay.
Chart 17338
Position: 57°27.50' N, 135°01.83' W
Anchor: 57°27.57' N, 135°01.55' W

*The best crab catch these cruisers ever had was right here, locally known as "Half-tide Neck," on the north tip of Moser Island, at half tide.*

Lindenberg Harbor provides good protection from northwest to easterly weather; it is open to the south and southwest. Moorage can be found deep in the harbor, north of the old pier complex ramp at the head of the cove. In heavy southeast weather, Appleton Cove is recommended.

This site was formerly used for log-loading; the bottom may still contain debris.

Anchor in about 7 fathoms over sand and gravel with newspaper kelp; fair-to-good holding with a well-set anchor.

## Sitkoh Bay (Chichagof Island)
Sitkoh Bay is northwest of the east entrance to Peril Strait.
Chart 17338
Entrance: 57°27.82' N, 134°50.97' W

Sitkoh Bay is open to the southeast and is deep and steep-to. Avoid rocks on the west shore near the marker.

## Florence Bay (Sitkoh Bay)
Florence Bay is inside Sitkoh Bay on the north shore.
Chart 17338
Position: 57°30.03' N, 134°52.96' W

Florence Bay is exposed to the southeast and is useful as temporary protection in strong northerly winds. Tuck in close to shore at the head of the bay.

## UPPER CHATHAM STRAIT

### Hawk Inlet (Admiralty Island)
Hawk Inlet, on the east side of Chatham Strait, lies 0.75 mile west of Young Bay on Stephens Passage.
Charts 17312, 17316, 17300
Entrance (Hawk Point bearing 025°T at 0.48 Nm): 58°05.38' N, 134°47.47' W
Anchor (head of inlet): 58°10.50' N, 134°44.67' W

The entrance is reported to have moderately swift currents. Greens Creek Mine marine terminal is located about 2 miles above the entrance at the former cannery site, with nav-aids marking the route. Favor the west shore at the narrows 0.3 mile northeast of Hawk Point. Anchorage in the basin at the head of the inlet is remote and bombproof. However, the entrance is shallow and narrow with a mid-channel rock and mud flats in all quarters. Favor the east shore. Currents add to the hazard. Use the most recent Chart 17312 as your guide.

Anchor (head of inlet) in 6 fathoms over mud and gravel with broken shells; fair-to-good holding.

### No Name Cove (Admiralty Island)
No Name Cove is 0.6 mile southwest of Piledriver Cove.
Charts 17312, 17300

Entrance: 58°04.80' N, 134°47.42' W
Anchor (No Name Cove): 58°04.52' N, 134°47.38' W

"No Name Cove" is located 0.5 mile south of the entrance to Hawk Inlet. Enter east of the islet where you can find good anchorage between the islet and the head of the bay. The cove offers good protection from southeasterly weather, but it is open to northwest chop.

Anchor in about 10 fathoms, over sand and shells with fair holding.

*Note:* Chart 17300 is a small-scale chart covering a large area with inadequate detail for coastal navigation.

### Wachusett Cove (Freshwater Bay)
Wachusett Cove, on the southwest side of Freshwater Bay, is 2.1 miles southwest of North Passage Point.
Chart 17300
Entrance: 57°49.85' N, 134°59.05' W
Anchor: 57°49.86' N, 134°59.75' W

Wachusett Cove is somewhat exposed to Chatham Strait weather but it is useful in fair weather. Pavlof Harbor is the preferred shelter.

Anchor in about 5 fathoms.

### Pavlof Harbor (Freshwater Bay)
Pavlof Harbor is 3 miles west of North Passage Point.
Chart 17300
Entrance: 57°50.95' N, 135°01.41' W
Anchor: 57°50.60' N, 135°01.64' W

Pavlof Harbor offers convenient shelter along this section of Chatham Strait. Pay close attention to the *Coast Pilot* directions to avoid a reef.

Anchor southeast of the pinnacle rock in about 7 fathoms.

### Cedar Cove (Freshwater Bay)
Cedar Cove, on the south side of Freshwater Bay, is 4 miles northwest of North Passage Point.
Chart 17300
Entrance: 57°52.33' N, 135°03.75' W
Anchor: 57°51.73' N, 135°03.00' W

Cedar Cove, which is almost landlocked, must be carefully entered west and south of the shoals extending northwest from the island that provides a natural breakwater. Avoid kelp patches and foul areas. Inside the cove there are depths of 10 fathoms.

### Tenakee Inlet (Chichagof Island)
Tenakee Inlet, on the west side of Chatham Strait, is 97 miles north of Cape Ommaney.
Charts 17320, 17300
Entrance: 57°47.25' N, 134°56.50' W

### Tenakee Springs (Tenakee Inlet)
Tenakee Springs lies on the north side of Tenakee Inlet, 9 miles inside the entrance.
Charts 17320, 17300
Tenakee Boat Harbor Light G"1": 57°46.64' N, 135°12.40' W

Tenakee Springs is a quaint village of approximately 100 people. A popular getaway for Juneau residents and cruising vessels, Tenakee Springs often serves as the beginning or end of kayak trips to and from Hoonah. The village is

*The colorful harbormaster in Tenakee Springs; his vest says: "Heaven doesn't want me. Hell is afraid I will take over."*

best known for its hot springs; these are located in a bathhouse at the center of the village, and are free though contributions for their upkeep are appreciated. Hours for use of the hot springs are posted on the bathhouse door. *Note:* women and men bathe separately without bathing suits!

The harbor, protected by two floating breakwaters, is located approximately 1/2 mile east of the center of the community. A light on the north shore, approximately 0.1 mile east of the harbor, marks a small islet close to the north shore. The small harbor is protected by two breakwaters. The harbor is easily entered from either end of the main breakwater that runs parallel to the shore. There is both assigned and transient moorage in the harbor. Call the Harbormaster on 16 for information and assignment. The harbor has four floats and a longer pier. If you tie to the pier, be sure to use batter boards or fenders and lines that you don't mind being coated with creosote. Except on holiday weekends, like the 4th of July, finding space is not generally a problem.

Fuel and water (untreated) are available at the community pier. There is a telephone at the head of the trail from the harbor to town and there are other telephones in town. No sewage facilities exist at the harbor. Because the town has no solid waste management facilities, boaters are encouraged to keep their solid waste aboard.

You can find supplies at the general store in town, as well as meals and accommodations. The Alaska Marine Highway System ferry stops in Tenakee on runs between Juneau and Sitka, and floatplane air service to Juneau is available. The ferry docks are immediately adjacent to the pier.

## Little Basket Bay (Chichagof Island)
Little Basket Bay is 1.4 miles south of Basket Bay.
Chart 17338
Position: 57°38.17' N, 134°53.00' W

Little Basket Bay is a small, shallow bight useful for temporary stops in fair weather.

## Kootznahoo Inlet (Admiralty Island) See on Chapter 5 Map
Kootznahoo Inlet, on the east shore of Chatham Strait, is 7.5 miles northeast of Peril Strait.
Chart 17339
Entrance: 57°31.25' N, 134°36.26' W

## Angoon and Kootznahoo Inlet Inner Harbor (Admiralty Island)
Angoon is bordered on its west side by Chatham Strait and on its east side by Kootznahoo Inlet.

*Floatplane dock in Kootznahoo Inlet, Angoon's inner harbor*

Chart 17339
Entrance (Danger Point Light bearing 195°T at 0.32 Nm): 57°31.25' N, 134°36.26' W

The Tlingit village of Angoon, population about 500, lies within the Admiralty Island National Monument. It is the only settlement on the island. Most services in Angoon are located in the inner harbor, inside Kootznahoo Inlet.

The entrance to the inner harbor, which lies between Danger Point and Kootznahoo Head, has numerous rocks and reefs. Transit to the inner harbor should be made at slack tide. Distance from the light at Danger Point to the inner harbor marina is 1.9 miles. Proceed into Kootznahoo Inlet past R"6" where you will see on your starboard first the seaplane float, then the Angoon Oil fuel dock, then the inner harbor floats.

*Note:* Boaters without expert local knowledge should not go beyond the waters of the inner harbor to Stillwater Anchorage, Mitchell Bay or Kanalku Bay, as these areas are uncharted and full of hazards.

Since Kootznahoo Inlet drains a large portion of west Admiralty Island, currents at the narrow entrance run to 7 knots. (Stillwater itself is just the opposite of its name—only 40-45 minutes of "still water.") Follow the chart carefully to avoid the many hazards. Boats over 60 feet are discouraged from entering. Night entry for any pleasure craft is not advisable.

*Angoon's small craft harbor inside Kootznahoo Inlet*

The inner harbor floats, which have room for just a couple of transient boats, are essentially filled with local vessels and are limited in length to 40 feet; vessels over 40 feet must anchor across from the floats and take a dinghy to the dock. Occasionally, the harbormaster can accommodate up to two 58-foot vessels at the inner harbor; call ahead to inquire about availability. Vessels over 60 feet are advised to anchor on the outside in Killisnoo Harbor, in Chatham Strait. For space availability, it's a good idea to call the harbormaster on VHF Ch 16 or 14 (907.788.3960) or city hall (907.788.3653) before you enter Kootznahoo Inlet.

Water and garbage disposal are the only services provided at the harbor floats. Diesel, gasoline and propane can be purchased at the Angoon Oil fuel dock (907.788.3436). The fuel dock is normally open during the summer season from Monday through Friday, 1000 to 1700. However, if you call the fuel dock or the harbormaster, special arrangements can be made. Groceries can be obtained at the small general store.

Frequently passed up by cruising boats, the villagers do everything possible to make your visit pleasant, and the area has now become particularly popular with kayakers and canoeists. The labyrinth of inlets and passages east of Angoon lead to the 32-mile long Cross-Admiralty canoe trail, which terminates at Mole Bay in Seymour Canal.

The village is served by regular air service and the State Ferry which calls twice a week year-round (once southbound, once northbound). The Ferry terminal is located in Killisnoo Harbor, approximately 1.9 miles SSE of Angoon, in Chatham Strait.

Killisnoo Harbor can provide convenient anchorage in stable weather, but it is not advisable in southeast weather.

Several lodges have also become popular for their cuisine, but phone well in advance for reservations. Shuttle service to and from Killisnoo Harbor, near the ferry dock, is usually provided by these lodges.

Kootznahoo Inlet Lodge (907.788.3501).
Favorite Bay Sportfishing Lodge (907.788.3344; www.favoritebay.com).
Whalers Cove Lodge in Killisnoo Harbor (907.788.3123; www.whalerscovelodge.com).

Anchor sites can be found in 5 fathoms, mid-channel east of the marina in Kootznahoo Inlet, avoiding the many rocks; or deep in Favorite Bay, 2.2 miles southeast of the marina in about 6 fathoms.

### Favorite Bay (Kootznahoo Inlet)
Favorite Bay is southeast of Angoon.
Chart 17339
Entrance (Sullivan Point bearing 015°T at 0.2 Nm): 57°29.70' N, 134°33.72' W

### Killisnoo Harbor (Admiralty Island)
Killisnoo Harbor, on the east side of Chatham Strait, is on the north side of the entrance to Hood Bay.
Charts 17339 (inset), 17320
Entrance (Light G"3" bearing 331°T at 0.11 Nm): 57°27.86' N, 134°33.86' W
Anchor: 57°27.97' N, 134°33.01' W

The Alaska State Ferry dock that serves the Angoon region is located in this harbor, 3 miles from town. Anchorage can be found on the east side of the harbor, northeast of the rocky kelp patch.

Anchor in 3 to 4 fathoms over a hard bottom with fair holding.

### Hood Bay (Admiralty Island)
Hood Bay, on the east side of Chatham Strait, is 25 miles north of Point Gardner.
Chart 17339
Entrance (mid-channel between buoys G"1" and R"2"): 57°25.29' N, 134°33.13' W

> Hood Bay has its entrance... between Distant Point and Killisnoo Island.... The bay is about 7 miles long from the entrance to the junction with both arms. (CP)

### North Arm (Hood Bay)
North Arm is 6 miles from the entrance to Hood Bay.
Chart 17339
Entrance: 57°22.74' N, 134°23.86' W
The head of the bay is reported to have a great combination of good anchoring and very good bear watching.

### South Arm (Hood Bay)
South Arm is immediately south of North Arm.
Chart 17339
Entrance: 57°22.47' N, 134°24.36' W

### Chaik Bay (Admiralty Island)
Chaik Bay, on the east side of Chatham Strait, is 19 miles north of Point Gardner.
Charts 17339, 17341
Entrance: 57°19.50' N, 134°35.48' W
Entrance (north arm): 57°20.06' N, 134°31.59' W
Entrance (south arm): 57°19.74' N, 134°31.63' W

There are numerous uncharted rocks in Chaik Bay which are a hazard to navigation. The mariner should use caution when navigating in this area. We have a report of a vessel going aground in this bay in an area that was indicated as 60 feet deep on the chart. It is worth saying again that the waters of Southeast Alaska are poorly charted. You must proceed slowly with an alert bow watch in areas like this. Read the notes on your charts.

### Whitewater Bay (Admiralty Island)
Whitewater Bay is 15 miles north of Point Gardner.
Charts 17341, 17320
Entrance: 57°15.84' N, 134°38.35' W
Anchor: 57°13.83' N, 134°33.16' W

Whitewater Bay requires vigilant piloting. Well-sheltered anchorage is reported at the head of the bay, about 0.18 Nm northeast of East Point. Note that all hazards are not charted and a skipper should verify that there is adequate swinging room. Avoid all kelp areas. The bottom is hard.

### Wilson Cove (Admiralty Island)
Wilson Cove, the east side of Chatham Strait, is immediately north of Point Wilson.
Chart 17320
Entrance: 57°09.16' N, 134°38.61' W

Although Wilson Cove is useful in easterly weather, we prefer Murder Cove, 8 miles to the south or Whitewater Bay, 7 miles north.

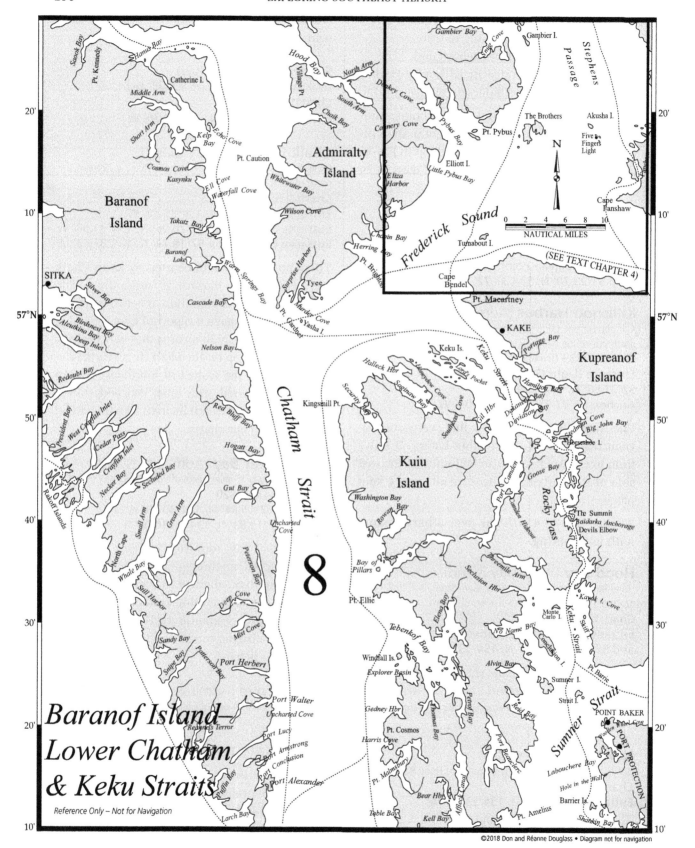

# 8

# BARANOF ISLAND, SOUTH OF SITKA; LOWER CHATHAM STRAIT & KEKU STRAIT

## INTRODUCTION

The west and east coasts of South Baranof Island, the west coast of Kuiu Island, and Keku Strait include some of the most stunningly beautiful and seldom-visited parts of Southeast Alaska. As a cruising area it is vast and mostly remote from civilization. If you are well prepared and ready for adventure, we encourage you to venture forth into these most pristine waters.

Along the Gulf of Alaska coast south of Sitka, the smooth-water route continues for the first 40 percent of the way to Cape Ommaney (the southern tip of Baranof Island), as hundreds of small off-lying islands and reefs provide protection. However, careful navigation is required to find your way among them, and large-scale charts are a must for safe transit of this coast.

As you proceed south, Goddard Hot Springs, is well worth a stop. Beyond this, Dorothy Narrows, a small, intricate route that opens up a large sheltered area for exploration, marks the end of navigational aids until Cape Ommaney. The Necker and Rakof islands of-

*Humpbacks in classic bubble-feeding activity*

fer some outstanding anchor sites that make perfect places for launching kayak and dinghy explorations of the rugged west coast.

South of Aspid and North capes, you are exposed to the full fury of whatever the Gulf of Alaska is dispensing; fair weather windows are required for transiting to the next safe anchorage. Fortunately, the distances are short and you can choose from a number of well-protected anchor sites: our favorites are in Necker Bay, Still Harbor, the small unnamed inlet we call Réanne's Terror, Redfish Bay, and Puffin Bay. You may also find refuge in Port Alexander, a small

Alaska frontier village that caters to fishing vessels and occasional pleasure craft inside of Cape Ommaney at the southern tip of Chatham Strait.

The east coast of Baranof Island has smaller inlets, which are no less striking. The mountains are higher and more precipitous and their peaks are covered with more snow than those of the west coast. Countless gullies are packed with snow to sea level into late summer. Beautiful waterfalls and unnamed rivers and creeks add to the uniqueness of this coast.

Breathtaking Red Bluff Bay and Gut Bay are "quintessential Southeast," where secure anchorage can be found deep within their bounds. The public float at Warm Springs Bay is a popular stop among pleasure boaters. From your boat or one of the hot tubs above the float you have a striking view of the beautiful falls.

The west coast of Kuiu Island, largely included within the Tebenkof Wilderness, has wonderful unspoiled bays and portages to explore. Wildlife is abundant and sport fishing is good.

Keku Strait connects Sumner Strait to Frederick Sound via infamous Rocky Pass. Kake, on the northeast corner of Keku Strait, is a thriving native community with public moorage floats, a fuel dock and grocery store. The Alaska Ferry

## WHO WAS BARANOF?

Baranof Island was named in 1805 by an Imperial Russian Navy captain, U.F. Lisianski, to honor Alexander Andreyevich Baranof (1747-1819), a Russian entrepreneur who was appointed as the first governor of the Russian fur trading colonies in Southeast Alaska.

The low-born Baranof was born near St. Petersburg but moved as a young man to Irkutsk, in Siberia, where he became a trader and tax collector. He did not make a success of this, however, and in 1790 as a means of escaping bankruptcy, he signed a five-year contract to become a manager with the Shelikhov Company, a Russian fur trading enterprise in Alaska that exploited Aleut and Tlingit natives as a labor force. In his first several years on the job Baranof moved the company's trading post at Three Saints Bay, on Kodiak Island, to the superior location of Kodiak, and established several new Russian settlements, including Voskresensk (now Seward), in Chugach Bay, another in Yakutat Bay, and Mikhailovsk, a few miles north of present-day Sitka. Baranof also fathered three children with his native mistress (whom he later married), and clashed with the local Russian Orthodox clergy.

Communications with Russia were almost nonexistent, and Baranof was surprised to learn in 1800 that instead of being replaced, as expected, he had been promoted to oversee of all of Shelikhov's interests in Alaska. By this time the company had acquired a monopoly over all fur trading in the region and was renamed the Russian-American Company. Under the patronage of Tsar Paul I, its charter included expanded colonization of coastal Alaska, coupled with the ongoing enslavement or suppression, through systematic violence, of the local Aleut and Tlingit inhabitants. After local Tlingits destroyed the settlement at Mikhailovsk in 1802, Baranof retaliated two years later with the support of the Russian Imperial Navy. The Battle of Sitka, as it became known, was the last of the major armed conflicts between Russians and natives in Alaska, and resulted in a rout of the Tlingits. Survivors fled, while Baranof, who was wounded in the battle, rebuilt the Russian settlement as New Archangel—later to become Sitka, and the capital of Russian America. Baranof was rewarded for his efforts by elevation to the middle ranks of the Russian nobility—an unprecedented achievement for the son of a merchant.

Under Baranof's leadership, the Russian-American Company established additional trading posts at Fort Ross, in what is now Sonoma County, California, and in Hawaii. However, the Alaskan settlements were dependent on British and American traders for food and materials, with bankruptcy and starvation being ever present threats. Baranof became increasingly unpopular among his own settlers, as well as the natives (against whose arrows he wore an undershirt of chain mail), although an audit commissioned in 1817 by his detractors revealed him to have been a scrupulous manager, and he himself never profited financially from his position.

Baranof retired from his managerial and gubernatorial duties in January 1818, at the age of 70, and departed Sitka at the end of that year for Russia. He became ill when his ship called en route into the Dutch colony of Batavia (now Jakarta, Indonesia), in March 1819, and died at sea shortly afterwards.

—AC

calls here, often bringing kayakers who want to explore the waters of Rocky Pass.

Between the years 1977 and 1982—after a narrow 5-foot-deep channel was dredged in

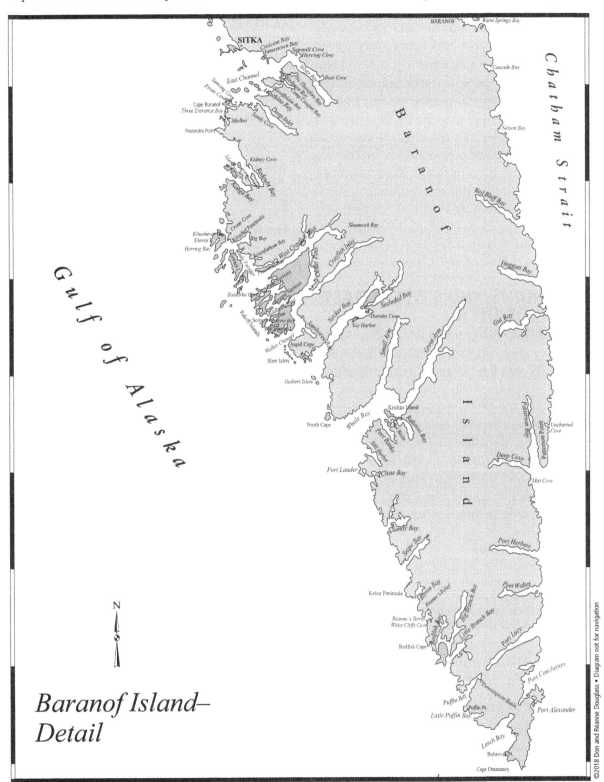

*Baranof Island– Detail*

Rocky Pass and marked with a system of poles set in concrete drums—many boats were lost or damaged; the poles were subsequently removed and the passage "closed." In the early 1990s, we spent many days reconstructing the route and found it a delightful area for exploration by small craft. In 1996, the U.S. Coast Guard reestablished a marker system that reopened this pristine area for those willing to meet its challenges. In more recent years, the USCG has added additional markers in the two most intricate areas in Rocky Pass. However, the 2017 *Coast Pilot* reports a narrowing channel with a controlling depth of 3.7 feet, and several cruisers have told us of insufficient depths. Plan to transit Rocky Pass only if you are confident in your skills, and use caution.

## BARANOF ISLAND'S WEST COAST, SOUTH OF SITKA

Most small vessels enter and exit Sitka via the smooth waters of Peril Strait and Salisbury Sound. Very few cruisers venture down Baranof Island's west coast because of its remoteness and direct exposure to the Gulf of Alaska. However, we have found good shelter and smooth sailing for much of the way. Passages with exposure to the open Pacific, such as Aspid and North capes and south of Point Lander to Ommaney Point, should be attempted only in fair weather.

### Eastern Channel
Eastern Channel is the main entrance to Sitka from the Gulf of Alaska.
Charts 17327, 17326
West entrance (Kulichkof Rock Light R"2" bearing 090°T at 1.2 Nm): 56°59.90' N, 135°29.21' W

### Eastern Anchorage (Baranof Island)
Eastern Anchorage is 0.4 mile southwest of Jamestown Bay.
Chart 17327
Position: 57°02.32' N, 135°18.46' W

Eastern Anchorage is used by cruise ships, but it is too exposed for small craft. Jamestown Bay, just north, is more protected (see Chapter 7).

### Silver Bay (Baranof Island)
Silver Bay, at the east end of Eastern Channel, is 3 miles southeast of Sitka.
Chart 17326
Entrance: 57°01.77' N, 135°14.86' W

As the logging industry retrenches, parts of Silver Bay, such as Herring Bay, may open up for recreational use. As always in areas of logging activity, beware of debris on the bottom which may hamper anchor set.

### Birdsnest Bay (Baranof Island)
Birdsnest Bay is between Camp Coogan Bay and No Thorofare Bay.
Chart 17326
Entrance: 57°00.58' N, 135°14.47' W

The best entrance to Birdsnest Bay is through the narrow channel from the west. Enter only with high tide. There is good shelter with narrow swinging room. Camp Coogan Bay is much easier to enter than Birdsnest Bay.

Anchor in 4 fathoms.

### Camp Coogan Bay (Baranof Island)
Camp Coogan Bay is 3.5 miles southeast of Sitka.
Chart 17326
Entrance: 57°00.93' N, 135°15.63' W
Anchor: 57°00.21' N, 135°13.51' W

Camp Coogan Bay, easily entered through a 100-yard-wide channel, offers very good protection with lots of swinging room over a large flat bottom. (Favor the south shore.)

Anchor in 8 fathoms over soft mud with fair-to-good holding.

### Aleutkina Bay (Baranof Island)
Aleutkina Bay is 2 miles west of Camp Coogan Bay.
Chart 17326
West entrance: 57°00.45' N, 135°19.72' W
East entrance: 57°00.82' N, 135°18.31' W
Anchor (large boats): 56°59.79' N, 135°17.28' W

Small craft will prefer the more sheltered and intimate Leesoffskaia Bay.

Anchor (large vessels) in 15 fathoms, mud bottom with fair holding.

*The channel on the north side of Entrance Island, Leesoffskaia Bay*

*Fish packer at Sandy Cove*

## Leesoffskaia Bay (Aleutkina Bay)
Leesoffskaia Bay is the east basin of Aleutkina Bay.
Chart 17326
Entrance: 56°59.97' N, 135°17.08' W
Anchor (Site #1): 57°00.25' N, 135°15.23' W
Anchor (Site #2): 57°00.30' N, 135°14.94' W

Leesoffskaia Bay is a good example of an intimate cove tucked behind a group of islands. It is an excellent landlocked, safe anchorage. We have seen small boats anchored in the narrow channel on the north side of the entrance island (very intimate!), as well as deep in the bay.

When you enter the bay, favor the north shore as the drying mud flat to the south nearly closes the entrance channel.

Anchor (Site #1): Anchor in 5 to 6 fathoms over mud and shells with good holding.

Anchor (Site #2): Anchor in 2 to 3 fathoms over mud and clamshells with good holding.

## Deep Inlet (Baranof Island)
Deep Inlet has a narrow entrance southeast of The Eckholms and the entrance to Eastern Channel.
Chart 17326
Entrance: 56°59.27' N, 135°18.57' W

Either Sandy Cove, at the entrance to Deep Cove, or Samsing Cove to the west are preferred anchor sites.

## Sandy Cove (Baranof Island)
Sandy Cove is 4.5 miles south of Sitka.
Chart 17326
Entrance: 56°59.30' N, 135°19.26' W
Anchor: 56°58.80' N, 135°18.97' W

There is good shelter in Sandy Cove. Fish buyers anchor here during gill net season. The bottom is covered with newspaper kelp, so holding is poor unless you set your anchor well.

Anchor in 7 to 10 fathoms over sand, some rocks and kelp with poor holding.

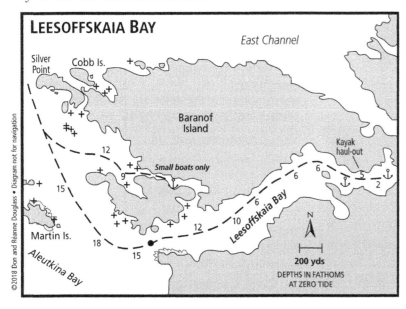

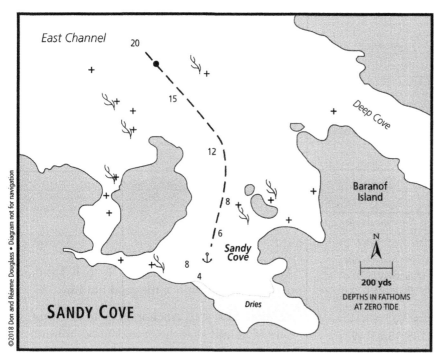

## Samsing Cove (Baranof Island)
Samsing Cove is 4 miles south of Sitka.
Chart 17326
Entrance: 56°59.32' N, 135°21.75' W
Anchor: 56°59.01' N, 135°21.60' W

Samsing Cove is the first of the three coves in the vicinity of Cape Burunof, and is well sheltered in all winds. It is small and cozy with a mostly flat bottom. It is also fairly easy to enter if you keep a mid-channel course until you are inside Easter Island, avoiding the off-lying rocks.

*Editor's Note:* The word *Burunof* is not a misspelling of Baranof, as one might think; rather, it comes from the Russian *Mys Burunof* (Cape of Breakers). The name Baranof was bestowed in 1805 by Imperial Russian Navy Captain U.F. Lisianski in honor of Alexander Andreyevich Baranof, the first governor of Russian America.

Anchor in 5 fathoms over mud and sand with good holding.

## Pirate Cove (Baranof Island)
Pirate Cove is 4 miles south of Sitka.
Chart 17326
Entrance: 56°59.36' N, 135°22.26' W
Anchor: 56°59.22' N, 135°22.26' W

Pirate Cove is the second of the three small scenic coves in the vicinity of Cape Burunof. It has less protection and swinging room than Samsing Cove and is open to northwest chop. As a temporary anchorage it is somewhat marginal.

Anchor mid-bay in 2 fathoms over mud and sand with fair holding.

## Three Entrance Bay (Baranof Island)
Three Entrance Bay is south of Cape Burunof.
Chart 17326
North entrance: 56°58.84' N, 135°23.12' W
Anchor: 56°58.76' N, 135°22.10' W

Three Entrance Bay, the third of the Cape Burunof coves, is well sheltered and has a wild aspect. Of the three entrances, we prefer the northern one; the south and middle entrances are foul. The northern entrance is narrow and intricate and should be attempted in fair weather only, as good visibility is required to avoid major offshore rocks.

Favor the north shore in the narrows, go

*North entrance to Three Entrance Bay*

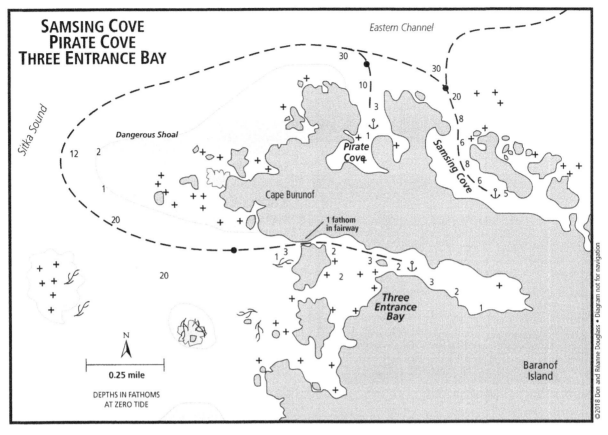

slowly, and watch for rocks—this part of the coast is one big rock pile!

Anchor as you choose in 2 to 3 fathoms over sand and gravel with fair holding.

## Mielkoi Cove (Baranof Island)
Mielkoi Cove is 1 mile south of Three Entrance Bay.
Chart 17326
Entrance: 56°58.24' N, 135°23.19' W

*Rapids at Redoubt Lake*

Mielkoi Cove is surrounded by islets and rocks and is uncharted. We have not explored the cove, but it looks like an interesting place.

## Koka Island Passage
Koka Island Passage is 8 miles south of Sitka.
Chart 17326
North entrance: 56°55.09' N, 135°22.93' W
South entrance: 56°54.19' N, 135°23.48' W

## Redoubt Bay (Baranof Island)
Redoubt Bay is 3 miles southeast of Povorotni Point.
Chart 17326
Entrance: 56°54.98' N, 135°20.72' W

Redoubt Bay is notable for Redoubt Lake at its far end. The rapids and falls are impressive. We found depths on the north side of the rapids to be greater than those charted. This is a good place to watch for spawning salmon jumping and heading upstream.

*North entrance to Redoubt Bay*

### Kidney Cove (Redoubt Bay)
Kidney Cove is on the north shore of Redoubt Bay.
Chart 17326
Entrance: 56°54.27' N, 135°19.27' W
Anchor: 56°54.55' N, 135°19.46' W

Kidney Cove provides a calm anchorage in west winds; it is a good place to anchor if you want to visit Redoubt Lake. There is a good view of 3,200-foot Mt. Dainishnikof from here and you may see bear roaming the shores. Kidney Cove is exposed to southerly weather but is otherwise sheltered.

Anchor in about 8 fathoms.

### Redoubt Lake (Redoubt Bay)
Redoubt Lake empties into the east arm of Redoubt Bay.
Chart 17326
Position (rapids): 56°53.19' N, 135°17.81' W

The falls from 10-mile-long Redoubt Lake make a roaring noise and create a lot of foam. There is a public mooring buoy in a nook on the west side of the falls out of the bulk of the current. The water is deeper here than charted. Stairs leading to the lake are east of the buoy. *Caution:* We had a large offset to the east when we charted our GPS position.

### Islet Passage
Islet Passage is 0.5 mile west of Redoubt Bay.
Chart 17326
North entrance: 56°54.66' N, 135°21.36' W
South entrance: 56°53.44' N, 135°21.16' W

### Kanga Bay (Baranof Island)
Kanga Bay is 1 mile southwest of Redoubt Bay.
Chart 17326
West entrance: 56°53.88' N, 135°22.92' W
Anchor: 56°52.82' N, 135°19.53' W

The inner basin of Kanga Bay provides good anchorage for larger boats, with lots of swinging room.

Anchor in 12 to 15 fathoms over soft mud with good holding.

### Crane Cove (Baranof Island)
Crane Cove is 0.4 mile southeast of Calligan Island.
Chart 17326
Entrance: 56°51.00' N, 135°23.07' W

Crane Cove is a tiny shallow cove more suited to sandhill cranes than small craft.

### Goddard Hot Springs Bay (Baranof Island)
Goddard Hot Springs Bay is 15 miles south of Sitka.
Chart 17326
North entrance (Torsar Island bearing 270°T at 0.35 Nm): 56°50.98' N, 135°24.59' W
South entrance (north entrance of Dorothy Narrows): 56°49.48' N, 135°22.81' W
Entrance (Goddard Hot Springs): 56°50.25' N, 135°23.46' W
Anchor (Goddard Hot Springs): 56°50.13' N, 135°22.81' W

Goddard Hot Springs are a real treat for all who explore Baranof Island's west coast. Don't miss this inviting place. The USFS installed wooden hot tubs inside the shelters, with large open windows to seaward. Two valves allow for temperature regulation—hot or very

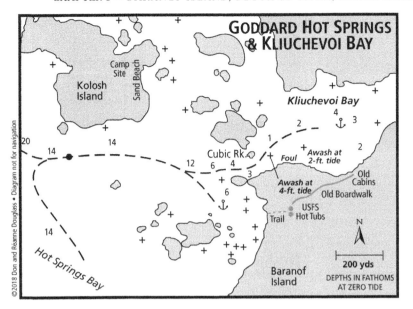

hot! You can easily land your dinghy on the sand and gravel beach; from here, a boardwalk leads to the tubs. There is an outhouse on the trail to the north, and an old open cement pool with a bathtub further up the hill.

The cove is small and foul with a rocky bottom and marginal holding (mud is reported in deeper water). The cove in front of the tub is used by local fishing boats from late afternoon to very early in the morning.

Anchor in 5 to 10 fathoms over sand, mud and kelp with fair holding. Set your anchor well so you can enjoy your hot tubbing. Kliuchevoi Bay to the northeast has better holding and shelter, but your boat is out of view while you're soaking.

### Kliuchevoi Bay (Baranof Island)
Kliuchevoi Bay is 0.3 mile north of Goddard Hot Springs.
Chart 17326
Entrance: 56°50.25' N, 135°22.85' W
Anchor: 56°50.32' N, 135°22.32' W

Kliuchevoi Bay, northeast of Goddard Hot Springs, is a small bay protected by islets and rock piles. It offers very good shelter and holding over a largely mud bottom with many clam shells; however, the entrance is narrow and shallow with numerous uncharted rocks. Pass south of "Cubic Rock" where you must make a dogleg, as shown on the diagram. At this point the passage is about 40 feet wide; a foul area lies along the southeast shore. Be extra cautious making this entrance; post a bow watch and proceed very slowly.

Anchor in 3 to 4 fathoms over mud with clamshells; very good holding.

### Dorothy Narrows
Dorothy Narrows, between Windy Passage and Hot Springs Bay, separates Baranof and Elovoi islands.
Chart 17326
North entrance: 56°49.48' N, 135°22.81' W
South entrance: 56°48.88' N, 135°22.71' W

Dorothy Narrows is the first of several narrows on the smooth-water route along the southwest

*U.S. Forest Service cabin with hot tub at Goddard Hot Springs Bay*

*Approaching Dorothy Narrows . . .*

*. . . while maintaining a sharp lookout!*

coast of Baranof Island. Small craft will have no problem maneuvering provided they post an alert bow watch and transit these channels slowly.

On a transit at zero tide, we found 1 fathom in the fairway from marker G"1" to the narrows, then a gradual deepening to 2½ fathoms, except for a 1-fathom shoal at the south entrance. Dorothy Narrows is not well charted, but you can see the soft bottom of sand, clam shells, and newspaper kelp, as well as lots of starfish.

The fairway in the narrows is about 60 feet wide. The biggest danger lies in cutting the corner north of marker G"1." Do not hug the marker, and stay east until you have passed the last of a series of rocks on the west shore. Favor the east shore a bit at the south entrance.

*Heading for a dip in the hot tub*

## Necker Islands
Necker Islands are located west of Goddard Hot Springs and north of West Crawfish Inlet.
Chart 17326

The Necker Islands are fun to explore by kayak. We have enjoyed staying in wild-looking yet secure Herring Bay when visiting them.

## Herring Bay (Elovoi Island)
Herring Bay indents the south side of Elovoi Island and is 2 miles south of Goddard Hot Springs.
Chart 17326
Entrance: 56°48.11' N, 135°24.54' W
Anchor: 56°49.07' N, 135°23.80' W

The head of Herring Bay offers very good protection; note the absence of logs on the beach. Although close to the Gulf of Alaska, in fair weather this little inlet makes a good base camp from which to explore a great variety of islets, rocks and tide-pools. Avoid foul areas and kelp when entering the bay. Once inside, you are landlocked and surrounded by old cedar forest.

Anchor in 3 fathoms over mud, sand, shells and kelp patches with good to very good holding.

## Symonds Bay and Rocky Cove (Biorka Island)
Symonds Bay is the cove on the north side of Biorka Island.
Chart 17326
Entrance: 56°51.98' N, 135°31.09' W
Anchor: 56°51.39' N, 135°31.05' W
Entrance (Rocky Cove): 56°50.53' N, 135°33.04' W

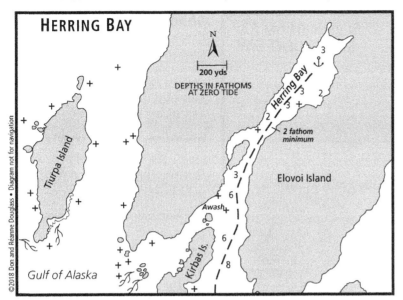

Biorka Island has a large aero beacon and antenna "farm." Symonds Bay offers good shelter from southerly weather with easy entry and good swinging room. Rocky Cove is uncharted and too exposed for anchorage.

*Green marker, G"1," north end of Dorothy Narrows*

Anchor (Symonds Bay) in 5 fathoms over sand with fair holding.

## Big Bay (Baranof Island)
Big Bay is at the northwest end of Windy Passage.
Chart 17326
Entrance: 56°48.80' N, 135°21.46' W
Anchor: 56°48.96' N, 135°19.62' W

Big Bay, well sheltered in the south arm, has easy entry and a lot of swinging room for large boats.

Anchor in 5 fathoms over mud with fair holding.

## Windy Passage
Windy Passage lies between Gornoi and Baranof islands.
Chart 17326
North entrance: 56°48.47' N, 135°21.65' W
South entrance: 56°46.44' N, 135°19.09' W

Windy Passage gets its name from the strong southeast winds that blow down its 5-mile length. VHF Weather Ch 1 fades in and out in this area.

## Sevenfathom Bay (Windy Passage)
Sevenfathom Bay, on the east side of Windy Passage, is 0.7 mile north of President Bay.
Chart 17326
Entrance: 56°47.52' N, 135°19.10' W
Anchor: 56°47.62' N, 135°18.23' W

Sevenfathom Bay and President Bay both offer very good anchorage for small craft at their head. In Sevenfathom Bay there is a USFS A-frame hut on the north shore and a public mooring buoy off the drying mud flat.

*Note:* The flat is much more extensive than indicated on the chart. For example, there is grass growing where the chart shows 2 fathoms!

Anchor in 6 fathoms over mud, sand, clamshells and some kelp.

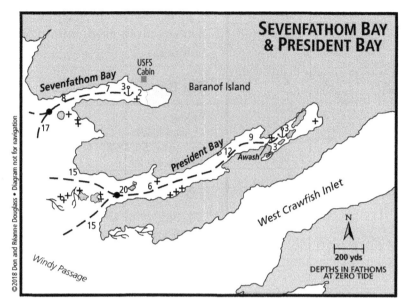

## Shamrock Bay (West Crawfish Inlet)
Shamrock Bay is 6 miles from the entrance to West Crawfish Inlet.
Chart 17326
Entrance: 56°49.82' N, 135°08.46' W

Shamrock Bay may provide good shelter, except for williwaws that sweep down the peaks overhead.

Anchor behind the islet at the head of the bay in 6 to 9 fathoms over gravel.

## Cedar Pass
Cedar Pass, between Lodge and Baranof islands, connects West Crawfish Inlet to Crawfish Inlet.
Chart 17326
North entrance: 56°48.53' N, 135°11.20' W
South entrance: 56°45.38' N, 135°11.58' W

We prefer the outside, smooth-water passage using First and Second Narrows west of Lodge Island.

## First Narrows (Rakof Islands)
First Narrows is between Lodge Island and Rakof Islands.
Chart 17326
Position: 56°45.40' N, 135°17.00' W

First and Second Narrows provide a secure route south to Walker Channel. We find a little less than 3 fathoms at zero tide in the fairway through the first narrows. Avoid an uncharted rock marked by kelp on the east shore of the northern entrance.

## Baidarka Cove (Rakof Islands)
Baidarka Cove is 6 miles south of Goddard Hot Springs.
Chart 17326
Entrance: 56°45.20' N, 135°17.00' W
Anchor: 56°44.89' N, 135°17.61' W

"Baidarka Cove" is formed by the three northernmost unnamed islands of the Rakof Islands. The cove offers good shelter in a rugged west coast setting,

## President Bay (Windy Passage)
President Bay is on the east side of Windy Passage, just inside the south entrance.
Chart 17326
Entrance: 56°46.90' N, 135°18.37' W
Anchor: 56°47.30' N, 135°16.21' W

We found good shelter at the head of President Bay in the small basin west of the islets and lagoon. Anchor north of the window between the islets and west of a rock pile. Avoid the rock awash on a 6-foot tide off the north entrance point to the inner basin.

Anchor in 3 to 4 fathoms over mud and clam shells with good holding.

*Necker Islands provide beautiful shelter.*

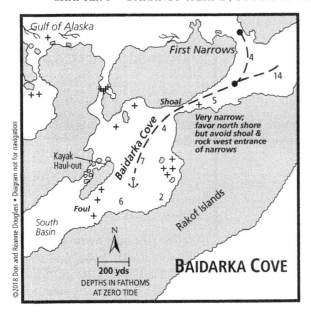

the north basin by a foul line of mussel-covered rocks. Enter only at high water by favoring the south shore about 45 feet off a bold white rock.

Weather reports on VHF Ch 1 can be heard from Baidarka Cove.

Anchor in 6 fathoms over mud with good holding.

### Second Narrows (Rakof Islands)
Second Narrows is between the southwest side of Lodge Island and Rakof Islands.
Chart 17326
Position: 56°44.08' N, 135°16.33' W

### Middle Channel (Rakof Islands)
Middle Channel, north of Beauchamp Island, leads to Crawfish Inlet, midway between Walker Channel and West Crawfish Inlet.
Chart 17326
Northeast entrance: 56°44.70' N, 135°12.98' W
Southwest entrance: 56°43.04' N, 135°17.77' W

Middle Channel provides access to Scow Bay, another of our favorite "West Coast" coves.

### Cameron Pass
Cameron Pass cuts across the northwest side of Beauchamp Island to Middle Channel.
Chart 17326
Northeast entrance: 56°43.20' N, 135°16.49' W
Southwest entrance: 56°41.80' N, 135°17.23' W

Cameron Pass connects Middle Channel to Scow Bay.

### Scow Bay (Beauchamp Island)
Scow Bay is on the west shore of Beauchamp Island.
Chart 17326
Entrance: 56°42.70' N, 135°16.46' W
Anchor (northeast cove): 56°43.47' N, 135°14.53' W

Scow Bay is a bombproof anchorage separated from the Gulf of Alaska by just a few low-lying islets and rocks. Shelter is good here and the contrast between the rugged coast and the bay's cedar-lined shores with many silver snags is impressive.

Avoid the rocks on the north shore as you

and is a natural base for kayaking. On entering the very narrow entrance, favor the north shore to avoid a dangerous rock that is awash on an 18-inch tide and extends over halfway from the south shore. The fairway carries a minimum of 3 fathoms.

Entry to the southwest basin is advisable only by dinghy or kayak. It is separated from

*Outer passage through the Rakof Islands*

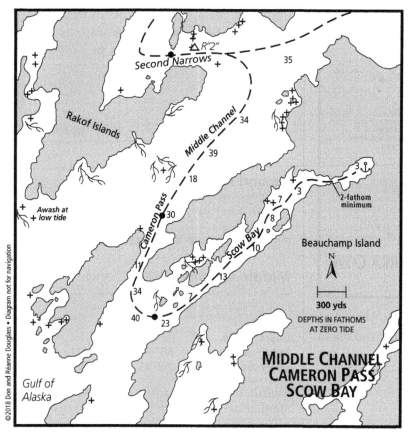

enter the inner basin; these rocks extend 60 percent of the way into the basin. Stay hard against the south shore about 5 to 10 feet off the tree limbs.

*Salmon for dinner again!*

Anchor in 3½ fathoms over brown mud, clamshells and some twigs with very good holding.

## Walker Channel
Walker Channel is the southeast entrance to Crawfish Inlet.
Chart 17326
West entrance: 56°41.41' N, 135°14.99' W
Northeast entrance: 56°44.60' N, 135°12.57' W

Walker Channel takes you out into the Gulf. Your progress southward from here involves hopping from one sheltered inlet to the next, rounding some imposing capes all the way to Cape Ommaney.

## Jamboree Bay (Walker Channel)
Jamboree Bay extends southeast from the head of Walker Channel.
Chart 17326
Entrance: 56°42.62' N, 135°11.62' W
Anchor: 56°41.91' N, 135°10.37' W

*In entering, keep in midchannel, and anchor near the head of the bay in 10 to 17 fathoms with good holding ground. SE winds sweep through the anchorage with considerable force. (CP)*

Anchored at the head of Jamboree Bay, you have little fetch in southeast winds. However, the bottom is rocky and of marginal holding.

Anchor in 10 fathoms over mud and rocks with marginal holding.

## Necker Bay (Baranof Island)
Necker Bay is 35 miles northwest of Cape Ommaney.
Chart 17328
Entrance: 56°39.37' N, 135°10.50' W

Necker Bay has several remote but good anchorages.

*Entrance Islets protect Still Harbor.*

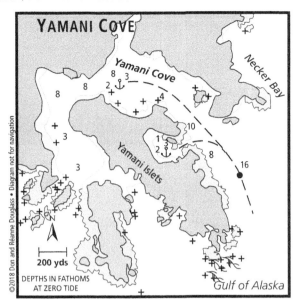

## Yamani Cove (Necker Bay)

Yamani Cove is on the north side of the entrance to Necker Bay and north of the Yamani Islets.
Chart 17328
Entrance: 56°40.30' N, 135°10.65' W
Anchor (east cove): 56°'40.32 N, 135°11.09' W
Anchor (north cove): 56°40.53' N, 135°11.35' W

Yamani Cove is a small cove with good shelter and an "outside feel." Enter east of the larger of the Yamani Islets and proceed to the cove on the islet's eastern side. From this site you have an excellent view of the Gulf of Alaska—including blowing foam! For the most protection, anchor along the north side of this islet.

Anchor (east cove) in about 2 fathoms over

---

## Still Harbor Disaster

### Don Douglass & Réanne Hemingway-Douglass

In 1979, Ward Eldridge, a Sitka shipwright, fell in love with *Merlin*, a derelict 73-foot Herreshoff schooner he'd seen in a Florida boatyard. Feeling sure he could restore the vessel, he bought her and spent the next six years rebuilding her from the keel up. Eleven years later, he brought her through the Panama Canal and up the West Coast to Sitka.

In 1999, Ward and his soon-to-be spouse, Kathy, set out a weekend for some R & R on *Merlin*. They anchored the schooner in Still Harbor, 35 miles south of Sitka, and launched their kayaks to do some exploring. When they returned several hours later, the masts were the only part of the vessel visible—the hull and superstructure lay below water. How could a boat of that size possibly just sink without warning?

Ward wondered if a seacock had failed; Kathy wondered if she'd forgotten to turn off the valve to the propane stove and an explosion had occurred.

Ward was devastated. Everything he owned, except what he'd taken in the kayak, was gone. With his VHF handheld, he made contact with a boat that took them back to Sitka. The next day, a friend took Ward back to Still Harbor where they dove the boat and recovered some of his belongings.

The community rallied around Ward, offering help and money. But when a second diver discovered a 5-foot round hole near the bottom of the hull, Ward speculated that a whale might have rammed *Merlin*. "Naively, I told people about my theory," he said, "and they thought I was nuts. I felt horrible."

Eventually, help outweighed the negative comments and, in a monumental community effort, the vessel was raised and towed to Sitka and set up in a boatyard where Ward and Kathy began the task of cleaning out *Merlin*'s interior. Imagine his relief when he discovered a piece of baleen, four by sixteen inches, wedged in the hull near the hole. Ward was exonerated, and *Merlin* was replanked and donated to the Sitka Maritime Heritage Society.

[*Note*: In the ensuing years, *Merlin* has passed into private hands. Ward and Kathy have both passed away.]

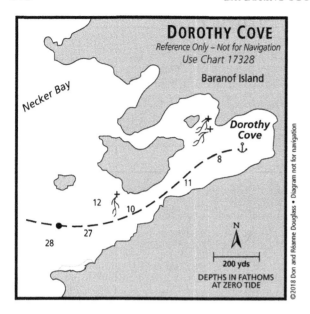

sand, gravel and newspaper kelp; holding is marginal unless you set your anchor well.

Anchor (north cove) in 2 to 8 fathoms over sand, gravel and kelp; fair-to-good holding with a well-set anchor.

## Dorothy Cove (Necker Bay)
Dorothy Cove is 6 miles above the entrance to Necker Bay.
Chart 17328
Entrance: 56°43.56' N, 135°03.51' W
Anchor: 56°43.78' N, 135°02.52' W

Dorothy Cove is a cozy anchorage in Necker Bay. The preferred anchorage is at the head of the bay; the site north of the islet may be even more snug.

Anchor in 7 fathoms over sand and gravel with good holding if anchor is well set.

## Secluded Bay (Necker Bay)
Secluded Bay is 0.7 miles north of Dorothy Cove.
Chart 17328
Entrance: 56°44.01' N, 135°03.72' W
Anchor: 56°44.43' N, 135°02.87' W

Secluded Bay is isolated and remote. It has an almost hidden south entrance. Call on Ch 16 or sound your horn if you think there might be opposing traffic. Passing and turning room is tight.

Anchor snuggled up against the unnamed islet in 4 fathoms over sand, mud and rocks with fair holding.

## North Cape (Baranof Island)
North Cape is 6 miles south of Aspid Cape and 30.5 miles northwest of Cape Ommaney.
Chart 17328
Position: (approximate) 56°35.75' N, 135°08.29' W

North Cape is exposed to the fury of southern storms from the Gulf of Alaska, as indicated by rocks washed bare of soil to a height of 150 feet. Still Harbor, 4 miles southeast of North Cape, provides very good shelter.

## Whale Bay (Baranof Island)
Whale Bay is 18 miles southeast of Goddard Hot Springs and 29 miles northwest of Cape Ommaney.
Chart 17328
Entrance: 56°34.38' N, 135°05.79' W

Whale Bay is roughly halfway between Sitka and Cape Ommaney. Anchorage can be found along the south shore of Whale Bay; however, we favor Still Harbor for both protection and convenience.

## Still Harbor (Whale Bay)
Still Harbor, at the entrance to Whale Bay, is 4 miles southeast of North Cape.
Chart 17328
Entrance: 56°33.91' N, 135°03.49' W
Anchor: 56°32.50' N, 135°00.96' W

> *Still Harbor... is about 1.5 miles N of Point Lauder.... The NE shore at the entrance is foul.*
> *The only anchorage is at the head of the harbor, and even there the swell is felt in heavy weather; this anchorage is not recommended.* (CP)

Still Harbor is indeed still; the entrance islets, reefs and rocks do a good job of knocking down the swells and dispersing their energy. (Our Petersburg fishing friend loves to anchor here.) We found no signs of shore stress from swell or chop and would feel free to call this a "summer home." Good anchorage can be found anywhere from north of island (30) to the head of the bay. We have seen lots of wildlife here. Avoid the rocks on the west shore;

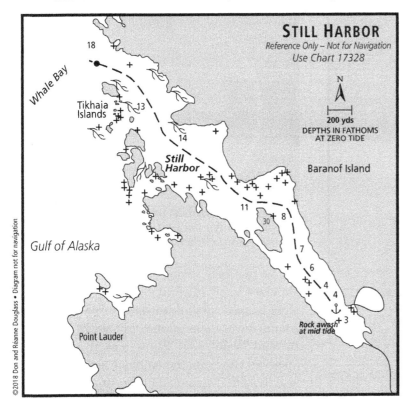

outside environment, where we can hear the surf pounding, yet we feel safe where there is no evidence of storm damage along shore—no logs at the head of the bay—and where the bottom is shallow, flat and sticky mud!

Anchor in 4 to 8 fathoms over sticky brown mud with very good holding.

## Kritoi Basin (Whale Bay)

Kritoi Basin is between Rakovoi Bay and Port Banks.
Chart 17328
Entrance: 56°36.14' N, 135°00.35' W
Anchor: 56°35.38' N, 134°59.31' W

Completely landlocked, Kritoi Basin is a little deep, but good, well-sheltered anchorage can be found anywhere along its shore. However, there is some shale bottom with poor holding. We prefer the south shore.

the southernmost rock extends farther from shore than charted!

The fishing boat, *Mary Gene,* rode out a 95-knot storm here in July 1996, proving that, when a storm is blowing in the Gulf, this anchorage may be underrated. Once again, we like the

Anchor in about 10 fathoms over brown mud, cobble and shale; fair-to-good holding if your anchor is well set.

## Sandy Bay (Baranof Island)

Sandy Bay is 6.5 miles south of Still Harbor and 21 miles north of Cape Ommaney.
Chart 17328
Entrance: 56°27.49' N, 134°59.96' W
Anchor (south shore, East Arm): 56°28.03' N, 134°58.43' W
Anchor (north shore, East Arm): 56°28.68' N, 134°57.90' W

The entrance to Sandy Bay is pure rock-bound coast. The picturesque sides of the cliffs are washed bare to a height of about 50 feet, and the waterfall is lovely.

The east arm of Sandy Bay has two anchor sites; however, neither is likely to be secure in a gale. Swells dissipate at East Arm. The south

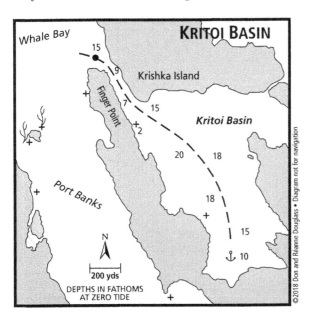

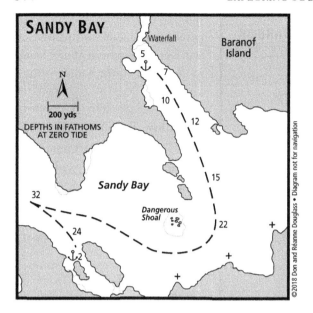

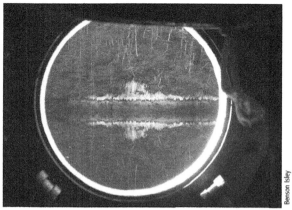

*Looking through the port hole at the perfect calm in Réanne's Relief*

shore is the more protected spot, but the fairway into the inner basin is only about 20 feet wide and is shoal with kelp.

Anchor (south shore, East Arm) in 6 fathoms over mud, sand, clams, rocks and kelp; fair holding.

Anchor (north shore, East Arm) in 4 to 6 fathoms over mud, sand and shells with good holding.

## Réanne's Terror (Baranof Island)

Réanne's Terror is 2.6 miles northwest of Redfish Cape.
Chart 17330
West entrance: 56°21.10' N, 134°54.51' W
South entrance: 56°20.94' N, 134°54.33' W
Entrance (Réanne's Relief): 56°21.47' N, 134°53.87' W
Anchor (Réanne's Relief): 56°21.50' N, 134°53.59' W
Entrance (White Cliffs Cove): 56°21.13' N, 134°53.45' W
Anchor (White Cliffs Cove): 56°20.85' N, 134°53.33' W

This cove is named informally after *Baidarka's* intrepid first mate. On our first visit to this bay, in the early 1990s, entering from the north appeared to be a formidable task. Heavy swells were heaped up and breaking on the entrance island, as well as along the north shore of Baranof Island, and foam spewed across the opening. However, the entrance was not as bad as it looked. Réanne held tight, and we scooted through the north opening in grand style.

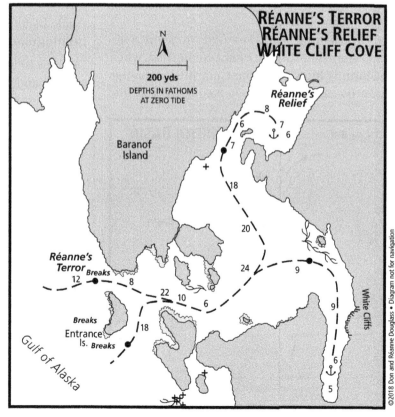

*Entrance to Réanne's Terror*

Since that first time, we have entered what we call "Réanne's Terror" many times in stable weather without fear on the first mate's part.

Under moderate conditions, you can enter either the north or the south side of the entrance island; the south entrance is wider and has less foam. Both entrances are deep, but they can be dangerous when large seas are running. The north entrance has 8 fathoms minimum in its fairway; the south has 15 fathoms minimum. Pleasure craft should have little trouble negotiating the turns required to enter Réanne's Terror. Note that we have found less water than Chart 17330 indicates.

Inside the bay—what relief! It is perfectly calm and the beauty is stunning—this is pristine wilderness at its best. You can anchor with complete shelter in the southeast cove, which we call "White Cliffs Cove," or in the north cove we call "Réanne's Relief." *Deception* reports this to be excellent anchorage that easily holds seven boats.

The bottom in Réanne's Relief is a thin layer of mud, so fair holding is about the best you can get. Using a shore tie in either of the two

*The photo says it all.*

*The terror lessening*

*Réanne's Relief at last*

coves would make the anchorage more comfortable and secure.

Anchor (Réanne's Relief) in 7 fathoms, soft brown mud bottom; fair-to-good holding.

Anchor (White Cliffs Cove) in about 8 fathoms over brown mud and clam shells with fair holding.

## Redfish Bay (Baranof Island)
Redfish Bay is 3 miles south of Réanne's Terror.
Chart 17330
Entrance (Redfish Point bearing 326°T at 0.25 Nm): 56°17.86' N, 134°52.28' W
Anchor (Granite Point Cove): 56°20.66' N, 134°51.98' W

The north arm of Redfish Bay leads to a good anchorage north of Granite Point. The first narrows is 100 yards wide; the second narrows is 25 yards wide.

Anchor in 8 to 10 fathoms over mud with fair holding. Easier anchorage in all but a serious blow can be found in Tenfathom Anchorage.

## Tenfathom Anchorage (Redfish Bay)
Tenfathom Anchorage is 0.6 mile east of Redfish Cape.
Chart 17330
Entrance: 56°18.80' N, 134°51.88' W
Anchor: 56°18.91' N, 134°51.43' W

Tenfathom Anchorage is well sheltered and

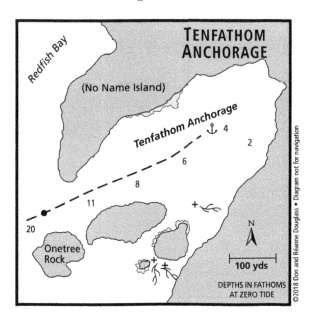

easy to enter. Some southerly swell enters the anchorage at high water via the south window.

Anchor in 10 to 12 fathoms over hard sand and mud with fair-to-good holding.

## Big Branch Bay (Baranof Island)
Big Branch Bay is just east of Redfish Bay.
Chart 17330
Entrance (light bearing 063°T at 0.2 Nm):
56°18.14′ N, 134°51.07′ W

## West Cove (Big Branch Bay)
West Cove is 1 mile north of the light at the mouth of Little Branch Bay.
Chart 17330
Entrance: 56°19.19′ N, 134°50.96′ W
Anchor: 56°19.61′ N, 134°51.21′ W

"West Cove" is what we call the anchor site in the west arm of Big Branch Bay; it is calm and well protected.

Anchor in 10 fathoms over sand and some newspaper kelp with fair holding if you set your anchor well.

## Puffin Bay (Baranof Island)
Puffin Bay's entrance is east of Sealion Rocks and 7 miles northwest of Cape Ommaney.
Chart 17330
Entrance: 56°15.00′ N, 134°48.59′ W

We found the small bight in Puffin Bay to be full of logs, indicating heavy pounding in southerly gales. Superior anchorage exists further up the bay in Forevergreen Basin.

## Forevergreen Basin (Baranof Island)
Forevergreen Basin is 2 miles inside Puffin Bay.
Chart 17330
Entrance: 56°16.62′ N, 134°46.28′ W
Anchor: 56°16.45′ N, 134°46.11′ W

"Forevergreen Basin" is our name for the unnamed basin south of Puffin Bay; the head offers excellent anchorage. We call this basin Forevergreen because we had such a good time here with our friend, fellow explorer and sometime crew, Professor Roderick Frazer Nash, owner of *Forevergreen*.

We consider this to be an excellent and secure (although small) anchor site. Williwaws may be strong at times, but the basin has little fetch and good holding. Wildlife viewing is good and fishing excellent. West winds, deflected down the high ridge to the east, become

*Heading inside Big Branch for a lunch stop*

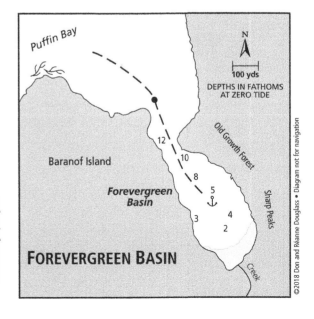

gentle breezes. Old-growth trees lie along the east shore below high sharp peaks.

Anchor in 6 fathoms over mud with good holding.

**Little Puffin Bay** (Baranof Island)
Little Puffin Bay is 1.5 miles south of Puffin Bay.
Chart 17330
Entrance: 56°13.75' N, 134°47.47' W

Little Puffin Bay is open to the west and should be considered a fair-weather anchorage only. The bottom appears to be a thin layer of sand over rocks with marginal holding.

**Cape Ommaney** (Baranof Island)
Cape Ommaney is the south tip of Baranof Island.
Chart 17330
Position (0.25 Nm south of cape, Wooden Island Light bearing 057°T at 0.44 Nm): 56°09.38' N, 134°40.32' W

*Caution:* Tide rips and turbulent seas are found off Cape Ommaney and Wooden Island.

# CHATHAM STRAIT AND BARANOF ISLAND'S EAST COAST (North to South)

The east coast of Baranof Island is infrequently visited but well worth exploring. Some excellent, well-sheltered coves and inlets run deep into the island's interior, with high snowy peaks that tower above. Port Alexander, at the south end of Baranof Island and five miles north of Cape Ommaney, has limited services, although there are a post office, public school and phone, and two exclusive fishing lodges. The hot tubs at Baranof Warm Springs and the raw beauty of Red Bluff Bay are particularly inviting.

**Kelp Bay** (Baranof Island)
Kelp Bay, on the northeast corner of Baranof Island, is 10.5 miles south of Peril Strait.
Chart 17337
Entrance (mid-channel South and North Point): 57°16.87' N, 134°50.65' W

*Humpback in Chatham Strait showing "stove bolt" markings on its head and the white underside of its long pectoral fin.*

CHAPTER 8 — BARANOF ISLAND, SOUTH OF SITKA; LOWER CHATHAM STRAIT & KEKU STRAIT   319

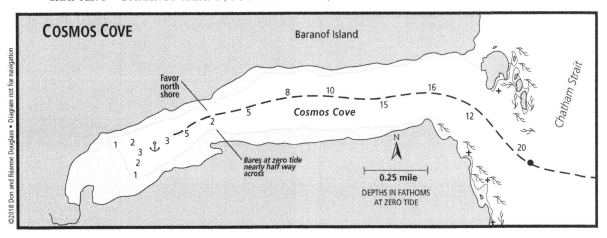

We prefer the excellent shelter and ease of entry found in Cosmos Cove, 2 miles south of Kelp Bay.

Chart 17337 carries the following cautionary note: "Exercise extreme caution when transiting the areas adjacent to Pond Island and southeast of Portage Point. Previously uncharted shoals and dangerous rocks have been located and others may exist."

*A whale research boat in Chatham Strait...*

*...with transponder for listening to whale sounds.*

### Echo Cove (Catherine Island)
Echo Cove is north of the entrance to Kelp Bay.
Chart 17337
Entrance: 57°17.25' N, 134°49.13' W
Anchor: 57°18.45' N, 134°49.72' W

> *Point Lull, the SE extremity of Catherine Island, forms the E side of Echo Cove, a narrow bight, which extends in a NNW direction. The cove is open to the S and affords temporary anchorage for small craft only. A submerged reef, marked by kelp, extends 0.6 mile S of Point Lull. Vessels transiting Echo Cove and The Basin in Kelp Bay should use caution or seek local knowledge.* (CP)

Pay attention to the cautions mentioned above in *Coast Pilot* on entering Kelp Bay. Echo Cove is convenient to Chatham Strait for temporary anchorage in fair weather. However, we prefer Cosmos or Ell coves.

### Cosmos Cove (Baranof Island)
Cosmos Cove, on the west side of Chatham Strait, is 2 miles south of Kelp Bay.
Chart 17337
Entrance: 57°14.41' N, 134°50.23' W
Anchor: 57°14.48' N, 134°52.79' W

Cosmos Cove is a large cove with a flat bottom that can be easily entered in all weather. When entering, favor the north shore midway into the cove; a shoal extends nearly halfway from the south side. A southerly wind can reduce the holding appreciably in this anchorage.

Anchor in 3 fathoms over soft mud, gravel, shell and grass with good holding.

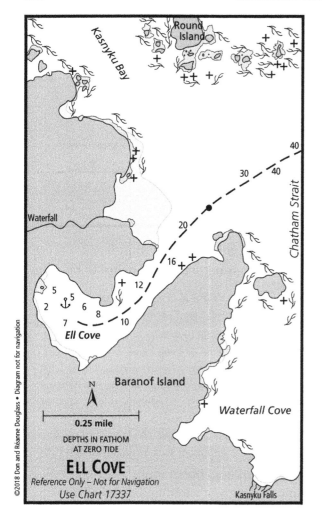

*Sign at Takatz Bay fish hatchery*

## Ell Cove (Baranof Island)

Ell Cove is 2.5 miles south of Cosmos Cove.
Chart 17337
Entrance: 57°12.14' N, 134°50.42' W
Anchor: 57°11.96' N, 134°51.02' W

We consider Ell Cove to be one of the best coves along Chatham Strait. Its name comes from its L-shape, which gives it full protection in all weather. It can be entered carefully in limited visibility by using radar.

The small cove has steep granite sides with cascades that descend from snowy ridges above. Old-growth spruce, cedar and hemlock cover its slopes. Immediately north of Ell Cove is a beautiful waterfall with a large sandy beach. Beware of the shoal that extends much farther from shore than is shown on the chart.

Wind direction inside the cove is not indicative of that blowing outside. Inside the cove, the wind tends to blow in circles without strength. There is no driftwood or any evidence of seas entering Ell Cove. Water temperature here is about 50°F.

Kasnyku Falls, an outstanding high cascade, is a half-mile to the south.

Anchor in 6 fathoms over soft mud with good holding.

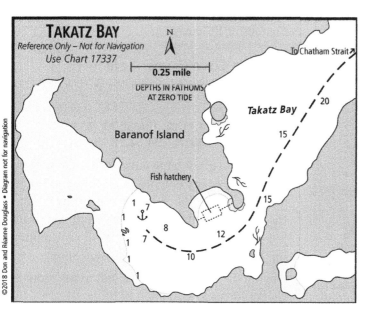

*Fish hatchery tanks*

## Waterfall Cove (Baranof Island)
Waterfall Cove is 6 miles north of Warm Springs Bay.
Chart 17337
Entrance: 57°11.82′ N, 134°49.84′ W
Anchor: 57°11.64′ N, 134°50.41′ W

Waterfall Cove is a good place to take a short break. Turn off your engine and enjoy the outstanding view of the 300- to 400-foot Kasnyku Falls cascading into the bay. The tiny cove at the head of the bay is marginal and too small for anchorage unless you use a shore tie; however, it is an excellent temporary anchorage in fair weather as it gives you the opportunity to get in your dinghy and appreciate the falls up close.

## Takatz Bay (Baranof Island)
Takatz Bay is 4 miles north of Warm Springs Bay.
Chart 17337
Entrance: 57°09.39′ N, 134°48.09′ W
Anchor: 57°08.11′ N, 134°51.44′ W

Deep in landlocked Takatz Bay, you can find excellent shelter from all weather. The basin is a large granite bowl surrounded by snowy peaks, and shows evidence of avalanches. A fish hatchery operates in the bight on the north side of the basin. The bay has easy access and a flat bottom.

The shoal at the head of the bay is steep-to and has been creeping eastward over time, so proceed slowly and carefully to the anchorage. The water is a translucent glacier melt with a visibility of less than 6 feet; summer water temperature is a cool 44° F.

Anchor north of the first small islet.

*A person waving at the lower left gives perspective to the towering Kasnyku Falls in Waterfall Cove.*

Anchor in 6 to 8 fathoms over soft mud with very good holding.

## Warm Springs Bay
(Baranof Island)
Warm Springs Bay is 7 miles northwest of Point Gardner.
Chart 17337
Entrance: 57°05.01′ N, 134°46.54′ W
Public float: 57°05.34′ N, 134°49.99′ W
Anchor (southwest arm): 57°04.46′ N, 134°49.65′ W
Anchor (Schooner Cove): 57°05.34′ N, 134°48.04′ W

Warm Springs Bay has a huge, beautiful 100-foot waterfall at its head which once provided hydropower for the residents of the tiny community of Baranof. Equally impressive are the natural hot springs, an easy half-mile walk from the public float. Rubber boots are recommended. Three natural hot pools tumble down the hillside adjacent to the river. The temperature in the pools is hot and hotter. Water from the hot springs is also piped to the more private, metal-tub bathhouses above the dock.

*Roaring waterfall at Warm Springs Bay.*

The main trail to the natural hot springs is mostly boardwalk with muddy spots. It continues past the hot pools a short distance west to Lake Baranof through stunted forest and tundra. Ground dogwood or bunchberry, salmonberry, wild violets and skunkweed cover the tundra in summer. The USFS maintains one of its recreational cabins at the far west end of the lake.

The bathhouses are open on the water side and have a magnificent view of the falls. Please respect the instructions and limit your soak to give others their turn. As this has become a popular

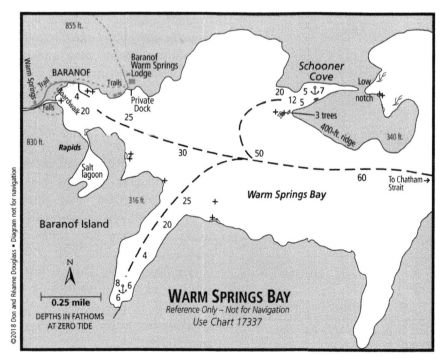

*The approach to the dock at the head of Baranof Warm Springs Bay*

*The natural hot pools right next to the waterfall*

*The boardwalk at Warm Springs Bay, Baranof Is.*

stop for cruisers, plan to arrive early in the day if you want a spot at the dock. The seine fleet can crowd the public float, and you might find more space during a fishery opening. You can also anchor nearby and take your dinghy in for the hot tubbing.

The 250-foot public float at the head of the bay receives strong east-flowing current from the river, so use caution when you dock. Friends recommend maneuvering at half tide or less, when the current from the falls is deflected by the rocks at the base of the falls. Avoid the large submerged rock approximately 6 feet off the east end of the float. There is untreated water at the float.

You can probably get a cell phone connec-

*The dock at Warm Springs Bay can become crowded very quickly; this is a very popular spot.*

*The author checks out one of the individual tubs in the bath house.*

tion while in Chatham Strait, outside the entrance to Warm Springs Bay. (Note the nearby Micro tower.) However, once you proceed deep into the bay the signal weakens because of the topography.

The salt lagoon across the bay to the south is fun to explore by dinghy or kayak. The opening is about 15 feet wide and carries 6 feet of water through its fairway at slack on a 14-foot tide. At other times, it is a waterfall! Inside the lagoon we have spotted seals, as well as harlequins, loons, and many other birds.

If our suggested anchor sites are full, try the bight just to the east of the lagoon. This anchorage has room for four or five boats.

Anchor (southwest arm) in 7 fathoms over gravel and kelp with fair holding.

Anchor (Schooner Cove) in 6 fathoms over a hard bottom; good holding with a well-set anchor.

## Cascade Bay (Baranof Island)
Cascade Bay is 3.4 miles south of Warm Springs Bay.
Chart 17320
Entrance: 57°01.56' N, 134°45.24' W

Cascade Bay is a beautiful anchorage with a huge waterfall in its northwest corner. The cove has a flat bottom of 25 fathoms nearly all the way to shore. There are rocks off the cascade, some of which bare at high water. A small shelf below a large snow bowl and avalanche chute provides a good kayak haul-out and campsite.

You can find temporary anchorage off this site below the snow bowl. The bottom is rocky with poor holding, so if you plan to spend any time here, it's a good idea to use a shore tie. Although southerly winds curl around the cove, there is little chop near shore.

---

## Bears—Where to Find Them
### Herb Nickles, Certified Alaska Naturalist

What types of bears can you see and what are the best islands or best reserves for viewing them?

Three species of bear are native to Alaska. Brown Bears, also known as Grizzly Bears, can be found from Southeast Alaska to the arctic. Black Bears are found throughout Alaska's forests. Polar Bears are only found in extreme northern and western Alaska.

Cruisers to Southeast Alaska are most likely to see the Black Bear (Ursus americanus). Although the species is primarily black in color, some individuals can be chocolate, red-brown or cinnamon. Black Bears with a creamy white fur occur on Kermode Island in Northern British Columbia. The Black Bear is generally solitary, except for a female with cubs, and primarily nocturnal. In Southeast Alaska, Black Bears occupy most islands with the exceptions of Admiralty, Baranof, Chichagof, and Kruzof. The best opportunity for viewing Black Bears from your vessel is on forested island beaches at sunset.

The Brown Bear (Ursus Arctos) is much larger than the Black Bear, ranging from 6 to 8 feet in length and weighing between 500 and 900 pounds. Brown Bear have a distinctive hump between their front shoulders.

Brown Bears occur throughout Southeast Alaska except on the islands south of Frederick Sound. They are abundant on islands with easily available food sources like Admiralty, Baranof, Chichagof, and Kruzof. The Brown Bear is most readily observed on Admiralty Island where the population density is as high as one bear per square mile. The Pack Creek viewing area in Admiralty Island National Monument is a popular location to view Brown Bears but requires a permit and fee paid in advance of your visit.

### Additional Resources:
Know Your Bear Facts: Alaska Department of Fish and Game https://www.adfg.alaska.gov/static/species/livingwithwildlife/bears/pdfs/know_your_bear_facts_brochure.pdf

Essentials of Traveling in Alaska's Bear Country: Alaska Department of Fish and Game http://www.adfg.alaska.gov/index.cfm?adfg=livingwithbears.bearcountry

Stan Price State Wildlife Sanctuary on Admiralty Island at: http://www.adfg.alaska.gov/index.cfm?adfg=stanprice.main

## Musings on Infinity in Southeast Alaska
### Linda Lewis—Journal Notes—M/V *Royal Sounder*

*Shades of shadows on the west side of Prince of Wales Island*

I have been on watch alone on the ocean during a gray dawn when I could see absolutely nothing but gray water for a full circle of the horizon. It was like being in a broad, flat pan, with just the edges curled up a bit—for 360 degrees. Why didn't I feel as though I was staring at infinity? Paradoxically, I felt closed in.

In Southeast Alaska, however, "infinity" means something. Because here there is perspective. I see multitudes of mountain peaks. I see shades of shadows—like a visual glissando. I see sky, and snow, and trees, and water. Now looking at this is something to set the mind afire.

Looking at *this* is musing on infinity.

*Mysterious, strange light shows*

*A layer of fog pours over the hill.*

## Nelson Bay (Baranof Island)

Nelson Bay is 8 miles south of Warm Springs Bay and 7 miles north of Red Bluff Bay.
Chart 17320
Entrance: 56°57.16' N, 134°44.06' W

> *Between Red Bluff Bay and Cascade Bay ... are four small bays where small craft may find a depth suitable for anchorage in smooth weather, but only one, Nelson Bay, has protection.*
>
> *Nelson Bay ... is an open bight at the head of which is a circular cove having two islets across the entrance. The entrance to the cove is between the N islet and the point N of it, and is 75 yards wide with a depth of 5 fathoms. The cove is 250 yards in diameter between the 10-fathom curves, and the general depth is 15 fathoms, soft bottom. This cove is suitable only for small craft.* (CP)

We have explored all four small bays mentioned in the *Coast Pilot* and found them all delightful, but uncharted. It is a pity that no large-scale chart exists of this area to allow common use without high risk.

## Red Bluff Bay (Baranof Island)

Red Bluff Bay is 6.8 miles south of Nelson Bay and 10 miles west of Kingsmill Point.
Chart 17336
Entrance: 56°50.37' N, 134°41.88' W
Anchor: 56°52.29' N, 134°47.06' W

Red Bluff Bay is perhaps the most spectacular combination of mountains, waterfalls and icefields in Southeast Alaska. From the entrance, the view of the high peaks of Baranof Island is breathtaking. Within this one bay we have counted nine waterfalls cascading off the surrounding massif. The entrance to the bay is unmistakable for the prominent, treeless red bluff on the north side of the fjord. Entry is made south of the islands, as indicated on the diagram. The bay is totally landlocked and shows no effect of outside chop or evidence of storm damage or logs along shore.

You can find anchorage off the ruins of the old cannery on the north shore opposite the large waterfall, in the double bight west of the cannery, or at the head of the inner basin. We

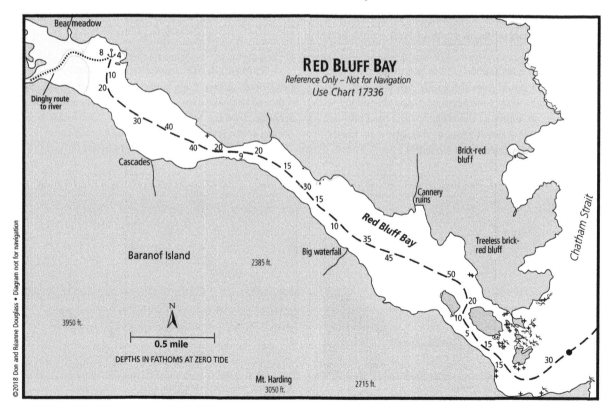

Copasetic *enters Red Bluff Bay*

prefer to anchor on the north side of a small islet at the head of the bay, opposite the large drying mud flat known locally as Bear Meadow. A large stream flowing out of a glacier-carved valley meanders across the grassy, sandy flats of this meadow. The lake upstream has great cutthroat fishing, but you need to watch out for brown bears along the riverbanks—this is their turf. Some pleasure boaters have told us of finding consistently excellent shrimping along the NW corner of the island marked with the number 85.

Red Bluff Bay shows no signs of human intrusion. This is pure wilderness—no logging, no urban noises, just the sound of the water cascading down the sides of the mountain.

Anchor in 4 fathoms over mud with good holding.

*A bucket full of shrimp caught in Red Bluff Bay*

## Hoggatt Bay (Baranof Island)
Hoggatt Bay is 4.5 miles south of Red Bluff Bay.
Chart 17336
Entrance: 56°46.27' N, 134°39.58' W

Hoggatt Bay is reported to have excellent shrimping and sport fishing

## Gut Bay (Baranof Island)
Gut Bay is 7 miles south of Red Bluff Bay.
Chart 17336
Entrance: 56°43.97' N, 134°38.36' W
Entrance (Mickie's Winter Basin): 56°42.59' N, 134°41.29' W
Anchor (Mickie's Winter Basin): 56°42.42' N, 134°41.36' W
Anchor (head of bay): 56°42.30' N, 134°44.45' W

Gut Bay is a beautiful place, well worth a visit by cruisers seeking a remote, quiet and protected anchorage. The entire bay is landlocked

*Waterfall in Red Bluff Bay*

and rather poorly charted. Except for occasional williwaws that blow off the surrounding snow-covered peaks (3,000 to 4,000 feet high) in unsettled weather, shelter is almost complete. There is no VHF radio reception inside Gut Bay; this and its deep, rocky bottom keep the bay from becoming a popular destination.

Mickie's Winter Basin is the best anchor site; the other is the narrow tongue of water at the far southwest corner of the bay. The entrance to Mickie's Winter Basin is shallow and narrow. We figure the fairway, which is roughly 30 feet wide, carries about 4 feet. Tidal range in the basin is less than that found outside, but due to restricted flow it occurs about an hour later than that listed for Sitka.

The shores are surrounded by thick forest to the water's edge. Steep bluffs and granite slopes rise abruptly to snow-filled cirques and avalanches chutes. To the south, Mt. Ada's stark pinnacles rise to 4,500 feet.

We found two disadvantages to Mickie's Winter Basin. The first is that the surrounding peaks limit the duration of direct sunlight, causing the basin to be a chilly 42° F during the day (This was in late June; Red Bluff Bay gets more sunlight). The second is that without radio reception, it is difficult to know what conditions exist outside in Chatham Strait.

There is a large grassy meadow at the head of the basin beyond a drying mud flat. Inside, the basin narrows (about 100 yards long) and depths increase to 4 to 5 fathoms before rising at the mud flats.

The tiny inlet at the far southwest end of Gut Bay has limited swinging room, but we have found that the current from the stream and the gentle breezes keep a boat lined up with the 150-foot wide channel. The view from this spot is similar to Mickie's Winter Basin—high granite bluffs with snow patches and cascades and little direct morning sun.

Anchor (Mickie's Winter Basin) in 3 to 4 fathoms over brown mud with roots and grass; fair-

---

## Icebound in Gut Bay
### Réanne Hemingway-Douglass

Somewhere in Michèle (Mickie) Demai's background lay a thirst for unusual adventure. You wouldn't have suspected it, though, if you had met her in Paris where she spent 15 years as a TV journalist, specializing in health problems. Her "secret garden," as she calls it, had always been the sea, and a dream to discover the last frontier of Alaska called to her. Not only to explore, but to experience a winter—a winter icebound—on *Nuage*, her 42-foot steel hulled sailboat!

Mickie had studied the charts of Alaska and discovered a little fjord on Baranof Island's east side—Gut Bay—well-sheltered and its waters fed by freshwater streams cold enough to ice over. She and her companion, Thomas, fell in love with the bay, and in September 1995, they sailed to Juneau to prepared *Nuage* for a long winter's night. Mickie prepared 120 jars of food; they took on extra water and fuel; propane; firewood; mountaineering equipment; they added insulation; they built a funny-looking cabin of plywood over the cockpit. Three months of preparations for five months in an icy retreat.

Every day in Gut Bay brought new fears—williwaws gusted to more than 80 miles an hour; avalanches roared down the mountainsides above the bay; ice cracked and groaned against the hull; the deck iced over.

But every day brought new delights, as well—the iridescent colors of the high-latitude winter sky; the pristine snow; the river otters that played on the ice near the boat. Mickie and Thomas reveled in their sanctuary. They maintained the boat; they read; they wrote; they chopped wood from the mountainsides; they skied across the frozen surface of the bay; they watched the wildlife—deer, ptarmigans, mink, bald eagles. The days sped by; they felt privileged to be a part of this wilderness.

April came. The ice began to melt and soon *Nuage* floated free again. Mickie and Thomas returned to sea, with a heightened sense of awareness, having tested their emotional strength. Gut Bay and Alaska captured the heart of a woman; a charming and unusual woman!

*Note:* We have called the anchorage where *Nuage* spent the winter "Mickie's Winter Basin" in honor of this unusual French woman.

to-good holding. Use a shore tie if williwaws are expected. You could also anchor outside the basin with more swinging room in 6 to 8 fathoms, soft mud bottom.

Anchor (head of bay) in 4 to 5 fathoms over soft brown mud with very good holding.

## Patterson Bay (Baranof Island)
Patterson Bay is 12 miles south of Gut Bay and 23 miles north of Cape Ommaney.
Chart 17335
Entrance: 56°32.44' N, 134°39.29' W

Patterson Bay is a stunning, narrow fjord with steep snowy peaks on all sides. 3,200-foot Mt. Cecil towers above the end of the bay. We have not explored the bay, but the stream outlet from Brentwood Lake seems to have created a sizeable flat area that could provide a good anchorage. The upper end of the bay is essentially landlocked, but this is williwaw terrain, so be careful in unstable weather.

## Deep Cove (Baranof Island)
Deep Cove is 1.1 miles west of Patterson Point.
Chart 17335
Entrance: 56°32.29' N, 134°40.21' W

Deep Cove has beautiful peaks along its south shore and a snowy ridge on its north shore. Although it is sheltered, we did not find any convenient anchor sites for small craft.

*Entrance to Mist Cove*

## Mist Cove (Baranof Island)
Mist Cove is 1.5 miles southwest of Patterson Point
Chart 17335
Entrance: 56°31.39' N, 134°39.87' W
Anchor: 56°30.98' N, 134°40.22' W

Mist Cove takes its name from the stunning high, thin cascade enveloped in blowing mist on its southwest side.

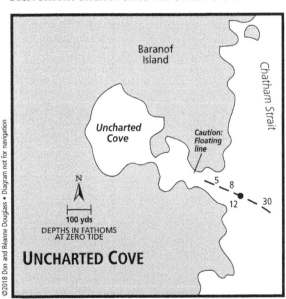

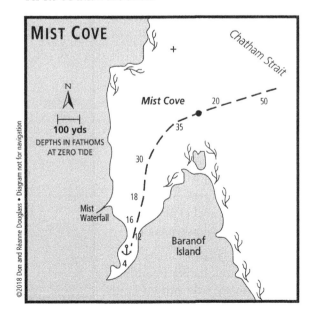

There is a small shelf with temporary anchorage below the falls. However, we have found better temporary anchorage deep in the south corner of the cove off the creek which has its source in Fawn Lake. The current here kept us facing in one direction. A steep USFS trail in good conditions leads to the head of the falls and on to the hatchery at Deer Lake.

Anchor in 5 to 10 fathoms over sand and gravel with fair holding.

## Little Port Walter (Port Walter)
Little Port Walter is west of the south entrance point to Port Walter.
Chart 17333
Entrance: 56°23.34' N, 134°38.22' W
Anchor: 56°22.88' N, 134°38.88' W

*NOAA Building at Little Port Walter*

*Little Port Walter... consists of an inner and outer harbor with a narrow connecting channel. The narrow channel... has a width of about 30 yards with a depth of 3¼ fathoms and is subject to shoaling. Vessels should enter the port between half and high tide only and preferably on a rising tide. They should pass along the SE side of the channel and make a slow turn to enter the inner harbor....*

*Good protected anchorage for small craft can be had in the inner harbor in 6 to 8 fathoms, mud bottom.* (CP)

Little Port Walter (inner harbor) is a very good cruising boat anchorage with a beautiful setting. The inner harbor, which is landlocked, has excellent shelter in all weather.

To enter the inner harbor, favor the west shore over a bar of about 3 fathoms at zero tide. The west shore has a three-story NOAA building with floats and a flag pole. Across a low lush valley, there are views of Baranof Island's snowy peaks.

Anchor in 7 fathoms on the middle of the inner harbor (avoiding the fish floats) over brown mud with good holding. The bottom is flat over a large area.

## Toledo Harbor (Baranof Island)
Toledo Harbor is 0.9 mile south of Port Walter Light 5.
Chart 17333
Entrance: 56°22.35' N, 134°37.86' W
Anchor: 56°22.40' N, 134°38.13' W

Toledo Harbor is a good pleasure-craft anchorage, close to Chatham Strait. We like to think the name for this tiny round cove came from someone who poked the nose of their boat inside and said, "Holy Toledo!"

The cove provides good protection for small craft in all weather, but swinging room is limited. Inside the basin, it is perfectly calm when

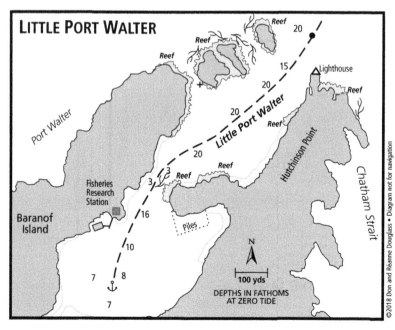

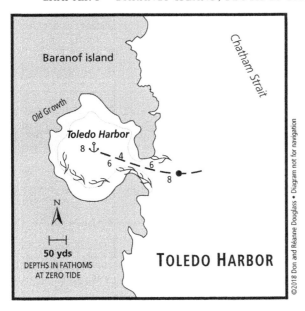

a northerly is blowing. The narrow entrance lies between patches of kelp on both shores; minimum depth in the fairway is about 3 fathoms.

Anchor in 7 fathoms over mud, avoiding the shoals; good holding.

## Port Lucy (Baranof Island)
Port Lucy is 10.5 miles north of Cape Ommaney.
Chart 17333
Entrance: 56°20.34' N, 134°38.64' W
Anchor: 56°17.38' N, 134°45.24' W

Protected anchorage can be found at the bitter end of Port Lucy over a large flat area.

Anchor in about 7 fathoms over a soft bottom.

## Port Armstrong (Baranof Island)
Port Armstrong is 3.5 miles north of Port Alexander.
Charts 17331
Entrance: 56°17.82' N, 134°38.60' W
Anchor: 56°17.50' N, 134°39.56' W

Port Armstrong has very good shelter from all weather. The entrance is fairly shallow, but the mid-channel fairway is clear and well protected. A resort is located on the creek on the north shore, with an oyster farm, private floats and a fish hatchery where the old charted wharf was once located.

Our preferred anchor site is in the southeast corner of the basin off a small pebble beach where there are two rusted tanks. Avoid the large rock awash on a 5-foot tide that extends from the north point of the basin.

Anchor in 6 to 10 fathoms over mud with good holding.

## Port Conclusion (Baranof Island)
Port Conclusion is 2.5 miles north of Port Alexander.
Chart 17331
Entrance: 56°16.77' N, 134°38.77' W
Position (Graveyard Cove): 56°16.20' N, 134°38.49' W
Position (John Bay): 56°16.67' N, 134°40.57' W

Port Conclusion was named by George Vancouver in 1793 as he concluded his exploration of the Northwest Coast. The best anchorage in Port Conclusion for small craft is Ship Cove.

## Ship Cove (Port Conclusion)
Ship Cove is 1.2 miles southwest of Point Conclusion.
Chart 17331
Entrance: 56°15.31' N, 134°40.04' W
Anchor: 56°15.37' N, 134°39.79' W

Ship Cove provides shelter for small craft over a flat, shallow bottom. A small plaque on the northwest side of this cove commemorates Vancouver's historic visit. A half-mile trail of unknown condition connects Ship Cove to the upper bay of Port Alexander.

Anchor in 2 to 3 fathoms, avoiding the kelp and shoals, over sand, gravel and mud with fair holding.

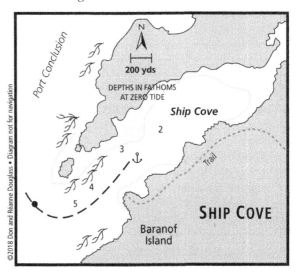

## Port Alexander (Baranof Island)

Port Alexander, near the south entrance to Chatham Strait, is 5 miles north of Cape Ommaney.

Chart 17331
Entrance (range): 56°14.39' N, 134°38.88' W
Public float: 56°14.80' N, 134°38.92' W

Port Alexander offers shelter for boaters working and cruising in the area of Cape Ommaney. The entrance is very narrow with only 2 fathoms in the fairway. The incorporated townsite has a public phone at the head of the gangway, a post office, a school, a small supply store and a few gift boutiques that sell handmade items. Some supplies can be obtained along the boardwalk. You may be able to purchase fuel for pleasure craft in season, but don't count

*A ghostly derelict*

on it. A 48-foot grid is west of the approach pier to the small-craft float. Laughing Raven

---

## A Wilderness Friend
### Réanne Hemingway-Douglass

Along the coast of Kuiu Island, I made a surprising new friend. We met by chance as *Baidarka* was slowly navigating a narrow, rock-filled inlet. I was on the bow, pointing the way through the rocks, when a shadow crossed my periphery vision.

"Don, look!" I yelled, stunned to see a woman standing on shore.

We'd been exploring for days without seeing another human. A few passing fishing boats here and there, but no houses, no structures. Imagine—in all this wilderness a human being!

"Do you live here? I asked.

"Yes, for 20 years."

"Just summers?"

"No, all year."

My friend, who shall remain nameless, moved to Petersburg with her young daughter after the death of her first husband. They spent 12 months in town and "hated it." Too many people!

She moved back to the secluded home with her daughter and second husband and his son, where they raised and home-schooled their combined family.

I imagined the response city teen-agers would have to their life, and the proverbial comment, "How boring!" No malls, no television, no movies, no Seven-Eleven to run to. Electricity and hot showers regulated by their generator; mail once a month when her husband crosses the strait by boat to the nearest village—much longer periods without mail in the winter.

"What do you do?" would be the next typical response.

And in her quiet, unassuming, almost shy manner, she would run down the list of things she does: Dig and can over 3,000 clams; make liverwurst and sausage out of the left-over venison; can the vegetables she grows in the summer; freeze the halibut and salmon they catch during the season (their quota is 700 lbs.). Before the winter sets in, she buys 350 lbs. of popping corn so she'll be able to feed the Canada geese that winter over every year. She knows them all by sight and has a name for each one. (One couple, a small male and a huge female, returned every season for five years.) She has a pet ferret to care for, too. He has white fur and pink eyes. "It's like having a permanent two-year old living with us," she comments.

And unlike city folk, my friend is decidedly attuned to nature. She knows all the habits of the wolves, the deer, the bear, the mink, the ferrets, the sea otters, the orcas and other whales. She can tell us all about the plants and the trees and the edible sea creatures. She sews and reads in her spare time, but she doesn't have much of that. Life is full and busy and, when the winter darkness sets in, she finds time to write me a long letter. In the spring, when the storms have abated, she'll mail it to me.

"Do you keep a journal?" I once asked her. Her ingenuousness struck me as refreshing.

"Yes, and someday I'd like to write a book . . . but I don't yet know how it ends."

Lodge offers fishing, lodging and meals. Call 907.568.2266 for information and reservations.

The public float is frequently crowded with fishing boats and live-aboards. Water at the float is untreated and must be boiled or treated for drinking; the water supply is also subject to shortages. The upper bay, which is filled with shoals, is used exclusively by locals in small boats. We do not recommend entering it.

## KUIU ISLAND'S WEST COAST

The west coast of Kuiu Island is a great place to view whales and sea otters and gaze across to the mountains of Baranof Island.

### Washington Bay (Kuiu Island)
Washington Bay, on the east side of Chatham Strait, is 9.5 miles south of Security Bay.
Chart 17370
Entrance: 56°42.99' N, 134°23.56' W

Washington Bay is easy to enter and offers an escape from the chop of Chatham Strait. However, it is too deep for convenient anchoring. The shore is steep-to; consider using a shore-tie. Both Rowan Bay, 5.5 miles to the south, and Security Bay, 9 miles to the north, are better anchorages.

### Rowan Bay (Kuiu Island)
Rowan Bay is 5.5 miles south of Washington Bay and 5 miles north of the Bay of Pillars.
Chart 17370
Entrance: 56°38.41' N, 134°18.14' W

The entrance to Rowan Bay has an irregular bottom with many surprises. Entering requires careful piloting and good visibility. Avoid the three dangerous rocks in the center of the entrance, and keep a sharp lookout as not all shoals and rocks are charted! The bay provides good shelter and comfortable anchorage on its south shore, providing you can avoid the numerous rocks. You may ask, "Why enter Rowan Bay when the Bay of Pillars provides more seclusion and even better shelter?" Answer: you stand a good chance of sighting bears, whales and sea otters.

Anchor in 6 fathoms over mud, shells and gravel with fair-to-good holding.

### Bay of Pillars and Honeymoon Basin (Kuiu Island)
Bay of Pillars is 18 miles south of Security Bay and 23 miles northeast of Port Alexander.
Chart 17370
Entrance: 56°34.87' N, 134°19.61' W
Anchor (inside first islands): 56°36.73' N, 134°12.88' W
Anchor (inner bay at portage trail): 56°38.71' N, 134°05.49' W
Entrance (Honeymoon Basin): 56°38.28' N, 134°06.37' W
Anchor (Honeymoon Basin): 56°37.63' N, 134°06.65' W

The Bay of Pillars offers very good shelter along the south shore behind the group of five small islands. Upon entering, avoid the large shoal off the south entrance, northwest of Point Ellis. There are numerous rock pillars throughout the bay that give it its name.

Excellent protection can be found in the inner bay; however, don't try entering without Chart 17370 and without reconnoitering first by dinghy. The narrows should be attempted only near slack water and with utmost caution

*Sea Ranger Resort in Bay of Pillars*

and skill. However, the rewards are great—wilderness and solitude with excellent shelter.

The narrows are poorly charted, requiring constant vigilance as you transit. We found 3 knots or more of ebb current and 2 knots of flood. The change of direction is delayed 60 to 90 minutes from high or low water on the outside.

Minimum fairway depths on a 5-foot tide were 4 fathoms at the west end of the narrows and the same amount as you approach the two islands at the east end of the narrows. The best route favors the north shore, north of those two islands, avoiding the islet with one tree on it and a rock just to the northeast that is awash at high water. Avoid the charted 1-fathom shoal by favoring the north shore until you reach the 10-fathom contour.

Once inside the inner basin, you discover true wilderness with eagles, blue herons, spotted harbor seals, sea otters and black bear.

Anchorage in the inner basin can be found off the east end at the Bay of Pillars portage trail #6M, marked by a board nailed to a tree. The mile-long trail leads to the bitter end of Port Camden on Keku Strait.

The most secure anchorage is found in the basin on the south side, which we call "Honeymoon Basin." This site is remote, quiet and wild, with a nice shallow bottom of brown mud with good holding and lots of swinging room. The shore is covered with old-growth forest backed by a high granite ridge. The rugged ridge to the east has a peak in the shape of an equilateral triangle, and there are snowy peaks to the south. Two creeks flow into the head of the basin; the westernmost flows through a low saddle.

Kayakers will find a good haul-out spot on a knoll on the eastern shore at the entrance to Honeymoon Basin.

Anchor (inside first islands) in 10 fathoms over a bottom of mud and clam shells; fair-to-good holding.

Anchor (inner basin at portage trail) in 9 fathoms over mud with shells; good holding.

Anchor near the head of Honeymoon Basin (east of a large silver snag) in 4 fathoms, brown mud with good holding.

### Tebenkof Bay (Kuiu Island)
Tebenkof Bay, just south of the Bay of Pillars, is entered between Point Ellis on the north and Swaine Point on the south.
Chart 17376
Entrance: 56°31.07' N, 134°16.82' W

Tebenkof Bay, surrounded by the Tebenkof Bay Wilderness area, holds wonderful surprises for exploring cruising boaters and kayakers. The entire bay is worth a week's stay in itself.

### Piledriver Cove (Tebenkof Bay)
Piledriver Cove is on the north side of Tebenkof Bay.
Chart 17376
Entrance: 56°32.42' N, 134°12.18' W

Piledriver Cove is a small indentation just south of Piledriver Mountain. Temporary anchorage can be found north of the mid-cove islet. The site is exposed to southwest winds.

### Happy Cove (Tebenkof Bay)
Happy Cove, on the north side of the Tebenkof Bay, is 1.2 miles north of Gap Point.
Chart 17376
Entrance: 56°29.97' N, 134°09.13' W
Anchor: 56°30.32' N, 134°08.74' W

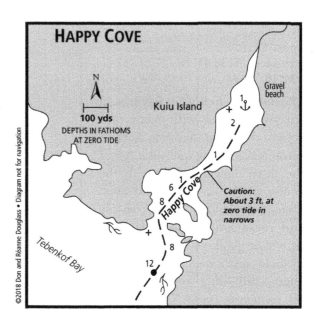

Happy Cove is a tiny uncharted indentation with pleasant anchorage in all but southerly gales; it has room for a couple of boats. The narrows has only 3 feet of water at zero tide, but the basin on the north side makes for happy anchoring.

Anchor in 2 to 3 fathoms over thick brown mud with very good holding if you set your anchor slowly.

## Elena Bay (Tebenkof Bay)
Elena Bay is the north arm of Tebenkof Bay.
Chart 17376
Entrance: 56°29.53' N, 134°06.33' W
Anchor (east side) : 56°30.50' N, 134°03.89' W

The head of Elena Bay, which is shallow, provides unlimited anchor sites for small craft. We prefer the east shore, north of island (70), avoiding rocks in the entrance.

Anchor in 4 fathoms over mud and sand with good holding.

## Shelter Cove (Tebenkof Bay)
Shelter Cove lies on the southeast side of Elena Bay.
Chart 17376
Entrance: 56°29.72' N, 134°04.09' W
Anchor: 56°28.82' N, 134°02.60' W
Anchor (inner basin): 56°27.94' N, 134°02.41' W

We find Shelter Cove very well sheltered, as well as wild and remote. The south part of the bay has a large flat bottom with plenty of swinging room.

The inner basin to the south has a difficult entrance. Reconnoiter the entrance to the basin before you enter. It is narrow and winding, with moderate current and about a half-fathom at zero tide. The channel starts close to the drying mud flat to avoid a rock awash at zero tide 100 yards from the west shore. Once you are a quarter-mile south of the rock, the basin opens up with 1 to 3 fathoms to the south end.

Anchor in 2 fathoms over soft brown mud with clam shells; good holding.

Anchor (inner basin) in 1 to 2 fathoms over brown mud with good holding.

## Eye of the Needle (Tebenkof Bay)
Eye of the Needle is 1.25 miles south of Elena Point.
Chart 17376
Entrance: 56°27.80' N, 134°05.22' W
Anchor (Site #1): 56°25.95' N, 134°03.00' W
Anchor (Site #2): 56°25.70' N, 134°02.85' W

"Eye of the Needle" is what we call a 2.5-mile-long narrow channel that leads through primeval wilderness and feels like

*A labyrinth of islands*

a passage in time. This is a special rainforest environment, a 5-mile round trip with optional anchor sites. This passage is best done in a smaller cruising vessel (under 35 feet) or one with a bow-thruster, as most of the needle is too narrow to turn around in. If you do attempt this channel, proceed at dead-slow speed—and in whispered voices.

In this peaceful place, the branches of old-growth trees sag nearly to the water's edge, laden with green moss. Bald eagles watch you from tree branches above. The mud in the shoals is slowly being covered with thick green lichen.

The average width of the channel is about 100 feet, less in the narrows. Favor the west shore until you near a dangerous rock halfway through the narrows; then use the center of the channel. After the first narrows, the channel widens. Continue to favor the west shore to avoid a large rock in the center that dries on a 6-foot tide. Anchor Site #1 is on the south side of that rock.

Anchor (Site #1) in 8 fathoms over mud and gravel with good holding.

Continuing south, you pass through the second narrows (60 feet wide), avoiding rocks on both shores, before you come to the *eye* of the needle. Favor the west shore to avoid both a big rock awash on a 4-foot tide and a bushy islet. South of this islet is anchor Site #2.

Anchor (Site #2) in 2 to 4 fathoms over mud and clam shells with good holding. At this point the channel shoals, so you need to turn around and retrace your route.

We went to the bitter end on a minus 2-foot tide, which allowed us a good view of bright red starfish and reflections of what we saw as "faces" on the rocks. Minimum depths in the fairway were 1½ fathoms in both the first and second narrows, and between 3 to 8 fathoms elsewhere.

## Petrof Bay and Cedar Bight (Tebenkof Bay)

Petrof Bay is the southeast arm of Tebenkof Bay.
Chart 17376
Entrance (Petrof Bay): 56°24.14' N, 134°03.72' W
Anchor (Petrof Bay): 56°22.09' N, 134°03.09' W
Entrance (Cedar Bight): 56°23.73' N, 134°04.61' W
Anchor (Cedar Bight): 56°22.97' N, 134°04.82' W

Petrof Bay and the smaller bay to the west, "Cedar Bight," offer good shelter over a flat, shallow bottom. The head of Petrof Bay is seldom used for anchorage because of its remoteness. However, if you choose this site, you may get a view of the sandhill cranes that nest along the creek. A trail—reportedly a good 2-mile walk—connects with Affleck Canal to the south.

For more coziness we prefer what we call Cedar Bight—the cove to the west—which has stands of cedar along its east shore, with hemlock and spruce on its west shore. Avoid the 1-fathom shoal and two mid-channel rocks not marked by kelp. The rapids in this cove are great for kayaking.

Anchor (Petrof Bay) in 3 fathoms over soft mud with very good holding.

Anchor (Cedar Bight) in 2 fathoms over brown mud with shells and small rocks; holding is good if you set your anchor well.

## Thetis Bay (Tebenkof Bay)

Thetis Bay is the southwest arm of Tebenkof Bay.
Chart 17376
Entrance: 56°25.03' N, 134°09.26' W
Anchor: 56°22.18' N, 134°10.30' W

Thetis Bay, which is surrounded by high ridges and peaks, offers very good protection from all weather. Tidal rapids flow in and out of the lagoon on the west shore and may give kayakers a chance to practice some whitewater techniques.

Anchor in 6 fathoms over sticky mud with very good holding.

## Orel Anchorage (Tebenkof Bay)
Orel Anchorage is 3 miles southeast of Explorer Basin.
Chart 17376
Entrance: 56°25.30' N, 134°08.34' W
Anchor: 56°24.86' N, 134°08.05' W

Orel Anchorage is a small landlocked anchorage, easy to get to and offering good protection from southerlies. Avoid the rocks on both sides of the entrance channel.

Anchor in 5 to 6 fathoms over mud in the center of the anchorage; good holding.

## Explorer Basin
Explorer Basin lies on the south side of Tebenkof Bay between Kuiu Island and the off-lying Windfall and Troller islands.
Chart 17376
West entrance (Swaine Point Passage): 56°26.14' N, 134°15.13' W
East entrance (Helianthus Passage): 56°26.96' N, 134°11.44' W
Anchor (southeast corner): 56°24.75' N, 134°11.18' W

Explorer Basin is well named. It's a great place to explore by kayak or dinghy. We have seen many sea otters here, two humpback whales and numerous sea lions. Enter south of Windfall Islands or via Helianthus Passage, known locally as Mail Boat Pass.

Anchorage can be found in the center of the Troller Islands or in the coves on the south side and southeast corner. Several small beaches on the islands are good for kayak haul-outs or camping.

Anchor (southeast corner) in 5 fathoms over a soft bottom with fair-to-good holding.

## Gedney Harbor (Kuiu Island)
Gedney Harbor is 2 miles northeast of Point Cosmos.
Chart 17376
Entrance: 56°22.26' N, 134°15.12' W
Anchor: 56°22.64' N, 134°14.25' W

Gedney Harbor is well protected in all weather by an island on its west side. This is a quiet place with no sign of chop. When you reach the head of the entrance channel, turn north and anchor in the lee of the large island on your port side.

Anchor in about 5 fathoms over soft sticky mud and sand with very good holding.

## Harris Cove (Kuiu Island)
Harris Cove is between Gedney Harbor and Port Malmesbury.
Chart 17376
Entrance: 56°19.12' N, 134°17.90' W

We have never found a good anchor site in Harris Cove, although shelter can be found on the south side next to the shore. We much prefer Gedney Harbor, 3.5 miles to the north (described above). At high water, a dinghy can enter the lagoon to the east of Harris Harbor from either the north or south end.

## Port Malmesbury (Kuiu Island)
Port Malmesbury is 13 miles east of Port Alexander.
Chart 17376
Entrance: 56°16.47' N, 134°17.48' W
Anchor (bitter end): 56°17.49' N, 134°09.60' W

We have found the best shelter for cruising boats in Port Malmesbury to be in the first arm to the northwest—the place we call "Mud Hole." We also like the basin at the far eastern end that has high peaks streaked by avalanche paths; this site offers good shelter, too, but it may be subject to williwaws in unsettled weather. Favor the southwest shore when entering the bitter end as a rocky patch extends 100 yards from shore. The scenery here is spectacular, with large old-growth trees and many giant silver snags. A striking, high peak towers above the head of the basin.

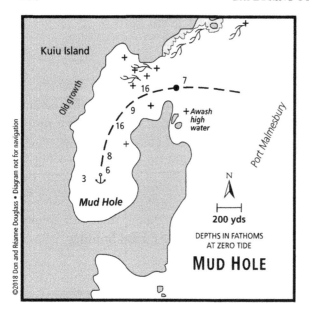

Anchor (bitter end) in 8 to 10 fathoms over soft brown mud with very good holding.

## Mud Hole (Port Malmesbury)
Mud Hole is 2.5 miles northeast of Point Harris Light in Port Malmesbury.
Chart 17376
Entrance: 56°18.57' N, 134°13.99' W
Anchor: 56°18.21' N, 134°14.58' W

Landlocked Mud Hole offers very good shelter from all weather, with adequate swinging room for several boats. The entrance has 4 fathoms in the fairway. Avoid rocks extending to mid-channel from the north shore. The swells from the southwest die off at a reef on the southeast side of the peninsula forming Mud Hole. We call this "Nursery Reef" because a dozen or more mother sea otters gathered to show off their babies as we slowly motored in.

Anchor in 6 to 8 fathoms over mud with very good holding.

## Table Bay (Kuiu Island)
Table Bay is 2 miles north of Point Crowley Light.
Chart 17386
Entrance: 56°08.96' N, 134°15.44' W
Entrance (landlocked cove): 56°10.02' N, 134°14.72' W

The east side of Table Bay is only a half-mile from Kell Bay in Affleck Canal. We prefer Port Malmesbury to those bays south of here.

## Crowley Bight (Kuiu Island)
Crowley Bight is 1.5 miles southeast of Point Crowley Light.
Chart 17386
Entrance: 56°06.10' N, 134°14.83' W

Crowley Bight is exposed in all but calm weather. (See Mud Hole above.)

## Howard Cove (Kuiu Island)
Howard Cove is 5 miles southeast of Point Crowley Light and 3 miles northwest of Cape Decision.
Chart 17386
Entrance: 56°02.39' N, 134°11.77' W

Howard Cove is full of kelp and useful only to boats fishing off Cape Decision in fair weather.

## Cape Decision (Kuiu Island)
Cape Decision is the south tip of Kuiu Island.
Chart 17386
Cape Decision (light brg 000°T at 0.50 Nm): 55°59.59' N, 134°08.16' W

Cape Decision connects Chatham Strait to Sumner Strait. Beware of breakers and strong tide rips south and east of the light.

# KEKU STRAIT FROM CONCLUSION ISLAND TO SUMNER STRAIT
*Note:* Please see West Sumner Strait in Chapter 9 for coves along Kuiu Island between Cape Decision and Reid Bay.

## Keku Strait
Keku Strait separates the west shore of Kupreanof Island from Kuiu Island and connects Sumner Strait with Frederick Sound via Rocky Pass.
Charts 17360, 17368, 17372
Note: Chart 17372 measures depths in feet.
South entrance (1.0 mile east of Conclusion Island and 3.6 miles northwest of Point Barrie): 56°27.83' N 133°45.03' W
North entrance (2.1 miles southwest of Pt. Macartney Light; 4.8 miles west of Kake): 56°59.57' N, 134°05.22' W

Keku Strait is an interesting alternative to busy Wrangell Narrows for small craft transiting from Sumner Strait to Frederick Strait or vice versa. It can be considered a complex rock pile through which saltwater flows, but it represents an appealing short cut for small craft heading between Ketchikan and Sitka. The large bays at either end of Keku Strait have some pristine and isolated anchorages that are well protected and seldom visited.

The middle 20-mile section of Keku Strait, called Rocky Pass, poses a variety of technical challenges to anyone who attempts it. Route markers reduce the uncertainty; however, Rocky Pass remains a wild, remote area requiring superior piloting skills. The channel is shallow with numerous mud flats on all sides and with strong currents in the narrows at Devils Elbow and The Summit. Thick kelp patches are found in many places.

We do not recommend Rocky Pass for larger boats or for skippers unsure of their piloting skills. Vessels over 30 feet may want to scout out the narrow parts of the route by dinghy before attempting a passage. However, since you can easily anchor almost anywhere in Rocky Pass, this scouting can be fun!

Traffic has increased over the past two decades, and you will likely see another boat or two in the Narrows. It's a good idea to give a Securité call when transiting the areas of limited visibility—especially The Summit and Devils Elbow.

Stories abound of good skippers who grounded or ruined their boats in Rocky Pass. When we first wrote about Rocky Pass, the USCG buoy tender, *Elderberry*—which was responsible for the area—had not visited the pass in over a decade, and they stated they would not be of help to stranded boats. Recent visitors report generally well-maintained markers; conversely, other visitors report missing markers. We have a report that a guided flotilla of sailboats grounded three vessels in Devil's Elbow in 2015.

Yes, it's challenging, but Rocky Pass remains a part of untouched Southeast Alaska—no clearcuts, no signs of civilization. If you have a chance to try it, and the skills to do it safely, by all means do so.

### No Name Bay (Kuiu Island)
No Name Bay is 3 miles west of Conclusion Island.
Chart 17360
Entrance: 56°29.85' N, 133°53.76' W
Anchor: 56°30.19' N, 133°57.55' W

No Name Bay has a narrow channel lined with islets and rocks and about a 2-fathom minimum in the fairway. Alvin Bay, west of Sumner Island, is considered the first choice by local fishermen for shelter along this part of Kuiu Island; No Name Bay is their second choice.

Anchor in 3 to 4 fathoms over a mixed bottom.

### Seclusion Harbor (Kuiu Island)
Seclusion Harbor is 4 miles northwest of Conclusion Island.
Chart 17360
Entrance: 56°32.94' N, 133°51.35' W

Seclusion Island has no large-scale chart. It has a tiny opening that appears to restrict its use. Locals recommend No Name Bay or Alvin Bay for shelter in foul weather.

### Threemile Arm (Kuiu Island)
Threemile Arm is 10 miles north of Alvin Bay.
Chart 17360
Entrance: 56°35.04' N, 133°49.37' W

*Threemile Arm ... makes off to the W at the NW end of the bay. Its entrance is obstructed by rocks. By proceeding with care, vessels can enter passing NE of the islet in the middle of the entrance, and find good protected anchorage in the middle of the arm in 5 to 8 fathoms, soft bottom.*

*In 1974, a survey revealed a rock awash in the middle of the arm in 56°35'45" N, 133°50'10" W.* (CP)

Threemile Arm is the northwest corner of the intricate islet/rock area north of Conclusion Island. Note the cautions above. We have not entered this area.

## Kayak Island Cove (Keku Strait)

Kayak Island Cove is on the west side of the islets at the south end of Rocky Pass.
Chart 17372 (depths measured in feet)
Entrance (1.6 miles northeast of Monte Carlo Island): 56°32.45' N, 133°43.01' W
Anchor: 56°32.87' N, 133°43.04' W

Kayak Island Cove is formed by a group of small islets and sandy beaches at the south end of Rocky Pass. It is an almost complete circle that offers temporary shelter for a lunch stop or a chance to explore the area. Primitive campsites lie along shell beaches among the islets, making it a great place for kayaks. We have stopped here on several occasions but never used it as an overnight anchorage; we would consider this in calm conditions only. The bottom is irregular and hard, with poor holding, and we once dragged anchor here in a stiff southerly breeze.

If you need shelter near the south entrance to Keku Strait, Point Baker fishermen have told us they prefer Alvin Cove first and No Name Bay second. Both Port Protection and Point Baker on the south side of Sumner Strait (Prince of Wales Island) have excellent shelter and are good places to wait for proper conditions, if you're northbound.

Strong ebb currents flowing south from Sumner Strait between Sumner Island and Point Baker can make for a rough-water cross-

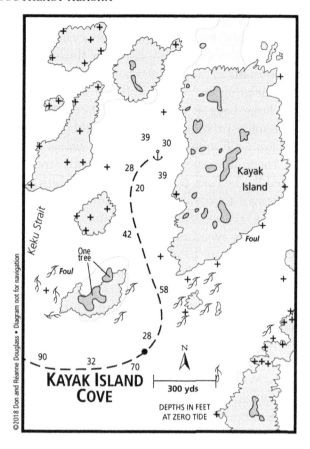

*Remember that on a southbound trip through Rocky Pass, as in this picture, the green markers must be kept to starboard.*

ing if the wind is blowing from the south. In this case, a short stop in either Alvin Cove or No Name Bay would be more prudent.

Anchor in 30 to 40 feet on the west side of the islets over a hard mixed bottom with poor holding.

## Rocky Pass (Keku Strait)

Rocky Pass lies between Kupreanof and Kuiu islands.
Chart 17372.
Note: Chart 17372 gives all depths in feet; our two diagrams on Rocky Pass also use feet.
South entrance (marker R"2" brg 025°T at 0.53 Nm) 56°33.43' N, 133°43.84' W
North entrance: (Entrance Island light brg 060°T at 0.18 Nm): 56°48.54' N, 133°48.11' W

*Authors' Note:* The Coast Guard re-marked Rocky Pass with all new navigation aids some time ago and they continue to add, maintain, and adjust the position of markers. It is essential that you use the most recent edition of

*Working our way through the kelp in Rocky Pass*

Chart 17372 (dated no earlier than 2011), with up-to-date corrections. We reprint a portion of the 2017 *Coast Pilot* information below. Always check for updates before making this passage.

*Rocky Pass has its south entrance about 8 miles north of Point Barrie. The east side of the entrance is bounded by foul ground and heavy kelp, offering a few bays for small boats.*

*A Federal project provides for a channel dredged to a depth of 5 feet through Devils Elbow and The Summit, the shallowest parts of the pass.*

*The pass is used by fishing vessels, cannery tenders, and tugs with log rafts. The draft which can be carried through depends on the tide. Because of strong currents, narrow channel, and sharp turns, it is advisable to make passage at or near high-water slack.*

*You can anchor almost anywhere in Rocky Pass.*

*The depths through Rocky Pass are generally shallow, and small craft can anchor practically anywhere with the aid of the chart. Larger craft can enter the south end of the pass for a distance of 2 miles until opposite Tunehean Creek and select anchorage according to draft, either to north or south of the midchannel reef off the mouth of the creek. At the north end of Rocky Pass, larger craft can anchor in Big John Bay, Stedman Cove, or in the channel as far south as 1 mile below High Island.*

*Devils Elbow about 14 miles north of Point Barrie, is the most dangerous part of the pass. The channel here makes a full right-angle turn. In 2007, the channel had a controlling depth of 3.7 feet with shoaling to 2.5 feet along the edge of the channel at Daybeacon 17.*

**Local magnetic disturbance:** *Differences of as much as 3° from the normal variation have been observed in the Devils Elbow in the vicinity of 50°38′N, 133°41′W. Differences of as much as 4° from normal variation have been observed in Keku Strait, north of The Summit, in the vicinity of 56°42′N, 133°44′W.*

**Tides:** *The range of tide at The Summit is about the same as at Ketchikan, but the time of tide occurs about ½ hour later than at Ketchikan. In the south and north bays of Keku Strait, the range of tide is about 0.8 of that at Ketchikan, and the time of tide is about the same as at Ketchikan. When proceeding in either direction, it is best to enter Rocky Pass about 1½ to 2 hours before high water. There are many places at each end of Rocky Pass where vessels waiting for the tide can anchor. Strangers should make passage on a rising tide and be careful to remain in the channel because of the many unmarked dangers close to the channel edge.*

**Currents:** *The flood current enters Keku Strait at both ends and meets in varying places between High Island and The Summit. At the entrance to Rocky Pass the tidal current has a velocity at strength of 0.9 to 1.2 knots.*

*At Devils Elbow the velocity of current is 1.8 to 2.4 knots, this being the strongest current encountered in the pass. Slack water occurs at practically high and low water. The period of slack at low water lasts only 5 or 10 minutes, and the current attains considerable velocity within a* half hour of this time. The high-water slack lasts considerably longer, and passage through Devils Elbow can easily be made within an hour before and after the high-water slack.

At The Summit strong currents set in within 1 hour of high-water slack attaining a velocity of about 2.6 knots. Through The Summit and the passages north of The Summit, the currents are quite variable because of frequent shallow depths and the intricate topography. High-water slack occurs near high water, but the ebb current runs for a considerable time after low water. (See the Tidal Current Tables for daily predictions.)

Rocky Pass is a special place enjoyed by increasing numbers of boaters. We have talked with skippers of boats as large as 50 feet who have successfully passed through Rocky Pass at high-water rising tide, after reconnoitering

## Rocky Pass Conquered!
### Linda Lewis & Dave Parker—M/V *Royal Sounder*

I finally got to accomplish what I considered my number one SE AK navigation challenge. As many things go, the anticipation was more nerve-wracking than the actual event. Everything went very smoothly on this 21 mile rocky, winding and shallow transit. We followed the Douglass guidebook's advice throughout. Because it was my holy grail, I was at the helm most of the trip. Dave did bow watch through the tricky parts, using the kelp for guidance and keeping a lookout for unanticipated rocks.

The number one issue for Rocky Pass is being in the right sections of the transit at the right times. Otherwise, the water is definitely too skinny and too fast. On our southbound trip—at high water slack—the lowest depth we encountered was 18 feet. We encountered that in the trickiest and shallowest sections (The Summit & Devils Elbow), as expected. We were happy with that depth.

We agree with Douglass that the currents run considerably faster than the *Coast Pilot* says. Our STWs and SOGs showed us a 3-4-knot current at the north entrance when we started down and I'll bet it was running 4-6-knots at that same time in the tricky places down the road. By the time we arrived at those sections it was high water slack at The Summit and running about 1 knot at Devils Elbow. As planned. We were happy that we got the timing right.

We were kept really busy. Eyes flicking from looking outside the boat, to spotting markers, to shifting to the depth sounder, to watching for kelp and unanticipated rocks, to following the course on the electronic chart, then back through the whole routine again. Even at a SOG of only 5 knots, I felt really busy at the helm.

We encountered considerable traffic during our passage on a Saturday in June, 2005. Four fishing boats popped out at The Summit and we encountered one pleasure boat after we started through. He was smaller than we were so he decided to beat a retreat and let us go through. The navigable channel is so narrow through places like The Summit and Devils Elbow that it would be very difficult to share—sort of like a one-lane road. I forgot to do a Securité call to warn that we were coming through; next time I won't forget. From our experience, it seems that more people may be using this passage.

It was a challenging and fun experience. In truth, we would not want to do it without using electronic charts. There is so much to look at to decide where you are that to pilot through using only visual cues for where to steer would be extremely difficult, if not downright hair-raising. The electronic charting was a great asset. (But we also always have our paper-chart backups sitting open and in the order of the day's trip.)

We found some additional extremely helpful markers have been put in place since the first edition of your book was published. Two are located in the area of the Summit (R"28" and R"24"), and one at Devils Elbow (R"14"). We also discovered that while our recently updated electronic chart collection (from a major vendor) had provided us with the newer edition raster chart of the area, the vector chart for this area did not get updated. The newer markers showed up on the raster view, but not the vector view. There is also a section right at The Devils Elbow where chart quilting problems appeared: the edges of the inset pieces of the chart don't line up nicely with the general chart. Electronic charting is wonderful, but also brings its challenges.

We jokingly said to each other that if they add a few more markers Rocky Pass will be like a mini Wrangell Narrows—only *lots* shallower. The markers are excellent. Transiting only at high water is no joke; we're believers. But with electronic charts, good timing, and good mariner's-eye watchfulness, this is a go-for-it transit for experienced cruisers. Other cruisers said it was doable and enjoyable. Now we can agree—from experience.

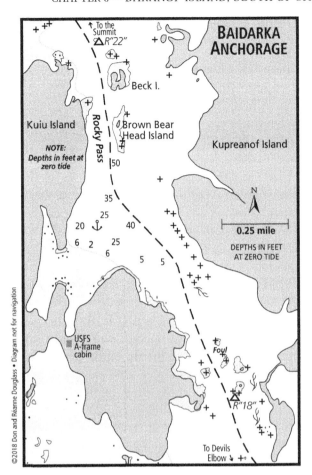

*Our first* Baidarka *in Baidarka Anchorage.*

both Devils Elbow and The Summit by dinghy first. With the dredged channels slowly silting in, you have as little as 2 feet depth at low water. We recommend that, before you commit to a passage of Rocky Pass, you talk with someone who has already made the trip in a boat similar to yours. The pass should be attempted only in good visibility and in fair weather.

Despite the presence of navigation aids, a transit of Rocky Pass is still not a piece of cake. It is a risky venture that requires careful small-boat handling in close quarters, coupled with good judgment. You should post alert lookouts on the bow and on the depth sounder, then proceed slowly, preferably on a rising tide, and be ready to stop or anchor on a moment's notice if need be.

On a northbound trip, you need to watch for mud banks along both sides of the route and avoid the rocks and heavy kelp in the fast-flowing Devils Elbow. The southern end of The Summit is frequently choked with kelp, and the dredged sections are shallow and slowly filling in. Avoid kelp when possible, and glide through slowly when you can't.

On a southbound trip, it is still somewhat difficult to find the north entrance to The Summit; the kelp is thick in many places. Use electronic charting or pre-set a GPS waypoint. Care should be taken on a flood tide not to get too close to the small island to the east near the south end of The Summit. When approaching Devils Elbow, it is easy to overshoot the sharp left turn required at the northwest entrance.

When making this almost-due-east dogleg, keep both G"17" and G"15" close to your starboard hand and R"14" on your port hand to avoid nasty rocks on the north side of the Narrows. Slow down and monitor your position carefully.

A transit of Rocky Pass should not be attempted without a copy of Chart 17372 (2011 or later), which shows the location of the nav-aids, including some newer aids that have been added at The Summit and at Devils Elbow.

We have noticed a flood current of an estimated 4 knots flowing north at Devils Elbow, and a flood of about 6 knots flowing south at The Summit along the edge of Summit Island. (This information is contrary to *Coast Pilot*, but it has been confirmed in conversation with U.S. Coast Guard personnel.) These currents can cause high closing-speeds or a loss of steerage. Otherwise, except for these short stretches, currents are moderate and the water is smooth.

GPS and electronic charting can help you identify turning points and make your transit of Rocky Pass feasible. A pre-drawn course line and waypoints on the latest edition of Chart 17372 are useful aids to prevent getting lost, as well as quick checks against your depth sounder readings. However, GPS variations and magnetic abnormalities are still too great to allow precisely following a GPS route. Added to these issues is the fact that the horizontal datum of the chart insets for The Summit and for Devils Elbow are NAD 27, not WGS 84 as for the rest of Chart 17372. If you are using paper charts and working with latitude and longitude from your GPS you should ideally re-set your GPS to NAD 27 for these sections. In reality, there is little time to do this, so paper-chart navigators working in conjunction with GPS coordinates should be extra cautious in these areas. Reaching The Summit at high tide and using good piloting skills (visual cues) are the critical elements for making this passage a safe one.

Rocky Pass is a wild place, so keep an alert bow watch and one eye on your depth sounder. Proceed accordingly and enjoy your explorations!

## Devils Elbow (Rocky Pass)
Devils Elbow is 5 miles north of the south entrance to Rocky Pass.
**Chart 17372 (depths in feet)**
South entrance: 56°37.89′ N, 133°41.11′ W
North entrance: 56°38.21′ N, 133°42.16′ W

When in Rocky Pass, use extra caution transiting the Devils Elbow. Upon entering Rocky Pass northbound, favor the Kuiu Island shore in a broad sweeping turn to the northeast. Favor the east shore to avoid the shoals southeast of Eagle Island. Passing G"11," maintain a mid-channel course and pass close to green markers G"13," G"15," and G"17" on your port side, keeping the red marker R"14" off to your starboard. Avoid the rocks on the foul north shore and all kelp patches by following a mid-channel course. Turn north as soon as the channel behind the peninsula opens up to avoid mid-channel rocks west of the tip of the peninsula. As noted in *Coast Pilot*, a 2007 survey found the channel had a controlling depth of 3.7 feet in the channel, with shoaling to 2.5 feet along the edge of the channel at Daybeacon 17. Some recent cruisers report even less depth here.

## Baidarka Anchorage (Rocky Pass)
Baidarka Anchorage is 0.35 mile south of Brown Bear Head Island.
**Chart 17372 (depths in feet)**
Anchor: 56°39.00′ N, 133°43.24′ W

You can anchor anywhere in Rocky Pass and should be prepared to do so quickly if conditions require it. Our favorite site is the small basin halfway between The Summit and Devils Elbow. The tides generally meet between these two parts of the pass, and what we call "Baidarka Anchorage" is a good place to anchor while you reconnoiter the challenges ahead, wait for the correct tide, or even remain overnight. We named this site after our first trusty trawler, which poked its bow (sometimes wrongly!) into the many excellent channels of Rocky Pass. We managed not to ground or leave any paint in Rocky Pass, but some of our transits have been rather exciting!

Baidarka Anchorage is protected from all weather and is out of the strong currents found in the channels to the north and south. At high water, you can take a dinghy trip to the USFS Devils Elbow cabin in the cove directly south. This is an excellent spot for photographing wild ducks, geese, mink, marten, wolves, and black bear.

Leaving Baidarka Anchorage heading north, we have passed Brown Bear Head Island on either side. If you use the west passage, stay close to the island for the deepest water.

Anchor off the steep-to flat in 25 feet over sand, mud and some gravel; holding is good if you set your anchor well.

## The Summit (Rocky Pass)
The Summit is 2.5 miles northwest of Devils Elbow.
Chart 17372 (depths in feet)
South entrance (100 yards northeast of G"23"): 56°39.98' N, 133°43.79' W
South entrance of dredged channel: 56°40.16' N, 133°44.01' W
North entrance (0.2 mile north of G"27"): 56°41.25' N, 133°44.16' W
North entrance (100 yards north of G"35," 0.6 mile south of High Island): 56°42.72' N, 133°44.13' W

This section of Rocky Pass is fully protected from outside influences; it has limited fetch, so there are no swells and little chop. For the most part, the waters are very calm and it is extremely quiet and peaceful.

As mentioned above, when heading north from Baidarka Anchorage, you can pass Brown Bear Head on either side. We prefer the west side, staying close to the island to avoid a 5-foot shoal off the west shore.

As you approach the south end of The Summit, you find a lot of kelp that hides numerous rocks and boulders. Stay close to G"23" to avoid the rocks near R"24." Turn north where the kelp opens up revealing a channel that points toward G"25."

There is generally less kelp on the surface at high water than at low water, and increased traffic is helping to keep the channels open. If you worry that the kelp you must pass through hides dangerous rocks, anchor for a few minutes and do some probing with your dinghy.

Caution: Rocks extend southeast from G"25," and across the fairway, north of G"23." Your route should follow an S-shaped curve in this area. Avoid the kelp patch at G"25;" there are underwater rocks close by on the east side. This is one of the shallowest and most kelp-ridden places in Rocky Pass. The channel through The Summit favors the east shore until you approach the north entrance.

On a southbound transit, the north entrance to The Summit is somewhat difficult to locate, but it can be identified by the dredged material thrown up on either side of the channel on the west side of the reef marked "awash at 1/2 tide" southeast of R"30."

Once inside the old dredged channel, you can generally see the bottom even in rainy weather. If you are passing through The Summit with a strong flood current flowing, be careful not to let your boat get set against the small islet on the west side of Summit Island. This is where we've found maximum current (up to 6 knots) and you will have little steerage as you try to motor slowly through.

Continuing northbound, once you pass the long thin reef marked "awash at 1/2 tide," keep the entire reef to your starboard until you pass R"30."

From here north, stay in the deep-water channel as indicated on the chart, then favor the Kuiu Island shore north of G"35," and pass the reef off 560-foot High Island. After passing Stadia Rock, favor Horseshoe Island shore. Stedman Cove is well sheltered and a good overnight anchorage.

Continuing westbound, favor Cucumber Reef to avoid the bad reef southwest of Stedman Cove entrance, then favor Entrance Island to avoid the long reef that extends from the south shore.

Once clear of Entrance Island, you leave Rocky Pass and can find good shelter in Dakaneek Bay, or head for the village of Kake. You can also head south into remote Port Camden or steam out through the Keku Islands to Frederick Sound.

Don't rush through this wonderful area. We encourage you to anchor overnight in Baidarka Anchorage and enjoy this special passage. Stopping for awhile can decrease your anxieties about timing The Summit and the Devils Elbow correctly and can increase your pleasure enormously.

## Stedman Cove (Horseshoe Island)

Stedman Cove, on the southwest shore of Horseshoe Island, is just inside the north entrance of Rocky Pass.
Chart 17372 (depths in feet)
Entrance (0.3 mile northeast of Cucumber Reef): 56°47.45' N, 133°45.18' W
Anchor: 56°48.04' N, 133°44.53' W

Stedman Cove, popular with crabbers and the site of an oyster farm, is a landlocked anchorage that offers excellent shelter from all weather. Avoid the shoal water off both the north and south sides of the cove. Be on the lookout for old floats and fishing platforms moored here, as well as for kelp patches on an otherwise soft bottom.

Anchor in 12 feet over soft sand and mud with very good holding.

## Big John Bay (Kupreanof Island)

Big John Bay is 2 miles east of Stedman Cove.
Chart 17372 (depths in feet)
Entrance (0.5 mile north of Beacon Island): 56°47.21' N, 133°43.25' W
Anchor: 56°47.93' N, 133°40.77' W

Anchor in 3 fathoms over sand and mud with isolated rocks.

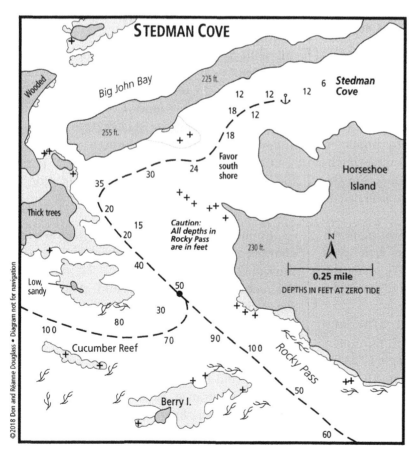

## Davidson Bay (Kupreanof Island)

Davidson Bay is 2.5 miles north of the north entrance to Rocky Pass.
Chart 17368
Entrance: 56°50.45' N, 133°51.00' W
Anchor: 56°50.99' N, 133°51.00' W

Davidson Bay, a large bay just east of Salt Point, is easy to enter, but it is open to southwest winds. The eastern section is a drying mud flat. Anchorage can be found in the corner of the bay off the drying mud flats, but better shelter can be found in Dakaneek Bay.

Anchor in 4 fathoms over sand with fair-to-good holding.

## Dakaneek Bay (Kupreanof Island)

Dakaneek Bay is 5 miles south of Kake at the head of Port Camden and 5 miles north of the north entrance to Rocky Pass.

# CHAPTER 8 — BARANOF ISLAND, SOUTH OF SITKA; LOWER CHATHAM STRAIT & KEKU STRAIT 347

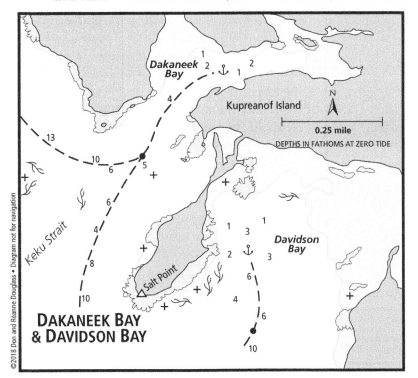

**Chart 17368**
Entrance: 56°51.36' N, 133°52.27' W
Anchor 56°51.87' N, 133°51.00' W

Dakaneek Bay, a small inlet on Kupreanof Island, is not listed in *Coast Pilot*. We find its shelter good and its access easy. You need to avoid two charted, isolated rocks in the entrance. (If you are southbound, this is a good place to stay while timing your approach to Rocky Pass.) Both Dakaneek and Davidson bays are good for crabbing.

Anchor off the drying mud flats in 2 fathoms over mud with good holding.

## Port Camden (Kuiu Island)
Port Camden, the large inlet west of Rocky Pass, is 10 miles south of Kake.
**Chart 17368**
Entrance: 56°48.41' N, 133°55.01' W

> Port Camden, the entrance to which is on the W side of Pup Island and 14 miles from Point Macartney, is an inlet 13 miles long and 1.5 miles wide for a distance of 5 miles from its entrance.... A good anchorage can be found in 20 fathoms in the wide part of Port Camden SW of Cam Island, favoring the SW shore of the inlet. Good anchorage, protected from all directions but the N, is available in 4 to 10 fathoms in the cove SE of Cam Island. Favor the W shore of the cove to avoid a large reef and a 3-fathom shoal to the N on the E side of the cove. An excellent anchorage for small boats can be had in a small cove on the E shore E of Cam Island. The entrance shoals to 2½ fathoms. Keep close to the W shore of the entrance. Beware of the reefs on the N side of the entrance to this cove. Anchorage in 4 fathoms, well protected on all sides, can be had. (CP)

Port Camden is full of black bear and, along with Goose Bay, is an excellent place to photograph them.

## Goose Bay (Port Camden)
Goose Bay is about 6 miles south of Point Camden.
**Chart 17368**
Entrance: 56°44.15' N, 133°52.65' W
Anchor: 56°44.65' N, 133°52.14' W

"Goose Bay" is the attractive landlocked bay on the east side of Port Camden Inlet. It offers excellent protection from all weather, and is close enough to Rocky Pass to allow an early-morning start on a southbound transit. We named this "Goose Bay" for a Canadian honker family that we saw along the shore. The area from Goose Bay to the head of Port Camden is a good place to see black bear and is reported to have very good "dungie" crab fishing.

There is plenty of swinging room in the bay, but avoid the rocks off the peninsula and the drying shoal to starboard at the entrance narrows.

Anchor in 4 fathoms over black mud and clamshells with excellent holding.

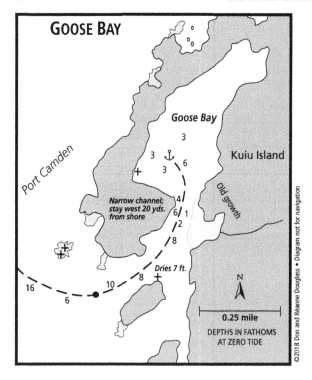

If you like an authentic old Alaskan atmosphere, Camden Hideout is a classic off-the-beaten-path place with no signs of weather. The entrance and basin are narrow and there is little turning room.

Favor the north shore inside the narrows. A small, 15-foot-deep basin at the head of the channel has enough room for one small boat. Although there is almost no swinging room, you hardly need to worry because it is so protected in here, but a stern-tie is a good idea. The water temperature is in the low-to-mid-sixties. You can anchor in the outer basin in 7 fathoms if a blow is expected.

Anchor in 2 fathoms over a mixed bottom with very good holding.

### Kadake Bay (Kuiu Island)
Kadake Bay is 2.2 miles southwest of Pup Island.
Chart 17368
Position: 56°48.59' N, 133°57.38' W

Kadake Bay is almost entirely filled with a drying mud flat. Some temporary anchorage can be found in its entrance channel.

### Gil Harbor (Kuiu Island)
Gil Harbor is 3.3 miles northwest of Pup Island.
Chart 17368
Entrance: 56°50.11' N, 133°59.06' W
Anchor: 56°49.64' N, 133°59.77' W

Gil Harbor is used by fishing boats as an anchorage, especially in southeast weather. Anchor deep in the harbor avoiding the numerous rocks in the northwest corner.

Anchor in 3 fathoms over sand and shells with good holding.

### Camden Hideout (Port Camden)
Camden Hideout is 2.5 miles southwest of Goose Bay.
Chart 17368 (inset)
Entrance: 56°43.14' N, 133°53.99' W
Anchor: 56°42.54' N, 133°54.96' W

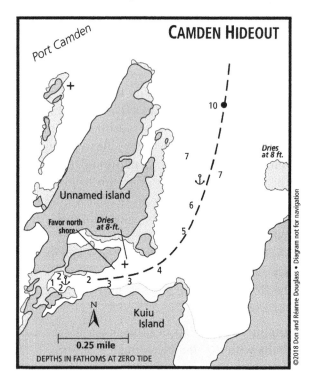

### Keku Islands (Keku Strait)
Keku Islands are on the southwest side of Keku Strait and 5 miles west of Kake.
Chart 17368

> *Keku Islands ... comprise a group of wooded islands, with outlying reefs, between which are no practicable channels.... Between Keku Islands and the reefs on the NE side is a channel about 1.5 miles wide and 8 miles long to Point*

Hamilton, with depths of 7 to 50 fathoms. S of Eva Island the channel is about 1 mile wide, between Point Hamilton and Hound Island, and leads between kelp-marked rocks and shoals on both sides. (CP)

The enchanted Keku Islands are full of surprises—a ridge of land uplifted in deep water provides a playground of islands, islets, reefs, and isolated rocks, unmarked with navigational aids and ripe for exploration.

Study Chart 17368 carefully and notice how quickly the depths of the water change without warning. The Keku Islands and Keku Strait have a warm and pleasant micro-climate that is quite agreeable for exploration and you're likely to see more whales than boats in this vicinity.

*Going ashore at Lord's Pocket*

## Kuiu Island Southeast Cove (Kuiu Island)
Kuiu Island Southwest Cove is 6 miles southwest of Kake.
Chart 17368
Position: 56°52.87' N, 134°01.77' W

"Southeast Cove" (a local name), is easy to get to and offers good protection in southeast weather. There are two large buoys here used by tugs to park barges and rafts. The cove is rather deep for small craft, except close to shore.

## Lord's Pocket (Payne Island)
Lord's Pocket is 5.5 miles southwest of Kake.
Chart 17368
West entrance: 56°56.47' N, 134°08.76' W
East entrance: 56°56.20' N, 134°05.50' W
South entrance: 56°56.16' N, 134°07.20' W
Anchor: 56°55.95' N, 134°05.41' W

"Lord's Pocket" is the local name for a centrally located anchorage on the southeast side of Payne Island that offers good protection from all weather. Entry is via Home League Pass on the south side of Payne Island, or through a window to the northeast. Skipper Paul Martin of Kake first told us about this

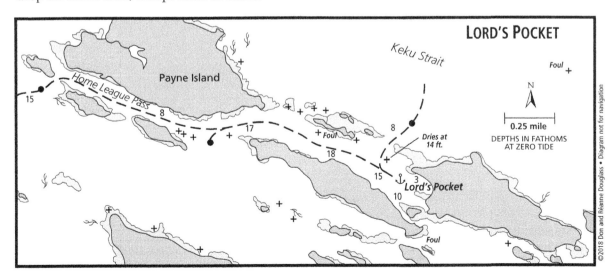

anchorage; however, we have also heard that it can be somewhat uncomfortable in strong northeast winds, especially at high tides.

Anchor in the southeast corner in 3 to 10 fathoms over mixed gravel with fair holding.

## Honeydew Cove (Kuiu Island)

Honeydew Cove, on the northeast corner of Kuiu Island, is due east across the peninsula from Halleck Harbor and 3 miles west of Lord's Pocket.
Chart 17368
East entrance: 56°55.01' N, 134°10.53' W
North entrance: 56°55.19' N, 134°11.00' W
Anchor: 56°54.96' N, 134°10.86' W

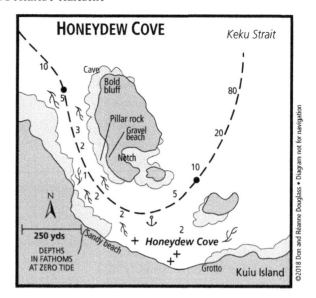

"Honeydew Cove," a small, otherwise unnamed bight, provides a picturesque anchorage with good protection in summer conditions, as well as good fishing and exploring. It is somewhat shallow and protected by kelp.

This cove is a favorite of Honeydew Murray, first mate on *Forevergreen*. She enjoys stretching her legs on the sandy beach and exploring the rocky bluffs, sculptured headlands, caves and shoreline of this remote, quiet spot.

Bull kelp (some strands 60 feet long or more) keeps the surface of the water calm. The water is so clear you can see the sandy, grassy bottom. As you row around, you can't help noticing the striking natural rock pillars. Overhead, we have seen bald eagles soaring while puffins scurried about the cove.

If Honeydew Cove is already occupied, consider anchoring one mile northwest, between the small wooded island and Kuiu Island, where there are sandy, shell beaches and high bluffs with shallow caves.

Anchor in 2 fathoms over sand and grass, avoiding the kelp patches and small rocks close to shore.

## Hamilton Bay (Kupreanof Island)

Hamilton Bay, on the southeast side of Point Hamilton, is 5 miles southeast of Kake.
Chart 17368
Entrance (0.6 mile northeast of Point Hamilton): 56°54.50' N, 133°53.08' W
Anchor (0.4 mile southeast of Little Hamilton Island): 56°53.33' N, 133°47.65' W

> Hamilton Bay . . . is a secure anchorage for vessels of any size. The entrance is clear in mid-channel, and extensive bare flats are at the head of the bay. Two large streams enter near the head. (CP)

*Kake boasts the tallest totem pole in southeast Alaska; public float is at right.*

*This large, well-stocked store in Kake is a welcome stop after wilderness cruising.*

Anchor in 5 fathoms over mud and shells with good holding.

**Portage Pass Bay** (Kupreanof Island)
Portage Pass Bay is 1.2 miles south of the Kake ferry docks.
Chart 17368
Northwest entrance (0.1 mile south of ferry docks): 56°57.53' N, 133°55.34' W
West entrance (0.5 mile northwest of Hamilton Island): 56°56.68' N, 133°56.41' W

Portage Pass Bay is a drying mud flat that connects Portage Bay to Hamilton Bay.

**Kake** (Kupreanof Island)
Kake is 5 miles southeast of Point Macartney.
Chart 17368 (inset)
South entrance: 56°58.22' N, 133°56.83' W
West entrance: 56°58.30' N, 133°57.18' W
Public float: 56°58.37' N, 133°56.75' W
Fuel dock: 56°57.76' N, 133°55.49' W

Kake, a Tlingit community of about 500, boasts Alaska's tallest totem pole (132.5 feet). The town has excellent cell phone coverage. The approaches to downtown Kake, as well as the public dock, two miles southeast of town, and Portage Bay, all lead through shallow waters, so monitor your depth sounder carefully. See *Coast Pilot* for information on routes and lists of hazards.

Avoid the shoal patch directly in line with the city pier and the very large shoal that extends from shore one-third of a mile between the city pier and the fuel dock.

Mooring possibilities are limited in Kake. From northwest to southeast you will find 1) the Kake city pier, with limited space for pleasure craft, but near the center of the village; 2) about a mile south, the Kake cannery docks, used for seafood unloading; 3) the former site of the Kake tribal fuel dock (it was destroyed in a storm in 2016); 4) the public cargo dock, used for large cargo; 5) the Alaska State ferry dock; 6) the Kake city float at Portage Bay. The Portage Bay floats are a city-owned marina about two miles south of town. Water, power, showers are available. Some cruisers recommend tying up here, and then dinghying the two miles to town. It is also possible to anchor between the Portage Bay floats and the city dock. Remain aware of ferry, sea plane, and commercial traffic. The Kake tribal fuel

*The fuel dock at Kake*

dock will be rebuilt over the next few seasons. Until then, recreational boaters can arrange a fuel truck delivery by calling the fuel station and making an appointment (907-785-3601).

Jill Princehouse on M/V *Passages* wrote us: "We were in Kake twice. The first time we stayed at the dock south of town. The second time we anchored out behind the islands. We enjoyed the anchorage and a gorgeous sunset but both times we used our dinghy to get around. The best place to hide a dinghy is behind the ferry dock because it's a short walk from there to the grocery store, south of the dock. For the post office and main village, the city dock is better."

The NOAA ship Fairweather *homeports in Ketchikan.*

## WEST FREDERICK SOUND FROM KEKU STRAIT (KAKE) TO KINGSMILL POINT

### Saginaw Bay (Kuiu Island)
Saginaw Bay is 11.7 miles west of Kake.
Chart 17368
Entrance: 56°55.37' N, 134°17.43' W

Saginaw Bay, entered south of Cornwallis Point, has a number of islets and isolated rocks. Anchorage can be found at its head near the drying mud flats or, more conveniently, along the north shore of Halleck Harbor.

A petroglyph on the cliff to the east of the entrance depicts a war party in canoes.

### Halleck Harbor (Saginaw Bay)
Halleck Harbor, on the northeast side of Saginaw Bay, is about 1.5 miles southeast of Cornwallis Point.
Chart 17368
Entrance: 56°54.96' N, 134°14.29' W
Anchor: 56°54.60' N, 134°12.36' W

Halleck Harbor has good protection from southerly weather in its southeast corner with room for several boats. It also has a petroglyph. We have heard it is also a good place to jig for halibut.

Anchor in 10 fathoms over hard sand and pebbles with fair-to-good holding.

### Security Bay (Kuiu Island)
Security Bay is 4.2 miles southwest of Saginaw Bay.
Chart 17368 (inset)
Entrance (0.25 mile west of Roadstead Island Light): 56°52.40' N, 134°22.90' W
Anchor (0.5 mile southeast of Cleft Island): 56°50.21' N, 134°19.34' W

The entrance to Security Bay is in a narrow channel west of Roadstead Island. Avoid the dangerous shoals and kelp patches north of Roadstead Island Light.

Good shelter can be found deep in the bay, away from the numerous foul areas, or in Cedar Bight.

Anchor in 10 fathoms over a hard mixed bottom with fair holding.

*Whale spouts can be seen from a long distance.*

## Cedar Bight (Security Bay)
Cedar Bight is east of Cleft Island.
Chart 17368
Entrance: 56°51.30' N, 134°20.76' W
Anchor: 56°50.88' N, 134°19.26' W

The entrance ledge at Cedar Bight can be passed on either the north or south side. Sheltered anchorage can be found deep in the bight, avoiding the ledges on the north shore north and east of Expedition Point.

Anchor over a hard mixed bottom with fair holding.

## Christmas Cove (Security Bay)
Christmas Cove is 0.6 Nm south of Roadstead Island Light.
Chart 17368
Entrance: 56°51.85' N, 134°22.57' W
Anchor: 56°51.54' N, 134°22.29' W

"Christmas Cove" is the local name for a tiny nook on the south end of Christmas Island. It is appropriate only for one or two small trawlers (under 30 feet). The entrance is via a very narrow, kelp-lined channel on the east side of Paralysis Point.

Christmas Cove is close to Frederick Sound and secure when you are well anchored inside, but is marginal for most cruising boats.

Anchor in 1½ fathoms over sand and mud with fair holding and very limited swinging room.

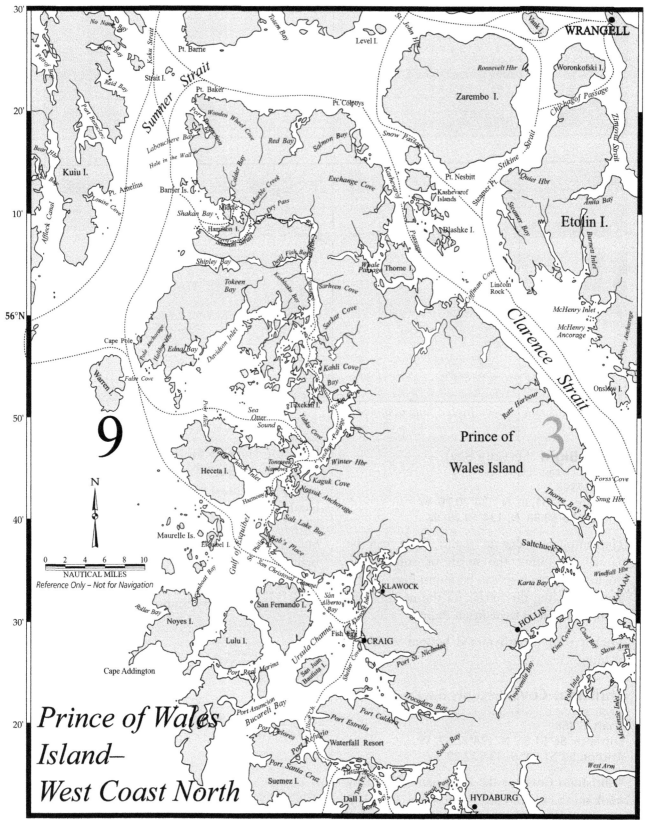

Prince of Wales Island– West Coast North

# 9

# WEST SUMNER STRAIT & PRINCE OF WALES ISLAND WEST COAST TO CRAIG

## INTRODUCTION

The west coast of Prince of Wales Island is one of the most beautiful regions in Southeast Alaska. Although it is perhaps the least explored, it offers wonderful opportunities for cruising boaters to get away from the more travelled waterways and enjoy the beauty in solitude. Hundreds of small islands create an "Outer Passage"—a smooth-water route through beautiful wilderness waters. Wildlife viewing along these shores is excellent as well: you may spot black bear, wolves, beaver, whales, seals, marten or mink, as well as eagles and numerous species of waterfowl.

*Harbor seal dining on squid*

Prince of Wales Island stretches from Sumner Strait to Dixon Entrance. It is 135 miles long with almost 1,000 miles of coastline in total. Heavy logging over the years has been a mixed blessing: more than a thousand miles of logging roads that denuded much of the terrain are now used by tourists and visitors who come to the island to fish, camp, kayak, mountain bike or sightsee by vehicle. A portion of the island has been set aside as South Prince of Wales Wilderness to preserve a truly pristine environment. Several west coast islands—Coronation and Warren islands, and the Maurelle group—are also designated Wilderness areas.

Heading south along the northwestern side of Prince of Wales, you come to Shakan Strait, whose waters curve around an arm of mountainous Kosciusko Island. From either side of the strait you have stunning views of high walls and rounded peaks.

Dry Pass, which connects Shakan Strait to El Capitan Passage, leads to perhaps the most

*One of the many fisherman active in the Pt. Baker area*

spectacular area along this coast—high granite walls with rounded domes that evoke Yosemite Valley. Numerous limestone caves have been discovered near the north end of El Capitan Passage. Cataloging of these, and exploration of new caves, is an ongoing process. El Capitan, the largest of the known caves, is reported to be the deepest (about 600 feet) in the United States.

From Shakan Bay through Sea Otter Sound to Craig, there are miles of wonderful cruising and sport fishing grounds. Prince of Wales Island is a sport fisherman's delight and you will find plenty of salmon and halibut along the coast, as well as rainbow, steelhead, and cutthroat trout in the island's many lakes and streams.

The climate is cool and moist, year-round. During the summer, temperatures range from 45°F to 70°F; winter temperatures are moderated by cloud cover and warm marine waters that range from 32°F to 42°F. Precipitation around the island ranges from 60 to over 200 inches per year.

The Alaska Marine Highway provides a daily 2.5-hour ferry ride from Ketchikan to Hollis, on the east side of Prince of Wales Island. Hollis is a turn-of-the-century gold mining town and logging camp with limited facilities. No scheduled public transport is available beyond here; however, a paved road links Hollis with the larger settlement of Craig, on the island's west coast. If you want to go hiking or explore the interior of Prince of Wales Island, you can rent a vehicle in Craig. Driving the island's extensive system of dirt roads can be an explorer's delight, but remember these are rough logging roads; be sure to give way to the logging trucks and check the fuel availability on your route.

Archaeological evidence suggests that Prince of Wales Island has been inhabited for at least 7,500 years. Two native tribes—the Tlingits and the Haida—are the most recent historical inhabitants. Klawock, pop. 854, is a Tlingit Village and the site of the island's only airport. Here it is possible to drop off or pick up crew. The town is home to an impressive collection of area totem poles and is the site of Alaska's first salmon cannery, which opened in 1878. From Klawock, it's a short cruise to the public float at neighboring Craig; this is the largest community on Prince of Wales Island, and offers plenty of commercial services—groceries, stores, banks, restaurants, shops and bars.

Further south, the Haida community of Hydaburg (see next chapter), has a wonderful totem park that is well worth a visit.

## WEST SUMNER STRAIT FROM PORT PROTECTION TO CORONATION AND WARREN ISLANDS

*Note:* No large-scale charts exist for parts of this coast, and some surveys date from before 1940, so navigate with due caution.

### Port Protection (Prince of Wales Island)
Port Protection is 1.5 miles south of Point Baker.
Chart 17378
Entrance: 56°20.21' N, 133°39.00' W

Port Protection, named by George Vancouver, is a small settlement with a State float that offers good shelter from all weather, as its name implies.

## Wooden Wheel Cove
(Port Protection)
Wooden Wheel Cove is 1 mile inside the entrance to Port Protection.
Chart 17378
Entrance: 56°19.77′ N, 133°36.92′ W
Public float: 56°19.40′ N, 133°36.79′ W

The public float (detached from shore) in Port Protection (Wooden Wheel Cove) is busy when the fishing fleet is in even though the float is poor condition. Rafting is encouraged; there is also a fish-loading pier. Wooden Wheel Trading Post (seasonal) has some provisions, fuel, showers, and a laundry.

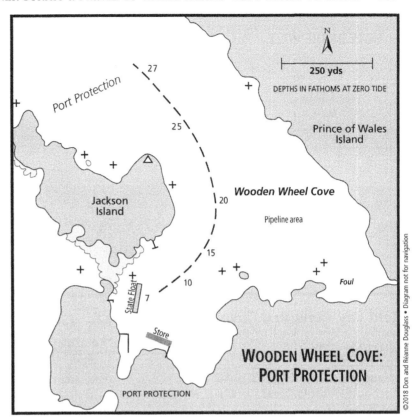

## Alvin Bay (Kuiu Island)
Alvin Bay, northwest of Sumner Island, is 11 miles northwest of Point Baker.
Chart 17360
Outer entrance (south tip Sumner Island brg 066°T at 0.80 Nm): 56°23.40′ N, 133°49.93′ W
Inner entrance (0.30 Nm east of channel): 56°26.12′ N, 133°53.61′ W
Anchor: 56°26.12′ N, 133°55.46′ W

Alvin Bay is one of the more sheltered anchorages on the west side of Sumner Strait. The entrance passage north of Sumner Island is passable, but it is encumbered with rocks. Caution: There is no large-scale chart for Alvin Bay and much of this coast. Avoid the entrance channel rocks and anchor near the center of the ¼-mile-wide bay.

Anchor in about 5 fathoms over mud and shell bottom with good holding.

## WHO WAS THE "PRINCE OF WALES"?

Prince of Wales is a title that dates back to the thirteenth century and is traditionally bestowed upon the (male) heir apparent to the British monarchy. The name "Prince of Wales" was given by George Vancouver in 1793 to all of what is now the Alexander Archipelago, but since 1825 it has applied only to the largest island in the group. The royal personage to whom it refers was George Augustus Frederick (1762-1830), eldest son of King George III, who was Prince of Wales in Vancouver's time, and who became King George IV upon his father's death in 1820. Before Vancouver's circumnavigation of Prince of Wales Island, it had been sighted and/or partially charted by other Europeans, including the Russian navigator Aleksei Chirikov (in 1741), several Spanish explorers (between 1774 and 1792), Captain James Cook (in 1779), and the Frenchman Jean-François de Galaup, better known as the Comte de La Pérouse (in 1786). The Tlingit name for Prince of Wales Island is "Taan" (sea lion).

—AC

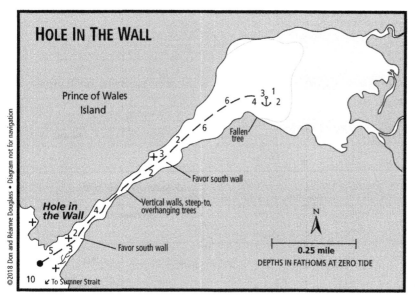

## Reid Bay, Peninsula Cove (Kuiu Island)
Reid Bay is 3 miles southwest of Sumner Island and 8 miles west of Point Baker.
Chart 17360
Entrance: 56°22.34' N, 133°51.46' W
Anchor (Peninsula Cove): 56°21.86' N, 133°52.64' W

Reid Bay is exposed to southeast winds and the chop of Sumner Strait. Its shores are ringed with submerged rocks, but small craft can find fair anchorage at the shore in what we call "Peninsula Cove." Anchor near the head of the cove, but avoid the rocks along shore.

Anchor (Peninsula Cove) in 5 to 8 fathoms over mud with rocks and kelp.

## Labouchere Bay (Prince of Wales Island)
Labouchere Bay is 4 miles south of Point Baker.
Chart 17378
Entrance: 56°18.12' N, 133°40.45' W
Anchor (south side of bay): 56°17.12' N, 133°39.16' W

Labouchere Bay is a landlocked bay with a number of islands, reefs and back bays to explore. According to the Forest Service, this area of Prince of Wales has the largest number of bears on the island. Within the many marvelous nooks and crannies, you can find a number of well-sheltered anchor sites. The most convenient anchorage is located on the south shore behind the largest of the islands. The bottom in Labouchere is highly irregular with isolated reefs.

Anchor (south side of bay) in 2 to 5 fathoms over sand, gravel and kelp with fair holding.

## Hole in the Wall (Prince of Wales Island)
Hole in the Wall is 1.8 miles south of Labouchere Bay.
Chart 17378
Entrance: 56°15.62' N, 133°38.74' W
Anchor: 56°16.06' N, 133°37.60' W

A breathtaking passage through clear aquamarine water, Hole in the Wall is a gem of the west coast of Prince of Wales Island. Threads of green moss and black lichen crisscross the fissured, convoluted base of granite that rises vertically along the entrance. Devil's claw, old-growth spruce, hemlock and cedar hang tenaciously to ledges high above, while delicate purple flowers line diagonal cracks in the rock.

The basin is landlocked and provides very good protection. Anchorage can be found tucked in behind the point in the southeast corner of the inner bay.

Anchor in 3 fathoms. Because the bottom is such soft black mud, use an extra light touch in setting your anchor; once set, it holds well.

*Entrance to Hole in the Wall*

## Port Beauclerc (Kuiu Island)

Port Beauclerc, on the west side of Sumner Strait, is 10 miles southwest of Point Baker.

Chart 17360
Entrance (Kuiu Island): 56°15.85' N, 133°52.88' W
Anchor (south arm): 56°15.65' N, 133°59.17' W

> Small-boat anchorage is available in the small cove W of the charted rock awash on the S side of this island, or in the cove on the Kuiu Island side S of the E end of Edwards Island.
>
> Anchorage may also be had in the S arm in 4 or 6 fathoms, mud bottom. Enter by the narrow passage S of Edwards Island and slightly favor the E shore of the arm to avoid a sunken rock, marked by kelp, 1 mile W of the W end of the narrow passage S of Edwards Island. On the E shore of the arm, 1 mile SE from the narrow passage, is a point close to a 3½-fathom spot.
>
> Caution: Where local knowledge is lacking, caution is advised in entering Port Beauclerc. (CP)

Port Beauclerc was named by Vancouver after Amelius Beauclerk, an English admiral; the French spelling was adopted at some later time. No large-scale chart exists for Port Beauclerc, so take precautions if you enter, and consult *Coast Pilot*.

Anchorage is reported off the islands northwest of Edwards Island, or deep in the south arm, which offers the most protection. Favor slightly east of mid-channel when entering the south arm to avoid the rock marked by kelp on the west shore.

Anchor (south arm) in 6 fathoms, mud bottom with fair holding.

## Louise Cove (Kuiu Island)

Louise Cove is on the west side of Point Amelius.

Chart 17386
Entrance: 56°11.49' N, 133°56.89' W

Use the larger-scale Chart 17386 available for this cove.

## Shakan Bay (Prince of Wales and Kosciusko islands)

Shakan Bay is 12 miles south of Point Baker.

Chart 17379
Entrance: 56°09.79' N, 133°39.60' W

The addition of Chart 17379 (2014) brings a welcome large-scale (1:10,000) view of Shakan Bay and Shakan Strait. The inset for El Capitan Passage on Chart 17389 (2014, 1:40:000) is also at 1:10,000.

Shakan Strait, along the south side of Shakan Bay, takes you to the north-end entrance of El Capitan Passage—a beautiful, well-marked transit which is not to be missed if you're cruising the west side of Prince of Wales Island.

## Shipley Bay (Kosciusko Island)

Shipley Bay is 4 miles south of Shakan Bay.

Chart 17387
Entrance: 56°05.87' N, 133°38.72' W
Anchor: 56°04.65' N, 133°32.13' W

When entering Shipley Bay, avoid the rocks and shoals extending from north to mid-channel. You can find good shelter in the cove. Avoid rocks and kelp on the north side of the cove.

*Looking back at the entrance to the narrow Hole in the Wall*

*A box from far across the ocean washes up on a remote beach on Prince of Wales Island.*

Anchor (cove west of point) in 3 fathoms over sand and mud with fair holding.

## Affleck Canal (Kuiu Island)
Affleck Canal, 14 miles long, is entered west of Point St. Albans and northwest of Fairway Island.
Chart 17386
Entrance: 56°04.86' N, 134°03.31' W

> The depths in general are great but very irregular, especially near the shores and at the head of the canal.
>
> A dangerous rock, covered 1 fathom, is in Affleck Canal, 1,300 yards 150° [true] from the center of Bush Islets. (CP)

Affleck Canal has a rocky bottom and only small-scale charts are available for the area. The west arm of Affleck Canal is called Kell Bay; the northwest arm is Bear Harbor.

## Kell Bay (Affleck Canal)
Kell Bay, on the west side of Affleck Canal, is 7 miles north of Fairway Island.
Chart 17386
Entrance: 56°09.35' N, 134°06.64' W
Entrance (southwest arm): 56°08.50' N, 134°09.84' W
Anchor (southwest arm): 56°08.29' N, 134°09.36' W
Anchor (southwest arm basin): 56°07.62' N, 134°10.34' W

The southwest shore of Kell Bay has a small landlocked arm that provides very good shelter to small craft behind the entrance islands or in the small basin at its head. Favor the west shore when you enter the basin.

Anchor (southwest arm behind the entrance islands) in 8 fathoms over mud with fair holding.

Anchor (southwest basin) in 4 to 6 fathoms over sand and gravel with fair-to-good holding.

## Bear Harbor (Affleck Canal)
Bear Harbor, on the west side of Affleck Canal, is 4 miles north of Kell Bay.
Chart 17386
Entrance: 56°13.51' N, 134°05.96' W
Entrance (middle arm): 56°13.89' N, 134°06.51' W
Anchor (west arm): 56°13.60' N, 134°07.32' W
Anchor (middle arm): 56°14.78' N, 134°06.67' W

Bear Harbor, like Kell Bay above, has very protected waters reached by narrow passages. The middle arm is landlocked, protected by small islands, and very good anchorage can be found near the head of the arm.

Anchor (west arm) in 16 fathoms over mud with fair holding.

Anchor (middle arm) in 5 to 10 fathoms over sand, mud and gravel with fair holding.

## Port McArthur (Kuiu Island)
Port McArthur is 4.5 miles north of Cape Decision.
Chart 17386
Entrance (Lemon Point Rock brg 246°T at 0.3 Nm): 56°04.48' N, 134°06.26' W
Anchor: 56°03.55' N, 134°07.12' W

> Port McArthur... is protected at the entrance by a group of islands and reefs, and it affords anchorage that is not secure because large swells run to the head of the bay. For small craft the most secure anchorage is in 4 fathoms behind South Island. (CP)

Anchor in 5 fathoms over mud, sand, gravel and kelp with fair holding

## Fishermans Harbor (Kosciusko Island)
Fishermans Harbor is 22 miles southwest of Port Protection
Chart 17402
Entrance: 55°58.62' N, 133°48.55' W

Please refer to the detailed directions in *Coast Pilot* to enter Fishermans Harbor.

## Pole Anchorage (Kosciusko Island)
Pole Anchorage is 1 mile south of Fishermans Harbor.
Chart 17402
Entrance: 55°58.23' N, 133°48.97' W
Anchor: 55°57.49' N, 133° 48.50' W

Refer to the directions in *Coast Pilot* to enter Pole Anchorage. Anchor in 10 fathoms over sand and mud surrounded by rocks and kelp, with fair holding.

## Coronation Island
Coronation Island is 5 miles south of Cape Decision and 20 miles southeast of Cape Ommaney.
Chart 17402

> *Coronation Island, west of Warren Island, is... divided into three peninsulas by Windy Bay on the W side and Aats Bay on the N side, the heads of which are separated by a range 1 mile in the center of the island.* (CP)

Coronation Island, due south of Cape Decision, and Warren Island, directly east of Coronation Island, both lie within designated Wilderness areas and are less frequently visited than other islands to the north and east. Coronation Island is located between Sumner and Chatham straits, but the area is subject to strong turbulent currents from Cape Decision through the Spanish Islands to Coronation Island, which may discourage some boaters.

The island was named more than two centuries ago by George Vancouver in honor of King George III's coronation—the very king against whom America waged its Revolutionary War.

Fishermen have long sought shelter along Coronation Island; pleasure boaters are also discovering its beauties—the white sand beach in Egg Harbor, pointed peaks, sea caves, and primitive forest untouched by chain saws. Animal life abounds here, too, both ashore and in the surrounding waters—deer and mountain goats, orcas, humpback whales and sea otters. A professional skipper who has frequently taken guests here told us that Coronation Island "... is not to be missed!" We agree!

## Egg Harbor (Coronation Island)
Egg Harbor, on the east side of Nation Point, is 22 miles from Port Alexander.
Chart 17402
Entrance (Nation Point brg 285°T at 0.45 Nm): 55°55.63' N, 134°19.38' W
Anchor: 55°54.77' N, 134°18.87' W

Egg Harbor is a lovely, deep cove on the northwest side of Coronation Island; it provides very good anchorage in most summer weather. The sandy bottom gradually shoals toward the head of the cove, and boats can anchor almost anywhere over the large flat bottom. A broad

---

### Exploring Coronation Island Wilderness
#### Barb Davis—S/V *Antares*

Egg Harbor is dominated by a 1,600-foot rock peak on its west side. A white sand beach that spreads out around the shore at the head of the bay is backed by magical, moss-covered forest. We explored the forest, following game trails that passed through 3-foot-deep moss. We spent a morning exploring the caves along the rocky shore, then began a climb to the peak, hand-over-foot, clawing our way up a mossy cliff toward the summit.

After hiking through primitive forest, we found ourselves at the top of a moon-like peak with crystal-clear views in every direction. We could see west to the Gulf of Alaska, north to the islands from which we had come, and east and south to the islands we had yet to explore, and we sighted a humpback whale feeding in the bay below.

By the time we got back to shore, we were exhausted and hungry, and all we could think about was what we'd have for dinner. But when we returned to the boat, we found it partially flooded with sea water from the head which had overflowed. (One of the cats must have dislodged the shut-off valve.) We spent the next hour bailing and mopping up with towels. After that, all we could think of was relaxing with a big glass of wine—forget dinner!

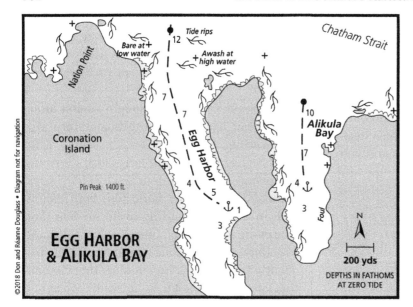

sandy beach backed by a lovely forest and many wild flowers affords excellent combing, and the steep hills promise good climbs and excellent views. Tunnels through the limestone connect beaches along the west shore.

Entering Egg Harbor, avoid the charted rocks, especially the rock on the east side of the channel awash at high water. During heavy northwesterlies (30 knots) the cove can become rolly, and it is not recommended during northerly storms. In northerly winds, Windy Bay offers the best protection on Coronation Island. Note that strong currents flowing out of Sumner Strait cause strong tide rips off all the islands south of Cape Decision.

Anchor in 3 fathoms over mud with fair-to-good holding.

## Alikula Bay (Coronation Island)

Alikula Bay is 0.75 mile east of Egg Harbor.
Chart 17402
Entrance: 55°55.36' N, 134°18.12' W
Anchor: 55°54.72' N, 134°18.15' W

Alikula Bay is much like Egg Harbor—a good anchorage but exposed to northerly gales and with more kelp.

Anchor in 5 fathoms over sand with fair holding.

## Aats Bay (Coronation Island)

Aats Bay is 2.5 miles east of Egg Harbor.
Chart 17402
Entrance: 55°55.11' N, 134°14.60' W
Anchor: 55°53.76' N, 134°13.94' W

Aats Bay is useful only for temporary anchorage in fair weather.

## Windy Bay (Coronation Island)

Windy Bay, on the west side of Coronation Island, is 3.2 miles south of Egg Harbor.
Chart 17402
Entrance: 55°51.78' N, 134°20.91' W
Anchor: 55°52.35' N, 134°17.53' W

From a half-mile offshore Windy Bay's entrance looks daunting: a series of reefs stretch nearly two-thirds of the way from north to south, almost blocking the entrance. The reefs act as a sort of breakwater, providing good shelter from the outside seas. However, on extreme high tides, swells break high over the reefs and surge can be felt all the way to the easternmost end of the bay.

Upon entering Windy Bay, favor the south shore to avoid the reefs and head to the southeastern end of the bay. Although depths throughout the entire bay are great and the shores steep-to, anchor sites can be found in 6 to 10 fathoms.

The view to the outside from behind the breaking reefs is spectacular and the steep rocky shores are lined with old-growth forests. We spotted deer and mountain goats from our anchor site, and sea otters peeked out at us from nearby kelp beds.

Anchor in 8 to 10 fathoms over a bottom of hard sand and rocks; fair-to good holding with a well-set anchor.

## False Cove (Warren Island)
False Cove is 1.5 miles north of Warren Cove.
Chart 17402
Entrance: 55°53.76' N, 133°50.29' W
Anchor: 55°53.82' N, 133°51.04' W

False Cove provides reasonable anchorage in fair weather during prevailing northwesterly wind. However, we prefer Warren Cove.

Anchor in 4 to 5 fathoms over sand with some kelp, fair holding.

## Warren Cove (Warren Island)
Warren Cove is on the east shore of Warren Island.
Chart 17402
Entrance: 55°52.36' N, 133°50.35' W
Anchor: 55°52.78' N, 133°51.66' W

Warren Cove's wide beach backed by rainforest is a delight to explore.

Anchor in 4 fathoms over sand with fair holding.

## Shakan Bay and El Capitan Passage
(Kosciusko and Hamilton Islands)
Shakan Bay is 12 miles south of Point Baker.
Charts 17379 (Shakan Bay) & 17387 (El Capitan Passage)
West entrance (Shakan Strait): 56°07.95' N, 133°34.75' W
El Capitan Cave USFS Dock (1.4 miles northwest of Aneskett Point): 56°09.66' N, 133°19.28' W

Shakan Bay has a number of shoals and rocks that require alert piloting; however, kelp marks

*Fishing boats at anchor in Egg Harbor*

most of these hazards. As mentioned previously, Charts 17379 and the inset to Chart 17387 provide large-scale (1:10,000) views of Shakan Bay and El Capitan Passage.

There is a small-boat passage to the inner bay north of Hamilton Island and west of Divide Island, which is a shortcut to Marble

*Shipwreck in Warren Cove*

*Pilothouse sits in sand at Warren Cove.*

Creek Cove or Calder Bay. This passage requires careful navigation. Shakan Strait, although longer, provides easier access to El Capitan Passage and can be navigated in limited visibility by radar.

El Capitan Cave, reported to be the deepest cave in the U.S., is located on the southern flank of 2,500-foot El Capitan Peak, on the north shore of El Capitan Passage east of Dry Pass. Cruising boaters can tie up at the USFS dock, walk across a parking lot and take a short but steep trail of stairs to the mouth of the cave. We have heard reports that the float is in poor condition, and currents can make landing difficult—use caution.

Note that the buoys in El Capitan Passage follow the standard color convention (red right returning) from south to north. In other words, if you are southbound, you must keep all red buoys to port and green ones to starboard.

## Marble Creek Cove (Prince of Wales Island)
Marble Creek is 8 miles southeast of Hole in the Wall.
Chart 17379
Entrance: 56°10.55' N, 133°28.83' W
Anchor: 56°10.58' N, 133°28.45' W

Surrounded by the huge, smooth granite domes of Mt. Calder to the northwest and the peaks towering on the north side of the strait, the inner waters of Shakan Strait invite inevitable comparison to Yosemite Valley. But here, there are no tourists, no roads, and if you're lucky, you'll see no more than one or two small boats. Aside from a marble quarry this is a lovely area.

Anchorage with fair protection can be taken off the ramp once used in logging operations. Due to soft mud, you must set your anchor with a light touch. Avoid the shoal that separates the north side of the bay from the creek outlet. Small boats can tuck in east of the ramp in 1 to 2 fathoms near the head of the bay with better protection from south and west winds.

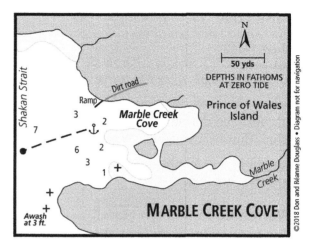

Anchor off the ramp in 5 fathoms over soft black mud with good holding.

## Calder Bay (Prince of Wales Island)
Calder Bay is 2 miles northwest of Marble Creek.
Chart 17379 & 17387
Entrance: 56°11.15' N, 133°31.61' W
Anchor: 56°11.42' N, 133°31.44' W

Calder Bay, at the base of Mt. Calder, has a large area for easy anchoring. It is somewhat exposed to south winds but the surrounding area is generally quiet and calm. Fellow cruisers have reported watching seven bears feeding in the large grassy area at its head. We have entered Calder Bay via the narrow passage north of Hamilton Island and west of Divide Island, which is shorter than Shakan Strait but requires caution and good visibility.

Anchor in 4 fathoms over sand with fair holding.

*Entrance to Marble Creek Cove*

## Prince of Wales Underground—El Capitan Cave

El Capitan Cave is one of more than 600 caves on Prince of Wales Island. Discovered in the 1970s, it is the largest known cave in Alaska, with several miles of maze-like limestone passages and numerous pits. One of these pits plunges more than 600 feet and is one of the deepest in the entire United States.

El Capitan Cave is also notable for finds of the fossilized remains of bears and other animals. In 1990, a spelunker named Kevin Allred discovered a pile of bear bones in a remote upper passage he named the Hibernaculum. Additional bones were found by paleontologists two years later in an adjacent chamber. The most prominent of these was the skeleton of a large female black bear. Intact and perfectly preserved, it appeared to be larger than a modern-day bear. Subsequent radiocarbon dating revealed the bones to be from 10,750 years ago, in the Late Pleistocene epoch, when bears and other animals were of generally greater size than they are now. The bones of several giant brown bears, dating back more than 12,000 years, have also been found in El Capitan Cave, along with the remains of red fox, caribou, wolverine, otter, and numerous smaller species (voles, bats, deer mice, etc.), the present-day descendants of which continue to use the cave as refuge to this day.

The entrance to the cave faces across El Capitan Passage. It is accessible by boat and float plane, and by car from Hollis and Craig. Boats may tie up at the Forest Service dock but at least one person should remain on board. Because of the inherent dangers and the general fragility of the cave, independent visits are not permitted, and a gate is in place to restrict access beyond the first 200 feet into the cave. However, the US Forest Service runs free tours during the summer months. A steep, 370-step wooden stairway ascends to the cave entrance from the boat dock. Tours last for about 2 hours. Call the Thorne Bay Ranger District (907-828-3304) at least two days ahead of time to reserve a place. For safety reasons, infants and children under seven years of age are not allowed. The ground within the cave is uneven and slippery. There are also low ceilings and pits (hard hats are provided). Wear sturdy shoes, warm clothing (the temperature inside the cave is around 40 degrees)—and bring a flashlight!

—AC

*The Forest Service dinghy dock—for access to the El Capitan Cave*

*Linda and Dave use the requisite hard hats, provided by the cave personnel.*

*It's a steep climb, but worth it.*

*This caver really got into the spirit!*

## El Capitan Passage (from Shakan Strait to Sea Otter Sound)

El Capitan Passage, between Kosciusko and Prince of Wales islands, extends about 18 miles from Shakan Strait to Sea Otter Sound.
Chart 17387 (inset)
West entrance (R"28" brg 000°T at 0.04 Nm):
56°09.14' N, 133°27.68' W

El Capitan Passage is the beautiful smooth-water route east of Kosciusko Island. It is well marked and gives little trouble to cruising boats that carefully monitor their progress on Chart 17387 at all stages of the tide.

Note our text outlines a north to south passage so that when you are southbound, the

*Smooth water at Entrance Cove*

*Transiting El Capitan southward; keeping all red buoys to port and all green buoys to starboard*

port-hand buoys are all red and count down from R"28" to R"2." Caution: Watch for shoals and mud flats on either side.

Small craft can find secure anchorage among a number of coves along either shore, or in the center of Dry Pass.

## Entrance Cove (El Capitan Passage)

Entrance Cove, on the south side of the passage, is just inside the entrance to El Capitan Passage and past a small islet.
Chart 17387 (inset)
Entrance: 56°09.25' N, 133°27.17' W
Anchor: 56°09.21' N, 133°27.18' W

"Entrance Cove" is what we call this small shallow cove that offers very good protection

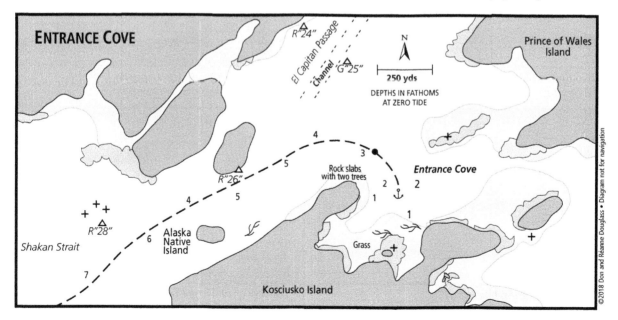

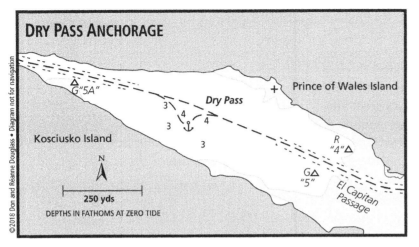

shallow throughout and offers plenty of swinging room. Alternatively, you can anchor in the larger basin, 0.3 mile west of the entrance to Dry Pass. This anchorage is the closest to the El Capitan Cave dinghy dock.

Anchor in 3 fathoms over mud with very good holding.

## Devilfish Bay (El Capitan Passage)

Devilfish Bay, on the west side of El Capitan Passage, is 3.5 miles south of Aneskett Point.
Chart 17387
Entrance: 56°05.31' N, 133°18.70' W
Anchor: 56°05.12' N, 133°22.68' W

from seas in any direction. The cove is located just east of what we call "Alaska Native Island" and south of green channel marker G"25," behind the spit.

Anchor in 1 to 2 fathoms over sand with kelp and grass with fair holding.

## Dry Pass Anchorage (El Capitan Passage)

Dry Pass Anchorage is 2.2 miles east of West Entrance.
Chart 17387 (inset)
Anchor: 56°09.63' N, 133°23.80' W

Dry Pass Anchorage is an excellent and very well-protected site in the center of El Capitan Passage, midway between the two easternmost dredged channels. (See *Coast Pilot* for dredged channel depths.) A 500-yard-long lagoon, it is

Devilfish Bay is a quiet, smooth, landlocked anchorage with shores covered with old-growth forest. The bay provides excellent protection from all sectors; when the wind is blowing from the south in El Capitan Passage, just a slight wind is felt from the west inside Devilfish Bay.

Some cruisers anchor in Devilfish Bay and then go by dinghy approximately 4.5 miles north to the USFS dock to tour El Capitan Cave. An Indian legend recounts that a giant devilfish rose out of the bay and washed away an entire village. When a group of researchers

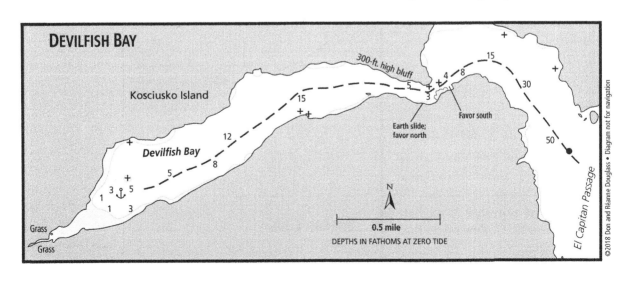

visited the bay in 1975, they were so overcome with "supernatural feelings of oppression, depression and alarm," they were convinced the area was cursed. However, we found the bay to be just the opposite—charming and lovely, with a touch of magic added when a great blue heron landed on our bow after we anchored. We spotted more leaping salmon in Devilfish Bay than we had seen anywhere else on the entire west coast. We like the bitter end of the bay, but the center has more swinging room.

Anchor in 3 fathoms at the head of the bay over mud and clam shells with very good holding.

## Sarheen Cove (El Capitan Passage)

Sarheen Cove, on the east shore of El Capitan Passage, is 3 miles southeast of Devilfish Bay.
Chart 17387
Entrance: 56°03.11' N, 133°16.14' W
Anchor: 56°03.00' N, 133°15.73' W

Sarheen Cove is a small indentation on Prince of Wales Island near the south end of El Capitan Passage. It is a good overnight anchor site, offering protection in most weather; southerlies generally blow by its entrance. By favoring the north shore on entering, you can avoid the large shoal on the south entrance point. The best protection is found close to the east shore.

Anchor in 5 fathoms over mud, rocks, shells and grass with good holding.

## Sarkar Cove (Prince of Wales Island)

Sarkar Cove, on the east side of El Capitan Passage, is 6 miles from Sea Otter Sound.
Chart 17403
Entrance: 55°57.76' N, 133°15.84' W
Anchor: 55°57.44' N, 133°15.02' W

Good protection from winds of all directions can be found in Sarkar Cove. El Capitan Lodge on the south shore provides sport fishing opportunities. Beware of float plane traffic.

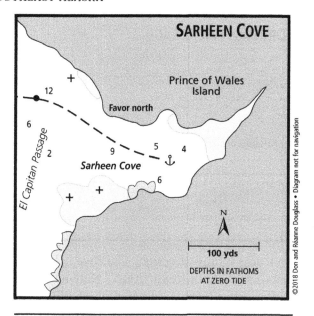

## Sarheen Cove
### From the First Mate's Diary
### Réanne Hemingway-Douglass

A Clark's nutcracker flies from treetop to treetop noisily warning the other birds of our approach. Soon a chorus of nutcrackers is clicking. Salmon cruise off the stream at the head of the cove, jumping—their silver bodies gleaming and curved—waiting, waiting for the rains to flood the creeks so they can head upstream to their natal ground.

Anchor deep in the cove in 6 fathoms over mud with good holding.

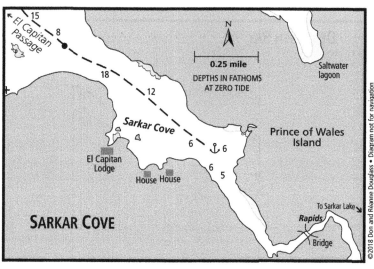

## New Tokeen (El Capitan Island)

New Tokeen is a small settlement on the west side of El Capitan Island near the south end of El Capitan Passage.

Chart 17403
Entrance: 55°56.15′ N, 133°19.79′ W

There is a mooring float for use of fishing vessels. Some supplies (fuel, water) may be available.

## Tuxekan Passage

Tuxekan Passage is on the east side of Tuxekan Island.

Charts 17403, 17404
North entrance (west of Kassan Islands): 55°55.47′ N, 133°17.64′ W
South entrance: 55°46.00′ N, 133°15.25′ W

*Kahli Cove looking south*

*Tuxekan Passage has its S entrance on the SE side of Karheen Passage, and extends N along the E side of Tuxekan Island for about 10 miles to El Capitan Passage. The shores are heavily wooded throughout its length, and are indented with numerous bights, coves, and bays that provide anchorage in any desired depth.* (CP)

## Kahli Cove (Prince of Wales Island)

Kahli Cove is 2 miles east of El Capitan Island.

Chart 17403
Entrance: 55°55.89′ N, 133°16.08′ W
Anchor: 55°55.27′ N, 133°15.63′ W

Kahli Cove is an intimate, well-protected anchorage west of Kassan Islands. Numerous islets and reefs at the south end provide total protection in a calm, quiet setting. Entry requires careful navigation and should not be attempted in poor visibility or by radar. When there is sufficient water, you can continue south through the narrow exit, but beware of the rock piles.

Anchor in 3 fathoms over a rocky bottom with poor-to-fair holding.

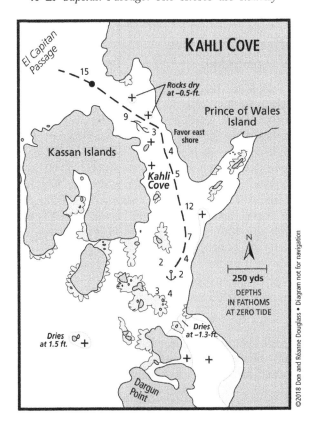

## Cyrus Cove (Orr Island)

Cyrus Cove is 5.5 miles northwest of Tuxekan Narrows and 7.5 miles east of Edna Bay.

Chart 17403
Entrance: 55°54.15′ N, 133°25.19′ W
Anchor (small vessels): 55°55.04′ N, 133°24.34′ W
Anchor (large vessels): 55°55.08′ N, 133°24.96′ W

Cyrus Cove provides welcome shelter in one

of the more remote and challenging navigation areas on the north coast of Prince of Wales Island. It is essentially landlocked, but is easy to enter in all conditions, with Owl Island providing a good lee.

When entering Cyrus Cove, favor the east shore at the narrows 0.5 miles inside the entrance to avoid a shoal that extends over half way out from the west shore.

Larger boats will find very good anchorage with adequate swinging room in the center of the cove in 8 to 12 fathoms, black mud bottom, with very good holding. Smaller vessels should curl around east into the landlocked east basin. Favor the north shore of the basin to avoid the rocks in the basin entrance on both shores, which narrow the entrance considerably. There is adequate swinging room for one or two boats, but avoid the rock pile and reef extending south near the head of the basin. The charted wharf ruins are no longer visible and you might want to avoid this spot because of possible submerged obstacles. Orr

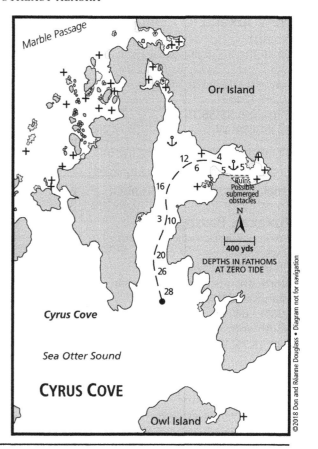

## Devilfish Bay—A Different Perspective
### Brian Pemberton, NW Explorations

What a great cruise we were having exploring the west side of Baranof Island, using *Exploring Southeast Alaska* as our only cruising guide, which had been spot-on. We had a great time at Réanne's Relief, then continued south along the coast, past Cape Ommaney, to seldom-visited Coronation Island, where we spent a wonderful couple of days.

On leaving Windy Bay we crossed Sumner Strait and set our course for Devilfish Bay in El Capitan Passage. I had chosen the site for the evening because the Douglass book reported it to be a good anchorage, and I was also intrigued by the interesting detail in their book about the superstitions natives held about Devilfish Bay.

After all seven of our boats were at anchor, we had a reception on our boat. By 1730, the wind was blowing consistently over 35 knots and gusting upward, so we started ferrying people back to their boats. Fortunately, we had our Grady White 22-foot boat with us, so despite the 2-3-foot seas, a lot of foam and wind, we delivered everyone safely to their boats.

Some of the boats that were rafted together started to drag after the winds reached a steady 50 knots. At that point, they split up and each set their anchor. Since we had a 46-foot Grand Banks rafted alongside our 49 footer, I decided now would be a good time to let out all the 500 feet of chain I'd been carrying all summer in my chain locker. So, with 10X scope, 500 feet of 3/8-foot chain, a 60-lb CQR, and an anchor bridal, we rode out the 55+ knots gale. Strangely, 100 yards north on the other side of the bay, there was virtually no wind at all.

When we raised our anchor the next morning, it took us over an hour to wash all the mud off the chain. We understood why we did not drag a bit—we had a great set!

So the lessons learned: 1) A lot of chain and scope is good! 2) Maybe the native folklore about mysteries we don't understand has merit. I know for sure that I will always use 10X scope in Devilfish Bay!

Island is fairly low so you might experience some wind but no significant williwaws.

Anchor (inner basin) in 5 fathoms over a mud and shell bottom with very good holding.

## Tuxekan Narrows
Tuxekan Narrows lies between Tuxekan and Prince of Wales islands.
Chart 17403
North entrance (Village Rock "VR" brg 074°T at 0.28 Nm): 55°53.28' N, 133°15.79' W
South entrance: 55°51.73' N, 133°13.07' W

The safest route through Tuxekan Narrows passes south and west of Village Rock at the north entrance to the narrows. The currents are weak—less than one knot—with flooding to the north and ebbing to the south.

## Nichin Cove (Tuxekan Island)
Nichin Cove is just south of Tuxekan Narrows.
Chart 17403
Entrance: 55°51.18' N, 133°13.42' W
Anchor: 55°50.94' N, 133°13.69' W

Nichin Cove provides convenient shelter from southerly winds. North of this point, the effect of southerlies is nil because of the many islands. In previous years Nichin Cove has been occupied by a large logging operation. Excellent temporary shelter from chop can be found deep in the cove just off the small float where swinging room is limited. Avoid the commercial operations and the large steel buoys marking the booming operation on the northwest side of the cove.

Anchor in 4 fathoms over sticky mud with very good holding.

## Yahku Cove (Tuxekan Island)
Yahku Cove is on the west side of Tuxekan Passage.
Chart 17403
Entrance: 55°47.55' N, 133°14.49' W
Anchor: 55°47.86' N, 133°14.52' W

*Baidarka's* first mate called tiny Yahku Cove "a Douglass find!" The rocky reef off the eastern entrance point acts effectively as a breakwa-

ter, and the moderate southerly chop from Tuxekan Passage does not enter the cove. If a strong southerly storm is expected, consider

*Heron fishing in the eel grass*

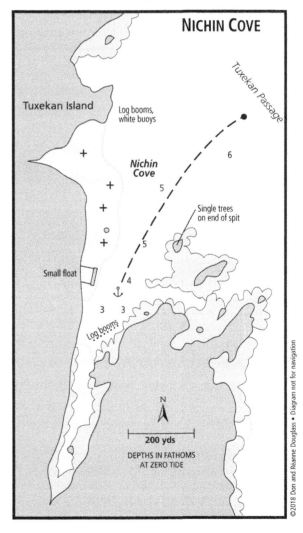

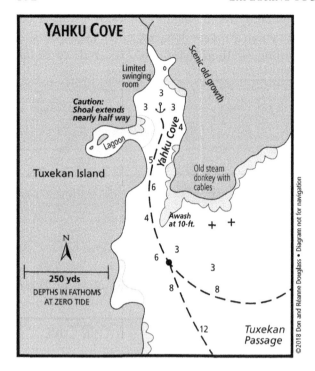

Winter Harbor or Kaguk Cove.

Almost landlocked, Yahku is surrounded by old-growth, mixed forest of spruce, cedar, hemlock and alder. Anchor just beyond the opening to the lagoon; swinging room is limited.

Anchor in 3 fathoms over sticky brown mud and clam shells with excellent holding.

## Davidson Inlet
Davidson Inlet is between Heceta and Kosciusko islands.
Chart 17403
Entrance (Surf Point Light brg 098°T at 1.10 Nm): 55°50.24' N, 133°39.87' W

## Holbrook Arm (Kosciusko Island)
Holbrook Arm is at the north end of Davidson Inlet.
Chart 17403
Entrance: 56°00.29' N, 133°29.51' W

Once the home of the village of Holbrook (abandoned), Holbrook Arm offers anchorage in moderate depths but it is open to the south.

## Tokeen Cove (Tokeen Bay)
Tokeen Cove is on the northwest end of Marble Island.
Chart 17403
Entrance: 55°59.76' N, 133°28.76' W
Anchor: 55°59.47' N, 133°28.33' W

Refer to *Coast Pilot*. Anchor in about 6 fathoms over a soft bottom with good holding.

## Sea Otter Sound
Sea Otter Sound extends west of Tuxekan Island and Karheen Passage to Davidson Inlet.
Chart 17403
Position (Gas Rock brg 247°T at 1.1 Nm): 55°51.17' N, 133°32.15' W

Sea Otter Sound is comparable to an inland sea, surrounded by an intricate group of islands, rocks and reefs. While secure anchor sites are somewhat scarce, the region is interesting to explore.

## Port Alice (Heceta Island)
Port Alice is on the south side of Davidson Inlet.
Chart 17403
Entrance: 55°49.97' N, 133°36.76' W
Anchor: 55°47.98' N, 133°35.73' W

Well-sheltered anchorage can be found at the head of the bay near the old log booms.

Anchor in 9 fathoms over mud and clam shells with good holding.

*A passenger on the anchor chain*

## Karheen Passage (Tuxekan Island)

Karheen Passage, on the southwest side of Tuxekan Island, extends from Tonowek Narrows to Sea Otter Sound.

Chart 17403
Northwest entrance: 55°50.35' N, 133°22.29' W
Southeast entrance (Kauda Point brg 012°T at 0.4 Nm): 55°46.03' N, 133°15.78' W

> *The SE part of the passage is characterized by islets, ledges, and generally broken ground, surrounded by comparatively deep water. . . . The channel is marked by a daybeacon, buoys, and an unlighted range as far as Karheen Cove and is used by vessels with a draft of about 17 feet.* (CP)

## Winter Harbor (Prince of Wales Island)

Winter Harbor is 1.5 miles from Yahku Cove on the east shore of Tuxekan Passage.

Chart 17403 & 17404
Entrance: 55°46.44' N, 133°14.08' W
Anchor: 55°46.22' N, 133°13.83' W

Winter Harbor provides very good shelter in strong southerlies. As in Nichin Cove, there has been an active logging operation in Winter Harbor. Temporary anchorage can be found nearby, but avoid the commercial operations at the head of the harbor. Larger cruising boats may find better southerly shelter in Kaguk Cove, 3 miles to the south.

Anchor in 3 fathoms over soft mud with shells; holding is good with a well-set anchor.

## Kaguk Cove (Prince of Wales Island)

Kaguk Cove, at the south end of Tuxekan Passage, is 2 miles southwest of Kauda Point.

Chart 17404
Entrance: 55°44.89' N, 133°16.96' W
Anchor: 55°44.35' N, 133°17.63' W

Kaguk Cove offers excellent shelter for all sizes of cruising boats.

Anchor in 5 fathoms over mud with good holding.

## Indian Garden Bay (Heceta Island)

Indian Garden Bay is at the north end of Tonowek Narrows.

Chart 17404
Entrance: 55°46.13' N, 133°19.79' W

Indian Garden Bay looks interesting and may provide good shelter. However, the cove is not well charted and it appears to have a rocky, irregular bottom.

## Tonowek Narrows

Tonowek Narrows, between Prince of Wales and Heceta islands, joins Tonowek Bay and Karheen Passage.

Chart 17404
North entrance (Green buoy "5" brg 300°T at 0.1 Nm): 55°47.11' N, 133°17.22' W
Southwest entrance: 55°45.22' N, 133°20.80' W

We have found that the flood current at Tonowek Narrows runs a snappy 4 to 6 knots. We've heard reports that the weathered totem pole at the southern tip of the island on the west side of the narrows is no longer visible. Avoid Point Swift Rock that dries at about 5 feet by following the marked channel immediately north.

The channel where Karheen Passage and Tuxekan Passage meet Tonowek Narrows is a rock pile. Substantial current and kelp patches require alert navigation. The flood flows north and the ebb flows south.

## Nossuk Anchorage (Prince of Wales Island)

Nossuk Anchorage, in the north part of Nossuk Bay, is 0.7 mile south of Tonowek Narrows.
Chart 17404
Entrance: 55°44.60' N, 133°21.04' W

*Nossuk Anchorage ... affords excellent anchorage in 10 fathoms, soft bottom. The N entrance is narrow; the chart shows the least depths. (CP)*

Nossuk Anchorage provides good shelter from chop, but contrary to *Coast Pilot*, we found that it has very irregular soundings, indicating a sharp rocky bottom. We would not risk fouling an anchor here and don't recommend it. If someone has located the soft bottom, we would like to know where it is! (We anchored in Nossuk Bay, instead.)

## Nossuk Bay (Prince of Wales Island)

Nossuk Bay, in the northeast part of Tonowek Bay, is 1.5 miles south of Tonowek Narrows.
Chart 17404
Entrance: 55°44.35' N, 133°22.02' W

Nossuk Bay has lots of shallow anchorages with ample swinging room, but watch for isolated rocks.

## No Name Cove (Nossuk Bay)

No Name Cove is the first cove on the southwest shore as you enter the bay.
Chart 17404
Entrance: 55°43.82' N, 133°22.01' W
Anchor: 55°43.68' N, 133°22.32' W

No Name Cove provides good anchorage in most weather.

Anchor in 6 fathoms over sand and gravel with fair holding.

## Harmony Islands Passage (Harmony Islands)

Harmony Islands Passage is the channel east of the Harmony Islands and east of the islands to the south, off the entrance to Salt Lake Bay.
Chart 17404
North entrance: 55°43.45' N, 133°23.77' W
South entrance (Blanquizal Island brg 125°T at 0.25 Nm): 55°37.16' N, 133°24.64' W

*Harmony Islands are a group of high, wooded islands. There are channels between the islands of this group, but they are made difficult by numerous dangers. Rocks that cover are off the S and W points of the group.*

*[Harmony Islands Passage] ... is used extensively by small craft plying between San Christoval Channel and Tonowek Narrows. The midchannel is safe and partially protected. (CP)*

"Harmony Islands Passage" is our name for the excellent smooth-water route described in *Coast Pilot*. To follow the passage, continue due south almost to the peninsula before turning west to Culebra Islands; the shoal south of the smallest Harmony Islands is larger than the area shown on the chart. The sheltered route continues inside St. Philip Island, but it is encumbered with mid-channel rocks near its south end and requires careful navigation.

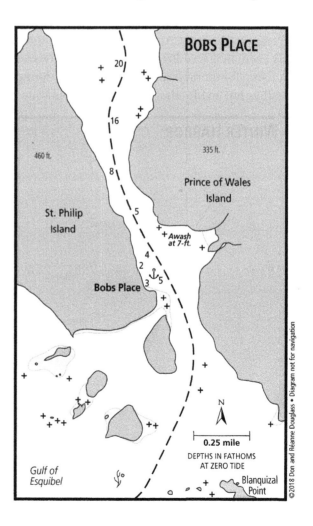

## Bobs Place (St. Philip Island)
Bobs Place is on the southeast corner of St. Philip Island.
Chart 17404
Anchor: 55°38.30' N, 133°24.36' W

Cruising boats can find additional shelter from southerly and westerly winds by passing inside St. Philip Island. Picturesque Bobs Place affords shelter, from all but a hard north or south blow, tucked behind the little hook on St. Philip Island, off the gravel and shell beach. There are some newspaper kelp patches here, so check your anchor set. On our last visit, we were unable to get our anchor to set, so we ventured on.

Anchor in 2 to 3 fathoms over soft sand with shell, kelp and grass; fair holding if you can get a set.

## Bocas de Finas
Bocas de Finas, the passage between the southwest coast of Heceta Island and the northeasternmost islands of the Maurelle group, leads from the junction of the Gulf of Esquibel with Tonowek Bay to Iphigenia Bay and the Pacific Ocean.
Chart 17404
Northwest entrance (Cape Lynch Light brg 058°T at 0.5 Nm): 55°46.59' N, 133°42.90' W
Southeast entrance (Desconocida Reef Light brg 025°T at 0.6 Nm): 55°40.77' N, 133°31.94' W

*Entering Launch Passage, Maurelle Islands*

## Maurelle Islands
The Maurelle Islands lie on the northwest side of the Gulf of Esquibel.
Chart 17404

The Maurelle Islands are a designated Wilderness. Within these islands, during stable weather, you can find surprisingly smooth waters and many small anchor sites. It is a perfect place to explore by kayak and dinghy. Our favorite anchor site in the region is Nagasay Cove on the north side of Esquibel Island.

---

## Learning to Carve
### Barb Davis—S/V *Antares*

With our last load of laundry in the dryer in Craig, Bill and I ventured across the street where we had seen a lean-to with a couple of people inside. As we neared, we noticed Alaska native people carving a totem pole. We hesitated a bit, not wanting to bother them, when the young women saw us and invited us to come in and take a look at their work. The pole, being carved from a 300-year-old cedar, was about 30 feet long and 36 inches in diameter and would be dedicated to the elders of Hydaburg.

Stan Marsden, a well-known carver, had been working on the pole for close to a year, and the raising was less than two weeks away. He had recruited his daughter and some friends to help, but they still had quite a bit of work left to do.

After spending some time talking with them, Stan asked us if we would like to help. He gave us the handmade tools and a quick lesson and away we went! I carved out the teeth of a raven while Bill planed the dorsal fin of a killer whale.

As we worked, Stan told us about another pole they had raised the previous year in Craig. It was in memory of his son who had died of a drug overdose. The entire town was involved in the carving and, on the day of the raising, 100 people helped carry it down the street to the park where it was to be raised. A three-day celebration was held, and everyone was invited. Stan explained that bringing everyone together for this event helped mend long-standing ill feelings.

As we were leaving, Stan invited us to attend the raising of the pole. We felt honored to be asked. Later when we walked down the street to view the other pole, it was the first time we understood the meaning behind the totem. It was a touching experience, and undoubtedly the most beautiful totem we had ever seen.

## Anguilla Bay (Anguilla Island)
Anguilla Bay is on the south side of Bocas de Finas.
Chart 17404
West entrance: 55°39.51' N, 133°36.38' W

Anguilla Bay is largely a rock pile, but we like the shelter and isolation found in Nagasay Cove. Use caution when plying the channels.

## Launch Passage
Launch Passage lies between Anguilla and Esquibel islands.
Chart 17404
East entrance: 55°39.05' N, 133°32.81' W

Narrow Launch Passage has some current and lots of kelp. Favor the south shore and use caution. If exiting Launch Passage by Anguilla Bay, avoid two dangerous rocks off the south tip of Anguilla Island that bare on a 2-foot tide.

## Nagasay Cove (Esquibel Island)
Nagasay Cove is on the north side of Esquibel Island.
Chart 17404
Anchor: 55°38.66' N, 133°33.93' W

Nagasay Cove, one of our favorites in this area, offers very good shelter in intimate, landlocked surroundings. Beware of the two large submerged rocks on the northeast side of the anchorage.

Anchor in 3 fathoms over sand and mud with good holding.

## San Lorenzo Islands, Hole in the Wall
San Lorenzo Islands, at the northeast end of Arriaga Passage, lie between Noyes Island and the Maurelle Islands.
Chart 17404
North entrance (Hole in the Wall): 55°36.24' N, 133°37.24' W
South entrance (Hole in the Wall): 55°35.25' N, 133°36.77' W

> *San Lorenzo Islands ... consists* [sic] *of two timbered islands separated by a narrow channel. This channel is locally known as Hole in the Wall.*
>
> *A submerged rock, which covers 4 feet, is about 150 feet off the W shore, opposite the vertical bluff. A depth of 3 fathoms can be carried past the rock on its NE side.* (CP)

Here is another Hole in the Wall experience for cruisers. Favor the east shore.

## Gulf of Esquibel
The Gulf of Esquibel is 8 miles long from Tonowek Bay to Noyes Island and 6 miles wide from the Maurelle Islands to San Fernando Island.
Chart 17404
Position: 55°35.00' N, 133°30.01' W

The gulf—a large bay sheltered by many islands from the Gulf of Alaska—can get brisk from westerly winds and chop. Garcia Cove on San Fernando Island is well protected.

## Steamboat Bay (Noyes Island)
Steamboat Bay is 3 miles east of Cape Ulitka Light.
Chart 17404
Entrance: 55°33.21' N, 133°38.16' W
Anchor: 55°32.00' N, 133°38.10' W

Fishing lodges occupy the shore of the bay. The wharf is private.

Anchor in about 12 fathoms over sand and gravel with fair holding.

## San Christoval Channel
San Christoval Channel, between Prince of Wales Island and San Fernando Island, connects San Alberto Bay to the Gulf of Esquibel.
Charts 17405, 17404
West entrance: 55°35.74' N, 133°23.49' W
Entrance (Larzatita Island brg 047°T at 0.2 Nm): 55°34.61' N, 133°20.31' W
Southeast entrance (San Christoval Rock buoy R"8" brg 300°T at 0.14 Nm): 55°33.61' N, 133°17.71' W

In transiting San Christoval Channel, we prefer to use the route along the south side of Larzatita Island, which is marked by mid-channel buoy "SC" and the range marks on Hermanos Islands. Cruising boats should experience few problems. We have found 3 knots of current, but we don't know where the upper limit lies. If you have a low-powered boat, wait for appropriate current.

## San Alberto Bay
San Alberto Bay is east of San Fernando Island.
Chart 17405
Position: 55°30.00' N, 133°15.01' W

A marked channel in the southeast part of San Alberto Bay leads to Klawock Inlet and village.

## Shinaku Inlet (Prince of Wales Island)
Shinaku Inlet, at the north end of San Alberto Bay, connects with Big Salt Lake and Klawock Inlet.
Chart 17405
West entrance: 55°34.25' N, 133°12.03' W
South entrance: 55°32.70' N, 133°10.51' W

## Klawock Inlet (Prince of Wales Island)
Klawock Inlet has the city of Craig at its south entrance and Big Salt Lake at its north end.
Chart 17405
West entrance (buoy G"1" brg 075°T at 0.12 Nm): 55°30.52' N, 133°11.42' W
South entrance (Craig Harbor, buoy G"3" brg 326°T at 0.1 Nm): 55°28.34' N, 133°09.52' W

## Klawock Harbor (Prince of Wales Island)
Klawock Harbor is 5 miles north of Craig.
Chart 17405
Entrance: 55°33.51' N, 133°06.50' W
Public floats: 55°33.26' N, 133°06.14' W

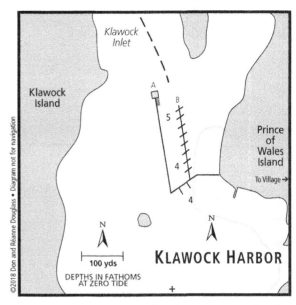

Klawock village—the site of Southeast's first cannery, established in 1878—has a small park with a remarkable collection of totems. If you do nothing else here, you should take a walk uphill from the harbor to visit the park. The totems, brought from abandoned communities on Prince of Wales Island, are beautiful examples of Northwest art. Some of them are quite unusual.

Klawock Harbor has two public floats with electricity. Fuel and water can be obtained at the cannery. Supplies are available at the village store (no alcohol). A paved road connects Klawock to Craig.

## Craig (Prince of Wales Island)
Craig is 55 miles southeast of Point Baker and 61 miles northwest of Cape Chacon. (Shelter Cove, known locally as South Cove, is on the southeast side of Craig Island.)
Chart 17405 (inset)
Position: (City float): 55°28.69' N, 133°09.10' W
Entrance (North Cove): 55°28.90' N, 133°08.64' W
Entrance (South Cove): 55°28.42' N, 133°08.70' W
Floats (North Cove): 55°28.71' N, 133°08.64' W
Floats (South Cove): 55°28.50' N, 133°08.59' W

Craig is the largest town on Prince of Wales Island and the major supply center for the southern end of the island. It is 31 miles by paved road from the ferry terminal at Hollis. The city has expanded its harbor facilities in recent years and welcomes visiting pleasure craft to its more than 220 slips. The Harbormaster office has showers. An additional harbor expansion was in the planning stages in 2018. There are two public marinas—South Cove Harbor and North Cove Harbor—both with power and water. The City Float at the west end of town has room for just 12 boats; it is quite crowded in fishing season and has no water. The town has full services: a marine supply store, several good cafes, and a bank (just above the City Float). Thompson House Market (a good mile from the City Float, or ¼ mile from South and North Cove Harbors) has kitchen supplies,

*Public floats at Klawock*

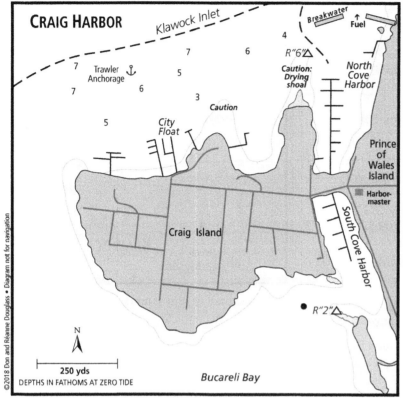

in addition to a nice selection of groceries. With advance notice they will deliver you and your purchases to the harbor. The post office and public telephones are next door to the market, as is the liquor store. You can find good anchorage anywhere in the bay north of Craig Island. *Note:* Most stores close on Sunday; Thompson's and the liquor store are exceptions.

Transients are usually assigned to the north end of North Cove Harbor. The fuel dock is located outside the North Cove Harbor area, beyond the breakwater to the north. There is a large, drying shoal east and south of R"6." Avoid this hazard by staying close to the docks. Enter the harbor slowly due to limited vision and turning room. This is a tricky spot, so stay alert. The harbormaster monitors Ch 16 (tel.: 907.826.3404; Website: www.craigak.com).

**Port Bagial** (Prince of Wales Island)
Port Bagial lies on the east side of Cape Suspiro.
Chart 17405
Entrance: 55°27.59' N, 133°08.01' W

Port Bagial is open to southerly weather.

---

## Dolphin Courage
### Don Douglass

A pod of dolphins swim in *Baidarka*'s bow wake, cheered on by our boisterous encouragement. One brave soul can't help but hover on either side of our stem, as if testing his nerve. He slows ever so slightly, until he makes gentle contact with our keel. Then, proving his superior control in touching a 50,000-pound bouncing trawler, he speeds off, perpendicular, performing a precision ritual few other dolphins have the courage to try.

*A carver's unique vision.*

## Port St. Nicholas (Prince of Wales Island)
Port St. Nicholas is 3 miles southeast of Craig.
Chart 17405
Entrance: 55°25.45' N, 133°06.04' W
Anchor: 55°27.13' N, 133°00.66' W

Port St. Nicholas is reported to provide anchorage near the head of the bay.

Anchor in about 8 fathoms over a soft bottom.

## Trocadero Bay (Big Harbor) (Prince of Wales Island)
Trocadero Bay is 5 miles southeast of Craig.
Chart 17405
Southwest entrance (mid-channel between Point Iphigenia and Madre de Dios Island): 55°23.10' N, 133°08.98' W
Northwest entrance (Culebrina Island brg 017°T at 0.45 Nm): 55°24.26' N, 133°04.93' W

*The totem park at Klawock includes this interesting combination.*

The entrance to Trocadero Bay is a cable area, but good anchorage may be found along the south shore, 0.9 and 1.8 miles from the head of the bay.

# Craig
### Michael Kampnich—Former Craig Harbormaster

Are you considering a trip to Southeast Alaska by boat? Maybe you're interested in getting a bit off the beaten track and away from the cruise ships? Then you may want to take a look at Craig and the west coast of Prince of Wales Island.

Craig, a community of 1,200 people, is the largest community on Prince of Wales Island. It is home-port and service center to the recreational and local commercial fishing fleet. Craig and the west coast area of POW Island also have much to offer anyone visiting the area, whether by boat or vehicle.

The west coast of Prince of Wales is a boating visitor's paradise. With hundreds of smaller islands scattered along the western shore, opportunities for cruising and exploring the many bays and passages are almost unlimited. Marine wildlife is abundant and viewing opportunities abound.

If you want to tie up and take a break, Craig has three harbors with over 200 slips that can be hot berthed along with designated transient moorage available and all the services expected. Vessels up to 150 feet can be accommodated with advance notice. On the floats you'll find a friendly, accommodating harbor staff. All basic accommodations are available at the harbors. The Craig Harbor Department is staffed seven days a week, year round, and monitors VHF 16 for all harbormaster calls. Shore side services include a laundromat, marine hardware stores, outboard and marine repair facilities, grocery stores, a post office, a library with Internet service for the public, a medical clinic, a dental office, two banks and an ATM, clothing stores, sport fish processing facilities and many other stores and shops that are all located within a 10-minute walk of the harbors.

There are also a number of smaller communities on the island that offer an opportunity to sample some of the different life styles of the island. Klawock, Hydaburg, Thorne Bay, Coffman Cove and Whale Pass are all accessible by road. Vehicle rentals are available in Craig. The native communities of Klawock (the Tlingit tribe) and Hydaburg and Kasaan (the Haida tribes) each have totem parks for interested visitors. Of two new totems carved by local resident, Stan Marsden, one was raised in the Hydaburg totem park. The other, the Healing Heart Totem Pole (the tallest in southeast Alaska), was raised here in Craig. Over the past 15 years a significant number of caves have been discovered in the northwestern area of the island. The Forest Service has daily tours during the summer of one of the most accessible caves, El Capitan. Craig has a number of 4th of July festivities, as do many of the communities on the island.

So stop in and see us. We'll meet you on the floats, catch a line and give you a hand tying up. If you'd like more information give us a call at 907.826.3404 or send us an email at: craighm@aptalaska.net. You can also learn more about Craig at www.craigak.com.

We have not made the portage to Kasaan Bay (Chapter 3), which follows a 5-mile-long canyon between two 2,000-foot peaks, and have no knowledge of its difficulty.

## Port Caldera (Prince of Wales Island)
Port Caldera is 6 miles south of Craig.
Chart 17405
Entrance: 55°22.86' N, 133°10.06' W
Anchor: 55°21.86' N, 133°09.68' W

Port Caldera is steep-to and useful only in strong southerlies or as a temporary anchorage for one or two small craft.

Anchor in about 10 fathoms over an unknown bottom.

## Cape Bartolome Light (Baker Island)
Cape Bartolome Light is 14 miles southwest of Port Estrella.
Chart 17406
Position (light brg 000°T at 1.0 Nm):
55°12.84' N, 133°36.92' W

## Port San Antonio (Baker Island)
Port San Antonio is about 2.0 miles north of Fortaleza Bay.
Chart 17406
Entrance (Point San Roque brg 043°T at 0.5 Nm): 55°19.72' N, 133°33.31' W
Entrance (north arm): 55°21.41' N, 133°35.48' W
Entrance (south arm): 55°21.06' N, 133°35.93' W
Anchor (north arm): 55°22.06' N, 133°35.32' W
Anchor (south arm): 55°20.14' N, 133°36.88' W

Port San Antonio has two arms, both surrounded by 2,000-foot peaks, which provide the best shelter on Baker Island for small craft. Williwaws may be present when gales blow

*The breakwater at the north end of North Cove Harbor is a barge, actively used for storage of fishing gear.*

*Craig has a very active fishing fleet.*

outside, but little chop or fetch enters the port. Avoid the dangerous mid-channel rock at the entrance that bares on a 1-foot tide. The north arm has a good, shallow bottom, but the south arm may be better in southeast winds.

*Sitting up high on land, this is a fitting landmark for Craig's North Harbor.*

*Shall we turn to port, where it's clear? Or starboard into the fog?*

[Port Dolores] *has generally broken bottom with a rocky reef, about 400 yards in extent, in its center about 0.4 mile inside the entrance. Its use is recommended only for small craft, and they can find anchorage in about 11 fathoms 0.4 mile from the head. The anchorage is exposed to W winds.* (CP)

Be forewarned: Dolores means "pains" or "sorrows" in Spanish.

Anchor (north arm) in 5 fathoms over mud with fair-to-good holding.

Anchor (south arm) in 10 fathoms over mud with good holding.

### Port Santa Cruz (Suemez Island)
Port Santa Cruz is 4.5 miles north of Cape Felix.
Chart 17406
Entrance (Labandera Rock brg 180°T at 0.25 Nm): 55°17.18' N, 133°27.54' W
Entrance (Indiada Cove): 55°16.51' N, 133°27.21' W
Anchor (Agueda Cove): 55°16.35' N, 133°25.98' W
Anchor (head of cove): 55°17.10' N, 133°24.65' W

Small craft can find protection from southeast winds in Agueda Cove or in the head of the cove. Indiada Cove appears to be full of kelp.

Anchor (Agueda Cove) in 6 to 10 fathoms over mud.

Anchor (head of cove) in 15 fathoms over mud.

### Port Dolores (Suemez Island)
Port Dolores is 4 miles northwest of Port Santa Cruz.
Chart 17406
Entrance: 55°20.21' N, 133°24.97' W
Anchor: 55°19.61' N, 133°23.47' W

Anchor 0.4 mile southeast of mid-bay islet in 10 fathoms over mud, sand, gravel with kelp; fair holding if you set your anchor well.

### Port Asumcion (Baker Island)
Port Asumcion is about 2.5 miles northeast of Port San Antonio.
Chart 17406
Entrance: 55°21.64' N, 133°30.13' W
Anchor: 55°22.32' N, 133°33.05' W

Port Asumcion offers good protection in all weather and is easy to enter. The bay is deep, however.

Anchor in 10 fathoms over sand with fair holding.

### Port Mayoral (Baker Island)
Port Mayoral lies between Baker Island and San Ignace Island.
Chart 17406
Entrance (south): 55°23.00' N, 133°27.13' W

Please note: Port Mayoral, Port Real Marina and Portillo Channel all lie in a wild, west-coast environment between Baker and San Fernando islands. This is an island area of many reefs, rocks and kelp beds. While it may offer excellent exploration and fishing, we can add nothing to Chart 17406.

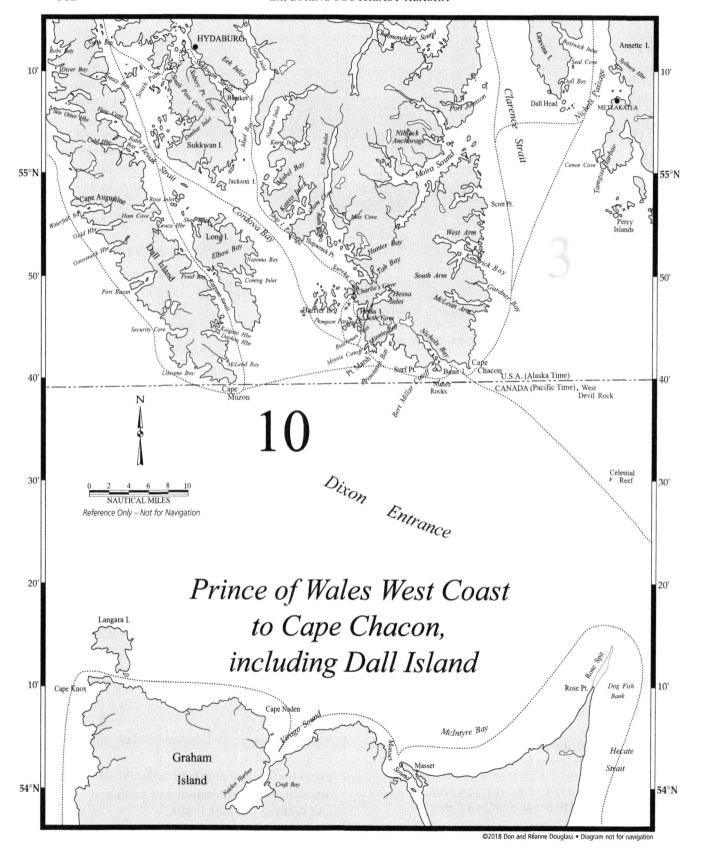

# 10

# PRINCE OF WALES ISLAND WEST COAST TO CAPE CHACON, INCLUDING DALL ISLAND

## INTRODUCTION

The southwestern tip of Prince of Wales Island, Dall Island, and Long Island, are remote places seldom visited by either pleasure craft or small fishing boats. This is a region you can explore to your heart's content and feel as if you are the first visitor since the early sailing ships encountered the Haida 200 years ago. However, in many cases, either there are no large-scale charts or the charts are inadequate or inaccurate. You must be skeptical and alert when entering these waters.

*A perfect picture of tranquility*

The route south of Craig, following the Prince of Wales shore, is a smooth-water route all the way to Point Marsh at the southwest tip of the island, with many islands that afford comfortable and quiet anchor sites for cruising boats. Hydaburg, with its magnificent totems and lovely setting, is a delightful place to visit. South of Hydaburg, you are on your own and should be as self-sufficient as possible. As you round Point Marsh, the open seas of Dixon Entrance predominate. The VHF radio weather repeater at Craig means that you are not completely isolated from outside contact.

South of Kassa Point, you enter the South Prince of Wales Wilderness—a region of islands and inlets preserved in their wild state that extends nearly all the way to Bert Millar Cutoff. These waters include Hunter Bay, Hessa Inlet and Little Brownson Bay, and it is difficult to imagine a more complex and isolated region to explore.

South of Tlevak Strait, the east shore of Dall Island and Kaigani Strait offer exciting waters all the way to Cape Muzon. This raw, undeveloped coastline is worth exploring; however, you need to watch for chart inaccuracies. The west coast of Dall Island is exposed to the full fury of the Gulf of Alaska when the winds blow, but in fair summer weather you can find a number of beautiful and sheltered inlets to explore.

So, in the spirit of expeditionary cruising, we offer what information we have found on this delightful area of the southwest corner of Southeast Alaska. We hope that visitors to this coast will help us add to the storehouse of knowledge for future boaters who seek the same beauty, solitude—and navigational guidance!

## WEST COAST PRINCE OF WALES TO CAPE CHACON

### Ulloa Channel

Ulloa Channel, 10 miles south of Craig, extends 9 miles from Bucareli Bay to Tlevak Narrows.

Chart 17407
North entrance (buoy R"2" bearing 072°T at 0.5 Nm): 55°21.28' N, 133°18.57' W
Southeast entrance (buoy R"4" bearing 000°T at 0.13 Nm): 55°15.90' N, 133°08.18' W

*The flood current in the channel sets SE, and the ebb NW. . . .*

*Anchorage in 10 to 15 fathoms, soft bottom, near Tlevak Narrows, can be had in Ulloa Channel, at the entrance to a small passage that is on the NW side of the largest island N of Ulloa Island, between it and the main shore of Prince of Wales Island.* (CP)

Ulloa Channel is the smooth-water route connecting Klawock and the Craig area to the cruising grounds of Hydaburg, Tlevak Strait, and Cordova Bay to the south.

### Port Refugio (Suemez Island)

Port Refugio, on the west side of Ulloa Channel, is opposite Waterfall.
Chart 17407
Entrance: 55°18.01' N, 133°17.90' W
Anchor: 55°16.91' N, 133°19.77' W

Excellent shelter from all weather can be found behind the island at the head of the bay. Large fish-buying vessels use the bay during the season, and floating logging communities sometimes moor here to harvest timber on Suemez Island.

We have found this a good place to watch black bear combing the tidal flats along the stream at the head of the bay.

Anchor in 5 fathoms over mud and gravel with fair-to-good holding.

### Waterfall (Prince of Wales Island)

Waterfall is 11.5 miles south of Craig.
Chart 17407
Entrance: 55°18.26' N, 133°14.86' W

Waterfall is a busy resort that is not set up to accommodate cruising boats. Some supplies may be available.

### Tlevak Narrows (The Skookum Chuck)

Tlevak Narrows, The Skookum Chuck, is 13 miles south of Craig and joins Ulloa Channel and Tlevak Strait.

# CHAPTER 10 — PRINCE OF WALES ISLAND WEST COAST TO CAPE CHACON, INCLUDING DALL ISLAND 385

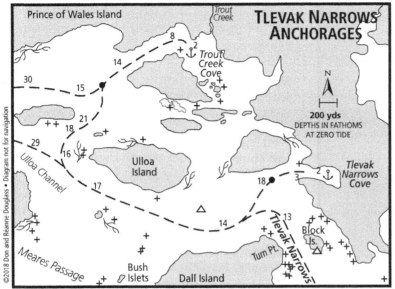

Chart 17407
Entrance (Trout Creek Cove): 55°16.78' N, 133°09.33' W
Anchor (Trout Creek Cove): 55°16.95' N, 133°08.37' W
Entrance (Tlevak Narrows Cove): 55°16.20' N, 133°07.38' W
Anchor (Tlevak Narrows Cove): 55°16.22' N, 133°06.82' W

Tlevak Narrows anchorages are well-sheltered coves out of the current of the narrows. Both coves are quiet with good trout fishing in the creek on the north shore.

Anchor (Trout Creek Cove) in 1½ fathoms over sand and mud with very good holding.

Anchor (Tlevak Narrows Cove) in 3 fathoms over sand with good holding.

Chart 17407
North entrance (Dall Island): 55°16.02' N, 133°07.59' W
South entrance (Lively Island Light bearing 000°T at 0.6 Nm): 55°13.11' N, 133°05.11' W

Tlevak Narrows runs at well over 5 knots at spring tides, with significant rips; flood currents flow east (see photo).

## Tlevak Narrows Anchorages
(Prince of Wales Island)
Tlevak Narrows Anchorages are 1 mile north of the north entrance of Tlevak Narrows.

## Soda Bay (Prince of Wales Island)
Soda Bay is 2 miles east of Tlevak Narrows.
Chart 17407
Entrance: 55°14.55' N, 133°02.73' W
Anchor (inner basin): 55°16.59' N, 132°55.75' W

Soda Bay, a large bay tucked in behind Shelikof Island, is out of both the current and chop. The half-mile-long inner basin is particularly safe and sheltered and has a large flat, shallow and sandy bottom. The basin has a complex entrance with about 5 fathoms carried through the narrow fairway channel. Two mini-coves are also west of the basin on the south shore. Caution: Avoid isolated rocks throughout the bay and survey the anchor site to verify that you have adequate swinging room.

Anchor in 3 fathoms over sand and mud and some gravel with fair holding.

*The* Coast Pilot *notes that this buoy (R"4") in Tlevak Narrows tows under during large tides.*

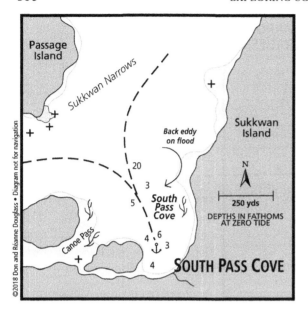

## North Pass
North Pass is 4 miles west of Hydaburg.
Chart 17407
Southwest entrance (Goat Island): 55°12.35' N, 132°56.74' W
East entrance (Goat Island): 55°13.70' N, 132°52.49' W

North Pass is an intricate waterway connecting North Tlevak Strait to Natzuhini Bay and Hydaburg. South Pass has fewer hazards and is the recommended route to Hydaburg.

## Natzuhini Bay (Prince of Wales Island)
Natzuhini Bay is 3 miles north of Hydaburg.
Chart 17407
Position: 55°15.42' N, 132°50.88' W

Natzuhini Bay is a large, landlocked rock pile best explored by kayak or dinghy.

## Goat Mouth Inlet (Goat Island)
Goat Mouth Inlet is north of the west entrance to South Pass.
Chart 17407
Entrance: 55°10.11' N, 132°54.23' W
Anchor: 55°11.43' N, 132°53.90' W

Goat Mouth Inlet appears to offer reasonable shelter at its head in fair weather but is partially exposed to southerly weather.

Anchor (deep in the inlet) in 8 to 10 fathoms over a mud bottom.

## South Pass
South Pass extends 3.5 miles northeast from Tlevak Strait to Sukkwan Narrows.
Chart 17407
West entrance: 55°10.07' N, 132°53.84' W
East entrance (at Sukkwan Narrows): 55°12.22' N, 132°50.20' W

South Pass is the standard route to and from Hydaburg. Many small anchor sites can be found on the east side of Goat Island. Caution: As you transit this rocky, narrow passage, be extremely vigilant. Keep buoys R"2" and R"4" to starboard as you make a northbound passage through South Pass to Hydaburg.

## South Pass Cove (Sukkwan Island)
South Pass Cove is 1 mile east of the west entrance to South Pass.
Chart 17407
Anchor: 55°10.00' N, 132°52.27' W

South Pass Cove offers good shelter, as shown in the diagram. Tucked in near the south shore, you avoid the back eddy that flows clockwise, outside, on flood currents. There is a small landing beach on the south shore and a canoe pass to the west.

*Réanne admiring a boat builder's work in Hydaburg*

Anchor in 4 fathoms over sand, gravel and kelp with fair holding.

## Hydaburg (Prince of Wales Island)
Hydaburg is 19 miles southeast of Craig.
Chart 17407
Public floats: 55°12.68' N, 132°49.79' W

Hydaburg is a small town of about 375 people. It is connected by road to Craig and the ferry terminal at Hollis. Facilities for cruising boats are few, although the docks received a substantial upgrade in 2015 and drinking water is now available at some floats. The village warrants a stop—particularly when the salmon are running. From the dock, you can watch the residents bringing in their catches and filleting them to smoke for their winter food stock. From the bridge over Hydaburg River, you can look down upon swarms of salmon

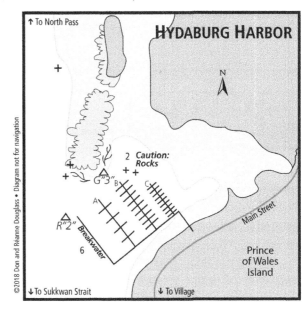

### Carrying a Totem Pole, Hydaburg Totem Park
#### Elsie Hulsizer

All around me, women laughed and cheered as we surged forward under the weight of the massive totem pole. Behind us drums beat and singers chanted.
We were in Hydaburg for the town's annual culture festival and I was helping village women carry a newly carved pole from the carving shed on the waterfront to the totem park in the center of town. The village men had raised three poles the day before and now it was the women's turn. They had won the privilege by beating the men in a game of tug-of-war. "They just pulled us across the line," a man told us in amazement.

Ninety women and girls marched forward holding the pole up on cross-braces, each with three women on each side.

"Keep going ladies! You're doing great," shouted the project leader. "You can't stop now. You have to reach the top of the hill." I looked ahead to see the road getting steeper and shifted my arms on the cross-brace to make sure I was carrying my share. To my right on the same cross-brace a teenage Haida girl walked proudly. She struggled to keep her hold on the pole, but that didn't stop a big grin spreading across her face.

Finally, we crested the hill. Men ran in to place sawhorses under the pole. On the order "lower the pole," we let down our cross-braces until they rested on the sawhorses. A cheer went up.

After the pole raising, we filed into the school gymnasium and feasted on salmon, halibut and herring roe. Afterwards, we watched Native dancers from Hydaburg, Ketchikan and Klawock perform. We were just visiting tourists but our hosts made us feel part of the community.

SE Alaska owes its totem parks to the New Deal of the Great Depression. From 1938 to 1941, the Civilian Conservation Corps (CCC) hired Native workers to create six new totem parks in Hydaburg, Ketchikan, Saxman, Kasaan, Wrangell, and Klawock. (Sitka already had a park with poles originally donated to fairs in St. Louis and Portland.) The workers rescued poles from abandoned villages. Depending on the state of the poles, they either restored or replicated them. They also carved additional poles.

The CCC poles are now deteriorating and Native villages are replacing them. Today's replacement poles are significantly better than the CCC poles with bolder, more authentic lines and more muted colors. A renaissance in Alaskan Native arts is underway.

SE Alaska's totem parks are one of the region's chief attractions, and they're getting better. Don't miss them. And if you have an opportunity to help carry or raise a pole, take it.

Hydaburg's annual culture festival is usually held during the last week in July.

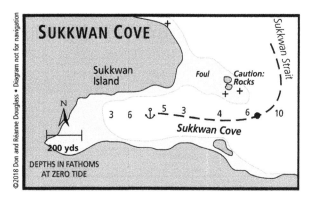

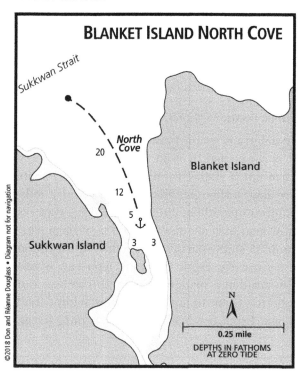

fighting to head upstream to their spawning grounds. School children drop lines along the river's edge to snag fish.

Above the floats there is a fine stand of old and well-cared-for totems, perhaps the best designs we've seen anywhere, and you can watch carvers at work. The town has a small store about 1/2 mile south of the harbor with limited supplies, and there is a post office.

## Sukkwan Strait

Sukkwan Strait extends 7 miles southeast from Hydaburg.
Chart 17431
North entrance: 55°12.22' N, 132°50.20' W
Southeast entrance: 55°07.87' N, 132°40.61' W

Sukkwan Strait connects Hydaburg to Cordova Bay to the south.

## Sukkwan Cove
(Sukkwan Island)
Sukkwan Cove is 2.2 miles south of Hydaburg.
Chart 17431
Entrance: 55°10.55' N, 132°48.53' W
Anchor: 55°10.56' N, 132°49.14' W

"Sukkwan Cove" is what we call the unnamed cove on the northeast corner of Sukkwan Island, west of Saltery Point. The cove offers fair protection in southeast winds and very good protection in all other winds.

Entry is easy, but the shoal at the north entrance, which has several rocks, extends a quarter-mile out. The bay may be full of crab pot floats, but it is shallow and has good swinging room.

Anchor in 4 fathoms over mud with good holding.

*Looking west from Hydaburg towards Sukkwan Narrows, which has a 13-foot depth at zero tide; check your tide tables and proceed carefully through here.*

## Blanket Island North Cove
(Blanket Island)
Blanket Island North Cove is on the north side of Blanket Island.
Chart 17431
Entrance: 55°08.53' N, 132°44.23' W
Anchor: 55°08.12' N, 132°43.98' W

You can find anchorage in what we call "Blanket Island North Cove." To avoid a southerly chop in Hetta Inlet, duck into the cove where it narrows just north of the first islet. The narrow passage is peaceful and fun to explore by kayak.

Anchor in 2 to 4 fathoms over sand, pebbles, shells and kelp with poor-to-fair holding.

## Hetta Inlet (Prince of Wales Island)
Hetta Inlet extends 5 miles north from Lime Point to the entrance of Sukkwan Strait, then 11 miles to Gould Island.
Chart 17431
Entrance (Lime Point bearing 090°T at 0.6 Nm): 55°03.24' N, 132°39.22' W

Hetta Inlet is the site of a number of abandoned mining operations; we prefer to anchor in Eek Inlet, at its south end.

At the head of Hetta Inlet (11 miles away), Gould Island nearly closes the inlet. However, you can pass through Sulzer Passage to get to Portage Bay—a spot not to be missed. See further description below under Sulzer Passage and Gould Passage and under Portage Bay.

## Eek Inlet (Hetta Inlet)
Eek Inlet is 0.6 mile north of Eek Point.
Chart 17431
Entrance: 55°08.72' N, 132°39.24' W
Anchor: 55°09.17' N, 132°39.69' W

*Artistic expertise seen in a Hydaburg totem*

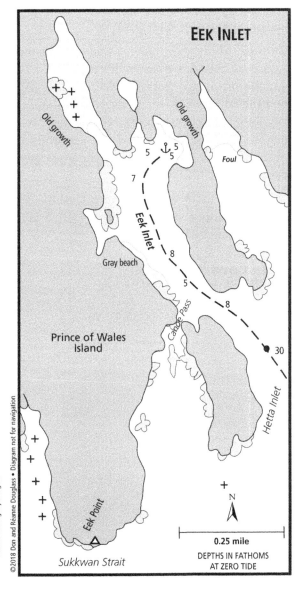

Despite its name, Eek Inlet offers good protection from all weather and is conveniently located at Hetta Inlet north of Cordova Bay. The inner basin on the east side is the best anchorage.

Enter Eek Inlet by passing east of the island and its off-lying rock, a half-mile east of Eek Point, as indicated in the diagram. This can be done carefully by radar if necessary.

Anchor in 5 fathoms over sand and gravel with fair holding.

## Mud Bay (Hetta Inlet)
Mud Bay is 2 miles north of Lime Point.
Chart 17431
Entrance: 55°05.15' N, 132°38.14' W
Anchor: 55°04.91' N, 132°37.86' W

Although Mud Bay's name sounds promising and *Coast Pilot* describes anchoring in 4 to 10 fathoms on a mud bottom, we disagree. We tried the bottom in several places and found it only hard and rocky; in addition, it is deep and steep-to. The anchorage offers protection from southerly winds only. Anchor, if you must, just east of the small islet.

Anchor in 6 to 10 fathoms over a hard, rocky bottom with poor-to-fair holding. Better yet, head for Mabel Bay.

## Hetta Cove (Hetta Inlet)
Hetta Cove is 3 miles northeast of Eek Inlet.
Chart 17431
Entrance: 55°10.16' N, 132°35.41' W

*Baidarka and friend cruising past Hydaburg*

*Local fishermen sometimes run their nets almost all the way across the fairway in places like Eek Inlet.*

Hetta cove has an inner basin that looks secure, but we have no further knowledge to add about anchoring here. Other cruisers have reported to us that it's worthwhile to follow the game trails or bushwhack along the stream to Hetta Lake, above the cove.

## Deer Bay (Hetta Inlet)
Deer Bay is 2 miles northwest of Copper Harbor.
Chart 17431
Entrance: 55°14.06' N, 132°40.55' W
Anchor: 55°14.41' N, 132°41.19' W

Deer Bay, on the west shore of Hetta Inlet, is a good place to anchor while you explore the bitter end of the inlet and Portage Bay. The M/V *Royal Sounder* found the bay to be true to its name. During their approach, two deer swam across the mouth of the bay.

Anchor in about 5 fathoms over mud and gravel with fair holding.

## Portage Bay (Hetta Inlet)
Portage Bay is the area north of Gould Island.
Chart 17431
Position: 55°16.80' N, 132°33.76' W

Prince of Wales Island is nearly cut in half by two deep inlets at this point. An old skid road that at one time supplied all the abandoned mill sites along this coast supposedly leads across 2.5 miles to the east side of Prince of Wales in the

*Hidden beauty along the trail to Hetta Lake.*

*Hiking the trail made smooth by the game in Hetta Cove; don't forget to make noise to keep the bears away (clap, sing, whistle).*

west arm of Cholmondeley Sound. Cruisers using our book told us they went by dinghy from their anchorage in nearby Deer Bay to Portage Bay to look for the remains of this skid road—but could not find it. What they did find, however, were wonderful broad vistas, a crystal clear mountain stream filled with fish, and animal prints in the mud. "Pristine" was the word they used for this fascinating place.

### Mabel Bay (Hassiah Inlet)
Mabel Bay is 16 miles southeast of Hydaburg.
Chart 17431
West entrance: 54°59.73′ N, 132°36.86′ W
North entrance: 54°59.98′ N, 132°35.12′ W
Anchor (south basin): 54°58.36′ N, 132°35.56′ W
Anchor (east basin): 54°59.10′ N, 132°33.12′ W

Scenic and landlocked, Mabel Bay offers excellent southerly protection. Choose between the east basin, which is slightly easier to enter, or the southern basin (avoid the rocky shoal

*Portage Bay—at the head of Hetta Inlet*

*Looking through crystal clear water to see lots of salmon only inches away*

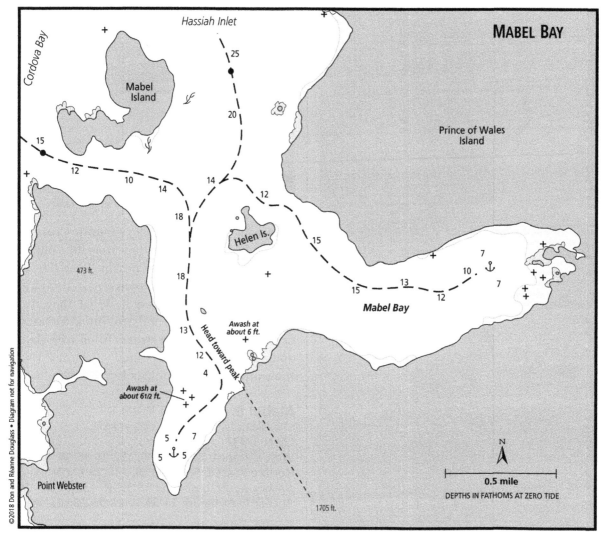

off the west shore). In a southeast storm, the wind may whistle across the trees in the southern basin, but it's a snug anchorage with plenty of swinging room.

Anchor (south basin) in 5 fathoms over a mixed bottom with fair-to-good holding.

Anchor (east basin) in 7 fathoms over a mixed bottom with fair-to-good holding.

## Cordova Bay
Cordova Bay extends from Lime Point to the northwest side of Dixon Entrance.
Chart 17400
North entrance (Mellen Rock Light bearing 270°T at 1.0 Nm): 55°01.59' N, 132°38.13' W
South entrance (Cape Muzon Light bearing 253°T at 5.5 Nm and Point Marsh bearing 082° at 8.5 Nm): 54°43.18' N, 132°33.62' W

Since Cordova Bay is open to the southeast, gales that blow with full force can create nasty chop.

## Elbow Bay (Long Island)
Elbow Bay is 4.5 miles west of Kassa Inlet.
Chart 17431
Entrance: 54°54.41' N, 132°39.02' W
Anchor (southeast arm): 54°53.79' N, 132°39.15' W

Elbow Bay offers very good shelter, deep in the largely landlocked bay. The entrance islands and reef off the north entrance point act as a natural breakwater in northerly winds.

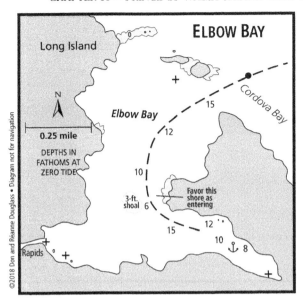

*Two deer swimming across the bow as if to greet these cruisers in Deer Bay*

The south peninsula provides complete shelter from southeast chop sometimes found in Cordova Bay. The lagoon and tidal rapids on the west shore offer a dynamic display of natural forces at work.

Long Island was once home to some of the largest cedars in Southeast Alaska. They are now a thing of the past as the clear cutting of Long Island is essentially complete.

Favor the south entrance point as you enter, and avoid the 3-foot shoal in the middle of the bay. Anchor deep in the southeast arm. The depths in Elbow Bay are somewhat irregular, and the bottom may be rocky with kelp in many places, so set your anchor well.

Anchor in 8 to 10 fathoms over a mixed bottom with fair-to-good holding.

## Natoma Bay (Long Island)

Natoma Bay is 3 miles south of Elbow Bay.

Chart 17409
Entrance: 54°51.01' N, 132°37.10' W
Anchor: 54°52.27' N, 132°38.02' W

Natoma Bay is a good lee when strong northwesterlies are blowing, but anything more than a moderate southerly makes for an exposed, rolly anchorage. The bay is shaped like a large crater, with isolated rocks and erratics littering the shoreline.

Anchor in 10 fathoms over mud with shells and rocks with fair holding. Be sure you set your anchor well.

## Coning Inlet (Long Island)

Coning Inlet is 4.5 miles south of Elbow Bay.

Chart 17409
Entrance: 54°49.51' N, 132°37.72' W

Coning Inlet, like Natoma Bay, is exposed to southeasterly weather. The lagoon at the head

*Climbing out on the other side*

*One last look back to check on the visitors*

*This entrance to the lagoon at Nutkwa Inlet needs to be transited only at high water slack, by shallow-draft boats.*

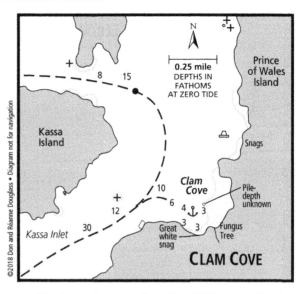

of Coning Inlet reaches to within 0.25 mile of Bolles Inlet on the other side of Long Island. Nina Cove is the preferable place to anchor in Coning Inlet.

## Nina Cove (Coning Inlet)
Nina Cove is on the south side of Coning Inlet at the entrance.
Chart 17409
Entrance: 54°49.44' N, 132°39.39' W
Anchor: 54°49.40' N, 132°40.58' W

Nina Cove is a small landlocked cove offering excellent shelter in all weather. This is a good place to stay while exploring the intricate system of lagoons that nearly cuts Long Island in half.

The entrance to Nina Cove is restricted; avoid the submerged rock off the small islet by favoring the east shore. The bottom of the cove is rocky sand and mud, so set your anchor well.

Anchor in 4 fathoms over sand, mud and some rocks with fair-to-good holding.

## Kassa Inlet (Prince of Wales Island)
Kassa Inlet is 4.5 miles northeast of Elbow Bay.
Chart 17431
Entrance: 54°55.62' N, 132°32.32' W

Kassa Inlet is a landlocked waterway with a couple of large islands in its center. Good protection is available at Clam Cove or northwest of Kassa Island.

## Clam Cove (Kassa Inlet)
Clam Cove is 2 miles inside Kassa Inlet.
Chart 17431
Anchor: 54°56.38' N, 132°28.63' W

Although it appears to be an open roadstead, Clam Cove provides good shelter from all quarters. Hook in behind the point where you will find it calm, even when a southwest wind blows outside in Cordova Bay. Anchor close to shore, avoiding the pile at unknown depth noted on the chart.

*The anchorage at Nutkwa Inlet*

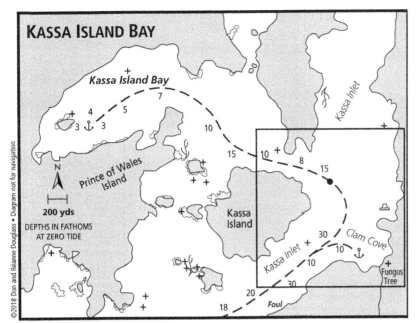

Kassa Island may offer a cozier anchor site for small craft.

Anchor in 3 to 5 fathoms over sand and mud with fair-to-good holding.

## Ship Island Passage
(Prince of Wales Island)
Ship Island Passage is 1 mile south of Kassa Inlet.

Chart 17431
North entrance: 54°55.20′ N, 132°31.99′ W
South entrance (Barbara Rock bearing 056°T at 0.26 Nm): 54°53.40′ N, 132°30.12′ W

*Small craft from Turn Point pass N of Bird Rocks and between Shipwreck Point and the island close-to. The narrow channel has a submerged rock. The pass to the W of the inner island is preferable; avoid the rock in the middle of the entrance.* (CP)

Ship Island Passage is a short, smooth-water route between Kassa Inlet and the entrance

Interesting to visitors, and visible from boats in the bight of the cove, is a great silvery white snag sporting a bright blue and white fungus known as Dryad's Saddle. This cove is also a favorite haunt of bald eagles.

The landlocked bay northwest of Kassa Island offers complete shelter during storms.

Anchor in 4 fathoms over sand, shells and grass with good holding.

## Kassa Island Bay (Kassa Inlet)
Kassa Island Cove is 1 mile northwest of Clam Cove.
Chart 17431
Entrance: 54°56.92′ N, 132°29.19′ W
Anchor: 54°57.24′ N, 132°31.79′ W

Kassa Island Bay, our name for the protected bay northwest of Kassa Island, offers great shelter over a large, mostly-flat bottom with unlimited swinging room. Avoid the kelp patches that indicate rocks. The intricate area immediately west of

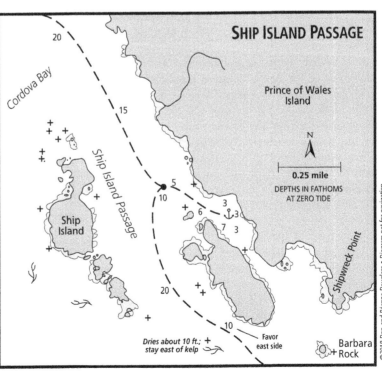

to Klakas Inlet. Temporary anchorage can be found near its south end. This marks the northern limit of the south Prince of Wales Wilderness Area.

## Ship Island Passage Cove (Ship Island)
Ship Island Passage Cove is 0.7 mile inside the south entrance to the passage.
Chart 17431
Entrance: 54°54.26' N, 132°30.84' W
Anchor: 54°54.14' N, 132°30.47' W

"Ship Island Passage Cove" is our name for the cove that makes a good rest stop or temporary anchorage in fair weather only. However, it can receive some chop, especially from the northwest. The bottom is a combination of rocks, sand, crushed shell and large kelp. Holding may vary from extremely poor to good, so check the set of your anchor carefully.

The southern exit to Ship Island Passage is narrow, and you should favor the east side next to the unnamed island located northwest of Barbara Rock. On the west side of the passage of the unnamed island. The rock dries on about a 10-foot tide.

Anchor in 3 to 5 fathoms over a mixed bottom with poor-to-fair holding.

*A rare, close encounter with Alaska's commanding eagle*

## Klakas Inlet
(Prince of Wales Island)
Klakas Inlet is 9.5 miles east of Elbow Bay.

---

## Bald Eagles
### Is the bald eagle still an endangered species?
### Herb Nickles, Certified Alaska Naturalist

Claims by fox farmers and fishermen of marauding eagles caused the Alaska Territorial Legislature in 1917 to impose a bounty on eagles. These claims were later found to be mainly false, but over 100,000 eagles were killed before the bounty was removed in 1953. However, the bald eagle's decline during the past half century was primarily due to reproductive failure caused by pesticides, such as DDT. Habitat destruction also contributed to shrinking populations in the Lower 48 states.

With statehood in 1959, the bald eagle in Alaska received federal protection under the Bald Eagle Protection Act of 1940. This act makes it illegal to kill or possess an eagle, alive or dead, or to possess any part of an eagle, including feathers. In 1972, the Alaska State Legislature established a stretch of the Chilkat River as critical bald eagle habitat to ensure protection of the large numbers found there in winter. In 1982, a portion of the surrounding area was established as the Alaska Chilkat Bald Eagle Preserve.

The bald eagle is well on its way to recovery in both Alaska and the lower 48 states. Recovery efforts have proven so successful that this uniquely American bird is no longer listed as threatened or endangered, although it is still protected by federal law.

### Additional Resources:
U.S. Fish & Wildlife Service—Bald Eagle Website: http://www.fws.gov/migratorybirds/BaldEagle.htm

Alaska Chilkat Bald Eagle Preserve: http://www.dnr.state.ak.us/parks/units/eagleprv.htm

Alaska Department of Fish & Game—Endangered Species: http://www.wc.adfg.state.ak.us/index.cfm?adfg=endangered.main

Used with permission from author: http://www.insidepassagenews.com/AlaskaFAQ/FAQ_15.html

Chart 17431
Entrance (mid-channel between Turn Island and Turn Point): 54°52.28' N, 132°22.87' W
Entrance (cove northeast of Klakas Island): 54°54.20' N, 132°23.00' W
Anchor (cove northeast of Klakas Island): 54°54.94' N, 132°22.13' W

> The main entrance to Klakas Inlet is E of Klakas Island; the deepest water favors the W side of the entrance. . . .
> Good anchorage in a depth of about 16 fathoms can be found E of a small wooded island about 1.5 miles ENE of the N end of Klakas Island. (CP)

The anchor site for Klakas Inlet mentioned above in *Coast Pilot* is a little exposed for our taste. We prefer Ruth Bay or Max Cove for more intimacy.

Anchor in about 7 fathoms over mud and shells with some rocks.

## Hunter Bay (Prince of Wales Island)
Hunter Bay extends 2.5 miles east of Turn Point.
Chart 17433
Entrance (Turn Point bearing 090°T at 0.3 Nm): 54°52.62' N, 132°22.33' W
Anchor: 54°52.23' N, 132°18.57' W

Hunter Bay, with Biscuit Lagoon, is a narrow, intriguing waterway leading to an isolated salt chuck at the head of its north arm. If southeast gales are forecast, set your anchor accordingly or use a stern-tie west of the islet, close in, on the south shore. All anchorages below peaks are subject to williwaws in gales or storms, and this place is no exception. Williwaws notwithstanding, Hunter Bay is a well-protected spot.

The features of Hunter Bay beg to be explored; if you do, be careful of tidal currents and avoid the mid-channel rocks on entering.

Anchor in 6 fathoms over mud and shells with good holding.

## Klinkwan Cove (Hunter Bay)
Klinkwan Cove is first cove on the north shore of Hunter Bay.
Chart 17433
Entrance: 54°52.83' N, 132°21.46' W

*Coast Pilot* advises against entering Klinkwan Cove, as it is full of rocks. However, it is a natural for exploring by kayak.

*Charlie's Cove, Barrier Islands*

*A stately parade of Mergansers, with one riding on mama . . .*

*. . . but when they get spooked, they all try to pile on.*

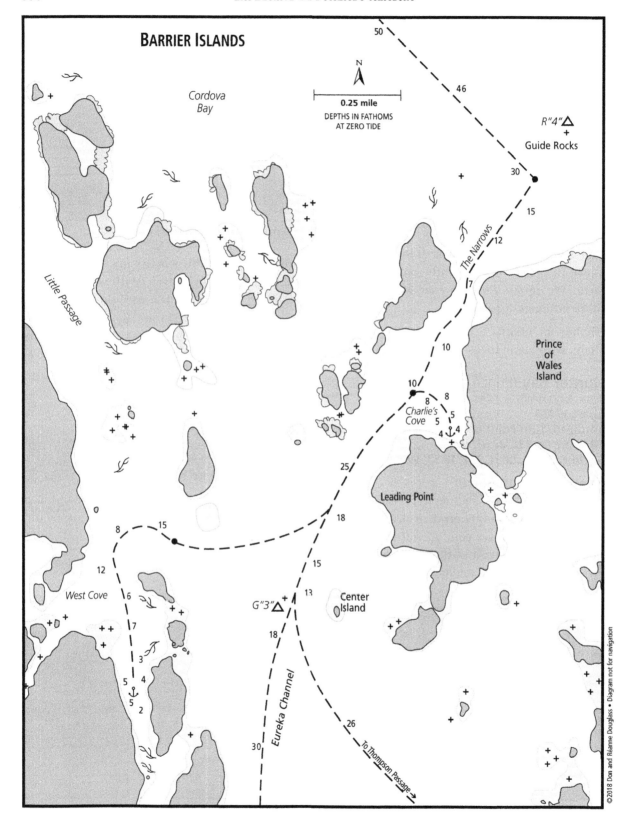

*That looks scary; did we make it out safely? (Dinghy exit from Biscuit Lagoon)*

*You bet we did; look at that smile on Réanne's face!*

## Biscuit Lagoon (Hunter Bay)
Biscuit Lagoon is at the head of the northeast arm of Hunter Bay.
Chart 17433
Entrance: 54°52.38' N, 132°19.78' W

Biscuit Lagoon is nearly cut off by a small island. It is passable only as noted in *Coast Pilot*. A large quantity of water passes through this narrow opening and to enter you need to time your passage at high water slack or you may be facing a waterfall. Avoid the rocks on the east side of the small entrance channel.

*Exploring the rocky shoreline in Biscuit Lagoon*

Depths within the lagoon are great, but the salt chuck at its head dries at low water. The shores of Biscuit Lagoon attract sandhill cranes as well as bear.

## Barrier Islands (Cordova Bay)
Barrier Islands lie 1 to 5 miles east of Round Islands Light and 4 to 8 miles northwest of Point Marsh.
Chart 17433
Position (Round Island Light): 54°46.68' N, 132°30.42' W

Approaches to the channels through the Barrier Islands pass about 0.5 mile both E and W of Black Rock. These two passages, Rocky Pass and Kelp Passage, continue E and W, respectively, of Middle Island and are useful only to small craft. It is possible to carry 2 fathoms of water through the W passage and 7 fathoms through the E.

The Barrier Islands provide a substantial break before you enter the southerly swell of Dixon Entrance. Covered with stubby, old-growth cedar, these numerous, low islands are alive with Clark's nutcrackers that raise a shrill

*Waterfall from High Lake, Hessa Inlet*

*The Barrier Islands offer some of the most beautiful scenery along the west side of Prince of Wales Island.*

cry upon your arrival. There are many beautiful inlets and bays to explore in this remote area.

## Eureka Channel
Eureka Channel is between Barrier Islands and Prince of Wales Island.
Chart 17433
North entrance (Guide Rocks R"4" bearing 060°T at 0.2 Nm): 54°49.43' N, 132°21.78' W
South entrance (Mexico Point bearing 142°T at 0.8 Nm): 54°46.02' N, 132°23.37' W

Eureka Channel is the scenic, smooth-water route heading south. The marker R"4" at Guide Rocks is the north entrance for this route. If Eureka Channel is used in conjunction with Thompson Passage or Buschmann Pass in fair weather, you should find smooth water until just north of Point Marsh, where you begin a turn east to Nichols Bay and Cape Chacon. Southwest swell and chop greatly diminish north of the Barrier Islands, but pick up quickly south of the islands. It's unwise to head south from Eureka Channel in the face of a southeast gale; there is no reliable shelter you can safely enter until you're on the east side of Prince of Wales Island. Shelter along Eureka Channel is marginal because the bottom tends to be rocky with poor holding. A shore tie will improve holding among the beautiful Barrier Islands.

## Charlie's Cove (Eureka Channel)
Chart 17433
Entrance: 54°48.77' N, 132°22.18' W
Anchor: 54°48.67' N, 132°22.07' W

We named "Charlie's Cove" after Charles E. Wood, author of the famous Charlie's Charts guides; he made this unnamed cove known to cruising boats via the description in his original *Charlie's Charts North to Alaska*. Charlie's Cove is a convenient stop-over offering good southerly protection when you tuck up against the small opening to the east.

Anchor in 4 fathoms over rock, gravel and kelp with poor-to-fair holding. Holding can be good if you set your anchor well.

## West Cove (Eureka Channel)
West Cove is 1 mile southwest of Charlie's Cove.
Chart 17433
Entrance: 54°48.28' N, 132°23.39' W
Anchor: 54°47.96' N, 132°23.72' W

Snug little West Cove is located on the west side of Eureka Channel west of marker G"3."

CHAPTER 10 — PRINCE OF WALES ISLAND WEST COAST TO CAPE CHACON, INCLUDING DALL ISLAND  401

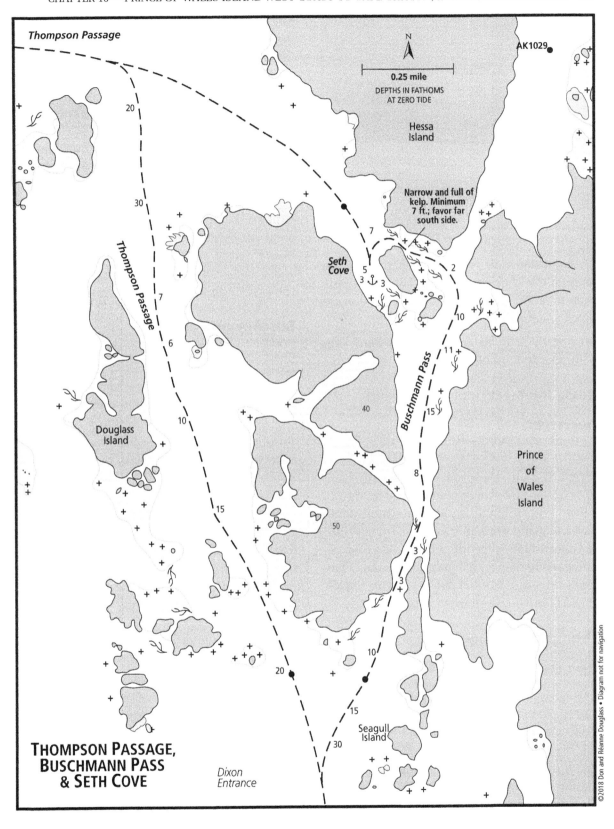

*Threading our way through Minnie Bay*

We found the cove was not as charted, so use caution. It is choked with kelp that allows little chop to enter. The bottom is poor, however, so check your anchor set.

Anchor in 5 fathoms over rock, gravel and kelp with poor-to-fair holding.

## Hessa Inlet (Prince of Wales Island)
Hessa Inlet is 5 miles east of the Barrier Islands.
Chart 17433
West entrance (northwest tip of Hessa Island bearing 150°T at 0.3 Nm): 54°47.37' N, 132°20.34' W

Hessa Inlet is a remote, landlocked waterway where you are unlikely to encounter other boats. In many ways, this southern tip of Prince of Wales Island is the ultimate frontier of expeditionary cruising in Southeast Alaska. Only small, highly maneuverable craft with experienced crew should consider exploring here.

## Thompson Passage
Thompson Passage is 0.5 mile west of Hessa Island.
Chart 17433
North entrance (Eureka Channel marker G"3" bearing 316°T at 0.8 Nm): 54°47.58' N, 132°22.03' W
South entrance (Seagull Island bearing 121°T at 0.3 Nm): 54°44.88' N, 132°19.93' W

Thompson Passage allows you put off entering the swell off Mexico Point. In fair weather, Thompson Passage lines up well with Minnie Cutoff to further avoid the swells off Point Marsh; however, you must be careful to avoid the many submerged and exposed rocks between these two points. The north entrance to Minnie Cutoff is encumbered with several breaking rocks; the entrance looks—and is—formidable in foul weather or when sizable swell is running.

If you have time to spare or you are seeking intimate surroundings, consider Buschmann Pass, which can be approached through the channel on the south side of Hessa Island. These small passages are fun and exciting to explore, but they should be navigated with great care and in fair weather with good visibility. Avoid the mid-channel rock near the south end of Thompson Passage by favoring the east shore.

## Buschmann Pass
Buschmann Pass connects Point Marsh to Hessa Inlet.
Chart 17433
North entrance (Whirlpool Point bearing 027°T at 0.3 Nm): 54°46.56' N, 132°18.80' W
South entrance (Seagull Island bearing 164°T at 0.16 Nm): 54°44.88' N, 132°19.54' W

Buschmann Pass is charted at small scale. It is narrow, very remote and with many rocks and strong, uncertain currents. Use extreme caution if you attempt a transit.

You can enter the north end of Buschmann Pass from Hessa Inlet south of Whirlpool Point. The north end is quite narrow and favors the Hessa Island shore. A moderate flood tide may be the best time to transit Buschmann Pass if you are southbound, as you will have more steering control.

If you are entering Buschmann Pass south of Hessa Island, east of what we call Seth Cove, reconnoiter the narrow, shallow pass before you attempt it. The bar is choked with kelp, and rocks awash on a 2-foot tide extend from the north shore to mid-channel. We found a tiny opening that favors the far south shore (stay about 30 feet from the south island). Let a moderate, east-flowing flood current carry you through the kelp and across the bar.

Buschmann Pass is a calm channel compared to the outside; however, it has considerable current flow at times. The pass has an enchanted feeling to it as it passes forested islets and heads directly for Dixon Entrance.

## Seth Cove (Barrier Islands)
Seth Cove is off the southwest tip of Hessa Island.
Chart 17433
Entrance: 54°46.07' N, 132°19.66' W
Anchor: 54°45.91' N, 132°19.59' W

"Seth Cove" is the small cove we named after our dedicated crew member, Seth Nickles, and the base from which we reconnoitered this area. It is protected from all southerly weather and is a calm place to stay until tides are favorable for an attempt to enter Buschmann Pass.

Anchor in 5 to 6 fathoms over rocks, clamshell and kelp with poor-to-fair holding; check your anchor set.

## Minnie Cutoff
Minnie Cutoff is just east of Point Marsh and 10 miles west of Cape Chacon.
Chart 17433
South entrance: 54°42.68' N, 132°18.09' W
North entrance: 54°43.74' N, 132°19.41' W

Minnie Cutoff, is used occasionally by experienced fishermen in small boats. It is not a place for the faint-hearted!

Entering Minnie Cutoff from the south on a northbound route is easier than on a southbound route. The northern entrance has several breaking rocks that are difficult to identify precisely. From the north, one glance will tell you this is not a cutoff to try in poor visibility or in foul weather when swells are running and whitewater breaks over the rocks and islets. The south entrance is less encumbered with rocks and has a navigation light.

We have entered from the north several times. On one passage (in stable weather), we found Minnie Cutoff so choked with kelp and submerged rocks that we had only about 30 feet on either side of *Baidarka*. Depth in the fairway east of island (90) is about 2 fathoms. Across from the entrance to Minnie Bay just south of island (90), there is a dangerous rock in the center of Minnie Cutoff awash on a 9-foot tide.

"Note B" on Chart 17433 states that all of Brownson Bay (and apparently Minnie Bay) is shallower than that stated on the chart, so

*Remnants of the past can be found all over the southeast forests.*

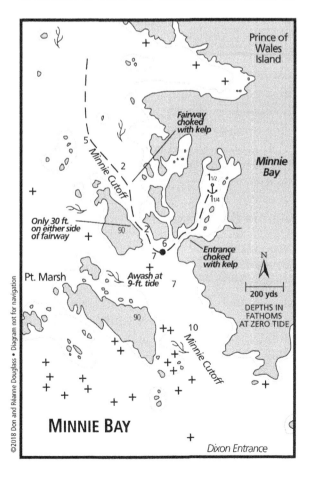

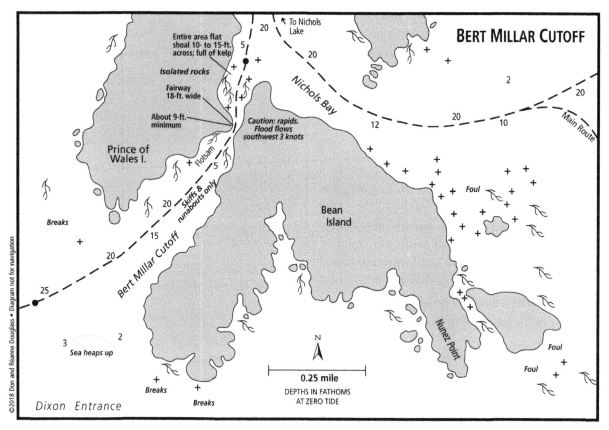

beware! If you're in doubt about using this cutoff, do the safest thing: round Point Marsh on the outside by staying a mile west and give a wide berth to the rocks off the point's northwest, southwest and south sides before you turn east. Only Bert Millar Cutoff, 7 miles to the east, has a more intimidating entrance.

## Minnie Bay (Prince of Wales Island)
Minnie Bay lies 1 mile northeast of Point Marsh.
Chart 17433
Entrance: 54°43.26′ N, 132°18.62′ W
Anchor: 54°43.46′ N, 132°18.36′ W

Minnie Bay is a lovely little cove with a restricted entrance choked with kelp (as with Minnie Cutoff). Entrance to the bay is made just south of island (90) by turning almost due east, avoiding kelp and rocks, then passing to the west side of three islets.

Depths throughout the entire bay do not exceed more than about one-and-a-half fathoms at zero tide, so it is appropriate only for boats with drafts of less than 4 feet. The bottom of the bay is rocky and irregular with patches of sand and kelp. No swell is felt within the bay.

Minnie Bay is charted at small scale, and Chart 17433 is helpful only for an overall view.

## Bert Millar Cutoff (Prince of Wales Island)
Bert Millar Cutoff, a tiny passage to Nichols Bay, is west of Bean Island and 3 miles west of Cape Chacon.
Chart 17433
South entrance: 54°41.15′ N, 132°07.71′ W
North entrance: 54°41.88′ N, 132°06.51′ W

Bert Millar Cutoff is used by sport fishing skiffs or small shallow draft runabouts with local knowledge. Entering from Dixon Entrance is particularly challenging with foam and breakers rolling in toward the cutoff. Beyond the entrance, the narrows is full of kelp, suggesting that few propeller boats of any size should use this route. It's a stunt passage for anything but a high-powered dinghy.

*The Bert Millar Cutoff is a stunt passage for small, high-powered skiffs.*

The entrance to Bert Millar Cutoff is considerably narrower than that described in *Coast Pilot*. We estimate the fairway to be only 18 feet wide between the rock walls. Scott Davis, in a high-tech rowing craft, found it too narrow to row through, and he let the current carry him through instead. There is zero margin of safety if any current is running or if anything goes wrong!

The current through the channel is mysterious. We went through Bert Millar in our 32-foot Nordic Tug, northbound on a flood and found ourselves face-to-face with a 6- to 9-inch waterfall flowing south! (A significant back eddy apparently runs for a couple of hours of flood off Cape Chacon and Nichols Bay.) With all hands poised to fend off, and with big fenders out on both sides of our 11-foot beam, we managed to squeak through with just a couple of feet to spare. Our depth sounder was useless in the kelp, but our bow crew said it appeared that we had 8 feet under the keel, which means we doubt there is 1¾ fathoms at zero tide in the tiny fairway. (Scott Davis reported he could see bottom all the way.)

As we headed into Nichols Bay, we turned around to study the tiny entrance and saw a great blue heron standing on kelp in the center of the channel we'd just come through and a fisheries skiff heading pell-mell out through the cutoff. If you want to see what Bert Millar is all about, we recommend that you enter Nichols Bay from the main route east of Bean Island and check it out by dinghy. Bert Millar is one of the few places we know of in Southeast Alaska to be honored with a full name.

## Nichols Bay (Prince of Wales Island)

Nichols Bay is 2.5 miles west of Cape Chacon.
Chart 17433
Entrance: 54°41.34' N, 132°03.89' W
Anchor (south): 54°42.87' N, 132°07.68' W
Anchor (central): 54°43.25' N, 132°08.12' W
Anchor (north): 54°44.45' N, 132°09.55' W

When entering Nichols Bay, we use the deeper channel on the south and west side of the three unnamed islands that nearly choke the entrance to the bay. The bay has three anchor sites, as indicated on the diagram. Our favorite is the south site, which is calm when 8-foot seas are running in Dixon Entrance. If a serious southeasterly blow approaches, we suggest anchoring at the central site just north of the peninsula that juts out on the west side of the bay, which appears to offer complete shelter. However, you will be sharing this site with a busy floating fishing lodge. The far north site has driftwood at its head, indicat-

*Checking out a classic Grumman that landed in Nichols Bay*

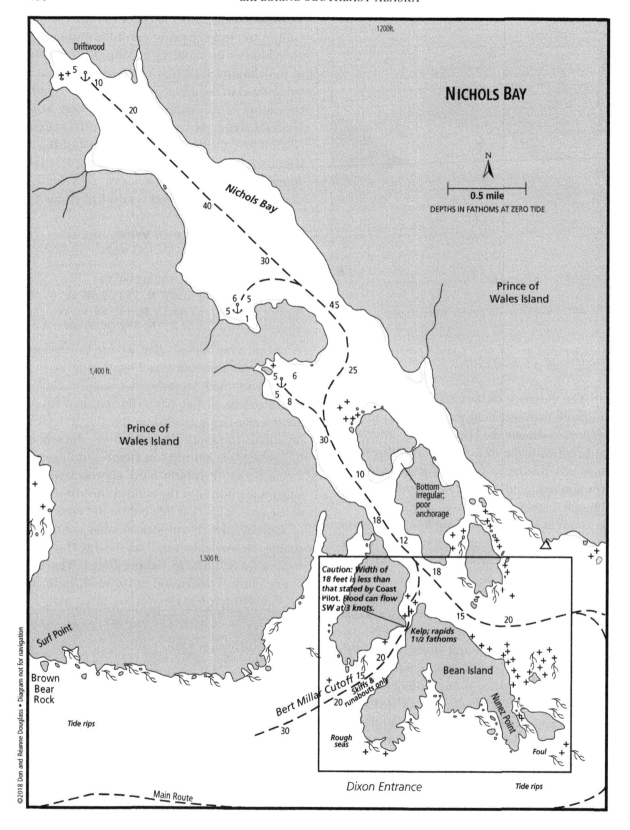

ing that, at times, southeast winds carry all the way up the bay. This northern anchor site is favored by boaters who like to explore the creek that drains Nichols Lake, three-quarters of a mile upstream.

Anchor (south) in 6 fathoms over sand and mud with fair-to-good holding.

Anchor (central) in 5 fathoms over sand and gravel with fair holding.

Anchor (north) in 5 fathoms over sand and mud with good holding.

## Cape Chacon (Prince of Wales Island)
Cape Chacon, the southeast point of Prince of Wales Island, is 23 miles east of Cape Muzon.
Chart 17433
Position (light bearing 335°T at 0.5 Nm):
54°40.91' N, 132°00.60' W

In addition to the back eddy off Cape Chacon mentioned for Bert Millar Cutoff, you may encounter tide rips along the south tip of Prince of Wales Island. Most fishing boats pass between Nunez Rocks and Nunez Point. Larger fishing boats return from Cordova Bay to Ketchikan via Cape Chacon, but because of Dixon Entrance's reputation for rough seas, most smaller fishing boats from the Craig area prefer to return to Ketchikan via El Capitan Passage and the north end of Prince of Wales Island. If you are unable to get U.S. weather on VHF, try the Canadian channels as they may have better reception in this area.

## TLEVAK AND KAIGANI STRAITS TO CAPE MUZON

### Tlevak Strait
Tlevak Strait extends 24 miles from Tlevak Narrows to Cordova Bay.
Chart 17400
North entrance (Lively Island
Light bearing 000°T at 0.6 Nm):
55°13.11' N, 133°05.11' W
Southeast entrance (Shoe Island
Light bearing 270°T at 1.7 Nm):
54°57.02' N, 132°41.71' W

*The direction of maximum flood current (and ebb) varies considerably as one progresses through the 24-mile-long Tlevak Strait. Maximum average currents range from 1.5 to 3.0 knots on the flood and 1.5 to 4.3 knots on the ebb; the strongest currents occurring in Tlevak Narrows. (CP)*

We have seen the flood current at 5 to 6 knots on spring tides in the narrows and, at times, it may even be higher! The current is much more moderate in the southern part of the bay.

Unfortunately, logging detracts from the beauty of the shoreline.

### North Bay (Dall Island)
North Bay is 2.8 miles south of Tlevak Narrows.
Chart 17407
Entrance: 55°13.12' N, 133°05.86' W
Anchor: 55°12.29' N, 133°07.61' W

Anchorage can be found in the southwest corner of North Bay.

Anchor in 8 fathoms over sand and gravel with fair holding.

### Farallon Bay (Dall Island)
Farallon Bay, on the west side of Tlevak Strait, is 1.5 miles southeast of North Bay.
Chart 17407
Entrance: 55°11.66' N, 133°04.62' W

Avoid the dangerous reef on the north entrance to Farallon Bay shown on the chart as a submerged rock.

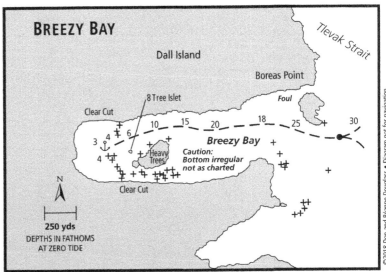

## Breezy Bay (Dall Island)
Breezy Bay is 4 miles south of Tlevak Narrows.
Chart 17407
Entrance: 55°09.58' N, 133°03.32' W
Anchor: 55°09.52' N, 133°06.43' W

We have found good fair-weather anchorage here and would consider it as an emergency shelter under some circumstances. The head of the bay in the lee of the large island is nearly landlocked. However, you need to avoid many charted and uncharted isolated rocks. As with much of Dall Island, the charting in these bays is incomplete or inaccurate, requiring vigilant piloting when entering. The beach is relatively log-free even though logging has left the shore in a shambles.

Anchor in 4 fathoms over an irregular rocky mixed bottom; fair-to-good holding with a well-set anchor.

## Island Bay (Sukkwan Island)
Island Bay is just north of Dunbar Inlet.
Chart 17408
Entrance: 55°05.57' N, 132°52.23' W
Anchor (north basin): 55°05.65' N, 132°51.40' W
Anchor: 55°05.32' N, 132°51.15' W

*Stellar Sea Lion*

Island Bay has a nice, intimate feel and anchor sites are limited only by your imagination.

Anchor (north basin) in 6 fathoms over a thin layer of mud with fair holding.

## Dunbar Inlet (Sukkwan Island)
Dunbar Inlet is 15 miles southeast of Tlevak Narrows.
Chart 17408
Entrance: 55°04.41' N, 132°52.32' W
Anchor (head of bay): 55°05.40' N, 132°48.95' W
Anchor: 55°05.20' N, 132°50.18' W

Dunbar Inlet has a somewhat tricky entrance. However, the effort is well worth it. There is good shelter from all weather and plenty of swinging room over a flat bottom. This is one of the better anchor sites in a southeast gale for the greater Tlevak Strait/Cordova Bay area.

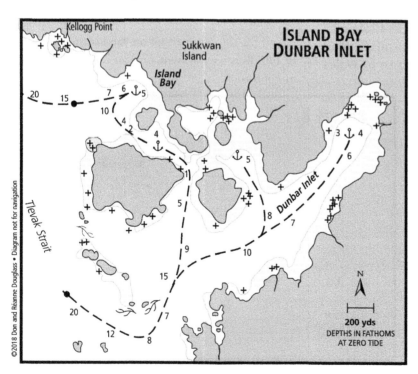

Anchor (head of bay) in 4 fathoms over sand and mud with good holding.

## Baldy Bay (Dall Island)
Baldy Bay is 2 miles southwest of the McFarland Islands.
Chart 17409
Entrance (View Cove Entrance Light bearing 000°T at 0.5 Nm): 55°02.65' N, 132°57.89' W

Baldy Bay is the largest inlet on the east shore of Dall Island. The large northwest arm is called View Cove. Coco Harbor is the well protected but deep arm to the west. Windy Cove, the south arm, is surrounded by high ridges.

Baldy Bay and its main arms are entered north of Reef Islands. Entrance Island can be passed on either side, but a mid-channel approach is required to avoid the off-lying rocks surrounding the island and along both shores. The anchorages in Baldy Bay are mostly deep and not strongly recommended. Because of the low pass in View Cove leading to the west side of Dall Island, winds rip through the area. We recommend Dunbar Inlet, 6 miles northeast, as a more satisfactory anchorage for small craft.

## View Cove (Dall Island)
View Cove is in Baldy Bay.
Chart 17408
Entrance: 55°03.42′ N, 132°59.52′ W

View Cove is open to the southeast; gales rip through the cove and into Manhattan Arm on the west side of Dall Island. Turn inside the reef light, north of a 7.5 fathom shoal, and find 10 fathoms. There is an old wharf on the north side below the clear-cut area. Karst formations are visible along the north shore.

*A classic fishing boat on the west side of Prince of Wales Island*

## Green Inlet (View Cove)
Green Inlet is on the south shore of View Cove.
Chart 17408
Entrance: 55°03.92′ N, 133°01.91′ W
Anchor: 55°03.52′ N, 133°02.23′ W

A sand bar awash at zero tide obstructs the entrance to Green Inlet, but inside is a well-protected anchorage for several small craft. Avoid the rocks at the inlet entrance.

Anchor in 3 fathoms over grass, mud and shells with fair-to-good holding.

## Windy Cove (Dall Island)
Windy Cove is 2 miles west northwest of High Point.
Chart 17408
Entrance: 55°02.15′ N, 133°01.58′ W

Windy Cove is landlocked. Although its name suggests the presence of williwaws, we would consider it for anchorage. The water is deep once you have passed the entrance bar. A mud shoal extends from the head of the cove to where 2.3 fathoms is shown on Chart 17408. A stern-tie to shore may be required.

## Reef Islands Inlet (Baldy Bay)
Reef Islands Inlet lies south of Reef Islands west of High Point.
Chart 17408
Entrance (View Cove Entrance Light bearing 000°T at 0.5 Nm): 55°02.65′ N, 132°57.89′ W
Entrance (West Arm, Reef Island Inlet): 55°01.57′ N, 132°58.81′ W
Anchor (East Arm): 55°00.91′ N, 132°58.90′ W
Anchor (West Arm, Reef Island Inlet): 55°00.82′ N, 132°59.85′ W

Reef Islands Inlet is the unnamed inlet south of Reef Islands and to the west of High Point.

The East Arm can accommodate just one or two small boats, and a shore tie may be needed. West Arm has slightly more swinging room. As you enter East Arm, favor the eastern shore to avoid the mid-channel rock in the center of the entrance.

Anchor (west arm) in 5 to 10 fathoms over mud with good holding.

Anchor (east arm) between the west islet and the avalanche chute in about 5 fathoms over

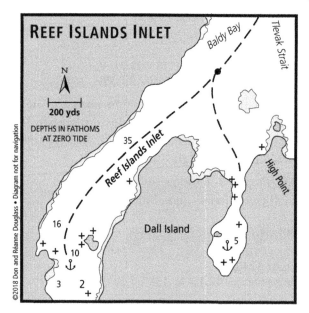

*The sad remains of better days*

mud with good holding but limited swinging room.

## Kaigani Strait

Kaigani Strait, south of Tlevak Strait, separates Long Island and the island groups to the northwest of it from Dall Island.
Charts 17408, 17400
North entrance: 55°00.28' N, 132°55.92' W
South entrance: 54°43.89' N, 132°39.09' W

## Howkan Narrows

Howkan Narrows lies at the south end of Kaigani Strait.
Chart 17409
North entrance (Howkan Narrows): 54°52.90' N, 132°50.00' W
South entrance (Howkan Narrows): 54°51.59' N, 132°48.34' W

Kaigani Strait and Howkan Narrows are small-craft waterways. The currents are moderate; watch for isolated shoals and turbulent water.

## Ham Cove (Dall Island)

Ham Cove is 0.8 mile west of the Channel Islands.
Chart 17408
Entrance: 54°53.09' N, 132°50.88' W
Anchor: 54°52.86' N, 132°51.25' W

Ham Cove is a small, rocky site with shallow water for small craft.

We like its shelter; however, swinging room is limited and finding the right place to anchor can be a challenge.

Anchor in 5 fathoms over sand, gravel and newspaper kelp with poor holding unless well set.

## American Bay (Dall Island)

American Bay is 12 miles north of Cape Muzon.
Chart 17409
Entrance: 54°51.05' N, 132°48.46' W
Anchor (east of Bay Islands): 54°51.10' N, 132°49.13' W
Anchor (west of Bay Islands): 54°50.99' N, 132°49.73' W

American Bay is somewhat sheltered by Howkan Narrows and anchorage can be found close-in along the north shore.

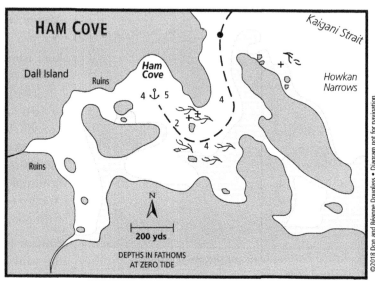

Anchor (either side of Bay Islands) in 5 to 10 fathoms.

### Bolles Inlet (Long Island)
Bolles Inlet is 2 miles east of American Bay.
Chart 17409
Entrance: 54°50.30′ N, 132°44.48′ W

Bolles Inlet is uncharted and looks quite interesting to explore. The east shore is just ¼ mile from Coning Inlet on the east side of Long Island.

### Pond Bay (Dall Island)
Pond Bay is 9 miles north of Cape Muzon.
Chart 17409
Entrance: 54°48.77′ N, 132°44.76′ W
Anchor: 54°48.49′ N, 132°46.66′ W

Pond Bay appears to provide good anchorage, except in southeast winds, but it is poorly charted. Its south shore, in the lee of the second or third island, may provide adequate shelter. The bottom appears rocky and lined with kelp, so more exploring is required. A stern-tie to shore would be advisable.

Anchor in about 10 fathoms over a thin layer of sand and mud with poor-to-fair holding.

### New Prop Cove (Dall Island)
New Prop Cove is 7 miles north of Cape Muzon.
Chart 17409
Entrance: 54°46.67′ N, 132°43.41′ W

"New Prop Cove" is our name for this small bight. The chart for the area is very poorly drawn and, to our dismay, we found a rocky pile lurking just below the surface on the north side of the entrance islet (110) and we had to limp into Ketchikan for repairs to our prop. The extensive reefs and kelp seem to provide good shelter for small craft along its south shore, but we suggest avoiding New Prop Cove until it is more adequately charted. South Kaigani Harbor is a better choice.

### South Kaigani Harbor (Dall Island)
South Kaigani Harbor is 5.5 miles north of Cape Muzon.
Chart 17409
Entrance: 54°45.18′ N, 132°43.41′ W
Anchor: 54°45.39′ N, 132°44.88′ W

The south basin of South Kaigani Harbor offers good shelter for two or three small vessels. *Coast Pilot* mentions several hazards. The south cove has been used in the past as a fly-in fishing resort and has a private float, buoy and pilings.

Locals say that the cove is secure in 40-knot southeast winds. We found anchoring near the center of the cove quite satisfactory.

Anchor in 6 fathoms over mud with good holding.

### Datzkoo Harbor (Dall Island)
Datzkoo Harbor is 5 miles north of Cape Muzon.
Chart 17409
Entrance: 54°44.41′ N, 132°43.17′ W
Anchor: 54°44.73′ N, 132°45.89′ W

An anchorage can be found 200 yards east of the small islet at the head of the bay.

Anchor in 10 to 12 fathoms over a soft, thin bottom with fair holding.

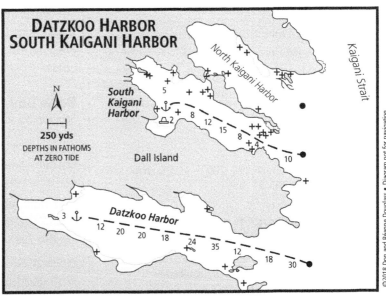

*The very beautiful Bobs Bay*

The west coast of Dall Island is exposed to the full force of the Gulf of Alaska. Its unique topography is similar to that of south Baranof Island. Bold headlands with karst formations here and there can be spotted through the trees along shore. Dall's many deep inlets surrounded by high peaks and ridges remain some of the least frequented cruising grounds and are an "undiscovered treasure." However, navigating along this coast is a constant challenge.

### Little Daykoo Harbor (Dall Island)
Little Daykoo Harbor is 2.5 miles north of Cape Muzon.
Chart 17409
Entrance: 54°42.35' N, 132°41.95' W

Little Daykoo Harbor may offer good shelter to small boats, but it looks like a rock pile to us.

### McLeod Bay (Dall Island)
McLeod Bay is 2 miles north of Cape Muzon.
Chart 17409
Entrance: 54°41.62' N, 132°41.90' W

The chart indicates that the bay is an unused submarine cable area. We cannot recommend this bay, since it's totally open to southeast winds and chop.

### Cape Muzon (Dall Island)
Cape Muzon is the south extremity of Dall Island.
Charts 17409, 17400
Position (Muzon Light brg 000°T at 1.0 Nm): 54°38.82' N, 132°41.51' W

## DALL ISLAND WEST COAST, FROM NORTH TO SOUTH
Dall Island is about 40 miles long from Eagle Point, its northwest extremity in Meares Passage, to Cape Muzon.
Chart 17400

### Meares Passage (Dall Island)
Meares Passage, at the northwest end of Dall Island, lies between Dall and Suemez islands.
Chart 17407
North entrance (between Suemez and Dall islands): 55°16.58' N, 133°11.69' W
South entrance (Diver Islands Light bearing 090°T at 0.9 Nm): 55°10.68' N, 133°17.52' W

Meares Passage connects Craig to the 40-mile-long west coast of Dall Island. Ocean swells are not prevalent until you are south of Millar Rocks and Divers islands. Meares Passage has obstructions at both ends, as noted on the chart.

### Bobs Bay (Dall Island)
Bobs Bay is 4 miles south of Meares Island.
Chart 17407
Entrance: 55°11.15' N, 133°14.73' W
Entrance (east arm): 55°11.64' N, 133°11.93' W
Anchor (east arm): 55°11.78' N, 133°10.12' W

Bobs Bay at the northwest end of Dall Island is an almost landlocked bay offering very good shelter deep in the East Arm.

Anchor in 4 to 8 fathoms over mud bottom with good holding.

## Diver Bay (Dall Island)
Diver Bay is 6 miles south of Meares Island.
Chart 17407
Entrance: 55°10.54' N, 133°14.45' W

## Hole in the Wall (Diver Bay)
Hole in the Wall is on the north side of Diver Bay.
Chart 17407
Entrance: 55°10.32' N, 133°12.39' W
Anchor: 55°10.50' N, 133°11.95' W

Hole in the Wall is a quintessential bowl-shaped Alaskan anchorage, fully protected from outside weather. Swells that decrease as you enter Diver Bay do not enter Hole in the Wall. As you traverse Diver Bay, watch carefully to avoid crab pots.

The entrance fairway to Hole in the Wall is about 40 feet wide with shallowest depths approximately 4 fathoms at its east end. Favor the north shore slightly to avoid a rocky spit at the east end. We prefer to anchor deep in the cove near the south shore in 2 to 3 fathoms, while local fishing boats tend to anchor along the north shore, closer to the entrance.

Anchor in 3 to 5 fathoms over sticky, soft, brown mud and sand with shells; very good holding.

## Foul Bay (Dall Island)
Foul Bay is 8 miles south of Meares Island.
Chart 17407
Entrance: 55°08.42' N, 133°13.50' W

Although some shelter may be available behind the reefs in Foul Bay, its entrance, which opens directly to the west, is intimidating and not often used even by local fishermen due to its threatening lee shore.

## Hook Arm (Sea Otter Harbor)
Hook Arm is the north arm of Sea Otter Harbor.
Chart 17408
Entrance: 55°06.86' N, 133°11.89' W
Anchor (Channel Island bight): 55°07.74' N, 133°09.89' W

Hook Arm, surrounded by high ridges 3 miles northeast of Cape Lookout, is a convenient shelter for exploring this part of the coast.

*Approaching Hole in the Wall*

---

# Port Bazan
## (First Mate's Diary)
### Réanne Hemingway-Douglass

The weather was picking by mid-afternoon today so, after passing up Welcome Cove (a shallow rock pile), we ran into Waterfall Bay, which is absolutely gorgeous. There's a lovely, high waterfall along the north side of the inlet and another smaller one at the head of the bay—hidden from view into until you're practically on it. The little bight of the bay into which this second cascade drops is where *Coast Pilot* says small craft could anchor. It was way too small for us, though, and we guess only a boat smaller than 30 feet could possibly fit.

We would have loved to spend the night there, soothed by the sound of the two falls, but the depths are too great for us to anchor conveniently. Our next try was Gooseneck Harbor, whose rock-infested entrance is harrowing. By the time we'd made three attempts to set anchor, williwaws were sending gusts of 30 to 35 knots and setting *Baidarka* toward the rocks. "I don't like this!" I shouted to Don. "Let's go on to Port Bazan."

So we raised anchor for the last time and brought up a 200-pound rock that took us 30 minutes to dislodge. When we finally anchored in Bazan it was 1608. Ten hours of work today. It's amazing how much mental energy we expend in a day like this. We had a Cup O' Soup tonight. I was too exhausted to cook.

### Manhattan Arm (Sea Otter Harbor)
Manhattan Arm is the southeast branch of Sea Otter Harbor.
Chart 17408
Entrance: 55°06.57' N, 133°11.71' W

Manhattan Arm lines up with View Cove on the east side of Dall Island to funnel southeast winds with great velocity.

### Sakie Bay (Dall Island)
Sakie Bay is 13 miles south of Meares Island.
Chart 17408
Entrance: 55°04.10' N, 133°13.35' W

Sakie Bay gets the full blast of northwesterlies, but it appears to offer fair shelter in southerly winds. Tide rips suggest an irregular bottom that has not been adequately surveyed. We would use Hook Arm or Waterfall Bay.

### Fisherman Cove (Dall Island)
Fisherman Cove is 15 miles south of Meares Island.
Chart 17408
Entrance: 55°01.23' N, 133°10.57' W
Anchor: 55°01.77' N, 133°10.05' W

Fisherman Cove offers temporary anchorage in fair summer weather only.

### Welcome Cove (Dall Island)
Welcome Cove is 1.5 miles north of Cape Augustine.
Chart 17408
Entrance: 54°58.38' N, 133°09.95' W

Welcome Cove is a misnomer as far as we are concerned. Not only is the cove poorly charted, but its entrance is so encumbered with rocks that, upon an attempt to reconnoiter in *Baidarka*, the bow watch (first mate) screamed, "Get out of here; it's too shallow!" Pass it up and leave it to small, local runabouts.

### Augustine Bay (Dall Island)
Augustine Bay is 18.5 miles south of Meares Island.
Chart 17408
Entrance: 54°57.57' N, 133°09.89' W

Anchor in 8 to 12 fathoms on the north side of Channel Island over a mixed bottom; fair-to-good holding.

Augustine Bay is open to the full force of Gulf of Alaska weather and is poorly charted. We do not recommend it as an anchorage.

### Waterfall Bay (Dall Island)
Waterfall Bay is 20 miles south of Meares Island.
Chart 17408
Entrance (Gourd Island bearing 070°T at 0.35 Nm): 54°56.54' N, 133°07.76' W
Anchor (north of north island): 54°57.04' N, 133°06.85' W
Anchor (east bight): 54°56.83' N, 133°03.08' W

Waterfall Bay, immediately south of Cape Augustine, is ringed by high peaks with steep-sided shores. Waterfall Bay is one of the most stunning inlets along Dall Island's west coast and deserves a stop. However, depths are so great that vessels under 70 feet may have trouble finding a good place to drop anchor. We have taken rest breaks here but, despite its beauty, we preferred not to remain overnight. The small bight at the head of the bay is suitable only for a single vessel under 30 feet.

### Gooseneck Harbor (Dall Island)
Gooseneck Harbor is 18 miles northwest of Cape Muzon and 23.5 miles south of Meares Island.
Chart 17408
Entrance: 54°53.01' N, 133°03.19' W
Anchor: 54°53.53' N, 133°00.50' W

> *The upper half of the harbor is mostly obstructed by bare rocks and ledges, and the head is especially foul. . . . In entering, follow the N shore at a distance of about 250 yards until about 1 mile inside. After rounding the point on the N side, find anchorage for small craft 100 yards off the N shore, 1.5 miles within the entrance.* (CP)

Gooseneck Harbor looks like our kind of place—landlocked by dozens of islets and rocks that cut down the swell, yet providing a scenic and vital view of what is occurring outside. High ridges surround the harbor bowl, deflecting the winds in unusual directions. Gooseneck Harbor is a lovely "bay of islands" and rocks topped with tufts of shrubs and small trees. However, its entrance is daunting and depths do not agree with those shown on the chart. (We found 3.2 fathoms where the chart shows 7 fathoms.)

In addition, the bottom is so rocky and irregular we could not get our 110-pound Bruce anchor to set despite several attempts. On our final try, we decided to move south to Port Bazan.

Anchor in about 7 fathoms over a very hard bottom with poor holding.

## Port Bazan (Dall Island)
Port Bazan is 14 miles northwest of Cape Muzon and 28 miles south of Meares Island.
Chart 17409
Northwest entrance: 54°49.57' N, 133°00.15' W
Anchor (in the lee of north center island):
54°50.63' N, 132°56.48' W

Port Bazan, on the south side of Cape Magdalena, is landlocked by large Dolgoi Island at its entrance. You can enter the port by passages on either the north or south side. A careful mid-channel course is required to avoid the submerged rocks lying along the route.

Once you are east of Dolgoi, the swells drop to nil, and very good shelter can be found on the north side of the north island.

Anchor in about 10 fathoms over brown, sticky (and stinky!) mud, with very good holding.

## Liscome Bay (Dall Island)
Liscome Bay is 5 miles northwest of Cape Muzon.
Chart 17409
Entrance: 54°41.38' N, 132°48.78' W
Anchor: 54°42.65' N, 132°48.94' W

Liscome Bay is sheltered from northwest weather, but it is open to the full effects of the south. Temporary anchorage for small craft is reported at the head of the bay.

Anchor in about 8 fathoms over an unrecorded bottom.

## FINIS
Congratulations!

If you have voyaged along Alaska's Inside Passage or down the rugged and isolated west coast, you have experienced one of Earth's premier cruising frontiers.

*Blow holes and flukes—the mighty whales are in action*

# Appendices and References

## APPENDIX A
### Suggested Itineraries for the Inside Passage to Alaska

Although this cruising guide begins in northern British Columbia and includes all of Southeast Alaska, we want to give you our suggested itineraries for cruising the Inside Passage all the way from Seattle, Washington, through Southeast Alaska. We hope you will consider this an added bonus to the book.

These itineraries are just examples of many possible schedules. The length of time you have available, your average cruising speeds and your choice of actual anchor sites will depend on the weather, as well as your own needs and values. We offer these ideas as a planning tool, not as something to follow rigidly.

The more time you can allow for your cruise, the better. Most boaters we've talked to wish they had allowed more time for the passage; many intend to, or actually do, return year after year.

As examples of some of the speediest passages possible, Alaska tugs run twenty-four hours a day, making the Seattle-Juneau-Seattle round-trip in fewer than ten days. A professional skipper who delivers small vessels from Anacortes to Juneau typically takes eight days, running at 10 knots during daylight hours.

For pleasure cruising, we find that less strenuous round-trips of four, six, eight and twelve weeks are most common, with average daily runs of 30 to 75 nautical miles the norm. Add more time if you have a slow boat, a small sailboat with an outboard, or if you simply want a more leisurely trip.

These suggested itineraries give typical daily runs and anchor sites, but they do not include layover days for shore activities, bad weather, or crew needs. You should plan for these contingencies, and adapt your schedule to the particular situation.

When conditions are favorable, you can frequently extend a day's run and accumulate layover days for the future. Then, if conditions deteriorate during a day's run, you can duck into a nearby cove without jeopardizing the overall pace of your trip. The lengthy daylight hours on the Inside Passage in summer (see Duration of Daylight in Appendix E) usually give you time to stop for a few hours to fish, to go ashore, or to take a rest at midday before you push on in the afternoon.

# "Ultra Marathon" Itinerary

**Rapid out-and-back trip to Juneau and Sitka**
**Four weeks (28 days) minimum**

*Features:*
Direct ferry route to Juneau with side trips to Tracy Arm to visit glaciers and icebergs, and to Sitka and major hot springs

*Total distance:*
2,030 miles

*Average daily run:*
75 miles

*Advantages:*
For fast boats having minimal time to "do Alaska"

*Feasibility:*
Suitable for well-equipped offshore cruising boats with a cruising speed in excess of 10 knots; good radar and GPS are mandatory.

*Best time:*
Mid-June to mid-July (longest days, least fog); requires stable weather conditions (see notes below under Planning Tips).

*Anchoring required:*
One-third of the time or less; this route offers the possibility of staying at marinas, government float docks or public mooring buoys a majority of the time.

| Day | Destination | Distance |
|---|---|---|
| Day 1 | Anacortes to Nanaimo | 78 mi. |
| Day 2 | to Campbell River | 84 mi. |
| Day 3 | to Port McNeill | 93 mi. |
| Day 4 | to Inner Warrior Cove | 85 mi. |
| Day 5 | to Goat Harbour | 78 mi. |
| Day 6 | to Lowe Inlet | 67 mi. |
| Day 7 | to Prince Rupert | 65 mi. |
| Day 8 | to Ketchikan | 85 mi. |
| Day 9 | to Wrangell | 95 mi. |
| Day 10 | to Entrance Island, Hobart Bay | 92 mi. |
| Day 11 | to Taku Harbor via Tracy Arm, Sawyer Glacier | 94 mi. |
| Day 12 | to Auke Bay via Juneau | 35 mi. |
| Day 13 | layover | |
| Day 14 | to Tenakee Hot Springs | 63 mi. |
| Day 15 | to Sitka via Peril Strait | 90 mi. |
| Day 16 | to Little Bear Cove | 32 mi. |
| Day 17 | to Baranof Warm Springs | 55 mi. |
| Day 18 | to Petersburg | 77 mi. |
| Day 19 | to Meyers Chuck via Wrangell Narrows | 79 mi. |
| Day 20 | to Ketchikan | 33 mi. |
| Day 21 | to Prince Rupert | 85 mi. |
| Day 22 | to Bishop Bay Hot Springs | 93 mi. |
| Day 23 | to Oliver Cove | 85 mi. |
| Day 24 | to Millbrook Cove | 78 mi. |
| Day 25 | to Port Neville | 97 mi. |
| Day 26 | to Campbell River | 50 mi. |
| Day 27 | to Nanaimo | 84 mi. |
| Day 28 | to Anacortes | 78 mi. |

# "The Highlights" Itinerary

**Fast round-trip to Juneau, Sitka and Glacier Bay**
**Six weeks (42 days) minimum**

*Features:*
Conventional ferry/cruise ship route including Tracy Arm and Glacier Bay to visit tidewater glaciers and icebergs, hot springs and Sitka

*Total Distance:*
2,156 miles

*Average daily run:*
53 miles

*Advantages:*
A fast trip for most small boats. Gives highlights of the Inside Passage for those with limited time; an introduction to scenic and historical opportunities.

*Feasibility:*
Suitable for well-equipped cruising boats with a cruising speed of 7 to 8 knots or more; radar necessary; GPS recommended.

*Best time:*
Early June to late-July (long days; least fog); requires stable weather conditions.

*Anchoring required:*
60 percent of the time

| Day 1 | Anacortes to Montague via Pender Island | 47 mi. |
|---|---|---|
| Day 2 | to Scottie Bay | 65 mi. |
| Day 3 | to Campbell River | 48 mi. |
| Day 4 | to Port Neville | 50 mi. |
| Day 5 | to Port Hardy | 61 mi. |
| Day 6 | to Fury Island Cove | 55 mi. |
| Day 7 | to Oliver Cove | 62 mi. |
| Day 8 | to Goat Harbour | 41 mi. |
| Day 9 | to Bishop Bay Hot Springs | 52 mi. |
| Day 10 | to East Inlet | 56 mi. |
| Day 11 | to Prince Rupert | 57 mi. |
| Day 12 | to Foggy Bay | 50 mi. |
| Day 13 | to Ketchikan | 34 mi. |
| Day 14 | to Santa Anna Inlet | 55 mi. |
| Day 15 | to Deception Cove via Wrangell | 57 mi. |
| Day 16 | to Entrance Island, Hobart Bay | 70 mi. |
| Day 17 | to Tracy Arm Cove via Sawyer Glacier | 48 mi. |
| Day 18 | to Juneau | 42 mi. |
| Day 19 | layover | |
| Day 20 | to Swanson Harbor | 51 mi. |
| Day 21 | to North Sandy Cove, Glacier Bay via headquarters | 59 mi. |
| Day 22 | to North Sandy Cove via Muir Glacier | 46 mi. |
| Day 23 | to Swanson Harbor | 51 mi. |
| Day 24 | to Appleton Cove | 65 mi. |
| Day 25 | to Sitka | 51 mi. |
| Day 26 | to Ell Cove | 68 mi. |
| Day 27 | to Portage Bay | 61 mi. |
| Day 28 | to St. John Harbor | 48 mi. |
| Day 29 | to Meyers Chuck | 54 mi. |
| Day 30 | to Ketchikan | 34 mi. |
| Day 31 | to Foggy Bay | 33 mi. |
| Day 32 | to Prince Rupert | 50 mi. |
| Day 33 | to Lowe Inlet | 60 mi. |
| Day 34 | to Goat Harbour | 61 mi. |
| Day 35 | to Oliver Cove | 38 mi. |
| Day 36 | to Fury Island | 55 mi. |
| Day 37 | to Blunden Harbour | 50 mi. |
| Day 38 | to Minstrel Island | 45 mi. |
| Day 39 | to Turn Island Cove | 45 mi. |
| Day 40 | to Sandy Island Marine Park | 57 mi. |
| Day 41 | to Pirates Cove | 62 mi. |
| Day 42 | to Anacortes | 62 mi. |

## "The Classic" Itinerary

**The full round-trip route to most scenic areas and introduction to the Outer Passage**
**Eight weeks (60 days) minimum**

*Features:*
Includes scenic routes such as Fiordland, Misty Fiords, Tracy Arm and Glacier Bay, Lynn Canal and Skagway; north portion of the Outer Passage from Glacier Bay to Milbanke Sound.

*Total distance:*
2,507 miles

*Average daily run:*
42 miles

*Advantages:*
Less hurried, but still a quick pace with a chance to explore some scenic, historic and out-of-the-way places; allows a wider choice of favorable transit times

*Feasibility:*
Suitable for well-equipped cruising boats with a cruising speed of 6 knots or more; radar and GPS recommended.

*Best time:*
Early June to late August (best weather, long days)

*Anchoring required:*
One-third of the time with a few nights at marinas or public floats

| Day 1 | Anacortes to Stuart Island | 32 mi. |
|---|---|---|
| Day 2 | to Pirates Cove | 36 mi. |
| Day 3 | to Scottie Bay | 43 mi. |
| Day 4 | to Mitlenatch Island | 37 mi. |
| Day 5 | to Turn Island Cove | 33 mi. |
| Day 6 | to Cutter Cove | 47 mi. |
| Day 7 | to Blunden Harbour | 45 mi. |
| Day 8 | to Millbrook Cove | 38 mi. |
| Day 9 | to Warrior Cove | 37 mi. |

| | | |
|---|---|---|
| Day 10 to Oliver Cove | 45 mi. |
| Day 11 to Windy Bay | 42 mi. |
| Day 12 to Bishop Bay Hot Springs | 51 mi. |
| Day 13 to Lowe Inlet | 45 mi. |
| Day 14 to Lawson Harbour | 43 mi. |
| Day 15 to Prince Rupert | 19 mi. |
| Day 16 to Tongass Island Cove | 43 mi. |
| Day 17 to Ketchikan | 52 mi. |
| Day 18 to Shoalwater Pass via Misty Fiords | 40 mi. |
| Day 19 to Yes Bay via Saks Cove | 60 mi. |
| Day 20 to Moser Bay | 40 mi. |
| Day 21 to Vixen Harbor | 41 mi. |
| Day 22 to Wrangell | 45 mi. |
| Day 23 to Ruth Cove | 63 mi. |
| Day 24 to Entrance Island, Hobart Bay | 47 mi. |
| Day 25 to Tracy Arm Cove via Sawyer Glacier | 70 mi. |
| Day 26 to Juneau | 42 mi. |
| Day 27 to Auke Bay | 15 mi. |
| Day 28 to Sullivan Island, Lynn Canal, Rescue Harbor | 43 mi. |
| Day 29 to Skagway | 32 mi. |
| Day 30 to Boat Harbor or St. James Bay | 48 mi. |
| Day 31 to Pleasant Island Bight | 47 mi. |
| Day 32 to North Sandy Cove, Glacier Bay | 38 mi. |
| Day 33 to North Sandy Cove via Muir Glacier | 45 mi. |
| Day 34 to North Inian Island | 38 mi. |
| Day 35 to Lost Cove, Lisianski Strait | 33 mi. |
| Day 36 to Double Cove | 26 mi. |
| Day 37 to Sitka | 44 mi. |
| Day 38 to "Annie's Pocket" | 34 mi. |
| Day 39 to Baranof Warm Springs | 53 mi. |
| Day 40 to Stedman Cove via Kake | 42 mi. |
| Day 41 to Port Protection via Rocky Pass | 38 mi. |
| Day 42 to Kahli Cove | 42 mi. |
| Day 43 to Craig | 42 mi. |
| Day 44 to Eek Inlet | 43 mi. |
| Day 45 to Charlie's Cove | 26 mi. |
| Day 46 to Nichols Bay | 20 mi. |
| Day 47 to Prince Rupert | 68 mi. |
| Day 48 to Captain Cove | 38 mi. |
| Day 49 to Patterson Inlet | 33 mi. |
| Day 50 to Helmcken Island Cove | 52 mi. |
| Day 51 to Kynumpt Harbour via Higgins Passage | 53 mi. |
| Day 52 to Goldstream Harbour | 41 mi. |
| Day 53 to Millbrook Cove | 30 mi. |
| Day 54 to Blunden Harbour | 38 mi. |
| Day 55 to Cutter Cove | 45 mi. |
| Day 56 to Turn Island Cove | 47 mi. |
| Day 57 to Sandy Island Marine Park | 53 mi. |
| Day 58 to Nanaimo | 49 mi. |
| Day 59 to Friday Harbor (or Roche Harbor) | 55 mi. |
| Day 60 to Anacortes | 20 mi. |

## "Dream" Itinerary

**Off-the-beaten-path round-trip with exposure to full Outer Passage**
**Three months (97 days or more) minimum**

*Features:*
Ultra-scenic route includes Nakwakto Rapids, the top hot springs, Fiordland, Misty Fiords, Tracy Arm and Glacier Bay, Lynn Canal and Skagway; full West Coast Outer Passage, including Vancouver Island's West Coast

*Total distance:*
3,006 miles

*Average daily run:*
31 miles

*Advantages:*
Self-paced immersion trip for those who want to do the Inside Passage to Alaska "right," with time to explore the West Coast Outer Passage and to visit the Northwest's secluded spots and major scenic and historical places; can be undertaken by most well-equipped cruising boats

*Feasibility:*
Suitable for boats equipped for extended travel with a cruising speed of 5 knots or more; radar and GPS recommended

*Best time:*
Mid-May to early September

Anchoring required:
80 percent or more of the time in secluded coves, off the beaten path; balance as desired at public mooring buoys or public floats

| | | | | | | |
|---|---|---|---|---|---|---|
| Day 1 | Anacortes to Stuart Island | 32 mi. | | Day 44 | to Skagway | 32 mi. |
| Day 2 | to Princess Bay, Wallace Island | 25 mi. | | Day 45 | to Boat Harbor or St. James Bay | 48 mi. |
| Day 3 | to Nanaimo | 28 mi. | | Day 46 | to Swanson Harbor | 29 mi. |
| Day 4 | to Scottie Bay | 33 mi. | | Day 47 | to Pleasant Island | 19 mi. |
| Day 5 | to Copeland Islands | 35 mi. | | Day 48 | to N. Sandy Cove | 40 mi. |
| Day 6 | to Thurston Bay via Yuculta Rapids | 43 mi. | | Day 49 | to N. Sandy Cove via Muir Glacier | 45 mi. |
| Day 7 | to Port Neville | 34 mi. | | Day 50 | to Russell Island Cove via Grand Pacific Glacier and Margerie Glacier | 52 mi. |
| Day 8 | to Mamalilaculla | 37 mi. | | | | |
| Day 9 | to Cypress Harbour | 25 mi. | | | | |
| Day 10 | to Blunden Harbour | 30 mi. | | Day 51 | to Blue Mouse Cove via Hopkins Glacier | 37 mi. |
| Day 11 | to Goose Point Cove (Nakwakto Rapids) | 18 mi. | | Day 52 | to North Inian Island | 46 mi. |
| Day 12 | to Miles Inlet via Seymour Inlet | 13 mi. | | Day 53 | to Lost Cove, Lisianski Strait | 33 mi. |
| Day 13 | to Millbrook Cove via Indian Island Cove | 29 mi. | | Day 54 | to Mirror Harbor, White Sulphur Springs | 12 mi. |
| Day 14 | to Joe's Bay, Fish Egg Inlet | 26 mi. | | Day 55 | to Double Cove | 20 mi. |
| Day 15 | to Codville Lagoon | 33 mi. | | Day 56 | to Whitestone Cove | 28 mi. |
| Day 16 | to Ocean Falls via McKenzie Rock | 46 mi. | | Day 57 | to Sitka | 15 mi. |
| | | | | Day 58 | to "Annie's Pocket" | 34 mi. |
| Day 17 | to Troup Narrows (Deer Passage) | 24 mi. | | Day 59 | to Ell Cove | 46 mi. |
| Day 18 | to Rescue Bay | 38 mi. | | Day 60 | to Baranof Warm Springs | 13 mi. |
| Day 19 | to Windy Bay via waterfall and Fiordland | 40 mi. | | Day 61 | to "Honeydew Cove" | 22 mi. |
| | | | | Day 62 | to "Baidarka Anchorage" via Kake | 34 mi. |
| Day 20 | to Swanson Bay | 23 mi. | | | | |
| Day 21 | to Bishop Hot Springs | 36 mi. | | Day 63 | to Hole in the Wall (Prince of Wales Island) | 28 mi. |
| Day 22 | to Sue Channel via Weewanie Hot Springs | 25 mi. | | | | |
| | | | | Day 64 | to Devilfish Bay | 28 mi. |
| Day 23 | to Coghlan Anchorage | 28 mi. | | Day 65 | to Bob's Place | 38 mi. |
| Day 24 | to East Inlet | 33 mi. | | Day 66 | to Craig via Klawock | 24 mi. |
| Day 25 | to Lawson Harbour | 33 mi. | | Day 67 | to South Pass Cove | 33 mi. |
| Day 26 | to Prince Rupert | 19 mi. | | Day 68 | to Charlie's Cove | 37 mi. |
| Day 27 | to Tongass Island Cove | 43 mi. | | Day 69 | to Nichols Bay | 20 mi. |
| Day 28 | to Foggy Bay via Very Inlet | 28 mi. | | Day 70 | to Prince Rupert via Duke Island and Foggy Bay if necessary | 68 mi. |
| Day 29 | to Ketchikan | 37 mi. | | | | |
| Day 30 | to Carp Island | 32 mi. | | Day 71 | to Captains Cove | 38 mi. |
| Day 31 | to Manzanita Bay via Rudyard Bay | 40 mi. | | Day 72 | to Patterson Inlet | 33 mi. |
| | | | | Day 73 | to Weinberg Inlet | 27 mi. |
| Day 32 | to Yes Bay | 48 mi. | | Day 74 | to Helmcken Island Cove | 30 mi. |
| Day 33 | to Meyers Chuck | 48 mi. | | Day 75 | to Oliver Cove | 45 mi. |
| Day 34 | to Frosty Bay | 25 mi. | | Day 76 | to Rock Inlet Cove | 42 mi. |
| Day 35 | to Wrangell | 30 mi. | | Day 77 | to Millbrook Cove (return to San Juans Islands via east or west coast of Vancouver Island. We suggest West Coast of Vancouver Island.) | 40 mi. |
| Day 36 | to Petersburg | 40 mi. | | | | |
| Day 37 | to Fanshaw | 38 mi. | | | | |
| Day 38 | to Tracy Arm Cove | 40 mi. | | | | |
| Day 39 | to Tracy Arm Cove via Sawyer Glacier | 40 mi. | | | | |
| | | | | Day 78 | to Bull Harbour | 33 mi. |
| Day 40 | to Taku Harbor | 25 mi. | | Day 79 | to Sea Otter Cove | 32 mi. |
| Day 41 | to Juneau | 20 mi. | | Day 80 | to Winter Harbour | 26 mi. |
| Day 42 | to Auke Bay | 19 mi. | | Day 81 | to Klaskino Inlet | 19 mi. |
| Day 43 | to Rescue Harbor | 43 mi. | | Day 82 | to Klaskish Inlet | 12 mi. |

## "Dream" Itinerary (Continued)

| | | |
|---|---|---|
| Day 83 to Baidarka Cove | 23 mi. | |
| Day 84 to Gay Passage | 10 mi. | |
| Day 85 to Petroglyph Cove | 17 mi. | |
| Day 86 to Queen Cove | 23 mi. | |
| Day 87 to Friendly Cove (Yuquot) | 30 mi. | |
| Day 88 to Hot Springs Cove | 30 mi. | |
| Day 89 to Little White Pine Cove | 19 mi. | |
| Day 90 to Adventure Cove via Tofino | 20 mi. | |
| Day 91 to Ucluelet | 32 mi. | |
| Day 92 to Broken Group | 12 mi. | |
| Day 93 to Dodger Pass via Broken Group | 15 mi. | |
| Day 94 to Port San Juan | 42 mi. | |
| Day 95 to Victoria | 53 mi. | |
| Day 96 layover | | |
| Day 97 to Anacortes | 40 mi. | |

## "Maxi-Dream" for Boats with Unlimited Time

Additional stops in British Columbia might include Smith and Rivers Inlets, Fish Egg Inlet, the west and east coasts of Prince of Wales Island, Queen Charlotte Islands, Queens Sound and the "backcountry" of Vancouver Island's West Coast. Consider adding these to your next trip. These areas are covered in other volumes in our Exploring series.

## Fuel Stops from Washington to Southeast Alaska for Cruising Boats

(Other fuel supplies may be available during fishing season—make local inquiry. Water is available at all stops and most have provisions.)

- Anacortes
- Friday Harbor
- Victoria
- Nanaimo
- Comox
- Lund
- Campbell River
- Blind Channel
- Port McNeill
- Port Hardy
- Bella Bella & Shearwater
- Klemtu
- Hartley Bay
- Prince Rupert
- Ketchikan
- Wrangell
- Prince of Wales east coast, Thorne Bay
- Petersburg
- Juneau
- Haines
- Skagway
- Hoonah
- Glacier Bay: Bartlett Cove
- Elfin Cove *(commercial diesel only)*
- Pelican
- Sitka
- Kake
- Point Baker
- Craig

## APPENDIX B
## Distances Table

**Inside Passage—Seattle, Washington, to Cape Spencer, Alaska**

From *United States Coast Pilot*, Vol. 8. 2006

| | Seattle, WA | Victoria, B.C. | Dixon Entrance, B.C. | Hyder, AK | Cape Chacon, AK | Metlakatla, AK | Ketchikan, AK | Craig, AK | Wrangell, AK | Cape Decision, AK | Port Alexander, AK | Petersburg, AK | Sitka, AK | Pelican, AK | Juneau, AK | Haines, AK | Skagway, AK | Gustavus, AK | Cape Spencer, AK |
|---|---|---|---|---|---|---|---|---|---|---|---|---|---|---|---|---|---|---|---|
| Seattle, WA 47°36.2'N., 122°20.3'W. | - | | | | | | | | | | | | | | | | | | |
| Victoria, B.C. 48°25.0'N., 123°28.5'W. | 72 | - | | | | | | | | | | | | | | | | | |
| Dixon Entrance, AK 54°28.0'N., 132°52.0'W. | 664 | 612 | - | | | | | | | | | | | | | | | | |
| Hyder, AK 55°54.2'N., 130°00.6'W. | 690 | 638 | 169 | - | | | | | | | | | | | | | | | |
| Cape Chacon, AK 54°40.6'N., 131°59.7'W. | 640 | 588 | 34 | 136 | - | | | | | | | | | | | | | | |
| Metlakatla, AK 55°07.8'N., 131°34.2'W. | 660 | 608 | 66 | 148 | 32 | - | | | | | | | | | | | | | |
| Ketchikan, AK 55°20.5'N., 131°38.7'W. | 659 | 608 | 79 | 144 | 45 | 16 | - | | | | | | | | | | | | |
| Craig, AK 55°28.7'N., 133°09.7'W. | 716 | 664 | 77 | 212 | 76 | 109 | 121 | - | | | | | | | | | | | |
| Wrangell, AK 56°28.2'N., 132°23.2'W. | 749 | 697 | 157 | 234 | 123 | 104 | 89 | 111 | - | | | | | | | | | | |
| Cape Decision, AK 55°59.4'N., 134°08.1'W. | 788 | 737 | 126 | 273 | 125 | 143 | 129 | 49 | 75 | - | | | | | | | | | |
| Port Alexander, AK 56°14.8'N., 134°38.8'W. | 812 | 761 | 150 | 297 | 149 | 167 | 153 | 73 | 99 | 24 | - | | | | | | | | |
| Petersburg, AK 56°48.9'N., 132°57.8'W. | 771 | 719 | 180 | 256 | 146 | 126 | 112 | 113 | 40 | 76 | 100 | - | | | | | | | |
| Sitka, AK 57°03.1'N., 135°20.5'W. | 883 | 832 | 221 | 368 | 220 | 238 | 224 | 144 | 170 | 95 | 82 | 159 | - | | | | | | |
| Pelican, AK 57°57.6'N., 136°13.8'W. | 989 | 937 | 332 | 464 | 331 | 334 | 320 | 255 | 248 | 206 | 186 | 207 | 79 | - | | | | | |
| Juneau, AK 58°17.9'N., 134°24.7'W. | 879 | 827 | 288 | 364 | 254 | 235 | 220 | 206 | 148 | 157 | 140 | 108 | 162 | 123 | - | | | | |
| Haines, AK 59°13.8'N., 135°26.1'W. | 950 | 898 | 359 | 435 | 325 | 305 | 291 | 253 | 219 | 204 | 186 | 179 | 276 | 136 | 88 | - | | | |
| Skagway, AK 59°26.8'N., 135°19.3'W. | 962 | 910 | 371 | 447 | 337 | 317 | 303 | 264 | 231 | 215 | 198 | 191 | 187 | 148 | 100 | 14 | - | | |
| Gustavus, AK 58°23.3'N., 135°43.6'W. | 938 | 886 | 290 | 423 | 289 | 293 | 278 | 213 | 208 | 164 | 147 | 166 | 136 | 45 | 82 | 96 | 106 | - | |
| Cape Spencer, AK 58°10.0'N., 136°38.3'W. | 976 | 924 | 319 | 451 | 318 | 321 | 307 | 242 | 235 | 193 | 173 | 195 | 85 | 18 | 110 | 124 | 136 | 32 | - |

# APPENDIX C
# Key VHF Radio Channels

## Emergency Contacts and Radio Information
Coast Guard Radio VHF Channel 16 (cellular—emergencies only) star(*)16
Rescue Co-ordination Center (emergencies only) 800-567-5111
Rescue Co-ordination Center (inquiries) 250-363-2333
Coast Guard Emergency/Pollution Response Hotline 800-889-8852
Provincial Environmental Emergency Program 800-663-3456

## Weather Channels
### Southeast Alaska
WX1 and WX2
Scroll through your VHF radio WX frequency channels until you pick up the best signal. See the "Mariner's Weather Guide" in the Introduction of this book to locate the transmitter stations as you listen.

### Seattle through B.C.
WX1—Seattle, Alert Bay, Comox, Klemtu
WX2—Calvert Island, Dundas Island
WX3—Bowen Island, Mt. Helmcken
WX4—Puget Sound, San Juan Islands

## VHF Channels for Vessel Traffic Services and Pleasure Craft Usage
(Vessels less than 20 meters in length are not required to participate in the Vessel Traffic System. However, in areas where large commercial vessels are operating, it is recommended to monitor the appropriate radio channel.)

- 5A  Vessel Traffic Service Seattle: Strait of Juan de Fuca west of Victoria
- 6   Intership Safety Communications only
- 9   Intership and ship-shore all vessels, working channel
- 11  Vessel Traffic Service Victoria: Strait of Juan de Fuca east of Victoria; Haro Strait; Boundary Passage; Gulf Islands; Southern Strait of Georgia
- 11  Vessel Traffic Service Prince Rupert: North of Cape Caution
- 12  Vessel Traffic Service Vancouver: Vancouver Harbour and Howe Sound
- **16  International Hailing Channel: Hailing, distress, urgent traffic, and safety calls only**
- 67  Intership and ship-shore: working channel
- 68  Intership and ship-shore: working channel
- 69  Intership and ship-shore: working channel
- 70  Digital Selective Calling (no voice)
- 71  Vessel Traffic Service Victoria: Northern Strait of Georgia to Cape Caution
- 71  Vessel Traffic Service Prince Rupert: Prince Rupert, Dixon Entrance and Chatham Sound
- 72  Intership: working channel
- 73  Intership and ship-shore, working channel
- 74  Vessel Traffic Service Prince Rupert: West of Vancouver Island
- 83  A Coast Guard Liaison: Primary Canadian Coast Guard Safety & Communications Channel

## Canadian Phone Contacts for Vessel Traffic Services
Victoria 250-363-6333
Prince Rupert 250-627-3074 or 250-627-3075
Canadian Coast Guard website for Radio Aids to Marine Navigation and Notices to Shipping: http://www.ccg-gcc.gc.ca/Marine-Communications/Home

## Canadian Marinas
Do not call marinas in Canada on Channel 16. They are not authorized to use 16. All marinas monitor a common frequency, depending on their geographical location.
- 68  South of Campbell River
- 73  Marinas Campbell River and north

# APPENDIX D
## Summer Wind Reports

The following wind report shows percentages of wind speeds for May through September for the area of East Dixon Entrance:

### Triple Island
*East Dixon Entrance, south of Dundas Island*

**May winds**
| | |
|---|---|
| less than 20 knots | 84 % |
| 20 to 30 knots | 15 % |
| greater than 34 knots | 1 % |

**June winds**
| | |
|---|---|
| less than 20 knots | 87 % |
| 20 to 30 knots | 13 % |
| greater than 34 knots | nil |

**July winds**
| | |
|---|---|
| less than 20 knots | 92 % |
| 20 to 30 knots | 8 % |
| greater than 34 knots | nil |

**August winds**
| | |
|---|---|
| less than 20 knots | 91 % |
| 20 to 30 knots | 9 % |
| greater than 34 knots | nil |

**September winds**
| | |
|---|---|
| less than 20 knots | 85 % |
| 20 to 30 knots | 14 % |
| greater than 34 knots | 1 % |

---

# APPENDIX E
## Duration of Daylight

Typical duration of daylight at 58° North (Juneau and Glacier Bay)

### June 15
*(Daylight Time at 135° W)*

| | | |
|---|---|---|
| Nautical (morning) | twilight | — |
| Civil | twilight | 0241 |
| Sunrise | | 0356 |
| Sunset | | 2205 |
| Civil | twilight | 2320 |
| Nautical (evening) | twilight | — |

Hours of daylight: 18 hours, 09 minutes
Hours of daylight and civil twilight:
    20 hours, 39 minutes
Hours of daylight and nautical twilight: 24 hours

### August 15
*(Daylight Time at 135° W)*

| | | |
|---|---|---|
| Nautical (morning) | twilight | 0327 |
| Civil | twilight | 0434 |
| Sunrise | | 0521 |
| Sunset | | 2046 |
| Civil | twilight | 2133 |
| Nautical (evening) | twilight | 2239 |

Hours of daylight: 15 hours, 25 minutes
Hours of daylight and civil twilight:
    16 hours, 59 minutes
Hours of daylight and nautical twilight:
    19 hours, 12 minutes

### Notes on Duration of Daylight Tables

1. *Civil twilight* is defined as that time when the sun is six degrees below the nominal horizon. At this time, the horizon is clearly visible, as are the brightest stars.

2. *Nautical twilight* is defined as that time when the sun is twelve degrees below the nominal horizon. At this time, the horizon is barely visible or fading from view.

3. Factors of local terrain, fog or moonlight can influence usable daylight or twilight hours.

4. See the Nautical Almanac for the formula to interpolate for exact times for various latitudes and longitudes.

## APPENDIX F
## Sources for Fishing Regulations

Southeast Alaska is home to some of the most productive fishing waters in the world and opportunities for quality fishing are endless.

The Alaska Department of Fish and Game publishes regulations for sport and commercial fishing for Alaska's many management areas. Visit the website at www.sf.adfg.state.ak.us to download the newest information for the areas you're interested in. Regulation pamphlets may also be obtained by contacting Alaska Department of Fish and Game, Sportfish Division, 2030 Sea Level Drive, Suite 205, Ketchikan, Alaska, 99901, or by calling 907.225.2859. The excellent has links to regulations by region and species.

Warnings of closures due to toxic Paralytic Shellfish Poison (PSP; see sidebar in Introduction) as well as local fishing closures/openings are broadcast on VHF weather channels. Fisheries open and close unexpectedly, so pay attention to the announcements.

## APPENDIX G
## Documenting Local Knowledge

1. Coves, bays or bights that seem to offer full or limited protection from different weather conditions are identified and visited by the authors.
2. Routes are sketched and photographed.
3. Perusal of a possible anchor site is made with a dual-frequency recording echo sounder; major underwater obstacles are identified; depth and flatness of the bottom over the expected swinging area are checked; depths are then recorded on the sketches.
4. A sample test of the bottom is made by using a small "lunch hook" attached to light line and six feet of chain for maximum responsiveness and feel of the bottom.
5. The response of the anchor to the bottom is noted (i.e., soft or hard mud, sand, gravel, rocky, etc.; also, digging power, bounce, foul with kelp, pull out, etc.)
6. Additional line is let out to fully set the anchor.
7. A pull-down, with the engine in reverse, is made against the anchor to test holding power of the bottom.
8. Upon retrieving the anchor, we inspect the residue on its flukes to verify bottom material, as well as the type of grass, kelp, etc.
9. Discussions are held with local residents and fishermen about anchorages, names, etc., and their comments noted on the sketches. In some cases rough drafts of the manuscript are sent to experts for review.
10. The information gathered from our tests or that submitted by local experts is consolidated and edited and becomes the local knowledge we have presented in our diagrams and text.

## APPENDIX H
## Sources of Books and Nautical Charts

Titles published by Fine Edge Nautical & Recreational Publishing can be found at most ship's chandlers and nautical bookstores. For a current list of titles, please go to www.FineEdge.com. For more titles from Réanne Hemingway-Douglass and Don Douglass, please visit www.caveartpress.com.

# APPENDIX I
# State and Federal Agencies and Visitor Information

The Tongass National Forest is the nation's largest. At more than 17 million acres, it's larger than West Virginia. The USDA National Forest Service manages a variety of recreational opportunities in the Tongass National Forest including the Admiralty Island and Misty Fiords National Monuments. Visit the USDA website https://www.fs.usda.gov/detail/tongass/about-forest/offices for more information including interactive maps and guidebooks for your intended destinations and activities.

**Tongass National Forest Supervisor's Offices**
Headquarters
648 Mission Street
Federal Building
Ketchikan, AK 99901-6591
Phone: 907-225-3101

**Tongass National Forest, Petersburg Supervisors Office**
123 Scow Bay Loop Road
PO Box 309
Petersburg, AK 99833-0309
Phone: 907-772-3841

**Tongass National Forest, Sitka Supervisors Office**
2108 Halibut Point Road
Sitka, AK 99835
Phone: 907-747-6671

**Tongass National Forest Ranger Districts**
Admiralty Island National Monument
8510 Mendenhall Loop Road
Juneau, AK 99801
Phone: 907-586-8800

**Craig Ranger District**
900 Main Street
PO Box 705
Craig, AK 99921-9998
Phone: 907-826-3271

**Hoonah Ranger District**
430 Airport Way
PO Box 135
Hoonah, AK 99829-0135
Phone: 907-945-3631

**Juneau Ranger District**
8510 Mendenhall Loop Road
Juneau, AK 99801
Phone: 907-586-8800

**Ketchikan Misty Fiords Ranger District**
3031 Tongass Avenue
Ketchikan, AK 99901-5743
Phone: 907-225-2148

**Petersburg Ranger District**
12 North Nordic Drive
PO Box 1328
Petersburg, AK 99833-1328
Phone: 907-772-3871

**Sitka Ranger District**
2108 Halibut Point Road
Sitka, AK 99835
Phone: 907-747-6671

**Thorne Bay Ranger District**
1312 Federal Way
PO Box 19001
Thorne Bay, AK 99919-0001
Phone: 907-828-3304

**Wrangell Ranger District**
525 Bennett Street
PO Box 51
Wrangell, AK 99929-0051
Phone: 907-874-2323

**Visitor Information**
Alaska Department of Fish and Game
http://www.adfg.alaska.gov/

**Alaska Geographic**
Partners with National Park Service, U.S. Fish and Wildlife Service, Bureau of Land Management, and the U.S. Forest Service to make information easily available:
https://www.akgeo.org/
Downloadable guides include *The Tongass National Forest Visitors Guide*
https://www.akgeo.org/wp-content/uploads/2016/06/Tongass-2016.pdf

**Alaska Marine Highway (Juneau and Prince Rupert)**
Phone: 800.642.0066
www.ferryalaska.com

**Alaska Marine Highway (Prince Rupert)**
Phone: 250.627.1744
www.ferryalaska.com

**Alaska Public Lands Information for Southeast Alaska (state and federal)**
https://www.alaskacenters.gov/destinations/regions/southeast

**Alaska State Vacation and Travel Information**
https://www.travelalaska.com/

**Alaska Wildlife Viewing Guidebooks**
http://www.adfg.alaska.gov/index.cfm?adfg=viewing.guidebooks

**Craig**
http://www.craigak.com/

**Glacier Bay National Park and Preserve**
P.O. Box 140, Gustavus, AK 99826
Telephone Visitor Information Station (May through September): 907.697.2627
Telephone (after hours; emergency): 907.697.2322
Telephone (October through April): 907.697.2230
www.nps.gov/glba

**Haines Convention and Visitors Bureau**
122 Second Ave.
Haines, AK 99827
Phone: 907.766.2234
www.haines.ak.us

**Hoonah Visitors Information**
http://www.visithoonah.com/

**Juneau Convention and Visitors Bureau**
800 Glacier Ave, Juneau, AK 99801
Phone: (907) 586-2201
https://www.traveljuneau.com/

**Kasaan**
http://kasaan.org/

**Ketchikan Visitors Bureau**
131 Front Street
Ketchikan, AK 99901
Phone: 907.225.6166
www.visit-ketchikan.com

**Petersburg Visitor Information Center**
A unique partnership between the USFS and the Petersburg Chamber of Commerce
19 Fram Street
Petersburg, AK 99833-0810
Phone: 907-772-4636
https://www.petersburg.org/

**Prince of Wales Island Chamber of Commerce & Visitor Information**
https://www.princeofwalescoc.org/

**Prince Rupert Convention and Visitors Bureau (British Columbia)**
200-215 Cowbay Road
Prince Rupert, B.C. V8J 3S1 Canada
Phone: 250.624.5637
https://visitprincerupert.com/
http://www.prince-rupert-tourism.com/

**Sitka Convention and Visitors Bureau**
303 Lincoln Street
Sitka, AK 99835
Phone: 907.747.5940
Web: www.sitka.org

**Skagway Convention and Visitors Bureau**
Box 1029
Skagway, AK 99840
Phone: 907.983.2854
Web: www.skagway.com

**Tenakee Springs**
http://www.tenakeespringsak.com/

**USFS Southeast Alaska Discovery Center**
50 Main Street
Ketchikan, AK 99901-6559
Phone: 907-228-6220
https://www.alaskacenters.gov/visitors-centers/ketchikan

**USFS Juneau Information Center**
101 Egan Drive
Juneau, AK 99801
Phone: 907.586.8800

**USFS Mendenhall Glacier Visitor Center**
Mendenhall Glacier
8510 Mendenhall Loop Road
Juneau, AK 99801
Phone: 907-789-0097

**Wrangell Visitor Center**
293 Campbell Drive (Nolan Center) Wrangell, AK 99929
Phone: 800.367.9745
http://www.wrangell.com/visitorservices

# Bibliography & References

There are many resources to help you have a safe, enjoyable, and fulfilling journey and this list incorporates a variety of references. Some of these are critically important to your vessel's safety (up-to-date *Canadian Sailing Directions* and U.S. *Coast Pilot*), some are valuable instruction manuals to bring with you on your voyage (Calder's *Boatowner's Mechanical and Electrical Manual* and *Marine Diesel Engines: Maintenance, Troubleshooting, and Repair*), and some will enrich your experience with discussions of the natural and human history of these remote lands and waters.

## Canadian *Sailing Directions:*

The Canadian Hydrographic Service issues *Sailing Directions PAC 200—General Information-Pacific Coast* for all B.C. areas. *Sailing Directions* booklets detailing specific geographical areas within B.C. are available as Print-On-Demand (POD). For Inside Passage cruisers, the areas of interest in northern B.C. waters can be found in: PAC 205E and PAC 206E.

http://www.charts.gc.ca/publications/sailingdirections-instructionsnautiques-eng.asp

In addition, updated Notices to Mariners are also available POD at https://www.notmar.gc.ca/index-en.php

U.S. Coast Pilot [From the official website]: https://www.nauticalcharts.noaa.gov/publications/coast-pilot/index.html

The *United States Coast Pilot*® consists of a series of nautical books that cover a variety of information important to navigators of coastal and intracoastal waters and the Great Lakes. Issued in nine volumes, they contain supplemental information that is difficult to portray on a nautical chart. Topics in the *Coast Pilot* include channel descriptions, anchorages, bridge and cable clearances, currents, tide and water levels, prominent features, pilotage, towage, weather, ice conditions, wharf descriptions, dangers, routes, traffic separation schemes, small-craft facilities, and Federal regulations applicable to navigation.

All *Coast Pilot* books are available to download for free from the Office of Coast Survey website. Hard copies of *Coast Pilot* can be purchased from NOAA Certified *Coast Pilot* Distributors and are up to date at the time of printing. Historical *Coast Pilots* are also available from the website if desired.

U.S. *Coast Pilot* information is updated weekly online. The prudent mariner will take note of updates by supplementing the most recent hard copy with downloads of the weekly updates.

## Books

Ashenfelter, Pete & Nancy. *Row to Alaska by Wind & Oar*. Anacortes, WA: Anderson Publishing Inc., 1994.

Bohn, Dave. *Glacier Bay, the Land and the Silence*, edited by David Brower, San Francisco: Sierra Club, 1967.

Boone, Louis, Jr. *Wrangell Narrows at a Glance*. Oregon City: Boone Maritime Press, 2012. [A valuable guide to transiting the Narrows by an Alaska State Ferry Master and Pilot. Sketches from the pilot's viewpoint direct the skipper from nav-aid to nav-aid. Captain Boone supplements his knowledgeable tips on navigating the turbulent currents of the Narrows with additional boat-handling information at www.WrangellNarrows.com.]

Burch, David. *Radar for Mariners*. San Francisco: International Marine / McGraw Hill, 2013. [Very complete and accessible information; includes CD for radar simulation practice.]

Calder, Nigel. *Boatowner's Mechanical and Electrical Manual*, 4th Edition. San Francisco: International Marine / McGraw-Hill, 2015. [No serious boater leaves port without it.]

Calder, Nigel. *Marine Diesel Engines: Maintenance, Troubleshooting, and Repair*, 3rd Edition. Camden, ME: International Marine / McGraw-Hill, 2006. [Everyone dependent on a diesel engine should be familiar with the material in this book.]

Caldwell, Francis E. & Donna L. Caldwell. *At Sea, Poems and Reflections*. Port Angeles, WA: Anchor Publishing: 2002.

Caldwell, Francis E. *Pacific Troller: Life on the Northwest Fishing Grounds*. Victoria: Trafford Publishing, 1978. [Reissue 2005. Short true adventures from Caldwell's fishing days in the Gulf of Alaska.]

Chapman, Frederic, Jonathan Eaton (Ed.). *Chapman Piloting, Seamanship & Small Boat Handling*, 68th Edition. New York: Hearst Marine Books, 2017. [Another classic that boaters should carry as a standard on board their vessel.]

Dauenhauer, Nora Marks, Richard Dauenhauer, and Lydia T. Black, Eds. *Anóoshi Lingít Aaní Ká / Russians in Tlingit America.* Seattle: University of Washington Press, 2008. [Fascinating scholarly volume presenting original Tlingit oral tradition and newly obtained primary source Russian documents detailing the Battles of Sitka, 1802 and 1804.]

DeArmond, R.N. & Patricia Roppel. *Baranof Island's Eastern Shore: The Waterfall Coast.* Sitka: Arrowhead Press, 1998. [Descriptions and historical details of Baranof's East Coast by two well-known Alaskan authors.]

Douglass, Don & Réanne Hemingway-Douglass. *Exploring the North Coast of British Columbia*, 3rd Edition. Anacortes, WA: Fine Edge Productions, 2017.

Douglass, Don & Réanne Hemingway-Douglass. *Exploring the San Juan and Gulf Islands.* 3rd Edition. Anacortes, WA: Fine Edge Productions, 2011.

Douglass, Don & Réanne Hemingway-Douglass. *Exploring the South Coast of British Columbia*, 2nd Edition. Anacortes, WA: Fine Edge Productions, 1999.

Douglass, Don & Réanne Hemingway-Douglass. *Exploring Vancouver Island's West Coast,* 2nd Edition. Anacortes, WA: Fine Edge Productions, 1999.

Duke, Bob. *Cruising To Alaska: Tips and Tactics.* Bellingham: Good Enough Publishing, 2004. [Interviews with seasoned Alaska boaters.]

Fox, William T. *At the Sea's Edge.* New York: Prentice Hall Press, 1983.

Goldschmidt, Walter R. & Theodore H. Haas. *Haa Aní / Our Land.* Seattle: University of Washington Press, 1946.

Hale, Robert, and Burroughs Bay, LLC., Eds. *Waggoner Cruising Guide.* Bellevue: Fine Edge Productions, published annually. [http://waggoner-guide.com/ Excellent for getting a boater as far as Prince Rupert.]

Hinz, Earl R. *The Complete Book of Anchoring and Mooring.* Maryland: Cornell Maritime Pres, 2001 reprint. [Highly recommended by Don Douglass as the best all-around book on anchoring.]

Horn, Elizabeth L. *Coastal Wildflowers of the Pacific Northwest.* Missoula, Montana: Mountain Press Publishing Company, 1994.

Hulsizer, Elsie. *Glaciers, Bears and Totems.* Madeira Park, B.C.: Harbour Publishing, 2010.

Kirchhoff, M. J. *Baranof Island.* Juneau: Alaska Cedar Press, 1990. [An illustrated history by one of the island's residents.]

Kozloff, Eugene N. *Plants and Animals of the Pacific Northwest.* Seattle: University of Washington Press, 1976. [Still one of the classic references for flora & fauna.]

Lawrence, Iain. *Sea Stories of the Inside Passage.* Bishop, CA: Fine Edge Productions, 1997.

Lochaas, Tom, Ed. *Treacherous Waters.* Camden, ME: International Marine / McGraw-Hill, 2003.

Miller, Robert H. *Kayaking the Inside Passage.* Woodstock: Countryman Press, 2005.

Monahan, Kevin. *Local Knowledge—A Skipper's Reference—Tacoma to Ketchikan*, Anacortes, WA. Fine Edge Productions, 2005.

Monahan, Kevin & Don Douglass. *The Radar Book: Effective Navigation and Collision Avoidance.* Anacortes, WA: Fine Edge Productions, 2008. [One of the best books on how to use your radar effectively.]

Monahan, Kevin & Don Douglass. *Proven Cruising Routes, Seattle to Ketchikan*, Vol. 1. Anacortes, WA: Fine Edge Productions, 2000.

Morton, Alexandra. *Listening to Whales—What the Orcas Have Taught Us.* New York: Ballantine Books, 2004.

Naske, Claus-M. & Herman E. Slotnick. *Alaska: A History of the 49th State,* 2nd Edition. Norman, OK: University of Oklahoma Press, 1987.

*Northwest Boat Travel.* Woodinville: Vernon Publishing Company, published annually. [Covers the entire Inside Passage, as well as Southeast Alaska.]

O'Clair, Rita M., Robert H. Armstrong, and Richard Carstensen. *The Nature of Southeast Alaska, A Guide to Plants, Animals, and Habitats.* Anchorage: Alaska Northwest Books, 2004.

Oppel, Frank, Ed. *Tales of Alaska and the Yukon.* Seacaucus, NJ: Castle, 1986. [Enjoyable reprints of original magazine articles and stories from 1885 to 1910 about Alaska, the Yukon, and British Columbia, with the original illustrations]

Peterson, Dale R. *Day By Day to Alaska*. Victoria, B.C.: Trafford, 2000. [Good reading for boaters with a vessel less than 28 feet in length.]

Piggott, Margaret. *Discover Southeast Alaska with Pack and Paddle*, 2nd Edition. Seattle: The Mountaineers, 1990.

Raban, Jonathan, *Passage to Juneau—A Sea and Its Meanings*. New York; Vintage Books, 2000.

Roppel, Patricia. *Land of Mists: Revillagigedo & Gravina Islands, Misty Fiords National Monument, Alaska*, 3rd Edition. Wrangell, AK: Farwest Research, 1998.

Roppel, Patricia. *Misty Fiords National Monument Wilderness*. Wrangell, AK: Farwest Research, 2000.

Snively, Gloria. *Exploring the Seashore in British Columbia, Washington and Oregon. A Guide to Shorebirds and Intertidal Plants and Animals.* West Vancouver: Gordon Soules Book Publishers Ltd., 1978, sixth printing, 1985.

Sweet, Bob. *The Weekend Navigator.* San Francisco: International Marine / McGraw-Hill, 2011. [Excellent, straight forward how-to book for GPS and electronics, now available in an updated second edition.]

Terdal, Leif G. *Small-Boat Cruising to Alaska*. Seattle: Hara Publishing, 2000. [Required reading for anyone attempting an Alaska cruise in a vessel less than 28 feet.]

*United States Coast Pilot,* Number 8. Washington, D.C.: U.S. Department of Commerce, NOAA, [Latest Edition].

Upton, Joe. *Journeys through the Inside Passage.* Anchorage: Alaska Northwest Books, 2000.

Upton, Joe. *The Coastal Companion: A Guide for the Alaska-bound Traveler.* Bainbridge Island: Coastal Publishing, 2004. [A mile-post guide interspersed with descriptions of Upton's experiences as an Alaskan fisherman.]

Upton, Joe. *Alaska Blues: A Season of Fishing the Inside Passage.* 2nd Edition. Seattle: Sasquatch Books, 1998. [Perhaps Upton's best of his true adventures.]

Wing, Charlie. *How Boat Things Work.* San Francisco: International Marine / McGraw-Hill, 2007. [Wonderfully clear explanations; particularly good book for the First Mate.]

Wise, Ken C. *Cruise of the Blue Flujin*. Fowlerville, Michigan: Wilderness Adventure Books, 1987. [Account of four Sea Scouts, including Don Douglass's uncle Phil, who canoed to Alaska in 1937.]

White, Helen & Maxcine Williams, Eds. *Alaska-Yukon Wild Flowers Guide.* Anchorage: Alaska Northwest Publishing Company, 1974.

Wood, Charles E. *Charlie's Charts North to Alaska*, 5rd Edition. Surrey, B.C.: Charlie's Charts, 2015.

## Acknowledgments

When it comes to exploring new horizons, we all stand on the shoulders of those who preceded us. This has been true since the first humans paddled down the coast of Southeast Alaska from Asia and since Cook, Quadra, Vancouver and others started their historic explorations. In doing our research of the harbors and coves of this beautiful water wilderness, we have those earlier explorers to thank, as well as those who have helped us along the waterways for decades.

We would like to express our thanks to the intrepid explorer-friends who've assisted us in collecting data for Southeast Alaska, either as crew on our vessel Research Vessel *Baidarka*, as companion boaters, or as "local knowledge" experts who have shared their "secrets" or photographs with us: Rod Nash, Herb and Wendy Nickles, Dave and Evie Frisby, Greg and Ilse Hine, Jean and Joel Gillingwators, Jean and Geneviève Doudeau, Barb and Bill Davis, Jack and Linda Shreiber, Carl and Carol Cederberg, Jill and Doug Princehouse, John Leone, Henry Wendt, Larry Johnson, Ward Eldridge and Kathy Kyle, Kevin Monahan, Bill Stanley, Frank and Margy Fletcher, Mike Youngblood, Mike and Claudia Herrick, Pat Roppell, Art and Linda Forbes, Larry Calvin, John Neal and Amanda Swan-Neal, Jim Kyle, Bruce and Margaret Evertz, Brian and Carol Pemberton, Chara Stewart, Clyde Ford, Bob Duke, David J. Shuler, Bob Berto, Dave Scott, Richard Friedman, David Parker, Dick and Nancy White, Carolyn and Tim De Cook, Jordan Roderick, John Grinter, Lorena and Leonard Landon, and Elsie and Steve Hulsizer.

Additional thanks go to the many harbormasters, park rangers, and their staff, who have given freely of their time to help keep us abreast of changes throughout the years: Ray Majeski, Lou McCall, John Stone, Mike Kampnich, Bob Clausen, David Duffey, Paul Dybdahl, Matt O'Boyle, Chris Brewton, Robert Venables, Chuck Young, and Stan Eliason. Thanks also go to Margaret Hazen and Wayne Clark for updates to Glacier Bay National Park and Preserve.

This new edition is due to the efforts of our editorial and production staff, Lisa Wright and Arlene Cook. Their critical eyes and thoughtful suggestions helped update this guide. Melanie Haage's design and layout work continues to enhance the accessibility of information in our *Exploring* guidebook series.

Our greatest appreciation goes to the myriad unnamed readers who have shared their tips or findings with us and who have given us encouragement to "keep exploring."

## About the Authors

Don Douglass and Réanne Hemingway-Douglass have logged more than 170,000 cruising miles over the past 30 years—from South America to Dutch Harbor in the Aleutians. They consider Alaskan waters as some of the finest in the world and they have spent many of their summers there on their research vessel, *Baidarka*.

Don, who began exploring Northwest waters in 1949 as a youth, has sailed the Inside Passage on everything from a 26-foot pleasure craft and commercial fishing boats to a Coast Guard icebreaker. He holds a BSEE degree from California State University and a Masters in Business Economics from Claremont Graduate University. Don holds honorary membership in the International Association of Cape Horners and he was elected to the Mountain Biking Hall of Fame as a founding father of the International Bicycling Association.

Réanne Hemingway-Douglass holds a BA degree in French from Pomona College. She attended Claremont Graduate University and the University of Grenoble, France. Her classic memoir, *Cape Horn: One Man's Dream, One Woman's Nightmare*, describes pitchpoling in the Great Southern Ocean. She is the first woman to have bicycled across Tierra del Fuego, an adventure she recounted in *Two Women Against the Wind*. Both books are available from www.caveartpress.com.

Together, the Douglasses have documented over 8,000 anchor sites between Mexico and the Gulf of Alaska. Their six highly acclaimed "Exploring" series guidebooks, published by FineEdge.com, and their cruising planning maps cover the waters from Baja, California to the Gulf of Alaska.

*Réanne Hemingway-Douglass and Don Douglass*

# Index

*Italicized names and page numbers refer to Sidebars.*

Aats Bay (Coronation Island), 362
*About Salmon: Alaska's Famous Fish, 91*
Adams Anchorage (Shelter Island), 182
Adams Inlet (Muir Inlet), 219
Admiralty Cove (Admiralty Island), 181
Affleck Canal (Kuiu Island), 360
Aiken Cove (North Arm), 93
Airport Small-craft Passenger Float (Ketchikan Harbor), 46
*Alaskan Eyes, 46*
Alava Bay (Revillagigedo Island), 54
Aleutkina Bay (Baranof Island), 300
Alikula Bay (Coronation Island), 362
Alvin Bay (Kuiu Island), 357
Amalga Harbor (Favorite Channel), 183
American Bay (Dall Island), 410
Anan Bay (Bradfield Canal), 78
*Anan Bay Bear and Wildlife Observatory, 80*
ANB Harbor, 281
Anchor Pass (Behm Canal), 61
*Anchoring Challenges in Southeast Alaska, 50*
Angoon and Kootznahoo Inlet Inner Harbor (Admiralty Island), 293
Anguilla Bay (Anguilla Island), 376
Anita Bay (Etolin Island), 74
Annette Bay (Annette Island), 36
Annie's Pocket (Baranof Island), 288
Appleton Cove (Rodman Bay), 289
Astrolabe Bay (Palma Bay), 238
Augustine Bay (Dall Island), 414
Auke Bay, 178
*Avoiding Fish Nets While Underway, 24*

Baht Harbor (Zarembo Island), 122
Baidarka Anchorage (Rocky Pass), 344
Baidarka Cove (Rakof Islands), 308
Baird Glacier Mud Flats (Thomas Bay), 144
Baker Cove (Goulding Harbor), 260
*Bald Eagles, 396*
Bald Headed Cove (Pennock Island), 46
Baldy Bay (Dall Island), 408
Bar Harbor (Ketchikan Harbor), 44
Baranof Island's West Coast, South of Sitka, 300
Barlow Cove (Mansfield Peninsula), 182
Barrier Islands (Cordova Bay), 399
Bartlett Cove (Glacier Bay), 211
Bat Cove (George Inlet), 39
Bay of Pillars and Honeymoon Basin (Kuiu Island), 333
Bear Bay and Baby Bear Bay (Baranof Island), 287
Bear Harbor (Affleck Canal), 360
Beardslee Islands (Glacier Bay), 212
*Bears—Where to Find Them, 324*
Beartrack Cove, 215
Beartrack Island, 216
Behm Canal and Misty Fiords National Monument, 53
Behm Narrows (Behm Canal), 61

Bell Arm (Behm Canal), 61
Benjamin Island Cove and Benjamin Island Bight (Benjamin Island), 185
Berg Bay (Blake Channel), 81
Berg Bay (Glacier Bay), 213
*Bering and Chirikov, 246*
Berners Bay (Lynn Canal), 187
Bert Millar Cutoff (Prince of Wales Island), 404
Bertha Bay (Chichagof Island), 255
Big Bay (Baranof Island), 307
Big Branch Bay (Baranof Island), 317
Big John Bay (Kupreanof Island), 346
Bingham Cove (Yakobi Island), 247
Birdsnest Bay (Baranof Island), 300
Biscuit Lagoon (Hunter Bay), 399
Black Bay (Chichagof Island), 261
Black Sand Cove (Gravina Island), 36
Blake Channel, 81
Blanket Island North Cove (Blanket Island), 389
Blashke Islands, 111
Blind Pass (Behm Canal), 61
Blue Mouse Cove (Gilbert Peninsula), 220
Boat Harbor (Lynn Canal), 185
Bobs Bay (Dall Island), 412
Bobs Place (St. Philip Island), 375
Bocas de Finas, 375
Boca de Quadra, 29
Bock Bight (Thomas Bay), 142
Bolles Inlet (Long Island), 411
Boussole Bay (Palma Bay), 237
Bradfield Canal, 78
Bradfield Canal to Blake Channel and Eastern Passage, 78
Bradshaw Cove (Chichagof Island), 285
Breezy Bay (Dall Island), 407
Bridget Cove (Lynn Canal), 186
Brown Cove, 141
Brundige Inlet (Dundas Island), 6
*Bull Rails Instead of Cleats for Securing Dock Lines, 96*
Bullhead Cove, 29
Burnett Inlet (Etolin Island), 108
Burroughs Bay (Behm Canal), 60
Buschmann Pass, 402

Caamano Point, 66
Calder Bay (Prince of Wales Island), 364
Camden Hideout (Port Camden), 348
Cameron Pass, 309
Camp Coogan Bay (Baranof Island), 300
Camp Cove (Ham Island), 37
Cannery Cove (Pybus Bay), 150
Canoe Cove (Annette Island), 35
Canoe Cove (Lisianski Strait), 251
Canoe Passage (Ernest Sound), 71
Cape Bartolome Light (Baker Island), 380
Cape Chacon (Prince of Wales Island), 407
Cape Decision (Kuiu Island), 338

Cape Edgecumbe Light (Kruzof Island), 284
Cape Fanshaw, 145
Cape Muzon (Dall Island), 412
Cape Ommaney (Baranof Island), 318
Cape Spencer, 233
Car Point Notch (Portland Canal), 17
Carp Island Cove (Behm Canal), 55
Carroll and George Inlets (Revillagigedo Island), 37
Carroll Inlet (Revillagigedo Island), 37
*Carrying a Totem Pole. Hydaburg Totem Park, 387*
Cascade Bay (Baranof Island), 324
Cascade Creek Bight (Thomas Bay), 143
Cascade Inlet, 34
Casey Moran Harbor (Ketchikan Harbor, labeled "City Floats" on charts), 44
Cat Passage, 31
Cedar Bight (Security Bay), 353
Cedar Cove (Freshwater Bay), 292
Cedar Pass, 308
Chaik Bay (Admiralty Island), 295
Chapin Bay (Admiralty Island), 148
Charlie's Cove (Eureka Channel), 400
Chatham Strait and Baranof Island's East Coast (North to South), 318
Checats Cove (Behm Canal), 57
Chichagof Bay (Prince of Wales Island), 90
Chicagof Island's West Coast, 251
Chichagof Pass, 117
Chickamin River (Behm Canal), 60
Chilkat Inlet (Lynn Canal), 192
Chilkoot Inlet (Lynn Canal), 193
Cholmondeley Sound (Prince of Wales Island), 97
Christmas Cove (Security Bay), 353
Circle Bay (Woronkofski Island), 117
Clam Cove (Gravina Island), 47
Clam Cove (Kassa Inlet), 395
Clare Island Cove (Niblack Anchorage), 94
Clarence Strait from Kasaan Peninsula to Sumner Strait, 66
*Clarence Strait South Entrance, 87*
Clark Bay (Twelvemile Arm), 103
Clarno Cove (North Arm), 93
Cleveland Passage, 146
*Clothing in Southeast Alaska, 86*
Clover Bay (Prince of Wales Island), 97
Clover Passage (Behm Canal), 66
Coal Bay (Kasaan Bay), 102
Coffman Cove (Prince of Wales Island), 109
Coho Cove (Thorne Arm), 37
Coning Inlet (Long Island), 393
Coon Cove (George Inlet), 39
Cordova Bay, 392
Coronation Island, 361
Cosmos Cove (Baranof Island), 319
Couverden Channel, 202

Couverden Island Cove (Couverden Island), 202
Cove 2 Miles Southeast of Lincoln Rock (Etolin Island), 109
Crab Bay (Annette Island), 34
*Craig, 379*
Craig (Prince of Wales Island), 377
Crane Cove (Baranof Island), 304
Crescent Harbor, 280
Cross Sound, 230
Crowley Bight (Kuiu Island), 338
Cuvacan Cove (Shelikof Bay), 283
Cyrus Cove (Orr Island), 369

Dakaneek Bay (Kupreanof Island), 346
Dall Bay (Gravina Island), 36
Dall Island West Coast, From North to South, 412
Danger Passage, 33
Datzkoo Harbor (Dall Island), 411
Davidson Bay (Kupreanof Island), 346
Davidson Inlet, 372
Davison Bay (Chichagof Island), 258
Dawes Glacier (Endicott Arm), 164
De Groff Bay (Krestof Island), 275
December Point Bight (Mitkof Island), 131
Deception Point Cove (Woewodski Island), 131
Deep Bay (Chichagof Island), 288
Deep Bay (Zarembo Island), 117
Deep Cove (Baranof Island), 329
Deep Inlet (Baranof Island), 301
Deer Bay (Hetta Inlet), 390
Deer Harbor (Yakobi Island), 248
Devilfish Bay (El Capitan Passage), 367
*Devilfish Bay—A Different Perspective, 370*
Devils Elbow (Rocky Pass), 344
Dewey Anchorage (Etolin Island), 107
Dicks Arm (Cross Sound), 233
Didrickson Bay (Portlock Harbor), 260
Diver Bay (Dall Island), 413
Dixon Harbor, Hankinson Cove, 236
*Dolphin Courage, 378*
Donkey Bay (Pybus Bay), 151
Dora Bay (Cholmondeley Sound), 97
Dorothy Cove (Necker Bay), 312
Dorothy Narrows, 305
Doty Cove (Admiralty Island), 172
Double Cove, Khaz Bay (Chichagof Island), 265
Douglas (Douglas Island), 176
Douglas Bay (Kupreanof Island), 126
Douglass Bay (Patterson Bay), 289
Dry Pass, 258
Dry Pass Anchorage (El Capitan Passage), 367
Dry Strait, 139
*Dry Strait—Good Judgment or Lack of Courage? 142*
Duke Island, 30
Dunbar Inlet (Sukkwan Island), 408
Duncan Bay Shortcut (west of Venn Passage), 6
Duncan Canal (Kupreanof Island), 125

Dundas Bay, Horsefly Bay and Mickey's Arm, 226

Eagle Harbor (Favorite Channel), 183
Earl Cove (Inian Islands), 229
East Channel (Krestof Sound), 275
Eastern Anchorage (Baranof Island), 300
Eastern Bay (Krestof Sound), 276
Eastern Channel, 300
Echo Cove (Berners Bay), 187
Echo Cove (Catherine Island), 319
Eek Inlet (Hetta Inlet), 389
Egg Harbor (Coronation Island), 361
El Capitan Passage (from Shakan Strait to Sea Otter Sound), 366
Elbow Bay (Long Island), 392
Elbow Passage, 263
*Eldred Rock Lighthouse, 192*
Elena Bay (Tebenkof Bay), 335
Elf Cove (Ford Arm), 266
*Elfin Cove, 231*
Elfin Cove (Chichagof Island), 231
Eliason and Thomsen Harbors (Sitka), 280
Eliza Harbor (Admiralty Island), 148
Ell Cove (Baranof Island), 320
Endicott Arm (Holkham Bay), 161
Entrance Cove (El Capitan Passage), 366
Ernest Sound to Wrangell Via Zimovia Strait, 69
Eureka Channel, 400
Exchange Cove (Exchange Island), 115
Excursion Inlet (Sawmill Bay), 207
Explorer Basin, 337
*Exploring Coronation Island Wilderness, 361*
Eye of the Needle (Tebenkof Bay), 335
*The Eyes Have It: Up Close on the Inside Passage, 114*

Falcon Arm (Slocum Arm), 266
False Cove (Warren Island), 363
Farallon Bay (Dall Island), 407
Farragut Bay, 144
Favorite Bay (Kootznahoo Inlet), 295
Favorite Channel, 182
Felice Strait, 34
Fern Harbor (Taylor Island), 228
Fingers Bay—North Arm (Whidbey Passage), 214
Fingers Bay—South Arm, 214
First Narrows (Rakof Islands), 308
Fish Bay (Baranof Island), 285
Fisherman Chuck (Etolin Island), 72
Fisherman Cove (Dall Island), 414
Fishermans Harbor (Kosciusko Island), 360
Fitzgibbon Cove (Behm Canal), 60
Flat Cove (Slocum Arm), 267
Florence Bay (Sitkoh Bay), 291
Flynn Cove (Chichagof Island), 206
Foggy Bay, Inner Cove, 27
Foggy Bay, Outer Cove, 26
Fool Inlet (Seymour Canal), 159
Ford Arm (Chichagof Island), 266

Fords Cove (Portland Canal), 18
*Fords Terror, 165*
Fords Terror (Endicott Arm), 161
Forevergreen Basin (Baranof Island), 317
Forevergreen Nook (Fords Terror), 163
Fortuna Strait, 270
Foul Bay (Dall Island), 413
*Fourth of July at Hoonah, 205*
Fox Island Cove (Fox Island), 22
Francis Anchorage (Farragut Bay), 144
Frederick Cove (West Arm), 96
Frederick Sound, East Section, 138
Frederick Sound, East to West, 138
French Harbor (Dutch Harbor), 96
Frosty Bay (Seward Passage), 71
Funter Bay (Mansfield Peninsula), 200

Gambier Bay—Snug Cove, North Cove, Good Island Nook, Good Island Inlet Basin, Last Chance Harbor (Admiralty Island), 156
Gardner Bay (Prince of Wales Island), 87
Gastineau Channel, 173
The Gate, 263
Gedney Harbor (Kuiu Island), 337
*George Vancouver, 112*
George Inlet (Revillagigedo Island), 39
Gil Harbor (Kuiu Island), 348
Gilanta Rocks, 23
Gilbert Bay (Port Snettisham), 170
Gilmer Bay (Kruzof Island), 282
Gilmer Cove (Neva Strait), 273
Glacier Bay National Park and Preserve, 208
*Glacier Bay National Park and Preserve Permits, 210*
Glacier Cove (Portland Canal), 19
*Glacier Ice Cruising—Keeping it Safe and Enjoyable, 166*
Gnat Cove (Carroll Inlet), 37
Goat Mouth Inlet (Goat Island), 386
Goddard Hot Springs Bay (Baranof Island), 304
Goleta Cove (Shelikof Bay), 283
Goose Bay (Polk Inlet), 100
Goose Bay (Port Camden), 347
Goose Cove (Baranof Island), 288
Gooseneck Harbor (Dall Island), 414
Goulding Harbor (Portlock Harbor), 260
Grand Pacific Glacier (Tarr Inlet), 223
Granite Cove (George Island), 233
Graves Harbor, 234
Green Inlet (View Cove), 409
Green Point Bight (Kupreanof Island), 132
Green Rocks / Christmas Tree Rock (Wrangell Narrows), 132
Greentop Harbor (Yakobi Island), 249
Guard Islands Light (Tongass Narrows), 47
Gulf of Esquibel, 376
Gustavus (Icy Passage), 208
Gut Bay (Baranof Island), 327
Gwent Cove (Pearse Canal), 14
*Haines, 194*

Haines (Chilkoot Inlet), 193
Haley Anchorage (Fish Bay), 285
Halfmoon Anchorage (Mitkof Island), 132
Halibut Bay (Portland Canal), 16
Halleck Harbor (Saginaw Bay), 352
Halliday Nook / Moira Cove (North Arm), 92
Ham Cove (Dall Island), 410
Ham Island Bight (Ham Island), 34
Hamilton Bay (Kupreanof Island), 350
Hanus Bay and Point Moses Cove (Baranof Island), 290
Happy Cove (Tebenkof Bay), 334
Happy Harbor (Kasaan Island), 101
Harbor Island (Holkham Bay), 161
Harmony Islands Passage (Harmony Islands), 374
Harris Cove (Kuiu Island), 337
Harris Island, 34
Hassler Harbor (Annette Island), 37
Hassler Pass and Gedney Pass (Behm Canal), 62
*Haul-out Grids in Southeast Alaska, 136*
Hawk Inlet (Admiralty Island), 291
Hayward Strait, 276
Helm Bay Float (Behm Canal), 66
Henry's Arm, 151
Herring Bay (Admiralty Island), 147
Herring Bay (Elovoi Island), 306
Hessa Inlet (Prince of Wales Island), 402
Hetta Cove (Hetta Inlet), 390
Hetta Inlet (Prince of Wales Island), 389
Hidden Bay (Prince of Wales Island), 89
Hidden Cove (Slocum Arm), 267
Hidden Inlet (Pearse Canal), 14
Hideaway Inlet (Clarno Cove), 93
Highfield Anchorage (Wrangell Island), 82
*A High-Latitude Emergency, 212*
Hobart Bay (Entrance Island), 155
Hoggatt Bay (Baranof Island), 327
Hoktaheen Cove (Yakobi Island), 248
Holbrook Arm (Kosciusko Island), 372
Hole in the Wall (Diver Bay), 413
Hole in the Wall (Prince of Wales Island), 358
Holkham Bay, 160
Hollis Anchorage (Twelvemile Arm), 103
Honeydew Cove (Kuiu Island), 350
Hood Bay (Admiralty Island), 295
Hook Arm (Sea Otter Harbor), 413
Hoonah (Port Frederick), 203
Hoonah Sound (Chichagof Island), 288
Howard Bay (Lynn Canal), 184
Howard Cove (Kuiu Island), 338
Howkan Narrows, 410
Hugh Miller Inlet (Glacier Bay), 219
Hunter Bay (Prince of Wales Island), 397
Hunter Cove (Muir Inlet), 219
Hydaburg (Prince of Wales Island), 387
*Hyder, 20*
Hyder (Portland Canal—U.S. side), 20
*Hypnotic Icebergs! 171*
*Icebound in Gut Bay, 328*

Icy Passage and Pleasant Island Cove, 207
Icy Point, 239
Icy Strait, 199
Icy Strait to Cross Sound, 199
Idaho Inlet (Chichagof Island), 225
Ideal Cove (Mitkof Island), 139
Ilin Bay and Constantine Cove (Islas Bay), 254
Imperial Passage, 259
Indian Garden Bay (Heceta Island), 373
Ingraham Bay (Prince of Wales Island), 90
Inian Cove (Inian Islands), 229
Inian Islands, 229
Island Bay (Sukkwan Island), 408
Island Cove and Wooded Knoll Cove (Slocum Arm), 267
Islas Bay (Chichagof Island), 253
Islet Passage, 304

Jamboree Bay (Walker Channel), 310
Jamestown Bay (Baranof Island), 281
*John Muir's Stickeen, 226*
Johns Hopkins Inlet (Glacier Bay), 222
Johnson Cove (Moira Sound), 95
Johnson Cove (Willoughby Island), 216
Judd Harbor (Duke Island), 30
*Juneau, 175*
Juneau (Gastineau Channel), 174

Kadake Bay (Kuiu Island), 348
Kaguk Cove (Prince of Wales Island), 373
Kah Shakes Cove, 28
Kah Sheets Bay (Kupreanof Island), 126
Kahli Cove (Prince of Wales Island), 369
Kaigani Strait, 410
Kake (Kupreanof Island), 351
Kakul Narrows (Peril Strait), 284
*Kaleidoscope Magic, 4*
Kalhagu Cove (Chilkat Inlet), 192
Kalinin Bay (Kruzof Island), 271
Kanga Bay (Baranof Island), 304
Karheen Passage (Tuxekan Island), 373
Karta Bay (Kasaan Bay), 102
Kasaan (Kasaan Bay), 101
Kasaan Bay (Prince of Wales Island), 98
Kashevarof Passage (Clarence Strait), 110
Kassa Inlet (Prince of Wales Island), 395
Kassa Island Bay (Kassa Inlet), 394
Kayak Island Cove (Keku Strait), 340
Keene Island Bay (Keene Island), 131
Kegan Cove (Moira Sound), 95
Keku Islands (Keku Strait), 348
Keku Strait, 338
Keku Strait from Conclusion Island to Sumner Strait, 338
Kelgaya Bay (Chilkoot Inlet), 193
Kell Bay (Affleck Canal), 360
Kelp Bay (Baranof Island), 318
Kelp Island Anchorage (Kelp Island), 30
Kendrick Bay (Prince of Wales Island), 88
Kendrick Islands, 88

*Ketchikan, 38*
Ketchikan (Revillagigedo Island), 41
Khaz Bay (Chichagof Island), 264
Khaz Head Anchorage, 270
Kidney Cove (Redoubt Bay), 304
Killisnoo Harbor (Admiralty Island), 295
Kimshan Cove (Chichagof Island), 262
Kina Cove (Kasaan Bay), 103
Kindergarten Bay (Etolin Island), 117
Kitkun Bay (Cholmondeley Sound), 97
Klag Bay, Chichagof Village Site (Chichagof Island), 263
Klawock Harbor (Prince of Wales Island), 377
Klawock Inlet (Prince of Wales Island), 377
Klinkwan Cove (Hunter Bay), 397
Kliuchevoi Bay (Baranof Island), 305
Kluanil Island Cove (Kasaan Bay), 99
Knudson Cove (Revillagigedo Island), 66
Koka Island Passage, 303
Kootznahoo Inlet (Admiralty Island) See on Chapter 5 Map, 293
Krestof Sound, 274
Kritoi Basin (Whale Bay), 313
Kuiu Island Southeast Cove (Kuiu Island), 349
Kuiu Island's West Coast, 333
Kukkan Passage, 262

*La Pérouse, 238*
Labouchere Bay (Prince of Wales Island), 358
Lake Anna and Sister Lake (Klag Bay), 263
Lake Bay (Stevenson Island), 110
Lamplugh Glacier (Johns Hopkins Inlet), 221
Launch Cove (Baranof Island), 287
Launch Passage, 376
Le Conte Bay, 140
*Learning to Carve, 375*
Leask Cove (George Inlet), 39
Lee Rock (Clarence Strait), 67
Leesoffskaia Bay (Aleutkina Bay), 301
Lemesurier Island—East Coast (Icy Strait), 224
Leo Anchorage (Chichagof Island), 270
*Lessons from Adverse Experiences, 261*
*Lessons from the Petersburg Birds, 134*
Letnikof Cove (Chilkat Inlet), 192
Limestone Inlet, 171
Lincoln Channel, 9
Lincoln Rock (Clarence Strait), 109
Lindenberg Harbor, 291
Liscome Bay (Dall Island), 415
Lisianski Inlet (Chichagof Island), 243
Lisianski Inside Passage, 251
Lisianski Strait, 245
Little Basket Bay (Chichagof Island), 293
Little Bay (Chichagof Island), 258
Little Coal Bay (Kasaan Bay), 102

Little Daykoo Harbor (Dall Island), 412
Little Duncan Bay (Kupreanof Island), 126
Little Goose Bay (Skowl Arm), 100
Little Port Walter (Port Walter), 330
Little Puffin Bay (Baranof Island), 318
Little Pybus Bay (Admiralty Island), 149
Long Bay and Taiya River, 199
Lord's Pocket (Payne Island), 349
Lost Cove (Lisianski Strait), 247
Louise Cove (Baranof Island), 284
Louise Cove (Kuiu Island), 359
Lucky Cove (Revillagigedo Island), 36
Lumber Cove (Chichagof Island), 253
Lutak Inlet (Chilkoot Inlet), 196
Lyman Anchorage (Prince of Wales Island), 103
Lynn Canal, 184
Lynn Canal North, 190

Mabel Bay (Hassiah Inlet), 391
Madan Bay (Eastern Passage), 82
Magnetic Cove (Union Bay), 69
Mainland Route across East Dixon Inlet via Portland Inlet, 8
Manhattan Arm (Sea Otter Harbor), 414
Manzanita Bay (Revillagigedo Island), 59
Manzanita Cove (Wales Island), 12
Maple Bay (Portland Canal), 18
Maquinna Cove (Muir Inlet), 219
Marble Creek Cove (Prince of Wales Island), 364
Margerie Glacier (Tarr Inlet), 223
Marguerite Bay (Traitors Cove), 64
Mary Island Anchorage (Mary Island), 33
Maurelle Islands, 375
McHenry Anchorage (Etolin Island), 107
McHenry Inlet (Etolin Island), 108
McKenzie Inlet (Skowl Arm), 100
McLean Arm (Prince of Wales Island), 87
McLeod Bay (Dall Island), 412
Meares Passage (Dall Island), 412
*Meditations on Passing Sumdum Glacier*, 160
Mendenhall Bar, 178
Menefee Anchorage (Moira Sound), 92
Merrifield Bay (Prince of Wales Island), 125
*Metlakatla*, 33
*Meyers Chuck*, 67
Meyers Chuck (Meyers Island), 67
Middle Channel (Rakof Islands), 309
Midway Rock (Wrangell Narrows), 130
Mielkoi Cove (Baranof Island), 303
Mills Bay, Lindeman Cove and Browns Bay (Kasaan Bay), 102
Mink Bay (Boca de Quadra), 30
Minnie Bay (Prince of Wales Island), 404
Minnie Cutoff, 403
*Mirror Harbor—A Piece of Cake?* 254
Mist Cove (Baranof Island), 329
Mite Cove (Lisianski Inlet), 243
Moira Sound (Prince of Wales Island), 92
Mole Harbor (Seymour Canal), 158
Morse Cove (Duke Island), 30
*Morse Cove Adventure*, 32
Moser Bay (Revillagigedo Island), 65

Moser Bay Bight (Revillagigedo Island), 65
Mosman Inlet (Etolin Island), 108
Mosquito Cove (Graves Harbor), 235
Moth Bay (Thorne Arm), 37
Mud Bay (Chichagof Island), 225
Mud Bay (Chilkoot Inlet), 193
Mud Bay (Hetta Inlet), 390
Mud Bay (Krestof Sound), 275
Mud Bay (Vank Island), 121
Mud Hole (Port Malmesbury), 338
Muir Glacier (Muir Inlet), 219
Muir Inlet (Glacier Bay), 218
Murder Cove (Admiralty Island), 147
Murphy Cove (Graves Harbor), 235
*Musings on Infinity in Southeast Alaska*, 325

Nadzaheen Cove (Annette Island), 37
Nagasay Cove (Esquibel Island), 376
Naha Bay (Revillagigedo Island), 64
Nahku Bay (Taiya Inlet), 198
Nakat Harbor, Baidarka Arm (Nakat Inlet), 22
Nakat Inlet, 22
Nakwasina Passage, 274
Nakwasina Sound, Beehive Island Cove, 274
Nanny Bay (Twelvemile Arm), 103
The Narrows, 82
Natoma Bay (Long Island), 393
Natzuhini Bay (Prince of Wales Island), 386
Necker Bay (Baranof Island), 310
Necker Islands, 306
Neets Bay, Fire Cove (Revillagigedo Island), 64
Neka Bay (Port Frederick), 206
Nelson Bay (Baranof Island), 326
Neva Strait, 273
New Eddystone Rock (Behm Canal), 57
New Prop Cove (Dall Island), 411
New Tokeen (El Capitan Island), 369
Niblack Anchorage (Moira Sound), 94
Nichin Cove (Tuxekan Island), 371
Nichols Bay (Prince of Wales Island), 405
Nichols Passage, 35
Nina Cove (Coning Inlet), 394
Nismeni Cove (Baranof Island), 289
No Name Bay (Kuiu Island), 339
No Name Cove (Admiralty Island), 291
No Name Cove (Nossuk Bay), 374
North Arm (Hood Bay), 295
North Arm (Moira Sound), 92
North Arm of Ingraham Bay (Prince of Wales Island), 90
North Bay (Dall Island), 407
North Cape (Baranof Island), 312
North Inian Pass, 228
North Pass, 386
North Sandy Cove (Glacier Bay), 216
North Sawyer and South Sawyer Glaciers (Tracy Arm), 169
Northern Stephens Passage, 180
Nossuk Anchorage (Prince of Wales Island), 374

Nossuk Bay (Prince of Wales Island), 374
Nowiskay Cove (North Arm), 92

Ogden Passage, 262
Olga Strait, 274
Olive Cove (Etolin Island), 73
Oliver Inlet (Admiralty Island), 180
*Orcas Finish Moose*, 209
Orel Anchorage (Tebenkof Bay), 337
Outer Passage South of Sitka, 281

*Pack Creek Brown Bears*, 159
Palma Bay, 237
Papkes Landing (Mitkof Island), 132
Patterson Bay (Baranof Island), 329
Pavlof Harbor (Freshwater Bay), 292
Pearl Harbor (Favorite Channel), 183
Pearl Harbour, 8
Pearse Canal, 10
Pelican (Lisianski Inlet), 243
Peril Strait (West to East), 284
*Petersburg*, 133
Petersburg (Mitkof Island), 134
Petersburg Creek (Kupreanof Island), 132
Petersen Islands (Ernest Sound), 70
Petrof Bay and Cedar Bight (Tebenkof Bay), 336
Piehle Passage, 267
*Piehle Passage—A Real Challenge for Experienced Mariners*, 270
Piledriver Cove (Tebenkof Bay), 334
Pinta Bay (Portlock Harbor), 260
Pirate Cove (Baranof Island), 302
Pleasant Bay (Seymour Canal), 157
Point Alava (Revillagigedo Island), 54
Point Astley, Wood Spit, 160
Point Baker (Prince of Wales Island), 125
Pole Anchorage (Kosciusko Island), 361
Polk Inlet (Skowl Arm), 100
Pond Bay (Dall Island), 411
Pond Bay (Duke Island), 31
Poor Man Bay (Kasaan Bay), 102
Porcupine Bay (Islas Bay), 254
Port Alexander (Baranof Island), 332
Port Alice (Heceta Island), 372
Port Althorp (Chichagof Island), 233
Port Armstrong (Baranof Island), 331
Port Asumcion (Baker Island), 381
Port Bagial (Prince of Wales Island), 378
*Port Bazan*, 413
Port Bazan (Dall Island), 415
Port Beauclerc (Kuiu Island), 359
Port Caldera (Prince of Wales Island), 380
Port Camden (Kuiu Island), 347
Port Chester (Annette Island), 35
Port Conclusion (Baranof Island), 331
Port Dolores (Suemez Island), 381
Port Frederick (Chichagof Island), 203
Port Houghton, 155
Port Krestof (Krestof Sound), 275
Port Lucy (Baranof Island), 331
Port Malmesbury (Kuiu Island), 337
Port Mary (Shelikof Bay), 284
Port Mayoral (Baker Island), 381
Port McArthur (Kuiu Island), 360

Port Protection (Prince of Wales Island), 356
Port Refugio (Suemez Island), 384
Port San Antonio (Baker Island), 380
Port Santa Cruz (Suemez Island), 381
Port Simpson (Lax Kw' Alaams), 8
Port Snettisham, 170
Port St. Nicholas (Prince of Wales Island), 379
Port Stewart (Behm Canal), 64
Port Tongass, 9
Portage Bay (Hetta Inlet), 390
Portage Bay (Kupreanof Island), 144
Portage Cove (Chilkoot Inlet), 193
Portage Pass Bay (Kupreanof Island), 351
Portland Canal, 15
Portlock Harbor (Chichagof Island), 259
President Bay (Windy Passage), 308
*Prince of Wales Underground—El Capitan Cave, 365*
Promisla Bay (Krestof Island), 276
Puffin Bay (Baranof Island), 317
Punchbowl Cove (Rudyerd Bay), 58
Pybus Bay (Admiralty Island), 150

Quiet Harbor (Etolin Island), 117

Radenbough Cove (Pennock Island), 47
Ratz Harbor (Prince of Wales Island), 106
Ray Anchorage (Duke Island), 30
Raymond and Wadding Coves (Behm Canal), 66
Read Island Cove (Farragut Bay), 144
Réanne's Terror (Baranof Island), 314
Red Bay (Prince of Wales Island), 123
Red Bluff Bay (Baranof Island), 326
Redfish Bay (Baranof Island), 316
Redoubt Bay (Baranof Island), 303
Redoubt Lake (Redoubt Bay), 304
Reef Harbor (Duke Island), 31
Reef Island (Portland Canal), 15
Reef Islands Inlet (Baldy Bay), 409
Regina Cove (Fillmore Island), 12
Reid Bay, Peninsula Cove (Kuiu Island), 358
Reid Inlet (Glacier Bay), 220
*Reid Inlet: A Matter of Perspective, 222*
Rendu Inlet (Glacier Bay), 220
Rescue Harbor (Sullivan Island), 190
*Respect the Bears!, 79*
Revillagigedo Channel, 23
Riggs Glacier (Muir Inlet), 219
Ripple Cove (Glacier Bay), 212
Rocky Bay, Cooney Cove (Etolin Island), 108
Rocky Pass (Keku Strait), 340
*Rocky Pass Conquered! 342*
Rod's Cove (Admiralty Island), 147
Rodman Bay (Baranof Island), 289
Roe Point Cove (Behm Canal), 55
Roosevelt Harbor (Zarembo Island), 117
Rough Channel, 264
Rowan Bay (Kuiu Island), 333
Rudyerd Bay (Behm Canal), 57

Rudyerd Bay, Upper Arm, 59
Rudyerd Island, Narrow Pass (Behm Canal), 54
Russell Island Passage (Russell Island), 222
*Russians in Alaska, 17*
Ruth Island Cove (Thomas Bay), 142
Ryus Bay (Duke Island), 34
Ryus Float (Ketchikan Harbor), 44

Saginaw Bay (Kuiu Island), 352
Saginaw Channel, 182
Sakie Bay (Dall Island), 414
Saks Cove (Behm Canal), 60
Salisbury Sound, 271
Salisbury Sound to Sitka—East Side of Kruzof Island, 271
Salmon Bay, 116
Salmonberry Cove (Chichagof Island), 284
Saltery Cove (Skowl Arm), 100
Samsing Cove (Baranof Island), 302
San Alberto Bay, 376
San Christoval Channel, 376
San Lorenzo Islands, Hole in the Wall, 376
Sandborn Canal (Port Houghton), 155
Sandfly Bay (Portland Canal), 16
Sandy Bay (Baranof Island), 313
Sandy Cove (Baranof Island), 301
Sanford Cove (Endicott Arm), 161
Santa Anna Inlet (Seward Passage), 71
Saook Bay (Baranof Island), 290
*Sarheen Cove, 368*
Sarheen Cove (El Capitan Passage), 368
Sarkar Cove (Prince of Wales Island), 368
Saxman Native Village (Revillagigedo Island), 41
Scenery Cove (Thomas Bay), 143
Schulze Cove, Piper Island (Fish Bay), 285
Scow Bay (Beauchamp Island), 309
Scow Bay (Mitkof Island), 132
*SE Alaska's Marinas, 13*
Sea Otter Sound, 372
Seal Cove (Gravina Island), 36
Sealing Cove (Japonski Island), 281
Sealion Cove (Kruzof Island), 281
Sebree Cove (Muir Inlet), 218
Secluded Bay (Necker Bay), 312
Seclusion Harbor (Kuiu Island), 339
Second Narrows (Rakof Islands), 309
Security Bay (Kuiu Island), 352
Sergius Narrows (Peril Strait), 286
Seth Cove (Barrier Islands), 403
Sevenfathom Bay (Windy Passage), 307
Seward Passage, 71
Seymour Canal (Admiralty Island), 157
Shag Cove (Geikie Inlet), 217
Shakan Bay (Prince of Wales and Kosciusko islands), 359
Shakan Bay and El Capitan Passage (Kosciusko and Hamilton Islands), 363
Shamrock Bay (West Crawfish Inlet), 308
Sharp Point (Revillagigedo Island), 56
Sheldon Cove (Donkey Bay), 151
Shelikof Bay (Kruzof Island), 283

Shelter Cove (Carroll Inlet), 38
Shelter Cove (Tebenkof Bay), 335
Shikosi Island Bight (Shikosi Island), 191
Shinaku Inlet (Prince of Wales Island), 377
Ship Cove (Port Conclusion), 331
Ship Island Passage (Ship Island), 395
Ship Island Passage Cove (Ship Island), 396
Shipley Bay (Kosciusko Island), 359
Shoalwater Pass (Behm Canal), 56
Shoemaker Bay Boat Harbor (Wrangell Island), 74
Short Arm (Kendrick Bay), 88
Short Bay and Bailey Bay (Bell Arm), 61
Short Finger Bay (Seymour Canal), 158
Shrimp Bay, Klu Bay (Revillagigedo Island), 62
Silver Bay (Baranof Island), 300
Sinitsin Cove (Kruzof Island), 273
*Sitka, 279*
Sitka (Baranof Island), 276
Sitkoh Bay (Chichagof Island), 291
*Skagway, 197*
Skagway (Taiya Inlet), 197
Skowl Arm (Kasaan Bay), 99
Slocum Arm (Chichagof Island), 266
Slocum Inlet, 173
Smeaton Bay (Behm Canal), 55
Smith Cove (Skowl Arm), 100
Smooth Channel, 264
Snail Point Bight (Behm Canal), 64
Snip Islands (Behm Canal), 59
Snow Passage (Clarence Strait), 116
Snug Anchorage (Prince of Wales Island), 106
Soapstone Cove (Lisianski Inlet), 243
Soda Bay (Prince of Wales Island), 385
Sokolof Island Cove (Sokolof Island), 121
Sore Finger Cove (Seymour Canal), 158
South Arm (Hood Bay), 295
South Arm (Kendrick Bay), 88
South Arm (Moira Sound), 95
South Inian Pass, 230
South Kaigani Harbor (Dall Island), 411
South Pass, 386
South Pass Cove (Sukkwan Island), 386
South Passage, 261
South Sandy Cove (Glacier Bay), 216
Southeast Alaska, 22
Southeast Cove (Port Snettisham), 170
Southwest Arm at Head of Port Frederick (Port Frederick), 206
Southwest Arm of Wales Harbour (Wales Island), 11
Spacious Bay (Behm Canal), 63
*Spanish Claims to Alaska, 121*
Spasski Bay (Chichagof Island), 203
Spiral Cove (Kasaan Bay), 99
Spokane Cove (Glacier Bay), 216
Squid Bay (Yakobi Island), 249
St. James Bay (Lynn Canal), 184
St. John Baptist Bay (Baranof Island), 274
St. John Harbor, 122
Stag Bay (Lisianski Strait), 246
Starrigavan Bay (Baranof Island), 276

Steamboat Bay, 146
Steamboat Bay (Noyes Island), 376
Steamer Bay (Etolin Island), 117
Stedman Cove (Horseshoe Island), 346
Stephens Passage, 154
Stewart (Portland Canal), 21
Stikine River, 138
Stikine Strait, 117
Still Harbor (Whale Bay), 312
*Still Harbor Disaster, 311*
Suicide Cove, 173
Sukkwan Cove (Sukkwan Island), 388
Sukkwan Strait, 388
Sukoi Inlet (Kruzof and Partofshikof islands), 273
Sukoi Islets (Frederick Sound), 141
Sullivan West Bight, 191
Suloia Bay (Chichagof Island), 286
The Summit (Rocky Pass), 345
Sumner Strait, North Shore, 125
Sumner Strait, West of Zarembo Island, 123
Sunny Cove (Cholmondeley Sound), 97
Surge Bay (Yakobi Island), 248
Surprise Harbor (Admiralty Island), 146
Surveyor Passage, 261
Swanson Harbor, 200
Sykes Cove (Behm Canal), 54
Sylburn Harbor (Annette Island), 35
Symonds Bay and Rocky Cove (Biorka Island), 306

Table Bay (Kuiu Island), 338
Taiya Inlet (Chilkoot Inlet), 196
Taiyasanka Harbor, 196
Takanis Bay (Yakobi Island), 248
Takatz Bay (Baranof Island), 321
Taku Harbor, 171
Taku Inlet, 173
Tamgas Harbor (Annette Island), 34
Tarr Inlet (Glacier Bay), 223
Tawak Passage and Gig Pass, 263
Taylor Bay (Cross Sound), 228
Tebenkof Bay (Kuiu Island), 334
Tee Harbor (Favorite Channel), 182
Tenakee Inlet (Chichagof Island), 292
Tenakee Springs (Tenakee Inlet), 292
Tenfathom Anchorage (Redfish Bay), 316
Thetis Bay (Tebenkof Bay), 336
Thomas Basin (Ketchikan Harbor), 43
Thomas Bay, 141
Thompson Passage, 402
Thoms Place (Wrangell Island), 72
Thorne Bay (Prince of Wales Island), 105
Three Entrance Bay (Baranof Island), 302
Threemile Arm (Kuiu Island), 339
Tidal Inlet (Glacier Bay), 220
Tlevak and Kaigani Straits to Cape Muzon, 407
Tlevak Narrows (The Skookum Chuck), 384
Tlevak Narrows Anchorages (Prince of Wales Island), 385
Tlevak Strait, 407
Tokeen Cove (Tokeen Bay), 372
Toledo Harbor (Baranof Island), 330
Tolstoi Bay, West Cove (Prince of Wales Island), 104
Tombstone Bay (Portland Canal), 18
Tongass Narrows, 39
*Tongass National Forest, 55*
Tongass Passage, 9
Tonowek Narrows, 373
Torch Bay, 236
Totem Bay (Kupreanof Island), 126
Tracy Arm (Holkham Bay), 164
Tracy Arm Cove (Tracy Arm), 167
Traitors Cove (Revillagigedo Island), 64
*Treacherous Waters, 183*
Tree Point, 23
Trocadero Bay (Big Harbor) (Prince of Wales Island), 379
Troller Anchorage (Lydonia Island), 260
Trollers Cove (Kasaan Bay), 98
Tsa Cove (George Inlet), 39
Turquoise Cove (Portland Canal), 18
Tuxekan Narrows, 371
Tuxekan Passage, 369
Twelvemile Bay (Twelvemile Arm), 103
Tyndall Cove (Geikie Inlet), 218

Ulloa Channel, 384
*Unexpected Creatures, 277*
Union Bay (Ernest Sound), 69
Upper Chatham Strait, 291
Ushk Bay (Chichagof Island), 288

Vanderbilt Reef (Lynn Canal), 186
Vank Island, 121
Venn Passage and Metlakatla Bay, B.C., 5
Very Inlet, 28
View Cove (Dall Island), 409
*Visiting the Anan Bear and Wildlife Observatory, 81*
Vixen Bay (Boca de Quadra), 30
Vixen Harbor (Ernest Sound), 69
Vixen Inlet, 70

Wachusett Cove (Freshwater Bay), 292
Wachusett Inlet (Muir Inlet), 219
Wales Harbour (Wales Island), 10
Wales Passage, 12
Wales Passage Cove (Pearse Island), 12
Walker Channel, 310
Walker Cove (Behm Canal), 59
Ward Cove (Revillagigedo Island), 47
Warm Springs Bay (Baranof Island), 322
Warren Cove (Warren Island), 363
Washington Bay (Kuiu Island), 333
Wasp Cove (Revillagigedo Island), 56
Waterfall (Prince of Wales Island), 384
Waterfall Bay (Dall Island), 414
Waterfall Cove (Baranof Island), 321
Waterfall Cove (Slocum Arm), 267
Weasel Cove (Boca de Quadra), 30
Welcome Cove (Dall Island), 414
West Arm (Cholmondeley Sound), 97
West Arm (Kendrick Bay), 88
West Arm (Moira Sound), 95
West Arm Anchorage (Fords Terror), 164
West Channel (Krestof Sound), 275
West Coast of Kruzof Island, 281
West Coast Prince of Wales to Cape Chacon, 384
West Cove (Big Branch Bay), 317
West Cove (Eureka Channel), 400
West Frederick Sound from Keku Strait (Kake) to Kingsmill Point, 352
West Sumner Strait From Port Protection to Coronation and Warren Islands, 356
Whale Bay (Baranof Island), 312
Whale Passage, 110
*Whale Songs, 124*
*A Whale's Tale, 272*
Whaletail Cove (Etolin Island), 73
*When Big Brother Can't Do the Job, 225*
Whiskey Bay (Pearse Island), 15
Whisky Cove (Pennock Island), 47
*White Knuckles, 179*
*White Pass & Yukon Route, 196*
White Sulphur Springs, West Arm, and Mirror Harbor (Bertha Bay), 255
Whitestone Cove (Baranof Island), 274
Whitewater Bay (Admiralty Island), 295
Whiting Harbor (Japonski Island), 276
*Who Was Baranof? 298*
*Who Was Casey Moran? 44*
*Who Was Chicagof? 251*
*Who Was Lisianski? 245*
*Who Was Prince Rupert, 3*
*Who Was the "Prince of Wales"? 357*
*A Wilderness Friend, 332*
William Cove (Tracy Arm), 168
William Henry Bay (Lynn Canal), 187
Willoughby Cove and Jacks Cove (Lemesurier Island), 225
Wilson Cove (Admiralty Island), 295
Windfall Harbor (Prince of Wales Island), 104
Windfall Harbor (Seymour Canal), 158
Windham Bay, 157
Windy Bay (Coronation Island), 362
Windy Cove (Dall Island), 409
Windy Passage, 307
Winter Harbor (Prince of Wales Island), 373
Winter Inlet (Pearse Island), 13
Woewodski Harbor (Admiralty Island), 148
Wood Lake Creek Outlet (Geikie Inlet), 218
Wooden Wheel Cove (Port Protection), 357
Woodpecker Cove (Mitkof Island), 122
*Wrangell, 77*
Wrangell (Wrangell Island), 75
Wrangell Narrows, 127
Wrangell to Petersbug Via Wrangell Narrows, 121

Yahku Cove (Tuxekan Island), 371
Yakobi Island's West Coast, 247
Yamani Cove (Necker Bay), 311
Yes Bay (Behm Canal), 62
Young Bay (Admiralty Island), 182

Zhilo Cove (Ilin Bay), 254
Zimovia Cove (Etolin Island), 72
Zimovia Strait, 72

# Enjoy these other publications from Fine Edge

### Exploring the Pacific Coast—San Diego to Seattle
Don Douglass and Réanne Hemingway-Douglass

All the places to tie up or anchor your boat from the Mexican border to Victoria/ Seattle. Over 500 of the best marinas and anchor sites, starting from San Diego to Santa Barbara—every anchor site in the beautiful Channel Islands, the greater SF Bay Area, the lower Columbia River, and the greater Puget Sound.

### Exploring the San Juan and Gulf Islands—2nd Ed.
*Cruising Paradise of the Pacific Northwest*
Don Douglass and Réanne Hemingway-Douglass

All the anchor sites in the paradise that straddles the U.S.-Canadian border, bounded by Deception Pass and Anacortes on the south, Nanaimo on the north, Victoria on the west, and Bellingham on the east.

### Exploring Vancouver Island's West Coast—2nd Ed.
Don Douglass and Réanne Hemingway-Douglass

With five great sounds, sixteen major inlets, and an abundance of spectacular wildlife, the largest island on the west coast of North America is a cruising paradise.

### Exploring the South Coast of British Columbia—2nd Ed.
*Gulf Islands & Desolation Sound to Port Hardy & Blunden Harbour*
Don Douglass and Réanne Hemingway-Douglass

"Clearly the most thorough, best produced and most useful [guides] available . . . particularly well thought out and painstakingly researched." — *NW Yachting*

### Exploring the North Coast of British Columbia
*Blunden Harbour to Dixon Entrance, Including Queen Charlotte Islands*
Don Douglass and Réanne Hemingway-Douglass

Describes previously uncharted Spiller Channel and Griffin Passage, the stunning scenery of Nakwakto Rapids and Seymour Inlet, Fish Egg Inlet, Queens Sound, and Hakai Recreation Area. Helps you plot a course for the beautiful South Moresby Island of the Queen Charlottes.

### Exploring the Virgin Islands
Joe Russell and Mark Bunzel

This cruising guide for the British and U.S. Virgin Islands features all the well-known anchorages, as well as many you have not seen before. Most shown with aerial photos, anchorage diagrams and GPS waypoints to make navigation in this cruising paradise easy.

### Exploring the Marquesas Islands
Joe Russell

Russell, who has lived and sailed in the Marquesas, documents the first cruising guide to this beautiful, little-known place. Includes history, language guide, chart diagrams, mileages and heading tables and archaeology. "A must reference for those wanting to thoroughly enjoy their first landfall on the famous Coconut Milk Run."—Earl Hinz, author, *Landfalls of Paradise—Cruising Guide to the Pacific Islands*

### Inside Passage Maps *North and South portions*
Now, for the first time, our maps include an index to all harbors and coves in this superb wilderness allowing you to customize your own routes.

### Exploring the Pacicific Coast Planning Map, *North & South*

### San Juan and Gulf Islands Nautical and Recreational Planning Map

# Enjoy these other publications from Fine Edge

## THE DREAMSPEAKER SERIES
### BY ANNE & LAURENCE YEADON-JONES

Volume 1: Gulf Islands & Vancouver Island
ISBN 978-1-932310-13-9

Volume 2: Desolation Sound & Discovery Islands
ISBN 978-1-932310-14-6

Volume 3: Vancouver, Howe Sound & the Sunshine Coast
ISBN 978-1-932310-15-3

Volume 4: The San Juan Islands
ISBN 978-1-932310-16-0

Volume 5: The Broughtons
ISBN 978-1-932310-17-7

*Ann and Laurence Yeadon-Jones' Dreamspeaker series are not only valuable resources filled with delightful hand-drawn maps, photos and important cruising information, they're also infused with a little bit of fun which makes them stand out from the others.*
—Peter A. Robson, editor, *Pacific Yachting Magazine*

ANNE & LAURENCE YEADON-JONES are experienced offshore and inshore sailors who voyaged from Southampton, England, in 1985 on their first adventure across the Atlantic Ocean. Over the last 17 years they have logged thousands of cruising hours charting, recording and photographing their travels, and exclusively along the beautifully rugged coastline and islands of the Pacific Northwest. Through their writing, charting and photography they endeavour to promote safe and enjoyable boating while profiling the uniqueness of coastal life.

Available at nautical bookstores,
West Marine and www.FineEdge.com

## FINE EDGE
*Nautical & Recreational Publishing*

# The Nautical Knowledge Series from Fine Edge

## Local Knowledge: A Skipper's Reference
*Tacoma to Ketchikan*
**Kevin Monahan**
A must-have reference for the skipper of any boat traveling the Inside Passage! Includes over 50 pages of handy distance tables and strategies for managing tides and currents in Johnstone Strait and Cordero Channel, time, distance and speed tables, weather data and much, much more!

## The Radar Book
**Kevin Monahan**
The complete picture on how to maximize the use of your marine radar system. By using practical examples, illustrated with screen displays and the corresponding charts, the newcomer to radar as well as the experienced mariner will learn how to tune a radar system, interpret the display in a variety of conditions, take advantage of all of the built-in features and use radar effectively as a real-time navigational tool.

## Keeping Your Boat Legal
*The Boating Legal Guide*
**Curt Epperson, JD, LLM**
This practical guide, written in a FAQ format, makes it easy to read and easy to find the information you need. It will help to understand today's legal requirements, insurance contract language and coverage, and to develop a system to organize your boats documents, maintain the proper records for insurance purposes and manage border crossings to Canada, Mexico or the Bahamas.

## GPS Instant Navigation, 2nd Edition
*A Practical Guide from Basics to Advanced Techniques*
**Kevin Monahan and Don Douglass**
In this clear, well-illustrated manual, mariners will find simple solutions to navigational challenges. Includes 150 detailed diagrams, which illustrate the many ways you can use GPS to solve classic piloting and navigation problems.

# For Your Reading Enjoyment

## Cape Horn
*One Man's Dream, One Woman's Nightmare—2nd Ed.*
**Réanne Hemingway-Douglass**
"This is the sea story to read if you read only one."—McGraw Hill, *International Marine Catalog* "Easily the hairy-chested adventure yarn of the decade, if not the half-century."
—Peter H. Spectre, *Wooden Boat*

## Unsinkable
**Dee Saunders**
Sunk by a freighter on their way to paradise, a cruising couple's strength and perseverance help them to rebuild their life and dreams.

## *Trekka* Round the World
**John Guzzwell**
Long out-of-print, this international classic is the story of Guzzwell's circumnavigation on his 20-foot yawl, *Trekka*. Includes previously unpublished photos and a foreword by America's renowned bluewater sailor-author Hal Roth.

## Destination Cortez Island
*A sailor's life along the BC Coast*
**June Cameron**
A nostalgic memoir of the lives of coastal pioneers—the old timers and their boats, that were essential in the days when the ocean was the only highway.

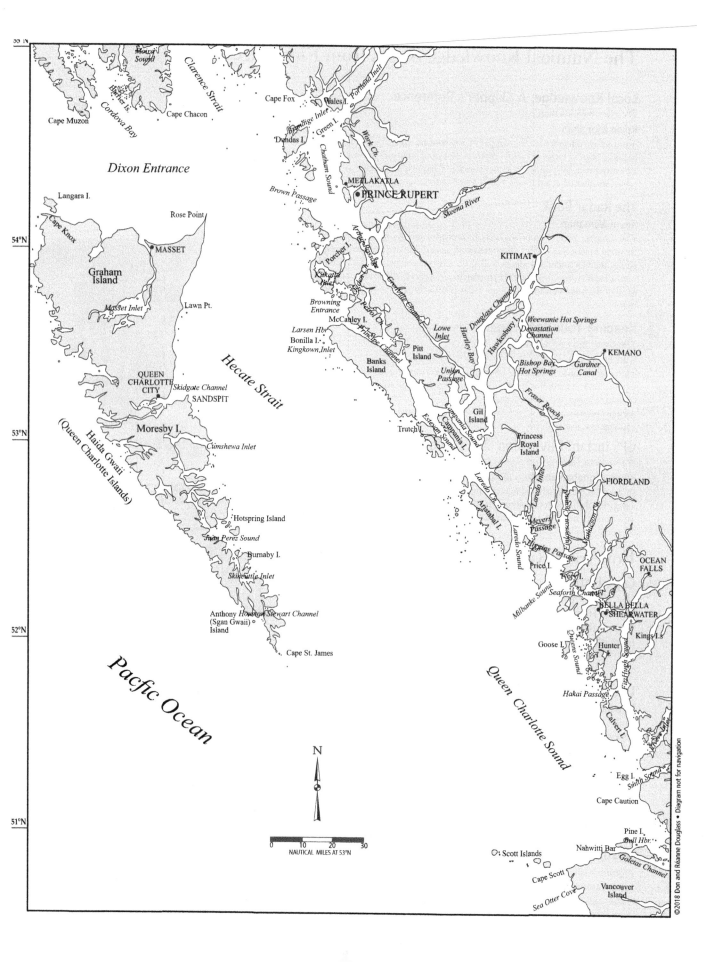